Doris Day

Doris Day

The Untold Story of the Girl Next Door

DAVID KAUFMAN

Distributed by Macmillan

Photo research by Ann Schneider
Designed by Jason Snyder

Library of Congress Cataloging-in-Publication Data

Kaufman, David, 1951–
Doris Day : the untold story of the girl next door / David Kaufman. —1st ed.
    p. cm.
Includes bibliographical references and index.
ISBN-13: 978-1-905264-30-8
ISBN-10: 1-905264-30-5
1. Day, Doris, 1924–. Motion picture actors and actresses—United States—Biography. 3. Singers—United States—Biography. I. Title.
PN2287.D324K38 2008
791.4302'8092—dc22
[B]
                                                      2008009410

To my parents, who taught me to recognize and appreciate joie de vivre in others . . . and to my partner, Ken Geist, who forever devises ways to make my already rich life all the more rewarding.

———— ✳ ————

Contents

✳

Introduction

✳

To begin with a paraphrase from Doris Day's most famous song, "Que Sera, Sera," when I was just a little boy growing up in a suburb of Cleveland, my parents took me to see Alfred Hitchcock's latest thriller, *The Man Who Knew Too Much*, at the Colony Theater at Shaker Square. Though it may seem like quite an adult film for a six-year-old, my overwhelming memory is of the great sense of relief I felt at the end, when Hank, the young boy who is kidnapped to maintain his parents' silence, is reunited with his mother, Jo, after he hears her singing the song destined to become the Doris Day classic.

The Man Who Knew Too Much was the first time I can remember identifying so thoroughly with a character in a movie. If I felt like Hank, it was because Jo's boundless love for her son reminded me so much of my mother's. Just as I knew that my mother would always be there for me, Jo would stop at nothing to get her son back. Jo was played, of course, by Doris Day, in one of her signature performances.

As a young person, I fell in love with Day all over again a few years later, when I saw her in *Please Don't Eat the Daisies*. It was later still, when I was sixteen or seventeen, that I first experienced what many consider Day's finest performance in her greatest film, *Love Me or Leave Me*. Though still young, I recognized *Love Me or Leave Me*—with Day playing Ruth Etting, another beloved American singer—for the masterpiece that it remains.

Decades later, while I was doing research for a possible biography of Ruth Etting, I discovered that her life paralleled Day's in a number of surprising ways, beginning with the fact that they both married their managers. Day's third husband, Marty Melcher, completely controlled every story about his wife and client, in the process of creating her image as the girl next door. Though she complied with Melcher's methods, Day vacillated between confirming and denying that she ever had anything to do with promoting such an image throughout her life. From the very first, Melcher treated Day like a commodity. According to colleagues, he even referred to her in business meetings as "Doris Day," rather than simply as "Doris" or "my wife."

Who was Doris Day? What was Doris Day? In the eight years I have worked on this biography—beginning in 2000, when I first met with Mitch Miller to talk about his decade as a Columbia Records executive who supervised Day during her heyday as a recording artist in the 1950s—I have learned that she was many things at once. She was, of course, a superb singer, whose first hit, "Sentimental Journey," during World War II, helped to define a fraught era. But following her years as a big band singer and her first and last nightclub act in 1947, Day's insecurity made it difficult for her to sing ever again for a live audience. She was a great movie star who, in the fifties and sixties, acted with some of the biggest names on the silver screen—Frank Sinatra, Jimmy Stewart, Rock Hudson, James Cagney, Cary Grant, Clark Gable, Jack Lemmon—to name but a few of her costars. (Day made thirty-nine movies in twenty years, and today, forty years after her retirement from film, she remains the number-one female star of all time.) Both on-screen and off, she was a bundle of energy with an innate tendency to exude both sexual and prim qualities simultaneously. It was this paradoxical if natural aspect of Day that made her a paradigm for her era, "the perennial virgin" who was at once voluptuous and innocent.

Like many great stars, Day remains an enigma. She started out as Doris Kappelhoff, a blonde German-American girl from Cincinnati who had a talent for dancing and singing, as well as an ambitious stage mother, Alma, who wanted to see her daughter succeed in show business, no matter the price. Day spent her forty-year career working as hard as her intimate controllers demanded at the expense of her own wishes for anything resembling a domestic existence. She came to feel disassociated from the icon she had become. Given her convoluted relationship with her image, it should come as no surprise that when comic actor Billy De Wolfe—one of her first colleagues and friends—nicknamed her Clara Bixby, the name stuck. As I discovered in the course of researching her story, pet names became desirable to Day since they permitted her to distance herself from "Doris Day." Amid the swirl of these made-up monikers—"Dodo," "Didi," "Eunice," and on and on—to this day she remains "Clara" to her closest friends. But no matter how difficult it was for her to be Doris Day, she has never failed to respond to many of her fans and even befriended a good number of them.

My interest in writing this biography was sparked by what is now a sharp visual memory from 1989. I was a theater critic living in Greenwich Village when I passed a used bookstore on West 4th Street displaying a copy of Day's memoir in the window. Written in 1975 with A. E. Hotchner, *Her Own Story* was filled with revelations. Day, whose natural exuberance and sunny disposition had brought cheer to her legions of fans throughout the world, had in fact led a life of disappointment and emotional turmoil. Despite her enormous success, Day had never had what she always wanted, which was a happy home life. Though she had portrayed a contented wife and mother time and again in her films, in truth, she was a tireless workaholic who had little or no time for her only son, Terry. Nor were any of her four marriages fulfilling. She had the galloping celebrity of Doris Day, but she was denied the anonymous life that Clara Bixby yearned for, which begins to explain why she always craved it.

Although a portrait of a fascinating person, *Her Own Story* lacked any useful perspective for placing Day in the larger context of her life, of her career, or of the culture in which she played such a significant role—a culture that ultimately left Day behind. As I learned while I continued to catch up with her early films, Day brought the same natural gifts to every role she played, and, contrary to conventional wisdom, she was never limited by type. But like the rest of the culture, Hollywood underwent significant changes in the sixties, even as Day—and, more specifically, Melcher—refused to change with it. Day did not swim in the revolutionary tides of the Hollywood that produced *Easy Rider, Bonnie and Clyde,* and *The Graduate.* In fact, Mike Nichols's *The Graduate* marks an important turning point in Day's story, the beginning of the end of her film career. Nichols offered Day the groundbreaking role of the predatory Mrs. Robinson, but Melcher, prude that he was, turned it down. Having helped create his wife's image as the girl next door, Melcher fought to maintain it to the end, long beyond its credibility. In 1967, when *The Graduate* arrived on the scene and altered the way we viewed American movies—no less than ourselves—Day appeared in the meaningless *Caprice* and the even more dreary *The Ballad of Josie.* Her following, final two films, *Where Were You When the Lights Went Out?* and *With Six You Get Eggroll,* were equally inane, dulling the American memory of her superior, earlier work. As a result, Day has been largely and unfairly neglected by cultural arbiters ever since.

During my work on this biography, I befriended five people who lived with and worked for Day at different periods in her life—among numerous other colleagues and fans who have shared their memories.

They have never imparted stories of their experiences with Day before now. Day herself knew about this book while it was being written, and she put up no obstacles to my completing it. I have been told by several of her intimates that in all likelihood she will never read it. As Day herself has said many times, she has only been able to put adversity behind her by not looking back, and she is reluctant to revisit the past.

In the course of writing her biography, I came to appreciate that Day has always been a creature of the moment, always striving to be as alive and vital in the present as possible. To an extraordinary degree, it is this vitality that comes across on the screen—even in the most banal of her films. And it is that life, lived in the here and now, over many decades, that I have endeavored to capture in re-creating her story.

1

"*Living Photographs*"

---✳︎---

"All charming people have something to conceal, usually
their total dependence on the appreciation of others."
—CYRIL CONNOLLY

"I have never thought of myself as a star. I'm a working lady
who tries to be as good as she can at what she does."
—DORIS DAY

When the technology for moving images was invented in the 1890s, motion pictures were referred to as "living photographs," and they transformed modern life forevermore. Arcades lined with personal viewing booths, called Kinetoscopes, sprang up in major cities across the United States, permitting anyone to step inside and, for the cost of a penny, observe scenic tours of exotic places, vaudevillian pratfalls, or inaugurations and other affairs of state. The silence in the booth made the experience all the more intimate and magical, its popularity leading to nickelodeons, where images were projected for assembled throngs.

One of the first nickelodeons was introduced in 1905 by Marcus Loew in Cincinnati, Ohio. Loew, whose name would become a fixture on many a cinema marquee, was visiting his Penny Hippodrome Arcade in Cincinnati's Fountain Square when he was approached by a man who told him about "a new idea in entertainment," across the river in Covington, Kentucky.

"I never got such a thrill in my life," Loew would recall two decades later. "The show was given in an old-fashioned brownstone house, and the proprietor had the hallways partitioned off with dry goods cases. He used to go to the window and sell the tickets to the children, then he went to the door and took the tickets, and after he did that he locked the door and went up and operated the machine. . . .The place was packed to suffocation. We wired at once for machines and started that Sunday in our arcade on the second floor. We took thirty feet of space and hired the chairs. The first day we played I believe there were seven or eight people short of five thousand and we did not advertise at all. The people simply poured into the arcade."

Though perhaps exaggerating to make his point, Loew could not be too hyperbolic about what he had stumbled upon. By 1910, it was estimated that no fewer than twenty-five million Americans were regular visitors at nickelodeons each week. Though the era has often been regarded as an innocent time in American history, such flickering images were often a welcome substitute for the hostile world just outside the screening rooms. But as film historian Kevin Brownlow revealed in his aptly named *Behind the Mask of Innocence,* many of these early movies actually depicted politically corrupt and morally bereft times. Because they dealt with such matters as alcoholism, drug abuse, and prostitution, their influence was feared far and wide. Chicago was the first to establish municipal censorship, in 1907, regulating what so many Americans were gawking at. The following year, the mayor of New York resorted to the far more extreme tactic of closing down all the nickelodeons in the city to protect its residents.

This was the cultural environment in which Alma Welz was born and came of age in Cincinnati. By the time Alma's only daughter, Doris, arrived in 1922, state censorship boards forbade showing newborn infants on-screen "because the movies are patronized by thousands of children who believe that babies are brought by the stork, and it would be criminal to undeceive them." People could still procure soft-core pornography, or "cooch reels," to observe in the privacy of their home. One of these, for instance, depicted a classroom of schoolgirls playing strip poker. When their teacher discovers them nude, she says, "Young ladies, may I remind you that this a finishing school? And you are all finished!"

The authorities were not the only ones concerned about what movie audiences were able to see. "I don't believe the motion picture playhouse the place to see gruesome, heartbreaking tragedies," wrote a reviewer of the 1912 film *In the Grip of Alcohol.* "I wouldn't want my little boy to look at that set of films. But that it teaches a terrible lesson, and may perhaps be a terrific force for good, I am not prepared to deny."

By 1929, a Florida filmgoer asked: "Why on earth does anybody want to see life represented on the screen as it is? How can they stand to see anything so monotonous? We all see these commonplace things every day of our lives and when we go to the theatre we want something unreal and beautiful to give us courage and hope to face the trials of this drab world of ours. . . . So please, Mr. Directors, give us not life as it is but as we would like it to be."

The vivacious Alma Welz preferred not the documentaries and propaganda films that were sprouting like mushrooms around her, but movies that portrayed life as she would have liked it to be. Alma's dreams appeared on the screen whenever she saw one particular actress, Doris Kenyon. A classic stage mother, Alma was so enamored of Kenyon's larger-than-life personality on-screen that she named her only daughter after her. Long after her retirement, Doris Day would say of her mother: "I think that she would have liked performing. . . . She never admitted to that, [but] I always felt that she was vicariously having this thrill through me."

* * *

Located in the southwest tip of Ohio across the river from Kentucky, Cincinnati was one of the first settlements in the Northwest Territory, founded in 1788. It became a common destination for German immigrants. By 1900, more than 100,000 inhabitants of the city—roughly a quarter of its population—were of German parentage. Two of these naturalized residents, Alma Welz and William Kappelhoff, would marry more than a decade later.

The red-haired Kappelhoff was the sixth of eight surviving children. He was born in Cincinnati on June 29, 1882. His father, Franz Joseph Wilhelm Kappelhoff (no doubt, originally "Kapellhof, meaning "chapel courtyard"), was from Warendorf, Westfalen, Germany, where he entered the world on August 8, 1843.

Franz Kappelhoff married Juliana Agnes Kreimer in 1874. After migrating to the United States, they had their first child, Frank, in 1876. By the turn of the century, the Kappelhoffs' large house on East 13th Street in Cincinnati served as a hostelry for seven male lodgers of German, Irish, and U.S. extraction. They included two barbers, a laborer, a baker, and a machinist. With so many boarders in their midst, the Kappelhoff children were highly disciplined to mind their manners and keep to themselves. Unfortunately, William learned his lesson only too well: he developed into a distant and withdrawn person, incapable of true affection.

Alma Sophia Welz was born in Cincinnati on July 6, 1895. Alma's father, Wilhelm Welz, came into the world on May 1, 1866, in Ötigheim, Baden, Germany; her mother, Anna Christina Mann, on March 21, 1863, in Muckenloch, Baden. She moved to the States in 1881 and married Wilhelm seven years later in Cincinnati. They had five children. Alma's elder brothers, William and Carl Ludwig, were born in 1889 and 1891, respectively. Her younger sister, Maria, arrived in 1898, and her younger brother, Frank, some years later. (Carl would become known as Charlie, and Maria as Marie.) According to the 1900 census, the family lived on Elm Street, when Wilhelm Welz was listed as a Teamster.

As an eldest daughter, Alma was reared to be a hausfrau, someone who saw to the needs of others and derived pleasure from maintaining an impeccably clean environment. Though Alma learned to look after her younger sister as they grew up, a competitive edge developed between the two girls. Both Alma and Marie would develop into large-boned, take-charge women. Doris's beloved Aunt Marie would marry once—and only briefly. She was so "mannish" in appearance and habits—Marie was a professional softball player—that her nephews and nieces would refer to her as "Uncle Marie" behind her back.

William Kappelhoff and Alma Welz were married by a Catholic priest at St. Mark's Church on Montgomery Road, on October 3, 1916. Their first child, Richard, was born the following year. With her own aspirations for public approval as the driving force, Alma enrolled her two-year-old son in a beauty contest, which he won. Sadly he died before his only sister was born. (Day, with typical modesty, would declare, "The only thing they could say about me as a baby was that I was healthy.") Alma's second child, Paul, was born on May 30, 1919. This was a time when "Hun-hating" was still prevalent, and German families were naturally tight knit in response. In the aftermath of World War I, America's mood shifted from optimism to fear and, with it, isolationism. Within such an environment, Alma and William Kappelhoff began to increase their own brood.

In 1921, when Alma was pregnant for the third and last time, she told her friends that she was hoping for a girl, and also hoping that her daughter would become an actress. When Doris was born on April 3, 1922, her brother Paul was three years old. (Doris Kenyon, the silent star after whom she was named, made a popular picture that year called *The Ruling Passion*, about a girl whose father becomes a millionaire through his invention of an automobile engine.) The Kappelhoffs were living with

Grandma Welz in her large ground-floor apartment at 3475 Greenlawn Street in Evanston, a suburb of Cincinnati. Anna Christina Welz, then fifty-nine, had been a widow for nearly fifteen years. Within this decidedly matriarchal environment, the already taciturn William Kappelhoff learned to keep his feelings to himself even more. If he had grown up surrounded by boarders in his home as a child, he was essentially living as one as an adult. He poured more and more of his energies into what he loved most: classical music.

Kappelhoff's interest in music was fostered by his hometown, long a music-oriented city. Musical development had begun in Cincinnati during the second decade of the nineteenth century. By 1825, musical academies and choral societies were prevalent and specialized in performing the works of Handel and Haydn. The sudden influx of German immigrants in the 1840s and after increased interest in classical music. A famous music hall was built in 1870 especially for *Sängerfeste* (choral or choir festivals). Confirming the important role that music would play in the city's development, half a century later Cincinnati would become "the center of the U.S. radio industry."

To keep up with the post–World War I economic boom sweeping the country, William Kappelhoff wore many musical hats while his daughter was growing up. He became a music coach in the public schools, gave private piano, violin, and voice lessons at home, and spent his nights as choral director at the largest of the *Gesangvereine*, or singing clubs, in Cincinnati. On Sundays, he took a busman's holiday and played the organ at St. Mark's Church. He had little or no time left for his daughter.

"It was an arduous program, and it did not make for a congenial home life," claimed a reporter, George Scullin, in 1957, in an extensive three-part series of articles devoted to Day's background. "Here you find the first clue to Doris' insistence today that she must have time to enjoy her family. There are to be more clues, all equally bitter."

In 1952, Day would share vivid recollections of recurring childhood nightmares, for which her father had no patience. Whenever she saw a bogeyman in the night and, screaming, went rushing down the hall to her parents' bedroom, the strict and unsympathetic William Kappelhoff would tell her, "Go back to bed at once. Let's have no more of this nonsense."

Trembling in her nightgown, the frightened little girl remained riveted outside her parents' closed bedroom door. She remembered hearing her father say, "That crazy girl, always imagining things." She would then wait in silent trepidation for him to fall back to sleep, before her mother would come to her rescue and escort her back to bed.

These late-night episodes probably occurred after Doris turned four, by which time the Kappelhoffs had moved into a duplex of their own, several blocks from where they had been living with Grandma Welz. "Some of the happy musical bedlam was lost in the move," claimed Scullin, after interviewing a number of Day's relatives and childhood friends in the mid-1950s. "Life became more ordered, more disciplined. Doris was entered in the nearby St. Mark's elementary school, and because of her exceptional aptitude for music her father started her out on a rigid program of piano instruction. He saw her as a gifted instrumentalist, with an uncanny ear for harmonics. . . . Her mother saw her as a gifted dancer, with an uncanny sense of rhythm and remarkable physical coordination. [For her own part,] Doris was too young to care."

"All the kids wanted to come to our house," Day recalled decades later. "It was a dark red brick house and sat up high off the street on a hill, with a long driveway back to the garage. It was a duplex. We lived on the first floor and had nine rooms and a tremendous attic to play in, also a fabulous basement for play, with one section that was my 'house' complete with kitchen cabinets, a stove big enough to cook dinner for all my dolls, not doll-sized, but girl-sized. Later my folks talked to a contractor and converted the attic into a darling apartment that I thought it would be heaven to live in, but we rented it to a widow and her son. It was a marvelous house."

While her father nurtured her musical ear, Doris's mother cultivated her natural rhythm by enrolling her in Harry Hessler's Mount Adams Dancing School in the afternoons. "To a large extent, Doris' popularity and exciting leadership in school can be explained as wish-fulfillment," claimed Scullin. "With her outside life so narrowly limited, school time became her playtime."

From the very beginning of her school career, Doris derived great pleasure from having a pet dog. According to Day, her first "little puppy" was given to her when she was five. "He belonged to my mother and me. His name was Tippy and I loved taking care of him." Doris was not only closer to but also very much like her mother. And, to all evidence, Alma widened the gulf between Doris and her father as a way of coping with her increasingly estranged relationship with her husband. Day recalled: "My mother tells me that I could be alone all day, for days, playing with my dolls, and playing house . . . and be happy about it."

Doris clearly inherited her mother's vivacity and lust for life. When she was growing up, Doris frequently displayed the unbridled vitality that would characterize her as an adult and come to define her screen persona. Indeed, this liveliness would regularly circumscribe the roles she played. Early in her film career, Day would tell a reporter: "When my mother would show me off to visitors I wasn't like other kids [who would] hang back. No, sirree! I'd do my stuff until mother would have to throw up her hands and say, 'That's enough, Doris, that's enough.'" When she was a teenager, Doris would tell her Uncle Frank, "You know, I've never met a stranger." She related to everyone she met and viewed them as equals.

A pivotal episode, when she was only five, demonstrates how quickly Doris became eager to please and not make waves. She was in kindergarten, waiting in the wings for her entrance in a school pageant. Her mother had made her costume and pinned her daughter into it just before the show. Though Doris had to go to the bathroom, rather than asking for help and risk missing her cue, she wet herself just before going on. The telltale stain on her red satin pants prompted giggles and then gales of laughter throughout the auditorium. "That was my debut in show business," a deadpan Day said in her memoir. "Wet pants Kappelhoff," she added, accentuating the embarrassment she felt as a child.

Day believed that this incident left her plagued with stage fright the rest of her life. Though a born performer, she would increasingly avoid the hazards of live performance, and came into her own only when acting for the camera. But even if Day appreciated how the humiliating episode of her youth left a permanent psychological scar, she failed to draw a less obvious, if more meaningful, connection: her evident need for approval—at any cost. She was already seeking from a public audience the attention her father denied her at home.

Her brother Paul recalled that when Doris was a flower girl at their aunt's wedding, his sister "was thrilled because she knew all eyes were focused on her. Never have you seen gleaming, starched ruffles worn with such poise and elegance. Following the ceremony and refreshments . . . do you think she sat down and wrinkled that beautiful dress? No one dared suggest it!"

According to classmate Margie Farfsing, Doris was "the pet of the first grade" and was very concerned about her appearance even when she was young. "We wore school uniforms and we all had to wear the belts around our middles like a string around a flour sack. But not Doris. . . . She wore her belt around her chest, real stylish. Got away with it, too."

"I got mad," Margie recalled years later. "It was always Doris who got to choose sides. All the girls listened to Doris. She just naturally took charge of things in whatever the gang was going to do. . . . I got tired of playing second fiddle to her all the time. Doris would be out teaching the boys how to play ball, and there I was, couldn't even kick the darn thing. My dad made me get a piece of old wood and kick it around after school until I thought I was pretty good. But never, not once, could I beat Doris.

"Most everybody liked Doris," continued Margie. "She was . . . always having fun and never mad at anybody. She was the instigator of a million things that we were never caught at, and even when we were caught flat-footed, nothing ever really came of it.

"I think the maddest she ever got was when one of the girls invented an intriguing little sucking noise she made with her teeth," Margie recalled. "Doris tried to do this until her face turned purple, but she never could. That's about the only thing I can remember Doris not being able to do."

Doris was close to her brother Paul, who called her "Doke" when they were growing up. In addition to wearing Paul's sweaters, Doris the tomboy also wanted to play with his friends. "When we wouldn't allow her to join our games, she'd hide our baseballs," Paul recalled. "The only time she got really mad was during the period she lost her baby teeth. Her face was a mass of freckles, she wore her hair in a Dutch bob and she looked just like a low-brow vaudeville comedian. I teased her unmercifully and she couldn't take it." In the winter, Doris would join them for snowball fights. "Doke, being the littlest, always got her face massaged in the snow," said Paul, who also remembered that Doris "was always getting in my hair."

Doris was evidently seeking from her brother the attention her taciturn father denied her. "Her father was one of those rigid, too-strict fathers, a Teutonic mixture of sentiment and discipline," recalled another grade-school classmate, Jane Carelton, "and I think Doris was afraid of him." But she also found a surrogate father in her Uncle Charlie, her mother's brother, who, with his wife, Lottie, had a bakery and restaurant at Cincinnati's Findley Market.

"Since my father had to practice a lot at nights and on Sundays, it was Uncle Charlie who took us to picnics and bazaars and on rides into the country Sunday afternoons," Day recalled, specifically remembering a doll with "dark, curly hair" that he tried to win for her at a fair. "He ended up buying the doll for me, and every Christmas my mother made her all new clothes."

As Uncle Charlie prospered with his baked goods, it would become a Welz tradition for nephews and nieces to help out in the bakery. "After school on Wednesdays and Saturdays, Uncle Charlie would sit me on a high stool with a piece of dough," recalled Day "I loved my bangs and never let them be cut until I couldn't see through them. Uncle Charlie said I looked like an ad for Dutch Boy paints. When I got to be twelve, Uncle Charlie promoted me to waiting on customers," she remembered with delight.

If William proved a halfhearted and thoughtless father, Alma more than compensated with her bottomless affection for her children. "My mother always sewed like an angel and she made all my clothes," Day said. Alma also always went trick-or-treating on Halloween with her daughter, who would recall the year her mother appeared costumed as Aunt Jemima with a "big pillow in her bosom." As far back as Doris could remember, Alma dressed up as the school Santa Claus: "[She] walked up and down each aisle and in a barrel-house basso asked what each of us wanted for Christmas, and had we been good little boys and girls." According to Doris, it was "a smart-aleck schoolmate" who told her that Santa Claus wasn't real. "None of us spoke to her for a whole year after she told us that."

The plucky Alma participated in her daughter's schooling in other crucial ways as well. She successfully campaigned for a free-milk program and spearheaded a movement for school uniforms to overcome class distinctions implied by attire. "Doris was an awful little snob when she was a schoolgirl, and always wanted to outdo the other kids in the matter of fashion," wrote a journalist years later. "This led her mother, who was president of the local PTA, to the conclusion that it wasn't right for children whose parents weren't all equally well off to vie with each other and cause themselves and others unhappiness. So Mrs. Day . . . put the idea in motion, and before long all the little girls, including high-hat Doris, wore the same cute uniform." The uniforms were "powder blue with white pique trim, the pocket had a flap and the belt went through the flap. In winter, [we wore] navy blue, with little buttons down the front and a beige collar." But it was as a stage mother that Alma really excelled and helped shape the future Doris Day; in addition to encouraging Doris to sing around the house, she applauded her daughter's portrayal of a duck in a Mother Goose play and also sent her to elocution school.

Day would tell Jane Ardmore in 1961: "Of course I used to dress up in my mother's clothes. Doesn't every little girl? I'll tell you what I wanted more than anything in the world. Four things: I wanted a brassiere, high heels, a permanent—for my straight yellow hair—and false teeth. These four things I wanted madly. My grandmother had upper and lower plates and I loved the sound of the click they made. I was so absorbed listening to her at the dinner table, I couldn't even eat."

Alma was fanatically clean, and Doris, in turn, would take such impulses to an even higher level, developing obsessive behavior patterns that would remain with her for most of her life. If she got her clothes dirty, she would change immediately—sometimes as many as three or four times a day, and sometimes bathe as often.

"Sometimes Doris changed dresses three times a day if she discovered some infinitesimal spot," Paul recalled. "As it gets very cold in Cincinnati, we were sent to school wearing long underwear. Doris inwardly rebelled. How she hated those tell-tale lumps under her long black stockings! The minute we arrived at school, she dashed into the cloak room and rolled the long underwear up above her knees. Just before she reached home—she rolled it back down again."

As a little girl, Doris loved roller-skating. She also coveted her brother's two-wheel bicycle and would recall the "unhappy Christmas" when she was eleven and her hopes of receiving her very own were dashed. "After that, I used to run all the way from school to beat my brother home so I could ride his bike. I'd come panting up the driveway—but the bike was always gone. He always got there first." Eventually, she did get a bike of her own, and Doris became an avid bike rider by her junior high days and would continue this preferred activity throughout much of her adult life.

* * *

Looking back on her childhood, Day would draw a picture of her father as a remote presence with whom she barely interacted, claiming that she was about eight when she realized how miserably her parents behaved with one another. "I so wanted loving things to happen between them, for them to show some affection toward each other . . . but there was nothing but quarrels, constant quarrels." That is, whenever he was home—which, according to Day, was rare.

Though he failed to find time for his daughter, Kappelhoff did make room in his rigorous schedule for a long, clandestine affair with Alma's best friend. Inadvertently, Doris would discover her father's secret before her mother did, a traumatic episode she would recall in painful detail. The event occurred on an evening when the Kappelhoffs were hosting a large party for family and friends. Since the soiree continued late into the night, Doris gave way to sleepiness and finally put herself to bed. When her father came tiptoeing through her bedroom to the spare room beyond—with paramour in tow—Doris pretended to be asleep and proceeded to hear the sounds of their lovemaking through the adjacent wall. When they concluded their session, Doris had to pretend even harder to be asleep—and to conceal her muffled sobs.

Some time later Alma drove Doris, her dancing partner, Jerry Doherty, and his mother, Frances, to a restaurant for a snack after a dance class. Instead of driving home afterward, however, Alma drove them to Avondale, a suburb of Cincinnati, where Day knew that her father's lover lived, having recently obtained a divorce and moved there. From the backseat of the car, Doris watched—along with her mother—as her father parked his own car and entered his lover's apartment building. Much later, thinking back on it as an adult, Day speculated that Alma might have received legal advice to have witnesses with her at the time. Justifiably, Day claimed that it was terribly wrong of her mother to have put her in the middle and used her in that way.

But even if Doris failed to recognize it as a child, Alma was often setting up barriers between her daughter and her husband and, in some perverse way, using Doris to punish William for their failed relationship. Day later emphasized that her stern father loved classical and choral music and despised many of the popular songs of the day. She described her parents battling over the radio dial, singling out a hit song of the Depression, "Life Is Just a Bowl of Cherries," which especially aggravated William. Fully aware of his antipathy to the song, Alma encouraged her daughter to sing it.

When he finally left the family, William didn't even try to say goodbye to his daughter. In her memoir, *Her Own Story*, Day describes the shocking afternoon her father left home for good. After Paul helped their father pack his bags, William left while his impressionable adolescent daughter hid behind the living room draperies, observing his departure with her nose pressed against the window. "My father got in the car and I watched it move away down the long driveway that ran along the side of our house. Then the car turned into the street and disappeared, and I felt that my life was disappearing with it."

If this sounds like an embroidered memory, the sentiment seems reliable and telling, for in the larger sense, the happy and settled life Day always desired did indeed disappear with the departure of the phantom father she never really had. When Day's parents separated in 1935, she was thirteen. While discussing her parents' divorce as an adult, Day claimed that being happily married "was the only real ambition I ever had—not to be a dancer or Hollywood movie star, but to be a housewife in a good marriage. Unfortunately, it was a dream that would elude me just as surely as it had eluded my mother." Throughout her life, Day would give expression to such feelings. She would also come to know what Alma already knew: that one can feel as isolated and lonely within a marriage as outside of one.

*   *   *

When William Kappelhoff left Alma, his daughter was in the seventh grade. For Doris, the breakup of her home was so traumatic she lost her religious faith and stopped attending church. Kappelhoff moved in with his sister, and his soon-to-be second wife, Freda Wingate, joined him. On standard grounds of "extreme cruelty and gross neglect of duty," Alma won her divorce from Kappelhoff on October 8, 1935—almost exactly nineteen years after they had married. She was to receive alimony from Kappelhoff for the support of her two children. But two months later, another court document declared Kappelhoff in "default for answer" and served a summons. Shortly after her divorce in 1936, forty-year-old Alma moved with the children from the nine-room house in Evanston to smaller and more affordable quarters in another Cincinnati suburb, College Hill, located on the opposite end of town.

Though Doris and Paul dutifully accompanied their father every Wednesday for dinner at their aunt's, it was more of a chore than a treat; during these visits Doris was on edge, fearful that "the other woman" would show up before they returned to the comfort and security of being home with Alma. But Doris was mature enough to be concerned about her mother's happiness as well. As Day would recall in an anecdote that captures Alma's grit and independence, "We kept trying to get my mother to go out on dates. One night she finally made a date and went to the garage to get her car, saying, 'If I want to come home, I'm coming home, and I'll come in my own car.' We all got on the neighbor's lawn, waving goodbye. Well, she came back about an hour later saying, 'He was the biggest bore.'"

Doris's home life actually became more enjoyable once her father departed the scene and her parents' constant bickering ceased. Alma regularly took her daughter to visit her aunt and uncle Hilda and Frank Welz, in Trenton, about forty miles from Cincinnati. Their rambling house had a large front porch with awnings, which meant "nobody could see anything" there, Day would recall years later. "I'd go out on the porch in my bare feet and sit in a rocker, and my mother and cousin Mary and her husband would come over and join us, and after a while somebody'd say, 'Let's go get some ice cream.'"

Visiting her aunt and uncle also allowed Doris to see the dog she had rescued from their negligent neighbors. The "big, young" pooch had lived in the neighbors' yard, and once, when they went on a weekend trip, the dog was left behind in the cold weather. "I've never forgotten it," Day declared about her first awareness of cruelty to animals. "I never spoke to them again. They left the dog to fend for himself, without water or food. He cried and we took him in. We took him away to my uncle and never said a word about it."

In his recollections of growing up with Doris, her brother Paul claimed, "Like Mom, Doris was never concerned beyond whatever the momentary problem might be. Her belief then is her present belief. 'If it's going to happen—it will.' As a result, she's always been able to think clearly." Paul also referred to Doris's tendency toward "preoccupation"—a severe case of daydreaming—as always having been "a family joke." If Doris inherited her mother's vivaciousness and eagerness to please, she also manifested her father's dark and brooding nature by suddenly becoming vacant and out of reach. This trait could be disconcerting for anyone who got close to her. According to Paul, such behavior first became apparent during her childhood.

"At home we'd gather around the dinner table and discuss the happenings of the day," Paul said. "Doris sat like a mouse and listened—only she wasn't listening. She'd go off into one of those blizzards and stare! 'Don't mind Doris,' Mom said as she served the soup. 'She isn't here right now—but she'll be back soon!'" In fact, young boyfriends had nicknamed her "Priscilla Preoccupied."

Doris recalled that the first boy who ever told her that he loved her was the druggist's son. But she far preferred one of her brother's friends, particularly because he proved beyond her reach. For a spell, she settled for the older brother of one of her playmates, even as she developed her tomboy tendencies. She also displayed her deeply sentimental nature by keeping the first corsage she ever received. She kept it for two years and was in tears when Alma finally made her throw it out.

When she was an adolescent, Doris once noticed a girl sitting alone on her front steps. Her name was Mary Goodwin, she was twelve, and her family had recently moved to Cincinnati. Doris sensed that Mary was feeling like an outsider and befriended her. "Hi!" Doris called out as she passed on her bicycle, sporting a visored cap. "Want to play softball with the gang?" Thus was the start of a great friendship. Alma would feed her love of movies by taking Doris and her new friend to the picture show every Saturday. "She had trouble separating us from our seats when the picture rolled around the second time," Mary recalled. Several times a year, the dutiful Alma also drove her daughter and friends forty-some miles to Middletown with its outdoor public swimming pool and picnic grounds.

Several of her friends felt that the adolescent Doris was mature for her age. "She was always dressing like a grown-up," said Margie Farfsing. "Always wearing her hair ribbon in some new way that all we girls wanted to copy. But she wasn't all little girl, believe me. She could keep up with any of the little boys we knew. She wouldn't look for trouble, but she was a little scrapper when she was pushed too far."

"Doke was an awful tomboy when she was eleven or twelve, but she seemed to have a deep-rooted sense of maturity that came to the surface early," recalled school friend Ginnie, who would eventually marry Doris's cousin Carl Welz. "She outgrew that silly, girlish stage long before any of the rest of us did. She was a hard worker, but with all that I never saw anybody who liked to have fun the way she did." Paul would also remember her as being "the little girl who always wanted to be a big girl. I can see her now—stomping down the street in Mom's high heels, wearing a big brimmed hat with a long skirt whipping around her ankles every inch of the way."

After school, Doris would spend hours with her girlfriends, sitting around the kitchen table and talking about their favorite movie stars. "I had a real mad crush on Clark Gable," Doris would recall about a Hollywood icon she never dreamed would one day be her co-star, "and I got his name into the conversation as often as possible." The movie-star-to-be had clearly inherited her mother's love of films. "I had a crush on show business even as a little girl," Day recalled. "Movie Star was my favorite game. I used to write in for pictures." Her banter with friends would continue until Alma was ready to prepare supper and would throw them all out of the kitchen.

According to Mary Goodwin, Day also inherited her famously infectious laugh from her mother. Alma's laugh was certainly distinctive. She was once a member of the audience for a live Jack Benny radio show, and the day after it aired, a friend called Alma to say she could detect her laughter during the program.

* * *

Once Doris's parents were divorced, her love for dancing became not just an after-school activity, but a "saving grace." Alma nurtured her daughter's interest in dance by enrolling her in the Geisler Studio of Dance and Stage Arts. Its program featuring an art deco cover, the Geisler Studio presented its Variety Revue of 1935 on Friday, May 24, with an 8:15 curtain. The first act consisted of seven segments, two of which featured the thirteen-year-old Doris Kappelhoff. She did a "Soft Shoe (Harmony)" in the "Divertissements" section, and she was listed as Sallie Sims in "The Old Gang" skit, in which Jerry Doherty, a boy who would become Doris's dancing partner, played Willie Klunk. Doris appeared on stage five times during the second half of the revue, performing a solo "Toe Dance" as well as a "Challenge Tap" duet with Jerry, and she was one of seven girls vying for "Gentleman" Jerry's attention in "The Girl I Met at Sherries." In addition to being listed as one of the girls in the "Hot Cha Chorus," she was also a "High Hatter" who performed "The Continental" with no less than George Geisler, the head of the studio. In fact, Doris was the only student among dozens so honored that evening.

That Friday night at least one other mother had ambitions for her child just as intense as Alma's for her daughter: Frances Doherty, whose son Jerry had just partnered so well with Doris. The two women agreed that their children would practice together regularly. With the Geisler imprimatur, they began performing at church functions and the like, ending their tap duets with typical "buck-and-wing" turns. "We were paid a few dollars for our performances, just about enough to cover our expenses," Day recalled.

According to her brother Paul: "As a rule when Doris was on the bill, Mom stayed backstage with her while I usually sat in the audience. Mom was concerned with getting Doris on and off, then back home to bed again. In their excitement, sometimes they'd forget about me! When they'd arrive home, Mom would look at Doris—Doris would look at Mom. 'Where's Paul?' they'd exclaim in the same breath. I was still sitting fast asleep in my seat when Mom rushed back to the auditorium. The janitors were sweeping up all around me! Mom gathered me up in her arms as if she had committed some unforgivable sin. The next morning at breakfast, we'd recall the incident and roar with laughter."

A big break came when Doris and Jerry won a $500 prize in a contest sponsored by a department store. With Alma at the wheel, the two mothers used the money to take their budding Ginger and Fred to Hollywood in the summer of 1937, the first extended trip of Day's life. (At the time, fifteen-year-old Doris was actually three years older than she would remember in her memoir.) No matter what restaurant they visited during their journey, Doris insisted on inspecting the kitchen before consenting to eat there. If it didn't meet her standards, she would make do with a safely packaged "container of milk"—no matter how hungry she was. "I suppose it was the result of the scrubbed and sweet-smelling kitchens of all my German relatives," she would explain in her memoir. "Whatever the reason, I was terribly finicky about the kitchens of the places we ate in."

The foursome arrived in a Hollywood teeming with activity. In part due to the Depression and the need for escapism, Hollywood was recovering far more rapidly than the rest of the country. In fact, America's film capital produced 778 feature films in 1937—the largest number since 1928. The fifteen-year-old Judy Garland made her "feature" debut in *Broadway Melody of 1938* at MGM, which netted $14.5 million that year. (Made in 1937, *Broadway Melody of 1938* is the film in which Garland plaintively sings "You Made Me Love You" to a photo of Clark Gable.) Shirley Temple made *Heidi* with Twentieth Century Fox, United Artists produced a hit for the ages with Fredric March and Janet Gaynor in *A Star Is Born,* and Warner Brothers would garner its first Best-Film-of-the-Year Academy Award for *The Life of Emile Zola.* Having gotten through the Depression on Cecil B. DeMille epics and Bing Crosby musicals, even Paramount Pictures was in the clear with a $3 million profit in 1937.

With their mothers, Doris and Jerry shared a one-room apartment for a month while they were enrolled at Fanchon & Marco Studios, where their dance instructor was Louis Da Pron. (At the time a bit player at Paramount, Da Pron would later come into prominence as a choreographer and make a dozen or so films with Donald O'Connor, among others.) "First, I had to see where the stars lived," Day recalled of their arrival in a deco-designed Hollywood. "My mother would drive us, we'd park on the street and just look. . . . My favorites then were that fabulous Jean Arthur, and Ginger Rogers. Such a marvelous face, and such a good actress!"

Alma's long-held dream for her daughter's film career suddenly seemed within their grasp. Emboldened by the responses both Doris and Jerry received for their dancing—and for their prospects in a dazzling Hollywood—Alma and Frances Doherty took their children back to Cincinnati to pack things up and return to Los Angeles for good. Such plans were foiled, however, on October 12, 1937, by a near-fatal car accident.

As with any legendary story, there are many variations as to what exactly occurred. "Someone gave a farewell party for mother in Hamilton, twenty miles away," Day recalled two decades after the party, which was hosted by Mr. and Mrs. Clarence Holden, at 258 Walnut Street, in Hamilton, fifteen miles north of the city. "About 10 o'clock, Lawrence [a boyfriend] phoned. 'Aunt Alma, can I drive up with Bud and his girl [Marion] and take Doris for a soda? Bud's got his dad's car.' We had sodas and sandwiches and started back to the party, yakking like mad. It was cold. The windows were steamy. We never did see the train that hit us," continued Day. "I remember the shock, the noise, the brown crepe dress I was wearing, the brown suede pumps that were ripped apart. When I tried to stand, my leg bent halfway up. I sat on the curb shaking my leg and thinking—how about dancing? Luckily, I fainted. . . . Bud had a broken leg and a concussion, and his girl had a concussion, but we were alive."

Whether Bud was called Albert or Lawrence was called Larry, in most versions of the story, Bud was driving the car with Marion beside him. Upon impact with the train at an apparently unguarded railroad crossing, their heads struck the windshield. Doris, who was sitting behind Bud, got herself out of the car, only to discover that her right leg had been shattered. Larry Doherty, Jerry's nineteen-year-old brother, who was sitting in the back with Doris, apparently sustained no injuries. As reported in the paper on October 14, the accident occurred shortly before midnight the previous day.

As reported in Day's memoir, the accident occurred on Friday, October 13, 1937. And, according to a local newspaper article, it was on a Wednesday, at midnight, "at Fifth and High streets" in Hamilton. Day was taken to Mercy Hospital. She was identified in the article as "a young Cincinnati dancer under contract to a Hollywood Studio, [and] relations said Miss Kappel was to have left for Hollywood in two weeks." The driver of the car, Albert Schroeder, told the Hamilton police that "he did not see the train in time to stop."

Doris sustained a double compound fracture in her right leg, requiring a steel pin and an "extra-heavy cast." Though she was told categorically she would never be able to dance again, the doctors withheld their prognosis about whether she would even be able to walk. During her convalescence, Doris spent more and more of her time listening to the radio and discovering favorite singers whom she would emulate, particularly Ella Fitzgerald. With a deliberate vibrato or tremor that moved around the notes, Day's young voice would especially evoke the Fitzgerald who recorded "You Showed Me the Way" in 1937.

Though another legend suggests that Doris quit high school because she needed to earn money, it was at least partly embarrassment over her crutches that compelled her to drop out. "I was in the way," explained the eager-to-please Day. "There was no place for my crutches under my desk, so someone was always tripping over them. They made a clatter when I put them down, and they made a clatter when I picked them up, and everyone was looking at me. Outside in the corridor between classes, everyone was rushing, and I could barely hobble. More than anything else, I was afraid someone would knock my crutches out from under me. I just couldn't take it."

It was during this time that Doris's Uncle Charlie sold his bakery to his brother and opened a tavern in the Price Hill section of Cincinnati. In exchange for room and board, Alma took charge of the kitchen, and Doris was happy in their new quarters above the tavern. "I couldn't have asked for a better place to convalesce," she said. "The jukebox was going all the time, and whenever I got hungry I just scooted down the stairs on my fanny, holding my crutches above my head, and helped myself in the kitchen." Her sense of false security brought hazards of its own, however. When she was dancing on her crutches, no less, she slipped and again broke her nearly healed right leg.

After her second cast and convalescence, Doris was goaded by her mother: "You could have a career," Alma said after her daughter related how depressed she was. "One thing these eight months have done for you, darling, is make your voice better and better."

In 1938, Doris had her breakthrough in a career that would eventually take her back to Hollywood as a warbler, by making her singing debut at Charlie Yee's Shanghai Inn, a second-floor Cantonese restaurant on East Fifth Street in downtown Cincinnati. She was still on crutches and earning $5 a night for her youthful singing, twice a night. Standing on both of her feet, she would use her crutches to tap out the rhythm, resembling an exotic bird or a puppeteer. "Sometimes my audience was little more than the overflowing Yee family, their round, smiling faces beaming appreciation and encouragement," Day recalled.

* * *

Alma further encouraged her daughter's newfound singing ambitions by taking her to vocal coach Grace Raine. As recalled by Day and Raine, their meeting was facilitated by Danny Engel, a "song plugger"—a promoter of new songs—who was a friend of Alma's. At first Raine refused to take Doris on. When she heard Doris sing, she told Alma: "It would be a waste of both my time and yours for Doris to take singing lessons. Frankly, and please don't think me unkind, Doris just hasn't any talent." Later, when she changed her mind, she was amazed by her student's progress.

In 1948, Day herself would say that she "studied voice for a year" before studying with Raine. In fact, she auditioned for a Saturday radio program on WCPO called *Carlem's Carnival* and sang for it regularly but without pay. "I got off to a bad start, though, by beginning with the classics, 'The Italian Street Song,' for one, if you please, but I soon discovered that I did not have a classical voice. . . . My next teacher, Miss Grace Raine, put me on the right track."

It was the persistent Alma who took her daughter once again to Raine, who finally changed her mind and accepted Doris as a pupil. "I had heard her sing a few times on the radio," Raine explained, "and she just didn't have it. But a song plugger told me that she was so beautiful that it didn't matter whether or not she could even carry a tune. So I took her [on] and gave her a special rate and got the surprise of my life when she showed really amazing progress after only three or four lessons."

"Don't crowd the microphone," Raine told Doris early on. "You're working too hard. Remember, an audience might not hear you gasp for air, but a microphone does." Raine recommended three lessons a week, but Alma could afford only one. A compromise was reached by breaking the single lesson into two half-hour sessions. "I never saw a girl work so hard in all my years of music," continued Raine, who had worked with Broadway singer Jane Froman. (Froman was portrayed by Susan Hayward in the 1952 film *With a Song in My Heart*.) "She would come in right on the dot and start to work without any fooling around. Most of the time her mother would come with her—she and a little brown and white spaniel—and Doris would sing with all her heart. Many times, her mother and the dog would lie down on the couch in the next room and go to sleep. I suppose she thought Doris would be less nervous that way. She had boundless faith in her daughter's ability."

Even as an injured adolescent, Doris was a tireless worker. Raine was particularly impressed by her energy and spirit. "What struck me most about Doris was her ability to always look on the bright side of things," Raine said. "Sometimes, in those days, there wasn't any bright side to look on." But in contrast with these sunny memories of Doris, Raine also reported that her pupil could be moody when she was disappointed with how she thought she sounded on a "recording device." "If Doris thought [the playback] was bad, she would cry her heart out and want to go home. . . . She took lessons from me for two years and I enjoyed all of it, even when she couldn't get her notes just right. She was trying to lower her voice—a terribly hard thing to do—and it was a strain on her. [But] she was a perfectionist."

Doris was also deeply distressed one day when she took her beloved dog, Tiny, for a walk and he "dashed away" into the street. Since she was still on crutches, she could not run after him. "There was a screech of brakes, and a sickening thud that I can hear to this day," she recalled decades later. Doris said she was "hurt . . . in a way that I would feel for the rest of my life." This event influenced Day's devotion in her retirement years—well over three decades later—to wounded and neglected animals.

2

"Day After Day"

———— ✳ ————

*"It's tough trying to act grown-up
when you don't know how."*
—DORIS DAY

*"The trouble with some women is they get all
excited about nothing—then marry him."*
—CHER

*I*f bands in the 1920s considered themselves complete with five, six,
or seven members, the dance-band craze of the next couple of decades typically required fifteen to twenty-five musicians. Ergo, the name
that evolved to categorically define them and their era: big bands. While
introducing white America to what had been predominantly black musical impulses, these big bands—under Benny Goodman, Glenn Miller,
Duke Ellington, Tommy Dorsey, Jimmy Dorsey, Artie Shaw, and Les
Brown, among others—made jazz far more popular and profitable than
anyone had anticipated.

In 1942, just before Doris Day herself emerged as a major singer, a
"slight, slender, visibly nervous" newcomer named Frank Sinatra caused
a singing sensation. A large clique of young female admirers shrieked for
nearly five minutes before he sang during a Benny Goodman show at New
York's Paramount Theater on Broadway. "Before," said tenor saxophonist
Ted Nash, "people went to see the band, and then they'd listen to a solo
now and then or a singer here and there. The singers were strictly secondary. But when Frank hit that screaming bunch of kids, the big bands just
went right into the background."

Having patterned his act on popular crooner Bing Crosby, Sinatra
paved the way for a number of other "single act" singers, including
Perry Como, Peggy Lee, Jo Stafford, and eventually Day—most of whom

became more significant than the bands for which they originally sang. As a lead singer, Day first replaced Ruby Wright—Barney Rapp's wife and longtime singer—who retired in 1939 to raise a family. "We held auditions in the Hotel Sinton," Rapp recalled. "Ruby, my wife, kept the score, but we must have heard about 200 singers. . . . Doris was among the first, and no matter who we heard after that, she was our girl."

A local Cincinnati bandleader, Barney Rapp suggested that Doris Kappelhoff change her less-than-felicitous surname to Day. Having already anglicized his name from Rappaport to hide his Jewish roots, Rapp told Doris that her last name took up "too much space on the marquee—can't have Kappelhoff." Doris agreed. Years later she claimed that she disliked the name Rapp had given her, one inspired by his admiration for her rendition of "Day After Day." "I hated it," said Day. "I thought it sounded really cheap. And I said, 'It sounds like I'm starring at the Gaiety Theater,' which was a burlesque house in Cincinnati."

Doris, of course, was long accustomed to many monikers. Like her father, her brother always called her Doke, and friends referred to her as Dodo or Didi. But performing under an assumed name would contribute to a growing disconnection or divide between Doris Kappelhoff and the star she would become.

Though not exactly a "burlesque house," Rapp's new establishment, the Sign of the Drum, was a supper club on the outskirts of Cincinnati, at 4430 Reading Road. Here Day didn't even have a makeshift dressing room. She had to slip into the "lovely new gown"—which her mother had made for her opening night—in the ladies' room, amid paint cans and other remnants of ongoing renovations. Day would recall in her memoir, *Her Own Story,* "I had just turned sixteen, but on the records I was listed as eighteen so that I could work in the club." She was actually seventeen when she started performing with Rapp's band—still quite young for such an adult job. As Day would tell a journalist years later about working with Rapp, "I looked pretty poised—on the outside. But I wasn't so poised inside. Between sets, I'd dash out to the powder room and cry all over . . . the attendant. It's tough trying to act grown-up when you don't know how."

"She had a voice of her own, mind you, but she was too young to have developed her own style," Rapp recalled nearly two decades later, emphasizing how timid and inaudible Doris was, at first. "I didn't know if she was holding up the microphone or if the mike was holding her up. . . . By the end of the first number, I could at least hear her. And by the end of the evening she was really giving out with the lyrics. [Didn't] sound much like the Doris Day we know now, but I want you to know that kid was a real hot singer."

In the earliest recordings of Day's voice, made from radio broadcasts, she is clearly trying to emulate her favorite singer, Ella Fitzgerald, singing "Ain't Misbehavin'," but also evokes early Billie Holiday. And in her jazzy rendition of "The Joint Is Really Jumpin' Down at Carnegie Hall," Day calls to mind the youthful Mary Martin.

When Day began singing for Cincinnati radio station WLW, one of her first assignments took her on a "one-night-stand circuits" tour with Bill McCluskey, who was in charge of the radio station's Artists Bureau. "It was at the Butler county fairground in Hamilton, Ohio, that she made her first appearance before a fair audience," McCluskey recalled. "It was a cold September night and the poor little girl was scared to death. She wasn't used to working a fair grandstand—and you couldn't blame her. The way the setup is, there are the stands where the people are, there is a big, open gap where the truck is, and out there almost beyond the *feel* of the audience the performers are. It is not an intimate setting. Some people need intimate settings to perform their best and Doris, at the time, was like that. I can remember her looking at me, nervous as a cat, and she said real low, 'Oh, Bill, the audience is so far away. What'll I do?' I said, 'Doris, you'll sing a darned snappy tune for your opening, it will go over big, and after that you'll sell 'em with a damn sweet one.' And that's what she did. They loved her."

Evidently, the earliest recordings of Day were made when she performed with Rapp and his New Englanders at the Sign of the Drum on June 17, 1939. As coproduced by the National Broadcasting Company (NBC), this was the first coast-to-coast broadcast of the band. After they opened with a swinging version of "Lady Be Good," Lee Johnson, the male vocalist, sang "Night Must Fall," "Beer Barrel Polka," and "If I Don't Care." Then Gordon Shaw, the announcer, introduced "Doris Day who has been sitting over here to my left, looking very fetching in her charming evening gown, and I suggest we put her to work right now to sing 'Little Sir Echo.'" As she offered a bouncy version of the song—followed by her encore, "I'm Happy About the Whole Thing," Day's seventeen-year-old voice was less shaded and supple than it would become. Also, the purity of expression and unembellished quality, both of which would in time make Day's voice at once familiar and remarkably fresh, were not yet apparent.

According to her memoir, Day sang with Rapp's band six nights a week, "from early evening to two in the morning." This required Alma to make the drive to and from the Sign of the Drum two times a night—to drop her daughter off, return home, and then pick her up seven or eight hours later. She was soon relieved of the responsibility when Doris discovered that Albert Paul Jorden, a trombonist in the band, also lived in Price Hill.

"It was one night soon after I began singing at this place that I asked [Al] if he would give me a ride home," Day would later tell a reporter. "I was earning twenty-five dollars a week and spending it all on clothes and I didn't have the carfare. He said yes, he'd take me home. And that began it. Not that we got along at first. We really didn't. I was young and very shy with boys. And he was bored with the girl-singer type."

In *Her Own Story*, Day explains that she eventually learned that the band's manager kept half her wages for himself (Rapp was paying her $50). From the very beginning of her career Day didn't pay much attention to financial matters.

Given her impression of him as a sullen personality, Doris was startled—and a little bit resistant—when the twenty-one-year-old Jorden asked her out. They had stopped performing for Rapp when he brought in another band to the Sign of the Drum, and there was no longer any reason for Jorden to be her chauffeur. But with his close-cropped black hair, fine physique, and handsome appearance, Day couldn't resist.

"The surprise was that Al Jorden as a date bore no resemblance to the surly Al Jorden who was my chauffeur," said Day. "He was amusing and relaxed and I had a really good time. I was baffled by the fact that a man who had been so consistently dreadful to me could have changed so completely. This Jekyll-Hyde switch from grump to charmer should have forewarned me about Al Jorden."

But Day's recollections of Jorden don't resemble reports from people who knew him then: that he was "a nice guy, very friendly and intelligent." The same colleagues also felt that Jorden had "only one real ambition in life: to earn enough money playing trombone so that he could quit the band business by the end of the next five or six years and open a business of some more steady sort, in Cincinnati, his hometown, and settle down." The fact that Doris herself wanted to settle down and raise a large family made the match even more appealing to her.

The youngest of four children, Jorden was born in 1917 in Cincinnati but spent some of his formative years across the river in Covington,

Kentucky, where his father, Albert M. Jorden, was a railroad engineer. Al was still living with his parents, who had moved back to Cincinnati, when Doris met him. He was also apparently something of a mama's boy. His mother, Ida Bell, was volubly opposed to his marrying Doris—or anyone. Nor could she have been too happy when her baby boy accepted an offer to perform with Gene Krupa's new band in New York.

Doris stopped seeing Jorden when he moved to New York. She resumed singing for Rapp and frequently went on the road with the band. She would later recall how grueling it was to travel fifty to one hundred miles from Cincinnati, some four nights a week, on a band bus. Day would actually travel as far away as Toronto with Rapp, when the band performed there for a druggists' convention.

"Being on the road is not easy, especially for one girl among a lot of guys," Day told George T. Simon, a critic for *Metronome* magazine. "There's no crying at night and missing mama and running home. So it makes you become a stronger person. You have to discipline yourself, musically and in every way. Being a band singer teaches you not only how to work in front of people but also how to deal with them."

"There were other factors that singers often had to overcome," Simon observed. "Out-of-tune pianos, not to mention out-of-tune bands and bands that played too loud, and PA systems that were so inadequate that the singers couldn't hear themselves at all. Then, too, there were purely physical problems, such as keeping one's throat in condition at all times (colds and lack of sleep were murder), looking well-dressed and well-groomed at all times despite the lack of money, getting sufficient sleep and finding adequate laundry and tailoring facilities." (As Day herself would recall, "I slept more hours in my bus seat than I did in a bed.")

Simon described the difficulties as being far worse for female vocalists, who "sometimes had to make up on bouncing buses and iron dresses in ladies' rooms. . . . A single girl among a pack of men certainly had her problems. If her leader was especially wolf-bent, as some of them were, the difficulties increased in proportion to his demands and/or his ardor. In addition, of course, there were the musicians themselves. The female vocalist had to be tactful in dealing not only with the men interested in extracurricular activities but also with the group as a whole in the usual day-to-day relationships."

"I often did eighteen shows a day with the band," Day recalled years later, "and then spent the night sleeping on a train seat as we made the jump to the next booking. I got so used to resting that way it didn't bother me at all. I would wake up in the morning without even a crick in my neck. I ate at any convenient hour of the day or night and sometimes I couldn't decide whether I was having breakfast, lunch, or dinner. We put on shows or traveled seven days a week, including holidays." This was all very challenging to someone with Day's cleanliness concerns. "The most wonderful thing in life, it seemed to me then, was to have a home that I could come back to every night, my own bed, and closets to hang my clothes in permanently." Day would also tell a radio interviewer: "New Year's Eve was the worst night, you know, when men would sit in my lap, on the bandstand, and climb on the piano, and throw drinks in my lap."

Frequently on the move in the early 1940s, Day was establishing her place as a big band singer even as the country emerged from the Great Depression and began to reaffirm itself as the world's most powerful nation. This was precisely when the United States entered the Second World War, following the attack on Pearl Harbor. The edginess and tension that accompanied this momentous national change were perfectly expressed in the jazzy sounds that filled American living rooms via radio broadcasts, both reflecting and relieving the anxious mood. Day's evolving, sentimentally tinged voice seemed to express the very heart of these shifting emotions, and propelled her through the career her mother wanted for her far more than Doris herself wanted. In spite of her growing success, Doris's overwhelming craving was to settle down.

* * *

Even though many would claim in the coming decades that Day sang with Fred Waring's band, she never did. When she left Rapp a second time, she recorded "With the Wind and the Rain in Your Hair," and sent a pressing to Bob Crosby, Bing's younger brother, who had formed his own band. Known as the Bobcats, it had a distinctive Dixieland sound. Bob Crosby wired Day, inviting her to join his troupe in Chicago, and she became one of three female vocalists singing for him in 1940. All of them—Day, Gloria DeHaven, and Kay Starr—would go on to enjoy bigger and better things.

But Day's time with Crosby proved short-lived. According to Day, she was asked to step aside when the Bobcats had a gig in New York, entailing a radio show and a new singer, Bonnie King. While emphasizing how much he liked her and saying he would have preferred for her to stay on, Crosby explained that the band's talent agency had imposed the change on him. Day was surprised and upset. But Crosby's bad news was offset by his also telling her that Les Brown wanted her for his band.

"A song plugger told me that there was a great singer I had to hear who came into town with the Bob Crosby band named Doris Day," Brown recalled. "They found out that she had given her notice. I sent for her . . . and this little girl shows up. I could see how scared she was. She told me that she wanted to go home, but I talked her into coming with me. I persuaded her to stay with us because I've always had clean-cut musicians in my band, and she wasn't afraid of them." Day began singing with Brown and his Duke Blue Devils in August 1940, earning $75 a week.

* * *

Brown's band had been formed at Duke University in the early 1930s— thus its name—and was comprised predominantly of college students. Though it broke up in the fall of 1937, the group re-formed the following year. It would later become known as "The Band of Renown," but Brown himself would promote it as the "Malted Milk Band," borrowing the phrase from a reporter. It was meant to convey an essentially "vanilla" or "white bread" sensibility, and to distinguish Brown's musicians from so many others, with their notorious reputation for drugs and alcohol. In retrospect, the name seems an early harbinger of Day's future image as the "girl next door," both sweet and an eternal virgin. As Brown said, "I liked Doris, really liked her. She was young and vulnerable and I felt responsible toward her as a father would feel toward a daughter."

There are recordings of Day made from a radio broadcast of Brown's band performing at the Glen Island Casino, in New Rochelle, N.Y., on October 25, 1940. She sings "There I Go" and "Maybe" in a voice more sultry and tentative than it would sound later. In a contemporary review of the band's performance at the New Rochelle club, George Simon observed: "And there's Doris Day, who for combined looks and voice has no apparent equal: she's pretty and fresh-looking, handles herself with unusual grace, and what's most important of all, sings with much natural feeling and in tune."

There is no doubt that with Brown's band, Day matured and became a thoroughly professional vocalist who helped, in no small way, to build the band's considerable reputation. It was Brown who pointed out that Day was singing with a slightly southern accent—Kentucky was, after all, just across the river from Cincinnati. "Instead of 'ah,' I want you to say,

'I,'" he told her shortly after she began singing for him. He would later place Day "in the company of Bing Crosby and Frank Sinatra. None of them can read a note of music, they depend on memory and ear, they are very fast reads; and I'd say that, next to Sinatra, Doris is the best in the business on selling a lyric."

Like radio itself, Day had infiltrated practically every American living room by 1940. But unfortunately, few live recordings of the singer survive from her broadcasts that year—in addition to "There I Go" and "Maybe," there is a melancholy Day singing "My Lost Horizon" with Brown. The deficiency is partly due to the doubling of licensing fees to radio stations by the American Society of Composers, Authors and Publishers (ASCAP) at the outset of the new decade. This led, in short order, to the stations forming their own rival agency, Broadcast Music Industry (BMI), and encouraging them to play recordings only by composers who joined forces with the new association. The two organizations have been in competition ever since.

While Day was singing with Brown's band, Al Jorden had hopped from Gene Krupa's band to Jimmy Dorsey's. (The fact that so many highly regarded bandleaders wanted Jorden is an indication of what a good player he was.) But Dorsey's band was touring all the time, and Day had to content herself with nothing but love letters from Jorden during much of this period. She was relieved to spend "every night" with him when their respective bands found themselves in New York during the spring of 1941, and Jorden proposed to her then. Given her ambition to be a wife and mother, as opposed to a singer, she seized the proposal—in spite of Brown's admonishing her that she would be throwing away a "glorious career."

Alma also opposed her daughter's giving up her career. Having gotten so far and so fast while still so young, how could Doris just let her singing career slip through her fingers in exchange for a marriage ring—especially now, with steady work clearly establishing her professional name? And who knew better than Alma how thankless marriage could be, let alone to a traveling band man? But for Doris, managing and raising a family was still her major aim in life. It might have stemmed from a highly competitive ambition to show her mother that she could succeed where her mother had failed. It was also the natural response to having a stage mother who drove her daughter to fulfill her own unrealized dreams.

As Day would tell journalist Jane Ardmore, Jorden "was the clean, handsome, Gene Kelly type, very intelligent, a marvelous musician, and he wrote the most darling letters. I couldn't wait to marry him. . . . Mother was all against it. She sensed that we weren't right for each other. I guess she felt too that it wasn't going to be so easy for me to give up my career and that was one thing Al insisted on. But it was OK with me: The only important thing was a husband and a family. Sharing life was the most important thing in the world."

"You've got to let kids do what they want," Day also recalled. "Maybe you are saving them, but they don't know it and they have to learn on their own. My mom knew Al and I weren't right for each other—first, because he wanted me to give up my singing when all my life I'd wanted a career; second, because I didn't have the slightest idea of what being a wife entailed. I was just wildly romantic. I wanted a husband. I wanted a family. Sharing was the only important thing in the world."

Before joining Jorden in New York, however, Day fulfilled her commitment to appear in Chicago that winter with Les Brown, a two-week engagement at Mike Todd's Theatre Café. Her renditions of four or five songs were to fill out the program of Gypsy Rose Lee—then at her prime as an "ecdysiast" or top-flight stripper—the evening's headliner. (Gypsy Rose Lee had a famous stage mother of her own, who would be immortalized as Mama Rose in the musical *Gypsy*.) Though Brown and his orchestra remained with the show in Chicago for six months, Day would leave them in March to marry Jorden.

She was replaced by an even younger singer, Betty Bonney, who made what is generally perceived as Les Brown's first hit record, "Joltin' Joe DiMaggio." According to George Simon, Brown's Band of Renown "really found itself" that coming summer, in 1941, and would go on to become Bob Hope's regular accompanist when he entertained the troops. For her part, Day floundered in her relationship with Jorden—from the very moment they married on April 17, 1941.

3

An Unsentimental Journey

---- ✴ ----

"I always feel a rise in my scalp or on the backs of my wrists
when something is special, whether it be song or man."
—DORIS DAY

D oris Day's first wedding was a sadly makeshift affair. It consisted of a quick ceremony at City Hall in New York, with Day clad in a beige dress, followed by a paltry reception between her husband's shows in a small and undistinguished room at the Edison Hotel in Manhattan's theater district—an inauspicious beginning to a thoroughly miserable union.

The newly married couple resided in a no less shabby, two-room furnished apartment at the Whitby—a 1920s building where Gene Krupa and Charlie Chaplin had once lived. As described by Day, the conditions at the Whitby in 1941 were truly squalid. But her memory—and her life-long obsession for a spic-and-span environment—might have led her to exaggerate.

Built directly across the street from the Martin Beck Theater on New York's West 45th Street, the Whitby was geared to accommodate visiting actors working in Broadway shows. Living with furniture and pots and pans that countless others had used was a major challenge for the compulsively fastidious Day. It was already challenge enough for her to assume the duties of a housewife. Up to then, Day had spent her whole life relying on Alma to take care of everything in or out of the kitchen.

"I had never cooked a meal in my life," Day would recall, "and I had to make a try by using a cookbook. I found that I could make most anything simply by following directions—but my timing was so bad I could never get things cooked at the same time! Finally, I became so wrought up by the time I had finished preparing a meal that I just couldn't eat a bite!"

Day's domestic problems were probably a letdown for Jorden. He had trouble understanding how his wife spent her days—or, more to the point, her nights—while he was working till two o'clock in the morning. His imagination roared out of control.

"What had been presented to me as love emerged as jealousy," Day remembered, "a pathologic jealousy that was destined to make a nightmare out of the next few years of my life." Though she had ignored earlier indications of Jorden's obsessive nature, there was no eluding it when, the day after they were married, she accompanied Billy Burton, the band's manager, to his office to receive a wedding present: a leather makeup case. Jorden stormed in after them, grabbed his wife's arm, and proceeded to drag her back to the Whitby.

"The minute we walked into our apartment, he spun me around and hit me in the face," Day recalled. "I put up my hands to protect myself but he hit me again and again, knocking me into the furniture and against the wall. All the while he was yelling at me, in uncontrollable rage, shrieking at me. 'You tramp, you no-good little whore. . .'

"We were married and discovered that we'd never really known each other at all," Day said. "I was in love with his letters. Around them, I'd fashioned a dream man. But my new husband was no dream; he was a live young man, very young and very jealous. We were miserable right from the beginning. We'd made a mistake and we were never alone to work it out, for we left at once on tour with Jimmy Dorsey. The other boys in the band were older, their wives were older and I had no idea what my duties as a wife were. I didn't know how to live with other people. Neither did Al. Our thinking was so young."

Day may have incurred Jorden's jealousy during their brief marriage in ways she would never be willing to acknowledge. She certainly was a far more sensual creature than her public image would ever allow. In 1962, Day would confide to a personal assistant that during her marriage to one of her first two husbands, she was simultaneously having an affair. Though nothing would justify the physical brutality that Day said Jorden inflicted on her, if he knew about an affair she was having, she clearly provided cause for jealousy.

Given Jorden's jealous outbursts—followed by his unctuous apologies—Day claims that she would have left him if she hadn't discovered, two months after their marriage, that she was pregnant. Jorden did what he could to induce an abortion, even, she later claimed, putting a gun to her belly and threatening to kill both mother and child unless she consented to get rid of the unborn baby. While in Cincinnati, Day and her mother hatched a plan: she would have her baby in New York and then leave Jorden during his next tour.

In her memoir, Day describes another terrifying episode when they were in Jorden's Mercury convertible, driving to a Dorsey gig in Buffalo and racing "110 miles per hour" on a "winding mountain road." As Jorden threatened to kill them both, the details she recalls are identical with the opening of *Julie*–the film Day later made with Louis Jourdan in 1956.

As she recalled in her memoir, there was yet another tawdry episode during a visit to Cincinnati, when Day and Jorden stayed with her in-laws. Late one night, Jorden began beating his wife in the bedroom, creating such a commotion that his parents were awakened and came to investigate the matter. Incredibly, Jorden's mother sympathized with her son. Incredible, too, that Day's unborn son survived a subsequent beating she described as "the worst of all," when she was in her eighth month of pregnancy.

Jorden was in Buffalo the night his wife's water broke, and, after enduring a difficult and prolonged labor, the nearly twenty-year-old Day gave birth to an eight-pound, one-ounce boy, midday on February 8, 1942, with her mother at her side. Day named him Terry in memory of *Terry and the Pirates*, a cartoon she loved during her childhood. Jorden saw the newborn for the first time two days later when he returned. It was then that Alma discovered a note in Jorden's pocket from a woman with whom he had just spent several days, during his Buffalo tour.

Day's plan to steal away from Jorden was thwarted when he quit the band and took his wife and son to Cincinnati and his ever-present mother-in-law. Not that Jorden had any interest in acting like a father. "One of the cruelest things he did was to forbid Doris to have the baby in the bedroom with them," Alma recalled. "The baby had to stay with me in my room all the time. There were times, I can tell you, when I was fearful that he might harm the poor little thing. I kept my eye on him all the time."

The Jordens moved into a small house next door to Day's Aunt Marie–a stocky, old-fashioned hausfrau–who would serve as a protector. Within a few weeks, after another of Jorden's violent outbursts, Day had the locks on the front door changed and placed his personal belongings on the porch. Safely situated with Terry at her aunt's, Day observed Jorden trying to enter the house, and she was surprised when he simply left. But she knew that she probably had not seen the last of her first husband. In his attempt to publicly account for their divorce many years later, Jorden would say: "There was a religious problem. I'm Protestant and Doris was Catholic. This made for a breach between us. . . . It was, at least, a part of the whole difficulty."

Day would have to become a working mother. But with a baby at home, she didn't want to subject herself to the frequent trips band singers were compelled to take. She sought and won a job with WLW, the far-reaching Cincinnati radio station, as a singer of sponsored shows. Day was willing to work for less than she had been earning as a band vocalist since the pay would be steady. Viewing her as the "hometown kid who had made good," the station manager leaped at the chance to employ her for $64 a week.

At WLW, Day had, in a sense, her first involvement with the movies, singing for *The Lion's Roar,* a fifteen-minute variety show sponsored by MGM to promote the film studio's latest films. With three backup singers, the program aired Monday through Friday at 6:30 p.m. Day also sang on the station's number-one show at 12:30 a.m., *Moon River,* a program that helped launch two other singers, Rosemary Clooney and Anita Ellis. (This was two decades before Henry Mancini composed his melancholy theme song of the same name for the film version of Truman Capote's *Breakfast at Tiffany's.*)

While Day's cousin, a lawyer, was working on her divorce, Jorden was stalking his wife. He followed her to and from the station, and kept showing up at restaurants where, after work, she had late-night suppers with friends. Eventually, Jorden confronted Day with a plea that they get back together, promising that things would be different this time. He even claimed he wanted to be a real father to Terry.

"It was really quite touching, what he had to say," observed Day, "but I had been through this too many times now for it to have any effect." Day was determined to put Jorden behind her. She was also determined to be a good mother, and—at first, at any rate—resisted Les Brown's entreaties when he invited her back as his lead singer. In addition to being happy in Cincinnati, "I really felt no ambition toward a career. I was perfectly content to get by, by singing on my radio shows," she recalled.

But with Alma pushing her, Day's lifelong ambivalence about working, when she just wanted to raise a family, seemed to prevail. After several at-home, Monday-night singing sessions with another local WLW group that called itself the Williams Brothers—including Andy, destined to have a major recording and TV career of his own—and after her new-found companions left Cincinnati for New York, Day was more inclined to accept Brown's latest request that she rejoin him and his band in Columbus. She also needed to earn money. As Day herself said, "Neither mother nor I asked for alimony when our marriages were dissolved."

"We were in Dayton, Ohio, and I told [Doris] that's as close as we'd be coming to Cincinnati, where she was living," Les Brown recalled, referring to his rehiring Day in 1943. "'So how about it?' I asked her. And when she couldn't quite seem to make up her mind because of her kid, I told her the band would send her son and her mother ahead to the Pennsylvania Hotel [in New York], where we were going to open in a few days, and fix them up there and everything if she'd join us right away in Ohio. That's when she agreed to come back."

The timing, however, was bad. Day resumed singing with the Band of Renown during a prolonged strike of the American Federation of Musicians. This prevented any recordings from being made, except for movies and "V Discs" ("Victory" discs)—a concession for soldiers abroad. The strike went into effect on August 1, 1942, and lasted until Decca and Capitol made individual settlements with the union in the fall of 1943, followed by Victor's and Columbia's negotiated agreements in November 1944. However, in addition to countless live radio broadcasts on shows with such names as *Spotlight Bands* and *One Night Stand,* there were also seemingly endless tours. "Whoever planned Les's tour was a sadist," Day would recall. "We played Canada in the dead of winter and Florida in August." There were also many engagements in and around New York, Chicago, Dallas, and Hollywood, in addition to stops in Kentucky, New Jersey, and elsewhere.

According to Day, whenever they remained somewhere for a week or more, she brought Alma and Terry to stay with her. Such an itinerant and haphazard existence had to be hard on the three of them. It was particularly exacerbated by Terry, who was a true terror during his "terrible twos." But, as described by Day, both she and her mother were either overly indulgent with the toddler or easily distracted. When they were staying at the Piccadilly Hotel in New York, he roamed down the hall and into other guest rooms, and eventually came back with their belongings. "We'd have to call the housekeeper to get them returned," explained Day. Terry would also fill containers with water and throw them out the window. The water bombs evoke an early episode in *Please Don't Eat the*

Daisies—a picture Day would make nearly two decades later, which may have inspired the memory.

"After Terry was born," Day recalled in 1961, "I'd either get home for Christmas or Mom and Terry would join me. Mother would come loaded down with all the baby equipment and jams and preserves and her own pots and pans, because she distrusted furnished apartments. They never had exactly what she needed to make exactly what she wanted, so she brought her own. With a toilet seat for Terry and her own roaster, she looked like 'Tobacco Road' when she got off the train. The boys in the band would all go down with me to meet the train—they were happy to see her, I can tell you, because at one time or another, she'd feed them all. And home cooking tasted awfully good to fellows on the road.

"Once when Terry was young and on a harness, he saw a horse and ran over to him and swung mother around and she broke her ankle on a grate," Day recalled. "We were living in a hotel and when I was away he would steal her crutches and . . . say, 'See Nana. I've got your crutches.'"

Alma would also remember doing the "one-night stand circuit" with her daughter: "We'd work a date, then pile into the car and drive to the next spot on the schedule. I used to do the driving, with Doris and three musicians as passengers. The musicians split expenses. After hotel bills and food we didn't have too much [left] over."

Day would remember her first Christmas with Les Brown's band and Alma and Terry in Boston. "We stayed at this small residential hotel where the guests had all lived for years and years and the rooms had crisscross curtains and fireplaces and big bay windows looking out on the snow. It snowed up a storm and I remember sitting at the desk, looking out and writing letters home. . . . We'd go out into the snow Christmas shopping with Warren Brown, Les' brother, who knew his way around town and guided us through the narrow, busy Christmas-y streets. . . . Mother bought me three evening dresses, the first real formals I'd had. They were so pretty, and we sang carols as we walked through the streets."

Day would also recall another Christmas she spent with the band, but without her mother or son. "I was in New York playing at the Penn Hotel and I'd be home ten days after Christmas," she said. "So it seemed wrong to have Mother and the baby come all the way to New York. We decided to wait and have our Christmas when I came home. . . . I guess I'd have cried my way right straight through the holiday if not for the boys in the band. They were wonderful. We had Christmas Eve off and they arranged a party. I was living at the Penn but the boys were all doubled up in some small hotel. Four of them threw their two rooms together and when we arrived there was a tree set up, little presents from all the boys to me, loads of delicatessen food, and we all took turns putting through long-distance calls to home."

It was while Day was staying at the Sherman Hotel in Chicago with the Les Brown band that Jorden tracked her down. Although he had joined the navy after their separation, he was still hoping they would get back together. Day reluctantly agreed to have dinner with him after a performance, and they proceeded to spend the night in her room. They both wept when she refused to take him back, but they also slept together that night. By the time Day saw Jorden next—for the last time, it would turn out, at a drugstore in Cincinnati—he had married Wiletta Extrom, with whom he would have a second son.

Day's divorce from Jorden was finalized in 1943, but the unhappy marriage had taken its toll. Years later, Les Brown would compare the young girl who sang for him before her marriage with the woman he observed after the separation. "She was a changed kid," he said. "Whereas she used to be scared but fascinated with life with the band, now she was moody and depressed. She cried a lot."

Day did look back at the early stages of her big-band days with nostalgia. "When I was with Les Brown's orchestra at the beginning of my career, I had a real ball," she told an interviewer in 1955, "because nobody knew who I was—and they just didn't care. But things change when you become known," she added ruefully, referring to the difficulties she would have coping with fame and media attention for the rest of her life.

*   *   *

While Day's touring with Les Brown's band was becoming more frequent, it put a stress on her continued regular programs at WLW. Another singer named Ann Perry was hired by the station to fill in for Day, before ultimately replacing her on both *The Lion's Roar* and *Moon River* shows. Perry's real name was Ethel Piermont. She was born in New York City in 1919. She was a fixture at WNEW in New York, when WLW offered her a job. "I didn't know exactly what it was I was going to do, at first," recalled Perry. "But then they said to me, 'You're going to replace Doris Day.'

" 'Replace her?' I thought to myself. 'How can I come near that voice?' It was a very hard pair of shoes to fill, because nobody was better than

she was. I loved the huskiness in her voice, and she had the most wonderful phrasing: she always knew just when to breathe and when to sing
the next lyric. And I was scared to death. I felt I would never be able to
match her."

When she first arrived at WLW, Perry would sit in the control room,
observing the shows and learning the routines. "The first few days she
was not terribly warm," recalled Perry of her lack of initial interactions
with Day. The first time they spoke, Perry said, "I can't understand it. I've
been here for three days, and you haven't said a word to me." Day jokingly responded, "I'm angry with you." When Perry asked, "Why?" Day
explained, "I have so much to do, and I understand you hadn't been
working—you could have come here and relieved me earlier." Perry tried
to counter with a joke of her own, when she rhetorically asked, "Have
you ever heard of a contract?"

From the very beginning, Perry noticed Day walking down the hall
arm-in-arm with an attractive man. "I always saw them leaving the studio
together, and I couldn't wait for her to leave, so I could get my hands on
him." He was another singer at WLW, named Norman Ruvell, who was
six years Day's senior.

"He was a delight, and a very nice guy. But he was not terribly interested in girls," added Perry, referring to his sexuality, as she confirmed
many years later while visiting him in L.A. on several occasions. When
Perry said, "Isn't it a shame about Norman," Day responded, "I don't
know what you're talking about." Perry quickly dropped the subject—
even though she felt that Day understood exactly what she had meant.

*   *   *

There are dozens of recordings of Day with Brown's band, made predominantly from radio broadcasts between 1944 and 1946. Typical of jazz
vocalists' techniques of the period, she plays with the pitch by circling
around it before closing in. She also already displays one of her hallmark effects: immaculate diction. If Day had impressed the critic George
Simon at the beginning of her band career, he became even more rhapsodic when writing in 1946 that "[she was] now THE band singer in the
field, who is singing better than ever and displaying great poise."

Day became a singing sensation of the war years and became identified with one of the biggest songs of the era, "Sentimental Journey,"
which she first performed at New York's Pennsylvania Hotel in 1944.

Though the song would be associated with her ever after, Day has given at least two diametrically opposed recollections about her first impression of it. She would tell A. E. Hotchner that as soon as Les Brown handed the sheet music to the band, "we all thought it was going to be a big hit." But she had told Simon earlier: "It was at one of those late-night rehearsals we used to have at the Hotel Pennsylvania. . . . Nobody was especially impressed. But after we played it on a couple of broadcasts, the mail started pouring in. Before that I don't think we'd even planned to record it."

Released in the beginning of 1945, Day's recording of "Sentimental Journey" would prove to be the perfect melding of song with singer, exploiting her naturally wistful voice to emotional effect. The tune was composed by one of the band's musical arrangers, Ben Homer, and tweaked by Brown himself. It had lyrics by Bud Green, who had written the words to "Flat Foot Floogie"—another Brown favorite. At least part of what fueled the melancholy song's initial success was its popularity with the GIs abroad, nostalgic for home, and with their wives, eager for their return. "Sentimental Journey" was number one for nine weeks on the *Billboard* charts, where it remained for several months. Not only did Day receive countless letters from soldiers, she joined the ranks of Betty Grable, Rita Hayworth, and Dorothy Lamour as one of their favorite pin-ups.

A sailor named Roy Scherer would recall being in the navy during the war and hearing Day's rendition of "Sentimental Journey" over the PA on a ship as it was leaving San Francisco for the South Pacific. "I can't possibly describe the emotions that choked up every guy on board ship that night. You didn't talk to your buddies. You just stood there with your eyes misted over, sort of slopping around in your emotion. I've never heard that record since that I am not transported back to the bay, standing at the railing of that troop transport," explained Scherer, who had no idea that he would eventually make three hit films with Day under a different name, Rock Hudson.

Day had another hit in 1944 with "My Dreams Are Getting Better All the Time," and then in 1945 with "You Won't Be Satisfied." It was also with Les Brown that Day recorded "The Christmas Song," the Mel Torme classic that begins with the familiar opening, "Chestnuts roasting on an open fire . . ."

Though Day would apparently forget it ever happened, Hollywood first took notice of her when she was Les Brown's leading singer. "I don't believe it's generally known that Columbia [Pictures] tested Doris back in 1945," her brother Paul recalled. "What happened was so typical of Doris. I remember her pacing back and forth on the roof of the El Mirador apartments in Hollywood. She was supposed to learn the lines for one scene. Instead she was memorizing the entire script! They liked the test despite her inexperience in acting and any other girl would have grabbed that contract. Not Doris! 'I don't think I'm ready,' she told the amazed heads at Columbia. 'I'll stay on with Les Brown.'"

But in 1948, Day indeed remembered that it was Max Arnow who "came up with the idea of a screen test" at Columbia Pictures. "I told him," Day said, "that I knew nothing about acting and that I was quite happy just singing with the band. But he left me some scenes from *Coquette*, which I was to learn. I was very casual about it all, studied the lines while I took sun baths on the roof, dropped into the studio and did the test. Despite my attitude, Columbia liked what they saw and were all for signing me, but my mother vetoed the idea." Alma felt the studio was trying to get her daughter too cheaply and that she could command more money. And Alma clearly was boss: she was her daughter's manager, no less than she was her mother.

Though Day would discover she had a natural facility for memorizing lines ("I have a photographic mind and it's very easy for me," she would declare, decades later), her obedience to her mother's wishes may have entailed more romantic reasons: there was a member of the band whom Day was unwilling to leave behind.

* * *

The war affected Day's life in at least one very specific—and significant—way. When Steve Madrick, the lead alto sax player of the Band of Renown, was drafted, Les Brown replaced him with George Weidler, who was asthmatic and ineligible for military service. According to Day, they began "noticing" each other several months after she rejoined Brown's band in 1943. According to a much earlier report, they first met when Weidler was playing sax for Stan Kenton in New York.

Regardless of the circumstances of their first meeting, at least part of the attraction for Day was that Weidler was "gentle" and "just the opposite of Al [Jorden]." He was also five feet, eleven inches tall, cared a good deal about his sartorial appearance, and was nearly four years younger than Day, who was all of twenty-one when they met. (In her memoir, she claims to have been in her "late teens.") Also, according to

Day, they quickly began sleeping together, and their sexual relationship was particularly good. In two years, the swarthy and mustachioed Weidler would become Day's second husband. One of six children, George Weidler's father, Alfred, was an architect. His mother, Margaret, was an opera singer, who first came to America with his four older siblings from Hamburg, Germany, aboard a ship that set sail on October 11, 1923. George was born in Los Angeles on January 11, 1926. A year younger, his sister Virginia became an extremely popular child film star, perhaps best known as Katharine Hepburn's precocious sister in *The Philadelphia Story* and as Norma Shearer's saccharine daughter in *The Women.*

Weidler had at least three things in common with Day. He was the offspring of German parents and had grown up in a musical environment, and they both delighted in playing cards while the bus shuttled them from one performance to another. And like Weidler, Day discovered that she enjoyed the consumption of alcohol—a common side effect of playing in a band. Weidler became, in fact, a heavy drinker. In contrast with Day's dynamism and her tendency to live in the moment, Weidler was a pensive intellectual, given to talking about philosophical and political matters. It remains difficult to say anything more conclusive about the man, who emerges as something of a cipher in Day's story—as he was, perhaps, also one in her life. (As Day herself would observe after their divorce, "If we had taken time to get acquainted instead of falling into each other's arms, our marriage might have been successful.")

As with Al Jorden before, any hopes of marrying Weidler had to be deferred. Underscoring the extent to which bands were in constant upheaval particularly during the war, Weidler relinquished his seat with Les Brown's troupe when Steve Madrick finished his tour of duty and returned to the States. As band bookings were becoming more sporadic, Weidler thought he would fare better in Los Angeles, fast becoming a center not only of movies but also of radio and recording studios. Once he returned home, however, he had to settle for weekend engagements before eventually joining Stan Kenton's band.

Day reunited with Weidler in the winter of 1945–46 when Brown's band performed at the Palladium in Hollywood. Cal Grayson interviewed her there, for what proved to be one of the longest feature articles on Day before her film career. He described a typical day for the singer: "Knocking herself out on the bandstand; making records in the middle of the night; pressing her own gowns; considering movie offers; bumping across country by bus on one-nighters; doing housework; signing autographs; shopping for clothes; listening to song pluggers. . . . Strictly speaking, Day's day is mostly night."

"My name may be Day," she told Grayson, "but I don't see much of it." According to the reporter, "[Day rises at noon], bathes and has her breakfast. If on [tour], a short walk with her three-year-old son, Terry, follows. . . . About five o'clock, she has her evening bath, begins fixing her hair and deciding on which gown she will wear that evening. She may or may not go out to dinner, depending on how much time she has, and how hungry she is. When the band begins to play, Doris sings at least two songs every set, or on an average of two tunes every fifteen minutes the band works. Between numbers she chats with dancers and signs autographs. [Day sings], in fact, until one or two o'clock in the morning. Then, when the city lies sleeping, Doris knocks off work. But she doesn't go home—not yet. She's been singing all evening—but not for her supper. She still has to have that. So, it's off to an all-night restaurant for food with her fellow entertainers."

Grayson also described how on rehearsal days, "Doris gets to work early—about two o'clock in the afternoon. At the Palladium, during the band's recent stay in Hollywood, Doris had to keep one eye on the music and one on son Terry at rehearsals. 'I'd be up on the bandstand singing away,' she chuckled, 'and I'd see him dart across the dance floor and out a door. I'd say, "Hold it, Les," then chase after Terry before going on with the tune. He knew every nook and cranny of the Palladium.'"

During a lunch at Lucey's (a popular Hollywood café), Day imparted one of the most revealing statements of her life to Grayson. "We are almost like brother and sister," she said about Terry. "In fact, a lot of people think Terry is my brother." And in fact they were both reared by the same woman—Alma—who was more than just a surrogate to Terry while his real mother worked.

There was another surprising revelation in Grayson's piece: "[Day] may talk contracts and screen tests with movie moguls. But tempting as the offers she received were, Doris decided to stick with the band, although she did attend the dramatic school at Columbia Pictures. Records helped in making her decision, Doris said. The tremendous success of the Les Brown platter, 'Sentimental Journey,' with Doris on the vocal, convinced her there is a quicker road to stardom on records."

In spite of her enthusiasm for remaining a singer, only some months, if not weeks, after her interview with Grayson, Day once again told Brown that she was leaving the band to devote her life to being a wife and mother. Again, Brown tried to dissuade her. And this time, she had more than just typical marriage-day jitters. "No bride ever went to her wedding with more misgivings," Day claimed in her memoir, without ever really explaining why. Though Day was poised to become emblematic of the all-American girl next door, here she was, all of twenty-three years old, and with a son, marrying for a second time.

George Weidler was barely twenty when they married. Unsure of himself and insecure at the time, he became more of a brother than a spouse. He may well have been too young and ill-suited for marriage. In her memoir, Day herself finds it "peculiar" that she can't recall the circumstances of their wedding. She was still performing with Brown's band in New York when—on March 30, 1946—they were married by a justice of the peace in Mount Vernon, just north of the city. Curiously, she has no idea why they went there—nor what, if anything, they did immediately afterward.

Brown was not the only one who had tried to discourage Day from marriage: a noted talent agent, Al Levy, encouraged her to pursue what he thought could be a dynamic career. Levy had seen Day perform with Les Brown's band numerous times and recognized her potential for stardom. During one of the band's performances at the Pennsylvania Hotel, Levy was sitting at a table with Manie Sacks, then head of A&R (Artists and Repertoire) for Columbia Records, where he managed all the recording artists, including Frank Sinatra. Levy sent Day a note, inviting her to join them after her performance, which she did. "Have you ever thought of going [out] on your own?" inquired the agent. "Not really," replied Day. "I'm going to get married soon." In her memoir Day would say, "I was not much interested in that, as I've never been fixed on a career—I was interested only to the extent that I could . . . be with George."

As the agent who had already helped establish Sinatra, Levy was a respected judge of singers with charisma. What Sinatra learned from Mabel Mercer, Day learned from her old teacher Grace Raine: that to "sell" a song, a singer has to convey it as if to one person. Al Levy would sell both Day and Sinatra to the entire world.

*   *   *

Though Day's second husband promptly returned to Los Angeles after their wedding, she did not follow him immediately. Despite her frequent claim that she wanted to be a housewife, Day was apparently more ambivalent about marriage than she realized. Certainly marrying Weidler didn't make much sense. If Day felt responsible for the financial support of her mother and Terry, why did she throw away a $500 weekly salary to marry Weidler? "George didn't have much money and I wouldn't have taken it from him if he had," she said. In the course of singing so many songs about romance, perhaps Day simply came to believe in the importance of love above all else. (As Hedda Hopper—the great gossip columnist of the day—would write about Day, "She was a girl who fell in love without pausing for breath.")

While Day gave Les Brown notice and continued to work with his band in the East, Weidler looked for both work and a new home in Los Angeles. Given the housing shortage during the postwar boom, they had to settle for a trailer in a makeshift and unappealing campsite on Sepulveda Boulevard. The conditions in Day's new home with Weidler proved as grim and dismaying as they had been at the Whitby, with Jorden in New York. A few years later, Day would tell a colleague stories about how depressed she was during her trailer-park days in Los Angeles. She spent her afternoons reading movie magazines and her mornings tiptoeing around discarded wine bottles strewn in the yard by hobos and Hollywood "wannabes." Moreover, since the Weidlers' trailer was far from the park's main office, it was difficult for them to receive phone calls.

"Al Levy came around quite often," recalled Day, "to tell me of things he hoped would open up for me, and to discuss my 'potential,' which he thought was fantastic." When he added she could be a "big star," Day replied, "I'm not interested." Levy's agency, Century Artists, was next door to Hedda Hopper's office in the Guaranty Building on Hollywood Boulevard. Even before he found his new client any work, "Al brought Doris to say hello as soon as he'd signed her," Hopper recalled, about her introduction to Day in *The Whole Truth and Nothing But*—her "behind-the-scenes stories of Hollywood and the people who made it famous." "She was a scared little creature, smothered in freckles, wearing scuffed-up shoes, skirt and sweater, but not a lick of make-up. For months she wore skirts and sweaters. When I asked her why she never wore a dress, she said: 'I can only afford skirts and sweaters.' Her first need was clothes. Al found a little dressmaker in Los Angeles to make her four evening dresses on Century Artists' money."

It was through Manie Sacks that, in the fall of 1946, Levy managed to get Day radio work with Bob Sweeny and Hal March, a pair of comics who had a show on CBS. (March went on to become host of the rigged hit TV show *The $64,000 Question.*) At least two live broadcast recordings of Day exist from her three months of work on the *Sweeny and March Radio Show*: a snappy version of "My Sugar Is So Refined" and a melancholy ballad, "I Know a Little Bit About a Lot of Things." According to Day, she didn't particularly like the job, because she felt exposed without a full band supporting her. On the other hand, Alma needed money for Terry, and Day was grateful to be taking home $89 a week. This is when Day might have met Jack Carson, who had played a good-natured oaf in movies since the late 1930s. Carson was also a regular on the *Sweeny and March* show. As divorced parents, they had a lot in common.

A guest star on Rudy Vallee's radio show in January 1947, Day sang "More Than You Know," "The Coffee Song," "Easy Street," and "Life Can Be Beautiful." Though Levy got Sacks to give Day her first recording contract—with Columbia Records—initially it didn't amount to much. But her agent kept insisting that Day could be a star. Day, however, was no less insistent that she didn't want anything even approaching stardom. "Whatever comes along, fine, as long as I can make enough money to take care of my family," she told Levy. "But don't try to build me up—I don't want any more than I've got right now."

Given their ongoing struggle to eke out a living, Weidler encouraged his wife to accept an offer for a "little something more," even though it would mean her spending a month in New York in the winter of 1947 without him. Billy Reed, a onetime vaudevillian and retired Broadway dancer, was opening an elegant if diminutive new midtown nightclub at 70 East 55th Street. Taking his cue from the physical space, Reed called it the Little Club, and he wanted Doris Day for his opening act.

New York's top nightclub at the time, the Copacabana, was covertly owned by mobster Frank Costello but run by Monte Proser, who invested in Reed's new club. Proser was also responsible for bringing Day and Reed together. The connection was based on a confluence of events involving Manie Sacks of Columbia Records and a New York lawyer named Sol Jaffee. Known for being both influential and comforting to his volatile stars, Sacks did all he could to help promising talent.

Proser was in Hollywood at the time, making a picture at the Goldwyn studios. According to Jaffee, "Sacks knew I was going to Hollywood to work with Proser and what he wanted me to do was to try to get Proser to give Doris Day a job." A makeshift audition was held on the Goldwyn lot. Proser felt that Day had a "nice" voice, but not big enough for the Copacabana. However, he thought she would be just right for the new, smaller club Billy Reed was managing. As Jaffee summarized the mini-saga, "The funny thing is neither of the two men who were instrumental in starting Doris on her way at the Little Club—Proser and I—had ever laid eyes on her before this strange New York–Hollywood ploy."

At first, Day said she wouldn't go, refusing to leave her husband. But after Levy spoke to him, Weidler consented. "Whatever it was Al said, George advised me to go," recalled Day. Levy, who had already persuaded Reed to pay Day $100 a week, purchased two train tickets: he wanted to accompany her to New York for her opening on February 25, 1947.

In addition to performing her obligatory hit "Sentimental Journey," Day's song list included such contemporary standards as "How About You?," "How Are Things in Glocca Morra?," "Too-Ra-Loo-Ra-Loo-Ra," "Little Girl Blue," and "Glad to Be Unhappy."

Two days after her opening night, Day made her first solo recording for Columbia Records, between 1:30 and 4:30 p.m., at Columbia's then-new cavernous studio in New York at 30th Street and Third Avenue. (The building had been a Greek Orthodox church.) Two of the six musicians who accompanied her were familiar faces from Bob Crosby's band. The session included "It Takes Time," "My Young and Foolish Heart," "Tell Me, Dream Face (What Am I to You?)," and "Pete"—the last a slow-dance number she also included in her set at the Little Club. The lyrics of "Pete" ("He never beats me/Never mistreats me") surely had a special resonance for Day, given her stormy relationship with Jorden. Though subtle to the point of being almost imperceptible, a large part of Day's universal appeal stemmed from a wistful, melancholy quality in her voice that made it immediately nostalgic and exploited her innate vulnerability. "Day's daisy voice was deceptive, a slightly bitter taste buried deep in the nectary," observed Gary Marmorstein in *The Label,* his history of Columbia Records. "Behind all the sunshine the voice harbored something dark and plangent."

The Little Club run would prove to be the first and last solo act Day ever performed in front of a live audience. Supported by only a small "combo" as opposed to a much larger band, she felt the audience's intense focus on her. Day's deep-seated anxieties about not looking or being good enough became excruciating. "Like Jo Stafford, she had stage fright," recalled Mitch Miller, the classically trained musician who, as the A&R boss at Columbia Records, would become one of the most significant influences on Day's singing career. "I was at the Little Club one night, and she was throwing up backstage before going on. The very idea of performing before an audience was too much for her."

However, she was a big hit with the smart New Yorkers who, still in a postwar celebratory mood, filled the seats. She received a rave review in the *Daily Mirror* on March 2: "The East Side nightclub sector was brightened this week by delightfully beautiful Doris Day," wrote Lee Mortimer. "I am no blonde-maniac, so when I say luscious Miss Day is one of the most gorgeous lasses around, I concede much. Doris has charm, personality, an easy grace and a fine, if not strong, voice which she knows how to use. The babe was a band vocalist from the West Coast. I have only one gripe. Like many outlanders, she overdresses for the big city. Beauty like hers should be simple and unadorned." The notice in *Variety* was decidedly more mixed: "Right now she's a shade too 'sweet,'" wrote the reviewer, who apparently found her insincere. "On the other hand [she is] a fetching personality who will more than hold her own in class or mass nighteries."

Day would never perform in a nightclub again and would always be nervous when called upon to sing in public. But given the revenue she generated, Reed invited Day to extend her run for a second month. Once again, however, Day's work was interfering with her private life. Day received a distressing letter from her husband, who was floundering as he watched his wife's career taking off. Unwilling to see himself as "Mr. Doris Day," Weidler asked for a divorce. (Warner Weidler claims that his brother's career was in far better shape at the time, suggesting that Day has mischaracterized it.)

Day attempted to phone Weidler, but failed to reach him. She was eager to return to Los Angeles and her young husband. But she was obliged to complete her monthlong commitment to Billy Reed, a circumstance that turned the rest of her run at the Little Club into, as she put it, "a battle with tragedy." She cried her way every night through "Glad to Be Unhappy," which includes some of Lorenz Hart's driest sallies on one-sided love: "Unrequited love's a bore/And I've got it pretty bad/But for someone you adore/It's a pleasure to be sad." This, of course, only added to Day's effectiveness with the number. As she would later claim, "I'm sure the audiences had never heard a performer so touched by her songs."

Desperately hoping to salvage her second marriage, Day returned to Los Angeles via train. But such hopes were quickly dashed when she discovered that Weidler had vacated their trailer and left no forwarding address. The fact that the trailer had been broken into suggested he had been gone for some time. That, at least, was one version of what had occurred; according to another, Weidler picked her up at the station and a tearful Day pleaded with her husband not to leave—but his mind was made up, and the two spent the night making their goodbyes. Weidler was apparently the first to appreciate that his soon-to-be ex-wife was poised to become a big star.

4

"Her Sex Sneaks Up On You"

✳

"Why-O, why-O, why-O? Why did I ever leave Ohio?"
—COMDEN AND GREEN

Though few would be aware of the distinction, Day's first Hollywood contract was drawn up with Michael Curtiz Productions as opposed to Warner Brothers, the studio where she would make her first seventeen films. Nor were many aware that the contract was every bit as exploitative as Sinatra's with Tommy Dorsey had been—a contract from which the mob famously extricated Sinatra. Unlike Sinatra, Day would have to abide by the servile conditions and indignities of her pact for its full, seven-year term, but not without resistance.

The top director at Warners since the silent era, Michael Curtiz had made some of the studio's biggest hits during the 1930s and 1940s, including *Captain Blood, The Sea Hawk, Casablanca, The Adventures of Robin Hood, Mildred Pierce,* and *Yankee Doodle Dandy.* Paul Henreid, who co-starred in *Casablanca,* said of the film's director, "He seemed able to handle any kind of picture—comedy, love story, Western, or giant historical epic."

Though Jack Warner was hardly known for his generosity, when Curtiz's own studio contract expired in the summer of 1946, he received a $50,000 bonus while they negotiated a far more handsome prize for him: his own production unit at Warners. The deal was finalized the following February, when Michael Curtiz Productions was established—with Curtiz as president, George J. Amy as vice president, and Ralph Herzog as "attorney for" Curtiz, to handle all legal matters. Under the terms of the arrangement, Curtiz earned 51 percent of the shares and Warners 49 percent. Thus Curtiz had the clout to have his way when casting problems emerged over *Romance on the High Seas*, slated to be the second film he made under his own banner. Initially, the musical was going to star Judy Garland, whose growing reputation for being unreliable made the powers-that-be at Warners choose Betty Hutton instead. But, as announced in the *New York Times* on April 16, 1947, the picture's director was "in a quandary" because Hutton was pregnant and "won't be available for the picture for two years. Jack Carson and Oscar Levant are ready to start the film and the following ladies are being considered for the part originally set for Hutton: Mary Martin, Lauren Bacall, Ginny Simms, Marion Hutton (Betty's sister) and Doris Day."

There are as many versions of how Day's name first joined that stellar list as there are men who claimed to be responsible for her big break into movies. (As film critic Rex Reed would succinctly say a half century after the fact, "I would love to know the true story about how she got heard the first time.") According to Day's memoir, she achieved her film breakthrough by singing at a party at Jule Styne's home in Beverly Hills. The composer and his lyricist, Sammy Cahn, urgently needed a star for their latest venture, *Romance on the High Seas*, and they referred the singing guest to Curtiz. But according to another version of the story, Styne had actually fallen for Day's voice when he heard her sing some weeks earlier at the Little Club in New York. And even if Cahn were at the subsequent party in Beverly Hills, he would later claim to have already been enamored of Day's voice through her recording of "Sentimental Journey"—and also to have been the one who introduced her to Al Levy in the first place. The Warners' archive further reveals that Day's screen test came some time later than she indicates and that her agent, Al Levy, was pivotal in reaching out to Curtiz on his own. Indeed, it's quite possible that Levy took Day to Styne's party only after he first approached Curtiz on his client's behalf.

Though Styne and Cahn would both receive credit for bringing Day to the attention of Curtiz, Cahn would try—nearly fifty years after the fact—to seize most of the credit himself. According to Cahn, when Curtiz was talking about Betty Hutton as Garland's replacement, he had been thinking only in "superstar" terms. But as soon as he heard that the director was considering Hutton's sister, Marion—who regularly sang for Glenn Miller—it meant that a band singer was suddenly a feasible candidate. Cahn claims that he then called Curtiz and said, "I know the best in the world. May I bring her?"

But proverbially, success has many fathers. According to Cahn, he accompanied Levy and his client when she went to audition for Curtiz. According to others, he did not. Years later, Day would tell her good friend Kaye Ballard that it was really Jack Carson, Day's costar-to-be in *Romance,* who facilitated the connection to Curtiz. This may not be as far-fetched as it sounds, since Carson was a regular player with Sweeny and March—who likely met Day when she worked on their radio show. This might also explain why Carson ultimately phoned Day to tell her that she got the part in *Romance*—as Day later claimed in her memoir.

Still another future colleague would claim that Sam Weiss, who supervised music at Warner Brothers, was instrumental in introducing Day to the studio. Weiss himself claimed: "I knew Doris very well from my band connections, long before she came to Hollywood. So it was inevitable that I wound up being a close friend of hers." Any one of these people may have been the "talent scout" who reportedly caught Day's act at the Little Club, liked what he saw, and contacted Levy to arrange a screen test with Curtiz.

Whoever was actually responsible, Curtiz was apparently introduced to Day—for "one of the most unlikely auditions in Hollywood history"—on or about March 27, 1947. That's the date, in any event, of a note the director wrote to Jack Warner, explaining that he wanted to break with movie musical tradition of working with an established film star and go with someone fresh and unknown to replace the sassy Hutton. When Al Levy showed up with Day to audition for Curtiz at his private bungalow on the Warners' lot, the director suddenly appeared in his outer office. "Not now," growled Curtiz, as Levy implored him to consider Day. But "a look costs you nothing," he thought to himself as he reconsidered the offer—and "often it pays much." He was "used to artificial girls with lips rouged," and Day struck him as "nice and real. Her hair has a western windblown something. She also looks sad. I like her. I invite them inside. I ask her about experience. Usually, you listen for an hour how they understudied Cornell, how they just missed a Broadway hit. 'Nothing,' she says. 'In school, when I was nine years old, I played a duck.'" According to Curtiz, he noticed that Levy was beginning "to sweat." "He thinks she doesn't sell me but her honesty sells me. She is sexy, too, but in an unsexy way. Her sex sneaks up on you." Curtiz proceeded to say, "If you feel sad . . . sing me a sad song." Day sang "Embraceable You" and broke out in tears while singing. In addition to the fresh wounds she felt over her breakup with Weidler, she also suddenly felt that her lack of experience meant she didn't stand a chance with Curtiz.

Day would recall crying even before she sang the song, when Curtiz asked her, "What makes you think you can act?" "I'm a singer—I didn't ask for this audition," she replied, as the tears came tumbling forth and she started to head for the door. "Come back here," said Curtiz. "I just wanted to see if you could cry." But Curtiz was obviously quite taken with Day. Rather than dismiss the tearful starlet then and there, he gave her another chance. She composed herself and proceeded to sing "What Do You Do on a Rainy Night in Rio?" Day was somewhat stiff as she sang, and Curtiz tried to get some life or movement out of her "by taking her hips into his hands and pushing her [from] side to side." Day told him, "I don't bounce around, I just sing."

Curtiz offered Day the screen test and the rudimentary version of a studio contract for appearing in *Romance on the High Seas*. Day's payment for the screen test would be "an exclusive option to employ" her at the rate of $500 per week for the first year, $750 for the second, $1,250 for the third, $1,750 for the fourth, $2,200 for the fifth, $2,250 for the sixth, and $2,500 for the seventh. To put Day's contractual salary into some kind of a perspective for 1947, Warners' Humphrey Bogart was Hollywood's highest-paid actor, earning $467,361 that year. And Deborah Kerr, a new British film star, received her first Hollywood contract that year, with MGM, for $3,000 a week.

Even though Day's rise to movie stardom was not quite as overnight as she later implied, it still came rapidly. After she signed the contract in mid-April she had her sound and photo tests all day at the studio on May 2. Already a veteran singer, Day was actually quite blasé about the test. "I'd been working before people much too long to be bothered by anything as easy as a screen test and I slept as I was being made-up," she recalled less than a year later. "The [makeup] girl was amazed [and] said most everyone was all keyed up before a test."

But Day would also reflect that she could hardly believe her screen test had been real. She wondered if there was any film in the camera, or if the whole thing had been a hoax. Day was probably aware of Curtiz's reputation for having his way with would-be stars. In his autobiography, *Casablanca* actor Paul Henreid claimed that Curtiz "was a practiced womanizer and was known to hire pretty young extras to whom he promised all sorts of things, including stardom, just to have them around and make passes at them at any odd hours when there was a break in the shooting. He would choose any private place on the set, usually behind some flat in a secluded area. He'd have the grips move a piece of furniture there, a couch, or even a mattress—almost anything to soften his lovemaking."

As Henreid further explained, Peter Lorre—also in *Casablanca* and a notorious practical joker—recruited a soundman to hook up a hidden microphone at one of Curtiz's favorite trysting sites. "We were all resting between takes one afternoon when suddenly, over the loudspeaker, we heard Mike moaning, 'Oh God! Oh no, no, no . . .' We were stunned. For a second we thought he was in pain, and we jumped up, but Peter Lorre, grinning like a madman, waved us back, and we realized what was going on. Mike's moaning became increasingly ecstatic: 'Oh yes, yes—oh God, yes.' And then: 'Take it all, take it all—my balls too!'" (Mitch Miller relayed this story with a slight variation, as the director ostensibly said, in his thick Hungarian accent, "Daun't fauget the balls, darlin, daun't fauget the balls.")

A year after seeing her screen test, Day would recall: "I sank down lower and lower in my seat . . . to make myself as small as possible, for I was sure now that nobody in this world would ever want to sign me for the movies. Then I suddenly realized that I had already been signed, and that I must have something or a big producer like Mr. Curtiz would never have hired me."

While negotiating the contract for his client, Levy had to give in order to get. On May 2, an internal letter from company vice president George Amy stipulated that Michael Curtiz Productions (MCP) would retain "exclusive rights on Miss Day's services, i.e., radio, nightclubs, personal and legitimate stage appearances. However, we will accord her full recording rights." As a cover note to the contract further explained, Day would receive only 50 percent of whatever money she earned for any "legitimate stage and radio activity" and MCP would receive the rest. A rider to the final version of Day's contract, dated May 15, is a potent reminder of just how much control the studios wielded over their contract players. It stipulated that the "Artist's" right to perform "shall be subject to the Producer's approval of the particular program upon which the Artist proposes to appear." This would apply even "during any 'lay off' periods or periods of suspension" (i.e., from filmmaking). Nor would Day receive any money above her weekly salary—"in the event that we loan your services to any other motion picture studio." While Curtiz would proceed to make four films with Day during the next three years, she would make thirteen more pictures with other directors at Warners—initially on "loan-out" from MCP.

At the last minute, it wasn't Judy Garland or Betty Hutton who was responsible, by default, for Day's big break—it was Lauren Bacall. On May 9, the *New York Times* announced that Bacall was in Mexico and "declined" to return to Hollywood for *Romance*, thus threatening her own contractual arrangements with Warners. But as explained three days later in the *Hollywood Examiner*, Bacall "doesn't want to make any more pictures, actually, if they interfere with her chance to spend time with Bogey." (Hubby Humphrey Bogart was then on location in Mexico, shooting *The Treasure of the Sierra Madre*.) But as the *Hollywood Examiner* elaborated: "Another reason [Bacall] didn't want to make *Romance* is because she felt she couldn't sing well enough."

Day was now poised for stardom. "The studio wanted a star name—Mary Martin, Lauren Bacall or Ginny Simms—for the role, but Mike [Curtiz] held out for Doris and got her," claimed one of the first announcements citing Day as the star of *Romance*. No matter what Al Levy had to relinquish in order to secure a seven-year movie contract for his client, he drove a shrewd bargain once Day was cast in her first film. A rider to her contract claimed that Day would get top billing "in all photoplays in which Artist appears [and] in type at least as large as that used to display the names of any other stars."

Under the headline "D-Day," a subsequent announcement underscored just how modest the girl from Cincinnati remained at the beginning of her film career: "As soon as Mike Curtiz signed Doris Day for *Romance on the High Seas*, she was asked what color she wanted for the walls and draperies of her star dressing room. She replied, 'I don't need a dressing room yet. I have no dresses.' When she was making her test, a wardrobe woman stooped down to change Doris's shoes. 'Oh, I can do that,' said the actress quickly. Seeing bicycles lined up outside the sound stage, she said, 'Oh, gee, I'd like to have one of those.' She was promised one if she landed a contract. So the first thing she requested after being signed was a bicycle." She even made the gossip columns. One of the first behind-the-scenes items about Day appeared on May 19, 1947, in the *Hollywood Citizen*, claiming that the "vocalist . . . disclosed that she had separated from her husband, George Weidler."

*   *   *

In retrospect, it seems almost preordained that in her first film role Day would play a character who assumes another's identity. Although Curtiz advised her to "just be" herself in every picture she would make and that she would prove a natural screen actress, the new public persona of Doris Day would become increasingly disassociated from her private self.

But Curtiz clearly recognized a potential star when he saw one. Having worked with the likes of Errol Flynn, Humphrey Bogart, Bette Davis, Cary Grant, and Joan Crawford, the director believed that movie stars were really personalities who transcended the roles that they played. When working with Ingrid Bergman on *Casablanca*, he warned the actress that she was "ruining her career" by emoting, and advised her to "simply be Ingrid Bergman and play the same role all the time."

Having recognized an elusive, larger-than-life quality in Day, Curtiz gave her similar advice. When he learned of his new starlet's plan to take lessons from the Warners' acting coach before shooting began on *Romance on the High Seas*, he admonished her against it. He understood that any so-called acting methods would risk making Day self-conscious and likely interfere with her natural gifts. "You have very strong personality," the director told Day in his broken English. "No matter what you do on screen, no matter what kind part you play, it will always be you. What I mean is, the Doris Day will always shine through the part. This will make you big important star."

In spite of Curtiz's reputation for being unpredictable, the making of *Romance on the High Seas* proved relatively clear sailing. With a sixty-day schedule, shooting began on June 2. Day was customarily on the job from 7 a.m. to 6 p.m. "For me," she would recall, "movie work meant a complete change in my way of living. Where the nightclub singer had gone to bed at two in the morning and awakened at two the next afternoon, the movie actress had to be up at 6:00 a.m., made-up and ready by 7:00. Of course I realized it had to be bed by nine o'clock, but I found I couldn't go to sleep at that hour. . . . I'd roll and toss and end up taking a long walk until I was tired, which was precisely at two in the morning. That meant that I was getting four long hours of sleep every night—*great!*"

She recalled, "How naive I was when I made my first picture. . . . I played a girl who took a trip to South America. I kept expecting the cast to take off for the high seas, but the whole thing was shot on Stage 4 at the studio!" Given that it was her first time working on a film, chalk lines were drawn on the set to ensure she would remain within camera range.

Day also suffered the jitters natural for a newcomer. As costar Oscar Levant would recall, "Doris was quite nervous when we were getting ready for shooting the scene where she sings while I accompany her at the piano. [She said,] 'I don't know how to do this.' I said, 'Let's go through it once,' and we did and she did it beautifully."

"On her solo numbers she had no difficulty in dominating the mike and the camera, just as she had dominated the audience as a night-club and radio singer, but when it came to asserting her starring role in a group scene she was always deferring to other actors," reporter George Scullin said a decade later. "Actually, she did not think she was making good, nor did she see any point in raising false hopes that she would ever make a second picture. Every day that she went to the set she was surprised to find herself still a member of the cast."

Given her relative ease as a singer, Day felt more comfortable the night of June 11, when she had her second Columbia recording session, from 8 to 11:15 p.m., at its Los Angeles studio on Vine Street. Her song list included "Just an Old Love of Mine," "A Chocolate Sundae on a Saturday Night," "When Tonight Is Just a Memory," and a postwar novelty, "I'm Still Sitting Under the Apple Tree."

In spite of her insecurity as a novice actress, Day's natural exuberance would be visible in practically every frame in which she appeared in *Romance on the High Seas.* And the young woman who had complained to Hedda Hopper about her lack of a wardrobe could gloat over the twenty-seven gowns that costumer Milo Anderson designed for her first film. But offscreen, it was a different matter, with Day depressed and nervous. While capturing her vivacity on film, Curtiz ironically took to calling his new star "Miss Lachrymose." Given her unease, Curtiz wisely discouraged her from seeing any of the daily rushes. On one occasion, when she was unhappy about how a scene went and asked to see how it came out, Curtiz told her, "I liked it . . . and that's good enough for you."

During the making of *Romance on the High Seas,* Day was staying at the comfortable, if far from luxurious, Plaza Hotel—a far cry from its New York namesake. It was popular with radio people because of its location on Vine Street, near the broadcast studios. Though Day had her lunches at Warners, she grew accustomed to having supper alone at the famed Brown Derby, just across the street from the Plaza. Over dinner and then back in her hotel room later, she would wallow in memories of her two failed marriages. Jane S. Carelton, a childhood friend, would recall "watching her shuffle into the lobby of the Plaza Hotel . . . a lonely, weary, tired girl, disillusion on her face."

Day would come to consider this period of her life a sob story.

Rather than return to her hotel room after dinner, she would walk down Hollywood Boulevard and look in the store windows, feeling vacant and empty. But during the shooting of her first film, Day bonded with her costar Jack Carson, the burly, six-foot-two, lovable lummox of 1940s B pictures, who helped educate her in the ways of the movie lot. "The man actually knows every trick that has ever been invented in Hollywood," Day would recall, "but instead of using 'em on me, he tipped me off to them. 'Get in the camera, honey,' he'd whisper, instead of shoving me out of the way. I wasn't even aware, half the time, where the thing was and so he'd even turn me to put me in range of the big Technicolor camera." She would also say that Carson taught her "more about acting than anyone" else even as she emphasized how "unselfish" and "adorable" he was to her.

"Jack had an innate strength, a vitality and joy that matched [Day's]," observed journalist Linda Griffith, who spent considerable time with both of them on the set of *Romance*. "You just couldn't be lonely when he was around. He was that kind of a man: a big, warm-hearted, all-American guy who gave the impression of being uncomplicated (like Doris), and easygoing, while actually he was very complex indeed (again like Doris). . . . In front of the camera they gave off their marvelous capacities for fun, their apple-pie brand of wholesome vitality. Off camera, they talked and talked and talked—about life and about God. It was obvious to those around them they were falling in love." "I'm crazy about Jack," Day told Griffith. "I don't think people were put into this world to be lonely, and when you're not married you're lonely."

A true affection developed with Carson. "Jack and Doris might have jumped into marriage," speculated Griffith, "if their respective histories had been a little different." Both had already been married twice, and Day, for one, was still smarting from her fresh breakup, wondering if she would ever again be able to make the commitment, which marriage—if not love—entailed. And if Day had Terry, Carson had two children from previous unions. He also had a drinking problem.

Years later, Carson would tell Griffith: "Doris was terribly upset about her divorce and I think the close friendship we developed was a welcome substitute for sitting alone in a hotel room. She didn't like being alone. She was bothered by that marriage breaking up and she was desperately looking for a religion to lean on."

Though Day was no longer a practicing Catholic, she was trying to reconnect to her spiritual side, hoping it would help her regain emotional strength and balance. Though she had been obliged to give up Weidler, in a little over a year she would adopt his newfound faith in Christian Science. And having served as an altar boy in an Episcopalian church during his childhood in Milwaukee, Carson considered himself deeply religious.

While Day lived at the Plaza Hotel and worked on *Romance on the High Seas*, she formed an enduring relationship with Ronnie Cowan, whose husband, Warren, was fast on his way to becoming one of the most powerful PR men in the history of Hollywood. (Ronnie and singer Dinah Shore had been roommates.) They met at Day's "first" Hollywood party, at radio mogul Atwater Kent's, which her press agent, Paul Marsh, compelled her to attend. Day and Cowan instantly hit it off and took to calling each other Zelda and Mabel. "In the early days of our friendship, Doris didn't have a car," recalled Ronnie Cowan, "so I'd pick her up at her hotel, and we'd go on progressive luncheons. We'd usually have soup at the Brown Derby and wind up at Schwab's Pharmacy for cheesecake."

"After they met, Doris and Ronnie became fast friends for the next twenty years," recalled Warren Cowan. "They each had the same kind of 'pixie' sense of humor, and they got along very, very well. You know, I don't know how many true friends Doris had. She had hundreds of acquaintances, but Ronnie was one of her closest friends." Throughout her life, Day would know a great many people but remain desperately lonely in spite of all the friendships.

*   *   *

Curtiz decided Day wouldn't do any dancing in her first picture, and put it off for a later one, when it would have more impact. While *Romance* was being filmed, the shrewd director made an important decision that would be a boon to Day's film career: the picture would end with Day's reprise of "It's Magic," instead of the negligible song "Two Lovers Met in the Night."

The film's final title was changed to *Romance on the High Seas* (from *Romance in High C*) on November 11, 1947, and it was released under the alternate name of *It's Magic* in England, where it would prove to be a huge success—and where Day would win the devotion of ever-widening and loyal fan clubs.

Though it may strike some as a relic from another era, *Romance on the High Seas* is an entertaining diversion—if not much else. (It remains to this day one of critic Rex Reed's favorite films. He continues to watch it with regularity and can cite line, chapter, and verse from many a scene.) The convoluted plot is built around mistaken identities, when Elvira Kent (Janis Paige) decides to send a stand-in for herself—Georgia Garrett (Day)—on a cruise, so she can remain in New York and spy on her husband. But no matter how lame the story, the film is really an excuse for the sprightly score by Jule Styne and Sammy Cahn, which turns decidedly Latin once the picture arrives south of the border. Curtiz might have dubbed his new discovery "Miss Lachrymose," but Day is nothing less than irrepressible from the first notes of her opening nightclub number, "I'm in Love, I'm in Love, I'm in Love." And if her exuberance evokes Betty Hutton, Day's beaming face and cascading blonde tresses make for an unmistakable resemblance to Ginger Rogers—as many a reviewer would point out.

A port of call in Cuba prompts a calypso number, "The Tourist Trade," as well as the film's big hit, "It's Magic," introduced in Spanish by a roving guitar player in a restaurant. He conveniently provides English lyrics to Georgia, who proceeds to sing them to Peter, at their table. The song, which she sings a second time in the picture, became Day's second enormous hit, after "Sentimental Journey."

With the ship's band, Day performs the film's jazzy swing number, "Put 'Em in a Box, Tie 'Em with a Ribbon," on the journey to Trinidad, during which Carson has his star turn with "Run, Run, Run" ("When you see a pretty woman . . ."), sung with a Jamaican accent and accompanied by another roaming band. For her final rendition of "It's Magic," Day's tight-fitting gown highlights her terrific figure, and she wields a chiffon kerchief in her hand, a conventional prop for singers of the period. Though the musical numbers were "created and directed" by Busby Berkeley, Warners' great choreographer of the 1930s, he was either loafing or slumming—or both. The only hint of his typically surreal techniques appears in the closing shot, as Georgia and Peter (Carson) perch atop a pedestal—like bride-and-groom figurines on a wedding cake—while a conga line of revelers swirls beneath them.

* * *

Shortly before the filming of *Romance on the High Seas* was completed on August 4, 1947, a full week ahead of schedule, Al Levy arranged another major assignment for Day. As confirmed by a contract dated July 22, she was to become the regular female vocalist on Frank Sinatra's *Your Hit*

Parade, a radio program sponsored by Lucky Strike, beginning on September 6, 1947. Once he realized her potential, Levy drew up a new contract with Day in September 1947 that increased his fees with escalating clauses, from 10 percent of her earnings up to $100,000, to 15 percent on earnings over $150,000, and 20 percent on any over $175,000. The agreement allowed Day to take on other jobs beyond *Your Hit Parade*. In August, she was a guest on Jack Smith's Procter & Gamble radio show for which she received $325 per appearance. But the terms of her contract with Curtiz mandated that half of her earnings from radio appearances went to MCP.

Day moved back to New York for the thirty-minute weekly show and remained with it for eleven weeks. According to Day, she "hated every minute of it . . . because I really disliked that kind of big-time radio program, performed live before a big audience in a big theater." She also hated being back in New York, even though she was staying at the upscale Plaza Hotel.

Day made a sprightly recording that fall of another song by Styne and Cahn, a polka from their Broadway hit *High Button Shoes*: "Poppa, Won't You Dance with Me." But even while her career as a singer seemed to be getting stronger and stronger, the American Tobacco Company declined to renew Day's contract for *Your Hit Parade*, reportedly because they felt her singing style was too similar to Sinatra's—whatever that meant. Perhaps the competitive Sinatra, in a move that proved to be at his own expense, pushed her out of the show. Its ratings began to drop several weeks after Day left—in January 1948 it was number eighteen on the Nielsen ratings—and continued to plummet over the course of the next year. By the spring of 1949, Sinatra was having problems of his own—with his sponsor, his show, his voice, and his love life. His spectacular comeback briefly preceded his signing a contract, five years later, to costar with Day in *Young at Heart*, her eighteenth picture.

Daydreamer

✳

*"Strip away the phony tinsel of Hollywood and
you find the real tinsel underneath."*

—OSCAR LEVANT

*"Any girl in the audience could be Doris Day,
and she could be any girl."*

—AL LEVY

Though Doris Day had been a last-minute replacement in her first film, from the beginning, director Michael Curtiz clearly recognized that he was working with a star in the making. Before the release of *Romance on the High Seas*, he cast her in his next musical project, and as the producer as well as director of Day's second film, the decision was entirely his. As early as July 7, 1947, the *Los Angeles Times* announced that Curtiz purchased the rights to *Forever and Always* for a "film musical" starring his "recent discovery, Doris Day." Though preliminary wardrobe and makeup tests were made in September, the real work on the film didn't begin until March 1948, by which time it had been renamed *My Dream Is Yours*.

My Dream Is Yours was a Technicolor reworking of *Twenty Million Sweethearts*, a trite Warners musical of 1934 starring Dick Powell and Ginger Rogers, which was itself based on *Hot Air*, a vaporous story by Jerry Wald and Paul Moss. ("Hot Air" was a colloquial reference to radio.) The updated screenplay by Harry Kurnitz and Dane Lussier featured characters that proved as generic as their names: Jack Carson played Doug Blake, a Hollywood talent scout and manager who, in the plot's opening gambit, loses his prime client, popular singer Gary Mitchell, to a new radio sponsor. In his search for a successor, Blake discovers Martha Gibson, played by Day.

As he said he would, Al Levy contributed quite a bit to the story, which may be why Curtiz promised to acknowledge him as associate producer—without, in the end, doing so. (According to the Screen Writers Guild, seven writers worked on *My Dream*—"exclusive" of H. Kurnitz's contribution.) Levy's contributions to the story might explain why some of the circumstances surrounding Gibson so strongly resemble Day's real life.

In order for Gibson to establish herself as a singer in Hollywood, she has to leave her little boy, Freddie, with her Uncle Charlie in New York—just as Day had left Terry with her mother in Cincinnati. (The most beloved uncle of Day's youth was named Charlie, as well.) Moreover, just as Day ostensibly got her big breakthrough into films by singing at a Hollywood party, so Gibson nearly gets hers the same way. Perhaps this film provided material for the legend of Day's discovery. As with a number of other incidents in Day's life, it sometimes becomes hard to separate fact from fiction. And if *My Dream Is Yours* is basically about the birth of a star, it confirmed Day's emergence as one.

As shot by Ernest Haller and Wilfred M. Cline, the film has a certain period focus on Hollywood: Not only does Gibson have lunch with the suave Mitchell at the Brown Derby, but the Coconut Grove figures prominently. Opening aerial shots of the California coastline gradually zoom in on deco Hollywood, as a voice-over prepares us for the film's self-mocking yet pretentious tone: "This is the mighty Pacific, its breakers coming to rest at last on the beaches of Southern California. To this unspoiled paradise came the great explorers. Kings and conquerors fought nature and themselves for a share of the treasures of this earth. The great American empire moved steadily west as man learned of the riches to be found here. A great city grew up as the land and sea gave up its riches to the newcomers. And when the earth could give no more, new kingdoms were carved out of air."

In one of the film's more quirky sequences, Blake begins to read a Bugs Bunny story to Freddie at bedtime, when the story suddenly springs to life as a dream sequence that finds Day and Carson cavorting with animated figures. Though it was not Curtiz's idea originally, he "had to fight for its retention against Warner's pressure for an all-cartoon scene."

Shooting began on March 29, 1948, when Day was on the set from 9:45 a.m. to 5:55 p.m. As conveyed in an April 15 note from Al Alleborn, who kept the daily production book, there was some tension on the set: "More than likely you will get a squawk from Curtiz about me and the entire company. . . . in back of all this crabbiness of Mike's and picking on everyone, especially [art director] Bob Haas and myself, is the fact he has [cinematographer] Ernie Haller (and I hope Ernie stays with the picture). Also, he has his brother, Dave, on the set and he always comes up with ideas and suggestions, which don't help matters." But according to Day, Curtiz "had a wild sense of humor and he loved making jokes. Then he would laugh at his own jokes and blush, he blushed all the time."

Harold E. Swisher, the motion picture editor of United Press Radio, visited the set to interview Day, whom he referred to as "the number one Cinderella in Hollywood today." "With her very first movie already in the hit class, Doris realizes she's a mighty lucky girl, and isn't afraid to say so. As she put it: 'I think I'm especially lucky because I recognize the fact that I've had good luck—and I hope I never forget it. I'm always asking myself, "Why did Michael Curtiz pick me?" And the answer always comes up, "It was just plain luck." As if to say she was afraid of losing her good fortune, Day pointed out a good-luck charm—an ebony figure of the Chinese god of Happiness—in her dressing room. "I rub his tummy every morning."

The production was declared finished on April 28, five days behind schedule. Even before *My Dream Is Yours* was released, a national survey of film exhibitors, conducted by the *Motion Picture Herald* in September, chose Day as one of ten "Stars of Tomorrow," on the basis of *Romance on the High Seas* alone. *American Magazine* also chose Day as a "Future Star" and featured her in a color photo, clad in a red plaid shirt, penny loafers, and blue jeans rolled up just below the knee. Seated on a lawn, she can be seen hugging a boxer puppy.

Not all the press proved welcoming, however. Louella Parsons got wind of Day's having missed work because she was ill while making *My Dream Is Yours* and reported it in her syndicated column. Parsons claimed that "Warner Brothers' newest sweetheart had become swell-headed and spoiled after her quick success, and was showing up three and four hours late for rehearsals on her second picture." Parsons's antipathy toward Day may have stemmed from the columnist's ongoing rivalry with Hedda Hopper, who had proved a Day enthusiast from the beginning.

*   *   *

With her second picture nearly completed, Day was feeling financially secure for the first time in her life. She was also eager to be reunited with her son and mother. In May 1948, she bought a modest, furnished house at 4523 Sancola, in North Hollywood, for $28,000. (It would eventually be torn down to make way for the Ventura Freeway.) Before Alma and Terry arrived, Day had filed for divorce from George Weidler. "Miss Day accuses Weidler of 'inflicting grievous mental and physical suffering' upon her, while she remained an 'always dutiful and loving wife,'" declared a story in the *Los Angeles Times*. "Separation took place on April 10, 1947, according to the petition prepared by Atty. Eugene S. Goodwin. The court was informed that a financial settlement was signed a year ago."

Two months later, Day had second thoughts. As reported, once again in the *Los Angeles Times*, "[She] wants to make sure she really desires a divorce from George Weidler before she steps into a courtroom." That, at any rate, was the reason she gave for failing to appear at the scheduled hearing. Day had not seen Weidler for approximately a year, when he called out of the blue, a week earlier, and suggested they get together. Since they had last seen each other, Day's life had been transformed by her growing success as a movie star. Now Weidler had become unrecognizable to Day. In place of the meek man who never seemed to know where he was headed—both literally and figuratively—was someone now very sure of himself.

"Something's happened to you," Day told Weidler. "I don't know what it is, George, but something's happened to you that I wish could happen to me. You're strong, and I always thought I was the strong one." Weidler explained that he had discovered Christian Science and how it had changed his life. The transformation in Weidler was compelling enough for Day herself to turn to Christian Science. Mary Baker Eddy's heal-thyself philosophy instantly appealed to Day, who, along with Weidler, had been a heavy smoker and an occasional drinker. Day was drawn to Christian Science "because I'd been thinking that I should be happier than I am," she would tell film scholar Molly Haskell decades later. "There has to be a better way, I thought. One ought to be able to control one's thinking instead of having depressions—one day you're up, the next you're down. I didn't want that kind of life, but I didn't know how to change it." Though Day would claim to be a practicing Christian Scientist, for the next few decades she would drift in and out of strictly abiding by its precepts.

Day recalled being nervous about the arrival of her son in North Hollywood that summer. "I wondered how it was going to be—having

Terry with me permanently," she said. "It came to me suddenly that the important things of life cannot be bought with money—only with humble effort. I now had the professional success for which I had been struggling. I was secure, financially, for the first time in my adult life. But here I was, more nervous than I had been the day I asked director Mike Curtiz for my first job in motion pictures, wondering what a six-year-old boy would think of me—his mother—and the home I had provided for him." Indeed, Day was so anxious about her reunion with Terry that she found a way of effectively postponing it, shipping him off to summer camp soon after he arrived. Many years later, Terry would claim that he had only a single memory of his mother before moving to Hollywood when seven years old. "The fact is, I wasn't quite sure who my mother was until I came to live with her," recalled Terry. "'Mother' was just a word, without meaning. My grandmother was my total parent."

It was shortly before they left Cincinnati that Alma relented and let her grandson get together with his father, Al Jorden, with or without Day's knowledge. It was the first time in a long while that Terry had laid eyes on his father, and it would prove to be the last.

On July 4, 1948, shortly after Day settled in her new home, Louella Parsons covered the news of Terry's arrival. Having recently been gratuitously nasty to the star, this time Parsons spoke of Day in glowing terms. When Day arrived at the studio for the interview, she was wearing a baseball cap. As Day explained, it was to keep her hair in place while she drove there in her "open car." According to Parsons's column, Day's son "Terry Jorden" had only just arrived in Hollywood and was living with his mother. Day felt compelled to say why she waited more than a year to be reunited with Terry. "You see, everything happened so fast. . . . I have never been on the stage. I had never made a picture. All I ever did was sing with a band, and on the radio."

Parsons boldly asked Day if she had had a real "romance" with Jack Carson while working on *My Dream Is Yours*. The budding star replied, "I was crazy about him. . . . We went out every night together, but then we both realized we weren't for each other, and since then we have been very good friends. He helped me a lot." When asked if she might ever get married again, Day told Parsons, "I don't think I'll marry. . . . Why should I—I've got my boy, and three times is out, you know."

Perhaps Day was more ambivalent about remarrying than she was willing to admit even to herself. While neighbors could glimpse Terry playing ball with his mother in their new yard on Sancola—at least while photographers were there to capture them at it—Alma wanted the boy to have a real father, and a part of his mother did, too.

*　　*　　*

Though made in the middle of 1947, *Romance on the High Seas* wouldn't be released until the following summer, when Day was establishing her first home in Hollywood. Within the booming record business in 1948, when Columbia introduced the "long-playing album" (i.e., 33 1/3 rpm), Peggy Lee's "Manana" was the number one song for nine weeks, as was Dinah Shore's "Buttons and Bows." Day would have four hits, including the number one "Love Somebody," her duet with Buddy Clark. On May 6, 1948, she reunited with Sinatra to record their popular version of Irving Berlin's "Let's Take an Old Fashioned Walk," a couple of days before the crooner began filming *Take Me Out to the Ball Game* at Metro. May 28 was Sinatra's last appearance on *Your Hit Parade*.

While Sinatra's singing career at Columbia was in something of a tailspin, Day's was just taking off—even if Al Levy's partners at first failed to realize it. The previous January (1948), *Look* magazine ran a feature on the upcoming movie star, predicting that she "has one of Hollywood's brightest futures. Although she is now an established singer—after a spot on NBC's Hit Parade with Sinatra—and is a Columbia recording artist, movies are a new kick." In addition to mentioning *Romance on the High Seas*, the article predicted "she'll make 'The '49ers' next" (a film that never came to be), and quoted Day as saying, "Of course I'm getting a house in Hollywood . . . I love it here."

Recognizing that Day had a fan base from her singing career, the publicity department at Warners promoted *Romance* by suggesting that distributors contact radio disc jockeys "about an 'ALL-DAY' program featuring tunes from the film"; a radio contest for listeners to "identify Doris Day recordings from a group of un-announced female vocalists"; or to sponsor a contest, "Find Doris Day Double—looks or singing ability. Finals on stage opening night!" In the cornball vernacular of the period, Day was promoted as "Gal-amorous" in the trailer for *Romance on the High Seas*. Indeed, there was so much advance buzz that Day received 130 fan letters at Warners by the end of February 1948, a good four months before her first film even opened. "Nobody had the instant stardom that Doris had," Rex Reed declared a half century later.

However, some critics found Day's ebullience and eagerness to please over-the-top, when they were initially exposed to it on celluloid. In his review of *Romance on the High Seas* for the *New York Times*, Bosley Crowther dismissed Day's performance as merely "bouncy." "Maybe [she] has ability and personality," he wrote, "but as shown in this picture at the Strand, she has no more than a vigorous disposition which hits the screen with a thud." Worse still, he added that while Warner Brothers was hoping to have landed a new Betty Hutton, Day lacked her "vital style." Nor did Crowther spare Curtiz, claiming that the director had "wasted the few minor talents that he had in a most provoking way."

But taking their cues from Warners' publicity department, the vast majority of the reviewers heralded the newcomer, recognizing some of the qualities that would eventually earn her celluloid fame as the number-one female star of the century. In the *Detroit News*, Al Weitschat wrote, "Miss Day lends a refreshing lift to a trite plot which sags noticeably whenever she isn't around." Orval Hopkins declared in the *Washington Post* that Day is "an engaging young singer and comedienne [who] gets off to a good start in this, her first picture . . ." John L. Scott was even more fulsome in the *Los Angeles Times*: "Miss Day is not only introduced but is practically the whole show on Warner theater screens. [She] reveals definite comedy talent in addition to her distinctive way of singing. . . . In her first role Miss Day is given arduous duty. She handles it expertly and should have quite a screen future."

Still others declared Day's film debut "impressive" and "brilliant." In the *New York World-Telegram*, Alton Cook was emphatic that Day was a hit, even if the film in which she made her debut was not: "Now that Miss Day's movie career has been launched, we certainly look forward to seeing her again—but with a fervent hope that fate will bless her with a better picture. Even a very talented girl needs help from her fellow workers." As the reviewers were sure to note, Day was famed as a vocalist and recording star, and many thought her superior to a film that seemed barely to contain her. Such judgments would become the case in critiques of a good number of the pictures she made in the early and later parts of her film career.

Perhaps no one was more impressed with Day's notices than Marty Melcher. Along with Dick Dorso, Melcher was one of Al Levy's partners at Century Artists. The first indication in the Warner Brothers archive of Melcher's involvement in Day's business affairs occurred in August 1947: a contract for a radio-show performance bore the signature of "Martin Melcher for Al Levy." Nearly a year later, and within a month of the opening of *Romance*, he would fail to accompany Patty Andrews, his wife, on her trip to London to perform at the Palladium with her sisters, collectively known as the Andrews Sisters.

According to Hedda Hopper, Melcher had been running the lights for the Andrews Sisters in the mid-1940s when Lew Levy, Maxine's husband (no relation to Al), advanced Dick Dorso funds to open Century Artists and get the pushy and crude Melcher "out from under his feet" and occupied with others. "Marty became the second partner in Century Artists as part of Lew's deal with Dorso [and] took on the sisters as clients." Though the world would come to believe they had been married for years, Melcher and Patty Andrews had been wed only nine months when *Romance on the High Seas* opened.

Melcher was poised to pounce once Weidler was legally removed from the scene. As he became a more involved, hands-on manager for Day, Melcher "got into the habit of dropping by Doris's home and having dinner with the family." Tentatively at first, Melcher made it his business to assume the man's role in the new Day household. He understood that one way to get to his client's heart was through Terry, whom he quickly befriended and took on a fishing trip. He knew that he also had to win over Alma, and showered his future mother-in-law with gifts. In the meantime, Melcher was still maintaining the façade of a happy relationship with his wife. On Day's birthday in 1951, Melcher would become her third husband.

*   *   *

One of the first of a growing avalanche of agreements for Doris Day— what would come to be known as "tie-ins"—was offered in a letter of July 7, 1948, to the Loft Candy Corporation, consenting to its use of Day's name and likeness to advertise its products. A letter signed by Day was sent the same day to Michael Curtiz Productions (MCP): "I request that you cancel any and all agreements and other arrangements which you heretofore may have made with Liggett & Myers Tobacco CO. and any and all other persons for my appearance on television programs advertising Chesterfield Cigarettes." In the coming years, Day would often say she gave up cigarettes and alcohol in conjunction with her growing interest in Christian Science.

Of far greater consequence was the contract drawn up with [Bob] Hope Productions on August 4, 1948, encompassing Day's services for one "thirty-minute radio program per week," as an "actress and/or singer, as we may direct." The contract went into effect on September 14 and covered 156 consecutive weeks: $1,000 each for the first fifty-two weeks, $1,350 for the next fifty-two, and $1,750 for the next fifty-two. Half of Day's earnings went to Michael Curtiz Productions. The show would be broadcast from Los Angeles by NBC.

Before her work with Bob Hope began, Day made another film. *It's a Great Feeling*, Day's third picture with Warners, was also her first with director David Butler, a former actor of the stage and silent screen who would become known for second-rate musicals. Butler would direct Day in five pictures, at least one of which, *Calamity Jane*, has a place among her best. *It's a Great Feeling*, however, proved to be rather conventional.

Since Day's contract was with Michael Curtiz Productions, a loan-out agreement was drawn up with Warner Brothers on August 19, 1948, when *It's a Great Feeling* still bore the original title, *Two Guys and a Gal*. The story by I.A.L. Diamond was basically a spoof of the Hollywood studio system, and more specifically of Warner Brothers. The opening narration says: "Just a few miles from Hollywood is the largest studio in the world, the home of Warner Brothers Pictures. This is the entrance to a world of glamour and enchantment."

Director David Butler as well as Curtiz would make cameo appearances in the film—along with, seemingly, everyone else on the Warner lot. A thick file of "Artists releases for services without compensation" in the archives includes signatures from Curtiz, Gary Cooper, Joan Crawford, Danny Kaye, Errol Flynn, Ronald Reagan, Jane Wyman, Patricia Neal, Eleanor Parker, Ray Heindorf, Raoul Walsh, and King Vidor. Even the two male leads, Jack Carson and Dennis Morgan, play themselves in the picture.

Day's hair tests for *It's a Great Feeling* were made as early as June 30, 1948, but the picture didn't get under way until August 23. Apart from an internal memo about Warner choreographer Leroy Prinz "getting restless," the production proceeded without incident. It was completed on October 16—a week ahead of schedule.

According to Butler, despite having already made two pictures with Curtiz, Day still lacked basic knowledge about performing before a camera. "[Doris] needed a lot of direction then, and she took it very well," Butler remembered. "She used to come in a door and run across the set so fast you couldn't pan with her. She [also] used to have a habit of letting people upstage her, which didn't go [well] with me because I had so much experience as an actor." Butler recognized, in other words, that Day was a naïf, in need of direction.

"Another thing that Doris Day needed experience with," continued Butler, "when they'd be sitting down in a two shot, and she'd have to look at the other party that she was acting with, she'd just turn her eyes and look. And when you do that, the camera picks up nothing but the whites of your eyes. But if you have had experience, you will just turn your head a little bit as you talk, and your eyes turn with you. Then you don't see the whites. You see the whole eye. So I used to explain those things to her, and she got very apt at it. She got to be very good . . . She has a lot of natural ability."

It's a Great Feeling was not only Day's third picture, but also her third with Jack Carson, with whom she had grown increasingly at ease. Carson noted that Day had by then become an avid practitioner of Christian Science and felt that she had "brightened" under its influence. "Of course, things changed rapidly for Doris," Carson said, looking back at their first three pictures together. "That first picture [*Romance on the High Seas*] really launched her. Two films later she was the star and I was the supporting player," he added, without a hint of resentment.

Day had stopped dating Carson and had begun seeing Ronald Reagan by the time work started on this picture. According to one Reagan biographer, Laurence Leamer, he had dinner with her about the time that Jane Wyman, his wife, filed for divorce, in May 1948. The actor "spent the evening talking about Janie," wrote Leamer, who added that Reagan's name was also "linked with Ruth Roman, Shirley Ballard, Kay Stewart and Ann Sothern."

Edmund Morris, Reagan's official biographer, would write: "My research cards show [Reagan] stepping out with at least sixteen different young and beautiful actresses, from Doris Day and Rhonda Fleming to the peachy and not-yet-legal Piper Laurie. God knows how many more there were or how many came back to spend the night with him in his hillside apartment, with its celestial view of the sparkling city. . . . He did admit, once, to sleeping with so many girls that the morning came when he did not know who one of them was."

Though Day doesn't appear in Reagan's 748-page autobiography, she recalled their dating: "There was a little place on La Cienega that had a small band and a small dance floor where he often took me. He danced well and he had a pleasant personality. So I inevitably enjoyed going out with Ronnie. When he wasn't dancing, he was talking. It really wasn't conversation, it was rather talking at you, sort of long discourses on subjects that interested him. I remember telling him that he should be touring the country making speeches." She recalled the view from his apartment: "I thought it was lovely, and I decided that that was the area where I wanted to live, high above the city lights with that celestial view." But she never would.

* * *

No sooner had she completed work on *It's a Great Feeling* than Day began performing with Bob Hope. She sang her first hit, "Sentimental Journey," on his radio show on October 19, 1948. Hope introduced Day variously as "America's heartthrob of the jukeboxes" and "Warner Bros. First Lady of Song." When his show aired on November 20, 1948, Day's lone song was her latest hit, "It's Magic." In the obligatory skit, Hope played a "college football hero . . . a triple-threat man [who] couldn't run, pass or kick." When he meets "Doris" in biology class, she says, "You're new in school, aren't you?" "How'd you know?" says Hope. "You're carrying books," replies Day. Three decades later, Day would recall: "I once did a radio show with Bob Hope, and was so nervous I was getting sick to my stomach, but Bob said, 'I don't believe you. Not after all the experience you've had.'"

As much as Day said she loved to work with Bob Hope, she also confided that once she began making films and stopped "working in front of people," it became increasingly "scary" for her to do so. Beyond recognizing that it was a "freaky thing" and that it was "horrible" for her, she couldn't really account for it or understand why she was so "nervous" about even the prospect of performing in front of people. But such insecurities would haunt her for the rest of her life.

Of course, Day sounded better than she imagined. On a broadcast of December 7, 1948, the *Bob Hope Show* introduced Day as "the cover-girl of *Modern Television and Radio* magazine." With the Les Brown band, she sang a plaintive rendition of "My Darling." For the humor skit, Day and Hope went on a Christmas shopping expedition for Bing Crosby, who was a guest star.

On Christmas, Day and Alma held an open-house party for Les Brown and some of his band members. "They came to cheer up mother," Day would tell Jane Ardmore, "because she was crying for Cincinnati." Later that week, Day was a guest star on Al Jolson's radio show, broadcast live

from Palm Springs on December 30. Before Day sang "It's Magic," her
host asked if Bob Hope ever made "any, you know, romantic advances."
"He kissed me once, but I'm never gonna let it happen again," replied
Day, as part of the prewritten, vaudevillian patter. "Why not?" inquired
Jolson. "[Because] he left a nose dent in my forehead."

Though the show seemed to go smoothly, there was at least one
behind-the-scenes glitch: Day's manager failed to secure the studio's advance permission for her participation—an infringement on her contract
with Michael Curtiz Productions and exactly the sort of misstep that
would lead to increasing ill will between Day and her employers. The
problem may have been that by then Melcher had taken control of Day
and her affairs, perhaps without having completely familiarized himself
with her contractual obligations. Her contract had been negotiated by Al
Levy—the man who had created Doris Day only to be slowly but surely
deposed by Melcher, who was clearly in over his head from the very beginning. Over the next two decades, many would come to despise having
to contend with the man's insecurity-disguised-as-arrogance.

6

"It Seems Like I've Always Known Him"

✳

---

*"And they'll say I'm naive/As a babe to believe/
Any fable I hear from a person in pants!"*

—OSCAR HAMMERSTEIN II

*"If this girl hits like I think she will, we can make
a whole business around her alone."*

—AL LEVY

"He was like a hometown boy," recalled Marty Melcher's cousin Helen Maislen, who went out with him when they were in high school. "I was amazed when he went on to Hollywood, and the life he had there. He was warm and friendly, very social. But I didn't think he was sophisticated enough to move in those circles. He didn't have any business education. He was a very small-town boy."

"All the Melcher boys were handsome," said Maislen's sister, Lillian Glickman. More than just handsome, Melcher grew to be six-foot-three. He would help create his future wife's all-American image and fed that image by looking—and playing—the part of the all-American man and husband.

Although Melcher later had a reputation as the Svengali to Doris Day, other aspects of his personality confirm that he could be as naive as she. Matthew Melcher was born on August 1, 1915, the child of a prominent Orthodox Jewish family in North Adams, Massachusetts. His later association with Day would make him something of a local celebrity: whenever he and Day visited his hometown, it was major news in the local papers with, for instance, an accompanying photo of Day raking leaves at her in-laws'. Several of Melcher's cousins saw him as a rube and a pushover, and his fame as a shrewd businessman of dubious tactics difficult to grasp. If anything, Melcher's assertive manner and aggressive negotiating methods were, perhaps, a defense against his insecurity. He had to labor to appear to be a "starker," or tough guy.

Melcher's father, Alter, came from Russia. His mother, Minnie—originally from Minsk—was only seventeen when she married Alter in 1905. A year later, Harmon, the first of seven children, was born. Alter was a shoemaker, who parlayed his trade into a dry goods and men's work-clothing store called Melcher's, on Center Street in downtown North Adams, where Matthew (Marty) worked during high school. Matthew, the sixth child, came right after Jack (nicknamed Yonny) and just before Sam, the youngest. Sophie was the only daughter. Another brother, Mendel, tragically was hit by a car in front of the store and killed when he was three. Of all his siblings, Marty would prove closest to Harry, the second born.

"All of us kids worked in the store, off and on," recalled ninety-three-year-old Jack Melcher in 2006, admitting that he was not very close to Marty when they were growing up. "We were two years apart, and that's a competitive age."

Yet another cousin, Harold Less, recalled that Minnie Melcher "had the door open all the time for anybody who wanted to come in and have a bite to eat. All those shamos [synagogue caretakers], who would travel from city to city, collecting money for their little congregations—they always stayed at the Melchers on weekends. She'd put them up and feed them. When you'd go over to visit, there would always be some guy with a big beard, dovening, in the living room."

Several relatives who were frequent guests at the Melchers would remember that the "welcoming" Minnie had "a good sense of humor," as opposed to Alter, who was "very quiet" and "kept to himself." The adult Marty Melcher would demonstrate the characteristics of both his parents, depending on his mood. Perhaps part of what drew Day and Melcher together was their similar experiences with parents, so very different from one another.

Melcher was a self-described "average student" in high school, where he turned his height to advantage by playing basketball. Shortly after graduating from Drury High in January of 1934, he moved to New York, where, in the midst of the Depression, he was fortunate enough to secure a job with Socony-Vacuum Oil Co. In 1959, a lengthy report on his background in his local town paper claimed that "he started at $18.80

per week and was being groomed for a career foreign sales job with the company in China. But after three years Mr. Melcher decided his fortune was to be found in Hollywood rather than the Orient. Once in the film capital he became a press agent and recalled handling such celebrities as Ben Blue and Martha Raye. From press agentry he went into radio packaging, from roughly 1937 to 1940, and then became a radio agent. In 1940 and 1941 the North Adams boy managed the singing Andrews Sisters, then at the height of their fame, and during this time was married to one of them, Patty Andrews." This, at least, was the hyperbole palmed off by Edward Matesky, in the *North Adams Transit.*

Melcher's cousin Matt Gabriner would recall seeing him at a night-club in Newark, New Jersey, in 1938 or 1939, with his first wife, who was also a singer. "But she was a wannabe," said Gabriner. ". . . No Patty Andrews or Doris Day." Gabriner also claimed that, typical of the times, Melcher "tried to pass himself off as not being Jewish." During World War II, he served as a sergeant in the Special Services branch in New York City, where one of his jobs was organizing shows for the army. Though he apparently worked with the Andrews Sisters as a road manager either before or after his service, he did not marry Patty Andrews until October 19, 1947—when they had a poolside wedding at Maxene Andrews's ranch. This was some months after Melcher had met Doris Day, and less than a year before he began to seize control of her career—betraying Patty Andrews in the process.

* * *

Though no one can dispute that Marty Melcher became the most significant figure in Doris Day's life, the circumstances behind the beginning of their complicated relationship are riddled with ambiguities and conflicting reports. The confusion was perpetrated by both Day and Melcher, who, at various points in their lives, would offer different accounts of how they met. They may have had good reason for muddying the waters to cover up Melcher's appropriation of the client of his partner, Al Levy, and making her his wife. Though Melcher had married Patty Andrews when she and her sisters were still one of the country's most popular singing groups, once he realized that Day, given her looks and her talent, had far greater cash potential, Melcher quickly switched allegiances. Levy had, after all, recently signed a contract anticipating earnings for Day beyond $175,000 a year. Day herself would come to downplay the notion

that their relationship was a romantic one, even—or maybe especially—at
the beginning.

In a town that famously micromanaged its stars' images by manipulating the media, Melcher would outdo the studios' publicity people by
controlling everything written about his wife and client, Doris Day. During Day's heyday, from the mid-1950s to the mid-1960s, she and Melcher
would grant interviews only to those publications that gave them final
approval of any article produced about her. One of their very first con-
trivances was the story of how they met.

Melcher initially appears in Day's memoir when she describes going
to his Century Artists office to register a complaint about Al Levy stalking her, which seems especially curious in light of everything else that
has been written about Day and Melcher's first encounter. When, late
in 1950—or several months before they were married—a reporter asked
them how they met, neither Day nor Melcher could remember: "Gosh,"
said Day, "he was my agent—and it seems like I've always known him."
Four years later, in what seems to be an otherwise reliable article based
on interviews with both Day and Melcher, Ida Zeitlin wrote: "The first
date [between Marty and Doris] wasn't a date. . . . To Melcher, it loomed
as a pain in the neck. 'I've been called out of town,' Levy told him. 'Will
you take Doris Day to her broadcast tonight, see that everything goes
smoothly?' Hooked, Marty canceled his plans as any agent must for a
profitable client, saw the job through, prepared to drive the girl home.
. . . Under her native friendliness, Marty thawed a little. He found this
blonde Miss Huckleberry Finn (as she'd been tagged by her fans) easy
to talk to. He found himself wanting to talk to her again, so he asked her
to dinner."

That same year, 1954, Melcher told yet another journalist that he was
involved in selecting Day's songs for her act at the Little Club and that
he had once pinch-hit for Al Levy and taken Day to a recording session.
"Neither of them was in the mood for romance," added Ernst Jacobi.

Again in 1954, Day told the *Daily News*: "One night Al was tied
up and asked Marty to escort me to a radio broadcast. That's how we
met." But in a piece to which she contributed in 1957 in the *American
Weekly*—which includes other erroneous claims—Day herself said that she
first met Melcher at the Little Club: "At rehearsals I sang and cried at
the same time. That's when I met Marty. He was head of the agency that
represented me and he happened to be in New York. He took charge of
rehearsals and was efficient and reassuring; but I heard what he told the

manager of the Little Club. 'Unload her,' he told him. 'We'd better not get involved.'"

In conflict with this startling and implausible claim is the certainty that it was Al Levy who accompanied his client Day to the Little Club in New York, just as it was Levy who continued to negotiate most, if not all, of her business affairs well into 1948. Nor does Day's assertion, in 1957, that Melcher was at the Little Club a decade earlier appear anywhere else. But as both Zeitlin's and Jacobi's earlier articles explain, it would have been only natural for Melcher to stand in for Levy at one event or another—and also to check out his partner's new client either at a singing engagement or on a movie set in 1947.

Given what transpired, Melcher's reported advice to "unload" Day is also surprising. But it reappears in several places, including what is, oddly enough, the most thorough and valid account of how Melcher developed his relationship with Day, by Hedda Hopper. The high-hatted Hollywood columnist's office was next door to Creative Artists, where she observed the developing dynamics among Day, Levy, and Melcher as they unfolded. According to Hopper, after Sinatra dropped Day from *Your Hit Parade* in December 1947, both Melcher and Dick Dorso, the third partner of Levy and Melcher's, complained about her being a drain on the firm. "Why do you waste your time on this dame?" they asked. "She's not the most beautiful girl in the world; she's loaded with freckles; she's got no clothes sense; she's going nowhere." (In fact, her first film—long finished by then—had yet to be released.) Comparing Day to Alice Faye, Levy told his partners, "People could identify themselves with Alice, and they can with Doris. . . . Because any girl in the audience could be Doris Day, and she could be any girl. . . . If this girl hits like I think she will, we can make a whole business around her alone."

According to Hopper, a crucial turning point occurred the following fall, when Levy asked Day to perform for a benefit at the Hollywood Bowl as a favor for a local disc jockey. "She agreed, as usual then, but didn't show up for rehearsal with the band," noted Hopper. "[Levy] telephoned to ask why. 'Marty says I don't have to do the benefit,' she answered. 'What's he got to do with it? [Levy asked.] He hasn't been in the picture much so far.' 'He told me you'll be traveling around a lot and getting other things. He said it will be best if he starts taking care of part of my business in case things come up when you're away.' 'That makes sense,' said Al. 'Okay.' That was the last time he had anything to do [with] Doris Day.

"[Levy] left for Century Artists' New York office with his wife, Ruth, shortly after," continued Hopper, "switching places with Dick Dorso. When the Andrews Sisters went to London for a big season at the Palladium [in July 1948], Marty Melcher stayed home and got to know Doris well. Later, his marriage to Patty Andrews ended in a heartbreaking divorce for her. . . . In New York on the Christmas Eve after he and Dorso had exchanged assignments, Al received a call from Melcher: 'I just want to tell you that as of now you're out of Century Artists. Doris and I have decided we don't need you, and that's it.'

"After Christmas, Al Levy walked down the hall to his Hollywood office and found a locksmith [had changed] the locks on the front door," continued Hopper. "Inside, Marty had his brother and sister occupying the place to prevent Al's moving back in."

Day herself would relate how Melcher began to take care of her financial matters about this time. "It seems his office was constantly getting my bills and overdrawn checks," she told journalist Jane Ardmore. "Al had gone to New York, and Marty called me in to explain that he would be handling my account: 'We'll chat about money—you're too easy with that check book.'"

However, it is Hopper's more thorough account of one of the most significant developments in Day's life that overwhelmingly suggests that Melcher betrayed not only his wife but also his partner in order to take over Doris Day and make her an even bigger meal ticket than he could have ever dreamed she would become. Though it appeared in print in 1963, or a good decade after the fact, Hopper's story was based on her conversations with Al Levy as the events occurred. Hopper, in fact, even wrote about the terms of Levy's contract with Day, giving him as much as 20 percent of her earnings, a further indication of just how much Levy had confided in the columnist.

Though Melcher was married to Andrews, "when he had a chance to better himself with a new client, Doris Day, who was starting to be big stuff at Warners, Marty couldn't get rid of Patty fast enough," declared Sam Weiss, who actively disliked Melcher and even kicked him out of his office when they first met. "[T]he only thing Marty loved was money. He loved Patty's money until Doris's money came along and then, because there was more of it, he loved Doris's money more."

Weiss also recalled the night he received an urgent call from Alma. "Sam," she said, "I'm scared to death. I'm alone in the house and Patty Andrews is at the door yelling that she wants to get in to get at Marty.

She's mad as hell." Weiss advised her not to open the door and said he would be right over. When he arrived, he discovered Andrews on the porch, wielding a baseball bat. "She was spitting fire," said Weiss. "There was no doubt, from the way she was swinging that club, that she meant to use it." Weiss kept his distance and, unobserved, waited until Andrews finally left.

There are also the related recollections of Annette Pearson, a secretary for Sam Friedman at Shapiro-Bernstein, a music publisher, whose Hollywood offices were on Vine Street. Pearson remembered leaving work late one afternoon, probably in the fall of 1948. "Marty was still married to Patty Andrews," said Pearson. "I came out to get my car, and there were Marty and Doris, making out in his car in the parking lot. I caught them, and he hated me so, after that.

"What a horrible man he was," continued Pearson. "And he completely controlled Doris. He came by one day, and without saying anything, he just walked into my boss's office, which was not allowed. My boss wasn't in, and Marty sat down at his desk and started making phone calls. I went in after him and said, 'Marty! Get out!'

"He looked at me, like I had lost my mind," continued Pearson. "He said, 'What do you mean?' I said, 'Nobody is allowed in Sammy's office.' And he got furious. He told me, 'You know, I'll have your job for this.' Then he stormed out. When Sammy got back and I told him what had happened, he said, 'Good for you.' And he told Marty, 'I can get along without you. But I can't get along without her.' Marty ruined poor Doris in so many ways, he really did. I think Marty was both physically and emotionally abusive."

* * *

According to Pearson, Alma made Christmas cookies and cakes for Day to give as presents to colleagues in the music business. But given Day's phenomenal overnight success, everyone found what was meant to be a personal gift to be a rather chintzy gesture. A similar anecdote illustrates Day's tendency to be absentminded, as Warner Brothers publicist Jerry Asher remembered a phone call he received from Alma. "I don't want to bother Doris," explained Day's mother, "so I hope you can help me. Before Christmas I baked fruitcakes for Doris to give to her studio friends. I've never heard a word, but I do hope everyone liked them." When Asher looked into the matter, he discovered that they were all "still in the trunk of Miss Preoccupied's car." As Day told Asher, "When I finally opened that trunk, those cakes were covered with moss. They looked like a group of little old men with long, green beards."

In fact, Alma's baked goods brought pleasure to many a palate, and within two years there was an announcement that her "best cookies" would be sold under the name of "Day Dreams." It would prove to be one of the countless projects involving the star's name that never saw the light of day.

The Beating of Publicity Drums

---- ✳ ----

"We were the only merchandise that got to leave the store at night."
—AVA GARDNER

Though every Hollywood studio was distressed by the momentous impact of television, they didn't know quite what to make of it at first. In 1948, the debut year of Day's first film, both the World Series and presidential nominating conventions were televised for the first time. Simultaneously, the number of filmgoers was plummeting: it fell by half between 1946 and 1953—from an estimated 90,000,000 per week to 45,900,000. The studios felt so threatened that they started behaving in irrational and self-destructive ways. "Contracts were written for actors," for instance, "that barred them from making any television appearances whatsoever for a specified period after the release of a picture—not even to plug the picture itself."

From the very beginning, however, Day's stardom was built on the familiarity and popularity of her voice. No matter how much the film industry was ailing or wherever her movie career might take her, her recording career was still in its infancy. And one career would play off the other very effectively, to help make her the all-time American icon she would become.

With her first film out and her second and third already made—but yet to be released—Day spent the month of January (1949) touring the country with "Bob Hope's All-Star Hollywood Show." It began in Fort Worth on January 5 and finished in Cleveland on the thirtieth—with stops in between in Louisiana, Florida, Georgia, Tennessee, Kentucky, and Pennsylvania. Hope's other guests included baritone Billy Farrell and comics Irene Ryan and Hy Averback. (Ryan would receive her greatest fame as Granny Clampett in TV's *The Beverly Hillbillies,* a little more than a decade later.) Looking back, Day would declare Averback "one of the funniest men in the whole world."

Decades later, Day explained that she developed a lifelong fear of flying after a number of near misses or "crises" during the many flights she took while touring with Bob Hope. There was one particular near-collision when they were landing in Pittsburgh, and, reportedly, even Hope "turned green."

After previewing *My Dream Is Yours* the previous fall, the studio decided to pull out all the stops promoting its new star. As reported by John L. Scott in the *Los Angeles Times,* "[She] returned a few days ago from a 27-city tour with Bob Hope's show, and seemed surprised to hear that J. L. Warner has decided to go all-out to make her the singing star of 1949.

"Miss Day either is a great actress or, as she insisted, she hadn't heard of the decision until we told her," continued the story. "Already the publicity drums are beginning to beat for the girl with the engaging smile, the come-hither voice and the quick quip." Scott then referred to two tantalizing forthcoming projects for Day, neither of which would be realized: "*Broadway Revisited,* in which she will divide top billing with Joan Crawford, Jack Carson, Virginia Mayo and Gordon MacRae, has been announced. There's also a good chance that she will co-star with MacRae, rising young male singer, in a musical version of *Brother Rat.* This, observers agree, would be a ten-strike."

More tom-toms could be heard in the *Daily News*: "After only one movie . . . Doris is No. 1 in the fan mail department at Warner Bros. She has two more flickers coming up. . . . She just returned from five weeks of personal appearances on the road with Bob Hope, having the time of her life. . . . Hope, she said, always managed to find an Army camp for unscheduled shows, which was fine by her any time of the day or night. 'But,' she said, 'he usually found them at 9 o'clock in the morning and by 9:30 I'd be singing and sounding like a frog.'"

"It's Magic," Day's hit song from *Romance on the High Seas,* was nominated for an Oscar, and she was home in time to sing it during the Academy Awards ceremony on March 24, 1949, the first to be telecast in its entirety. After explaining that the nominees for the best song would be "interspersed" throughout the event, as opposed to "bunched together," emcee Robert Montgomery announced that "the lovely newcomer . . . Miss Doris Day" would sing the song she sang in her first picture. Clad in a white, sashed, floor-length gown offset by evening gloves and a pearl necklace, Day exhibited a placid expression without betraying any of the considerable anxiety she felt about performing before such a large audience. Nor was any trepidation conveyed by Day's crystalline voice, as her bouncy hairdo glistened and an overhead and occasionally visible microphone at moments cast a shadow on her still pudgy cheeks. She curtsied gracefully as Montgomery, thanking her, vainly tried for a stab at humor: "If Jule Styne and Sammy Cahn—who wrote that little number—have any quarrel with that, they may rise and leave quietly."

A couple of weeks later—or shortly before *My Dream Is Yours* opened at the Warners Downtown in Los Angeles (April 15)—the *Sunday Mirror* featured it as the Movie of the Week with a full-page item by Jack Thompson, who wrote: "Warner Brothers seem singularly fortunate in Doris Day, who stars in their latest musical. . . . She has looks, an appealing voice and acting ability. She shouldn't miss." More thoroughly synchronized with her singing career than ever before, an ad for the picture was geared to promote Day the singer by proclaiming: "THE GIRL WHOSE VOICE MAKES MILLIONS OF RECORDS WHIRL NOW BRINGS YOU AN ALL-TIME RECORD IN MUSICAL SCREEN ENTERTAINMENT FROM WARNER BROS.!"

All of the advance publicity for the star-to-be paid off. While the critical response to *My Dream Is Yours* proved decidedly mixed, most of the reviewers reveled in the ongoing "discovery" of Day. Following so close on the heels of her first picture, they recognized that she was a talent to be reckoned with. "The voice of Doris Day should be well known to one and all by now," said Darr Smith in the *Daily News*. "However, it is now to be reported that the little blonde with the bulldog jaw is also something of an actress." In the *Hollywood Reporter*, C. Young claimed that Day "gives everything she has—which is plenty," but came down hard on Curtiz for "expect[ing] her to carry so many of the musical numbers, especially when they lack production values and consist essentially of solo singing spots." ". . . Another ordinary musical that except for the presence of Doris Day, and her engaging screen personality, to say nothing of her talent, would be shrugged off by most moviegoers," offered the reviewer of L.A.'s *Citizen News*. "But Miss Day brings 'something' to the screen that proves quite fascinating to movie audiences."

In his review for the *New York Herald Tribune*, the more discerning Otis L. Guernsey Jr. found the film "relentlessly average." He also built Day up, at first, only to bring her down a peg or two: "Unquestionably

Miss Day has what is called 'talent' in Los Angeles," wrote Guernsey. "Her native good looks are gilded by long, bright blonde tresses; she has a certain swagger that gives the illusion of vivacity in certain scenes, and her sense of rhythm does much for a husky voice in the film's many swing numbers."

But then he proceeded to denigrate her as he continued: "Miss Day bears an exact resemblance to many other so-called movie musical stars—it is all there, from the drug store voice to the flat, one dimensional performance, and she is even a near ringer for Esther Williams without the red hair. Miss Day bears the same old rubber stamp imprint of the producer's inexperienced 'find' and the make-up man's stereotype, with all the freshness of a wax flower and the individuality of a fan magazine cover."

Despite Guernsey's reservations, Day's performance in *My Dream* displayed far more variety and a wider acting range than she had demonstrated in her first. And with her shoulder-length, cascading blonde tresses and prominent cheeks, she proved more evocative of Ginger Rogers than of Esther Williams—as many others—including Day herself—would attest.

Like *Romance on the High Seas*, *My Dream Is Yours* earned more than $650,000, a respectable amount for a studio picture at the time. Curtiz's deal with Jack Warner provided him with a weekly stipend of $3,500, in addition to 25 percent of his films' profits. The veteran supporting player Adolph Menjou was guaranteed $35,000 for four weeks' work, while Day, fast becoming a star, was earning a fraction of that at her contractual rate of $750 a week. Meanwhile, that same year, another Warners contract player by the name of Bette Davis earned $364,000.

When the reviews of *My Dream Is Yours* came out, Day was in the midst of another tour with Bob Hope, earning an additional $1,000 per week. But the terms of her oppressive contract with Curtiz meant she had to pay him half of those earnings.

Within a couple of months of Day's return from her tour with Bob Hope, *It's a Great Feeling* was released. Half a century later, the response to this, her third picture, seems far more positive than it warranted. On the other hand, many of the reviews correctly emphasized how refreshing it was for a motion picture studio to be so tongue-in-cheek about its own practices. "Hollywood, usually deadly serious about itself, has turned out a picture which laughs loudly at the antics of one movie studio," observed Eileen Creelman in the *New York Sun*. "It is just a slightly lunatic stroll about a studio, with no feelings spared. It gives every evidence of having been written as it strolled along."

Yet again, Day won the critical approval denied the film itself. "Those feuding inseparables, Dennis Morgan and Jack Carson, are lucky enough to have Doris Day to scrap over," claimed Dorothy Masters in the *Daily News*. "Although there's not much story, the boys fare well enough without relying largely on their acrimonious dialogue to keep the customers entertained." But even if the *New York Herald Tribune*'s Joe Pihodna found the film itself a "sleeper" and "a rare Warner production," he proved notably underwhelmed by the studio's new star: "Doris Day made this reviewer uncomfortable by insisting that she couldn't act throughout the proceedings. This sort of confession is too close to the truth for comfort."

Day was already more of an actress than she received credit for. One is aware of a beginner better than her material. But too many critics of the day assumed that she was primarily a singer and that acting remained, for the most part, beyond her abilities. They had no idea what she was capable of as an actress, and wouldn't for some years.

* * *

To help promote *It's a Great Feeling*, Day was interviewed by Elizabeth Wilson for *New Liberty*. "A press agent once told me to tell interviewers that I didn't finish school on account of my accident," Day told Wilson. "But that isn't true. I had to go to work. We were poorer than Okies." There were at least three other significant revelations: "Telephones are her pet aversion," reported Wilson. "She rarely answers them, and hardly ever returns a call." Also, "On a personal-appearance trip recently she ran into George Weidler. They patched things up and they are going to try married life again. 'See?' she says. 'Everything comes out all right.' . . . And recently, when Doris went on a shopping spree at Magnin's, she was so delighted with the service one of the saleswomen gave her, that the saleslady now lives in the Day house."

On "grounds of desertion," Day's "default divorce" from Weidler would be finalized, in fact, on May 31, 1949—or four months after the article appeared—and any notion of their getting together again before then had proved short-lived. Without complications and without alimony, Day's divorce was handled by Melcher's attorney, Jerome B. Rosenthal, who would become known for manipulating his clients like an invisible puppeteer. Having been admitted to the State Bar of California in 1946, Rosenthal quickly established himself as an attorney for up-and-coming movie stars. He was featured in a story by Virginia MacPherson for United Press two years later, presenting him as "a handsome young man with about 20 clients" and "with prowess in applying psychology, reconciling parties, and juggling clients' finances." "You do a lot more than handle their divorces," Rosenthal told MacPherson. "You're a father confessor, a high-finance wizard, a movie critic, and a conscience." By 1949 Rosenthal was already skimming 5 percent off the top of all of Day's earnings—in addition to his lawyer's fees.

As Elizabeth Wilson suggested, Day indeed had more work than time on her hands at the beginning of 1949, when she hired that salesgirl from Magnin's by the name of Lee Levine. Levine became the first in a long parade of personal assistants over the next six decades. She acted as a private secretary, opening mail, paying bills, fielding unwelcome calls, and doing whatever was needed around the house. "Lee likes doing all the things Doris hates," wrote Pauline Swanson in an article on Day that featured photos of Terry with his mother. When asked if she intended to marry again, Day told Swanson: "Sure I need a man. . . . I think it's that I get so tired of making decisions." She reflected, perhaps mindful of her mother, "I don't want to turn into a dominating woman. I hate dominating women. Don't get me wrong. I don't want a husband who will also be a boss. That went out with high button shoes. But just somebody to whom I could say, now and then, 'whataya think, honey?' . . . you know. . . ." Perhaps mindful of Melcher, she added that it would probably happen "in about six months."

If for much of her life Day would shun phones and fail to return calls—she would increasingly rely on assistants to handle them—another behavioral pattern emerged during this, the early part of her film career. As reported in the Press Book for *It's a Great Feeling*: "Doris Day rated herself today as Hollywood's No. 1 anti-night-life girl. She doesn't own a single evening gown. You can't get her to put her foot into a supper club. 'I spent almost every night for eight years in evening gowns in night clubs and I don't want any part of either of them again in my private life,' Day explained. 'Of course, when movie roles call for me to dress up, I naturally comply,' she continued. 'That's part of my work. But dressing up just for the sake of dressing up—that's not for me. I'd rather have a trim sports dress, or a pair of slacks, than the most beautiful evening gown in the world.'"

Though Day did not dare to discuss in public her insecurities concerning her personal appearance—which were particularly pronounced in the beginning of her film career—she would recall almost quitting because of them. "I remember when I was first at Warner Brothers, Curtiz got to the point where every time I saw him, he would say, 'I want you to lose weight. I want your cheeks to be hollow,'" Day told journalist Jane Ardmore years later. "I thought he was absolutely right. I'd only been in pictures a short while and every day when I saw the rushes, I'd look at [myself] and burst into tears. And I'd tell Marty—we weren't married [yet]—I'd say I've just got to quit. I'm not right for pictures. I'm not glamorous and I'm not pretty or photogenic.

"And of course my face was loaded with freckles and by the time the make-up man finished covering them up, I felt like I had on a plaster mask," Day continued. "Until I'd gotten into pictures, I'd never thought [about] what I looked like, and I developed a complex a mile wide. I think I would have given my soul to look like Hedy Lamarr. And then all of a sudden the fan mail started coming in. It was bewildering because the letters said, 'I wish I could look like you. . . . I'd like to have a nose like yours. . . . You're so healthy looking, and I love freckles. Why don't you wear them on the screen? . . . How I wish I had your personality.' Those letters really helped me. They proved something that to me was almost a revelation—that almost everyone wishes they were someone else, which is just what I wanted. I began to realize that whatever it was they liked about me had nothing to do with the way I looked, that how people look doesn't matter, it's what's inside that counts."

* * *

Young Man with a Horn was based on the life of Bix Beiderbecke, generally considered the first great white jazz trumpeter, who died at the age of twenty-eight from alcoholism in 1931. Dorothy Baker crafted a novel of the same name out of his life in 1945, and producer Jerry Wald persuaded Warners to secure the screen rights. After failing to get James Stewart for the lead, Wald had Ronald Reagan in mind. However, Kirk Douglas, who had suddenly established himself as a star, became the more desirable choice. Curtiz was signed as the director.

A writer at Warners before he became a major producer at the studio, Wald had collaborated with Curtiz on a number of films, including the mid-40s classic *Mildred Pierce*, starring Joan Crawford. He would also come to be perceived as the model for the ruthless filmmaker at the center of Budd Schulberg's scathing novel about Hollywood back-stabbing, *What Makes Sammy Run?* Clearly Wald could be every bit as shrewd as his fictional counterpart. Among the first to recognize Day's potential as a dramatic actress, he was the first to cast her as such. According to Curtiz biographer James Robertson, Wald had "envisaged" Day in a "serious role" after he observed her working on the set of *Romance on the High Seas.*

Although Warner Brothers "waited for the right time and the right young man to bring the life of one of the '20s great trumpeters to the screen," the protracted development of *Young Man* was, in fact, due to an ongoing conflict between Jack Warner and Wald. His eye on the box office, Warner wanted the film to have a conventionally happy ending. Wald preferred to remain true to the conclusion of Baker's novel, with the protagonist's ignominious death. With three different writers involved in shaping the script, the ending became something of a compromise. After a preview screening, Douglas tried to restore the fatal ending. But, as backed by Wald, a typically ambiguous Curtiz ending was retained as a tactful compromise.

Following tests in late June, filming got under way on July 11, 1949, and would be completed on August 27—on schedule—except for a few location shots in New York filmed in early September. Though Day received the costar billing stipulated in her contract with MCP, she was only a featured player, portraying a singer named Jo Jordan. (Jordan was actually a black character in Baker's novel, but as Kirk Douglas succinctly stated in his memoir, "You couldn't do that then.") Evidently, Day resented the demotion, which may have contributed to her incompatibility with Douglas. For his part, Douglas may have had misgivings about working with someone considered a singer rather than an actress.

"Kirk was civil to me and that's about all," Day would say later. "But then Kirk never makes much of an effort toward anyone else. He's pretty wrapped up in himself. . . . *Young Man with a Horn* was one of the few utterly joyless experiences I had in films."

While recalling his work with Day, Douglas remarked: "That face that she shows the world—smiling, only talking good, happy, tuned into God—as far as I'm concerned, that's just a mask. I haven't a clue as to what's underneath. Doris is just about the remotest person I know."

Curiously, it wasn't some publicity report but rather the Production Notes for the film that reported that Day "put down her pretty little foot and notified Perc Westmore, head of studio makeup, that she didn't want any phony glamour, that she wanted to show her freckles, her turned-up nose, and look exactly like Doris Day. Which isn't bad. Westmore effected a compromise with her and Miss Day's freckles are at least partially hidden by makeup."

Shortly before she began working on *Young Man*, Day met with Don Allen for her cover story in *Motion Picture* magazine. "Whether Doris will marry again soon is a matter of much speculation," claimed Allen. "The gossip columnists insist, however, that she and agent Martin Melcher are romantically inclined. They have been seen together on several occasions." Melcher tried to deflect the rumors by explaining: "I am a talent agent and a business manager. One of my clients is Doris Day. Naturally, in order to transact her business, it is necessary for us to be together in public." But the columnists knew what they were talking about, and Melcher's affair with his "client" was by this time a reality.

All Talking, No Singing, No Dancing

---- ✳ ----

"The myth of Hollywood is far less than the reality."
—DAVID BROWN, PRODUCER

While Day's contract with Michael Curtiz Productions was still in effect, Warner Brothers purchased controlling stock of MCP from Curtiz at the end of 1948, in essence taking control of the star. (The stock agreement was dated December 31.) Day's status was reported two months later in the *Los Angeles Times*: "Mike Curtiz signed her for pictures and when the director decided to rejoin Warners, the studio took over her contract."

"The evil of studio bookkeeping is not a new thing," claimed Curtiz's stepson, John Meredyth Lucas, who had served as dialogue director on *Romance on the High Seas*. "But with the combination of that and other efforts, Warners was finally able to put Mike [Curtiz] in a position that was untenable. They offered to buy the company from him, tendering what they called a generous profit to buy out all his rights including Doris Day's contract. Day, they told him, was worthless. They were going to let her go. Mike reluctantly signed the agreement. The Warners had Doris Day's contract and had a superstar."

Though Day was technically "laid off" in the fall of 1948 and free of any responsibilities at Warners, she agreed to be available "without compensation" for interviews and other "publicity work." She also appeared on "the new" Frank Sinatra radio show several times in September, and in December returned to Bob Hope's radio show.

On October 24, Warners placed Day on salary for the day and she returned to the studio to discuss a film about to go into production. According to an internal memo, she was called in for an interview with the

producer, Jerry Wald, and the director, Stuart Heisler, regarding a picture
then called *Storm Center*. In *Her Own Story*, Day would claim that she
"didn't hesitate in accepting" the role. In 1957, however, she would recall
telling Wald that the nonsinging part was too serious and dramatic for
her. "I don't think I can handle it," she said. Wald replied: "Well, I think
you can." Though Day declared herself eager to work with her idol Ginger Rogers, she must have been ambivalent about not being the star, instead playing Lucy, the kid sister to Rogers's Marsha. In fact, Rogers was,
herself, a last-minute replacement for Lauren Bacall, whom Jack Warner
had suspended for the sixth time, for refusing to make the picture. A
good year earlier, there was talk of starting the picture with Jane Wyman
as the star, and Bette Davis was later suggested as the potential lead.

As written by celebrated novelist Daniel Fuchs and Richard Brooks
(the future writer and director of *Elmer Gantry*), *Storm Warning* was a
retelling of Tennessee Williams's *A Streetcar Named Desire* with a significant embellishment to the drama: the Ku Klux Klan. Wald, for one, took
the picture very seriously, with lengthy memos to Fuchs recommending script changes. Once the picture was in production, Wald fired off a
memo to Warner recommending possible title changes, each ending with
an exclamation point: *Cause for Alarm!*, *The Violent Friends!*, *The Fallen!*,
The Outraged City!, *Outcry!*, *Winner Take Nothing!*, *Thunder in the Night!*,
and *The End of the Line!* He would also prove a very hands-on producer.
"We saw Miss Day's wardrobe tests on Saturday," Wald wrote costumer
Milo Anderson. "We don't want her to wear slacks. The simpler you keep
her dressed, the better. We're afraid that the slacks and the chest expan-
sion destroy the character of the girl we're trying to establish with her."
In another note to Anderson, with an accompanying picture of Day in
costume, he wrote: "Don't like this robe. I know it isn't expensive, but it
looks it. Let's get something a little more drab—something that seems to
have been worn for a couple of years." And in a memo to makeup man
Perc Westmore, Wald advised: "Outside of the dip in the front of Doris
Day's hair-do, her hair will be excellent for 'Storm Center.' The dip makes
the hair seem artificial, especially since we're anxious to have a marked
contrast between Miss Rogers and Doris. Heisler and I feel that elimina-
tion of it will make her look just right."

Marsha Mitchell, played by Rogers, is a dress model from New York
who goes to Rock Point, a fictitious town, apparently in the Deep South,
to visit her sister, Lucy, a waitress at a "recreation center," or bowling
alley and restaurant, played by Day. Lucy's husband, Hank, is a hunk in

the Stanley Kowalski mold; though Hank sports a white T-shirt, unlike Stanley's, it's not torn and sweat-stained. He is a Klansman and, in the opening scene, Marsha observes him and his brethren murdering a white reporter who had been investigating their activities. The other main character is Burt Rainey, the local DA. Rainey has been eager to rid the town of "a bunch of hoodlums dressed up in sheets" and learns that Marsha has witnessed their latest crime.

Even with the knowledge that her husband has killed a man, the vapid Lucy says, "I don't care what he's done. I'm not gonna leave him." Torn about turning in her brother-in-law, Marsha nonetheless agrees at first to go home to New York, but Rainey compels her to remain and appear in court, where she backs away from identifying either Hank or the Klan. "The people who live around here never see anything or hear anything," says Rainey to Marsha. "I thought that you, being a stranger here, might have better eyesight."

The role of Burt was typecast with Ronald Reagan, who received second billing in the opening credits—after Rogers and before Day. Though both Jose Ferrer and Marlon Brando were under consideration, Hank would be played by rugged-looking Steve Cochran. According to the publicity Production Notes for the film, "Broadway's" Cochran had last appeared on stage as Mae West's muscled costar in *Diamond Lil.*

Lucy's willingness to forgive Hank finally comes to an end after she discovers him attempting to rape Marsha—another echo of Stanley Kowalski and Blanche DuBois. In the final Klan meeting, Hank shoots and kills his wife—making *Storm Warning* the only film in which a character played by Day dies.

After a meeting at the studio in August, Fuchs, in a three-page memo, acknowledged various problems with the script: "The theme is not developed. The story is repetitious—i.e., Mae refuses to talk. The theme is not resolved. We go outside the story of Mae to Hank's breakdown for the ending." Emphasizing that "the kind of story we have to work out is a thriller," Fuchs made an extraordinary claim, comparing *Storm Warning* to the Hitchcock classic *Rebecca*: "Like Mae Larsen in our story, Joan Fontaine was plunged into a set of circumstances that were both mysterious and ugly. Like Mae, Joan Fontaine soon discovered that a person she loved was a murderer. . . . Like Mae, Fontaine soon found herself in danger."

Day's technical layoff was rescinded on October 28, when she started studying her script, prior to the beginning of production on November 15, 1949. The starting date was actually moved up to accommodate Rogers, who had a previous commitment. The cast and crew spent two weeks in December shooting on location in Corona, California. A sleepy little town sixty miles north of Hollywood, it was selected for its central intersection, which featured a courthouse, a library, a gas station, and a church-cum-funeral home. ("The story of any man's life is on four corners, such as those in Corona," explained Heisler. "There before you—law and order, education, religion, death, and gas and oil.")

The production book lists Day's first appearance on the shoot as December 7, when she drove in her own car to the Corona location. She received a call on Saturday, December 10, instructing her to report for work on Monday at 9 a.m. After phoning in sick that morning, she missed Tuesday as well. This prompted Jack Warner to fire off a finger-wagging, internal note: "If Doris Day is well enough to appear on the Bob Hope radio show tonight, we want to take her off payroll for the two days she has not reported for work here. You can ascertain from her doctor or have our doctor call hers to find out what her condition is. Also, find out what notice she gave our Production Department that she would not report yesterday morning and what it is costing us to work without her."

It may well be that a healthy Day was playing the prima donna, as opposed to really being ill. Having played a subservient role in *Young Man with a Horn* and now again in *Storm Warning*, she was beginning to realize that her contract made her something of an indentured servant, and relations between her and Jack Warner were coming to a head. In her memoir, Day recalls having had only "one serious encounter" with Warner. It was when she confronted him in his "cavernous, rococo office" over a script she didn't want to do. Though she fails to identify the film, to all evidence it was *The West Point Story*, a picture that Day would make half a year after completing *Storm Warning*, even though *West Point Story* would be released first.

While emphasizing that Day was "making her debut in an all-acting assignment," a press release for *Storm Warning* added that "within the space of a few years she has stepped to number one spot, over all others on Warner Bros.' lot, in the amount of fan mail received each month." Though it might seem odd for a studio head to cast one of his biggest stars in secondary roles, such as the role of Lucy, the fact was that Day's stardom rested upon her highly regarded vocalism. From Warner's perspective, it made perfect sense to test her in the dramatic waters of secondary nonsinging roles before casting her in starring straight roles. For

Day, the gambit paid off handsomely: It was on the basis of seeing her in *Storm Warning* that Alfred Hitchcock would tell Day at a party that he wanted to work with her. This would lead, four or five years later, to one of Day's finest pictures, *The Man Who Knew Too Much*.

While working on *Storm Warning*, Day told a columnist that she resented the studio's previous attempts to make her into a glamorous type. "I don't have it," Day explained. "It isn't here. They put a wig on me, they crimp some false eyelashes onto me, they arch my eyebrows clear up to here, and they stuff me full of padding. All I look like is something that looks like it is trying to look like a Hollywood glamour girl. In other words: nothing! . . . I don't want any young girls going home and crying themselves to sleep on their pillow because they are not as beautiful as they think I am," added Day, the proto-feminist. "I'm a plain dame like they are and if I succeed at something in a picture despite being as plain as they are, then that gives them hope that they can succeed, too."

Storm Warning was completed on January 21, 1950, three days behind schedule: "shot 45 days on a 42 day shooting schedule," stipulated the production book for the picture. Day proceeded to make two more movies in rapid succession, both of which would be released before *Storm Warning*: *Tea for Two* and *The West Point Story*. *Storm Warning* was held up nearly an entire year—perhaps because its controversial subject matter required a more careful and sensitive marketing campaign. Special advance screenings of the picture were held for "representative invitation audiences," including, among others, the head of the Anti-Defamation League, chiefs of police, local newspaper publishers, local editors in chief, P.T.A. presidents, district attorneys, county and city judges, and columnists. "The boys at the Warner office in New York think it's one of the greatest pictures they've ever seen," Wald wrote in a letter, after one of the first screenings, in April 1950. "You can take bets right now that Rogers can't help but get an Academy nomination for this picture."

Amid other publicity assignments that spring, Day made a short for the Veterans of Foreign Wars and participated in promoting the Society for Crippled Children. This was while she was back where she belonged: making another musical (*Tea for Two*) and, once again, the star.

✳　✳　✳

Since Warners had long held the rights to the popular 1925 Broadway musical *No! No! Nanette!*, with Day on the payroll it was only natural to make a film version. *Nanette* was rechristened *Tea for Two*, after one of the show's most enduring songs. The original score by Vincent Youmans and Irving Caesar included yet another great popular classic: "I Want to Be Happy." The film version would toss out most of the show's songs in favor of inter-polating still more period standards by, among others, the Gershwins, Al Dubin, and Harry Warren. Liberties were taken with the story, framing it as a flashback to the Great Depression, when, in fact, the original was set during the boom preceding it.

The revamped plot concerned a show within the show called *No! No! Nanette!* and the conventional problem of raising the funds to put it on the boards. Producer-director Larry Blair (Billy De Wolfe) knows that his fiancée, Nanette Carter (Day), is both stagestruck and extremely wealthy. Her doting uncle Max (S. Z. Sakall) manages Nanette's fortune. Without the heart to tell her they've lost everything in the 1929 crash, Max con-cocts a scheme that promises her the requisite $25,000 if she wins a bet he knows she will lose: She has to say "no" to everything she's asked over a twenty-four-hour period. This leads to any number of misunderstand-ings between Nanette and everyone else, including songwriter Jimmy Smith (Gordon MacRae) and Tommy Trainer (Gene Nelson), the star of the show within the show.

As before, a loan-out agreement had been drawn up with Michael Curtiz Productions for Day to make *Tea for Two*, her sixth picture—albeit the fifth to be released—and the second directed by David Butler. After a few weeks of rehearsals, filming began on March 23, 1950. *Tea for Two* would mark the first time Day received top billing. It was also the first film she made with both MacRae and Nelson—not to mention Billy De Wolfe, who would become one of her dearest friends. Two decades later, she would remember that it was "as enjoyable as any picture I ever made." According to Butler, "there had been a great improvement" in Day's grasp of how to perform before a camera.

A year older than Day, MacRae was also a contract player at Warners. Though he had been known for his warbling on radio, on albums, and in Broadway musicals, his first picture, *The Big Punch* (1948), featured him in a nonsinging role. He remained primarily a singer who could act. But given his all-American good looks and his fine baritone, MacRae and Day became ideal partners who would go on to make four more pictures to-gether in rapid succession. Their affable costar Nelson was a hoofer and actor whose Hollywood career had started at Fox. However, like MacRae, he was on Broadway in a musical revue in 1948 when a talent scout from Warners noticed him. Nelson also became a contract player whose first film for the studio was *The Daughter of Rosie O'Grady*. A rat-a-tat-tat tap dancer, Nelson—though neither a Fred Astaire nor a Gene Kelly—had flair and cinematic charm. Warners also employed his wife, Miriam—whom he introduced to everyone as "My better *half-Nelson*"—as a dance assistant.

As Jack Warners's "dance" man, LeRoy Prinz continued to receive credit as choreographer for *Tea for Two*. But, according to Miriam Nelson, it was really her husband who developed the steps for the numbers. "Gene and I worked out ideas together: I would take [Day's] part before she ever came on the set, and he and I would dance together.

"LeRoy Prinz had a great flair for explaining a number to the bosses: he made it up as he went along," recalled Miriam. "He'd say, 'Well, I envision twenty-four girls on staircases, and they're dressed in gold and red. . . .' He'd make up all this stuff. And it sounded wonderful, so it would be okay'ed by Jack Warner. But then, we had to make this pure fantasy happen. He had several assistants. And we'd work on things together.

"Eddie Prinz [LeRoy's brother] was more of a dancer," Miriam continued. "At one point, LeRoy wanted an actor to jump off this little cliff, but he was afraid to do it. So LeRoy turned to his brother, saying, 'Well, Eddie will show you,' as he gave Eddie a shove, and he went over the cliff."

Since she had broken her leg as a teenager, Day was skittish about dancing for the first time in front of a camera. But according to Miriam, "It came back very quickly to her. I don't remember her ever not being able to do something I showed her. She was a good tapper. She showed me some things that she had learned from her teacher when she was just a kid, and there was one step in particular that we used in 'I Know That You Know.'"

Miriam subsequently incorporated the step into one of her routines, and then passed it on to other tap dancers, who, thanks to their mentor, referred to it as "the Doris Day step." "It's a combination that you repeat three times, and it had a good rhythm to it," explained Miriam. "It was very fast and it had a lot of taps and riffs."

While she was working on the picture, Day told James Padgitt of the *Dallas Herald* about her discovery that she could dance again: "Call it progress in reverse. . . . I thought I was through forever with a dancing career when I broke my leg in an automobile accident. . . . Not knowing what else to do I took up vocal lessons. Now look what's happened—I'm dancing."

Day also told Padgitt that she "tentatively" listed dancing as one of her "accomplishments" when she signed with Curtiz. "[But] I wasn't sure about my leg, even after all this time," Day explained. "Then when *Tea for Two* came along I was asked if I would like to take a crack at some tap routines with Gene Nelson as partner. In a week and a half of rehearsals, going for eight hours every day, I've picked up the dancing that I never thought could be mine again. I'm in the groove once more, rarin' to go!" According to Padgitt, Day was "exuberant" over current developments. "I'm having every opportunity to prove my versatility," she told the reporter.

Padgitt also relayed that Day had phoned ballerina Vera Ellen after "winding up" her first production number for the film *I Know That You Know*. "Vera Ellen and I went to dancing school in Cincinnati," said Day. "When I had to bow out, Vera went on to great fame. I told her, 'I've got two more routines with Gene in the picture, so look out, Vera, you've got competition. This kid is in business again.' If the day ever dawns that I can dance as beautifully as Vera Ellen, I'll sing at the top of my lungs with joy. Meanwhile, I'll continue singing and . . . dancing."

Another reporter who visited the set, Betty Craig from the *Denver Post*, wrote that doctors examined Day before giving their approval for her to dance in the picture. "She looks so unbelievably happy while she [dances] that it is quite evident Doris has missed her dancing since she became an important singer on the screen," Craig observed. More than half a century later, Miriam would say, "Breaking her leg was the best thing that could have happened to [Day], because she became a singer and then a star. She might never have had that [trajectory], if she hadn't had the accident."

Miriam became a friend of Day's. "We used to giggle a lot," Miriam said. "She loved to laugh, and I do too. As a matter of fact, when I'd be on the set, she could be doing a dramatic scene. . . . But if I were standing by the camera, she'd just look at me and break out laughing. The director would say to me, 'What did you do?' I kept saying, 'I didn't do anything.' And he'd respond, 'Don't stand by the camera,' or 'Don't be in Doris's sight line.' So I had to stand out of the light so she couldn't see me watching her."

It didn't take much to get them going. "Once we decided to spend the whole day, in between shots, talking about penny candy," continued Nelson. "She'd come up with, 'Do you remember those yellow banana things that were actually marshmallows?' We'd laugh about that. Of course, we went through candy corn and jellybeans right away. And then I remembered those little wax bottles that you'd bite the top off, and they had different flavored syrups inside. And that's the way she was."

Nelson's behavior with Day was similar to Ronnie Cowan's. "I know some hostesses who refuse to invite us both to the same party," Cowan recalled in 1957. "We have twin funny bones and when something strikes us as highly amusing we're off. We don't need much prompting, or we have a stand-by act we lapse into.

"I had thought that all movie stars were sophisticated," Nelson said. "But that wasn't true at all—and especially not of Doris. She was very down-to-earth and talked to everybody, and laughed with everybody. We just had a good time."

Day also hit it off with her costar Gordon MacRae, but she developed a more meaningful and lasting relationship with the flamboyant, and obviously gay, Billy De Wolfe. They bonded instantly because of their shared love of nicknames. Dubbing colleagues with quirky monikers was their way of making them their own. According to Miriam, De Wolfe invented a fresh nickname for practically everyone involved with *Tea for Two*. "He called me Anastasia Gonzales, because I looked Latin," said Nelson. "He called Gene, 'Norton,' I think, and Gordon MacRae was 'Melvyn'—although it might have been the other way around. [It was, indeed, the reverse.] I keep mixing them up, because they never stuck."

One nickname that did stick was De Wolfe's for Day: Clara Bixby. Day's most intimate friends have referred to her as Clara ever since. According to Nelson, all the letters and postcards she received from Day were signed "Clara." Day identified herself as Clara on the phone to Miriam. And Miriam still refers to Day as Clara in conversation. Day, in turn, called Miriam "Mim," and De Wolfe "Spike."

The crews would come up with two other epithets for Day on the set: "Nora Neat" and "Dorothy Detail." Though she apparently embraced these descriptive names with the same enthusiasm that she had the many others she accrued over the years—Dodo, Doke, Didi, and, of course, Clara Bixby—her lifelong fascination with nicknames may have had a less benign aspect to it, particularly since she encouraged her closest friends to call her Clara instead of Doris. (Within this context, it must be remembered that "Day" itself was an invented name, which she disliked from the beginning.) "Clara" became a palpable way of differentiating herself from Doris Day, of disassociating herself from the person the public knew.

Indeed, Day increasingly failed to relate to the film star she was becoming. With friends, she preferred an alias, because she came to feel more and more alienated from the image engulfing her, a distorted portrait reflected, captured, and refracted in a public hall of mirrors. But as much as Day disavowed her image to herself and her friends, she would also collude in maintaining it for the sake of her career.

*　　*　　*

The wisecracking character actress Eve Arden was another contract player at Warners who appeared in both *My Dream Is Yours* and *Tea for Two* with Day. In her autobiography, Arden recalled Day advising her to "look for a man who will be your lover as well as your friend." At the time, Day was openly declaring her desire to marry again—in particular so that her son might have a father. Columnists had begun to devote more space to reporting that Day and Marty Melcher were "romantically inclined." But with the phony coyness that circumscribed their "just friends" celebrity love-dance, Melcher would only acknowledge that she was "one" of his clients.

It was true that Day's relationship with Melcher had begun as a friendship. She did not fall madly in love with him—as she had with her first two husbands. "When it came to romance I thought only in terms of explosions," Day maintained. "It never occurred to me, for example, that friendship with a man like Marty could ripen into love. How could I possibly love him when I liked him so much? Wouldn't you think I'd know better after having been through two Fourth of Julys?"

Yet, in the end, she did submit to Melcher's advances. On April 7, journalist Harrison Carroll would announce the couple's marriage plans in the *Herald*. Under the headline, "DORIS, MARTY ADMIT PLANS TO WED BUT SAY THERE WILL BE NO RUSH," he wrote: "Now that Patti Andrews has been awarded an interlocutory decree, her ex, Marty Melcher, and Doris Day, can be candid about their romantic plans. The two looked very happy as they conferred in Doris' dressing room . . . at Warners. They admitted—the first time to my knowledge—that they will wed but said there will be no rush. They'll wait until 'matters are straightened out.' If that means until Patti's divorce is final, they'll have to wait almost a year."

Melcher had a friend in Miriam Nelson. "I remember a lot of people didn't like Marty, but I did," she said. "He was fun to be around." As she also recalled, "Doris and Marty always seemed to be having fun. I don't remember ever seeing them angry." It should be added, however, that this was relatively early in their relationship.

Despite juggling the shooting schedule of *Tea for Two* to accommodate the stars' radio responsibilities—MacRae to *Railroad Hour* and Day to the *Bob Hope Show*—*Tea for Two* still wrapped up on May 13, 1950, five days ahead of schedule. Within a matter of weeks, Day would buy—for $40,000—Martha Raye's house at 131 S. Valley in Toluca Lake, a small community where Bob Hope and Walt Disney lived. A two-story Colonial, Day's new home was white clapboard with dark green shutters flanking the windows. It was on a quiet, tree-lined block with a dead end, which made it ideal for children—and there were plenty of them around for Terry to befriend. Ideal, too, was its location, a couple of short blocks from the Warners lot.

"The place was a wreck," recalled Day, who proceeded to redecorate to her own tastes. She removed the wall-to-wall mirrors in the living room and covered the kitchen walls with a cheerful, ivy-patterned paper. Day often claimed that she would have been an interior decorator, if not for her career in show business. But she had problems finding the time to oversee the work, and Melcher took control. "They were using green wood and cheap plaster," Day complained. "They were taking advantage of me in all sorts of ways. Marty stopped everything and took over."

According to a detailed report, Day "liked yellow, printed fabrics, and paintings and comfortable furnishings. Her traditional furniture and accessories were accented by the occasional antique." The dining room, for instance, featured a scenic wall covering depicting idle strollers in the English countryside. The custom-made dining-room table was surrounded by French provincial chairs, covered in striped silk. The console was home to two Georgian silver candelabra, and the center of the table displayed a Lowestoft bowl on a silver stand, above which hung an antique crystal chandelier. Terry's bedroom had wallpaper depicting duck hunters aiming their guns and displaying their bounty.

Since Day loved cookouts, she built an enormous pit and grill for barbecues on one side of a swimming pool placed in the large backyard; on the other side, she set up a pair of volleyball and badminton courts. She also added extra showers for the swimming-pool guests and a sun porch. With so much to offer her guests, the Toluca Lake home became a playground for Day's most intimate friends. It also became a magnet for the neighborhood children to play with Terry. Day even had a drinking fountain installed beside the volleyball court—perhaps to discourage the kids from traipsing through the kitchen and aggravating her phobias about cleanliness.

During the year and a half of their courtship, Melcher accompanied Day to many an antique shop and auction as she continued to find objects for her new home, and especially additions to her milk glass collection. He helped paint the living-room walls a "Williamsburg green," laid bricks on the patio, and put up trellises around the pool. "Marty wooed me with a hammer in one hand and a paint brush in the other," Day later told a reporter. "Sometimes I think he got the idea of marrying me out of a Sears-Roebuck catalogue."

While securing her new home gave Day a stability she had always yearned for, her image as the "girl next door" simultaneously came into sharper focus. Day was promoted as just that in Hedda Hopper's column, on July 23, 1950. This was no small feat for a woman who, by her mid-twenties, had already divorced twice and was rearing a son without a father. "Her greatest quality, besides her talent," Melcher told Hopper, "is her complete naturalness. She puts living ahead of her career. And as for her voice, I think [Christian Science guru] Martin Broones described it aptly. He said, 'It's like the music you get from a wonderfully mellow cello.'"

While confirming that Day was "head over heels in love" with Melcher, Hopper also divulged that she was earning "better than a quarter of a million" dollars a year, that she was about to "branch out into straight dramatic parts," and that her favorite song was "I Love You Just the Way You Are"—"which, incidentally, she has never recorded." The columnist also emphasized that, unlike many other stars, Day was direct: "She'd rather say 'Hi' than 'Hello' and she'll never have any delusions of grandeur. Happiness and a sunny disposition come in the door with her."

✳   ✳   ✳

After getting third billing on both *Young Man with a Horn* and *Storm Warning*, Day felt wonderful about being a star once again in *Tea for Two*, and her high spirits came through in her exuberant performance. That temporary return to prestige, however, made her next assignment all the more difficult to accept. When she discovered that her role in *The West Point Story* would be subservient not only to James Cagney's but also to Virginia Mayo's, Day evidently stormed Jack Warner's office, asking to be removed from the picture. When that didn't work, Mayo reported, "Doris Day wanted her husband to get me out and her in. She wanted to be the only female and to get me out of the picture and combine our roles."

Despite any behind-the-scenes or unspoken fight between its female costars, *The West Point Story* was definitely Cagney's picture. His first musical in eight years, it marked his own bold and passionate attempt to recapture the enormous success he had had in 1942 with *Yankee Doodle Dandy*, which earned him an Oscar for his performance as Broadway all-star George M. Cohan. According to Cagney biographer John MacCabe, Warners gave him final approval of script, cast, and director of *The West Point Story*. The scenario was loosely based on an anecdote concerning Cohan's living as a cadet at West Point in order to prepare for one of his stage musicals. Though ultimately disappointing, the film would not be without its charms—even though Day would never acknowledge them.

Cagney played Elwin Bixby, a has-been musical director who spends a month at West Point directing an annual student production. Mayo is Eve Dillon, Bixby's choreographic assistant and apparent lover. The hostilities between Bixby and Eve—and the ambiguities in their relation-ship—are part of why *The West Point Story* proves so dissatisfying a film. In that respect, Day may have been giving better advice than she realized when she suggested amalgamating her character with that of Eve.

From the very beginning, the plot doesn't fall into place as much as it stumbles along. Bixby is recruited by Harry Eberhart, a big-time Broadway producer, to take on the West Point assignment. Tom Fletch-er (Gordon MacRae), the cadet who has written the upcoming show with classmate Hal Courtland (Gene Nelson), is Eberhart's nephew. Given Fletcher's glorious baritone, Eberhart knows just what a fine Broadway career he might have. But "the chump wants to be an army officer. Now what kind of a career is that?" asks Eberhart of Bixby. As Bixby tells Eve after they've started working with Tom: "There's gold in them there tonsils."

It's not Bixby but Tom Fletcher who is a takeoff on George M. Co-han, but while Cohan was a Broadway writer and performer famous for his jingoism, Tom is a patriot who resists realizing his dramatic capaci-ties. Bixby's real job is to persuade Tom to forgo his planned military career and realize his Broadway potential. To that end, Bixby recruits Jan Wilson (Day) from Hollywood. Bixby had discovered Jan when she was "buried" in an Eberhart chorus and helped turn her into the movie star she has become. When Jan explains what she's giving up to join the show in West Point, she could be describing Day's routine at the time: "I've got two recording dates, three personal appearances, radio broadcasts, interviews." And after she cancels some previously scheduled appearances to remain on the East Coast, her studio manager evokes Jack Warner as he says: "I'll tell you about your personal life: You haven't got one. You've got a contract."

Though Day doesn't appear until well into the scenario, once she does, there's no evidence of her having had any misgivings about her role. With her first number, "Ten Thousand Sheep," she exudes a new-found confidence and maturity as a singer, and her natural ebullience acts like a shot of adrenaline in the film's limp arm. Day also gives a rousing rendition of the "Military Polka," and MacRae proves, again, a fine-voiced and virile costar in several numbers, including "By the Kissing Rock." His resonant voice dominates the large cadet numbers, such as "The Corps."

The filming of *West Point Story* began the first week in June 1950. It was while she was working on this picture that Day settled into her new home in Toluca Lake.

*   *   *

As Day prepared to marry Melcher, Don Allen reported: "Terry takes a rather proprietary attitude toward Marty Melcher. He will tell you that he was the first to recognize Melcher's sterling qualities, and therefore he, Terry, was directly responsible for the forthcoming nuptials. Doris says this is quite true," Allen continued. "Terry and Marty have been great pals ever since they first met. And Terry used to swell his chest and speak proudly and often of, 'My mommy's agent.'"

Apparently eight-year-old Terry even had influence on his mother's contemplating a third marriage. "Marty used to come to dinner," Day told reporter Jim Henaghan. "and one night I noticed that after we were seated at the table, Terry moved his place mat and chair so close to Marty's that the poor man could hardly bend his arm. I asked Terry what he was doing that for, and he said, 'I like him.' Maybe that was when I first knew I liked him more than just as a good manager."

Henaghan went on to say of her decision to marry: "Terry and his grandmother may not have been watching and listening through a crack in the bedroom door, but they knew what was going on. They [had] stage-managed most of it."

"You didn't marry me because you loved me," Day later recalled telling Melcher. "You were just after Mom and Terry!" Though she was teasing, giving yet another interviewer fodder for print, there was a significant element of truth to the statement. Given Day's ambivalence about another marriage, Melcher had no choice but to capture her through her son and mother. Like much of Hollywood, Melcher was only too aware of Day's having gone on record a number of times about her reluctance, following two failed unions, to marry again.

It was only natural that Terry proved the catalyst for his mother's developing more than a professional relationship with her agent. Now that the boy was finally living with his mother, he wanted her to provide him with a father. An unspoken subtext to the formation of the Melcher trio is that Terry was simultaneously getting to know both his mother and his future stepfather. If anything, he appeared to have had a decided preference for Melcher—at first, at any rate. Moreover, since Day was on edge about suddenly having to become a mother to her son, Melcher's participation in the process made matters easier.

Years later, Day would declare: "I wasn't even really a mother until Marty. My mother was the mother to Terry and me. I didn't really become a mother until I became Marty's wife—then for the first time I was ready to be a woman, a wife, and a mother."

In one of the more concise assessments of what the Melchers were really about, another reporter, Kirtley Baskette, wrote: "Make believe is their business and home is where they leave it behind." But such a point of view hardly revealed the true picture. To foster Day's lucrative career, the Melchers had begun to create a scenario about an ideal home life, and pawn it off to the media as being real.

In fact, certain themes emerging in these early reports on the Melchers' "happy" home life would resurface again and again in the parade of movie magazines that captured the minutiae of Day's daily routine. If the primary subject concerned the general happiness the Melchers enjoyed, the articles' more specific anecdotes provided an "inside" look: Day was an unusually heavy eater unconcerned about her figure; Melcher was a fix-it man; he married Day only because of Terry's playing a "persistent cupid" angling for him as a father; Alma thoroughly approved of Melcher; the Melchers were quiet, stay-at-home types, indifferent to parties amid the increasingly bustling, night-life community of Hollywood. "When you don't drink, know any gossip or care about hearing any, what's there to do at a party?" Day asked rhetorically. In truth, she was really reluctant to go to parties because of her basic shyness, her overwhelming need to please, and her ultimately feeling that she never could.

Given her steady cultivation of the girl-next-door image, yet another surprising but consistent notion was that Day never had any interest in preparing food or washing the dishes. Early on, she attributed this to her mother: "Why should I compete in the kitchen when mom lives with us and knows all the answers?" Day, however, could manage hot dogs and hamburgers on the grill, that is, when Melcher wasn't using it for steaks, clad in his white apron with the word "GENIUS" emblazoned on front. And Day, who would become famous for taking numerous daily showers, was also obsessive regarding the decoration of her home.

* * *

Though Day's recording career was already firmly established at Columbia Records, it was further fueled by the arrival on February 15, 1950, of A&R man Mitch Miller, who would continue to supervise her for the next decade. Having learned the music business at Mercury, Miller proceeded to mastermind the recordings of not only Day, but also Tony Bennett, Frankie Laine, Rosemary Clooney, Johnnie Ray, Johnny Mathis, and many other pop singers of the era.

A graduate of the Eastman School in Rochester, New York, Mitchell William Miller was introduced to Columbia by his onetime classmate Goddard Lieberson, executive vice president of the studio. Miller was essentially a replacement for Manie Sacks, who had been so instrumental in Day's start. Sacks resented having to suddenly report to Lieberson and "departed in a huff."

While acknowledging that "Doris had already made it before I came to Columbia," Miller was well aware of his advantages. "I had it all over the other producers. One, I knew music. Second, I knew the psychology of the listener. You have to remember, there was no video back then, so the artists had to project an image in the listener's mind. And Doris Day was the girl-next-door with a smile in her voice. And I had to find the songs for her. She did a lot of things for me that you wouldn't expect of her. I would look for things that would be a change of pace and surprise the listeners."

For better and for worse, Miller indeed became famous for having his singers perform novelty numbers. "Columbia came from number four to number one in two years," Miller subsequently boasted. "We had eight

of the 'Top Ten' bestsellers in the country some weeks." Though he became a genius for navigating the ever-burgeoning sea of popular music
during the 1950s, Miller was also a dictatorial A&R man who imposed his
tastes on those he supervised, sometimes against their will. He specifically recalled that Day did not want to record "A Guy Is a Guy," which
she nonetheless did in 1952.

"The enormous success of the label under Miller's guidance earned
him the respect of the CBS executives, as well as a tremendous measure
of power that, combined with his penchant for control, could be in-
timidating for an artist," Charles Granata observed in an in-depth study
of Sinatra's recording career. With his black goatee and twinkling eye,
Miller could appear impish. But he was far more calculating and shrewd
than his appearance might imply—devilish, really. He also got a reputation for being outspoken. Miller would further become known for the
singers he brought together on duets. "I came up with pairings," Miller
explained, as he described "putting" Day with Johnnie Ray. "I called it
'sweet surprise.'"

From the beginning, Day reminded Miller of Mildred Bailey. "There
was a [similarly] dangerous quality in the voice, because it was so vulnerable." He found Day "very easy to work with. She came in prepared. A
lot of [singers], since they didn't know how to read music, would always
think that if you came in prepared, you would lose spontaneity. Don't
forget, there was no editing, no taping—you went direct to disc. So you
had to have producers who knew how to capture that. They could have
sung well, but have had a lousy recording balance." But not Day, who,
Miller emphasized, worked hard: "She was never sick or missed a recording session."

Though headquartered in New York, Miller made forays to Los Angeles for Columbia Records. He recalled occasionally visiting the Melchers'
house and playing volleyball. "Doris was always sunny and bright and
happy. But when Marty was around, she didn't talk as much. Marty did
all the talking." According to Miller, Alma was a "lusty dame." "Alma had
a code-word for bullshit, 'bruntz,' and Doris picked up on it," he added.

Miller boasted that when composers brought songs to him at Columbia Records: "If I'd promise them an artist, they would hold the song
until I made the record. Then they'd go out and get an advance from a
publisher." Some years later, when Robert Allen gave "Everybody Loves
a Lover" to Miller, he recalled: "I played it for Doris, and she said she
wanted to do it. But then, Marty came to me—without her knowing it, I'm

sure—and said, 'She'll only do it if I can publish the song.' Then, when I talked to Bob Allen, he said, 'Hell no, I'm going to publish it myself. I wrote the song—why should I give it to him?' So I told Marty, and he said, she won't do it. But the very next day, I got a call from Doris, and she said, 'I'm not going to walk away from a hit. I'm going to do the song.'" In a decade of working with Day, this was the only instance Miller could think of when she defied Melcher's wishes.

Not only was the song destined to become one of Day's biggest hit singles, but the sentiment of the lyric can be viewed as her personal anthem: "Everybody loves a lover/I'm a lover/Everybody loves me . . . That's why I feel/just like a Pollyanna."

✳   ✳   ✳

When first planned, *Lullaby of Broadway* was to star June Haver, and on May 6, 1950, the studio announced Dennis Morgan as her "likely" leading man. Gene Nelson's name replaced Morgan's within a week, however, and the title was changed to *Just Off Broadway* before finally becoming *Lullaby of Broadway*, on July 17. Several weeks later, a story in the *Examiner* claimed that Haver asked to be removed from the project: "She says she isn't up to the strenuous dance routines and big musical numbers so soon after [an] illness." Two days later, the *Hollywood Reporter* cited Doris Day as Haver's successor: "The picture was to have started this week, but may be postponed several days to permit Miss Day to wind [up] her current role in 'The West Point Story.'"

If Day remained upset about her secondary role in *The West Point Story*, she was also unhappy about being cast in *Lullaby of Broadway*, given its taxing dance numbers—as opposed to the easier dance routines she recently enjoyed in *Tea for Two*. She did not keep an appointment to see studio executive Bill Jacobs at 10 a.m. on August 14 but, instead, requested a meeting with Steve Trilling, Warners' head of production, the next day, "regarding her role." In spite of the broken leg she had sustained in her youth, Day had proven to the world—and to herself—that she could dance, and she should have felt up to the requirements of *Lullaby*. Moreover, she should have been comfortable with the prospect of learning her routines, once again, from her costar Gene Nelson and his wife, Miriam. In truth, however, Day had only a couple of opportunities to strut her stuff in *Tea for Two*: in "Oh Me, Oh My, Oh You" and in the closing dance version of the title song. But now, in view of the elaborate dance steps planned for *Lullaby*, she was anxious about the heavy work involved. "Marty Melcher kicked like seven steers to keep Doris Day out of 'Lullaby,'" *Variety* reported. In one of the first complaints she ever made about working on a picture while shooting, Day would tell a reporter, "In musicals, you're never through. It's always, 'Run down to the shed and work on your dances.' Other people get to go home. Not us. I don't find dancing easy."

In addition to the Melchers' reservations about the "strenuous dance routines" in *Lullaby*, their relations with Warner Brothers continued to deteriorate during the summer. On June 14, 1950, a studio executive, Alex Evelove, talked to Melcher about several ongoing disputes concerning Day's contract—one of which touched upon an interview she was to have with Martin Block on his WNEW radio program. Evelove wrote a sharply worded internal memo to studio executive Roy Obringer on June 14, 1950, explaining the "gist" of their "conversations." While providing powerful testimony to just how much the studio tried to maintain control over its stars, the memo also offers keen insights into how nasty and aggressive Melcher could become in his business negotiations.

"I told Melcher that Miss Day required studio approval for the Martin Block transcription and that such approval was not forthcoming, because it was against our policy," explained Evelove. "Before that, [Melcher] had told Cohn that he would like to have Doris out of her contract with Warner Bros., because he could sell her for $100,000 elsewhere. Also, that we, the studio, had pushed the girl around. . . . Melcher started talking lawyers immediately and denying my statement. He accused me of threatening him with that factual statement, and he, himself, threatened to publicize the matter and said that I could tell upstairs that she was tired of being pushed around, etc., etc. He also threatened to make the Martin Block recording without our approval." The "etc., etc.," suggests just how common—and predictable—Melcher's behavior had become.

As instructed by Jack Warner, Evelove requested a script for the broadcast from Melcher. "He said that the show would be an ad lib show," reported Evelove. "I then asked him for an outline or gist of the program, he said I should get it from Martin Block. Then he said it had already been recorded, but quickly denied this when I said, 'That takes care of it,' and started to hang up. He said further that they would make any disc jockey appearances they pleased without studio consultation, and I understood that he told Bill Orr [secretary to MCP and Jack Warner's onetime son-in-law] that Doris had already done such without

studio approval. He said that such a transcription in connection with
her Columbia Records did not require studio approval. Each time that I
talked to him yesterday, I told him the studio does not look with favor
on Doris' failure to attend our star previews." Beneath all this contention
rested two facts: Day had become a major star at Warner Brothers, and
both Melcher and the studio had to get along as best they could.

It's impossible to say whether Day was aware of any of these behind-
the-scenes squabbles. But there can be no doubt that, even beyond the
typical star behavior, she always preferred that others go to the front
lines and fight her battles—be it her mother, her manager, her husband,
or eventually, even, her son. As with many, Day's natural preference was
to remain as oblivious as possible to anything unpleasant. But in going so
far to avoid any unpleasantness in her career, Day paid a far greater price
than she bargained for: She relinquished all oversight of her professional
future, inviting her original protectors to become her abusers, stealing
her blind.

✳   ✳   ✳

Rehearsals for *Lullaby of Broadway* began on August 21. In an atypically
immodest moment, Gene Nelson said, "Somebody gave me a red T-shirt
once with the inscription, 'I Didn't Know It Was Impossible When I Did
It.' I think that sums up my whole creative philosophy in dance choreography. If it isn't a challenge, it's not worth doing."

More than a half century later, Miriam Nelson would explain why the
title number in *Lullaby* was considerably more arduous than anything
they had attempted in *Tea for Two*. "Gene was fearless," recalled Nelson.
"He was going down the stairs backwards—which means, you can't see
where you're going. You have to put your foot down behind you, and
then turn. And I was afraid to do it. So I would do it very slow. I never
did it up to tempo. So when Clara came in to learn the routine, I would
say, now you put your right foot down here, then you turn, and you put
your left foot here. And I never did it fast myself. But she learned it and
she did do it fast. And it wasn't until the picture was finished that I told
her, 'Well, you did something I couldn't do.'"

The production began filming on August 31 and ended on November 17—two days behind schedule. It took three weeks to shoot the party
sequence, during which Billy De Wolfe and Ann Triola performed "You're
Dependable," and Day and Nelson sang and danced their way through

"Zing Went the Strings of My Heart." "[Director] David Butler was very experienced at doing musicals," observed Miriam Nelson, who recalled his easygoing ways. "He could have done it in his sleep. In fact, he loved sports, and many times he'd be sitting in his director's chair with this little radio by his ear, listening to the ball games, while he was doing a scene. He was always very nice. I was never aware of any conflicts."

Whatever reservations Day may have had at first about doing *Lullaby*, she gave it her all once work started. "She was professional, and she felt her position very greatly as time went on," Butler would recall. "I knew her from the time she was scared to death until the time she got to know everything. . . . She always knew her lines. She always looked well. She always took care of herself. And I can't say enough nice things about Doris Day."

While working on *Lullaby*, the Nelsons frequently accompanied Day to her new home for lunch. "We used to go over to her house a lot," Miriam remembered. "She'd say, 'Come on, my mom has just made some potato salad, so when we break for lunch, we'll all go over there.'" During rehearsals, they would bring their bathing suits and swim in the pool. But once shooting began they had to be careful about their makeup, so painstakingly applied in the morning, and swimming was ruled out. Miriam recalled that whenever they swam, Smudgie and Beanie, Day's black and white standard poodles, frolicked with them. (Day sometimes called them Mildred and Ralph.) "Smudgie would take a flying leap off of the board—all four legs straight out, doing a belly flop. And then he'd swim to the stairs, come out, and go and do it again. But Beanie was nervous," said Miriam, "he'd just run around barking at us while we were in the pool."

Smudgie was one of the first dogs in need that Day rescued. One day, she had had to step over him when she went to have her picture taken at Landsdowne Studio in Hollywood. "He's always lying in the way," said the apologetic photographer. "Frankly, I don't know what to do with him. My landlady won't let me take him home and this is no place for a dog. I may have to give him to the pound." That was all Day needed to hear to take Smudgie home.

"Terry was always sitting at the piano, playing," Miriam recalled. As proud as his mother was of him, "I remember Clara saying once about Terry, 'Poor thing: he's got my teeth.'" Day was apparently self-conscious about her overbite, and, according to Nelson, "felt that she showed too many of her teeth when she smiled."

When the Nelsons began going over to Day's new home in Toluca
Lake, Melcher was still a sidelined agent and not the constant presence
he would become. The media did what they could to connect Day to
other potential beaus. The spring 1950 issue of the magazine *Radio
Album* ran a two-page photo spread on the new film star, documenting her "Busy Day" and revealing that "Doris's name has been linked
romantically with singer Frankie Laine"—even though there's no further
evidence for such a connection. The magazine also claimed that Day was
on Bob Hope's radio show "every Tuesday night at 9," which involved
early afternoon rehearsals. The large, central photo depicted Alma at
the front door, sending her daughter off in the morning to confront her
"hectic schedule."

A number of other behind-the-scene developments during the filming of *Lullaby* confirmed how quickly Day was becoming a megastar.
Louella Parsons paid Day $750 to appear on her show and promote *Tea
for Two*. Their session was recorded on September 6, for an airing four
days later. It was also during this period that the American Veterans
Association launched its nationwide campaign to supply identification
tags indicating people's blood type. Having given President Truman the
first tag to generate attendant publicity, the association presented the
second to Day on the set of *Lullaby*. She also did very well in another
popularity contest involving public figures: When *Life* conducted a poll
asking schoolchildren, "What person of whom you have heard or read
would you like most to be?" she was topped only by General Douglas
MacArthur and Florence Nightingale.

Day's success as a singer was broadcast in an ad in *Billboard*, which
included a large photo of a wistful Day and a note bearing her signature:
"Dear Disk Jockeys: I am very grateful and honored to be your number
one girl again this year. Fondly, Doris Day. P.S. My sincere thanks to
Columbia Records." Another sign of her growing fame was that the private plans of Day and Melcher were becoming increasingly more public.
Under the headline "Marty Melcher to Adopt Doris Day's Son After Wedding," Harrison Carroll wrote in the *Herald*: "That is one of the reasons
why Marty hasn't tried to speed up his freedom from Patty Andrews. He
and Doris want everything to be in order with the courts here. So they
are waiting until Patty's divorce from Melcher becomes final next spring.
On the 'Lullaby . . .' set, Doris declares emphatically: 'When we do get
married, it will be a wedding with all the trimmings.'"

Parsons would announce that Day and Melcher were to be wed in

Santa Barbara, on April 3, 1951–the future bride's birthday. "Only her close relatives will be present and the bride and groom will honeymoon far away from Hollywood traveling by motor." Parsons also claimed that Day and Nelson's next Warners' picture would be *Sons o' Guns,* based on a twenty-year-old Broadway hit of the same name. "New songs will be written and the play brought up to date," explained Parsons. It was one of those countless Hollywood projects that never came to pass.

By the time work began on *Lullaby of Broadway, Tea for Two* was being promoted before its release on September 1, along with advance publicity about Day's coming "eight-side album" for Columbia Records of the film's songs. As reported by a Hollywood paper, "Doris Day showed up at the press preview [on July 25] of 'Tea For Two,' posed for the lensers in the lobby, then sneaked out of a side door a few minutes before the movie started." Reviewers were, for the most part, delighted with her performance and emphasized her deepening accomplishments as an actress. "The picture, old and new parts alike, is so ingratiating that this observer felt the glow of pleasure ordinarily reserved for users of advertised products," claimed Archer Winston in the *New York Post.* "Miss Day demands a footnote. She has always been a pretty good singer, having done that for a living before the movies tapped her. Now she's a better singer, and a much better, more relaxed actress," he added, before declaring the film to be "the best Warner Bros. musical made in a decade, and that covers a lot of territory."

In the *Los Angeles Times,* John L. Scott found it "[a] charming piece of musical froth. . . . MacRae and Doris warble delightfully through several of the film's songs, and Nelson scores with a stair dance." In the *Daily Mirror,* Frank Quinn hailed "a light-hearted filmusical, melodic and nostalgic. Warners tied it up in a neat little Technicolor package for relaxing." The *Hollywood Reporter* offered a dissenting view, as did Wanda Hale in the *Daily News.* Though she liked the songs, Hale found the picture "a tiresome piece of entertainment, with flat humor, inadequate performances and an all-around amateurish air."

In spite of such criticism, the film gave the studio one of its four top moneymakers of the year and did much to increase Day's fan base: she was clearly confirming her stardom. As Gene Handsaker reported in an AP "Newsfeature": "Hollywood–Data on delightful, de-lovely Doris Day: She gets the most fan mail of anybody at Warner Brothers–about 1,500 letters a week. The ones that please her most say their writers saw one of her pictures several times. The record is 14 sittings through 'Tea for Two' by a fan she knows only as Joe. Another Day devotee sends her candy. Eight soldiers in Korea mailed her a recording on which they voiced their esteem. Another group of fighters there dispatched $50 with a request that she send them a crank-type phonograph and all the records . . . their money would buy."

✳   ✳   ✳

In light of Day's success in *Tea for Two*, Warners suddenly felt compelled to make amends for her secondary billing in *The West Point Story*. The quick solution was to feature both Day's name and image before Virginia Mayo's in the film's trailer. As a song written for it claims: "First there's Cagney, full of that nimble wit/And for songs there's Doris Day/ There's Virginia Mayo, who scores a hit/And your favorite, Gordon MacRae. . . ." Her billing in the opening credits, however, comes after both Mayo's and Cagney's—but before MacRae's and Nelson's. The publicity concentrated on playing up comparisons with *Yankee Doodle Dandy*, calling *The West Point Story* "Dandier" in some ads, "Dandiest" in others. With a photo of Day and Terry leaving their home dressed in rain gear, the Press Book featured a tie-in with Standard Oiled Clothing Co., "Manufacturers of slickers for women and children," and did not fail to include a long list of stores across the country prepared in advance for the "tie-in!"

When the film opened in December, the reviewers tended to admire Cagney far more than the film, which could barely contain the energy of his performance. "If everything about 'The West Point Story' were anywhere near as good as Jimmy Cagney is in it, this Warner musical show . . . would be the top musical of the year," opined Bosley Crowther in the *New York Times*. According to Crowther, whenever Cagney was not on screen, "the thing sags in woeful fashion, the romance becomes absurd and the patriotic chest-thumping becomes so much chorus-boy parade." "One could wish that either Cagney or his producers could imagine something better for him to do," chimed in Otis L. Guernsey Jr., in the *New York Herald Tribune*, "but until this happens he is still very much of a show in himself." While referring to "the tortuous, hard-to-follow story," Philip K. Scheuer in the *L.A. Times* wrote, "[T]he composite result is only spasmodically successful." Though *Variety* began by declaring it "worthwhile entertainment with a good general box-office outlook," the reviewer would ultimately criticize the producer and director for permitting "the picture to be unnecessarily long in footage, making it difficult to sustain the interest over the entire course without a few sags."

Having been opposed to making the picture in the first place, Day herself would later deem it "another one of my un-favorites," dismissing the story as "strange" and having too many characters that failed to add up.

*   *   *

Along with Ginger Rogers, Steve Cochran, and Ronald Reagan, Day was slated to appear in Miami for the world premiere of *Storm Warning* on January 17, 1951. But as Hedda Hopper announced in her column, Day came "down with the flu [and] had to cancel her scheduled appearance." Cochran, for his part, showed up with a broken leg. When the film was finally released in February, it was promoted as "provocative" and "shocking." "UNDER THE WHITE HOOD HE WAS PURE YELLOW," screamed the copy for an ad, depicting a hooded man whipping a cowering Ginger Rogers, while Day looks on, aghast. The film seems neither as sensational nor as realistic as it apparently did upon its release; rather, it now unfolds like a sanctimonious pulp melodrama concocted to exploit an incendiary topic. In fact, the Klan's two victims in the picture are not African Americans, but a white man and a white woman.

Though the role of Lucy took advantage of Day's natural exuberance as well as her ability to cry on cue, too often she hovers awkwardly in the background; like a benched player watching others at bat, she gives the impression of inexperience and of being out of her element in this dramatic part. At times, she has a vacant stare that makes her seem disconnected from the other characters—as well as from her own. Rogers, who was nearing forty, appears a little too old to be playing Day's sister—perhaps the reason for her nervous performance. And if Reagan is his usual, mediocre self, even worse is the obviously overemoting Cochran. Indeed, he gives a performance of such staggering fraudulence that it's difficult to comprehend how more than one reviewer could have referred to the film as documentary-like—except that they probably took their cues from Warners' publicity department.

"Ku Klux Klan hoodlums ... are the special angry target of this slashing, outspoken, semi-documentary motion picture," read the notice in *Cue*. "The brothers Warner have made many such films in the past; this one is among their best. In addition, [it] is first-rate melodrama—a grim and gripping story."

Fred Hift, critic of the *Motion Picture Herald*, probably best captured the spirit behind the response to the film with his jingoistic opening: "In these troubled days, with democracy on the defense, a picture like 'Storm Warning' must be considered a real tribute not only to the people who made it, but also [to] the country in which it could be made. For here is a film about the Ku Klux Klan that pulls no punches and delivers a telling blow against mob action such as the Klan encourages."

Today, the other advance trade reviews seem no less over-the-top and difficult to fathom without a vigorous reminder of the pre–civil rights environment within which the film was released. "A semi-factual presentation that avoids shouting its points, and a good marquee lineup of names, should rate it attention in most playdates," trumpeted *Variety*. "The Jerry Wald production is presented in a matter-of-fact manner that strengthens both the melodrama and the moral it poses. . . . Unexpected and very good is the offbeat assignment of the sister, as done by Doris Day." *Film Daily* welcomed a picture that "permits a fine selection of players to demonstrate their talents with excellent results. There is nothing light or frivolous here. . . . It is a bitterly realistic yarn that Stuart Heisler has very capably brought to the screen."

In the *L.A. Times*, Edwin Schallert claimed that the picture "pulls no punches in being a ruthless expose of the Ku Klux Klan," even as he pointed out, "This might have been quite a picture in the days when the Klan was at the flood tide as an organization. It comes now when it is much nearer the ebb, localized." In the *Examiner* Dorothy Manners found it "[a]bsorbing, biting and violent drama . . . an extraordinarily engrossing film . . . Both musical comedy queens turn in performances that would stack up with Bette Davis or Olivia De Havilland."

The serious tone with which Warners promoted the film clearly paid off with the vast majority of the press. And the uniformly positive response to Day prompted Warners to quickly announce that she was being given three more "straight dramatic" roles. In *Helen Scott*, she was to play a doctor in a New England town; in *The Fuse*, a newspaper reporter; and in *The Moment I Saw You*, a New York housewife. None of these projects was ever realized.

*   *   *

Lullaby of Broadway was released a couple months after *Storm Warning*, reaffirming Day's real star power as a musical dynamo. The film's title song, written by Harry Warren and Al Dubin, had won an Oscar when it was introduced in *The Gold Diggers of 1935*, also produced by Warner Brothers. The score featured a number of other songs promoted as "All-Time Favorites": "Just One of Those Things," "Somebody Loves Me," and "You're Getting to be a Habit with Me." When the picture opened, many recognized the trite and innocuous story for what it was: an excuse to string the musical numbers together. Written by Earl Baldwin, the premise of the story recalls Apple Annie, the colorful Damon Runyon figure first captured on film in 1933 by Frank Capra in *Lady for a Day*. (In 1961, Capra would remake the film—his last—as *A Pocketful of Miracles*, with Bette Davis as the lead.) The plot of *Lullaby* pivots around subterfuge and mistaken identity, when would-be stage actress Melinda Howard (Day) comes from London to New York under the belief that her mother, Jessica (Gladys George), is a Broadway star. Jessica's colleagues do their best to prevent Melinda from learning that she has become an alcoholic has-been relegated to performing in dives. For the scheme to work, they tell Melinda that Adolph Hubbell (S. Z. Sakall)—the owner of the mansion in which they're all servants—is renting it from Jessica. While Hubbell has lecherous eyes on Melinda, he's married to a domineering wife, played by the blustery character actress Florence Bates. Melinda, in turn, falls in love with Tom Farnham (Gene Nelson), a star dancer. Not only did the film reunite Day and the bumbling Sakall for the fourth time, it also included the Page Cavanaugh Trio in their first film appearance since *Romance on the High Seas*.

While the marketing campaign featured "Disc Jockey Contests," Warners joined with Columbia Records in what they called "one of the biggest promotional tie-ups in recent years." With Day on hand as "hostess," there was a special preview showing at the Academy Awards Theater for "1,000 music-store sales personnel and all the disc jockeys from this area." The Press Book for the ninety-two-minute film also made the "IMPORTANT" announcement of "A Columbia First!": "The Album Comes in Three Speeds! 78 RPM—33 1/3 RPM—45 RPM." Since this was their third film together—following *Tea for Two* and *The West Point Story*—Day and Nelson were billed as "America's newest sweethearts."

After attending a preview of the film, Jimmy Starr gave his readers in the *Herald* another kind of preview—of the predominantly ecstatic reviews Day was about to receive. "Although I've seen her in several pictures, I never realized before what a terrific triple-threat gal Doris Day really is," wrote Starr. "I had always enjoyed her singing on the screen and on recordings, but until 'Lullaby' came along I had no idea that she is one of the town's best dancers. . . . In the recent 'Storm Warning' Doris well proved herself a capable actress of dramatic roles . . . she sparked 'Lullaby' with a combination of singing and dancing that brought applause from a jaded preview audience. . . .

"I had the impression that I was seeing someone entirely new to the movies," Starr continued. "Warner Brothers should look hard and long for the proper material for Doris . . . there's a gold mine in her varied talents and they should be displayed always to the best advantage. . . . After seeing Doris in 'Lullaby' I can honestly say that I think she's the best music bet in the picture business."

"Let me tell you about this lovely Day, who is building in the movies," exclaimed Jim O'Connor in the *New York Journal-American* when the film was released. "She's a looker; blonde; blue-eyed; nicely stacked in the right places; peaches and cream complexion; full bosomed; leggy; caressive lips; graceful of foot; teeth as white as white and twice as bright. And the kid can sing!" In her review for the *Examiner*, Louella Parsons wrote: "To me, any picture with Doris Day is sold before it has started. I just like her. All she has to do is open her mouth to sing and I'm her fan."

Though the production numbers were hardly as "lavish" as Kate Cameron found them in her review in the *Daily News*, the infectious songs feature top-drawer choreography and dancing, which more than justify the lame screenplay. In addition, onetime leading actress Gladys George infuses the film with emotional weight in her moving portrayal of Jessica Howard—a.k.a. "Greenwich Village Gertie."

The mayor of Cincinnati proclaimed March 28, 1951, "Doris Day's Day," and Warners persuaded other cities—including Boston, Buffalo, and Los Angeles—to do so as well in conjunction with the opening of the picture. According to the *Hollywood Reporter* the stunt worked, and the film enjoyed "top business in 125 key city situations, in addition to a number of smaller spots over the country. . . . The picture is presently outgrossing nearly all previous Warners' Technicolor musical releases."

✳ ✳ ✳

Conceived of as a vehicle for Warners' new musical star, *On Moonlight Bay* marked Day's third picture with Gordon MacRae and the first where her permanent image as the "girl next door" began to emerge. Based on a trilogy of *Penrod* stories by Booth Tarkington, the film shifts focus from the twelve-year-old character, Penrod, to his older sister, Marjorie, and her budding romance with neighbor Bill Sherman. As George Morris observed in his later-day study of Day's films: "Her Marjorie Winfield is a formative role in the development of a persona that was increasing in popularity with every picture." The coveted juvenile part of Wesley Winfield went to Billy Gray (who, within a few years, would become Bud on TV's *Father Knows Best*). Papa George Winfield was played by stalwart character actor Leon Ames, Mama by Rosemary DeCamp, and the sassy Winfield housekeeper, Stella, by Mary Wickes.

"[Mel] Shavelson and [Jack] Rose, who conceived the idea of reviving the Tarkington stories because of advice from studio field men that 'family' pictures are still eminently salable, identified the Tarkington characters by name in the first draft of the scenario," claimed a story in the *New York Times*. "The studio chieftains ordered the names changed to prevent recognition of the story source."

Set in a small town in Indiana in 1917, the real focus of *On Moonlight Bay* remains on the tried and true, white-picket-fence verities of a bygone era in American history, a time "when folks were learning the Grizzly Bear, the Bunny Hop and the Turkey Trot, and a fellow felt more like an animal trainer than a dancer," declared the trailer for the film. Like MGM's *Meet Me in St. Louis*, which it emulated, *On Moonlight Bay* evokes a needlepoint sampler come to life. It is also the first picture to present Day as a tomboy. "I'd like my daughter to become a wife—not a second baseman," says George Winfield. Not only does Marjorie play baseball with the boys, she also wins a Kewpie doll with her perfect ball tossing at an amusement park booth. When Mom helps Marjorie put on her "first party dress," she tells her to stop "walking like a first baseman."

On the verge of turning twenty-nine when she made the film, Day was playing a character nearly half her age, and she did what she could to compensate for the discrepancy. She went on a rigorous diet of yogurt and wheat germ to slim down for the part. The property man even took her new regimen into account when preparing a table for the party scene in the film, using blackstrap molasses and whole wheat flour for the pastry, yogurt for the white layers in the cake, and chocolates filled with cottage cheese.

If *On Moonlight Bay* would prove pure escapist fare, Americans suddenly had a good deal to escape from. When filming began at Warners in January, TV cameras were positioned in the backyard of Mrs. Ruth Colhoun, "a Los Angeles mother of three," to capture the construction of one of the first atomic-bomb shelters. "On hand were cheering starlets, studio flacks . . . and representatives from the construction company that would dig the $1,995 underground cubicle at the edge of Mrs. Colhoun's patio and provide it with beige-painted concrete walls, green carpeting and storage space for canned food," according to one report. "It will make a wonderful place for the children to play in," Mrs. Colhoun told reporters, "and it will be a good storehouse, too. I do a lot of canning and bottling in the summer, you know."

At the time schoolchildren were being subjected to A-bomb drills in their classrooms, crouching under their desks, probably fearful of being smashed to smithereens. "The Day and MacRae youngsters took the drill in stride," reported a studio release, which also described Gordon MacRae's upcoming "personal appearance" at the El Rancho hotel in Las Vegas. Having already performed there in the fall, MacRae was hoping "to advance the opening date" of his second appearance to March 1: "before the A-bomb tests are concluded [nearby.] The singer wants to see an A-bomb explosion."

Filming *On Moonlight Bay* ran over schedule, well into March, after director Roy Del Ruth came down with a virus. Though veteran director Raoul Walsh took over for Del Ruth, other members of the company came down with the virus as well, including Day, who missed a week of work. Once back at the studio, she was visited by the president and vice president of her fan club: Jan Olliffe, a bank clerk, and Pat Doyle, a secretary, who both lived in Oakland. "At the suggestion of Doris Day, girl members of her fan club make a practice of visiting military hospitals in their areas to talk with hospitalized veterans," explained a press release. "If they happen to find a vet who is a strong Doris Day fan, they notify the star and she sends the vet an album of her recordings."

Melcher had jewelers visit his wife-to-be on the set to help her select her wedding ring, which was framed in an antique setting. Day also welcomed her brother Paul and his wife when they moved to Hollywood in late January. After trying to eke out a living as a salesman, Paul was to become an "associate" in Melcher's new music business. His wife of three and half years, Shirley Ann, née Schuchart, a former switchboard operator, was to assist him. Though Melcher never relinquished control or gave Paul any real authority, Paul did handle many of the practical details involved in his sister's singing career.

* * *

Look magazine helped promote *On Moonlight Bay* with a four-page picture spread. Warners also held advance screenings for disc jockeys and record distributors in key cities, including Los Angeles, where Day, though she procured nine tickets for relatives to attend a preview, chose not to appear.

When it was released in July, *On Moonlight Bay* was perceived as Day's most extravagant musical yet. In the *Hollywood Citizen-News*, Margaret Harford reserved special praise for Day, who "remains one of the screen's freshest personalities and she is charming in this film." While pronouncing the movie "a grand show" and "delightful entertainment," a reviewer for *Cue* concurred, claiming that Day "does one of the nicest jobs of her bright career." "The picture is strictly summer-weight material—thin, porous and not at all wrinkleproof, but comfortably loose and light," quipped the reviewer in *Time*, who added: "Actress Day does not quite pass for an 18-year-old, but her freshness keeps her in character."

A three-page publicity release issued by Warners offered lively quotes from Day, renouncing "the red carpet treatment," which stars typically received. "I resolved early that even though a lot of others around me lost their heads, I wouldn't lose mine." The release continued: "To help her stay the Doris Day before fame and fortune struck, and to guard against the insidious influence of the red carpet, Doris associates with her pre-Hollywood friends from Cincinnati whenever she can."

"I enjoy talking to them because I can be completely myself," Day explained. "I also like to talk to people, total strangers, whom I meet while shopping in markets or department stores. Sometimes they recognize me after a while, and then they change. I can tell when that [happens,] because they start looking at me as a curiosity."

As a gesture toward the many veterans who had done so much for her singing career, Day made a tour of service hospitals in the San Francisco Bay area. She serenaded them with "It's Magic," "Sentimental Journey," and "A Bushel and a Peck," and had the pleasure of learning from one soldier that he had been aboard the U.S.S. *Valley Forge* when Day was voted "The Girl We're Fighting For."

A Cunning Suitor

---------------------------------- ✳ ----------------------------------

*"Personally, I think if a woman hasn't met the right
man by the time she's 24, she may be lucky."*
—DEBORAH KERR

A s Day's marriage date of April 3 was fast approaching, Warners told
its star to take as long a honeymoon as she wished. The couple
planned on spending five weeks in New York and New England—until
Melcher realized that he could not afford more than two weeks away from
his new music business. They also talked about eloping to Las Vegas, and
then visiting friends in Omaha—Dr. and Mrs. Leon McGoogan—"by way
of Colorado," before deciding to go by train to New Orleans instead. It
was even announced that Day had hired "Vivien Leigh's New Orleans
guide" for a tour of the French Quarter, where she hoped to locate some
"antique window shutters" for her new house. She also hoped to complete all her recording dates for *On Moonlight Bay* by March 15, 1951,
"to give her time to shop for a trousseau. "Otherwise," Doris said with a
sigh, "I'll have to get married in blue jeans." Day had her eye on a green
organdy outfit for her wedding day, but ultimately decided to wear a suit
from her closet, in which Melcher had never seen her.

But once Day finished shooting *On Moonlight Bay*, she had to be
available for any necessary retakes, not to mention demands from the
publicity department. Moreover, by then Day and Melcher had been
living together—for how long, it's hard to say. In truth, a honeymoon
seemed beside the point. But mindful of the publicity surrounding just
about everything her daughter did, Alma pointed out it wouldn't look
"proper" without at least the gesture of one. For years, many a movie
magazine would report that Alma "had to shoo them out of the house for
their honeymoon." Alma—it was even reported—packed their bags.

Long after Patty Andrews received her divorce from Marty on March 31, 1950 (she asked for neither alimony nor community property), the Melchers were finally married on Day's birthday, April 3, 1951—when the bride was twenty-nine, the groom thirty-five—"but not without some difficulty," reported the *L.A. Times*. "The couple appeared at the Burbank branch of the County Clerk's office, but found it closed. They drove to Van Nuys in a fruitless attempt to find a place where they might obtain a license." They returned to Burbank, where they were married by justice of the peace Leonard Hammer, and where *Los Angeles Times* reporter Dick Turpin was "pressed into service" as their witness.

There is a photo of the beaming couple on a wooden bench, beneath a sign: "County Clerk/Marriage Licenses/Justice Court." This was actually a Warner Brothers publicity photo, sent out with the caption: "IT'S OFFICIAL—Marriage of . . . star Doris Day to her business manager, Marty Melcher, long awaited by Hollywood, took place yesterday (April 3) on her birthday in a quiet ceremony at the Burbank City hall. The singing actress had completed her role in 'On Moonlight Bay,' only the previous day. They will leave shortly on a honeymoon by motor."

As if to underscore just how mundane the event was for them, the about-to-be newlyweds had an hour or so to kill in Burbank before Hammer found time to marry them. While waiting, they stopped at LaChance's, a dry goods store, where Day picked out material for new curtains. They spent their wedding night at home, where Alma prepared their meal.

They then enjoyed a posed, all-American honeymoon at the El Tovar Hotel in Grand Canyon. They intended to break up the drive by spending their first night in Phoenix. But without consulting a road map, Melcher got lost and they had to make do with a vacancy they found in Imperial Valley, one of the most blazingly hot desert spots in Southern California. It was at an extremely shabby looking motel where the bed was too short for the six-foot-three Melcher. They proceeded to spend a rainy night in Phoenix on their way back to Los Angeles, and later told the press that they cut their honeymoon short because they wanted to be with Terry. Though it was work that had compelled the Melchers to rush home, another story had been concocted for the media, as usual.

But Melcher was indeed trying to become more like a father to the nine-year-old Terry, whom he would soon adopt. In addition to playing ball with Terry and teaching him how to ride a bike, Melcher had also begun to instill the value of money in the boy. He gave him a dollar a week for keeping the family's shoes shined and for putting back all of the pool gear at the end of the day. Terry's fastidious mother would have insisted her son do it for free but recognized the wisdom behind Melcher's methods. Melcher also helped Terry rig a clothesline pully from his bedroom to a neighbor's bedroom, so he could whisk off a private note before going to sleep. Terry was typically in bed the same time as his parents, 9 p.m.

* * *

As Day's star rose ever higher, Melcher was increasingly aggravated by the terms of her four-year-old contract that so limited her earnings from Warners. Tensions between the studio and the star's bulldog manager were growing. In an urgent, internal WB memo dated May 1 and addressed to Evelove, a studio executive, Ben Cohn explained how a pushy Melcher called him "late in the afternoon today" and said, "I know I am a little late in calling you, but Doris Day is doing two disc jockey shows today—Ira Cook on KECA and Johnnie Grant on KMPC—so I'm asking you now for a clearance. . . . While you're getting a clearance, you might tell the studio she is going to do the Jack Kirkwood show tomorrow. . . . In addition, we are setting up several other disc jockey appearances." Cohn added that he had to remind Melcher "a second time" that the studio's permission was required for such appearances.

Still another internal memo dated May 1 indicates how unhappy the studio was over a story Melcher had arranged for *Motion Picture* magazine to do without securing the publicity department's approval. After "inadvertently" learning about the article, the studio contacted Lou Larkin, the man scheduled to write it. "Larkin replied that he was a personal friend of Melcher's, had already had preliminary discussions with him on doing a story, and Marty had agreed to cooperate if he could pick it up, catch-as-catch-can, at his office," explained the memo. "There appears to be complete double dealing on the part of both Melcher and the magazine," it continued. Worse yet, the Melchers had already been photographed for the piece, while "[w]e have been trying to get layouts of Marty and Doris for the past four months. We have not been able to get them to agree to pose for the art."

Melcher was also seizing control of the home front. When he advertised for a housekeeper, the most important addition of all to the new homestead arrived in the fall of 1951: Katherine Sartin Mattox, known as "Katie." Sartin had no idea who Doris Day was. "I remember the 'Mister'

[Marty] saying, 'Katie can you cook?' And then he mentioned some fancy French name [for a dish]. I said, 'I have no idea what that is. But if you tell me what's in it, I can cook it. I can cook anything.'" Sartin, a large black woman with salt-of-the-earth values and a no-nonsense manner, instantly endeared herself to practically everyone she met. She was hired primarily as a cook—although Alma would continue to receive credit for the household meals in most publicity stories. In the eyes of several people who would work for Day, Sartin truly became Terry's mother—even if Alma continued to act that role as well. At least one later insider felt that Day became far closer to Sartin than she had ever been to Alma.

As Terry grew out of his clothes, the frugal Alma shipped them to her nephew's son, two years younger than Terry. "They fit me perfectly," recalled Paul Welz, before adding proudly, "I was the best-dressed kid around."

*　　　*　　　*

Starlift, Day's ninth picture, was thrown together in a month—and it looks it. There's no point in even summarizing the plot, since it keeps veering off in so many directions that the film is incomprehensible. Day herself knew it was ridiculous, redeemed only by the fun she had working with Ruth Roman, a would-be leading actress who quickly came to settle for character parts. Day recalled just how much she and Ruth Roman enjoyed playing themselves, even howling with laughter when they worked on this absurd picture. With good reason, they also wondered why the picture was being made. But even if she "didn't care much" for the film, Day emphasized that she "had a good time."

The picture grew out of Roman's experiences at Travis Air Force Base near San Francisco, where she entertained troops both before they shipped out for the Korean War and then when they returned, many of them wounded. After Roman persuaded other Hollywood stars to join her in a rotating fashion, the army termed the program "Operation Starlift," which became Warners' working title for the picture. "When the studio decided to make the film, I was asked for 'human interest stories' of what I had experienced . . . with the G.I.'s," Roman explained. "One of the situations was a love interest"—in the film realized by Janice Rule, as a Hollywood starlet, and Ron Hagerthy, as an air force corporal.

Along with Day, *Starlift* would feature Gordon MacRae, Virginia Mayo, Gene Nelson, and Roman—all playing themselves. But like *Hol-*

lywood Canteen, an earlier Warners war picture, *Starlift* was top-heavy with stars making guest or cameo appearances: James Cagney, Gary Cooper, Virginia Gibson, Phil Harris, Frank Lovejoy, Lucille Norman, Louella Parsons, Randolph Scott, Jane Wyman, and Patrice Wymore (Mrs. Errol Flynn). The plan was for all the stars to go to their hometowns and promote the "star-studded extravaganza." It says a good deal about Day's status at Warners that her name would appear first on the list of on-screen credits and in all the ads, which proclaimed: "All of Hollywood's Wonders Are In It! Most of the Warner Stars Are In It! All of Hollywood's Heart Is In It!"

Day's work on the picture began on May 21, 1951, and ended on June 20. She missed a day of shooting when she had a swollen jaw, the result of a wisdom-tooth extraction. One day, she was visited on the set by a new friend, Charlotte Greenwood, the tall and slender comedienne. Greenwood's husband, Martin Broones, had become the Melchers' spiritual leader in the teachings of Christian Science. "The Melchers and the Broones are constantly together—at one another's home for dinner, at the theater, and attend the same church," explained a press release. They also played volleyball regularly at the Melchers' home, where the glass-enclosed patio facing the court was turned into an "eating room" for guests.

In addition to the Broones and the Nelsons, the regulars on the volleyball court included the MacRaes and singers Jack Smith and Jo Stafford. The stars brought their own skills to the game. "Gordon [MacRae] likes to sing while he plays and everybody gets to listening and joining in," Day said. "He sort of sabotages our games, as a result. Gene [Nelson] is so light on his feet and so acrobatic that it's exciting to watch him play. What happens is you're so busy keeping an eye on Gene that you forget your own game."

Though more PR fluff, Day may be viewed as anticipating the woman's liberation movement by more than a decade with her advice to "Housewives of America, and the rest of the world for that matter, [who] should go out and get themselves a part-time job. Just staying at home doing the washing, ironing and mending is pretty dull routine. . . . A wife needs the mental stimulus of an outside interest, just like a husband who goes forth each day to the office.

"I think it's a healthy thing," Day added. "Boredom is the greatest destroyer of marriage because it's the root of most evils, in the first place. In the case of marriage, the woman, confined unrelievedly to her four walls, can well get off the beam without even realizing what has happened to her. I think the antidote for the illness is 'keeping busy,' but busy at something contrasting to housework and all it entails. . . . If you're financially well-off, you don't need to accept a salary for your efforts but can work for the fun of it."

Day even suggested a "good-neighbor policy" for mothers who could not afford babysitters. "It would operate like this," Day explained. "Neighbor A would watch over Neighbor B's offspring one afternoon and Neighbor B would return the favor the next . . . I have my home, which I love," Day continued, "and I have my job, which means a lot to me. Neither interferes with the other, because I won't permit it."

Day was far too busy to have to deal with the boredom she warned against. Yet this working wife would become increasingly aware that her marriage to Melcher was a sham, more of a business relationship than an emotional union between husband and wife.

✳　✳　✳

Day was now working double-time at Warners, beginning *I'll See You in My Dreams* even as she was finishing *Starlift.* But from her perspective, making movies was far preferable to touring with a band. "In pictures we work six days a week," Day explained in a studio press release, "have three meals at normal hours, change clothes in clean, warm dressing rooms—and go home when day's work is done. That, to me, is heaven."

Day reacted quickly to dispel the rumor that she would replace Mary Martin in the Broadway production of *South Pacific.* "I am one film actress," said Day, "who has no interest in doing a stage production. I dislike repetition and doing the same role night after night would drive me crazy. . . . I like to do my work during the day, and spend my nights at home, and you can't do that on the stage."

Yet, increasingly, her stardom was interfering with her life. One Sunday, when Day wanted to "get in the car and go somewhere" for the sake of doing something, Melcher pointed out that the traffic would be bumper to bumper. Worse yet, there would be a crowd wherever they went, and the movie star—just three years into her career—would end up spending her day signing autographs—only to return home exhausted.

I'll See You in My Dreams, Day's tenth picture, was a biographical film about lyricist Gus Kahn, who wrote more than 500 songs. These included some of America's most beloved, such as "My Blue Heaven,"

"Mammy," "I'm Just Wild About Harry," "Yes Sir, That's My Baby," "It Had to Be You," and "Carolina in the Morning."

When Curtiz was approached to direct the film, he balked at first, conveying his reluctance in a letter. "I have read the 'Gus Kahn Story' over and over again, and I am a little discouraged about it," Curtiz wrote. "It's the same story we've been seeing for years and years—the struggling composer and/or lyricist and the song plugger who helps them. We see them with their families and then they become successful. The story is not strong enough on its own. . . . The conflicts seem to me to be weak, probably because the authors are attempting to stick to the real life story."

Among his specific complaints, Curtiz felt that the script didn't provide enough "opportunities" for big production numbers—"except for the New York 'Whoopee' sequence." He then added, rather surprisingly: "I don't think Doris Day singing a number now and then is going to be entertaining enough." The director also felt that Gordon MacRae—Jack Warner's choice for Day's costar—was simply wrong as Kahn. "I think it would be much better if you would assign me to some other story which is more in my line," he argued in his closing paragraph. "I have no intention of causing unpleasantness because I would like to work and work right away, but I would like to do a story which I feel I can make into a successful picture."

Though the letter was addressed to studio producer Steve Trilling, Curtiz asked him to share it with Warner. His imploring tone tends to confirm that, in recent years, the once big money earner had lost a lot of his power at Warner Bros.

Ironically, *I'll See You in My Dreams* proved the studio's second most successful film of 1952, and Day's performance was recognized as perhaps the finest of her early career. Curtiz, who, in the end, had given in to the studio, sharpened the script, bolstering the arc of the story and injecting it with a fervor rarely found in his musicals.

Hedda Hopper's column had announced that Day would be starring in the film. The pedestrian working title, *The Gus Kahn Story*, was dropped for the marginally better *Wish I Had a Girl*, based on one of Kahn's songs. The final title of *I'll See You in My Dreams*, taken from another Kahn song, was decided upon in early July 1951, just before production commenced. Though shooting was scheduled to begin on July 16, a memo dated a week earlier demonstrates just how vague Curtiz's plans for the film had remained: "For your information and the record,

Doris Day so far is the only principal set for this production. We now have 87 pages of script." What would ultimately prove to be a solid film—superior to many other bio flicks of the period—was written by Mel Shavelson and Jack Rose. It was, in fact, their ninth consecutive screenplay—and their third for Day, following *It's a Great Feeling* and *On Moonlight Bay*. It would also be the fourth and last picture Curtiz directed with the star whom he had discovered.

The wide range of types on the "advance tentative" list of actors to play Gus Kahn suggests that, at the beginning of the project, the studio had little grasp of the nature of his character or, indeed, appearance: Gordon MacRae, Red Skelton, Jeff Chandler, David Wayne, James Stewart, Richard Conte, Arthur Kennedy, John Lund, Dana Andrews, and, as late as June 13, Van Johnson and Ralph Meeker were all under consideration. Gene Nelson took a screen test for the part, and Frank Lovejoy, ultimately cast as Kahn's regular collaborator, Walter Donaldson, was also on the list.

Before finally offering the part to Danny Thomas, Jack Warner demanded that the nightclub performer have his large nose altered. Though the real Gus Kahn was reportedly "intensely shy," Thomas, much less so, stood his ground and won his first major role without undergoing cosmetic surgery. Warner relented when others pointed out that Kahn was not a particularly attractive man.

According to one publicity report, shortly before his death in 1941, Kahn had been one of the "greatest early boosters" of Thomas, when the singer was just beginning to establish himself as a nightclub performer at the 5100 Club in Chicago, Kahn's hometown: "[Kahn would] frequently catch Thomas's act and would always have a talk with him afterwards."

Spanning a thirty-year period beginning in 1910, the episodic *I'll See You in My Dreams* recalls another era when, in the opening shot, Kahn arrives on horseback at Wabash Avenue. He's bringing his lyrics to a music publishing house, where Grace LeBoy (Day) works as a "demonstrator," who gives voice to songs for prospective publication. Grace reluctantly looks at Kahn's lyrics during her lunch break and advises him: "Do you know why you write a popular song? Because most boys and girls don't know how to say 'I love you.' So you've got to say it for them—in thirty-two bars of music: no more, no less."

Though Grace proceeds to write the music for Kahn's early songs, she is wise enough to admit, "My tunes are not in the same class as your lyrics," as she encourages him to collaborate with more established composers. Kahn emerges as something of a self-deprecating bungler who needs his wife-to-be, Grace, to goad him on: from getting him to wear a tie to tending to every facet of developing his career. The film clearly paints Grace as a manipulative, domineering wife.

The use of Grace Kahn as a "technical advisor" on the set lent the film its strong sense of verisimilitude, as did the casting of several minor parts. Thomas's daughter played Kahn's fifteen-year-old offspring, and onetime Les Brown vocalist Ray Kellogg donned a fat suit to portray the "husky" John McCormack, who sings "Memories." Grace Kahn and her son Donald appear in the banquet scene at the end of the picture, which involved 120 extras. "Yesterday Mrs. Kahn was in the unique position of applauding herself in a sequence," said a report. "When Doris finishes singing the camera centers on the real Mrs. Kahn applauding Doris." The testimonial dinner was shot in the same room at the Beverly Wilshire Hotel in which the actual banquet had taken place in 1939.

After shooting commenced on July 25, Day worked hard, long days. She rose at 5:45 every morning in order to arrive at the studio promptly an hour later for makeup and hairdressing. Among the numerous publicity tidbits, it was announced that for her early arrival at the studio, Day would lay out her clothes the night before.

Meanwhile, her star as a singer continued to rise. She was proclaimed the "most popular singer" in England, where her records had recently been "outselling those of any other singer." The star's Canadian fans included fifty disc jockeys and movie critics who signed a "three by four foot post-card" for Day, hand-delivered to her at the studio by a Canadian film exhibitor.

Still another press release declared Day "the most popular pin-up girl of the U.S. servicemen during the Korean War." She was celebrated as the "favorite motion picture star" at Keesler Air Force Base in Mississippi, as "The Girl Who Most Helped to Brighten our Sentence in the Army" at Camp McCoy in Wisconsin, and as "The Girl We Would Like to Spend the 12 to 4 Watch With" at the Naval Ordinance Depot in Keyport, Washington. A press report boasted that Day had been chosen by "so many Army, Navy, Air Corps and Marine units in the United States, Korea, Alaska, Japan, Guam and Germany that an exact count" could not be kept. And the local USO office identified "the number-one request of service men visiting Hollywood" as "How can I meet Doris Day?" or "How can I get a picture of Doris Day?" Clearly at the top of her game, Day received the spontaneous applause of cast and crew on the set of *Dreams* when she finished her blackface rendition of "Toot, Toot Tootsie."

While Curtiz shot the book scenes with one production unit, Leroy Prinz simultaneously shot the musical episodes with another, putting "12 male dancers, 11 female, and 6 showgirls" through their paces. Curtiz participated in the musical decisions as well. It was Curtiz who realized how effective it might be for Thomas to sing "It Had to Be You" directly to Day on camera, rather than prerecording the number.

Day's recollection of doing that particular scene not only reinforced how emotional it had been for her, but also underscored how often she called upon personal experiences when working on a picture. Grace has just given birth to her baby daughter in the hospital, and Gus arrives the morning after the delivery. "He sits on the bed beside me, holds my hands and, full of tenderness and love, sings 'Pretty Baby,'" Day recalled in her memoir. (The song, in fact, was "It Had to Be You.") She disclosed that she "couldn't help but cry" when Thomas started singing the song to her: she instantly thought about Terry's birth and how "unfulfilled" she had felt at the time, since his father, Al Jorden, was not there.

Though *Dreams* finished on schedule, Curtiz's position with Warners continued to erode. An internal memo to Trilling, dated August 11, claimed: "I told Mike Curtiz, on the set this morning, what you told me to tell him. In other words, that he was overshooting, and he said to me, 'How can I be over-shooting when my Producer is always telling me that I am not making enough shots and not covering things enough?'"

Marketing plans for the film relied heavily on the release of the soundtrack, which Columbia brought out as a boxed album, available at three speeds. Beginning with Omaha and Kansas City, the Melchers set out on a "cross-country motor tour," so Day could "confer" on the air with disc jockeys. *Dreams* was chosen as the Christmas attraction at Radio City Music Hall, where it broke all records, and there was also a benefit premiere in Chicago on December 27, 1951, attended by both Grace Kahn and Danny Thomas.

The reviews of *Dreams* tended to focus on the film's sentimentality. "[The picture] treads a nostalgic path through the catalog of the late Gus Kahn's lyrics, offering entertainment that twangs at the heart and memory chords," explained the critic of *Variety*. "Miss Day sells the Kahn tunes given her with a wallop and lends likeable competence to the portrayal of Grace." The reviewer for the *New York Times*, a bit more circumspect, gave Day credit for "a good, solid job" and lauded the "sweetness" of her singing.

The trade reviews were more unbridled. "A dream of a movie, warm and tender," gushed *Photoplay*. "Danny Thomas as Kahn infuses his role with a down-to-earth appeal that knocks at every heart. Doris Day as the wife, who literally pushed her husband to fame, is equally fine."

"'Dreams' has a warmth that few musicals possess," proclaimed *Film Bulletin*. "As the wife, Doris Day is in top form, singing the songs with verve and showmanship." *Variety* reported that the picture took the "No. 1 spot nationally" during its initial release, "Xmas–New Year's week." Day comes across as even better than these initial reviewers allowed. She sustains the viewers' sympathy for Grace even as she conveys the bossy aspects of her character's personality—the naturally ebullient Day effortlessly straddles these opposing impulses. She even tugs at the heartstrings with facial expressions alone, when, late in the scenario, Kahn, about to leave her, announces he's fed up with her controlling tactics.

As with *Young Man with a Horn*, the musical numbers in *I'll See You in My Dreams* seem incidental to its dramatic story. Both pictures underscored what a first-rate actress Day had become in serious roles; in not a single moment of *Dreams* does she appear self-conscious or even seem to be acting at all. Moreover, both of these films exploit her extraordinary ability to project a song. And as with her dramatic performance, there is nothing forced or unnatural about Day's singing, which here seems to have reached yet another new peak. Her renditions of "Pretty Baby," "I Wish I Had a Girl," "The One I Love Belongs to Somebody Else," and the title song—as well as her duets with Thomas, "Ain't We Got Fun" and "Makin' Whoopee"—display a newfound interpretive maturity that does not interfere with the honey-dewed, husky purity of her voice.

Day also ages credibly as Grace. Given the many different fashions in the expansive time frame of the film, she had thirty-five wardrobe changes, the role challenging her hairdresser, Gertrude Wheeler, to create at least ten hairdos. Thomas is a tad less persuasive negotiating Kahn's aging. As Curtiz biographer Robertson wrote, Curtiz "soon realized that Thomas was no actor, but covered up this central defect with a portrait of Kahn as a weak man dependent upon his wife, thus allowing Thomas to indulge some of his talent for light-heartedness without a descent into outright comedy. This ploy almost works in that Thomas shows up as merely irritating some of the time and as adequate for most of it instead of miscast throughout." Still, Day and Thomas made for a winning, on-screen couple, and the film earned $1,758,000.

Day continued to promote the film with the debut, on March 28, 1952, of her own radio program, *The Doris Day Show*, produced by Melcher and aired by CBS. Her guests the first night were both Danny Thomas and the real Mrs. Gus Kahn. Subsequent guests would include songwriter Frank Loesser, singer Jack Smith, Kirk Douglas, Gordon Mac-Rae, Ray Bolger, Donald O'Connor, and Liberace. "We have lots of fun at the piano on my show," Day told Hedda Hopper a month later. "We go into impromptu vocals just the way we do at home when friends gather for an informal evening."

✳ ✳ ✳

Given the success of *I'll See You in My Dreams*, Warner Brothers announced that they would be remaking the first talkie, *The Jazz Singer*, with their "winning team" of costars Doris Day and Danny Thomas. "I wouldn't care if they re-titled it 'Mrs. Jazz Singer,' just as long as they put Doris in it," Thomas said, though he did not get his wish. Curtiz and Thomas did remake the film in 1953, but with Peggy Lee, in her first starring role, instead of Day. The director may have been hoping to strike Hollywood gold twice, but popular singer Lee would never become the equal of Day as a film star.

Day did become involved in another *Winning Team*, however, even if it would prove far from what the film's title suggested. It was a biography of Grover Cleveland Alexander, one of the greatest pitchers in the history of baseball, whose career flagged because he had epilepsy and recurring bouts of double vision—all while his early fans at first dismissed him as a hopeless alcoholic. "The greatest control pitcher of all-time" turned into "a stumbling has-been." The biopic begins his story of past greatness at a carnival sideshow, in which he appears as "Alex the Great," sandwiched between a fire-eater and a flea circus. He would rally from this low point with a comeback climaxed by his winning the championship for the St. Louis Cardinals from the New York Yankees in the 1926 World Series.

Based on a nine-page story by Jack Sher that appeared in the April 1950 issue of *Sport* magazine, the picture was originally called *Alex the Great*, then *Alexander*, and, next, *The Big League*. The final "title change memo" was dated February 19, 1952. The picture was assigned to Bryan Foy, the eldest of vaudeville's "Seven Little Foys." Whether it was the director or the material that Day objected to, she let the studio know that she did not want to participate in the project. She may have been opposed to playing an unsympathetic character who abandons her husband when he needs her the most. A wire, dated November 26, 1951, reminded the star of her "contract of employment" and added that she was "hereby directed to report to Mr. Foy at his office at our studio at Burbank, California, at 10:00 a.m. Tuesday, November 27."

After both Day and Ronald Reagan showed up at the studio for tests on December 7, shooting began on the twelfth, and concluded on January 28—one day behind schedule. The real Mrs. Grover Cleveland Alexander, Aimée, served as the film's "technical advisor"—and later went on tour to promote it. Foy filled out the cast with a number of major league players. The Cleveland Indians star pitcher Bob Lemon—a future manager of the New York Yankees—was on hand to coach Reagan. The production sustained at least one injury and several delays: "Reagan, whose right leg was broken in a charity baseball game three years ago, narrowly escaped the same injury to his left leg in a sequence," a production note recorded. "Jerry Priddy, Detroit second baseman, stepped on him accidentally and the big leaguer's spikes inflicted a painful laceration which kept Reagan hobbling for days." Another note explained: "California's most unusual winter in some 330 years upset the shooting schedule for the picture several times. Games had to be postponed because of rain and soggy fields and once because of heavy frost."

Though Day missed a few days because of a cold, the filming was uneventful. The picture would further establish Day as an actress, as opposed to a singer, but it nonetheless squeezed in a song, "Old Saint Nicholas," sung while the family decorates a tree on Christmas Eve. This set a precedent for Day—to offer a song or two in her nonmusical pictures—which Melcher would always argue for in view of the lucrative publishing rights.

As written by Ted Sherdeman, Seelag Lester, and Merwin Gerard, Aimée Alexander complains early in the scenario that she can't "compete against [her husband's] love for baseball" and "can't give him all the things that he wants and needs." After his professional debut in 1911, when he's declared Rookie of the Year, the years zip by as Aimée keeps a scrapbook of her husband's exploits. When Alex develops vision problems, Aimée believes the gossip that drinking is the cause. In her most melodramatic moment, Aimée says, "I haven't helped by staying. Maybe I can help by going away"—as she leaves him. Then, desperate to find

Alex, she is reduced to tears when she discovers him telling his story as a pathetic carnival sideshow act. This is all before the film's exciting climax, when Alexander regains his stature and proves instrumental in leading the Cardinals to victory in the World Series.

Day's less-than-sparkling performance seems to have reflected her resistance to making the film in the first place. Reagan, of course, was never much of an actor. (When, in the following decade, Reagan was running for governor of California, Jack Warner was approached to contribute to his campaign. "No, no, no. Dennis Morgan for governor. Ronald Reagan as the friend," responded Warner, as if he were casting a movie, at the same time keeping his billfold tightly closed.) Despite her top billing, Day, without a more gifted partner, foundered in the part. Whatever sparks ignited when they saw each other offscreen failed to catch fire before the cameras.

The Winning Team proves as dull and misconceived today as it was seen to be when it opened in June 1952. While dismissing Reagan as "passable as a ballplayer and okay as the man," *Variety* called it a "conventionally-treated screen biography." Day—"on whose name rests the film's chief marquee draw"—fared much better with the trade paper, which concluded that she had contributed "a sincere, moving portrayal of Alexander's wife." "'The Winning Team' loses out through sand-lot writing and direction and a rookie performance by Ronald Reagan in the leading role," wrote a reviewer in *Time. Newsweek* saw the film as "most persuasive when it interjects actual newsreel shots of the 1926 series, and the somewhat blurred and dimming sequences conjure up the roar and tension of the actual occasion."

Despite this misfire, filmgoers were hurling more and more kisses Day's way: as the Press Book for *The Winning Team* reported about the response to her previous role as Mrs. Gus Kahn: "There was no mistaking the fact that the lovely blonde lady had stepped into big time acting. New fame resulted and she has appeared on more magazine covers possibly than any other Hollywood star, her fan mail quadrupled, and Doris had readied herself for even greater roles."

In conjunction with her winning *Photoplay*'s Gold Medal for being "the most popular actress of the year," the magazine featured her "Life Story" in its March issue. When she learned of the award, tears formed in her eyes. After a silent pause, she said with genuine incredulity, "I've won this just for entertaining people?" The eight-page article accompanied Day's photo on the cover, with her characteristic smile.

The May issue of *Modern Screen* celebrated the Melchers' first anniversary as "the happiest chapter" in Day's still young life and Melcher as "something of a hero" to Terry. Written by Jim Burton, the piece presented the pair as "very much like that young couple down the block from you." Beneath the fluffy banter, however, one can begin to detect strain between the Melchers, even this early in their relationship. For one thing, Day complained that whenever they "go into Beverly Hills and do a bit of shopping, [it was never to satisfy her] dreams of silk and leather and gold" at Saks or Magnins, but to a hardware store. And while acknowledging that the Melchers "do not open their home wide to journalistic sightseers" and that "an army of magazine writers fret about how unavailable they are," Burton offered at least one surprising revelation. "Everything that Marty repaired worked fine afterwards, because Doris would call in the proper mechanic the next day to fix it right—and Marty, not knowing this, swaggered about among his accomplishments like a victory-drunk genius." This performance was part of Melcher's ongoing effort to overcome his country bumpkin roots and present himself as the all-American male and husband. It's worth noting that at this point Melcher was describing himself as "an agent whose main interest is music publishing" and that he was not yet primed to take over his wife's film career.

Michael Curtiz Productions extended Day's contract for fifty weeks on March 28 ("at $2,250 per week, beginning on May 8, 1952"); it was to run for two years. Given this pending deadline and Day's growing success, her handlers had been renegotiating her future situation with Warners. Following a conversation with Lew Wasserman of MCA (Music Corporation of American), Jack Warner wrote a memo on January 22, 1952, stipulating that Day's new contract would be for five years with an option for two more: "During the five year period Day could make two pictures on percentage for her own company, or something along this order."

According to a subsequent memo in the Warner Brothers archives, by November 13, 1952, "numerous conversations regarding a new deal for Doris Day" had taken place. On November 21, Jack Warner received a telegram from Wasserman: After explaining that the Doris Day "proposal to Warners" followed "numerous meetings" with Melcher, his lawyer, Jerry Rosenthal, and MCA, Wasserman added, "Furthermore at no time that I can remember have we ever used any one deal as a pattern for our business relationship." This amounts to one of the first indications of a proposed Doris Day "corporation," to be established under the studio's aegis.

It was Lew Wasserman, as opposed to Melcher, who was in the midst of transforming the way Hollywood conducted business. In 1950, Wasserman engineered a two-picture deal for his client Jimmy Stewart, who would receive a percentage of the profits on each, revolutionizing the way stars were paid. If the stars' power grew at the studios' expense, Day was on the verge of becoming a part of the revolution. But a good deal more haggling over her future business arrangements would ensue throughout 1953. In the end, Melcher would extricate his wife from the clutches of Jack Warner, even if the maneuver would ultimately benefit Rosenthal the most. Day, the breadwinner for all of them, was simply a pawn in their machinations.

"Dynamite" Doris

---- ✳ ----

*"I don't think she ever had any idea of how great she was.
She just thought that was the way she was supposed to be."*
—DONALD SADDLER

April in Paris, Day's twelfth picture in five years, maintained a pace that was taking its toll. While she was making the film, MCA sent a letter to Warner Brothers requesting "a minimum period of 6 weeks" vacation for its client, after completing the picture: "She has been working constantly, going from one picture to another, and feels that it is impossible for her to continue to do so without a period of time off." *April in Paris* was also Day's third film with director David Butler. A studio press release of December 19, 1951, heralded her starring role in the picture. Though the following month Gordon MacRae was announced as her costar, this was not to be. Having recently directed Ray Bolger in *Where's Charley?* Butler, instead, cast this actor—a gifted clown, but inappropriate as a romantic lead—to the tune of $125,000, which *Variety* declared to be "his top pic salary to date." If Bolger's bulging eyes and angular nose—coupled with his edgy, fey mannerisms—made him an ideal Scarecrow in *The Wizard of Oz* and a perfect transvestite in *Where's Charley?*, he was a poor choice as Day's costar.

The misguided casting created another opportunity for critics to judge Warners as being well beneath MGM's standards. As reported in the *Daily News,* "Ray Bolger, who wasn't judged pretty enough to be starred along Gene Kelly lines when he was at MGM, is back in Hollywood as a Warner star and grinning about passing the romantic test at long last." Of course, Bolger himself took a more positive view of the casting decision: "Hollywood has changed its feelings entirely. The handsome, stereotyped leading men aren't getting the jobs. Hollywood has discovered that the prettiest girls don't always marry the handsomest men. Danny Thomas proved it in 'I'll See You in My Dreams.' Nobody noticed his nose."

Yet again built around a case of mistaken identity and set, in part, on a cruise ship, the formulaic story of *April in Paris* is vaguely reminiscent of Day's first film, *Romance on the High Seas*. Day plays Ethel ("Dynamite") Jackson, a Broadway chorus girl who by error receives an invitation to represent the American Theater at a French festival in Paris. Bolger portrays S. Winthtrop Putnam, a D.C. bureaucrat sent to New York to explain that the invitation was really meant for renowned actress Ethel Barrymore. But once it's suggested that a lowly chorus girl is more symbolic of American democracy, Jackson is delegated the U.S. representative after all. Putnam joins her on the transatlantic journey, and inevitably they fall in love. There are, of course, the predictable complications. For one, Putnam is already engaged to a state official's daughter; for another, a French entertainer and waiter on the ship, Philippe Fouquet (Claude Dauphin), has designs of his own on Jackson.

No matter how trite the story, *April in Paris* had a lively score. Having previously written the popular title number with E. Y. Harburg, Vernon Duke was commissioned to compose seven songs for the picture, most of them with lyrics by Sammy Cahn. Knowing full well that Day's endorsement would sell just about any number, the lyricist did his best to curry favor in an awkward note to her, dated March 12: ". . . wishing you a most pleasant and wonderful assignment. I am especially proud to be connected in my small capacity. The best of everything. Sammy Cahn."

Production on the picture began just after Day was named the "Queen of National Smile Week" by the Association of Greeting Card Advertising Managers. Though LeRoy Prinz received screen credit for the choreography, his brother Eddie, yet again, supervised the dancers. However, the real creative work belonged this time to Donald Saddler. A half century later, Saddler would recall, "The only thing I can remember about Eddie Prinz is that he used to be in LeRoy's office sometimes, and if you went there, they were playing cards. Prinz was very close with the front office, and very secure at Warners. His brother had another job there. He had come from Broadway, where they did routines." In the course of working with Saddler, Day grew very fond of him. In addition to doing two more pictures with Day, he would become a friend who remained in touch over the years.

Saddler was born in Van Nuys in 1920 and raised in Los Angeles. He first studied dance there, with Nico Charisse, who would marry his young student Cyd. Saddler next worked with the Uruguayan Carmalita Maracci, who had a reputation for being one of the finest dance instructors on the West Coast. Saddler moved to New York in 1939 and, in short order, helped cofound a dance company called Ballet Theater, which eventually became American Ballet Theatre. Like so many other theater artists who came to New York in the mid-twentieth century, Saddler ended up in Hollywood through his involvement with Broadway shows. After performing for two years in *High Button Shoes,* Saddler was cast in a low-profile musical revue called *Bless You All,* starring Jules Munshin and Pearl Bailey and choreographed by the stalwart dance captain Helen Tamaris.

"When it was closing, Tamaris came to me and said, 'You know, Donald, I'm going to Hollywood to do a film with Bing Crosby and Jane Wyman,'" Saddler recalled of his first involvement with a motion picture: *Just for You,* made at Paramount in 1952. "Why don't you come with me and be my assistant?" Tamaris asked. In addition to working with Tamaris on the film's big number, he also created a solo for Jane Wyman: "Helen came to me and said, 'Why don't you work with Jane?'" Saddler remained grateful to Wyman for "a big plug" when she ran into LeRoy Prinz at the Warners commissary and became no less indebted to Prinz: "LeRoy sent for me, and said, 'I'm doing a movie called "April in Paris." I'll give you the ideas, but you stage it, and then shoot it.' And in the process, he taught me all that he knew about the camera."

Saddler's first day on the set with Day, was February 21, 1952. They rehearsed on the "Prinz unit" until March 15, even as production began for Butler on the twelfth and finished on June 7. At the outset, Saddler told Day: "I would love to have some time with you alone, just so I could try out some steps to see how you respond to the music. I could get a head start that way." Day responded, "Wonderful, wonderful." "That was when we began going into the studio together," added Saddler, recalling their first get-together.

"A lot of people in her position are very nervous about working with a new director or a new choreographer because they think, 'That person doesn't know me, and they can destroy me.' But there was instantly a nice rapport. And after a while, I could think ahead, because I knew how she moved, and it proved a great asset. I always made her feel that if a step wasn't right, then I'd just give her another one. And she was Warner Brothers–trained, where sometimes they would just go on the set, improvise the number, and shoot it," which, Saddler maintained, could produce sloppy results.

If one of a choreographer's principal goals was to know a dancer's limitations, Saddler detected few in Day. "Of all the stars and principals I've ever danced with, I think she was one of the most gifted," continued Saddler. "I don't think she ever had any idea of how great she was. She just thought that was the way she was supposed to be. But when she was working, she was in her own world. Her real world wasn't as magical as the world she went into. It's hard to explain, but you know it when you see it—the power of it. She could do anything.

"When you showed her something, she would immediately perform it. So you knew if it was going to work for her or not. She would take it and go with it, and that's a truly great talent. She just threw herself into it. And you knew exactly what it was going to be like. With a lot of other stars, sometimes you have to wait for the curtain to go up to really see them do it. But with Doris, if she couldn't take a step I gave her and make something out of it—or make it her own—then it was the step's fault, because she had perfect rhythm. She was one of the great talents."

When they were about to work on the opening number, "It Must Be Good," which involved a dozen or so chorus girls, Day displayed her customary anxiety and modesty. "Doris came to me and said, 'Would you do it with me first, because I don't want all those professional dancers to have to stand around while you're teaching me what you've already taught them?' She was a little insecure about being a star, in front of all the chorus girls, who, she believed, had a lot more technique than she did."

Saddler earned $250 a week at Warner Brothers. One particular memory reinforces the studio's reputation for stinginess: LeRoy Prinz advised Saddler always to tell Day how good each take was: "Because we only do single takes here," Prinz confessed. However, the star and her dance coach worked out a special system for getting around this restriction. Day told Saddler, 'If we're shooting a number, and you don't think it came out well, let's have a signal. And then I'll say, 'I think I made a mistake. I'd like to do it again.'" Whenever he felt something was wrong with a shoot, Saddler would utter the obligatory words of praise, but gaze down at the floor. "And I would be right beside the camera," he explained, "so I was always in her view."

The studio's parsimonious tactics prevailed for the rollicking number "Ring the Bell Tonight," set in the cruise ship's kitchen. Though a relatively lengthy and elaborate production number, it was both staged and shot in a single day, and much of it was improvised.

Though Day's character was nicknamed Dynamite, there were no visible sparks between her and Bolger, on-screen or off. "Doris had a lot more fun with [French star] Claude Dauphin. He was easygoing, and they reacted well together," said Saddler, who also remembered Bolger, primarily a tap dancer, asking him for some more nuanced ballet steps in a number. If Day proved a quick study with Saddler, Bolger was the opposite. "The next day he couldn't remember a thing we had done," Saddler remarked. "He'd always fall back on a set routine, which he had been doing for years."

There were fireworks of a different sort on the set, however, when Butler, in earshot of everyone, confronted Bolger over stealing a scene from his costar; and also when Dauphin, as a waiter, poured too much brandy over a flaming dish and singed his eyebrows. The gentlemanly Saddler noted that Day did nothing to disguise her disapproval of LeRoy Prinz, who could be vulgar and crude, offending her with his cursing.

Basically a parody of American bureaucracy, the film prompted an extraordinary letter from a married couple, the Irwins, from West Los Angeles, sent to Warners via Joseph Breen of the Motion Picture Producers Association. Dated January 23, 1953, and written in green ink, the letter showed their McCarthyite sympathies.

"The story was very weak and certainly very distasteful. In fact it had a slight but obvious reaking [*sic*] of so-called 'Communistic inspired' dialogue and actions throughout the entire picture. We are sure—if it wasn't—the Communists could not have done a more impressive job. . . . Believe us, we're not trying to use Communism as the 'scape-goat' but in all sincerity it would be an extremely clever way for them to get their point across.

". . . This picture was most degrading for women and men alike. . . . In fact almost every picture we have seen lately or are exposed to— through no fault of our own is 1. Sex 2. Sex 3. And more Sex. . . . As for future viewing of Doris Day (the reason we attended the movie) we are all deeply disappointed and we hope she wakes up—before she is another one of the Hollywood puppets."

Though Breen had not previously raised any matters of hidden Communist agendas in *April in Paris*, his preliminary letters to Warner had cited another of the Irwins' complaints: "several instances of unacceptably sex-suggestive dialogue and situations which could not be approved."

In keeping with Day's growing popularity, she had by now entered what critic Stanley Kauffmann dubbed an artist's "Age of the Larynx," that is, when the number of interviews given seems to consume as much time as required to accomplish the work. Indeed, as the *Hollywood Reporter* reported in the middle of June 1952: "Doris Day, beginning today, will devote an entire week to interviews by columnists and slick and fan mag correspondents. The interviews, averaging six a day, will embrace her latest Warners film, 'April in Paris.'"

Reviewers tended to agree that the film was mildly entertaining. "It is an average round of comedy, songs and dances . . . with the name of Doris Day to give it a marquee advantage," concluded *Variety*. "Fairly pleasant, breezy filmusical, short on story but long on laughs," echoed the *Hollywood Reporter*. Philip K. Scheuer criticized "the rambling, much too complicated plot" in the *L.A. Times*, while Kay Proctor accurately summed it up in the *L.A. Examiner*: "It's easy on the eyes . . . easy on the ears . . . and guaranteed not to make you think!"

* * *

Given the success they had with Doris Day and Gordon MacRae in *On Moonlight Bay*, Warners made a sequel, also based on Booth Tarkington's *Penrod* stories and set in the post–World War I era. As announced in *Variety* on May 1, 1952–which humorously claimed that Warners was also using "the same moon"–the two stars were back on board for *By the Light of the Silvery Moon*–as was much of the rest of the cast. With Day once again portraying Marjorie Winfield, Leon Ames returned as her father, Rosemary DeCamp as her mother, and familiar character actress Mary Wickes as the Winfield housekeeper and cook, Stella. Billy Gray was making a comeback as Marjorie's younger, mischievous brother, Wesley. Even the mongrel dog, Corky, returned for *Silvery Moon*, cavorting on the same set.

With its white-picket-fence and front-porch verities, *Silvery Moon* sealed Day's archetypal image as the all-American girl next door. The film also sealed Day's image as a tomboy. It opens with Stella introducing filmgoers to the Winfield family: "The Winfields have two children: a boy and a girl," explains Stella, as the camera pans to a "tin lizzie," and the person who's been repairing the buggy slides out from underneath. "That's the girl," Stella adds with a definite edge to her voice, as Marjorie comes into view, clad in a man's overalls and plaid flannel shirt–obligatory grease stains on her cheeks. George Winfield calls his eighteen-year-old daughter "a grease monkey," as opposed to "a charming, feminine young lady." And later, when he hears that she's marrying Bill Sherman, George pointedly remarks, with a twinkle in his eye, that he feels as if he's "losing a son"—not a daughter. In a scene in which Marjorie sports a man's hunting jacket and fur cap, George says, "Look at her. No wonder men leave town—a fine picture of grace, beauty, and femininity."

Silvery Moon helped established Day as more than just a movie star; she became an important American figure who, in many a role, anticipated the women's movement by at least a decade. Marjorie, for example, is disappointed to learn that Bill wants to put off their marriage until he's gainfully employed and accumulates a little "nest egg." When she counters that they could marry sooner if she were also working, Bill offers a conventional reply: "The business world's a man's world, Marjorie, and women have no right forsaking their sacred heritage to meddle in it. Now they're even meddling in politics." To send the point home, this scene occurs after they leave a dance, the car breaks down, and Marjorie makes the repairs, soiling her ball gown in the process.

The *Hollywood Reporter* announced that Donald Saddler, who had worked so closely and so well with Day on *April in Paris*, would return to Warners to assist LeRoy Prinz on the film. As soon as she learned that Saddler was going to be part of *Silvery Moon*, Day personally called Steve Trilling, head of production at Warner Brothers, to insist that the choreographer receive screen credit this time, in lieu of Prinz, who really contributed less and less to her efforts. Shortly afterward, Prinz candidly told Saddler, "You know, Doris is not very fond of me." But in a more comradely spirit, the studio dance head also told the upstart, "I want you to know, I'll be around, and if I can help you in any way, I will." The irony is that Saddler had worked even more diligently when he was choreographing *April in Paris*—which had more lavish production numbers—without receiving any credit. (Saddler singled out "King Chanticleer" in *Silvery Moon* as the most elaborate number he ever choreographed for Day.)

Saddler genially accommodated her idiosyncratic ways of rehearsing: "I quickly learned to let her talk about whatever was on her mind when she'd come to class at the studio. Whether it was something about Terry, or something that had happened at home, she had to get it out of her system. Because if she didn't, and I was about to show her the next step, she would stop me and say, 'Oh, you know what happened?' She was like a little girl, always eager to report something. But if I let her get it out, then when we started [practicing at] the barre, our work could be nonstop."

When the subject of Christian Science first arose, Day told Saddler that Charlotte Greenwood, the gangly comedienne and dancer, was Marty's "practitioner" (or guide) and that Greenwood's husband, Martin Broones, functioned as her own. Saddler noticed not even a hint on Day's part of wanting to proselytize him. A dashing, cultured, bright, and considerate gentleman, Saddler was unlike the men Day was accustomed to dealing with in the cutthroat music world and Hollywood. But even if few of Day's associates liked Melcher, Saddler did. He also had the distinct impression that Day did not want her husband interfering with their time in the studio. "I don't think Doris would have liked his being there," said Saddler. "We had this wonderful rapport of working together, and just talking through things."

The ragtime "Chanticleer" number had been Saddler's idea. When he first brought it to Day's attention, early in the planning stages, she was put off by a foreign word she did not know. Nor did she seem any more disposed to the song when Saddler explained that "chanticleer" was the French word for rooster. She turned keen only when Saddler proposed a minstrel number instead, but they quickly realized it would alienate African-Americans. When Saddler later reintroduced the idea for "Chanticleer," Day had no memory of having rejected it. Saddler then worked first with the other dancers, whom he had portray barnyard animals, and the big number was ready for the star. She joined them to work on the scene the day before it was shot. "Doris always made it so easy," said Saddler. "She just jumped into it so wonderfully. She loved the number because she was kind of tomboyish, anyway. Everything she did was of the moment and real."

Since the film's editor, Irene Morra, knew how important the "Chanticleer" number was to Saddler, she invited him to participate in the edit, and he was grateful she did. More typical for Warners, the bouncy "Ain't We Got Fun" duet that occurs earlier in the picture was improvised and staged right on the set with Day and MacRae. "Of course, they were both so wonderful, that it rolled out easily," said Saddler.

With David Butler again at the helm, production on *Silvery Moon* ran smoothly, beginning on August 11 and even finishing a day ahead of schedule (on October 14). Jan Olliffe, the president of the national Doris Day fan club, once again visited Day on the set. The twenty-two-year-old Olliffe "greatly resembles the star," the publicity department announced. As a surprise for Terry, Day rode home for lunch one day in the film's 1919 Model-T Ford. He had recently taken on a neighborhood paper route. Gordon MacRae's eight-year-old daughter, Meredith, had a more temporary job that summer, ice-skating with her father in the picture.

Saddler pointed out that one of the ice skaters in the rousing finale of the title song was Larry Kert, who, only four years later, would originate on Broadway the role of Tony in *West Side Story*. And the actor wielding the red megaphone, out on the studio's frozen lake, was another name-in-the-making: Merv Griffin.

Indeed, after seeing Griffin perform in Las Vegas, the Melchers were responsible for getting him a contract with Warner Brothers. "When we played Las Vegas, we did a whole floor show, featuring the Freddy Martin Band, where we all performed," recalled Griffin, who had had a big hit with a novelty song, "I've Got a Lovely Bunch of Coconuts," in 1950. "We had wonderful material. You have to understand, there were only three hotels on the strip, at that time. I was at the Last Frontier. Next door was El Rancho Vegas, and up, where we thought was far too far away, was Bugsy Siegel's the Flamingo. That's when this little boy came up to me after the show, and said, 'My mommy wants to make a movie with you.' And I thought, 'Oh, yeah, little kid?' I said, 'Who's your mama?' And he said, 'Doris Day.' And then, there she was, with Marty. I eventually tested, and they put me under contract."

At the time, William Orr was the head of casting at Warners. "He gave a big party at his house," Griffin recalled. "There was a reception line and all of a sudden, there was Gordon MacRae, and behind him was Sammy Cahn, the great songwriter. So Gordon said, 'Oh, Merv, I admire your records so much. What are you doing in Hollywood?' I kind of looked surprised, as I said, 'I just signed with Warner Brothers.' And then Sammy Cahn leaned in and said, 'Yeah. He's going to take your place, Gordon.' And I thought, 'Oh my God.' Gordon looked really upset.

"I got a call from the casting office, saying I was in *By the Light of the Silvery Moon*," Griffin recalled, "and telling me to see David Butler, who was a great friend of my uncle's. So I showed up on the day of my shooting. Strangely enough, I was like an MC in the skating-rink scene—I did that twice in movies at Warner Brothers and then ended up as an MC in life."

Saddler, meanwhile, became an occasional volleyball player at the Melchers on weekends. During one of his visits, Day told him about a soda fountain they were having installed for free and complained about the commercial she had to do to get it. "You know Marty and all his angles," she said with a sigh.

As they were completing work on *Silvery Moon*, Saddler received an invitation to choreograph Rosalind Russell in *Wonderful Town* on Broadway. He wistfully recalled taking up the subject with Day, either before or after a volleyball game, in the library. "I know that the next picture is *Calamity Jane*," Saddler told her, "and if you don't want me to go to New York, I won't." Though Day liked the affable and elegant Saddler and admired what he did for her, she knew that he was classically trained and wasting his talents with the churned-out work at Warners. She encouraged him to go to New York. "It may be two or three months before we even start *Calamity Jane*," Day pointed out. "Maybe you can do it and be back in time. But one way or the other, you've got to do a Broadway show." She added that she would come to New York to see it—and she did.

Given Day's ongoing and rollicking success, Warners planned to make *Calamity Jane* her most expensive picture to date. "The studio is giving her the real grand treatment for the [film]," Hedda Hopper wrote in her column, "which is going to be the biggest and classiest musical she's had up to date. And being the No. 1 feminine box-office attraction, she deserves it."

✳ ✳ ✳

The marketing for *Silvery Moon* focused on the movie's tried-and-true family values, and a promotional campaign encouraged newspaper delivery ("carrier") boys to see the film with their mothers. When it opened at Radio City Music Hall in April 1953—as part of the twenty-first Annual Gala Easter show—reviewers tended to mimic the advance hype: "It's a harmless, entertaining, tuneful bit of nonsense that's no strain on the brain but a tonic to the senses," said a *Seattle Times* reviewer. "Choice, long-tested corn of the Booth Tarkington variety. It is further guaranteed by the presence of the incredibly blond Doris Day, alternately tomboyish and marvelously, flamboyantly and tunefully feminine," wrote Archer Winsten in the *New York Post*. "If you want this reviewer's personal reaction, it is that few blonds seem gayer, or have whiter teeth, or sing more zestfully than Doris Day." "Miss Day is thoroughly charming in the feminine lead and seems to sing better than ever, which is saying a lot for the always good singing star," offered the *Hollywood Reporter*. Even the curmudgeonly Bosley Crowther declared it "agreeably melodious" in the *New York Times* and the *New York Tribune*'s professorial Otis L. Guernsey

Jr. termed it "a spun-sugar musical, prettily pink to go with the season of bunnies, lilies and new bonnets, generous-looking in Technicolor."

Day herself considered *Moonlight Bay* and *Silvery Moon* among her favorite films, because of the era they were set in, when "everything was sweet." Describing herself as an "old-fashioned person" and "an old-fashioned girl," she emphasized her basic nostalgia as she added: "I really wish that I'd lived then."

Day's archetypal portrayals of the all-American girl next door in *On Moonlight Bay* and followed so closely in *By the Light of the Silvery Moon* branded her for good as such in the cultural landscape. Hugh Hefner chose the year of *Silvery Moon*—1953—to launch *Playboy*, a magazine that became an institution by presenting a monthly centerfold he described simply as "the girl next door with her clothes off." Day, however, despite her reputation, was really the inverse: Though fully clothed in all of her films, she was far, far from the "girl next door" she was perceived to be.

The tight-fitting blue overalls worn by Day in the "Chanticleer" number emphasize her large derriere more prominently than ever before and help explain why Bob Hope nicknamed her "J.B."; though Hope often called her "J.B." in public, only insiders knew its meaning: "Jut Butt."

*   *   *

While the pace of Day's filmmaking at Warners showed no signs of slackening, her family life at least acquired some outward stability. In July 1952, Melcher adopted the ten-year-old Terry, giving him his surname. Unlike so many other aspects of the Melchers' home life, this was done quietly and without publicity. And now he was running his own music company, called Daywin, with her brother Paul's help in the office. Always the dutiful mother hen, Alma had to be pleased that her only surviving son, with his own family, now lived near her in Los Angeles. Much later Day would come to realize—and acknowledge—that mixing business with family matters was a major mistake, essentially demeaning both.

Day's childhood pal Mary Goodwin had also recently moved from Cincinnati to Los Angeles. Goodwin contacted the star via the studio to renew their friendship. During the rare periods when Day wasn't working on a picture, Goodwin became a regular visitor and her shopping companion.

In an article for *Photoplay*, Goodwin described "a typical day" in the Melcher household. "I arrive at Doris' for a morning visit," she wrote.

"Doris is busy seeing her Marty off to the office, with seven of Terry's friends under his feet. In the next couple of hours there are a succession of people passing through: the upholsterers bringing in furniture and taking other pieces away, the gardener, Terry's music teacher, a magazine writer who is waiting to interview Doris in the midst of the confusion, photographers from the studio, some fan club officials from Seattle."

Day and Goodwin usually had lunch together at the Smoke House, a no-frills eatery directly across the street from the Warners lot. Day was known to be a basic, meat-and-potatoes gal. But Goodwin described Day's habit of studying the plates on neighboring tables and then driving the waiters crazy as she changed her mind time and again, even while placing an order.

After lunch came the shopping expeditions. "There's nothing in the world Doris likes better than shopping, though quite often she doesn't buy a thing," wrote Goodwin. "Doris is a careful buyer and a careful spender. She adores sales and has an infallible knack for spotting good 'buys.'"

Goodwin also described Day as being more than just fastidious and, in fact, as positively phobic about "neatness and order." Goodwin even observed her childhood friend telling Terry not to touch the wallpaper or walk on the carpet. "In desperation, Terry came up with the idea of hanging a rope outside his bedroom window, so he can shinny up and down." Goodwin spoke—as many did—of the kitchen as the room in which the Melchers, their friends, and visitors usually congregated—just as had been the case when Day was growing up in Cincinnati.

Goodwin presented two particularly intriguing, if contradictory, perceptions of Day that were passed on to her by Melcher. For one, Melcher saw Day as a "human periscope" because of her "innate curiosity. She must know what goes on around her all the time." Melcher also recognized that "Doris is the first to admit that she 'tunes out' on people. She can quite suddenly forget that you're there. [And] she will swear she told you something last week which she had remarked to someone else, or vice versa. Her close associates know better than to expect her to meet them for lunch unless they've checked with her an hour before."

11

"Secret Love"

———————— ✳ ————————

"I think Calamity Jane *is the real me."*
—DORIS DAY

Since its premiere in 1953, *Calamity Jane* was considered a consolation prize for Day, after she failed to bag the title role in *Annie Get Your Gun*. According to some reports, MGM was eager that Day portray Annie Oakley as a loan-out, and Day was eager to take on the role she seemed born to play. But Jack Warner, fearful that his new star would quickly discover how a first-class studio functioned—and resent the relatively miserly working conditions at Warners—declined to lend her.

Yet the matter remains equivocal: if *Calamity Jane* was written for Day as a recompense, it seems odd that Michael Curtiz announced the film as one of her upcoming projects long before *Annie Get Your Gun* emerged as a possible project at another studio. Curtiz had bought the rights to *Calamity* some time after he made *Romance on the High Seas* with his new discovery. "Both Doris and Curtiz have previous chores before they get around to [making] this," Dorothy Manners said in the *Chicago Herald American* on June 22, 1948. "But 'Calamity' is first up on the Michael Curtiz production for 1949."

In the end *Calamity Jane* proved vastly superior to *Annie Get Your Gun*. Along with Day herself, many regard it as one of her best films. "I think 'Calamity Jane' is the real me," she said in a BBC documentary. And she would tell another interviewer: "I am Calamity Jane, didn't you know that?"

In his insightful book on Day's movies, George Morris is on target when describing *Calamity Jane* as "Day's definitive characterization during the first epoch of her stardom. The tomboy aspect of Day's persona receives full expression here, but her swaggering bravado conceals a feminine vulnerability essential for audience sympathy. Day is never masculine or abrasive; she brings dimension to the role by capturing the contradictions in Calamity's character, her brusque, independent nature as well as that softer side of her which yearns ultimately for emotional commitment to a man."

Calamity Jane was Day's tenth musical for Warners and her fifth with David Butler as director. Though he, too, felt that Day was at her peak, Butler did think she had become a tad uppity: "By the time we did 'Calamity Jane,' Doris had reached the height of her profession. She was great in it. She was very matter of fact about what she wanted to do. . . . This was the time when she might come into a scene, and you'd want her to walk over to the mantelpiece, but she'd want to stop at the table. Then we'd shoot it her way, and afterwards she'd say, 'It might be best to go to the mantel.' Those were little situations. They didn't mean anything, except that they made you feel that she was starting to feel her oats a little, starting to want to direct, as I've found out so many people do. Now, I'm very fond of Doris Day. I love her. She's great, and I can't say enough about her ability. But most people, when they get a little up to stardom, there are very few of them who act the same as they did when they were starting, somehow or other. But I guess that's the way of the beast."

The real Calamity Jane was the product of a much rougher era than a Doris Day musical of the 1950s could ever hope to portray. Martha Jane Canary received the nickname "Calamity" because of her fortitude during a crisis, when, in 1872, she rescued a U.S. army captain in the midst of an Indian uprising at Goose Creek Camp, South Dakota.

Though the rollicking musical movie of 1953 played down this all-important episode in her life, another anecdote, relayed by Buffalo Bill Cody, suggests that screenwriter James O'Hanlon and lyricist Paul Francis Webster carefully studied the life of the actual Martha Canary and made accurate references to her in their fictionalized scenario. "In 1876, Jane, by a daring feat, saved the lives of six passengers on a stage coach traveling from Deadwood to Wild Birch, in the Black hills country," recalled Cody, famous for embellishing his stories. "The stage was surrounded by Indians, and the driver, Jack McCall, was wounded by an arrow. Although the other six passengers were men, not one of them had nerve enough to take the ribbons [i.e., the reins]. Seeing the situation, Jane mounted the driver's seat without a moment's hesitation and brought the stage safely and in good time to Wild Birch."

The film's opening has Day's Calamity riding shotgun on a stagecoach as she sings, "Oh, the Deadwood Stage is a headin' on over the hills. . . ." There are, of course, inevitable and glaring discrepancies between movie and fact: whereas the real Canary was a large, dark-haired, homely alcoholic, the film's Calamity is confined to Day's smaller frame and is blonde, attractive, and partial to "sarsapparilly."

A big picture that would prove an enormous success for the studio, *Calamity Jane* required Day to learn all sorts of rugged skills, such as horseback riding and handling a whip. Her rehearsals were rigorous. For example, on December 6 she worked with a "stagecoach" at a ranch and then proceeded to the studio to practice riding and whip cracking for more than three hours. She devoted the following week to improving her horseback riding. Production began on December 20, 1952, and continued through March 23, 1953, when it finished seven days late. As many as eighty-three extras and fifty-six horses were employed.

Jack Warner received another letter from Joseph Breen, vice president and director of the Production Code Administration of the Motion Picture Association of America, itemizing censorship concerns about upholding the moral standards of the day. One item warned that "[t]he lady who winks flirtatiously at Calamity should not resemble a street-walker." Moreover, "Katie [played by Allyn McLerie] should not strip down to the more intimate garments of feminine apparel such as panties and brassiere." But the most interesting caveat admonished, "We repeat our previous caution regarding the characterization of Francis Fryer [who performs in drag at a saloon]. He should not be on the effeminate side."

Despite Breen's stipulated wish, the "flirtatiously" winking extra—who mistakes Calamity for a man on the sidewalks of Chicago—most definitely evokes a prostitute in the finished film. But when muscular character actor Dick Wesson, as Francis Fryer, dons a dress to impersonate a female saloon singer, he is decidedly not "effeminate." This subplot about a cross-dressing performer only seems to accentuate that *Calamity Jane* is, in essence, the story of a pioneering transvestite who seems like "just one of the boys."

Though she thinks she's in love with a U.S. cavalryman, Lt. Danny Gilmartin (Philip Carery), Calamity spends most of the film sparring with Bill Hickok (Howard Keel)—whom she marries in the end. She has by then been thoroughly feminized by Katie Brown, the would-be singer fetched by Calamity from Chicago to replace Francis Fryer at Deadwood's Golden Garter Saloon. "I may have made a mistake about his gender, but not his talent," says the proprietor of the saloon, after Fryer sings "I've Got a Heart Full of Honey" and his wig accidentally comes off, exposing him as a man and prompting pandemonium in the auditorium.

Though it is, of course, good clean fun and family entertainment, *Calamity Jane* has a deeper subtext as it examines impersonation and gender. Not only does Calamity dress like a man and Fryer like a woman, but Katie decides to impersonate Adelaide Adams when Calamity mistakes her for that headlining star. Indeed, when she firsts meet Calamity, Katie in turn mistakes her for a man, prompting gales of laughter from "Calam," who reflects, "Come to think of it, that ain't so funny."

Having already told Calamity, "If ya ever crawled out of that deer-hide and dolled up a bit, I got a hunch you'd be a passably pretty gal," Bill Hickok admonishes, "You dress, talk, ride and shoot like a man, but you think like a female." Moreover, as pointed out in *The Celluloid Closet*, a documentary about hidden homosexual references in Hollywood films, lesbian undercurrents in the plot build to a crescendo when Day sings "Secret Love," clad in a buckskin suit and cowboy hat while riding a horse. Consider the lyrics: "Once I had a secret love . . ."

Day gave her speaking voice a deeper timbre throughout the film. "I lowered my voice and stuck out my chin a little," she explained in her memoir. She also offered the most athletic performance of her career to date, climbing over the stagecoach, leaping onto the bar in the saloon, and sliding along it several times, twirling her gun. Day recalled the trauma of nearly dying in the course of filming *Calamity*. In the scene in which she's lassoed and hoisted aloft, the rope was wound so tight that she had difficulty breathing. Given all the guns going off and the commotion below, no one heard her screams. By the time she was let down, she had almost passed out for lack of air. They had to rework the harness and reshoot the scene.

If Day was one of the film's greatest assets, its original score was another, with infectious tunes by Sammy Fain and nimble lyrics by Paul Francis Webster. There wasn't a dud among the songs. While "I Can Do Without You" was highly reminiscent of "Anything You Can Do" from *Annie Get Your Gun*, and "I Just Got Back from the Windy City" evoked "Everything's Up to Date in Kansas City" from *Oklahoma*, Fain and Webster produced a hit for the ages with "Secret Love." The song instantly went to the top of the charts and remained there for practically half a year, ultimately winning the Oscar. It would forever after be identified with Day, along with "Sentimental Journey," "It's Magic," and "Que Sera, Sera."

A month before *Calamity Jane* opened, Hedda Hopper proclaimed it "by far the best picture Doris Day ever made." With a lot of accompanying hoopla, the film premiered on November 1, 1953, in the Black Hills state of South Dakota, where the picture is set and where the real Calamity Jane is buried. The mayor of Rapid City declared November 1 through 7 "Calamity Jane Week," and parades were held in Rapid City and Lead. According to a local paper, "Bands, Indians, stage coaches and other attractions [added] color to the parade," and newsreel cameras were on hand to capture the pageantry.

The film opened around the nation to a generally ecstatic response, and Day received some of her best notices yet. "A rollicking musical filled with humor, vitality and surefire song hits, 'Calamity Jane' stands out as one of Warners' brightest filmusicals [*sic*] to explode on the screen," gushed Milton Luban in the *Hollywood Reporter*, "with Doris Day in the title role delivering what easily may be her most sparkling performance to date."

"Doris Day has given Warners one of its best—if not the best musical in years . . . the Day gal converts an ordinary story into topflight entertainment," wrote a critic in *Film Bulletin*. Philip K. Scheuer concurred in the *Los Angeles Times*: "In 'Calamity Jane,' Warners borrows as unblushingly from 'Oklahoma!' and 'Annie Get Your Gun' as Doris Day, the Calamity, borrows from the men's wardrobe. But, imitative or not, the Technicolor musical . . . adds up to the liveliest from the studio in a long while and easily Miss Day's most effective to date."

Irene Thirer in the *New York Post* deemed it "a lusty, zestful musical comedy interpretation of the gun-totin' gal of the old West. If you're partial to Doris' talents as we are, you'll find this a veritable field Day, and you'll have much fun watching the vivacious blond cavort all over the screen." In addition to the many accolades the film received, Butler won a *Photoplay* award for *Calamity*, as did Day, who was "picked by moviegoers as one of the nation's most popular actresses."

Having already released boxed albums of the scores of *By the Light of the Silvery Moon, Moonlight Bay, Lullaby of Broadway, Tea for Two,* and *Young Man with a Horn,* Columbia issued *Calamity Jane* as both a 45 and a 78 set. (By 1954, the 45-rpm record had gained in popularity as the 78-rpm was being phased out.) Not only did "Secret Love" become a top single of 1954, *Calamity Jane* also emerged as one of the top ten albums of the year.

* * *

While Day worked on *Calamity Jane,* Melcher and Wasserman were busy negotiating her new financial arrangements with Warner Brothers, which entailed two contracts. The terms of the "corporation" to be forged were spelled out in a letter dated April 4, 1953, over the signature of Warners' Roy Obringer. Even though Day's contract with Michael Curtiz Productions had a full year to run, one being drawn up stipulated that she would make one picture a year "for a period of five years" and receive $150,000 per film, plus "10% of the gross proceeds in excess of $2,500,000." Obringer sent Jack Warner a follow-up memo two days later, demonstrating just how completely the studio intended to maintain its control: "I again discussed with Lew Wasserman the 15-year distribution period on the Day Corporation pictures and also the fact that while there would be an attempt of mutual agreement on story, director, dance director, leading man, music and songs, the company would have final say on both the Day-Warner Bros. contract and the Warner Bros.-Day Corporation contract."

Though Day's contract with Michael Curtiz Productions had been re-newed ("for 52 weeks at $2,500 per") on March 30, 1953, it was terminat-ed on July 29 to allow Day to enter into a new "employment agreement" with the studio. Warners was trying to settle for a two-year contract—as opposed to the initial five-year commitment to Michael Curtiz Produc-tions—but the terms proved far less than the Melchers had been seeking. In fact, they were virtually the same as they had been under the initial contract with Curtiz: Day would make two pictures each year at her then regular rate of $2,500 per week. As Obringer highlighted in an August 29 memo, Day would be earning $11,250 for her next picture, *Lucky Me*, a far cry from the $150,000 the Melchers had been seeking. But to all evidence, this new agreement would not prove binding—even if it had ever been signed. By striving to retain too much control—and on the same stingy terms as before—Warners would forfeit one of its star players in a little more than a year.

Given Day's status, Melcher had gained ever more negotiating pow-ers for his wife. "Doris Day, having climbed to the No. 1 feminine spot on the list of the 10 top-money making stars, is getting a new contract—and thereon hangs a tale," claimed a gossip item in the *Cleveland Plain Dealer*. "Doris wants TV rights and other concessions and, as she is about the hottest property in town, she'll probably get them." She would eventu-ally be getting concessions she wanted from any number of studios, as opposed to Warners. In fact, Doris Day was well on her way to becoming the number one female box-office film star of all time.

12

"There's No Place Like Home"

---------- ✳ ----------

"I'm nothing special. . . . I'm no different than anybody else."
—DORIS DAY

"Her blue eyes have always been sad eyes."
—JANE CARLETON

The physical demands of Day's performance in *Calamity Jane* exhausted her and prompted the Melchers to take their first real vacation shortly after the completion of the picture, in late March 1953. They went by train to Chicago and then drove east to visit relatives, as well as for a short stay in New York to promote *By the Light of the Silvery Moon*. In North Adams, Massachusetts, where Day met her in-laws for the first time, they stayed with Melcher's brother Harold and his wife, Celia, in their large home on Marion Avenue. "Harry and Seal had a long driveway," recalled their sister-in-law, Marilyn Less. "Everybody just went in the back door and I remember one morning when we arrived, there was Doris Day scrambling eggs in the kitchen." It was such family doings—and in particular, her mother-in-law's cooking—that Day recalled with relish: "When the family gathers at the old home, they feel so sorry for the absent members not being there to taste Minnie's potato pancakes."

Though the Melcher "mishpocheh" was steeped in Jewish customs, some of Marty's relatives bent over backwards to approve of his marriage to Day and his becoming a Christian Scientist: "He went to Hollywood, and we accepted anything he did," said Lillian Glickman. Another cousin, David Towler, claimed that to this family of Orthodox Jews, "the whole thing was meshugge [i.e., crazy]."

Half a century later, Melcher's brother Jack would say: "As far as his becoming a Christian Scientist, everybody looked the other way. We never discussed it. Marty and Doris kept to themselves. They wanted it that way, and everybody respected their thoughts on the matter." If the head of the household had any misgivings about his son marrying a shiksa, he took them to his grave several months after meeting his new daughter-in-law. Alter Melcher died on July 28, 1953.

During her stay in New England, Day loved the scenic drive to Manchester, Vermont, an hour and a half from North Adams. They visited Melcher's eldest brother, Harmon, and his wife in Athens, New York, where Day had a bizarre and touching experience. After dinner, while Marty and Doris were upstairs talking, they suddenly heard muffled voices coming from just outside. "We looked out the window, and the big tree was loaded with children, peeking in," recalled Day, who went outside to sign autographs. "There seemed to be hundreds of them. There was no yelling and pushing and screaming. They were polite and well-behaved. They'd never seen a movie star before and simply wanted to say hello because they felt curious and friendly. I really felt humble."

In Cincinnati, Melcher drove his wife to what had been the Sign of the Drum, the club where Day had her first singing job with Barney Rapp. She was now dismayed to discover that it had become a "dilapidated-looking" clothing factory. Day again displayed her characteristic modesty when, staying with her aunt and uncle near Cincinnati, she opened the door for the morning mail. As the postman stared at her in tongue-tied disbelief, Day said: "What's the matter? I'm nothing special. Look, I go to work just like you do. I'm no different than anybody else." She would spend a good deal of her life desperately trying to believe that, persevering in denial that stardom had put her in an exalted category.

When the Melchers went to New York, they attended *Wonderful Town* on Broadway. "They took me to Lindy's after the performance," recalled Donald Saddler, who had choreographed the production. "And she loved the show. But you could tell that she didn't really like New York. It had brought back memories of when she was singing at the Little Club. So they didn't stay in New York very long."

After returning to Los Angeles, the Melchers continued their vacation, driving up the coast for an extended weekend. Day had already given more than six hundred interviews to "well-meaning writers who were only allowed an hour at most, during lunch-time at the studio." At Melcher's behest, Day gave journalist Carl Schroeder special treat-

ment. Along with his photographer, Bob Beerman, he accompanied the
Melchers to the Monterey Peninsula, a trip that would provide material
for an extensive article in the September issue of *Modern Screen*. The four
spent a weekend at the Del Monte Lodge and went on outings together,
in particular to Carmel. Thus even her vacation became another form of
work; Schroeder and Beerman tagged along with the Melchers as they
went sightseeing, shopping, and dining. They were even on hand when
Day signaled the start of a yacht race by firing a miniature silver pistol
and when she had her first professional tennis lesson. ("Final Score?
Love, all," read an accompanying photo caption.)

Under the obvious title "Sentimental Journey," Schroeder's piece began with a lame joke about attempting to follow the Melchers from Los
Angeles in their Oldsmobile convertible, as planned, only to discover that
they decided to take their Cadillac instead. Day told Schroeder that in
spite of her fame, at heart she remained a small-town girl: "Sure, I live
in Hollywood, and I'm certain people must get a funny idea, sometimes,
reading about all the so-called glamour. I am an actress, true, and proud
of it, but I'm more of my home town of Cincinnati than Hollywood, and
that's not trying to compare the respective merits of either place."

Straining to give his article some degree of candor, Schroeder reported that the Melchers had recently had a heated argument, though
neither seemed to remember how it had started. "If we can't see it my
way, I'm going to pack up and leave," shouted Melcher. After Day replied,
"Go ahead, see if I care," the eleven-year-old Terry chimed in, "If Marty
goes, I go too."

Along with Schroeder, the couple toured Carmel's famous 17-Mile
Drive and Pebble Beach, incorporating one of the world's most famous
golf courses. Day read a plaque quoting Robert Louis Stevenson, who
considered the site "the finest meeting place of land and water in existence," a description that planted the seeds for her permanent move there
later in life.

Day recovered some privacy when the Melchers drove to San Fran-
cisco and Schroeder and Beerman returned to Los Angeles. She was back
in Los Angeles by May 19, 1953, in time to promote *By the Light of the
Silvery Moon* on Tennessee Ernie Ford's radio show. The first week in
July, she also had sessions with eight disc jockeys and was back at Warner
Brothers on August 5, when she rode her bike to the studio and recorded
"Secret Love." Destined to win an Oscar and become one of Day's biggest
hits, "Secret Love" was famously recorded in a single take that consumed

all of three minutes. According to Day, Ray Heindorf, head of the music department at Warners, "was a brilliant musician. . . . He just knew when I wanted to breathe, when I wanted to stop, when I wanted to slow down, when I wanted to pick up."

The Melchers now had more privacy at home, as well. Alma, once an ever-hovering presence, had moved out of Toluca Lake into her own place nearby. "Even so, everything is organized and I have nothing to worry about," Day told an interviewer. "I always plan the menus. Mother does the shopping for us still, and we have a cook from New Orleans who prepares wonderful meals and keeps things in order."

As reported in the issue of *Modern Screen* documenting the last leg of the Melchers' recent vacation, Gene Nelson and Jane Powell had fallen in love in the spring while making *Three Sailors and a Girl* at Warners. In order to marry, both had to divorce their respective spouses. Since Powell had two children and Nelson one, the gossip columnists were a-twitter over the scandal, and Day was concerned about its impact on Gene's wife, Miriam.

"After Gene and I broke up, Doris and Marty were so nice to me," Miriam Nelson recalled. "They took me out a lot. They would call me and say, 'We've just split a watermelon, come on over and have some.' Another time, they called and said, 'Put your best bib and tucker on, we're going to take you to a big party.' And I said, 'I can't go to a party that I haven't been invited to.' And they'd say, 'We're inviting you.' That's the way they were."

Day urged Nelson to find someone and remarry. "I remember Doris gave me a pep talk. She said I should start dating, because it had been a while since Gene and I had broken up. She said, 'You don't want to be known as a wallflower, or have people feeling sorry for you. You have to get out there and date.' But I didn't feel ready, and didn't want to go out.

"One day I was over at their house," continued Nelson. "And Marty was down playing volleyball in the backyard, and I was up in Doris's bedroom, overlooking the game. We were looking out the window, talking about all these guys playing ball. I remember they kept watering down their lemonades—they'd drink some, and then add water from the hose.

"Then Doris said, 'Well, look at all those guys down there. Which one do you want?' And I asked which ones were available. There were a lot of music people there, like Paul Weston, who was married [to Jo Stafford], and somebody else who was going steady. And I said, 'What about that tall, dark and handsome one.' She said, 'Oh yeah. . . . He's an up-and-coming executive at CBS.' So I said, 'Okay. I pick him.'"

His name was Jack Meyers, and the Melchers arranged for him to have dinner with Nelson. They married and remained together until Meyers's death, nearly twenty-five years later. As Nelson recalled, "Doris always felt that she was too big, and she once told me that she liked having a tall man. My [second] husband was the same size as Marty, and Doris said, 'Isn't it nice having tall men—we can wear high heels, and get away with it.'"

A cofounder of a charitable organization for children called SHARE, Nelson also remembered that Day attended one of its early benefits, probably in 1953. "Dean Martin was on hand, walking around with a microphone in his hand trying to [recruit] people to sing. When he put the mike in front of Doris, she did it, but she hated having to do it. And she resisted going to another SHARE show, because she was so afraid that somebody might ask her to sing again. People always wanted her to sing, but she wasn't comfortable with it."

Day attended the event in the company of Warren Cowan, who remembered her nervousness about singing before a live audience. "Doris, who to this day is underrated as a singer, could get up, and sing in front of a [film] studio audience with no problem. But she couldn't sing in a public setting. It made her very nervous. One night Ronnie and I took Marty and Doris to the SHARE show. It was held every year, and wives of celebrities would dance—they were like the Rockettes: Lucille Ball, Janet Leigh and Bob Stack's wife. . . . After the dance, there was an auction, and somebody bid a thousand dollars for Doris to sing a song. And I'll never forget it: She grabbed my hand and squeezed it very hard before going up to the piano. It was at Ciro's nightclub, and there must have been 800 people there. I remember saying to Marty, as she was walking down to the stage, 'I can't tell you how sorry I am that I put her in this position.' And he said, 'Don't worry: She's like a cat that always lands on its feet.' She sang 'It Had to Be You,'" continued Cowan, "and it was one of the most memorable moments I've ever had in my experience in show business. It was the only time that I ever heard Doris sing in public, and it was magnificent." Though Day did appear at SHARE events in the future, she never sang at one again.

When Hedda Hopper asked Day why she was so frightened of performing before a live audience, she replied: "I don't know. . . . I'm never nervous making a picture. There could be 4,000 extras around and they don't bother me at all. If they could fill night clubs with extras, I'd be in business."

*   *   *

In 1953, after five years of tirelessly grinding out one film after another, and just when she was supposed to begin work on her sixteenth, Doris Day suffered a physical collapse. It would seem that, after her first real vacation in the spring, her body began to rebel. Day would recall in her memoir her first awareness of having difficulty breathing while driving with Marty to Irvine Park, where Terry had spent a week with his Boy Scout troop. "I tried to take a full breath but I couldn't," claimed Day. "Short gasps were all I could manage. I felt a rise of panic. I kept my face averted so that Marty couldn't see what trouble I was having. I really felt that I was going to suffocate."

It's telling that instead of appealing to Melcher for help, at first Day felt compelled to hide the problem from him. He was becoming more of a taskmaster and less of a husband, and she clearly feared his reaction. However, this wasn't just a passing malady, but a condition that would put Day out of commission. This indisposition prevented her from contributing to publicity for *Calamity Jane* and culminated in her refusal to perform "Secret Love" at the Academy Awards. Such refusals prompted a backlash from the press that, in turn, exacerbated her mysterious ailment. Even more significant, her uneasiness delayed work on her next film, *Lucky Me*, by more than a month.

"Doris had been working very hard," her good friend Ronnie Cowan recalled. "She became extremely tense, and the Hollywood Women's Press Club voted her [its Sour Apple Award for being] the Most Uncooperative Actress of the Year. She brooded about that, and then she found she had trouble breathing. We'd go shopping, and she'd gasp, and I'd have to find a paper bag for her to breathe into. Finally, I learned that she had developed a lump in her breast, and it had thrown her into a panic. Not only did she have a fear of cancer, but she felt she would be betraying her faith by going to a doctor. Marty was very patient with her and persuaded her it would be all right to see a surgeon. The lump in her breast turned out to be a benign cyst, which required only very minor surgery."

Given Day's fatigue after *Calamity Jane*, Warners had insisted that, before beginning work on *Lucky Me*, she have a complete physical. The doctor discovered that small cyst on her left breast. But even after it was removed and found to be benign, Day's anxiety continued. On September 22, *Variety* reported, "Not such a GOOD MORNING or Day for Doris who is bedded with a breathing ailment. She's continuing laboratory tests at home after spending two days at St. Joseph's. 'Lucky Me's' delayed."

Four days later, Melcher attempted damage control and found a willing mouthpiece in Hedda Hopper, who refuted the *Variety* item in her syndicated column: "Marty Melcher tells me that Doris Day isn't really sick. She has a heavy cold, but 'Lucky Me' won't be held." Then, on October 1, the *Los Angeles Times* announced that the star was "suffering from nervous exhaustion," and the *Hollywood Reporter* explained, "Doris Day will rest a few weeks before starting 'Lucky Me.' . . . The studio said the delay resulted on the advice of Miss Day's medico. The singing star was hospitalized with minor surgery last week." The ambiguous terms of such reports left her fans mystified about her malady.

Though entirely speculative, one of the more perceptive diagnoses of Day's condition appeared in the January issue of *Modern Screen.* It was written by Jane Carleton, who was a classmate of Day's in Cincinnati. "I am not a physician and I do not know the underlying causes of the psychoneuroses, but in the case of Doris Day I honestly think that this girl is unhappy because she doesn't want a career but is trapped by one. Against her own inclination, she has become big business.

"I've watched her give out with that gay, deceiving, flip air of enjoyment," continued Carleton. "But to me, her blue eyes have always been sad eyes. This girl has never hungered for fame or money or adoration. All she has ever wanted is to leave the rat race, to get away from it, to settle down with her husband and family in a nice, middle-class neighborhood."

"The pictures and records which had given her fame and fortune had also taken their toll in energy," said a reporter in the *Los Angeles Times* on September 11, before resorting to a hypothetical analysis: "In addition, she was suffering from the most common actress-mother-housewife ailment: inability to cope with all the demands on her time. She demanded perfection from herself in each area of her life."

In retrospect, Day's prolonged delay in starting work on *Lucky Me* might have stemmed from more than just her health problems. Her physical symptoms may have reflected in part the sudden instability of her position at Warner Brothers. Day had signed a "release" from her original 1947 contract with MCP on July 27, 1953, and was poised to sign "a new contract of employment" with the studio, committing her to two pictures a year at her old rate of $2,500 per week—as opposed to the $150,000 per-picture deal that Melcher had been striving for and come to expect.

But Melcher was still in the process of negotiating the creation of his own company, Arwin. His plan was to gain for his wife a share of the film profits as well. In her column on October 19, 1953, Hedda Hopper reported: "Marty Melcher and Jack Warner have been in business huddles for some weeks. The result is a new production company headed by Marty on the Warner lot." Day's delaying work on *Lucky Me* was possibly a tactic of her husband's. Hopper added that Melcher's first picture under the new arrangement would be *Yankee Doodle Girl*, written by his partner, Dick Dorso, and starring Day. Though the film was never made, the Melchers' company, Arwin Productions, would materialize by the following spring. Part of the deal with Warners included an agreement—signed on August 15, 1953—stipulating that Arwin would retain the publishing rights to any songs introduced in Day's pictures.

Despite reports to the contrary, a new contract between Day and Warner Brothers, so long under negotiation, was apparently never concluded. She made both *Lucky Me* and her next picture for the studio, *Young at Heart*, under special arrangements. And even as Warners' dealings with Day underwent changes, the studio's long-term relationship with Michael Curtiz was coming to an end. Curtiz had made eleven pictures under the banner of his own production unit on the Warner Brothers lot. Within a few years, Warners would claim that *I'll See You in My Dreams* was the only picture under this special agreement to have turned a profit and that Curtiz's ten other films had lost a total of $4.6 million. Alarmed and mortified, Curtiz took the studio to court to salvage what he could of his broken reputation—if not of their working relationship.

"I never dreamed I would be battling . . . against the studio with which I spent twenty-six years and for whom I made eighty-seven pictures," Curtiz wrote Jack Warner in January 1954. "I was always faithful to Warners in doing my very best with whatever material the studio entrusted to me. . . . You know in your heart, Jack, that whatever story you assigned to me, I worked my heart out without any regard to whether it was a 'big' or a 'little' picture or whether the story should ever have been purchased in the first place."

✳   ✳   ✳

Though work on *Lucky Me* didn't begin until November 1953, in an interoffice memo of December 29, 1952, producer Walter MacEwen had recommended extensive rewrites of the script, initially called *Sally*. "I also feel that too much is made of Sally's superstitions throughout," MacEwen wrote to Steve Trilling, Warners' production chief. "A little bit of this goes a long way, and too much of it tends to make a dope of Sally. It should be used just enough to complicate her relationship with Blair." Unfortunately, Trilling did not sufficiently abide by MacEwen's advice, and the picture would misfire in many respects. When she read the script, Day declared herself "dismayed at how bad it was."

Preliminary plans called for *Lucky Me* to be shot in the then-popular 3-D mode, yet another device intended to combat the recent inroads that television had made into the ailing motion picture industry. (While making *Calamity Jane*, Day was asked her thoughts about her future prospects on television: "I think TV is here to stay," she responded. "I think my future in television will be on film.") Though *Lucky Me* has nothing else distinctive—or distinguished—about it, the film does hold cinematic distinction as the first musical shot in CinemaScope. This wide-screen technique, invented in France, had recently been perfected and copyrighted by Fox. In an attempt to exploit the trend, Warners prominently displayed the newfangled word in ads for the film.

After a month of dance rehearsals without Day, shooting began on November 5, 1953. However, because Day's condition remained touch-and-go and her husband's negotiations with the studio were still up in the air, the production suffered further delays. By November 28, *Lucky Me* was five days behind its latest revised schedule. Day was due on the set at 1:30 that afternoon. "At 1:40 her husband called and said Miss Day was ill and would not be in," reads a terse note in the production book. Day stayed at home again on December 17 and 18, but ultimately showed up on the day before Christmas (from 10 to 1) as well as the day after. According to the studio's production notes, on February 10, 1954: "Doris Day became ill while in Makeup and went home at 7:30 AM. 30 Extras were cancelled on Weather Permitting call."

One of the bit players in the climactic party scene was a stunning twenty-three-year-old woman from Kulm, North Dakota. Her name was Angie Dickinson. "I won a television contest, called Jack Rourke's Beauty Parade, on local television, in 1953," recalled Dickinson. "And the winner was going to get, among other things, a part in a Warner Brothers movie. And they came through: It was a part—not very big: I was just one step above an extra. That was my absolute, bare beginning, and I was thrilled to death. I was so overcome with my good fortune and also respectful of an arena that I was not familiar with, and just kept my polite distance. I got to sit around and talk with Phil Silvers."

According to Dickinson, she had two lines, one of which was dropped. The one retained was: "Happy birthday, Uncle Otis." "I don't know how I could remember it all this time," she added more than fifty years later. She did not recall Melcher being on the set. "The only thing I remember, other than hanging around and being thrilled to death, was a man telling me: 'You're not standing there anymore, move over here now.' He said, '[Doris] doesn't want you that close to her—you're too pretty.'"

When Day performed before the cameras, she gave no indication that anything was wrong with her health. However, instead of mingling as usual with cast and crew between takes, she spent most of her free time alone in her dressing room, with strict orders not to be disturbed. (As Dickinson put it, Day "was not a 'hanging-around' person.") She did, however, make one significant acquaintance while working on *Lucky Me*: Judy Garland, who was filming *A Star Is Born* on the Warners lot. Day and Garland related strongly to each other. As Garland biographer David Shipman pointed out, they "both had been in show business since an early age and had hardly known any other life." Garland had her "laughing until I actually doubled over," Day observed. "Unhappy as she was, there was something straight about Judy that I truly admired. . . . I can't overemphasize the appeal of a person like that, especially in a place like Hollywood that is so shot through with phonies and pretenders." Indeed, like Day, Garland had a basic goodness that made her vulnerable to abuse from those she trusted. Shipman conveyed Day's observation "that Garland had much less confidence in her manager-husband than she had in hers—which must be one of the great ironies of show business: after her husband's death, Day discovered that he had cheated her out of her fortune."

Apart from her newfound friendship with Garland, making *Lucky Me* became a wretched business for Day. (To be sure, her illness did not help matters.) The film brings to mind a Dick Powell–Ruby Keeler scenario from an earlier decade and provides a perfect example of what the studio factory system churned out at its height. Day plays Candy Williams, a chorus girl obsessed with superstitions. Her colleagues in the picture were Phil Silvers, Eddie Foy Jr., and Nancy Walker, players whose talents reveal the film's roots in vaudeville and burlesque. (Silvers had been a headliner at the famed Minsky's for six years.)

According to Robert Cummings, Day chose him as her leading man. "When I first met [Doris] I didn't know who she was," he recalled. "I was doing a tense, dramatic scene in 'Dial M For Murder.' I looked up past the camera and hot lights to see a fuzzy figure in a white sharkskin slack suit, perched atop an eight-foot stepladder." Day continued to observe Cummings at work on the Hitchcock thriller. "It never occurred to her to make the grand entrance, sweep on the set, and be introduced," continued Cummings. "She simply doesn't behave like an 'artiste.'"

The semblance of a plot commences when the troupe's show within a show, "Parisian Pretties," fails, and the characters find themselves stranded in Miami without money. To pay for an expensive French dinner in a hotel restaurant, they are pressed into kitchen duty. A typical Hollywood expository formula leads to Candy's meeting—and falling in love with—hotel guest Dick Carson (Cummings), a famous songwriter working on a new Broadway show.

The ever-effervescent Day makes her entrance at the beginning of the film, dancing down the street and into the opening number, "Superstition Song." According to the press department, it required two weeks of rehearsal and several days to shoot the scene, one of the most "extensive" musical numbers in Warners history—"geographically speaking," the publicists blabbered. While Candy dances past storefronts en route to the theater, Day was in fact making her way from one end of the studio's expansive Burbank lot to the other; as she sings such lines as "Three on a match isn't good/So make a circle, knock on wood," she sidesteps an open ladder, avoids stepping on cracks in the sidewalk, and sharply veers to avoid a black cat in her path.

Following their success with *Calamity Jane*, Sammy Fain and Paul Francis Webster were recruited to write ten new songs for *Lucky Me*— with far less lilting results. But the studio, clearly banking on the score to sell the film, was pulling strings to control Columbia Records' release of the soundtrack in conjunction with the film's release. But even if the Press Book—with its reproductions of the sheet music covers—encouraged exhibitors to "See Columbia Records Distribs," "Run Disc Jockey Contests," and "Give Records as Prizes," the music was, in essence, standard pastiche, embracing ballads ("Love You Dearly"), love songs ("I Speak to the Stars"), and novelty numbers ("Superstition Song")—none of which entered the repertoire.

Lucky Me has little to recommend it other than Day—in spite of recent, reported maladies—being at her peak as Candy Williams. She may be a little fuller in the face and torso than before, but she appears thriving and robust, offering a delightful Scottish brogue in "Blue Bells of Broadway" and—in a black wig—hilariously impersonating a British aristocrat. Though reviewers recognized the picture for the trifle it is, they reveled in Day's "breezy" performance and the "sparks" it emitted.

And Day's achievement came without much support from her cohorts. Even if Day is at her beguiling best after Cummings tackles her—widening her eyes along with her ire—she was acting in a vacuum; long past his heyday as an attractive leading man, Cummings was woefully miscast as Dick Carson. He is awkward in the part, his affability appears forced, and he frequently brings to mind the proverbial deer blinded by headlights. It's intriguing to imagine how the film might have fared with someone else in the part. In fact, at least one other actor had been under consideration.

"They tested me for the role in 'Lucky Me,'" Merv Griffin remembered. "But I was too young looking and they gave it to Bob Cummings. I was crushed. Instead, they gave me 'So This Is Love' with Kathryn Grayson. And while we were shooting, Doris was working on the lot, too. She came by my dressing room and said, 'How's it going?' Well, I was thrilled. She said, 'Are you happy?' And I said, 'Oh, yes! And I thank you for all your input.' That was really our first chat together."

Nor did Day's other costar Phil Silvers bring very much to *Lucky Me*. Fifty years later, his comic "shtick" seems too intense and dated. Moreover, the publicity material suggestion that Silvers was another love interest for Day in *Lucky Me* was simply absurd. It recalled Ray Bolger's weakness as Day's costar in *April in Paris*. With surprising candor, the Press Book quoted Silvers's acknowledgment that "the prospects of his ever playing a romantic lead are virtually non-existent."

The film was further handicapped by Jack Donohue's work as director. He had recently worked magic for the studio when he staged the musical numbers for *Calamity Jane*, and a couple of years earlier he had scored well on Broadway by guiding Silvers through his paces in the Broadway version of *Top Banana*. Though a veteran stage dancer, Donohue had neither the experience nor the skills for directing a film.

The reviews reflected the film's many deficiencies. "Doris Day is not as lucky in her latest screen sortie as its title suggests," wrote Otis L. Guernsey Jr. in the *New York Herald Tribune*. "She dances and warbles her way through 'Lucky Me' at the Paramount as though every song were a show-stopper and every twist of the backstage story a happy surprise.

She has bounce but her hollow CinemaScope vehicle has none. It leaves her all spruced up for enchantment, madly waving a wand on whose tip some one has forgotten to attach the magic star." Archer Winston was a bit less snooty in his otherwise accurate notice in the *New York Post*: "[It] glitters harmlessly without ever dazzling [and is] bounded on one side by avoidance of originality and on the other by adherence to the accepted formulas."

Ironically, Day herself finally received a good review in the *New York Times*—the one paper consistently critical of her—for one of her worst films thus far: "With the help of director Jack Donohue, who tosses her pieces of driftwood, she bobs up persistently as the most elastic—and most lovely—of the stranded song-and-dance team. She is breezy, bright and lyric when the spirits of the others are most low." But as author George Morris succinctly put it, *"Lucky Me* tries hard to be spontaneous and original but succeeds only in looking forced and tired."

* * *

While *Lucky Me* was being promoted, Day tried to take it easy and did not join her costars for its world premiere in Miami, the picture's location. But she helped publicize the film in other ways. A press photo of Day appeared in papers across the nation, showing her on a ladder, painting her "two-foot-high" signature on a twenty-five-by-thirty-five-foot billboard in Hollywood. (The "world's largest portrait," insisted the publicists.) A press release on Day's birthday, also the Melchers' third anniversary, announced that the couple had gone to Palm Springs "for an indefinite stay." Melcher's gift, "to the star of 'Lucky Me,' is an unlimited account at the salon of Miss Day's favorite designer, Howard Shoup. She already has ordered six evening gowns."

In order to ease the burdens on Day, the Melchers had been talking about hiring someone to help with her everyday matters. In Palm Springs she had befriended a blonde woman, Ruth Gordon, who was staying at the same hotel. Day admired her short coiffure and asked where she had her hair done. Back home in Los Angeles, Day phoned Gordon to ask if they might go to the hairdresser together. Gordon eagerly agreed. While they lunched and then went shopping, the star sized up her new friend and decided to hire her as a chauffeur for trips to and from the studio and also as an all-purpose companion. Gordon became the first of a long line of women Day would employ as confidential assistants.

An issue of *Photoplay* (May 1954) appealed to Day's fans with an article titled "You Can Help Doris Get Well!" along with a coupon to be clipped and returned with their "best wishes" to the star. The piece relayed the "nagging, insistent" rumors about her illness, before quoting Melcher's attempt to manipulate the media: "The report that Doris Day is in a state of collapse is not true," he said. "It never was true. The history of Doris Day proves it isn't true." His last remark conveys Melcher's view of "Doris Day" as an object, a commodity to be exploited.

"Doris Day did return to work," resumed the unsigned article in *Photoplay*, "but not the Doris Hollywood had known. Her sets, in the past, had been alive with her own special kind of radiance. They had bustled with activity—Doris being interviewed between scenes, posing happily for pictures, welcoming guests. Now the door to the 'Lucky Me' sound stage spelled out a forbidding message in large red letters: NO VISITORS. And Doris herself has been wan, sometimes tearful, almost always solitary."

After describing some well-rehearsed anecdotes of her life—the broken leg, the failed marriages, the tearful screen test—and mentioning that she received 15,000 letters a month, the piece ended with what seems like valid insights to "the key to the Doris Day illness. She is normal. She is human. It's possible that the very same people who unwittingly helped build the legend of Doris Day have just as unwittingly begun to tear it down. It is a legend that, for Doris' own good, should never have been created . . . for living it twenty-four hours a day could easily have proved too much, even for a Superwoman. And Doris is human—flesh and heart."

Three months later, under the title "I'm Well Again," the May issue of *Photoplay* featured a reproduction of a handwritten letter from Day. It was addressed to the fans that had sent her their get-well wishes. "I want you all to know that I am boundlessly grateful for your interest in my health," Day, or her handlers, wrote. She explained that "Marty and my doctor and I decided that for the good of the picture and for my own continued well-being I should find more time to relax from the necessary and ever-present tension of the film sets." After pointing out that each of the many musical numbers required "a couple of weeks workout in itself, this [i.e., breathing time] seemed like a sensible idea, and I tried to maintain a more restful schedule during the production." The accompanying photos in the four-page spread confirmed her comments, one showing Day in the surf, another of the Melchers picnicking on the beach.

Though Day was in the public eye less during the spring of 1954, she made her first appearance on the popular Sunday night CBS quiz show *What's My Line?* on June 10. Day was a "mystery challenger," questioned by the blindfolded Bennett Cerf, Arlene Francis, Steve Allen, and Dorothy Kilgallen. As she provided her "yes" or "no" answers, Day disguised her voice with a high, thin squeal. When Kilgallen asked, "Might you be described as a glamour girl, rather than a terribly serious actress?" Host John Daly answered for Day: "Uh huh." Steve Allen, at one point, asked whether she was Marilyn Maxwell. It was Arlene Francis who correctly guessed that it was Day. After the panel determined her identity, Daly presented Day with Columbia's "millionth" pressing of "Secret Love"—a "gold record" in a frame. Daly then added how much he had enjoyed her picture *Young at Heart*, to which Day replied that the picture had yet to be made.

Young at Heart would be Day's next—and last—picture at Warners, before she set out to work with other studios. (Day would return to make what would be her final film with Warners, *The Pajama Game*, according to her own terms.) *Young at Heart* also marked the first film made with the Melchers' independent production company, Arwin, which was still establishing itself. "The setup gives the star and her husband a new kind of freedom and authority, and Doris is basking in the delight of being partly her own boss," a story in the *Los Angeles Times* observed. "Warner Bros. supply the financing, and simultaneously give us a free hand in management," explained Melcher. "We have the chance to develop our own ideas and present them to [Warners], with a complete outline of our financial needs."

Given the impact of television, for years studios had been unloading their contract players. And with Lew Wasserman leading the pack, the seismic changes between studios and their stars had come to a head: like many another star, Day could now call the shots to her own advantage—or, rather, Melcher did so on her behalf. "I simply couldn't take on business details of an operation like ours, no more than I can plan out a whole picture," Day chimed in. "What I like is to arrive when everything is ready, and then offer suggestions from my own point of view. I haven't the creative mind to build from the ground up." She further explained that her "secret ambition," in light of her newfound independence, was to "develop my dramatic talent on the screen. . . . I got encouragement from Alfred Hitchcock, who told me he was going to make a picture in which I would appear."

Having met Day at a party and told her he wanted to work with her, Hitchcock would hire her to make *The Man Who Knew Too Much* a year after the formation of her own company had been announced. "I was so nervous before I met Hitchcock," Day told Hedda Hopper. "I'd always admired him as a director and had no idea what I would say to him. I figured the best policy was honesty, so I told him how shy I am. You know what, Hedda, he told me he was the same way. Said he actually doesn't like to go into studio commissaries, then told me he was nervous about meeting me. Isn't that wonderful?"

Day was suddenly very active again, though the work was beginning to seem more and more a substitute for an empty and aimless existence. Day told Hopper that she "can't wait to finish a picture," given all the other things she hoped to accomplish. "But the first day I'm home I start asking, 'What do I do?' I begin following the housekeeper around until she says, 'Go outside and sit in the sun—it'll do you good.' She just wants to get rid of me. I sit in the sun 10 minutes, then start studying the house. First thing I do is rearrange all the pictures."

13

"Fairy Tales Can Come True"

---　✳　---

"Half the time I let Doris have her way; the rest of the time I give in."
—MARTY MELCHER

Young at Heart, Doris Day's seventeenth film at Warner Brothers, was a landmark in at least one respect: It was the first to bear the name of the company created by Marty Melcher—Arwin Productions. The picture was a musical remake of a highly regarded Warners movie called *Four Daughters* (1938). That tearjerker was based on a *Cosmopolitan* magazine story by Fannie Hurst, the best-selling author perhaps most widely known for *Imitation of Life*.

Four Daughters was a popular and critical hit, earning five Academy Award nominations, including for Best Picture, Best Director for Michael Curtiz, and Best Supporting Actor for New York stage actor John Garfield, in a seething performance that established him as a movie star. (Garfield's first major film role had been intended for Errol Flynn.) The film spawned two sequels in rapid succession: *Four Wives* in 1939 and *Four Mothers* in 1940. All three pictures featured the same three actresses: the Lane sisters—Priscilla, Rosemary, and Lola. Gale Page played the fourth sister.

With a screenplay by Julius J. Epstein and Lenore Coffee, *Four Daughters* tells the tale of widower Adam Lemp (Claude Rains), a music professor who lives with his "eligible" daughters, and also with his salt-of-the-earth elderly sister, Etta (May Robson). The story is set in Connecticut, here typifying small-town U.S.A. just before the suburbs evolved and permanently altered the landscape. While the titular sisters are primed for marriage, Ann (Priscilla Lane), "the baby," falls in love with Felix Dietz, a composer of "modern tone poems." But when she

learns that her sister Emma also loves him, the self-sacrificing Ann marries Mickey Borden (Garfield), an embittered and moody outsider. Ann
clearly hopes to turn his miserable existence around, but her sacrifice
proves misspent when Mickey kills himself.

As conceived by Fannie Hurst and portrayed by John Garfield, Mickey was a complex character whose cynicism lends *Four Daughters* a subtle
complexity that far transcends the story's sentimental core. Though Epstein and Coffee are credited with the screenplay of *Young at Heart,* Liam
O'Brien's "adaptation" of it proved far more extensive than such a credit
implies. Not only were the "four daughters" reduced to three, but the
writers permitted Barney Sloan (Frank Sinatra)—originally Mickey—to
survive. Inexplicably, O'Brien changed all the characters' names: Ann
Lemp becomes Laurie Tuttle (Day), Felix Dietz became Alex Burke (Gig
Young), Aunt Etta was Aunt Jessie (Ethel Barrymore), and Emma was
Amy Tuttle (Alison Fraser). The eldest daughter became Fran (Dorothy
Malone) and her betrothed, Bob (Alan Hale Jr.). The father of the household, Gregory Tuttle, was played by Robert Keith.

Young at Heart is a better film than either its reception or its reputation suggests. Its biggest liability stemmed from the decision to give
the otherwise heartrending saga a happy ending—without making any
other adjustments that might have helped justify the change. Nor does
the film's revised title have much to do with what unfolds on-screen. By
1954, Hollywood was well aware that a familiar theme song could help
sell a movie, and Warners had one ready-made with "Young at Heart."
Carolyn Leigh's opening lyric for Johnny Richard's popular tune provided an instant signal that the story's tragic ending had been altered:
"Fairy tales can come true/It can happen to you."

Sinatra, who undertook the difficult role of Barney, had reached the
nadir of his career in the years immediately leading up to *Young at Heart.*
A year earlier, his wife, Ava Gardner, had to implore Harry Cohn, the head
of Columbia, to cast the crooner in *From Here to Eternity,* and he willingly
tackled the assignment for a paltry $8,000—far from the $125,000 he had
commanded.

Sinatra's rendition of "Young at Heart" (released in February 1954)
became his first hit single in seven years—giving his career a much-need-
ed shot in the arm. "Old Blue Eyes" also received an even bigger boost
the following month, when he won his first Oscar for *From Here to Eternity.* Though he had made well over a dozen pictures before reestablish-

ing himself in that World War II soap opera, it provided him with his first serious role. *Young at Heart* would be his second.

In fact, it was Sinatra who demanded that *Young at Heart* conclude on an optimistic note. He was, however, less committed to the film's title. In a typed memo to Jack Warner, dated July 15, Sinatra wrote: "I still think 'Someone to Watch Over Me' is a better title." Of course, the narcissistic Sinatra would have preferred the title of that Gershwin song since it would have placed his character at the center of the film's attention—rather than among the members of the larger ensemble. But it also would have been the better choice, since "Someone to Watch Over Me" describes just what the film is about.

Another working title for the film was *Sister Act*, which was closer to the original, *Four Daughters*. It's all the more surprising that an alternative name was not ultimately selected, considering that Alperson Pictures Corporation "protested" the use of the title as presenting a "harmful conflict" with *its* 1938 picture, *The Young in Heart*, and also considering that NBC was working on a television show titled *Young at Heart*.

In a letter dated July 26, Joseph Breen—the officious vice president and director of the Production Code Administration of the Motion Picture Association of America—offered his censorship suggestions for the film-in-progress and urged Warners to opt for a happier ending: "As presently written, it appears that Barney is deliberately trying to commit suicide in scene 87 and following. We suggest that you stress the fact that Barney is temporarily 'out of his mind' during this sequence and that he smashes his car as a result of his insane driving rather than deliberately turning off his windshield wipers during the snow storm." Underscoring just how much control the MPAA could wield at the time, Breen also requested a preview of "all lyrics to be used in this production."

As of July 21, the budget for *Young at Heart* was set at $1,110,000. Since the entire cast received $277,199, it says much about Sinatra's revitalized reputation that he commanded $85,000, or nearly a third of the total. While her new contract with Warners was pending, Day outdid Sinatra with her $100,000 fee—especially impressive, since, as today, male stars typically received considerably more than their female counterparts. Costars Ethel Barrymore and Gig Young each received $25,000 for *Heart*, a good deal more than the studio considered paying either Lucille Watson ($15,000) or Fay Bainter ($10,000) to play Aunt Jessie. It was also noticeably less than the $35,000 Melvyn Douglas wanted to play Tuttle.

Poor Dorothy Malone had to settle for $1,250, and Alan Hale Jr. received a measly $850. (Among the other budget items, "women's wardrobe" was assigned $21,379.) All things considered, *Young at Heart* was one of the few pictures made under Jack Warner's eagle eye that ultimately cost a good deal more than first allocated.

Though plans were made for six days of preproduction and rehearsals and forty-one days of shooting—commencing on July 22—the picture ultimately came in ten days behind schedule. (With a day off for Labor Day, the cameras stopped rolling on September 21.) The biggest problem was Sinatra, who frequently arrived late on the set—sometimes by half an hour, and at least once by two hours. (According to Day, he, in fact, missed several mornings entirely—even though these daily absences are not reflected in the daily production records.) Sinatra was also supposed to make a guest appearance on the Red Skelton show, but phoned at the last minute with the excuse that he couldn't appear because the shooting schedule had run over.

Sinatra had further problems getting along with a number of people during the filming. Having recently regained his footing as a megastar, he made up for lost time and became more imperious and arrogant than ever. He had the first cameraman, Charles Lang, replaced by Ted McCord, who started work on August 13, exactly two weeks before Sinatra himself finished his involvement with the film. (McCord received credit for the cinematography.) As Day speculated, the problem may have been the "impatient" Sinatra's chafing at Lang's taking too much time with his camera setups. But even more vexing for Day, Sinatra, the recent Oscar winner, had Melcher ousted from the set of *Young at Heart*, Melcher's first undertaking as a producer.

In keeping with his new contract, Melcher attempted to get the rights to "You, My Love," "the new song submitted by Frank Sinatra" for the picture. Sinatra, of course, had considerable clout, and when he made a fuss over the matter, Jack Warner was called in to mediate. Sam Weiss, a music publisher, witnessed the exchange, during which Sinatra informed Warner that he would leave the picture "if that creep Melcher is anywhere on the Warners lot. I've heard too many rotten things about him and I don't want him around."

An internal memo sought to clarify the issue: when Warners agreed that Arwin Productions would retain the publishing rights to the songs in Day's pictures, "[i]t was the intention of the agreement that this clause was to apply to songs sung by Doris Day," not other singers. "Saw M.

Melcher my office 8/6/54," begins a note that Jack Warner made on a July 30 letter from Melcher's MCA agent, concerning the Sinatra song. "Agreed leave matter entirely my hands and would if necessary as last resort allow Sinatra publish and have copyright on song." It helped Warner, who needed to pacify the hot-tempered Sinatra. When the negotiations for *Young at Heart* were drawn up, they stipulated that "the said Martin Melcher . . . shall have no production authority over said photoplay and shall not be connected with . . . any production capacity whatsoever."

Mitch Miller, too, remembered the fight between Melcher and Sinatra—and suggested that Melcher was highly "overmatched." "It was not hard to dislike Marty Melcher," Miller also said. "I never had any respect for him." It was during *Young at Heart* that Melcher had a dinner date with Jimmy Van Heusen only to receive a call from the songwriter an hour before, canceling. Referring to Sinatra, Van Heusen explained, "The monster called—and I have to go see him." "Frank was like a gangster who demanded that everyone be at his beck and call," added Miller, as he recalled the anecdote. "There isn't anyone in his life that he didn't, finally, cross off."

✳ ✳ ✳

Michael Freedland, one of Sinatra's biographers, said: "With Ava [Gardner] having gone, there was no reason not to cash in on the morose Frank, the one who was lost and lonely. . . . 'One For My Baby' was one of those perfect lachrymose numbers that sounded so right simply because the singer knew how to hold a glass and a half-smoked cigarette as well as he knew how to hold a tune. He had done it before, but never with such intensity. The other song that made its mark in the picture [*Young at Heart*] was perhaps the most beautiful number Sinatra ever performed: Gershwin's 'Someone to Watch Over Me.'"

Though Melcher had no choice but to make himself scarce on the set of *Young at Heart*, he continued pulling strings behind the scenes. The script called for his wife to sing a number called "Ready, Willing and Able" during a scene on the beach. Since Day was overly self-conscious about a slight curvature to her right leg, broken in her youth, she resisted being filmed in a bathing suit. Melcher had a brainstorm: Knowing that his wife completely trusted Donald Saddler, he decided to involve the suave dance director in the project. "Marty phoned me," recalled Saddler, "and said, 'We're doing *Young at Heart*, and there's a little musical sequence at a picnic on the beach. Even though there's not much dancing in the scene, Doris would like to have it staged—she doesn't want to improvise it. Do you have any time?'"

Once Saddler agreed to participate, Melcher recruited him to help persuade Day to don "swim shorts" for the scene. Saddler assured her that he would carefully monitor the camera angles. And during the shoot on the beach above Malibu, Saddler did just that: He saw to it that Day danced in profile. "Doris had great legs," he explained, "but she had a 'thing' about it. One muscle formation was slightly thinner than the other, and if she stood facing you, you could see the difference, a slight curve to the one leg." When Day first appeared in her bathing shorts, members of the crew whistled at her. Though such a reaction suggests that she had nothing to worry about, it may, in fact, have been arranged by Melcher to reassure his wife. Saddler recalled Day showing up on the set wearing an open-collar shirt and a pair of blue jeans. When he complimented her on her ensemble, she said, "The jeans are Terry's, you know."

During the brief time that Saddler was involved with *Young at Heart*, the great ballet dancer Alicia Markova arrived in town, and he invited her to lunch at the Warner Brothers commissary. Afterward, Saddler asked Day whether she would like to meet Markova and prepared her by saying, "She's one of our greatest Giselles." He recalled that "Doris became like an overexcited child. When I brought Alicia to Doris's trailer, she said, 'I'm so sorry I've never seen you do *Giselle*.' They chatted for a bit. And Alicia was impressed that a movie star even knew who she was." Saddler mentioned that Markova knew Ethel Barrymore and wanted to say hello to the majestic stage actress. Day invited both her choreographer and the ballerina to the set, and as soon as Barrymore saw Markova arrive, she arose from her chair and crossed the sound stage to greet her. "Can you believe it?" Day remarked to Saddler. "She's never out of that chair. I mean, we have to cart her around everywhere." (As publicity for the picture would divulge: "Ethel Barrymore made her acting debut before any of her co-actors in Warners *Young at Heart* were born.")

It had been nearly two years since Barrymore had made a picture, and working on this one was plainly a trial. Though Sinatra could be no less callous and gangster-like with women than with men, he could also display great generosity and comradeship. When he learned that Barrymore was turning seventy-five on August 15, he had a cake brought in the day before so that the entire cast could celebrate with her. Another indication of his occasional chivalrous spirit surfaced when a stagehand tossed Day a box of tissues after she cried for a scene, and it hit her forehead. "Frank lunged for the guy, scolding, 'Don't ever do that! You don't throw things at a lady, understand?' Doris Day said later, 'Over the years, whenever I pull a Kleenex out of a box, I think of Frank.'"

Sinatra was not the only one who delayed the making of *Young at Heart*. With the picture already six days behind schedule, the entire company was dismissed on September 11 because "Miss Barrymore became too ill to work." And even though Day was on the set most days from 9 a.m. to 5:50 p.m., on September 14 "Doris Day could only do one long shot because of her bad lip." And the following day: "Company [only] rehearsed today because of Miss Day's swollen lip."

"I didn't really find that film exciting to make," Day recalled years later. "I'd like to maybe work with [Sinatra] now, I would enjoy it more. And maybe he would feel that way, too. At that point in time I don't think either one of us enjoyed it all that much, but we probably would now." But at the time, she simply denied rumors that she and her co-star had any problems. On September 20, the penultimate day of the shoot, reporter Kendis Rochlen visited the set. "Doris Day gave me a bright smile and a quick denial when I asked her if it were true that she and Frank Sinatra were considerably less than friendly while making 'Young at Heart,'" Rochlen reported in her column in the *Mirror*. "'Why, of course we got along. There was no feud,' Doris insisted. But I noticed she was quick to change the subject."

In contrast with Day's sunny report, "one crew member" told Rochlen: "Frank can be plenty charming if he wants to. But he didn't win any popularity contests this time. He acted like he thought everyone else was a jerk. He and Doris didn't exactly fight—it was more [a matter of] what they did not say to each other. They sort of steered clear of each other between scenes."

When Rochlen asked Day about Melcher, she replied, "He's sweet, considerate and understanding. He takes care of the business affairs. I have no head for figures—can't even keep a checkbook straight. What's more I don't want to learn. I don't even know how much I make.

"When you've been as broke as I've been," Day said, "you learn to count your change before leaving [the store]. But even now, with years of what I guess you'd call success behind me, I can't believe in the 'big' money. If it's change of a ten-dollar bill, I'm fine. But if it's a deal involving thousands of dollars, Marty has to handle it. I just can't imagine that much money."

* * *

With the formation of their own company behind them, the Melchers proceeded to negotiate "a production-distribution arrangement" with the studio. Under this agreement, Day's next picture would be "a musical with a Western background" called *Nothing but a Woman*, the story to deal "with the misadventures of a suffragette on a Western speaking tour who unwittingly hires a bandit as her protector." This was yet another movie that never reached the screen. But now Day was no longer obligated to Warners, and Melcher was free to pitch her services elsewhere.

A strong indication of just how much Day had already come to represent America to the world arrived in the form of a press announcement, during the McCarthy hearings, that the "typically American" star had been chosen to "broadcast to inhabitants of Iron Curtain countries over the most powerful American propaganda radio station in Europe. Radio Luxemburg, which is capable of reaching more people in more countries controlled by the Reds than any other, revealed that Miss Day is the first American entertainer to be asked to broadcast to its listeners. She will sing and talk about living conditions in America."

Since Day and Sinatra were major recording artists, the marketing plans for *Young at Heart* made much of an annual poll of 4,150 disc jockeys that selected them as the top female and male vocalists of the previous year. The ad's tagline for the picture was straightforward—"Together For the First Time! Terrific From the First Moment." A marketing suggestion in the Press Book encouraged "a letter-writing contest asking eligible males 'Why I Would Like a Date with "Doris"' . . . Prize entrant gets his wish . . . a date with a local model named Doris."

After a press preview on December 8 at the Wiltern Theater, *Young at Heart* premiered in Fort Worth on Christmas Eve, 1954, the general release following in mid-January. The film received mostly mixed to negative reviews. Practically every critic complained about how the new version of the plot was a whitewash of the original. According to the *Saturday Review*, "Hollywood has not lost its knack for making indifferent new pictures out of good old pictures."

"The sentiments of this wide-eyed romance have become a bit tarnished with age, and the present performance of it is not as crisp as the first one was," opined Bosley Crowther in the *New York Times*. "Miss Day is sometimes much too bubbly. . . . But even so," he continued, "Miss Day

above: The natural-born performer—smiling and eager to please from the very beginning. (1)

top right: With her mop of hair, the three-year-old Doris poses within the protective embrace of her brother Paul. (2)

bottom right: Doris and her first dancing partner, Jerry Doherty, before the car accident in 1937 that compelled her to become a singer. (3)

Photo credits appear on page 627 of the main text.

left: Doris Day and her first husband-to-be, trombonist Al Jorden. His gangly hands were used as weapons against her on a number of occasions. (4)

below: A typically animated Day makes a point to Bob Crosby, Bing's brother. She was briefly the lead singer for Bob Crosby's Bobcats in 1940. (5)

left: Les Brown, his "Band of Renown," and their star singer—circa 1945, after she had her first number-one hit with them, "Sentimental Journey." (6)

above: Bandleader
Stan Kenton and Day
gazing at her dapper
second husband,
George Weidler,
with apparent
fondness. (7)

right: A publicity
shot for Day's first
and last cabaret
act at The Little
Club, New York
City, February,
1947—just before
the Hollywood
transformation. (8)

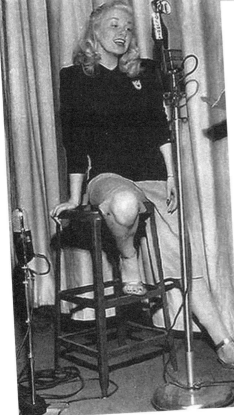

above: Day leaning on the shoulder of Michael Curtiz, the Warner Brothers director who cast her in her first film, *Romance on the High Seas,* and put her under contract in 1947. That's co-star and early paramour Jack Carson, on the left. (9)

left: With a microphone that's almost as large as her head, Day makes one of her first of more than 600 recordings. (10)

above: Hamming
it up with Sinatra
and posing for the
camera, during a
Your Hit Parade
show in the winter
of 1947. (11)

right: A plump
Day mops the
brow of comedian
Ben Blue, as singer
Peggy Lee fans
him. (1948) (12)

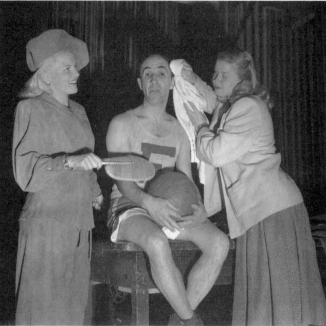

above: Whooping it up with Bob Hope and the boys on a plane on a U.S. tour in early 1948. After they came close to crashing on several occasions, Day would shun flying for much of the rest of her life, compelling her to turn down a number of films that entailed on-location shooting. (13)

right: Day and comic actor Billy De Wolfe in a scene from *Tea for Two*. After instantly befriending Day early in her film career, De Wolfe nicknamed her "Clara," the name she uses with friends to this day. (14)

Performing a handstand for the camera on the
diving board in her Hollywood backyard, 1950 (15).

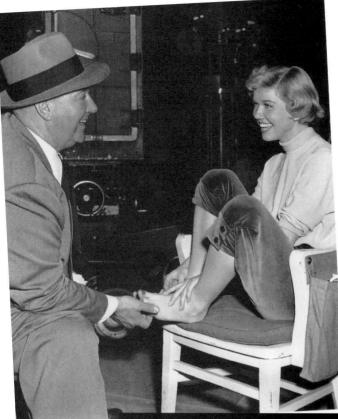

left: Stalwart director David Butler tickles his star's tootsies on the set of *Tea for Two,* the second of five Warner Brothers' films he made with Day. (Spring 1950.) (16)

above: R to L: Day, Louella Parsons and Nancy Davis all look upon Ronald Reagan as he gazes up to a higher authority. (17)

left: Though divorced, hoofers Miriam and Gene Nelson donned their best smiles for dinner at a charitable benefit in 1954. Day matched Miriam with her next husband. (18)

right: Day sharing a happy moment with her Columbia A & R man, Mitch Miller (L), and prominent arranger and conductor, Percy Faith (R). (19)

left: Day with her eight-year-old son, Terry Jorden, soon to become Terry Melcher, when adopted by her third husband. (20)

left: Day with Marty Melcher: The newlyweds on their PR-driven honeymoon in Grand Canyon, April, 1951. (21)

right: Posing on the set of *Calamity Jane* with her most beloved of helpers: mother Alma (second from right), Aunt Marie (far right) and at-home cook Katie Sarten (far left). The woman in the middle is Katie's niece. (22)

Working in the studio with choreographer and classical dancer, Donald Saddler: "Of all the stars and principals I've ever danced with, I think she was one of the most gifted." Circa 1952. (23)

left: Five-time co-star Gordon MacRae gives Day some golf instructions. (24)

below: To promote her 1953 film *Lucky Me,* Day signed her 30-foot image on a billboard on Wilshire Blvd. The photo ran in papers throughout the country. (25)

right: While Day was making *Lucky Me,* she befriended Judy Garland, who was working at Warners on *A Star Is Born.* Here they are having a grand time with Garland's co-star, James Mason. (26)

above: Day and Gig Young comforting the elderly and ailing Ethel Barrymore on the set of *Young at Heart.* When choreographer Donald Saddler brought ballerina Alicia Markova to visit during the making of the picture, Barrymore arose from her chair and crossed the sound stage to greet her. "Can you believe it?" Day remarked to Saddler. "She's never out of that chair—I mean, we have to cart her around everywhere." (27)

left: Mother and daughter reverse roles, as Doris combs Alma's hair in her MGM dressing room during the making of *Love Me or Leave Me*. (28)

right: Alfred Hitchcock cracks a rare smile with his two stars of *The Man Who Knew Too Much*, Day and James Stewart. (29)

left: In Cincinnati for the premiere of *Julie* in 1956, Day saw her father for the first time since she was a teenager and William Kappelhoff left his family behind for "another woman." (30)

above: That's Harvey Evans in the middle, holding Day aloft during the rousing "Seven and a Half Cents" number in *The Pajama Game:* "She was my idol, and then ironically, about a year after I graduated high school, I was holding her ass in *The Pajama Game.*" (31)

above: With husband Marty Melcher to her right and knitting needles in her lap, Day was candidly captured at Columbia's recording studio, between takes. (32)

right: A pensive Day having an unguarded moment in the recording studio. (1957) According to A & R man James Harbert, Day did not like recording with an orchestra. "She often said, 'Why don't we just record this with you and me at the piano? I feel very free when I'm singing with you. And then you can take it and add the orchestra.' Dragging her to recording sessions became one of my responsibilities." (33)

is attractive when she casually bounces around, before she becomes a soul-saver and one-girl society for the prevention of cruelty to strays."

After complimenting Day's and Sinatra's voices, Archer Winston wrote in the *New York Post*: "No objection is here made to their performances, which are also equal or superior to the now thoroughly confused roles. It's always disheartening to see a film end poorly after a good beginning."

Young at Heart might strike some as a trite artifact of its era, when the so-called nuclear family supposedly nurtured the kind of love that could vanquish any adversity. Though at first it does seem terminally sweet, it takes a darker turn as soon as Barney arrives on-screen with his relentlessly cynical attitude. And, as *Daily News* critic Wanda Hale wrote, Day, in a rare serious performance, proved utterly up to the task. Besides, in spite of the reviews, the film proved popular, and Day's short hairdo as Laurie established a new fashion.

Though there was little chemistry between Day and the five-foot, ten-inch Sinatra—who weighed only 135 pounds at the time—his scrawniness contributed to his effectiveness as Barney. To emphasize Barney's shabbiness and to give him a "slept-in-his-clothes" look, director Douglas encouraged Sinatra to leave his suit on whenever he took a nap on the set. And like Day, he was at his peak as a vocalist. In addition to a new song by Mack Gordon and James Van Heusen—the lilting "You, My Love"—Sinatra sang several standards in the film: "Just One of Those Things," "One for My Baby," and "Someone to Watch Over Me."

The picture was promoted with yet another cover story on Day in the February issue of *Photoplay*. This piece, by Ernst Jacobi, reads as if it had been paid for by Arwin Productions, with a full-page ad for the film and a four-color spread featuring Day promoting Lustre-Creme Shampoo, the caption referring to her appearance in *Young at Heart*.

Jacobi interviewed the Melchers over lunch on the Warner Brothers lot, where the couple ate steaks with fries and consumed a strange concoction of their own invention, tomato juice and buttermilk. He subsequently met individually with Melcher and Day, ostensibly to get candid impressions from each about the other. But the portrait he draws of their idyllic relationship can only be summarized as sheer fantasy—if not his, then theirs.

Jacobi gets close to some kind of truth when he accounts for their mutual attraction by declaring them "a study in contrasts, a composition in black and white. Marty—a good deal handsomer than he appears in snapshots—is very dark, the perfect foil for Doris' fairness. Where Doris is bubbling over with enthusiasm, is straightforward and direct, Marty is wry, suave, very calm and restrained." When asked the "secret of their success in marriage," Melcher jokingly told Jacobi, "It's very simple. . . . Half the time I let Doris have her way; the rest of the time I give in." In contrast with Melcher's witticism, it's rather telling that the agent had his wife sign a contract that very year, codifying their professional relationship—nearly five years after they were married—and favoring him much more than her. But if Melcher would come to be viewed as a monster who took advantage of his wife and client, Day herself would tell Jacobi: "At times he'll make a pretense of being cynical, but underneath it he's one of the softest, gentlest men I've ever known."

Day's next picture—about a leading American singer married to her manager—contained several striking parallels with her own life. In her portrayal of Ruth Etting in *Love Me or Leave Me*, Day would give what many think is her greatest performance in her greatest film.

14

"A Perfect Motion Picture"

✳

"That lack of guile photographs."
—JAMES CAGNEY

As soon as Melcher no longer had to conform to some studio's notion of Day's girl-next-door image, he shredded it and made her into a sex symbol—something much closer to the sensual woman she actually was. This calculated ploy worked on more levels than even Melcher anticipated. He found an ideal vehicle for this new Doris Day in *Love Me or Leave Me*. She responded with a performance that many regard as her finest achievement.

During April 1952, plans for *Love Me or Leave Me*, which told the story of singer Ruth Etting, were put on hold, while MGM awaited "approval from the principals in the Ruth Etting deal." Ruth Etting was a major exponent of early jazz and blues, her career powerfully fueled by the success of two different but related industries: radio and record albums. At her height during the Great Depression, not only were there Ruth Etting records and sheet music, but she also had dolls, hats, and even ice-cream sundaes named after her. She also made dozens of "soundies," or short movie recordings of songs to accompany feature films. In addition to Etting, the two other "principals" represented in *Love Me or Leave Me* were her manager and first husband, Martin Snyder, and her accompanist and second husband, Myrl Alderman. Snyder, a two-bit Chicago hoodlum, was known as Moe the Gimp, because of a limp that resulted from a childhood bout with polio. Snyder's arm-twisting gave his "Ruthie's" career its start in Chicago, and then compelled her to marry him. But it was the vulnerable quality in Etting's voice that helped make her one of the most popular singers in American history.

In order to secure permission for their story to be filmed, Snyder received $55,000 from MGM and Etting far more. A memorandum, written upon the conclusion of negotiations in July, reveals that the studio was "at liberty to do with the names, and with each of the names, whatever we desire." As usual with Hollywood scenarios, broad liberties were taken in bringing Etting's story to the screen. (Daniel Fuchs, who would win an Oscar for his "story" idea, emphasized that the screenplay strayed from the truth of Etting's life.) Still, the plot remained far more faithful to real events than most film biographies. The movie made it clear that Etting married Snyder only out of a sense of obligation and that it was really her pianist, Alderman, whom she truly loved. (Myrl Alderman would be renamed Johnny in the picture.) Snyder was physically abusive to Etting, and he ultimately made front-page news by shooting Alderman, whom Etting eventually married. The scandal involving one of the nation's biggest stars ended Etting's career in the mid-1930s.

Given the racier aspects of the story, Breen and his production code office were furiously raising objections with MGM throughout 1953 and 1954. One of the first complaints was that the "demand for [Ruth's] body is stated too often, and much too bluntly." Next came the more severe pronouncement that the entire story was unacceptable because "it is one of an illicit relationship, without the necessary compensating moral values required by the Code." For her part, Etting "refused to approve" several versions "because the scripts contained an inference that she was engaged in an illicit relationship with a character known as 'The Gimp,' whereas in real life they were husband and wife."

At the time, Day seemed to be cast against type. But she must have identified with the singer whose husband was her manager—and also abusive. Like Al Jorden, Moe Snyder was insanely jealous and resorted to fisticuffs to express his passion for his wife. And, like Marty Melcher, Snyder devoted his energies to promoting and exploiting his wife's natural talents. As Etting's agent, Snyder controlled every aspect of her career—often acting like a bully. In the same way that Sinatra banned Melcher from the set of *Young at Heart*, when Etting performed in Ziegfeld's Broadway theater, the great impresario refused the domineering Snyder backstage privileges. In the film, when Snyder tells a Ziegfeld choreographer, "I'm her manager. She never made a move I didn't tell her"—one can almost hear Melcher speaking. The more one examines the parallels between, on the one hand, Etting and Snyder and, on the other, Day and at least two of her husbands, the more the film appears to unfold in a remarkably parallel universe.

Although *Love Me or Leave Me* was a cinematic reflection of many facets of Day's life, the studio, in fact, first offered the role of Etting to at least two other actresses. Still smarting over the fact that her singing voice had been dubbed in *Show Boat*—and unwilling to subject herself to such a public affront again—Ava Gardner turned down the role, even when George Cukor was slated to direct it. (When, after the film's release, Gardner asked Cukor whether he regretted their both having decided not to do the picture, he responded that if they had made it, it wouldn't have turned out as well.) Jane Russell, too, refused the part in order to make a different biographical film, *I'll Cry Tomorrow* (which, in the end, she failed to make).

Hedda Hopper erroneously announced in her column that Jane Powell had been cast as Etting. Perhaps at her own instigation, Powell had been under consideration and even auditioned for the role. After Day won the part, Powell sent producer Joe Pasternak a telegram on July 2, thanking him for "the privilege of testing for it."

After Gardner and Russell turned down the part, Pasternak said he had "to beg" Day to do the film. "There was apparently something in that picture that reminded her of something she didn't want to be reminded of," said the producer. "We could never figure out what it was. But she did it and gave the finest performance of her career."

Day's $200,000 salary for her first picture with a studio other than Warner Brothers reveals how big a star she had become by 1954. Melcher's most shrewd maneuver had been to secure MGM's agreement to pay Day's recording company (Arwin) for any use of her "voice [taken] from the sound track, or otherwise." He also reduced Day's anxiety about working at a new studio by having MGM hire her personal wardrobe girl (Marie Blancard), hairdresser (Merele Stoltz), and makeup man (Kester Sweeney). Further, producer Pasternak promised to use Joe Ruttenberg, MGM's top cinematographer, who had won an Oscar for *Mrs. Miniver.* (In the end, Ruttenberg did not work on the film.) MGM had to agree to delay production until late October so that Day might take a month's vacation after completing "principal photography" on *Young at Heart.* She was in the midst of wrapping up that movie at Warners even as her MGM contract was being finalized. But then, the casting of James Cagney as Moe the Gimp would delay production still another month.

Cagney had been sent a copy of the script while he was making *Mister Roberts* on location in the South Pacific. "I took one read-through and said, 'My God, yes. We go with this one.' There was nothing to be added, nothing to be taken away. It was in fact that extremely rare thing, the perfect script." Cagney was so keen to do the picture that for the first time since becoming a star in the 1930s, he accepted second billing, after Day.

Even though he had worked with Day on *The West Point Story,* Cagney did not grasp the depth of her talent until they began working together on the Etting story. "I saw something in her I hadn't noticed before," Cagney recalled. "She had matured into a really exceptional actress, and I told her so. I said, 'You know, girl, you have a quality that I've seen but twice before,'" he added, before specifying Pauline Lord and Laurette Taylor, two great and famous stage actresses. "Both these ladies could really get in there and do it with everything," he gushed. "They could take you apart playing a scene. Now, you're the third one." As he further tried to define the quality he had seen in these actresses, Cagney wrote: "wide open as a barn door, no guile at all. *Un*shrewd. In all of these people there is a beautiful basic simplicity showing from the lack of guile. And that lack of guile photographs." Cagney's attempt to describe the quintessence of Day's special gift exactly paralleled Michael Curtiz's observation when he first worked with the budding actress in 1947.

The preproduction schedule for *Love Me or Leave Me* committed Day to forty-one "Work" and thirty-nine "Rehearse & Record" days, a sharp contrast with Cagney and his thirty-six "Work" days and no rehearsals. This MGM musical was clearly a lavish departure from the cut-rate films Day had made at Warners. In fact, the total budget for the film rose from $2,346,000 to $2,587,000, mostly because a dozen rehearsal days were added along with nine days for the shoot. Director Charles Vidor was to receive $115,000. Day's costumes alone came to $40,000, while Percy Faith received $10,000 for his "exclusive services as conductor and/or arranger."

Rehearsals began on November 19 and continued through December 4, 1954, when production began, continuing through February 8. Day worked exceptionally hard on the picture. Reportedly, she had only half a day off during the first seven weeks of shooting. But she also had fun making the film: "I had a lot of glasses with a big nose attached in my dressing room," she said. "I drove [Vidor] crazy. I would get all dressed up in a beautiful dress and picture hat and come out with these glasses on. He would say, 'Get the hell out of here.' We were always hysterical in my dressing room."

Though *Love Me or Leave Me* would emerge as a fictionalized version of Ruth Etting's life—for example, she never was the dancehall hostess as the film portrays her—pains were taken to be accurate in a number of respects. Johnny Green, the musical director at MGM, sent Etting a letter on March 11, 1954, inquiring about how her repertory of songs had developed. Alderman replied a week later on Etting's behalf: "Ruth doesn't 'play' much typewriter and I am little better but here goes." He proceeded to report that Etting's first "big" songs in Chicago nightclubs were "I Cried for You," "The One I Love Belongs to Somebody Else"— which Day had already sung in *I'll See You in My Dreams*—and "What Can I Say, Dear, After I Say I'm Sorry." Day would sing the first and last in the film. Etting's earliest hit recording was "Back in Your Own Back Yard," and a number of other songs featured by her included "Shakin' the Blues Away," "Love Me or Leave Me," and "Ten Cents a Dance." The film would feature thirteen songs from the past, in addition to two new numbers: "I'll Never Stop Loving You" and "Never Look Back." Day's plaintive rendition of the latter would become a hit single that remained on the charts for nineteen weeks, and one of the film's most striking images shows her clad in an aqua-blue, beaded dress as she sings "Shakin' the Blues Away."

In his letter, Alderman also wrote of the public humiliation the couple had suffered over the years. "We shall appreciate your regarding [this] address as confidential," he wrote, "inasmuch as we have endured all the troubles we desire." There was a postscript, too, revealing yet another way in which the film would depart from reality: "Ruth's break with Ziegfeld came as a result of her recording of 'Blue Skies' which Irving Berlin heard and contacted her to go to New York." In other words, it was Berlin who got Etting her part in the Ziegfeld Follies, not Synder, who makes it happen in the movie version.

Apart from the Follies segment, the entire film was shot in sequence, an unusual procedure that may well have enhanced the performances. Among numerous behind-the-scenes tidbits, the legs used as a backdrop in the Ziegfeld number belonged to none other than Cyd Charisse, who was legendary for her gams. Also, producer Joe Pasternak had a walk-on role as one of the fans who visit Etting backstage.

While working on *Love Me or Leave Me* Day called the Hungarian Vidor Basci, meaning "uncle" in his native language. According to Vidor, Day had "uncertain confidence in her own abilities" and refused to see the daily rushes of what had been shot. "On the few occasions when she has looked at herself on screen she has suffered, she tells me, intense and foolish embarrassment," Vidor said in an interview after the movie came out, adding, "She was shy about taking off enough clothes to play the Etting part, [and I] had to convince her it was dramatically right to undress a little."

"I was frightened at what the wide screen would do to my face," Day confided to Lydia Lane of the *Los Angeles Times.* "But after I saw my test, and everyone liked it so much, I felt better." In an even more revealing statement, Day told Lane: "When I first started in pictures I couldn't stand to see myself on the screen. I told Marty, 'I'm not pretty enough for pictures.'" After recalling that Melcher tried to reassure her ("It's the impact of your personality and your talent that counts"), Day resumed: "If you don't feel that you are pretty, don't worry about it. . . . Just try to make up for it with other things [like] character. . . . Being warm, dependable, sincere, considerate, interested."

MGM's hopes for the success of *Love Me or Leave Me* were quickly boosted by responses to the advance screenings. Dore Schary sent a telegram to Pasternak after the film's preview on April 5: "Preview last night tremendous smash. [Preview] cards extraordinary. There is some cutting to be done but all minor. Congratulations and thanks." Top MGM producer Sol C. Siegel, who attended the preview, sent Pasternak a letter the following day: "Dear Joe: I was invited last night to the preview of your wonderful picture. . . . Congratulations on a first-rate job of showmanship and 'producing' in the real sense of the word." Personal encomiums to Pasternak followed on the part of other industry insiders: "One of the finest musicals I have ever seen," wrote director Henry Koster. "It is not only thoroughly entertaining, but done with such wonderful craftsmanship and imagination that it deserves all the praise in the world. The acting is superb. I don't think James Cagney has ever done a finer performance, nor has Doris Day. Every bit was turned out with brilliant know-how. . . . I hate Charlie Vidor."

"I don't know whether there is such a thing as a perfect motion picture but if there is, you have made it," cheered bestselling author Sidney Sheldon. "It's a wonderful story with real people and moving situations, produced in flawless taste."

An advance story in the *Motion Picture Herald* proclaimed "performances that command Academy Award attention" and announced that "[t]he grapevine from California has proved magnificently right again with the arrival in New York this week of the print of 'Love Me or Leave Me.' Everything you've heard about this turbulent drama, excitingly attuned to today's box-office, is true. A public preview was held at

Loew's Lexington theatre, the same place where 'Blackboard Jungle' was sneaked. The response was identical. A thrilled, spell-bound audience acclaimed a big, new dramatic hit.

"She [Day] not only plumbs new depths as an actress, but takes us there with her," continued the story. "Like any worthwhile performance, it is at once internal and external. It also encourages us to identify and empathize with Day's Etting—as opposed to merely feeling sympathy towards her." When she was a TV talk-show guest for the first time (in 1970, on Merv Griffin's show), even the self-deprecating Day spoke of *Love Me* as her favorite of all her films.

A two-page spread in *Life* magazine declared the "unsavory romantic story" of Etting and Snyder "the least likely subject for a movie musical to be tried in a long time. But MGM has made 'Love Me or Leave Me' into a fine, untypical musical by sticking pretty faithfully to that story."

Hedda Hopper added to the advance reaction by declaring, in a feature on the front page of the Sunday arts section of the *Los Angeles Times*, "Personally, [Day's] a far cry from the girl next door. The extrovert of the screen is in real life a shy somebody whose sunny smile covers a multitude of moods. She's sensitive, takes her work seriously and doesn't know what to do with herself when she's not before a camera. Doris came of age in 'Love Me or Leave Me.' . . . As Doris says, 'It's the most grown-up thing I've done—it's womanly instead of girly-girly.'" Hopper's subsequent sentence, however, was the real eye-opener: "When Doris finished this picture on a loanout, she asked for and got her release from Warners, figuring it was time she got out on her own." Even before the "top-notch" *Love Me or Leave Me* opened, the *Los Angeles Times* reported that the early press response had prompted MGM to offer her $1 million for four pictures.

Most of the ads featured Day in her "Shakin' the Blues Away" gown; others showed Cagney on the verge of slapping her. In addition to full-page ads in *Life, Look, Cosmopolitan*, and, according to the Press Book, "all the fan magazines," marketing plans for the picture included an interview with Day to be made available to disc jockeys and to recount "the fabulous career of Ruth Etting." Day went so far as to make 135 different tape recordings that greeted "individually by name" the DJs listed by city in the extensive Press Book. More than two thousand of them received not only the movie soundtrack but also an album of *The Original Records of Ruth Etting*, to prompt a "'ready-to-go' show."

There were tie-ins with a new Doris Day coloring book as well as a Doris Day "cut-out dolls" book—both published by Whitman Co. and described as "perennially one of the five-and-ten cent stores' best sellers." In addition to the typical flags and banners, distributors could buy a four-page, two-color "herald" (newspaper supplement)—chock-full of not only stills from the picture but also copy (available for "$5.50 per 1000") to be used as inserts in local newspapers. A cute takeoff on the title was suggested for "co-op newspaper ads": "He'll LOVE YOU. . . Not LEAVE YOU! Shop Locally for these Beauty-Aid specials!" And finally: a follow-up, twelve-page "Supplement to the Pressbook" containing fresh ads exploiting the almost uniform praise. "The Picture That the Critics Say Is Academy Award Stuff!" screamed the oversize copy on one of the full-page ads.

When *Love Me or Leave Me* opened the last week in May, the mainstream reviewers concurred with the advance praise. "[A] stinging but entertaining film," observed Bosley Crowther in the *New York Times*. "Best of all for everybody, it has Doris Day to play the role of the blonde and bewitching Miss Etting and it has James Cagney to play The Gimp. [They] do their jobs extremely well and make an uncommonly interesting and dramatic couple for a musical film. . . . When Mr. Cagney finally slaps Miss Day in the face, the audience reacts to the shameful violence with genuine and audible gasps. . . . And, of course, it is hard to think of anyone better qualified to do the job of singing Miss Etting's old numbers than the lovely and lyrical Miss Day. [She] has the voice and the feeling to do justice to the sentiments in this film."

Alton Cook was even more emphatic in the *New York World-Telegram and Sun*: "One of the most strongly dramatic musical movies ever filmed. Superlatives cluster around this movie, so [let's] take them one at a time. To begin with, we have Doris Day in the first role that could reveal that she is an actress of emotional force as well as the sweet little ingénue. Miss Day is an astounding revelation."

"A tremendously powerful drama," added William K. Zinsser in the *New York Herald Tribune*. "Cagney has created a fascinating portrait of the Gimp. . . . Doris Day graduates out of her world of peppy collegiate revels with this picture, and the change is all to the good. She gives a mature performance, bubbly over her success and depressed by her sordid marriage. . . . M-G-M deserves great credit for telling it candidly without the syrup that makes most Hollywood musicals so harrowingly sweet."

Filmgoers rousingly agreed. As reported in the trade papers, the picture grossed $170,662 in its first week at Radio City Music Hall, yet another breakthrough. The film was voted one of the year's ten best pictures "by the nation's critics and radio and television commentators," but it was not nominated for a Best Picture Oscar. For decades, many would view the Academy's failure to nominate Day for her portrayal of Etting as one of its biggest oversights. (The 1955 Best Actress award went to Anna Magnani for *The Rose Tattoo*.) Cagney did receive a Best Actor nomination but lost to Ernest Borgnine for *Marty*, which also won the award for Best Picture. Cagney's biographer John McCaber acknowledged that "[i]t is one of those rare instances when the Cagney strength is fully matched by another performer. [It] is a dual triumph of acting in surprisingly equal balance. It is not Doris Day's picture . . . nor is it his, but a superb example of costarring."

✳   ✳   ✳

As engineered by Melcher, the massive change in his wife's image was promoted with a cover story in the October issue of *Photoplay*. She appeared curled up in a rattan chair, wearing a pink blouse and blue pedal pushers, her face beaming. Mike Connolly's story inside bore his regular headline, "Impertinent Interview." "How do you feel about being sexy for the first time in pictures?" Connolly asked at the top of the piece. Likening the sensation to "a shot in the arm," Day emphasized that *Love Me or Leave Me* was her first picture away from Warners, her "home lot," where she had been confined to "All American Girl roles. . . . I've discovered that I like to do things with some depth . . . that use the emotions," Day added, before resorting to cliché: "When I first came to M-G-M, I was like the little bird whose mother pushes her out of the nest."

In this remarkably unguarded interview, Day talked about what she perceived as the adverse effects of fame. "I made pictures, one after another, for three years at Warners before I stepped out of Burbank to make a personal appearance tour with one of Bob Hope's troupes. By then, people knew who I was. I couldn't get used to the way they stared at me. . . . I kept thinking, 'Oh gosh, I wonder if my hair is combed right' or 'What is the matter with me that they should stare so?' And then I went into a shell. I'm just now coming out of the shell. I've pulled myself together and now I realize that it wouldn't be normal if people didn't stare at a movie star and ask for her autograph.

"I've always been shy with strangers," she continued. "After I get to know people, I'm not shy. But I'm terribly afraid of the first meeting." Day spoke forthrightly and almost self-consciously here about one of her principal traits: her need to please others, which prompted her more or less constant fear of disappointing them.

The same issue of *Photoplay* included a gossip item that might have been a publicist's plant but is nonetheless revealing: the assertion that, despite his "pestering" her to let him see *Love Me or Leave Me*, "Doris doesn't dare let the 13-year-old Terry see it." The notice played up Day as a new sex symbol, in other words, while simultaneously restoring her more wholesome image. Still another reporter quoted Day as saying that during this period, Terry had taken to calling her "Sis," as opposed to "Mom." The child in Day would always be prominent and obvious to anyone percep-tive, including her own young son.

Looking back on her breakthrough in *Love Me or Leave Me*, Day would ask Cameron Shipp, in the cover story of *Cosmopolitan* magazine (spring, 1956): "Why do I always have to be the girl-next-door? I don't think I ever was." Day now began disowning the image she had worked so hard to help create in the first place.

15

"Whatever Will Be, Will Be"

✳

"They held the cameras for me, and when the tears finally came, they shot. There was really no technique involved."
—DORIS DAY

When Doris Day met Alfred Hitchcock at a party and he told her he wanted to make a picture with her, she was rightfully excited by the prospect. The master of suspense had already established himself as one of the most distinguished directors of international cinema. Now, several years later, he remained true to his word and cast Day as the distraught mother, Jo McKenna, in *The Man Who Knew Too Much*, eliciting from her one of her strongest performances.

Known for his careful preparation and artful eye, Hitchcock was at the peak of his considerable powers in the mid-1950s, having recently made *Rear Window* and *To Catch a Thief,* two masterpieces. *The Man Who Knew Too Much* was a remake of a British film of the same name (starring Leslie Banks and Edna Best), which he had made in 1934. The script was rewritten by Angus McPhail and the director's new discovery, John Michael Hayes, who had already penned *Rear Window* (with Grace Kelly and Jimmy Stewart) and *To Catch a Thief* (with Grace Kelly and Cary Grant). With his customary wit, Hitchcock would comment to French filmmaker François Truffaut, concerning his two versions of *The Man Who Knew Too Much*, that "the first . . . was the work of a talented amateur; the second was made by a professional."

Although at one point a new title (*Into Thin Air*) was considered, the story remained basically the same: While vacationing abroad, a husband and wife learn about an assassination plot, and their child is kidnapped to maintain their silence. The setting was changed from Switzerland to

Morocco, a far more exotic and precarious environment, and their child became a son, Hank, instead of a daughter. Hank's mother, Jo, is a retired singer; his father, Ben McKenna, an American doctor. (Chris Olsen, who played Hank, was also Day's son in *I'll See You in My Dreams.*)

"[Hitchcock] was not content merely to improve the form, to probe the characters, or to update the story," observed French filmmakers Eric Rohmer and Claude Chabrol, who, like Truffaut, were enamored of the director and wrote a joint study of his work. "What we are given is a veritable transfiguration. In its new form, this film is one of those in which the Hitchcockian mythology finds its purest, if not its most obvious expression."

Given his notorious obsession with "cool" blondes, Day was a surprising choice for Hitchcock. Though blonde, she was far from cool. The director shrewdly understood, however, that Day's innocent image also made her ideal for playing a mother and wife in peril. Shrewd, too, to have chosen Day to play opposite Jimmy Stewart, who had already been cast. The personification of small-town civic virtue, Stewart was the male equivalent of Day. After she first met him at a party given by Alan Ladd and his wife, Day told Melcher how much she liked the all-American film star, and, moreover, hoped to make a picture with him. Having been likened to Huckleberry Finn in the beginning of her film career because of her freckles, Day was now finding her Tom Sawyer in Stewart.

The Man Who Knew Too Much was the most complicated and peripatetic picture of Day's career, with location shooting in London and North Africa. Though filming would not begin until May 13, 1955, in Marrakech, the Melchers decided first to explore some of Europe, an itinerary that included Day's appearance at the Cannes Film Festival during the last week of April. With Terry in tow, they left Los Angeles on March 28 on the transcontinental SuperChief train, arriving in New York three days later. There, Melcher gave his wife a gold bracelet on her birthday, with four lucky charms, one for each year of their marriage. Howard Thompson interviewed the couple for a feature in the *New York Times*. "I know I'll love working with [Hitchcock], because I've found out he's as shy as I am," Day told Thompson. "Oh, yes, I'm shy," she repeated. "I'm full of confidence in front of the camera. Otherwise . . . I know I've been accused of being overly sensitive," she added, referring to her refusal to sing "My Secret Love" at the Academy Awards.

On April 6, the Melchers boarded the *Queen Elizabeth* for their crossing to Europe. (In her stateroom, Day discovered flowers awaiting her from "Hitch," the accompanying card wishing her "Love and a sickless Voyage.") As scheduled, they had six days to relax in London before pressing on to France.

But the stay hardly proved restful. "The reception for Miss Day in London has been sensational with as many as 200 to 300 children assembling every day at the Savoy Hotel to see her. Special arrangements were made to have her give them autographs at 7:30 in the morning so the crowd might later be dispersed." "It's one of the loveliest cities I've ever seen," Day would say about the British capital, specifying her particular fondness for Green Park. While Melcher and Terry took in the landmarks, Day went shopping.

They spent several nights in Paris, where they stayed at the Hotel George V before boarding a train for Cannes to explore the Riviera for two weeks and attend the film festival. (*Marty*, starring Ernest Borgnine, won the Palme d'Or that year, as it had the Oscar.) The French government supplied the Melchers with a chauffered car. They visited Monte Carlo, Nice, San Remo, and Marseilles. On the beach in Cannes, Day was spotted wearing a bikini. The skimpy suits, still not common around the world, had become all the rage on the Riviera by the mid-1950s. Bikinis would not become popular in the United States for another five years, when the gimmicky 1960 pop hit "Itsy Bitsy Teeny Weenie Yellow Polka Dot Bikini" confirmed its arrival in the mainstream. On May 12, the Melchers went by ship from Cannes to Casablanca and then to Marrakech by car. The forty-eight-day shooting schedule allocated nine days in Morocco, seventeen in London, and the rest at the Paramount lot. Ultimately, filming ran over by an astonishing thirty-four days. The cast assembled for the first time in the patio of the Mamounia Hotel in Marrakech, where both Day and Stewart stayed and took most of their meals. (The hotel's restaurant provided the setting for the scene in which the McKennas dine with the British couple that subsequently kidnaps Hank.)

"None of us knew one another very well before that," Day told a reporter, "but by the time the picture was finished, we were all fast friends. At this first meeting, however, Hitchcock gave us a serious talk. We needn't worry very much about the native uprisings, he said. We were almost safe. Almost. I tried not to think about it. After all, why should the Moroccan Arabs be any different from the Hollywood-extra Arabs?"

As she continues, Day reveals a typical American's naive attitude toward the Third World and recalls the frightened teenager leaving Ohio for the first time and setting out for California, albeit with her mother.

"That went over big with me," Day said, referring to Hitchock's remarks about native uprisings, "until I saw a pair of piercing black eyes looking at me over a face mask. I nearly ran to hide in a corner." Day became "a little scared . . . about the way my son Terry was bargaining with the natives. One day I saw him talking to a murderous-looking character. Pretty soon, though, he ran over to Marty and said, 'Dad, that fellow has a knife I want, but it costs too much. I've been working on him for three days now. In a couple more I'll practically get it for free!' You know, he did!"

Day also became dismayed by the "ungodly" heat, and by the crushing poverty in French Morocco. "There wasn't much she could do about the poverty," said Hitchcock biographer Patrick McGilligan, "but as an animal lover the star used her clout to demand that all the hoofed and feathered creatures used in the production be well fed on the film budget."

Accustomed to shooting a scene in one or two takes at Warners, Day was totally unfamiliar with the kind of painstaking filmmaking for which Hitchcock was famous. The fact that some scenes required thirty or more takes—coupled with the director giving her no instructions whatsoever—made her extremely apprehensive. Aware that Stewart had already made both *Rope* and *Rear Window* with Hitchcock, the frequently insecure Day asked her costar if the director was leaving her to her own devices because he was unhappy with her work. Stewart tried to reassure her, saying that Hitchcock told actors what to do only if they were going astray. In spite of his reputation, Hitchcock was basically a benign director.

"In the beginning," recalled Stewart, "it certainly threw Doris for a loop. Doris surprised a lot of people with her acting in 'The Man Who Knew Too Much,' but she didn't surprise Hitch, who knew what to expect from her." (It was her dramatic work in *Storm Warning* that prompted Hitchcock to work with Day.) Their warming relationship helped relieve her anxieties, to a point. "I loved him personally," Day remembered. "We would go to dinner and laugh, and he was warm and loving, just really sweet. But I didn't understand him on the set."

The Moroccan sequences used more than three hundred extras and took much longer to shoot than expected. (The total revised budget for the picture was $1,580,000, with $704,250 allocated for the cast and $111,100 for extras.) Given her eating habits, Day was severely challenged by Moroccan cuisine and had to make special arrangements with the hotel's kitchen. Between the problems presented by the food and the heat, she fell out of sorts and had to keep to her room for a couple of days.

When the cast and crew reassembled in London on May 28 for location shooting at the Royal Albert Hall and the Savoy Hotel, Alma joined her daughter before moving on, by herself, to visit relatives in Germany. Day appeared at a big press bash in London, held jointly by Warners, MGM, Paramount, and Columbia Records. (Even before the release of *Love Me or Leave Me*, it was prematurely announced that Day had a $1 million four-picture deal with MGM—one of which would pair her again with James Cagney—though negotiations with MGM proved inconclusive.) She also did an interview with John Ellison for his BBC radio program *In Town Tonight.* Day talked about her work on the Hitchcock film and sang eight bars of "Ready, Willing and Able" to help promote *Young at Heart,* then showing in London. Ellison deliberately entered provocative territory when he mentioned that she had been observed wearing a bikini in Cannes. Clearly startled, Day tittered before rushing to explain that she felt "overdressed" on the beach in her regular suit and had bought a bikini at a local shop.

Day did not know that Melcher had primed Ellison to ask her about the bikini, part of his larger scheme to alter his wife's image with *Love Me or Leave Me.* After Day concluded the program by singing "Secret Love," Ellison sprang another surprise: Leading members of the Doris Day Fan Club of Great Britain—including its president, Julia Coleman, and secretary, John Smith—popped in to present her with a silver tea set, "for all the joy you've given [our members] over the past eight years." Day later recalled, "I was so overcome I broke up."

Day met with the throng of the club's members on June 19 for a proper English tea at the Savoy Hotel. With a tape recorder running, she signed photos while Melcher tried to manage the crowd. "Let her breathe," he can be heard imploring.

"We used to organize big outings for the film premieres," recalled Sheila Smith, an early member of the fan club, now on the verge of becoming one of its London branch managers. "We'd take everybody by coach, and advertise [the event]." The fan club maintained itself and evolved over the years—until the present day—confirmation that her British fans were "more loyal" than American ones. Looking back on her session with her British fans, Day observed, "It seemed they knew more about me than I did myself," an admission suggesting just how distant she felt from her image, even as early as 1955, or that she had a talent for forgetting her past.

✳   ✳   ✳

Back in Hollywood—where some of the most emotionally wrenching scenes in *The Man Who Knew Too Much* were yet to be shot—Day insisted on finally confronting Hitchcock to discuss her nagging feeling that he was not giving her enough direction. This meeting, uncharacteristic of Day, is a powerful indication of just how important the film had become for her. It featured her first dramatic role for a studio other than Warners, and she was eager to confirm her acting abilities.

Hitchcock tried to put her mind at rest. "But, dear Doris, you've done nothing to elicit comment from me," confirming precisely what Stewart had told her earlier. "You have been doing what I felt was right for the film and that's why I haven't told you anything."

What many consider the most effective scene of Day's career as an actress—when Ben gives Jo a sleeping pill before telling her that their boy is missing—was shot at Paramount in a single day, during the first week in August. "Now, I'm supposed to cry, but not hysterically, because according to the script I've been taking sedatives," recalled Day. "I tried to do this scene. I really tried, but I simply couldn't. 'It just isn't there,' I told Mr. Hitchcock," Day said, recalling their preliminary work on the scene in the morning, before the cameras started to roll. They broke for lunch, and Day returned to her dressing room, where, "for the first time in ages," she said, "I couldn't eat."

Having grown accustomed to the advice of her Warners wardrobe mistress, Marie, Day had kept her on after leaving the studio to become an independent actress. Marie reassured Day after her trial run for the scene, "Look, Doris. You're a professional. You're going to do this. Just don't think about it."

"After lunch I went back to the set and we got it in the first take," Day said. "They held the cameras for me, and when the tears finally came, they shot. There was really no technique involved." Modest as usual, Day downplayed her considerable technique. After seeing the picture, Donald Saddler told Day he found her so convincing in the scene that he forgot who she was. Day explained, "I just thought to myself, what if it was Terry?" Apparently without realizing it, Day was using Method acting, so in vogue at the time. "What happened to me in that scene seemed very real,"

Day recalled. "I actually experienced the feeling that I was losing my little son to a kidnapper. I was living that ordeal." After an advance private screening, when Hitchcock was asked how he "got such a performance" out of Day, he replied, in his typically terse manner, "It wasn't me. It was Doris." Hitchcock was not only shy, like Day, but equally modest.

As for the all-important scream Day had to muster for the climactic scene, when Jo notices the assassin's gun peeking through the curtains at Royal Albert Hall: "One really good scream can give [me] a Charlie horse in my voice for weeks. So if they can't turn up the volume of my scream, I'm going to insist that they loop [or edit] it—with a double," she maintained before the film's release.

Day's own scream was ultimately used in the scene, which Hitchcock biographer Donald Spoto holds up as "the quintessential summary of his method and one of the most astonishingly beautiful and successful suspense episodes in the history of the medium. A wordless, twelve-minute . . . sequence, it gives full scope to what Hitchcock has called 'pure cinema.'"

Besides featuring one of Day's best performances, *The Man Who Knew Too Much* also introduced her most singular vocal legacy, the song "Que Sera, Sera." The song contributed greatly to the film's enduring importance. Jay Livingston and Ray Evans wrote the infectious tune especially for Day. The song was actually commissioned by Hitchcock, who had never done such a thing before. He met with Livingston and Evans to explain the pivotal importance of the song to the story: the kidnapped Hank is reunited with his mother when he hears her singing it. The songwriting team proceeded to write, in a matter of hours, what became an internationally familiar work. However, the composers waited several days before delivering it. They did not want Hitchcock to know how quickly and easily it had come to them.

Given "Que Sera, Sera"'s phenomenal popularity, it is astonishing to learn that at first Day rejected it as too simple and childlike and that Melcher had to insist on her doing it. "Que Sera, Sera" would become Day's theme song, forever identified with her. Its advocating a trust in fate, a reliance on "whatever will be, will be," came to encapsulate Day's personal philosophy.

Having just introduced the Italian expression "Que Sera, Sera" in his 1954 film *The Barefoot Contessa*, Joseph Mankiewicz—the highly literate film writer and director—deeply resented the success of the song, feeling that Livingston and Evans had stolen the idea. ("Que Sera, Sera" was the

motto on a nobleman's mausoleum in the opening and closing scenes of
Contessa—a Humphrey Bogart and Ava Gardner vehicle that was a critical
and financial flop.) Under its alternate title, "Whatever Will Be, Will Be,"
the song would win an Oscar and become Day's sixth recording to sell
more than a million copies. She would sing it again in *Please Don't Eat
the Daisies* (1960) and *The Glass Bottom Boat* (1966). And more than a
decade later, she would make it the theme song of her TV show, which
ran for five years.

✳   ✳   ✳

Life magazine featured *The Man Who Knew Too Much* in two issues, de-
voting the "first to its exotic, exciting background and then to its hair-
raising entertainment qualities," the Press Book announced. The second
article revealed that for the all-important climax in Royal Albert Hall,
Hitchcock employed not only the London Symphony Orchestra but also
a 350-member chorus.

A Paramount press release quoted Day on the notion that in this film
she had suddenly become an actress. "I don't know why anyone should
be surprised," she said. "Singing roles naturally limit an actress so far as
the type role and story is [*sic*] concerned. But once she's accepted as an
'actress' who sings—rather than as a 'singer' who tries to act—her career
has greater possibilities."

To further promote the picture, Day did a good number of so-called
tie-up ads: one for Bolex Home Movie Camera, another for Page & Shaw
Candy, and two for Lux Soap and Lustre Crème Shampoo. She also
wrote an extensive article on her costar Jimmy Stewart for one of the
movie magazines—though it was probably written by publicists. Their
performing at the piano together, the article relates, "became a pleasant
ritual throughout the making of the picture. Frequently between takes,
when there was a piano handy, Jimmy would drift over and start tinkling,
and pretty soon I would follow."

Although the words might have been put in her mouth by a publicist,
the article includes at least one observation that seems to express Day's
true feelings about being a star—as well as her roots in the Depression:
"Before I met Jimmy, I often wondered about the secret of his abiding
popularity. After all, the average movie star—male or female—doesn't have
half the security of a hairdresser or makeup man. It simply isn't as easy

to wear as well under the withering glare of the spotlight as it is in the shade behind the scenes."

Day became quite blunt with another reporter when she described her reaction to seeing herself in the picture. "In some of the terror scenes I looked just awful. My mouth was crooked, my hair was all mussed, my eyes were swollen, my dress was like a sack. If I had seen the rushes of that—well, I'll tell you one thing. I'd have marched in to Hitchcock and told him he was ruining me." Day explained that she understood her character was "supposed to look awful. . . . But me, personally I don't like to see myself looking like that. As I say, if I had seen the rushes, the next time we played such a scene I'd have settled my dress, combed my hair and kept my mouth straight. Consciously or subconsciously, I'd be trying to make me, Doris Day, look pretty instead of making that woman look real," Day continued, inadvertently referring to Method acting again. "So I don't look at the rushes. As long as it's a picture about that woman, I keep myself out of it."

In a related comment, Hollywood's legendary costume designer Edith Head complimented Day for having "a natural flair for style" and being the "easiest star" she had ever worked with—all the more impressive considering that, during her extensive reign in Hollywood, Head had worked with practically every one of the great stars. "But designing her costumes for 'The Man Who Knew Too Much' was difficult. I had to make her reasonably drab [and] it was hard work," added Head, describing a costumer's typical lament.

But both Hitchcock and Head knew exactly what they were doing with Day. As Paramount executive Don Hartman wrote to fellow executive Russell Holman in a telegram of October 11, 1955: "Ran 'The Man Who Knew Too Much' today in rough form without dubbing and scoring and think it is one of Hitchcock's and Jimmy Stewart's best pictures. Doris Day is every bit as good as in 'Love Me Or Leave Me.' . . . I prophesy now with safety that this is another in the long list of Paramount smash hits."

*　*　*

When *The Man Who Knew Too Much* opened in the summer of 1956, the reviews emphasized Day's breakthrough as a dramatic actress, even as they confirmed that Hitchcock had made another suspense picture for the ages. "Doris Day is surprisingly effective as the mother who is frantic about her child. She also has a dandy sequence in which she signals the boy with a song," Bosley Crowther wrote in the *New York Times*. "Even in mammoth VistaVision, the old Hitchcock thriller-stuff has punch."

The *Daily News*, too, spoke well of Day's achievement: "Mrs. Mc-Kenna is remarkably well played by Doris Day, who, until she appeared in the role of Ruth Etting in 'Love Me or Leave Me,' was considered just a pretty girl who had a way with a song. She is now rapidly developing into a fine actress."

"Hitchcock fans have reached the 'show-me' point where they practically challenge him to bring forth enough new cinema inventiveness to hold them on the edge of their seats all through the show, and in his latest Paramount production the old master of suspense and mystery proves he has plenty of tricks left in his bag," offered Don Gillette in the *Hollywood Reporter*. Placing the role in the larger spectrum of Day's entire film career, author George Morris would call Jo McKenna "the most challenging part" she had undertaken, adding that "the actress responded with a performance of nerve-shattering intensity."

With Day at the top of her game and now liberated from Warner Brothers, Melcher was busy hatching new deals for this new and important dramatic star who could still do musicals as well. Several tantalizing projects were announced, but unfortunately never made, including MGM's *New Girl in Town*, a musical version of Eugene O'Neill's *Anna Christie*. A two-picture deal was also in the offing with RKO, where plans were under way for Day to appear in *Love Affair* and *Stage Door*, costarring Carol Channing.

With *The Man Who Knew Too Much* completed, the Melchers found relaxation in Palm Springs, where they spent a week at the Marion Davies Desert Inn. In addition to playing golf and tennis—and lolling in the sun—Day and Terry rented a tandem bicycle and went riding. While Day shopped for clothes, Melcher acquired a membership at the Tamarisk Country Club, as well as a plot of land near the golf course, where they hoped to build their dream house. Along with Marilyn Maxwell and Rhonda Fleming, the Melchers attended Lena Horne's cabaret act on her opening night at the Coconut Grove and congratulated her after the performance.

"We go out more than we used to," Day told Dorothy O'Leary for her cover story in *Screen* magazine. "We like to go out to dinner with a few friends, then come back [home] or to someone else's house to 'chew the fat.' If we don't go out, I like to get in bed early and watch TV. Since I'm not doing so many pictures now, I can sleep later some of the time, and you know, I'm beginning to enjoy that!"

Though they never exactly became the famed rat pack, the Melchers enjoyed dinners out with Jerry Lewis and his wife, Patti; Dick Powell and June Allyson; Danny Thomas and his wife, Rose Marie; Donna Reed and her husband, Tony Owen; and Jack and Mary Benny. Melcher was the ringleader, so Benny presented him with a whistle on a chain, and Jerry Lewis gave him a basketball, declaring him the coach of their team. Lewis had also taken to calling Day "Sylvia." The name, he said, "has the ring of a great actress." Lewis and his wife also presented Day with their own version of an Oscar for her performance in *The Man Who Knew Too Much*. "It was a gold loving cup engraved with our sentiments," Lewis said, joking. "When we gave it to her, she got so misty-eyed we thought she was going to flood the place."

Donna Reed recalled a surprise birthday party that Day gave for Melcher: "While 25 of us patiently waited at the Beverly Hills Club, Doris was giving her greatest performance. For some reason, Marty decided he was too tired to go out to dinner. When Doris finally got him to the party, and we all shouted 'Happy Birthday,' he was the most amazed man. It seems he'd never had a surprise party. He walked around most of the evening smiling—in a delighted daze."

Robert Cummings, who also attended the party, remembered: "Pastel place mats, flickering candles, and freshly cut garden flowers. Everything was all pink and Doris Day–looking." The romantic mood suddenly turned silly, however, when Jerry Lewis started indulging in his typical antics, and his plate went flying across the dinner table.

Before work began on *Julie*, Day's next picture, the Melchers spent a weekend taking Terry to Alisal, a 20,000-acre cattle ranch about one hundred miles north of Los Angeles. The ranch was popular with urban dwellers who wanted "cowboy" life. Befriending the ranch hands, Terry particularly enjoyed helping them with their chores. Day and Melcher got into the spirit of the place; the three rode horseback for two hours on a Saturday morning, and had their breakfast in an isolated clearing in the wooded hills.

Terry had so much fun that he cried when he had to say goodbye to his new friends. He also announced that he wanted to become a cowboy himself. His wise mother said she would give the idea her blessings as long as he finished college first. But as a proud Day told yet another reporter, the thirteen-year-old Terry "loves music and plays piano very well. He thinks that he'd like to be in show business someday, either in production or the music end." The Melchers converted their garage into "a big playroom for Terry and his friends" journalist Dorothy O'Leary further reported. "It was wood-paneled and featured its own soda bar, TV set, ping-pong table, and movie projector."

Day continued to confirm her reputation as an overeater. "We seldom have a phone conversation when I don't hear her munching on something," recalled Ronnie Cowan. In Europe with Marty, she wrote long letters to Cowan, describing not the sights but their meals, and Marty teased her about this correspondence: "more like a cook book than a travelog," he said. "I just happen to be one of those lucky people . . . who can eat anything without having to measure my waistline all the time," Day boasted. She also bragged about going through a large jar of peanut butter in her dressing room in a single week, during the making of *The Man Who Knew Too Much*, and then explained that she had to "smuggle" chocolates, which Marty wanted her to avoid, when they went to Palm Springs.

Once again, Day revealed just how much she was hiding from Melcher. "You know, Marty and I are going to Palm Springs for a few days," Day blurted out during an interview. "Marty doesn't like me to eat chocolates, says I'm like Ray Milland in 'The Lost Weekend' about them. But if I sneak them into my [bag] I can grab a few every time he stops for gas. Matter of fact, I think I'll ride in the back seat so I can really gorge myself!'"

16

Day Noir

---- ✳ ----

"If this is what married life is going to be,
then we have nothing—absolutely nothing!"
—FROM *JULIE*

While promoting her recently completed *The Man Who Knew Too Much,* Day told an interviewer about her upcoming project, *Julie*: "We're going to Pebble Beach," she said, referring to the picturesque site in Carmel, to which she would relocate upon retiring in 1980. "[Carmel] just delights me," Day continued, "because I'm taking up golf, and there are some wonderful courses up there. I'll be working with Arwin Productions, which is our own company, and don't ask me what Arwin means; I haven't the slightest idea. Andrew Stone is doing the picture, and it's going to be quite an adventure."

Julie, Arwin's second picture with MGM, was specifically chosen to further establish Day's credentials as a dramatic actress. Though she would sing the film's theme, no songs were awkwardly folded into the story. Originally, there were plans for Day to sing a duet with her co-star Louis Jourdan—the suave, French heartthrob—but they were abandoned. *Julie* would also be the first film that Melcher produced on his own, and, according to Day, the new dynamic permanently altered their relationship.

Referring to the film's working title, *If I Can't Have You,* the *Los Angeles Times* announced that the production would be made with director Andrew Stone's customary "documentary technique . . . with all scenes shot on actual locations." Having started his career by directing such lightweight musicals as *The Great Victor Herbert* and *Stormy Weather,* Stone turned to much heavier subject matter. And with location shooting, he frequently achieved a gritty authenticity in such films as *The Steel Trap* and *The Decks Ran Red. Julie* would prove no exception. If Stone's previous picture, *The Night Holds Terror*, had been made for $75,000, the $750,000 allocated for *Julie* indicates a significant advance in the director's standing—even if nearly half the budget, or $310,000, went to its two stars.

Julie was based on an actual murder case in Lyon County, Iowa, in 1900. A highly regarded and prosperous farmer of Garfield township, August Schroeder, was discovered one morning by his wife, Dora, hanging from a rafter in his barn. Those who knew Schroeder had trouble believing him a suicide. The unfolding of the case would eventually justify their suspicions.

After Schroeder's death, Dora married his farmhand Charles Rocker. A court case in the spring of 1904 revealed not only Rocker's attempt to kill his own child with Dora but also his murder of Schroeder. Though Dora was accused of collaborating with Rocker, she was found to be "entirely innocent of the killing of her former husband and as a matter of fact [was] unaware that he came to his death feloniously until told by Rocker some time since."

In addition to resetting the story in California, Stone updated and completely revamped it. Day plays Julie Benton, an airline hostess. Her husband, Lyle—portrayed by Louis Jourdan—is a classical pianist. Insanely jealous, not only does he attempt, in the opening scene, to kill himself and Julie in a car crash, he later admits to the murder of her first husband, Bob.

"How can you humiliate me like this?. . . In front of all those people," a livid Julie asks in her opening monologue, as she's leaving a country club and driving a convertible along a twisting, coastal road, with Lyle in the passenger seat. She continues: "It's unforgivable. Is it because he's a cousin of Bob's?" The "he" is Cliff Henderson (Barry Sullivan), the man who will aid Julie in her attempt to elude Lyle, once he has announced his intention to murder her. "Well," Julie continues, "if this is what married life is going to be, then we have nothing—absolutely nothing!"

Julie's implicit threat prompts Lyle to place his left foot over her right on the accelerator, and press down, causing the car to careen out of control. The film opens on this note of high suspense and proceeds to sustain it for practically its entire 109 minutes, culminating with Julie forced to land a plane after Lyle has shot the pilot.

When, earlier in the picture, Julie seeks protection from the police, she is told, "If we called in every guy who threatened his wife, we'd need a jail the size of the Pentagon." After she's advised to flee and change her identity, an incensed Julie reflects: "He admitted to killing my husband. He admits that he wants to kill me, and nobody can help me do anything."

The role of Julie Benton, a "woman in jeopardy," offered Day a particular challenge, given her first, brutal marriage to the physically abusive Al Jorden, whose jealousy prompted him to threaten her at gunpoint—and in a car, no less. Referring to her twenty-three tearful scenes in the film, Day told costar Barry Sullivan, "When I resolved to go in for dramatic roles, I hadn't bargained on this."

In her dedication to coming off well in her husband's first film as sole producer, Day had to not only confront her fear of flying, but train as an "airline hostess" with Transocean Airlines in San Francisco, enduring three days of in-flight filming for the climactic scene. "I held my breath and shut my eyes as long as I could," Day recalled. "By the time I had my eyes open again we were airborne. I kept telling myself that I wasn't scared, that I was actually enjoying the feel of flying." In addition, in order to make the most of the star's time during the complicated shooting schedule, Day was shuttled from one site to another via helicopter, compounding her fear.

Julie was shot at forty-eight locations including twenty-five towns and cities along the California coast: "From north of San Francisco to south of San Diego," explained a publicity item, "in each instance . . . the scene [was filmed] exactly where it was supposed to have happened." The use of such "live sets" compelled Melcher to take out forty-four insurance policies—amounting to $500,000 of coverage. Many of the sites were located by Virginia Stone, who worked closely with her husband on most of his films and, in the case of *Julie*, received credit as assistant to the film's producer as well as the editor.

Filming the car chase along the famous 17-Mile Drive in Carmel consumed three days—in addition to two weeks of aerial filming with three DC-6 aircraft—and required two helicopters, a speed launch, two camera towers, the two cars that appear on-screen, and two camera cars. A report given the press told of an injured Hollywood stuntman: standing in for Barry Sullivan, he leaped from the car Jourdan was driving and "rolled some 75 feet into a ravine."

The MGM Press Book for the film includes two odd items about bit players. The first concerns Gordon H. Scherer, an Ohio congressman and member of the House Un-American Activities Committee. He was visiting Los Angeles in connection with hearings and one afternoon happened to return to his hotel, where a scene was being shot.

"I saw all these people and lights and things," Scherer told a reporter, "so I stopped to gawk for a few minutes. A man who said he was the director came up to me, put a cigarette in my mouth and told me to turn around and start talking to the strangers around me. I told him I didn't smoke and he said, 'Oh yes, in my pictures you do.' So the lawmaker smoked," the Press Book continued. "They shot the scene 15 times and two hours and two packages of cigarettes later, Rep. Scherer ended his motion picture acting career. He never did get to meet Miss Day."

The second anecdote describes a hitchhiker named John Koehler. A would-be actor from Seattle, Koehler was making his way to Hollywood to break into films when the Melchers stopped their car, gave him a lift, and then got him a part as an extra in the picture.

Since Day was convinced that the camera added five pounds to her figure, she was in the habit of watching her diet whenever she worked on a film. During the *Julie* period, her breakfast consisted of fruit, soft-boiled eggs, and Sanka. Lunch, in her dressing room, was usually a small steak and salad. She would also fit in a catnap, if she could, to prepare for the wrenching emotional exercise that *Julie* proved to be.

That year, Day's birthday fell on a Sunday, and the entire cast and crew helped her celebrate with an enormous cake, which became yet another photo opportunity. Given her self-acknowledged "tendency in dramatic pictures to speak in low tones," Day received a unique gift from sound engineer Frank Scheid. "He's always after me to talk louder," Day told reporters, "so he presented me with a caricature of himself boasting mammoth rubber ears. The card read: 'I'm all ears, but I still can't hear you.'"

April 3 marked the Melchers' fifth anniversary, but its celebration was a bit of a sham. While Melcher had gained complete control of the property that was Doris Day, his relationship with his wife was unraveling. As pressure on him to succeed increased, he sacrificed Day, his wife, to Day, his client. Though they would do their best to maintain a happy and united front before the world, by 1956 their marriage had become what it may have been for Melcher all along: a business arrangement.

Day would hint at this when, the following year, she told the always sympathetic journalist Jane Ardmore that making *Julie* was the "worst" experience of her film career to date. "It was the first time I couldn't come home and tell Marty my problems: You can't tell the producer," she said. "He suddenly became a company man." Without knowing the cause, Day suffered heavy hemorrhaging that commenced a couple weeks into the shooting in Carmel and a "constant, rather intense stabbing pain" in her stomach. Though she pleaded with Melcher to return to Los Angeles so her condition might be properly diagnosed, it would have entailed shutting down the film and he simply refused. While he kept insisting that his wife heal herself according to the tenets of Christian Science, she completed the picture only by enduring weeks of "bleeding," "pain," and "loss of energy and weight." As far as Day was concerned, Melcher had become a far more ardent Christian Scientist than she had ever been.

Day's growing estrangement from Melcher might have been what compelled her to turn to her suave costar Louis Jourdan for emotional support. Day always denied publicly that she had an affair with Jourdan, and Jourdan has never acknowledged it. But even if they did not have a physical affair, Day's memoir describes what certainly had become an affair of the heart and mind, her words emphasizing just how intimate they became and acknowledging that Melcher suspected them of an affair, maintaining that he was "very jealous" of Jourdan.

"Louis and I had long talks about our problems, about life in Hollywood, about Paris, about our children, about Life in the larger sense. We would take long walks on the beautiful Carmel beach, chatting by the hour," said Day, who "frankly" admitted that she "enjoyed being with Louis much more than with Marty. Of course Marty sensed this, and that too was part of his jealousy." Nor was the irony lost on Day, when he started to behave like Julie's jealous husband in the film.

Fifty years later, while reflecting on *Julie* and Doris Day, Jourdan said: "Both Doris and I hated the director. I also disliked her husband, and I was surprised to discover [that] she did, too." Jourdan was also amazed to discover Day "wanting to be sexy," since it so contradicted her famous, girl-next-door image.

Day herself remarked of Melcher, "The romance goes out the window when you suddenly feel that you're married to your father." Day confided that, in contrast to the wonderful bond she developed with Jourdan, Melcher was "not a conversationalist" and "never really talked about us." In fact, five years into their marriage, her relationship with her husband was "changing." He was becoming more "tyrannical" with Terry; moreover, with growing control over her career, he was also showing a "tyrannical side" as a producer.

Whatever happiness Day derived from her intimacy with Jourdan, her physical problems during the making of *Julie* had been well beyond his consolations. The film completed (on May 15), she returned to Los

Angeles and immediately saw her gynecologist, Dr. Willard Crosley. He discovered an intestinal tumor the size of a "grapefruit," which had to be removed at once. The complicated, four-hour operation at Glendale Memorial Hospital also included a hysterectomy. Fortunately, the tumor proved to be benign.

*   *   *

Things had been changing for the Melchers even before Louis Jourdan entered the picture. Whatever positive image they kept projecting for the sake of public consumption in movie magazines, the true tenor of their marriage became manifest in an unusual legal "Agreement" drawn up between "Doris Day" and "Martin Melcher" and dated December 28, 1955. Long before prenuptial agreements became standard among Hollywood celebrities, the Melchers entered into something far more rare: a postnuptial arrangement. The document, a business contract couched in armchair legalese, underscores that after four and a half years, the Melchers' union had become more professional than marital. At the top of the document, the "Artist"—Day—is described as "a professional performer of renown in various phases of the entertainment field, including, without limitation, motion pictures, radio, phonograph records, etc.; and wants to engage manager as stated below." The "Manager"—Melcher—is described as "experienced as a manager in all phases of theatrical and related fields, and wants to act as manager, as stated below."

That the agreement was drawn up so long into their marriage suggests just how insecure Melcher had become. On the other hand, the terms certainly favored the manager. They stipulated, for instance, that the "Artist will not engage any other personal manager, [but that the] Manager may represent or act as personal manager for persons other than Artist." Even more curiously, another item basically undermined what Melcher actually did for his wife/client: "Manager is not required to and will not seek employment or engagements for Artist, and will not perform any of the functions of a 'Theatrical Agent,' an 'Artist's Manager' or an 'Investment Counselor.'" It was geared, in other words, to protect Melcher from legal restraints, even while ensuring his all-too-accommodating wife's legal obligations to him.

Melcher had, in fact, become less a husband than a boss to his wife, even as he ceded more control of their affairs to his lawyer, Jerome Rosenthal. The agreement becomes all the more meaningful in the context of other legal documents that would emerge and figure prominently in the unprecedented lawsuit Day would bring against Rosenthal after Melcher's death in 1968. On May 11, 1956, the Melchers signed retainer agreements with Rosenthal. "These 'simple' agreements gave Rosenthal a 10 percent interest in virtually everything the Melchers owned and earned," explained a court judgment several decades later. "Rosenthal had already represented the Melchers as an attorney for several years prior to May 11, 1956, and had an obligation to provide a full disclosure of the true implications of the agreements. He never adequately informed them, and he didn't advise them to obtain independent legal advice. They signed the agreements in all innocence and as a result of undue influence."

Pointing out that Melcher's office was adjacent to Rosenthal's, the judgment also declared that they had mutual daily meetings and conferences. "By virtue of the attorney-client relationship, Rosenthal's status as an attorney, and his claim to business acumen, Melcher was awed and developed a false sense of security concerning his ability to rely and depend on the advice rendered by Rosenthal regarding Melcher's legal and business affairs. The 1956 retainer agreements converted Rosenthal from mere attorney into business adviser and tax planner. They gave him the contractual basis for ascendancy over the Melchers' financial affairs." Though Day knew that she was, in truth, working very hard for her husband—and grew, increasingly, to resent it—she had no idea they were both really working primarily for Jerome Rosenthal.

*　　*　　*

When *Julie* was about to be released, *Life* magazine devoted a two-page photo spread to help promote the film, with five stills featuring Day either sobbing or on the run. Marketing plans included Day's attending the movie's premiere in Cincinnati, her hometown, early in October. Warren Cowan, in charge of the campaign, accompanied the Melchers to Ohio.

"Before we took off for the Cincinnati premiere of 'Julie' I talked with my brother Paul and asked him to call our father, [to] tell him that I was coming and that I'd love to see him," Day recalled in a piece that appeared under her own signature in *The American Weekly* the following year. William Kappelhoff visited Day's hotel on the morning of her arrival. It was the first time that Day had seen her father since her adolescence—the first time they had met, in other words, since she had become Doris Day.

Her hectic schedule of interviews and other events was hardly con-
ducive for them to become reacquainted. They agreed to meet later that
afternoon, at an old German bar and grill that Kappelhoff owned, in
what had become Cincinnati's black ghetto. Accompanied by Melcher
and Cowan, she felt almost ashamed to arrive there in a chauffeured
Cadillac provided by MGM. But the occasion proved festive, with a "Welcome Doris" sign on the front door, bunting strung along the bar, the
jukebox playing nothing but Day songs, and the beer flowing nonstop.
Day met Luvenia Williams Bennett, who ran the grill for her father and
was rendered speechless when her father told her of his plan to marry
this "lovely black lady," nearly fourteen years his junior. Day remembered
her smile as "one of the sweetest."

After its premiere in Cincinnati and then Cleveland, *Julie* opened
during November in theaters and drive-ins across the country. While
some critics found the film's verisimilitude chilling, others considered
the scenario phony and melodramatic. "The casting of Miss Day in her
role is its own justification: she looks [the part] and makes you share
her harrowing ordeal," responded Philip K. Scheuer in his rave review
for the *Los Angeles Times*. "Its feeling of documentary, on-the-spot real-
ism reaches and holds an extraordinary pitch of tension, in both filming
and tight intercutting. Any picture you can think of would be hard put
to match 'Julie''s 95 minutes of unalloyed, unrelieved suspense, and that
goes for 'Diabolique,' 'Wages of Fear,' 'The Bad Seed,' the individual and
collected works of Hitchcock," he said before comparing it favorably to
the one film Day had made with the master of suspense. "Stone tells his
story straight, using amazingly few artifices and stripping away the gloss,
the 'gingerbread,' that surrounded Miss Day in her previous suspense
movie, Hitchcock's 'The Man Who Knew Too Much.'"

"Doris Day is concentrating on more dramatic roles and less singing
and is proving herself very capable of building a new career as a 'straight'
actress," Gus Dallas wrote in *Motion Picture Daily*. "In 'Julie' she reaches
a high level of serious acting and fulfills the promise she showed in the
recently released 'The Man Who Knew Too Much.' [It's] a thriller which
gives her ample opportunity to run the gamut of emotions." The critics
for the *Hollywood Reporter* and *Variety* were far less disposed to the film,
saying, respectively, "A chase melodrama marred by several disputable
situations" and "Suspenseful ingredients are piled up well enough, but
'Julie' goes overboard both on plot and length."

Given what she had to endure while working on *Julie,* the bravura performance that Day delivered is all the more remarkable. She is particularly effective portraying Julie's duplicity, when she begins to suspect that Lyle has killed her first husband. In *Julie,* Day once again demonstrated her gifts as an actress, not just as a singing star. If *Julie* is the closest Day ever came to film noir, the film also has the aura of authenticity associated with cinéma vérité, a quality that had as much to do with Fred Jackman's camera work as with Stone's directorial techniques. The locations would heighten the sense of reality of a film that sometimes looks and sounds like a documentary, rather than the black-and-white Hollywood thriller it actually is. But this, too, was an Andrew Stone signature or hallmark. Stone the director perfectly understood how to realize Stone the writer's coarse and realistic dialogue.

Jourdan, however, proves simply fraudulent as Lyle. He conveys the character's weakness but none of the "savage fury" and "violent love" inherent in the character. Jourdan sadly diminishes what otherwise might have been a thriller for the ages. But *Julie* nonetheless proved to be far better than either its reputation or its roots in formulaic melodrama would allow. It was made for less than $1 million and proved profitable for the studio. Stone would earn a much-deserved Oscar nomination for his original screenplay and no-nonsense dialogue. Leith Stevens and Tom Adair also received a nomination for the picture's haunting theme song, wistfully sung by Day. (Adair's forced lyrics hardly seem worthy of any award.) The song deliberately emulated the popular theme to a more classic noir film, *Laura.*

＊　　＊　　＊

Day's growing popularity in Great Britain prompted the rerelease there of her first picture, *Romance on the High Seas* (spring, 1956) under the alternate title *It's Magic.* In response to a "birthday tape" made by her British fan club and sent to her belatedly, Day returned the gift with a tape of her own, made on October 28. It includes the evident starts and stops of a recorder, as well as prompts from Melcher. "Hi kids, this is DoDo," it began. "We decided to send you a letter on tape . . . and I thought that you could all get together and play it back. . . . We just got up a little bit ago, I'm ashamed to say, about 11 o'clock, and it's raining, for a change. . . . And we're sitting in our playroom . . . and looking out and we have a little fire going. The dogs are here, and, um, my mother is here, and Marty is here. And we're just kind of sitting around and having a real lazy Sunday."

Day eventually explained that Terry was not home—he was fishing with a friend. "There's a lake at the end of our street," she said, before betraying some mistrust of her adolescent son, who had once fallen in the water and then tracked "the slime and wet" into the house, much to his mother's chagrin: "And that's where they are, I hope." Beyond divulging that Terry was enrolled at a military academy, Day claimed he had grown considerably since they were in London sixteen months ago and, in fact, was now taller than she.

When Marty took over the microphone, he proved remarkably candid as he recalled the first time they got together with the British fans for tea on a Sunday afternoon: "You were all very nervous and you sat around, and nobody knew what to say or when to say it. And Doris tried to make you comfortable. And nobody even could drink their tea. You all were such wonderful kids, and we never forgot it." He subsequently returned "the mike" to "Miss Doris, DiDi Day, DoDo, take it away." The tape was the first of many that Day would make for her fans.

✳   ✳   ✳

Early in 1957, based on a poll of more than 750 musicians, composers, and directors, *Down Beat* magazine cited Doris Day as "the top musical personality" of the previous year. Choosing Day was made all the more irresistible by the recent release of *Day by Day*. The first of Day's sixteen so-called concept albums, it was built around a theme that had nothing to do with any of her films. (It was recorded in only three sessions during September 1956, consuming a total of ten and a half hours.) Both *Day by Day* and its follow-up album, inevitably titled *Day by Night*, figure among her finest work. Their success rested not only upon Day's vivid sense of a song's meaning but also upon Paul Weston's lush orchestrations embellishing her pristine voice.

Before becoming a top conductor and arranger at Columbia, Weston had been the first musical director at Capitol Records, where he collaborated with his wife, Jo Stafford, as well as with Betty Hutton, Margaret Whiting, Gordon MacRae, and Dean Martin. Earlier, he had worked with Dinah Shore, when she was just starting out, and had done some arrangements for Bob Crosby's band. Weston joined Columbia Records in 1950 and became the West Coast director of artists and repertoire. It is significant that *Day by Day* was made with Weston, as opposed to Day's more usual supervisor at Columbia Records, Mitch Miller. There was an ongoing conflict between Weston, who favored standards, and Miller, who continually imposed novelties on Columbia's recording artists.

According to the record liner notes, Day herself selected each of the dozen songs on *Day by Day*. Practically every one is a standard, and they share a leitmotif of rueful feelings over lost love, a theme Day understood only too well: "The Song Is You," "Hello, My Lover, Goodbye," "But Not for Me," "I Remember You," "I Hadn't Anyone Till You," "But Beautiful," "Autumn Leaves," "Don't Take Your Love from Me," "There Will Never Be Another You," "Gone With the Wind," "The Gypsy in My Soul," "Day by Day." (The fact that Day chose all these songs herself lends yet a third meaning to the album's title.) Weston's arrangements are, in a word, intimate, while Day's voice is at its best: simple and direct—which is to say, unadorned yet expressive. To be sure, more than one of these songs became even more popular because of Day's fresh interpretations of 1956.

For the second year in a row, DJs across the country, in a poll conducted by *Billboard*, named Day the "most popular girl singer." That same year, the Laurel Awards poll, taken by *Motion Picture Exhibitor*, a trade paper, declared her the "top star"—along with Rock Hudson. Female follow-ups were Susan Hayward, Ava Gardner, Audrey Hepburn, Kim Novak, Deborah Kerr, Elizabeth Taylor, Cyd Charisse, Marilyn Monroe, and Eleanor Parker. In the first of three installments of what was being billed as "Doris Day's Complete Life Story," journalist George Scullin perfectly summarized the paradox Day presented: "Doris Day is one of the most written about and least known of all the big stars in Hollywood." Although Scullin promised to get beyond her "friendly, smiling, healthy, all-American girl" image, much of her real story would continue to remain private.

"If Doris weren't more complicated than that, she'd be the all-American girl from next door, all right, but she'd still be living there," Scullin wrote. A New York journalist who met with Day in Beverly Hills, Scullin did succeed in getting his subject to be extremely forthright when she told him, "I can't bear to look at my rushes or my pictures, so I don't think I deserve it when nice things are said [about me]. It's somebody else." And while she encouraged Scullin to talk to others she had worked with, Day divulged a surprising thought: "They know more about me than I know myself. I've told my own story so often, maybe I'm getting in a rut."

The week after *Julie* opened in New York, where it set a box-office record, Scullin talked to Melcher, who was remarkably candid about the problems he was having as the producer of his wife's film. "In most businesses, when a husband-and-wife team win a point, they win it together. But in our case, if Doris won, I lost. And if I won, Doris lost. Now you take a situation like that home with you. Instead of the star going home to get some sympathy from her husband, and the producer going home to weep on his wife's shoulder, we'd go home together. And there, over a wonderful dinner, we'd sit, not too happy." Fully aware of the Melchers' domestic problems, Rosenthal had them sign a power-of-attorney document on December 7, giving him total control over their legal and financial matters.

"I'm Not at All in Love"

✳
---

*"Unless somebody takes this lady to the hospital right
this minute, I am going to walk off this picture.
Either she goes to a hospital, or I go. Thank you."*
—DORIS DAY

After her departure from Warner Brothers Day quickly established
herself as one of the finest screen actresses of her generation.
However, it seems fitting that she did return to her home studio to make
one of her best musical films. Based on a smash Broadway hit that opened
at the St. James Theater on May 13, 1954, *The Pajama Game* provided
Day with a role that might have been written for her. While her last three
characters—Ruth Etting in *Love Me or Leave Me*, Jo McKenna in *The Man
Who Knew Too Much*, and the title character in *Julie*—had each emphasized Day's vulnerable qualities, her Babe Williams in *The Pajama Game*
revealed her hard and fiercely independent side. A working woman, Babe
will not even permit her budding romance with a factory foreman to get
in the way of her proto-feminist principles—or her job. Though it may be
oversimplifying the analogy, Day could be as outgoing as her mother and
as withdrawn as her father—depending on the situation. Moreover, she
could draw upon both contrary temperaments at the same time, perhaps
never with such winning effect as in *The Pajama Game*.

The Broadway musical *The Pajama Game* was based on a 1953 novel
by Richard Bissell titled *7 and ½ Cents*—to some extent incorporating the
author's own experiences at an Iowa pajama factory beset by union problems. They prove particularly thorny for a budding romance between the
head of the grievance committee, Babe Williams, and the factory's new
superintendent, Sid Sorokin. As cowritten by Bissell and Broadway veteran George Abbott, the show's book became the backdrop for a glorious score by an exciting new team, Richard Adler and Jerry Ross, whose

joint mentor, Frank Loesser, contributed more than a note and lyric or two to this, their first musical. For it—and with or without Loesser—Adler and Ross wrote a number of hits: "Hey, There," "Hernando's Hideaway," "Steam Heat," "There Once Was a Man," "Once-a-Year Day," and "Small Talk." The songwriting duo's next show, *Damn Yankees*, would prove to be their last. Shortly after its Broadway opening in 1955, the twenty-nine-year-old Ross succumbed to a chronic bronchial condition. But he left behind a song that would gain a place among Day's biggest hits after she recorded it in the spring of 1958, "Everybody Loves a Lover," a pop tune which was not written for either show.

Producing their musicals quickly and cheaply, Warner Brothers always remained in the shadow of MGM, which, after all, was responsible for such classics as *The Wizard of Oz, On the Town, The Band Wagon, Meet Me in St. Louis, Singin' in the Rain, An American in Paris,* and many others. But the brothers Warner had their doubts about the prospects of motion pictures in the mid-1950s. Given their recent success with the TV series *Cheyenne,* the studio had set about making four additional Western series—*Maverick, Colt #45, Sugarfoot,* and *Lawman*—in the spring of 1956, when Jack's three brothers sold the majority of their stock holdings to the First National Bank of Boston for $20 million. Compared with the 17,000 movie houses in the United States, there would be more than 40 million TV sets in American homes by 1957.

Yet despite such misgivings about the financial potential for a big musical film, the studio did put a lot of money into *The Pajama Game.* Warners paid Bissell $750,000 for the rights to *7 and ½ Cents* and even employed MGM's Stanley Donen to coproduce and codirect the picture. Having already directed *Singin' in the Rain,* as well as *On the Town, Funny Face,* and *Seven Brides for Seven Brothers,* Donen had proven himself a master of the genre and he was able to command a top fee. The famous Day was going to make her return to Warners with this picture, and the studio was finally going to treat her fittingly.

Following his phone conversation with George Abbott on May 5, 1955, Jack Warner wrote a note revealing that it was Abbott who wanted to bring Donen on board as his coproducer and codirector of *The Pajama Game* ("... wants us to find out how much Donen gets from Metro"). Warner's notes named Marlon Brando as Abbott's "first choice" for Sid Sorokin—Brando's first musical film, *Guys and Dolls,* was on the verge of release—and Gordon MacRae as his "second."

Another interesting item in the May 5 communiqué found Warner suggesting a salary of "approximately" $2,000 per week for Carol Haney. The beatniks had permeated the mainstream by 1954, and Haney was clearly an exponent of their movement—with her self-dubbed "idiot boy" hairdo and her impish manner. Though she played the secondary role of Gladys Hotchkiss in the Broadway production of *The Pajama Game,* Haney was also the show's lead dancer and practically stole the limelight from its stars, Janis Paige and John Raitt—especially due to the inventive and red-hot choreography, the work of a new kid on Broadway by the name of Bob Fosse. (Haney's understudy on Broadway was an unknown dancer first spotted at the St. James Theater by Paramount producer Hal B. Wallis—Shirley MacLaine.)

While Haney was apparently the only surefire casting decision from the outset, over the next few months George Abbott came up with very different ideas for the leads. In a follow-up letter to Warner, dated September 28, Abbott wrote: "Do you think it essential and/or advisable to have Hollywood stars for Sid and Babe? Have you anyone in mind? Do you think Sinatra would be good, and would he be available? A suggestion that has come up many times is that we try to get Sinatra and Doris Day."

Warner shot off a rapid response to Abbott from Claridge's Hotel in London. "I think Sinatra and Doris Day would make a fine combination if they could be secured on a deal within reason." In the end, Warner's primary allegiance was always to his wallet. Warner devoted most of his two-and-half-page typed letter to discussing cuts, so the film version would not be "overlong." While approving of the musical cuts, which Abbott had already made, he favored "the possibility of a new song . . . as we could get a great deal of air time on a new hit song which would plug the picture, and aid in the exploitation." While three numbers from the original score were ultimately eliminated ("A New Town Is a Blue Town," "Her Is," and "Think of the Time I Save"), it was Warner who wanted to retain the reprise of "Hey There," "the top song of the show." Adler did write a new song for Day, "The Man Who Invented Love." Though she recorded the number while the camera was rolling, it proved lackluster and, in the end, her reprisal of "Hey There" (also recorded live) took its place.

On March 17, 1956, Louella Parsons announced in the *Los Angeles Examiner* that Day had just signed a contract to play Babe Williams. "I'd like to go back to Warners," Day told Parsons, "and I'd like to do a musical next, because I've [now done] comedy and straight drama." Day did not report that Warners was paying her the handsome sum of $250,000 for the picture.

An internal memo to Jack Warner, dated March 27, indicates that Bing Crosby was under consideration as her costar. But the fifty-three-year-old crooner knocked himself out of the running by demanding "$200,000 against 5 percent of the gross, in addition to 25 percent of the gross for his company." On April 26, Parsons wrote that Howard Keel was going to be Day's costar, and added, "Doris likes the music in 'Pajama Game' so much [that] she drives around with the album playing the tunes on her car phonograph." (An internal document indicates that they were considering paying Keel $100,000.)

Casting considerations for *Pajama Game* were not the only Day-related news items making their way into the columns during this dazzling period for the star. In the *Mirror-News*, Dick Williams wrote, "Doris Day, whose career has zoomed since she became a free-lancer, is probably the hottest femme star in town right now." Going beyond *The Pajama Game*, he announced her plans for "remakes" of *Love Affair* and *Stage Door* at RKO—as well as a deal with MGM for "several films," including a musical version of *Anna Christie*, to be called *Christie*. On May 12, Parsons announced that Day had just signed a $1,050,000 recording contract with Columbia Records, "reportedly one of the largest [deals] made in the record business with a singer," another newspaper contributed. And four days later, Hedda Hopper announced that Day's "picture price these days is $300,000," adding, "[s]he and Marty Melcher are working overtime to tie up a 'South Pacific' deal with Rodgers and Hammerstein." Hopper reported that the Melchers were hoping to purchase a house in Beverly Hills and saw one "they liked a lot." The owner told the Melchers that the home had been built by Ruth Etting and that one across the street belonged to Grace Kahn—both of whom Day had played in films.

Day's fans would always regret that she never did play Nellie Forbush in the film version of *South Pacific*, but very few ever knew that one of the greatest teams of American songwriters had also contemplated writing a score specifically for her—without ever doing it, alas. *Variety* announced that Melcher was negotiating a two-picture deal with Rodgers and Hammerstein: "Talks are understood to have stemmed from Richard Rodgers' long-held belief that Miss Day should play the role of Ensign Nellie Forbush." The stage play would be "converted . . . some time next year" and "be followed by another musical. Later, it's understood, would be a dramatic property for which Rodgers & Hammerstein would turn out a special score, rather than a property already tuned. Miss Day would star in the latter film as well."

Columnist Sheilah Graham divulged that Arwin had offered $2 million for the movie rights to *South Pacific*—without stipulating how much Day's salary would be. The Melchers "were dying for Doris to do 'South Pacific,'" recalled Mitch Miller. "She was made to order for it and Marty thought he was going to hold them up for a lot of money. But they said 'fuck you': They went with Mitzi Gaynor, instead. I remember, Doris was upset at the time."

"It's the first film Doris has ever said, 'This I want to do,'" Graham said. "There's only one guy she wants to do it with—Cary Grant—who, believe it or not, has a good singing voice. It sounds like a very Enchanted Evening in the cinema. . . . To go back to 'Pajama Game,' Rock Hudson was first choice for the male lead but he absolutely will not sing outside of the bathtub." These are the first references to either Grant or Hudson as possible leading men for Day, though each would become her costar some years later.

In the same column, Graham was one of the first to report that John Raitt would re-create his stage role of Sid Sorokin in the screen version of *The Pajama Game*. She also said that Day would receive "more than $250,000" for the picture and added, "When Doris started at this studio eight years ago, her salary was $250 a week." But Raitt's participation was not as certain as Graham implied in her column late in May. As late as July 12, Jack Warner received a Western Union telegram: "LATEST DEVEL-OPMENT PAJAMA GAME DONEN MUCHLY PREFERS WANTS TO SETTLE FOR JOHN RAITT/DORIS DAY SAW TESTS LAST NIGHT AND PUTTING MILDLY NOT KEEN ANYONE/SHE TALKED DONEN ASKED IF ANY CHANCE DEAN MARTIN OR EVEN GORDON MACRAE/NOW ARRANGING PROBABILITY RAITT COMING COAST MAKE TEST WITH DORIS DAY STANLEY DONEN DIRECTING JULY 30."

Casting Raitt would save Warners a good deal of money. The total budget for the film was approved at $2,562,000, and the distribution of the salaries left no doubt who the star was. Day received $250,000 compared to Raitt's paltry $25,000. Even Haney and Eddie Foy Jr. commanded more than Raitt—$30,000 and $28,000, respectively. The budget also allocated $110,000 for Donen, $100,000 for Abbott, and $25,000 for Fosse. According to the terms Melcher negotiated for his wife, she was committed to "15 weeks plus 2 weeks free." Also, "Miss Day will hold story conferences and other consultations on Saturdays during the term (without pay) with producer and/or director at her home or at other places arranged for, as may be desired or required."

A light baritone with a strong voice, Raitt brought his wife and three children—including future singer Bonnie—from New York and rented a house in Toluca Lake once owned by Jack Webb. The virile Raitt would also prove a winning costar for Day—even if his prospects for a film career beyond *Pajama Game* never amounted to much. But Day had ulterior motives for initially wanting just about anybody but Raitt as her costar. While fourteen members of the original Broadway cast were imported to Hollywood to make the film version, Day was the only principal player who was new to the roster. If one of her ambitions was to please others at any cost, quite naturally she felt like an outsider—and something of an interloper and a spoiler—who had displaced Janis Paige from the *Pajama Game* "family." It's telling that Day would prove utterly dismissive of this, one of her best films, claiming it was "an arduous assignment [because] I had to fit into a polished company that had been together for two years."

In another recollection, she referred to her "great trepidation" about making the picture, which indicates that her insecurity over her talents continued unabated—despite all the polls putting her at number one and all the sensational notices she had been receiving for her recent films. Characteristically, Day also told a reporter for *Family Weekly*, "I don't know if I can handle the songs. . . . They require an Ethel Merman type," which clearly Day could not relate to being—nor was she one. Day had also anticipated that she would have difficulty tackling the vigorous dance steps the film required. Beneath it all, Day was echoing the popular notion that the real singing and dancing pros worked in Broadway shows and not in Hollywood musicals.

As Haney would explain to Arthur Knight for an article promoting the picture in *Dance Magazine*, "Warners took over what amounted to a package—'The Pajama Game' as presented . . . on the stage, with most of the same performers, the same choreographer. . . . Aside from redoing some of the dances and trimming a couple of scenes for time reasons— like my dream dance with Eddie Foy—the show was left virtually intact."

"Doris just jumped in and just fit with everybody, and that was difficult because [we] all had been together for at least a year," recalled John Raitt. "She brought all of her quality, that we all love in her, to that role."

"Doris Day was the star, but she was right there with us every day, and very approachable," said Harvey Evans, one of the dancers in the picture, who, like Day, had not been in the stage production. "She was just terrific, and couldn't have been a nicer human being." Shortly after working on *Pajama Game*, Evans appeared in *Silk Stockings*, which starred Fred Astaire. In contrast with Day, Evans recalled, "Fred Astaire was really quite distant. You know, we didn't get to know him until shooting day, and then he just 'bopped' out of his trailer looking 30 years younger than he did during the rehearsal, the day before."

Evans, whose original surname was Hohnecker, was, at the time, an eighteen-year-old song-and-dance man who had just toured with the road company of *Damn Yankees*, when Fosse recognized his potential and cast him in the film version of *Pajama Game*. He appears in the "Hernando's Hideaway" number as the man in search of "Poopsie"; he's clad in a blue-and-white striped shirt in the "Once-a-Year Day" number; and in the rousing "Seven and a Half Cents" conclusion, he's the middle dancer of the three holding Day aloft. (As Evans said, "She was my idol, and then ironically, about a year after I graduated high school, I was holding her ass in 'The Pajama Game.'")

On the set, Evans told Day that he, too, was from Cincinnati, and that he had also studied with Grace Raine. "We sort of befriended each other," said Evans, who explained that Day "didn't stay in her dressing room or trailer—she was just always around. Because of the rep-company feeling of this movie, rehearsing it first and then being with all those principals all the time, it was quite an astonishing job."

Rehearsals for *The Pajama Game* began on November 1. On the second day, Day bruised a couple ribs while working with Raitt on the number "There Once Was a Man." He may have inhabited his role a little too completely: Sid tells Babe, "Personally, I think a little physical punishment is good for people." Day was subsequently out "ill" for several days. When she returned to work on November 7, according to the production book, Day "came in and watched the rehearsals and rehearsed dialogue, only, as she had been advised by her doctor not to rehearse any singing or dancing until the injury to her side had improved." She resumed song rehearsals two days later, however, and production on the picture finally began in earnest on November 28.

Day wrote an undated thank-you note to Jack Warner on her gray stationery with its lime-green trim and the inscribed motto, "Merci beaucoup": "Dear J.L.—Your flowers are so beautiful! Do come down and see them—*and me*!!! Thank you very much—I love being home again. Doris." There was also a welcome-home party for her on the set, with a cake featuring nineteen candles. *Pajama Game* was the star's eighteenth picture, and the extra candle represented the studio's wish that she would soon return and make another with them.

But the making of *Pajama Game* would prove a far less genteel experience than Day's note or the cake implied. "As the shooting went on, we were aware that Stanley Donen was rushing this film and being sloppy with it," Evans recalled. "And he wasn't pleasant. There was a rumor that he was getting a thousand dollars a day, for every day that he came in ahead of schedule."

Such an incentive encouraged Donen to behave just like Eddie Foy's Hinesie, the foreman at the pajama factory, who, in the show's opening number, compels everyone to "hurry up" and is always "racing with the clock." And incredible as it sounds, he completed the picture twenty-two days ahead of schedule. "It seemed to us like it was greed, pure and simple," continued Evans. "That's why we're not wearing make-up in some scenes, and why we couldn't have another take, sometimes."

Broadway designers William and Jean Eckart had been invited to design the costumes for the film. The husband-and-wife team was very excited about their first venture in Hollywood, only to be terribly disappointed once they arrived. "We had done a lot of costume sketches for 'The Pajama Game' in New York, many of which were for costumes for the chorus," recalled Jean Eckart. "But when we arrived at Warner Brothers they couldn't understand why we wanted to have costumes built. They had intended on pulling the chorus costumes from stock." The Eckarts came "to realize that the Hollywood they'd dreamed of no longer existed."

While the costume budget allocated only $3,150 for Babe and $824 for Sid, to cut corners still further, the dancers indeed wore stock costumes from the wardrobe department—which led to at least one delightful discovery. "There was a plain red jacket with J. Dean in it," recalled Evans, "and we realized it was James Dean's jacket from *Rebel Without a Cause*." The male dancers took turns wearing the treasured item.

The Pajama Game is about a pending union strike over pay, and for the dancers, life began to imitate art on the set. They were receiving a weekly salary of $157.50, in addition to "15% overtime adjustments for lifts, throws, catches and upgraded dance work." But they were also being used to play the factory workers—"when we were not in a musical number," explained Evans. "And we'd get paid as an extra—which was a lot less . . . There were so many times we were used as extras, but when we were shooting 'Once-a-Year Day' in Hollenbeck Park, a group of us discovered a vacant house across from it, and we would go hide there, so they couldn't find us."

With the support of the Screen Actors Guild, another dancer, Lynn Bernay, led them on a strike to Jack Warner's office. "As we were singing and dancing about a strike, we struck Warner's office," Evans remembered, "and we got our money."

Evans observed that it was clear to everyone that Carol Haney was having major physical problems. "When you watch 'Steam Heat,' you can see that she's not really up to par," he said. Haney's fragile condition became more apparent on Christmas Eve, a Monday, when twenty-two male and thirty female dancers worked on "Hernando's Hideaway" from 7:45 in the morning until 6:05 that night.

"Carol Haney just looked awful," said Evans. "They were using this bee's-wax fog for the number, which was horrible to breathe. And she was sitting alone in the booth that they filmed her at. Then Doris walked onto the soundstage. She saw Carol sitting there, went over to her, sat down, and talked with her for about five minutes. Then Doris quietly walked to the middle of the soundstage and said, 'Could I please have everyone's attention.' And slowly everyone stopped what they were doing, and the place was suddenly quiet: It was just like Norma Desmond's arrival on the [Cecil B. DeMille] set in *Sunset Boulevard.* Then, pointing to Carol Haney, Doris said, 'Unless somebody takes this lady to the hospital right this minute, I am going to walk off this picture. Either she goes to a hospital, or I go. Thank you.' And then Doris walked away." The daily production book confirmed Day's intervention: "1:00–2:00—Miss Carol Haney had to leave set because of illness. . . . Production 10 days ahead of schedule."

Donen's mandate to beat the timetable proved difficult for one and all. In the hospital, it was discovered that Haney was diabetic. So in a very real sense, Day saved Haney's life. "She totally became our hero for doing that," Evans recalled. "Even Fosse wasn't standing up for us, as we were being pushed and shoved and rushed through everything."

Sending Haney to the hospital might appear to contradict Day's commitment to Christian Science. Yet it would have been only natural for her to have second thoughts about its tenets, given her own surgery a few months earlier. Day's passionate defense of Haney had been powerfully fueled by her own recent experience with a ruthless man—Melcher—who would not let her see a doctor because of cost overruns that would have ensued during the filming of *Julie* in Carmel.

But like everyone—except, perhaps, Jack Warner—Day was fed up with Donen's speed-demon tactics as a director. And, as always, she felt that the individual in need should come first, over any other pressing concerns for the larger project. What's even more telling about the episode is that Day apparently felt emboldened enough by her recent successes—and apparently for the first time aware of her clout—to assert herself in an aggressive fashion. Then, too, Melcher wasn't around as much as he used to be to handle the unpleasant matters for her. (Evans doesn't recall ever seeing him on the set of *The Pajama Game*.)

Donen's self-interest in finishing the picture ahead of schedule proved relentless. The day after Christmas, when Haney had been safely ensconced in the hospital, the entire company had to make up for its day off, and worked—incredibly—from 5 p.m. until 4 a.m. Haney did not return until January 14, 1957, when they shot a "retake" of "Hernando's Hideaway," completed the next day: "Shot 27 days on a 49-day schedule," proclaimed a note in the production book: "Co. closed down for two holidays and one week due to illness of Miss Haney."

Donen had one legitimate gripe of his own: George Abbott played tennis every day and contributed nothing to warrant his credit as a co-director. "I don't recall Abbott ever directing, or saying anything, or even being behind a camera," Evans recalled. Another of his memories concerned Day's ongoing insecurity about her legs: "We were aware that she was a feisty star who had a disagreement with Abbott and Donen about the pajama top they wanted her to wear in the end, because she didn't think her legs looked good enough, and didn't want them to show. But eventually they talked her into it, and God knows, her legs were gorgeous."

Another censorious party did not want Day's legs to be shown in the picture. After reading the script, Geoffrey M. Shurlock of the Motion Picture Association of America wrote to Warners: "It is unacceptable to show Sid wearing only the pajama bottoms and Babe only the pajama top. This costuming, we feel, is unacceptably sex-suggestive and so too is Babe's line, 'Two can sleep as cheap as one.'"

Fortunately, neither Donen nor Warner obeyed Shurlock or Day's wishes. (Nor could Shurlock have been too happy about some of the ad copy for the film: "Boss Vows: 'I'll Get to the Bottom of This!'") In addition to their exciting and nuanced performances, Raitt's muscled torso and Day's gorgeous figure contributed a good deal to their making such an attractive—and convincing—on-screen couple. Babe tells Sid at the picnic that she's "a very cold, hard-boiled doll," and Day perfectly captures her character's tough-as-nails stance right from the beginning, chomping on an apple in a very unlady-like way—her masculine hairdo adding to the effect—as she's on the verge of singing "I'm Not at All in Love." But in the end, she also perfectly conveys Babe's vulnerability as she melts in Sid's arms.

Evans observed why Day became known as "Miss Lachrymose" while she was at work on the scene in which Babe, having short-circuited the factory's power by jamming a cloth in her sewing machine, finds herself fired: "Doris had done it beautifully, and then they had to re-light it, or something. And she walked to a corner of the set and had her back to all of us, and I thought, 'What is she doing?' And then, when they said they were ready to shoot, Doris turned around, and you could see where the tears were forming in her eyes. She was 'motivating,' and it was the first time I had ever seen anyone do that. . . . And it was unbelievably thrilling for me."

David Butler, Day's five-time director who had last worked with her on *Calamity Jane,* took credit for giving her an important lesson about holding back her tears. "I told her one time that I had heard D. W. Griffith tell Lillian Gish, 'You'll get much more sympathy from an audience if you can have your eyes filled with tears and hold them in there. Don't let them drop down your cheek.' Doris was sensational at that. Her eyes would fill up with tears and you'd very, very seldom see the tears drop."

Shortly before work on *The Pajama Game* began, the Melchers found a house they liked in Beverly Hills. Located at 713 North Crescent Drive, the house belonged to Los Angeles Symphony conductor Alfred Wallenstein. A block and a half south of Sunset Boulevard and the Beverly Hills Hotel and just across the street from Louis Jourdan's French provincial–style house, beyond the large backyard was Dinah Shore's house. Doris Kenyon, the actress after whom the infant Day was named, had once lived on the same block.

The Melchers' new abode was a one-level, Spanish-style affair built in 1922, and it was much larger than it appeared from the street. Like many other homes in the area, it also had a self-contained guesthouse with a fireplace. Though it cost the Melchers $150,000, they spent considerably more on extensive renovations. With its wide acreage, the property, more than the house, appealed to them. ("The house itself was rather strange looking," Day would say on a tape prepared for her British fans.) They thoroughly modernized the house, spending almost a year doing so. By the time the alterations were finished, the 30,000-square-foot lot included a pool, spa, covered patio, and an enormous backyard useful to the many pets ultimately residing there. The property also had numerous fruit trees from which Katie, the cook, would pluck the makings of breakfast juice.

During the renovations, the Melchers rented a house on Palm Drive in Beverly Hills. "I . . . told somebody that this was the perfect setting for Halloween," Day said of her temporary residence. "The place looks like it's haunted. . . . We don't have very much furniture here, because everything is being upholstered and being changed for the new house. And we're kind of camping out, as we say: Just a place to hang our hats. And I must say that Katherine, our housekeeper, is not very happy with this place."

*   *   *

In her advance review of *Pajama Game* in *Show Business,* a trade publication, Sylvia Ashton wrote that the film actually "improved [on the Broadway show] in practically every department. . . . It rollicks, it sparkles, it sings, it dances—it moves as few musical movies, particularly adaptations do. . . . Miss Day's wholesome beauty, newly achieved concept of dramatic values and first-rate singing seem to set the pace."

Another preliminary trade review by James Powers in the *Hollywood Reporter* was equally ecstatic: "With zip and zest and a proper, precise knowledge of what a musical comedy is intended to be, George Abbott and Stanley Donen have staged the best one of the year for Warners." This was all the more impressive, given that *Funny Face, Silk Stockings,* and *Pal Joey* had also been introduced that year. As Powers further wrote, *Pajama Game* was "a romp, a lark, a frolic, a spree of singing, dancing, humor and romance, a triumph in every department. . . . Doris Day heads the fine cast and she does a superlative job. . . . Miss Day, freckled, short blonde locks and all, is as pretty as a Fourth of July picnic and as spirited. . . . John Raitt, vigorous, virile and handsome, scores a fine success." While predicting that the picture would be "a socko" box office entry, *Variety's* critic had special praise for the "beauteous Doris Day . . . always authoritative with a song and now a poised picture personality as she was/is on disks, is an appealing looker. She makes her chore even a shade more believable than Raitt."

Before the film's premiere at Radio City Music Hall on August 30, 1957, the *New York Times* reported that Warners was participating with "ten other companies" in a $2,500,000 advertising and promotional campaign for *Pajama Game*. Another newspaper pointed out that Weldon Pajamas, a "technical advisor" for the picture, was, ironically, a nonunion firm.

With Terry in tow, the Melchers went to New York to promote the film during the first two weeks of September 1957. If Warners continued to be upset—like the rest of the industry—by viewers defecting to television, Day did her best to win some of them back by appearing on *What's My Line?*, for the second time. Though she again played the "mystery challenger," the panelists—Arlene Francis, Dorothy Kilgallen, Bennett Cerf, and Robert Young (sitting in for Ernie Kovacs)—this time determined her identity a lot more quickly.

After a "perfectly hectic two weeks" in New York, Melcher took his wife to North Adams for "what they had hoped would be a quiet weekend stay" with his brother Harry. "But Miss Day was recognized yesterday in visits to the Sterling & Francine Clark Art Institute and a gift shop in Williamstown," the local paper reported, "and word of their presence quickly spread." While taking a Sunday night stroll, Day discovered a stray cat in a tree and took it home to her brother-in-law. The next morning, the Melchers drove the fifteen-year-old Terry to his new private school, Loomis Academy, in Connecticut, on their way back to New York, where they were to spend another week before heading home to Beverly Hills.

When *Pajama Game* opened, *Variety* pronounced it the "box-office champ among the Broadway first-run films . . . racking up a terrific $106,000 for four days [during] its second session at the Music Hall." The *New York World-Telegram and Sun* reported that the film was part of the "First Test" of a "Pay-TV . . . Living Room" experiment—in Bartlesville, Oklahoma: "Curious neighbors crowded into the living rooms of some of the 300 customers who yesterday paid to see the movies 'Pajama Game' and 'Mississippi Gambler' on their TV sets," said one report.

The Pajama Game Broadway company wasn't alone in resenting that Day had usurped the role that Janis Paige had made her own on stage. So did Bosley Crowther. But he also widely embraced Day's performance in his review in the *New York Times*: "It is fresh, funny, lively and tuneful. Indeed in certain respects—such as when they all go on the factory picnic—it is even more lively than it was on the stage. . . . The whole thing is splendid, the color is gay and strong and even Miss Day, the interloper, is right in the spirit of things." The film received across-the-board raves. Even as demanding a critic as William K. Zinsser wrote, in the *New York Herald Tribune*, that "[e]verything about the show, in fact, looks fresh. . . . Raitt and Miss Day make an attractive, if somewhat boy-and-girl-next-door pair in the throes of love. . . . The duets between [them] are staged with imagination and humor."

Given the customary delay in foreign distribution, *Pajama Game* did not open in Great Britain until the winter. The Doris Day fan club convened on December 16 for a party and screening at the Warner Theatre in Leicester Square. The club's subsequent quarterly newsletter reported: the "[d]ress was strictly pajamas . . . natch!" The spring newsletter also included the announcement that Sheila Smith and Mavis Eede had taken over the duties of secretary from John Smith, whose "pressure of work at the office and recent engagement" had compelled him to resign in the fall of 1957. "In case you are wondering whether the London Branch is now in good hands, we would like to add that we have both been helping John for over a year, and dealt with the majority of his correspondence," wrote the new team of secretaries in a letter for the issue. Sheila Smith would eventually move into Day's guesthouse in Beverly Hills to help out with her daily routine.

In a tape made on December 2 for the club's upcoming get-together, Day explained how she had recently hired a woman, Shirley Kappel, as her secretary. "Oh, boy, what a life-saver she is," said Day. "I can sit down and just get these letters out so fast. . . . You'll all be hearing from me much more from now on." After mentioning that she and Marty had spent the last weekend in Palm Springs, Day added that Alma was in Cincinnati for the past three months but was returning in a week or so—in ample time to help the Melchers move into their new Beverly Hills house on Crescent Drive.

Finally, the busy Day seized the opportunity to plug her latest album, which she said she had "just finished" with Frank DeVol—*Hooray for Hollywood.* She called it "a 24-sided album," referring to the number of songs. Day's atypically slow and sultry version of the familiar title song is an implicitly sarcastic rendition that stresses the lyrics' barely disguised cynicism ("where you're terrific if you're even good"). Given her nagging feeling that her film career and stardom were denying her the quiet home life she yearned for, perhaps she located even more contempt in the lyrics than the songwriters intended.

*   *   *

Although Doris Day would later claim that, after the "arduous assignment" of *The Pajama Game*, she "would have taken a few months off if the opportunity to perform with [Clark] Gable hadn't presented itself," she had, in fact, committed herself to making *Teacher's Pet* months before work on *The Pajama Game* even began. Nor was Gable the first actor approached to play the scruffy city newspaper editor at the heart of the story. "In that era, if you had a male comedy role, there was one name that always meant something, and that was Cary Grant," said Fay Kanin, who cowrote the Oscar-nominated screenplay of *Teacher's Pet* with her husband, Michael. "So we said how about Cary Grant? They tried him, but he wasn't available. Then we said, how about Jimmy Stewart? He wasn't available either."

While acknowledging that Gable was "too old" to be Day's costar, Fay Kanin said, simply, "But he was Clark Gable. I remember that we were very excited when he accepted the role." One of Hollywood's biggest stars, Gable was making his first comedy in more than two decades. According to Kanin, *Teacher's Pet* was originally written as a "straight drama" and "a serious play about 'the self-made man.' But then, it didn't sell. It just sat there," she recalled, adding that *Born Yesterday*, a major hit play by her brother-in-law, Garson Kanin, inspired her and her husband to convert *Teacher's Pet* into a comedy.

"'Born Yesterday' was a serious subject, treated as a comedy," Kanin elaborated. "And so I said to Michael, 'You know, that's a helluva good idea. I think what's wrong with "Teacher's Pet" is that we didn't have fun with it.' So we took it out, and we rewrote it as a comedy, and we sent it out. And it was sold immediately to George Seaton and William Perlberg who bought it for Doris Day before any man was cast." The team of Perlberg and Seaton reportedly "took less than forty-eight hours to decide on buying the script."

Seaton had made his mark in a number of classic films, having co-written *A Day at the Races* and *The Song of Bernadette*—among other pictures—before directing, most notably, *Miracle on 34th Street* and *The Country Girl*. He had worked with producer William Perlberg on *Bernadette* as early as 1943, but they didn't become a regular team until 1952, when they became especially known for their on-location filming.

Plans for the picture reaffirmed Day's growing status as a star of the first magnitude. According to the "agreement" between Day and Paramount, she was to receive $220,000 for sixteen weeks' work, in addition to $12,500 for any additional week and 5 percent of the gross after $5,500,000. Still another sign of Day's stardom was her announcement after finishing *Pajama Game* that she wouldn't be doing publicity work for several weeks. "I plan to pull a Garbo every so often, now," Day confided. An obvious advantage to being a freelance star—as opposed to a contractual studio slave—was the freedom to set her own rules. Indeed, Day's position had become so firmly established that seventeen requests for interviews and nine photo sittings awaited her once the moratorium was lifted.

In the film, Day played Erica Stone, a pert and no-nonsense journalism professor who doesn't realize that her star pupil is a practicing city editor pretending to be a student. Production began on April 17 and closed down on June 21—ten days behind schedule. From the beginning, Perlberg and Seaton strove to make *Teacher's Pet* as realistic as possible. One of the principal sets was a replica of the *New York World-Telegram and Sun*'s newsroom. The paper's real-life city editor, Norton Mockridge, served as a technical adviser to Seaton and played an assistant editor in the film. The decision to shoot in black-and-white contributed to the picture's documentary-like feeling. In preparation, Day audited several journalism classes at U.C.L.A. over the course of a week. To add to the picture's verisimilitude—as well as for publicity purposes—copies of the script were sent to city editors of every newspaper in the country with a circulation of over 100,000, and their advice was sought. More than two hundred journalists were invited to appear in the scenes shot in the fictitious city room.

From 156 "affirmative replies," 49 were selected by chance drawing from a drum. Their trip to Hollywood would include air travel, hotel, and minimum guild wages for a week's work. In addition to such PR stunts, Paramount shrewdly recruited other studios to help defray the costs. During their stay, the journalists were also guests of Columbia, Warners, MGM, Twentieth Century Fox, and Allied Artists at dinners and screenings, which, not so incidentally, helped promote their own films. Approximately twenty more local journalists took part in both the picture and the festivities. During the summer, some weeks before the Melchers moved into their new Beverly Hills home—as yet unfurnished—it became the scene of a barbecue for the newsmen, described as an "empty house" affair. The event was held on Saturday, May 11, and included "some 40 Hollywood stars." (Though, in fact, it had been planned for the backyard, an atypical downpour forced the guests to take shelter in the wide-open spaces of the empty rooms.)

Recalling her adolescent crush on costar Gable, Day remarked, "When I started making 'Teacher's Pet' with Clark, I was so thrilled I felt as though I were high-school age again. And he was every bit as nice as I had imagined him to be." Day would also remember that Gable "was anything but macho, he was the gentlest, dearest man, and very humble. It was wonderful to see. After a take, he was like a little boy: He would say to George Seaton, our director, 'George, are you sure that I gave you what you wanted?' . . . and George would say, 'Oh, Clark, it was very good. It was just right on.'" Day could have been describing herself, for the most part, when she observed in an interview: "Underneath it all [Clark] was delicate, I think, and didn't know how he was adored in this world. He had no idea. He was insecure."

Director Seaton said he felt "there were times when Doris seemed a bit nervous playing opposite the great Gable." But Fay Kanin confirmed Day's impressions of him: "When he came on the set the first day, he was so unlike a big, self-important movie star. He came on modestly. He didn't ask for any special privileges. He was so terrific. I had dealt with movie stars, and he didn't act that way at all."

Though the film turned out well, Gable does appear too old for Day. There is even a self-conscious—if unspoken—joke regarding his age: While Erica and Jim are dancing a standard cheek-to-cheek in the pivotal nightclub scene, the band suddenly switches to a mambo, and he has to bow out. Moreover, given Gable's puffy appearance, it's hard to credit Day's choosing him over the far more suave Gig Young as Hugo. As Mamie Van Doren—a stripper in the picture, who is relegated to dumb-blonde lines—observes about Hugo, "He's dreamy. He must be from Hollywood."

Though the Kanins' bright dialogue contributed much to making the picture a huge hit, there is something too formulaic about the disparities between Erica and Jim. It might have been easier to accept Erica's edu-cated refinement in contrast with Jim's street smarts and coarseness had her boyfriend not been such a highbrow. On the other hand, *Teacher's Pet* makes a compelling argument that not only do opposites attract, but espe-cially when brought to such irresistible winning life by Day and Gable.

Once assigned to the picture, legendary costume designer Edith Head accompanied Day on a shopping expedition for accessories at Bull-ocks Department Store on Wilshire Boulevard, where the star was accosted by other shoppers as she selected a pair of shoes, a purse, and a belt. (She also had lunch at one of her favorite nearby restaurants, Biff's, an unassuming establishment reminiscent of restaurants in Cincinnati.) Day so loved the simple, form-fitting black sheath dress designed by Head for the nightclub scene that the studio let her keep it.

The screenwriter Ted Berkman visited the Paramount set and was stunned by just how much Day had been transformed since he saw her eight years earlier on the arm of John Huston at the Academy Awards. "They were a most unlikely couple, clearly pasted together by some beleaguered studio publicity department," Berkman wrote in his memoir. "Huston was brilliant, acerbic, the quintessential creative rebel bored by Hollywood ritual but fascinated by the possibilities of the screen medium. Day was plump, freckled, inarticulate, a gawky youngster being groomed to exploit her honeyed singing voice." Now Berkman was struck by the "svelte, poised star," who had been "completely redesigned. Like a tenement building converted to an elegant mansion, only the shell remained. Everything that could be changed had been: hair-do, eyebrows, carriage. The paunchy mid-section and overstuffed derriere were gone, streamlined, at heaven knows what cost in money and self-discipline. It was an extraordinary testimonial to Hollywood's skill at fabricating an image."

While working on *Teacher's Pet*, Day made another tape for her British fans. In addition to mentioning Alma's visit to the set that afternoon, she explained that David Toff—her British music publisher—had been to dinner earlier that week and that her mother was away for the weekend. Day's encomiums to Clark Gable were interrupted by a phone call from Gig Young and his wife: "They just called to say that they're out in the Valley having dinner and they'd like to stop by," she explained. Day said she would be finishing work on *Teacher's Pet* on June 14—the very day of Terry's return home from school. As usual, she promised to return to Britain before long.

✳ ✳ ✳

In response to the observation in Mamie Van Doren's memoir that Day was curt and never said a word to her on the set, Day told Christopher Frayling of the BBC: "She is really not well. This lady is making that up. And that's too bad. I feel sorry for her [having] to say something like that. . . . I don't behave like that." But there were periods in Day's life when she kept very much to herself in her dressing room and emerged only for work, as was the case during the filming of *Teacher's Pet.*

Having suffered with epileptic-like seizures after being hit on the head by a baseball in his youth, Day's brother Paul died of a cerebral hemorrhage at thirty-eight—five days after her birthday (1957), and just before work on *Teacher's Pet* began. "Paul's death hit Doris very hard," a studio representative announced. "Doris isn't the snooty type, who sashays off to her dressing room the minute the cameras stop turning. No, she'll stay on the set, munching candy bars and yacking it up with the crew. But this time it was different. She'd just sit. Her thoughts seemed to be miles away. She wouldn't see the press. And sometimes she'd cry. We got kind of scared. We thought, maybe she's making herself sick. Like that time back in 1954 . . . when she was afraid she had cancer."

"When Marty suggested he come into this business, I was worried about it," Day remarked a year or two before her brother's death. "I didn't think he knew enough about the business. I was against it. [But] I couldn't have been more wrong. He's absolutely marvelous. The disc jockeys think he's the greatest. He's a real blessing to us, promoting sheet music and our records. . . . He's patient [and] loyal." Looking back on his death in her memoir, Day said, "My mother and I felt his death very deeply, and I know I would have been laid low by it if I had not been committed to start photography on a picture with Clark Gable."

Music publisher Sam Weiss felt very strongly that Melcher had been a "factor" in Paul's death, given "the way I saw Marty treat Paul, ruin his spirit, his self-respect, treat him like shit, and there was Paul doing more work for Doris than Marty did in his whole life. . . . Paul had a wife and two kids but Marty wouldn't pay him enough to live on. Doris adored Paul and if she had known the way Marty was treating him, starving him on the salary he paid Paul from money that Doris earned, well, I think Doris would have pitched Marty out on his ear." Indeed, though Paul was Day's brother and worked hard for her, he could never just show up at the Melchers' house, but had to make an appointment first.

According to Fay Kanin, Melcher was "not really around" when they were making *Teacher's Pet.* But knowing only too well that his wife's albums helped sell her pictures—and that her pictures promoted the sale of her albums—Melcher was instrumental in the decision that a song be added for Day in the film, giving Arwin the rights to publish it. "From the beginning, we said there were to be no songs for Doris Day," Kanin recalled—the point being to really make it a nonsinging part and capitalize on her abilities as an actress in the marketing of the film. "Then all of a sudden, she decided she wanted to have one." The recording of the film's title song would prove a big winner for Day, as well as for its composer, Joe Lubin. His other number, "The Girl Who Invented Rock and Roll," works best in the nightclub scene, when Mamie Van Doren introduces it as the stripper, Peggy. Day's subsequent parody only makes an already tacky song sound even tackier.

Melcher's absence from the *Teacher's Pet* set was partly due to his work on *The Green-Eyed Blonde*—the only movie he would produce without his wife. Also known under the alternative title *Blonde and Dangerous*, the 76-minute, black-and-white B movie was directed by Bernard Girard and written by the highly admired Dalton Trumbo. A prominent member of the "Hollywood 10," who was on Senator Joseph McCarthy's blacklist due to Communist sympathies, Trumbo's screenplay for *The Brave One*, written under the pseudonym Robert Rich, had recently won an Oscar. The more humorously named Sally Stubblefield received credit for the script of *Green-Eyed Blonde*.

Made with Warners, *Green-Eyed Blonde* featured a no-name cast, including "talented newcomer" Susan Oliver, Linda Plowman, Beverly Long, Norma Jean Nilsson—"and a host of fighting, kicking, scratching boys-and-girls-gone-wild." Riddled with exclamation points, the ad copy conveyed a pulp paperback novel brought to the screen: "The Story of a Teen-Age Fire-Bomb!" "Girls on a Rumble!" "She Dates Her Guys Through a Barbed-Wire Fence!" "An Illegitimate Baby—And She Won't Tell Who the Father Is!" "It's Shameful But It's Real! The Naked Truth Told by a Girl Who Lived in a Home for Unwed Mothers!" Melcher had been drawn to such material in the wake of the recent success of several pictures about juvenile delinquents, including *Blackboard Jungle*, *Rebel Without a Cause*, and *The Wild One*. But it's telling that his contribution to the genre would be the most cheap and tasteless of the lot.

* * *

The Hollywood premiere of *Teacher's Pet*, on March 20, 1958, was an all-star event. Though Gable attended, Day did not. She did, however, undertake the daunting chore of recording 506 forty-second personal messages to disc jockeys to promote the recording of the title song: "It took eleven sessions, totaling 8 hours and six minutes to record the material," a PR item reported. Day also went to Chicago to promote the film with "a whirlwind 14-hour press, radio, TV and fan signing campaign. . . . Miss Day opened her crowded campaign by visiting 12 disc jockeys starting at 7 a.m. She then lunched with movie columnists, spent the mid-afternoon as hostess for a 'coke' party for 26 senior and junior high school editors. From 5:30 until 9 p.m. she guested on several television shows. At 9:15 she appeared in the lobby of the Woods Theater for an autograph party preceding the final show of the day." She also went on to New York to promote the picture.

The reviewers were suitably impressed with the film. "The normal relationship between teacher and pupil plays truant in this hilarious, yet thought-provoking film," offered Samuel D. Berns in *Motion Picture Daily*. *Variety's* reviewer was equally smitten: "[The picture] might sound on hasty re-cap to be yet another version of 'The Front Page.' Actually there is rich new life and liveliness, and even a fresh approach with humor and heartiness in [the] original screenplay. Clark Gable and Doris Day give it solid star appeal. . . . Miss Day, who apparently can do almost any kind of role is as bright and fresh as a newly set stick of type." Jack Moffitt was even more ecstatic in the *Hollywood Reporter*: "Humming with sex like an open night wire to Reno . . . Miss Day [gives] a performance full of expert shadings. One of her most deft acting chores contrasts her classroom cordiality to her supposed student with her all-out feminine warmness for her psychology boy friend, Gig Young." The film "is more fun than the funnies and, for all the drolleries of its dialogue, emerges as a serious 'think piece' about newspapers," observed Philip K. Scheuer in the *Los Angeles Times*. "While Director Seaton's emphasis is on dialogue, his players make the most of its subtleties. Gable and Miss Day hit it off delightfully together."

Along with Tony Curtis, Day received a "Henrietta" award for being the world's "favorite" actor and actress on February 26 from the Hollywood Foreign Press. The Golden Globe Award for Best Actress went to Joanne Woodward for *The Three Faces of Eve* and for best film to *The Bridge on the River Kwai*, which would, the following month, emerge as the major Oscar winner. For the first time, Day was a presenter at the Academy Awards, held on March 26, 1958, at the RKO Pantages Theatre. Jimmy Stewart, one of the five hosts for this, the thirtieth annual presentation, had costarred with Day in *The Man Who Knew Too Much*. Two of the other hosts, Jack Lemmon and David Niven, were about to become costars in, respectively, *It Happened to Jane* and *Please Don't Eat the Daisies.* But Day made her appearance with yet another costar, Clark Gable, seventy-five minutes into the program, when the host was Bob Hope, recently returned from a visit to Russia. Hope announced that the Best Writing awards would be presented by "two of our great actors, two of our most popular motion picture stars, here in Hollywood." The tune of "Teacher's Pet" could be heard as they emerged onstage.

"It's an honor, Bob, to be presenting the writing awards tonight," said Day, clad in a sparkling white, shoulder-strapped dress and evening gloves, her eyebrows heavily painted. "Bob, I know from experience that writers are the hardest workers in Hollywood," Gable added. "Yeah," cracked Hope, "if they worked a little harder, Clark, I wouldn't have to go to Moscow to get laughs." When Day recited the nominations for Best Original Screenplay, her enunciation of the numerous Italian names involved with Fellini's *I Vitelloni* proved impeccable. The winner, however, was the easily pronounced George Wells, for *Designing Woman.*

✳   ✳   ✳

The Melchers went to New York in the middle of April to discuss possible film projects. They also picked up Terry from the Loomis School in Connecticut and spent the weekend with Marty's brother in North Adams. After returning Terry to school on Monday, they checked out possible locations in Connecticut for Day's next film, *It Happened to Jane,* before returning to New York for more business conferences.

When it finally happened in the early spring of 1958, the Melchers' long-planned move to Crescent Drive was well documented in one of the rare movie magazine articles about Day that was not designed to promote one of her pictures. "We loved [the house] the very first time we clapped eyes on it," said Day. "We drove by once fourteen months ago when it was still a Spanish-type place, not the way we wanted it at all then. But we could 'see' into what it could be—our dream place." After adding that they "remodeled ninety percent—inside and out," Melcher revealed a more practical aspect to making it their dream house: "Its location here in Beverly Hills is perfect," he said. "It's near [both] Doris' studio and my office."

"We had bought the house in winter, and the yard had been merely a tangle of bare branches," Day also recalled. "We moved in during spring. I opened the back door into a yard full of blossoms—the pink and white blossoms of peach, pear and plum trees. We didn't know that the yard contained the fruit trees I had always wanted."

As revealed by one of the photos illustrating the article, at least one prominent aspect of the ranch-style home's original Spanish design remained—a tiered, brick courtyard in the rear, with a large sycamore tree in the center. Day would grow especially fond of gazing at the tree as she lay in bed late at night, letting her mind drift off to sleep. With five bedrooms, six bathrooms, and walk-in closets, the house also featured an enormous kitchen, considered very high-tech with its island cabinets and up-to-the-minute appliances. Here Day would conduct many an interview in the coming years.

While focusing on what the residence would become most famous for—the Melchers' "ice cream bar," in lieu of an alcoholic one—the three-page feature also provided Day with the opportunity to crow about her very own "office-den, something I've been dying to have. It's hi-fied all over and is painted white with grass-cloth material on the walls"—walls that would be lined with framed awards and other memorabilia. The living room featured a fireplace with a nearby window seat beneath slatted shutters, and it housed two large sofas, plaid upholstered chairs, plus paintings and posters on the wall. The Melchers brought their French provincial dining room set with them from Toluca Lake.

With Louis Jourdan living across the street on Crescent, another new neighbor was a former client of Melcher's, the lyricist Paul Francis Webster, who lived two doors down, at 709. He and Sammy Fain had written the songs for *Calamity Jane* and *Lucky Me*. Webster's son, Guy, had befriended Terry when they both lived in Toluca Lake. "I knew Marty when he used to represent my father," recalled Guy Webster, who was seventeen in 1958. "Marty was a bit of a vulgarian and not a particularly nice person. When he became a stepfather, he was never warm, cozy or friendly to Terry. He viewed Terry as a bump in the road."

When the Melchers moved to Crescent, Webster remembered, "Terry was my next-door neighbor, and we became best friends. We used to throw oranges from our back yards at each other—over the house in between. They were like torpedoes, which we used to dodge." Webster also recalled that his father had written a song, "The Twelfth of Never," for Day to sing in *Julie*. "But Louis Jourdan didn't like it. He kept telling Doris, 'It's not right for you,' so she never used it. We got Johnny Mathis to sing it, and it became a big hit that year. When Marty wanted my dad to write another song for Doris, he wanted a kickback," continued Webster, "carpeting for his new house in Beverly Hills. My father said, 'Are you kidding. I don't do that sort of thing.' They didn't work together after that, and they became less friendly."

*   *   *

Although his towering influence on the music world would ultimately bring Day's recording career to a close in less than a decade, Elvis Presley and Day executed PR nods to each other during the period of her move into her new home. Indeed, they became honorary members of each other's fan club. "Hi," wrote Presley in his letter of acceptance, which appeared in the spring 1958 issue of her British fan club's newsletter. "Thanks for inviting me to join your Club for one of my very favorite vocalists. I have asked the President of my Official Club to write the necessary article and I will do my best to write you a proper letter myself as soon as I have time. (I don't know yet exactly when I'm going in the Army—so I have been rushing through a pretty tight schedule in case they call me suddenly.) I'm very proud that Miss Day has accepted the invitation to join our club."

The newsletter did not mention that neighbors could glimpse Terry's sixteenth-birthday present in the new driveway at Crescent: a candy-apple-green Chevy with a stick shift, for what journalist Hortense Rich described as his "wild, uncontrollable drag-racing." "When I went through the hot rod craze, [my mother] almost went out of her mind," Terry recalled several years later. "She refused to get in the car with me, but once circumstances forced her to let me drive her to an important appointment in my car. My mother doesn't like to drive when she's on her way to a recording session. When she's about to sing, she has to be completely relaxed. On a recording day, she does very little talking, and when it's time to go to the studio my father usually drives her there so that she can rest.

"I think she finally said yes in order to give me a sense of importance," he continued. "On the way to Hollywood, my engine shook and sounded like a jet airplane. To me, this was normal, but my mother began to look pretty unhappy about it. . . . [B]y the time we reached the studio, my mother was pretty well shaken up. 'Never again, Terry,' she said."

Several months after moving into her new house, Day was invited to write up her idea of an "ideal day." Predicated on a fantasy of having the power "to make time stand still for 24 hours," the article certainly reflected what might be deemed her philosophy of life: to live in the moment. "I wouldn't think about the day to follow or the day before." After spending her ideal morning with her husband and son, she would play tennis with champion Pancho Gonzales before lunch. "After lunch, I'd like to revisit all the places I have enjoyed. And I'd hope that—for this one day—I could wish myself across oceans and continents." In addition to visiting galleries in Madrid and Paris, Day would return to what she considered "the most beautiful place in the world: the beach at Eden-Roc on the French Riviera." After swimming in the Mediterranean with Melcher, Day would spend the afternoon shopping in London with Alma.

"Dinner would be a time for good conversation, and, as my dinner companion, I would choose Adlai Stevenson," she stated, referring to the Democratic presidential candidate and going completely against her predominantly conservative and Republican viewpoints. "He is a man of intelligence and wit and deep concern for people, and I have only been able to talk to him for five or ten minutes in crowded rooms. Then I would want fun and excitement and gaiety. I'd want to see 'My Fair Lady' again, and catch a late show of Frank Sinatra's. I'd want him to sing just for Marty and me!" Given Sinatra's attitude toward Melcher, that last wish was just about as likely as the rest of Day's dream day. After a hot bath and late-night snack, she would drift off to sleep, soothed by the sycamore tree outside her bedroom window.

"Sticking Keys and Farting Poodles"

✳

"She's as wholesome as wheat germ, as bubbly as champagne."
—JACK MOFFITT

When Day began working on *The Tunnel of Love*, her twenty-third picture—and her only film directed by Gene Kelly—she sent her British fans a letter: "I am sitting on the set having my hair curled in my luncheon break, so I thought I would write to you," she wrote on January 30, 1958. "First of all, Glenn Ford is not in 'The Tunnel of Love' with me, and I am sure you'll all be very surprised to hear this. Richard Widmark is my co-star now."

By emphasizing how surprised her fans would be by this news, Day was inadvertently predicting an important reason for the film's failure. No matter what one's opinion of Day's performance as the stalwart Isolde Poole, the volatile and edgy Widmark was seriously miscast as her subservient husband, Augie. During an extensive interview (1986) looking back on his career, the actor himself would tell film historian Michael Buckley that accepting the part had been "an error."

"It was something that happened at the last minute," he elaborated. "Glenn Ford was supposed to do it and bowed out. My lawyer was handling the people who were putting together 'Tunnel of Love,' so they asked me if I'd do it. I said, 'Okay, if I can have a week's rehearsal.' About the second day, Doris Day said, 'Oh, screw this rehearsal—let's shoot it!' I was no good and neither was the movie," the remarkably honest Widmark added. "It could've been [better] with the right actor. You've got to have kind of a weaker guy playing it. I was wrong for the role."

Indeed, a publicity report at the time of the film's release reveals his defensiveness about having been miscast. "I used to do lots of romantic comedy back in my salad days on the stage," Widmark told a studio publicist. "As a matter of fact, my Broadway debut was in George Abbott's 'Kiss and Tell,' and later on I had a long run in 'Dream Girl.'" However, during the next eleven years, Widmark sealed his reputation as a trigger-happy heavy, in no fewer than thirty pictures.

"Dick Widmark was completely wrong for the part," recalled Elizabeth Wilson, who played Miss MacCracken in the picture. Along with Elisabeth Fraser, Wilson was in the original Broadway version of *Tunnel of Love*, a hit play by Joseph Fields that starred Tom Ewell as Augie. (Though Fields received credit for the screen adaptation, his collaborator, Jerome Chodorv, blacklisted at the time, did not.) "I got the part, as did Liz Fraser, and we went out to California together," Wilson continued. "We were informed almost immediately that there was going to be a big delay. Joe Fields, who had produced and directed, was going to direct the film. But then, he didn't. They put me on salary and then we had to wait six weeks or so for Gene Kelly to show up and start the picture."

The film was further undermined by the decision to alter the play's risqué ending. In the stage version, a question remains whether or not Augie actually fathered a baby with another woman that he and Isolde adopt. In the film, the uncertainty is eliminated. Cleaned up for the mainstream Hollywood audience of 1958, the film lost its edge.

Production began on January 22, 1958, and concluded during the first week in March. "I don't think Dick Widmark was a happy camper," Wilson continued. "I don't think Doris was particularly happy, either. I think she needed somebody to talk to, and she felt comfortable with me. Dick Widmark and I bonded, too. And Gene Kelly was really gentle and very supportive. But I think maybe it was because we all just needed each other. Let's face it, it was a strange kind of comedy. The film just didn't feel right [when we were making it]. It didn't feel like the play at all. The work was just empty. I can remember Gene Kelly trying to keep a sense of humor. At one point, he picked up a girl and was dancing around with her."

Kelly told both Day and Widmark that they looked Swedish and took to calling Day Brunhilda. Day could also find consolation in MGM's having assigned her the same dressing room that she had when filming *Love Me or Leave Me*. This time, she got around the studio by bicycle—"from sound stage to wardrobe to commissary," reported a publicity release. Nearly a decade later, Day would say of Widmark: "Well, he's very quiet. You don't really get to know Dick too well, because he's kind of introverted. But he has great strength and great simplicity." Wilson considered the "very laid-back" Widmark radically different from Day. "There was something so natural about Doris," said Wilson. "That was her great gift. She was a non-actress." Even though Wilson had no memory of Melcher's presence during filming, she met him a number of times at the house on Crescent. "I remember, we used to go to her house. We were invited quite often. Whoever I would be with, we would drink before, because we weren't allowed to there. But they had a lot of open-houses and parties." Wilson also recalled the time Day drove the two of them to lunch. "One of her recordings came on the radio, and she was very cool about it. She smiled, but she made some criticisms about the way it was recorded."

A trailer for *The Tunnel of Love* heralded it as "The Battle of the Sexes in the Suburbs." The Press Book described the film as the story of a "couple with a charming reconverted barn in the suburbs but no baby in the bassinet." Based on a box-office hit—both on Broadway and on tour—the film earned the reprimands of snobbish commentators for being a "commercial success," perhaps the reason for the ecstatic, over-the-top predictions of the trade reviews. "One of the year's funniest pictures," wrote the reviewer in *Variety,* "undoubtedly the raciest, most ribald treatment of sex in pictures in years. It's a cinch for socko [box office]."

"It's a rollicking sampling of the Kinsey report with laughing gas used to anesthetize all the more serious problems," Jack Moffitt wrote in the *Hollywood Reporter.* Neither the mainstream critics nor posterity has been as kind to the misfired film. With his usually harsh if perspicacious judgments, critic Leslie Halliwell deemed it a "[t]asteless and not very funny comedy, somewhat miscast." And the ever-reliable George Morris accurately dismissed the picture in a lone paragraph in his study of Day's movies, calling it "one of the star's weakest."

Shortly after the shooting of *Tunnel* was concluded, Day recorded *Cuttin' Capers,* an album done under the supervision of Frank DeVol, in November 1958. Columbia Records held Day up as the number-one American record seller in foreign countries, at the time. "People don't have to understand your words to know what you sing," she told syndicated columnist Sidney Skolsky. "The important thing is to *feel* what the lyrics say, not just to say them." The album copy for *Cuttin' Capers* offered "a sheaf of songs that deal with various euphoric states in various euphoric manners." The finger-snapping title song was by Joe Lubin, who had written the equally bouncy "Teacher's Pet," and there were also more familiar classics such as "Makin' Whoopee," "Steppin' Out with My Baby," "Let's Take a Walk Around the Block," and "I'm Sitting on Top of the World." If Day's rendition of "Fit as a Fiddle" was recorded in the remarkably slow tempo she preferred, her "Why Don't We Do This More Often" has all the nimble, kittenish allure of Marilyn Monroe, whose seductive voice Day seemed to be emulating.

This is in sharp contrast with Day's film image. Though she would say, time and again, that she never understood where her "good-girl" image came from, she insisted on maintaining it when she had lunch at the Brown Derby with Susan Serisawa, a high school senior and "guest" reporter for the *Los Angeles Times*. "In looking for Doris in future pictures, seek the 'nice-type' girl you're so accustomed to seeing her play," wrote Serisawa. "And because she's aware that her fans like to see her as the 'good' girl, it's doubtful if she'll ever go siren. After all, 'who wants to see Gary Cooper as the villain?' as Doris put it." When asked by another reporter if she cultivated her "wholesome" image, Day replied: "The audience won't accept me any other way—downbeat or neurotic or psychopathic. It might be kind of fun doing a bad girl; most actresses like to play that kind of part and many of them can get away with it. But I can't. In a million years, they wouldn't believe it."

*   *   *

Among the next projects United Artists had in mind for Day was a film version of *Roar Like a Dove*, a play by Lesley Storm. It concerned an American woman married to a Scottish lord. Having given birth to six daughters, she refuses her husband's request to try yet again for a male heir—until the final curtain. *Roar* was a hit in London, and the Melchers intended to travel there and confer with Storm as soon as work on *Tunnel* was finished. The film was to be made in England. "I've planned to take my son out of school in April . . . and have him tutored in England so he can be with me," Day told Hedda Hopper. "I'd like to take Smudgie, my poodle, also; he's getting on now, is sensitive and misses me." It is probably just as well that these plans collapsed; *Roar Like a Dove* would prove an instant flop when it opened on Broadway five years later.

After the completion of *Tunnel*, the Melchers headed to New York with Alma in tow. En route, they spent a night in Cincinnati, staying with Day's Aunt Hilda and Uncle Frank. "When I got there, they had all the German kind of food I was raised on," recalled Day. "And then my Aunt

Marie would come over in the morning with half the local bakery in her arms and put it all on the table and I'd have a piece of everything."

In her memoir, Day recalled, "There was a lot of antiblack talk in their neighborhood because blacks were starting to move into the area." Under the circumstances, it was daring of Day, during this, her latest visit, to invite her father to come by. She hadn't been in touch with him since the premiere of *Julie* in Cincinnati, several years earlier, when she first met his barmaid, Luvenia Williams Bennett. Day claimed that her "heart sank" when he showed up with Luvenia and another black woman in the car. Tellingly, they remained in the car when he went in the house to see his daughter.

According to Day, her parents had not seen each other in twenty years. He said hello to Alma, but beyond that remained uncommunicative. Day's usually gutsy mother quickly fled. Kappelhoff's visit was predictably tense, "strained," and abrupt. After escorting her father to the door and maintaining a safe distance on the porch, Day almost immediately regretted her failure to go to the car and greet the two black women. It was the last time she ever saw her father.

* * *

In his attempt to help Doris Day find a new rehearsal pianist, Sam Weiss introduced her to James Harbert, a young composer and accompanist. "Sam told me, 'Go out to Doris Day's house and play her a number of your new songs. She wants to meet you,'" recalled Harbert. "I played her a couple of songs, and both she and Marty were impressed. It was Marty who said, 'You know, Doris badly needs a pianist.'"

The twenty-nine-year-old Harbert was classically trained, a graduate of Philadelphia's Curtis Institute of Music, which had schooled such distinguished composers as Leonard Bernstein, Gian Carlo Menotti, Samuel Barber, and Mark Blitzstein. While studying at Curtis, Harbert accompanied a student who would go on to become a great operatic soprano. "I worked with Anna Moffo three days a week," recalled Harbert. "I taught her Verdi. I remember once, when we were both exhausted, and Anna said there was a 'Doris Day' movie [*Young Man with a Horn*] playing: 'Why don't we go see it?'" Moffo added: "You know, she's my favorite singer of all time. First of all, her intonation is so wonderful. But it's also the way she can read a lyric."

When he met the Melchers in the winter of 1957, Harbert was working with Frank Sinatra and was also a regular piano player at Sinatra's
restaurant Puccini's, on Beverly Drive in Beverly Hills. Harbert started rehearsing with Day in the den of her new house on Crescent. "There was
a little spinet piano which had been given to Marty for free," he recalled.
"And it was just terrible. Some of the keys would stick. And the two huge
dogs [Smudgie and Beanie] would come and sit on my feet, so I couldn't
raise my feet for the pedals. And then they would break wind, after which
Doris would say, 'Bad doggie.' I'd have to tickle their scrotums with my
feet to get them to move away." (Since she couldn't face the fact that they
were aging, Day had been saying for years that Smudgie and Beanie were
three and five, respectively. "They've been three and five almost as long
as Jack Benny has been thirty-nine," quipped a reporter.)

While Day began working with Harbert, her husband was lining up
her next movie, *The Wreck of the Old 97,* for Columbia Pictures. Her costar, Jack Lemmon, wasn't confirmed as such until March 1958, or five
months after her name was first attached to the project. Retitled *That
Jane from Maine* and finally released as *It Happened to Jane,* the picture
was a rare Day film made on location. Shooting began in the spring and
continued into the summer in Chester, Connecticut, which stood in for
Cape Anne, Maine. Day remarked, "Connecticut looks more like Maine
than Maine does."

With his natural bent for playing everyman characters and his down-
to-earth demeanor, Lemmon was a natural match for Day. Though it
was Lemmon's eleventh film, *Jane* arrived relatively early in what would
amount to an unusually long movie career. Considering how well they
played together—and, in fact, became friends—it's surprising that they
never made another picture together.

In *It Happened to Jane,* Day plays Jane Osgood, a small-town widow
who runs a lobster business while raising two youngsters—one of whom
was portrayed by Mickey Rooney's son Teddy. (When she first saw him,
Day was struck by his close resemblance to Terry.) Written by Norman
Katkov, the screenplay quickly establishes the story's principal conflict,
when a shipment of three hundred lobsters that Jane sent off to a restaurant is returned. The negligent railroad failed to deliver them in a timely
fashion and they expired on board. Though lawyer and friend George
Denham (Lemmon) institutes an "open and shut case," certain that his
"Janie" will be reimbursed, they have to battle the miserly railroad tycoon,

Harry Foster Malone, "the meanest man in the world" played by innovative TV comic Ernie Kovacs with all but a twirl of a villainous mustache.

The film found a natural director in Richard Quine, whose earlier picture *The Solid Gold Cadillac* also concerned a feisty woman fighting a large corporation. The publicity for *Jane* billed it as a "modern-day David and Goliath story," invoking *Mr. Deeds Goes to Town*, and setting forth Day's Jane as a Frank Capra–like heroine. To win the public's sympathy, Jane appears on several familiar television shows of the day, including *I've Got a Secret*. (Ads for the film prominently listed well-known TV personalities as guest stars: Bill Cullen, Dave Garroway, Jayne Meadows, Gary Moore, Henry Morgan, Bob Paige, and Betsy Palmer.)

With Terry and Alma—and Terry's friend Rick—accompanying them, the Melchers stayed in Chester in a two-story house overlooking the Connecticut River, while Day worked on the picture. Lemmon roomed with Quine and Kovacs in a seventeeth-century house. "At three o'clock every afternoon, Dick Quine would let us off for the day—whether Columbia ever found out I don't know," recalled Steve Forrest, who portrayed Larry Hall, a newspaper reporter who falls for Jane. "There was a beautiful trout stream nearby, and the trout were absolutely teeming. So most of us would go trout-fishing. Jack wouldn't. He would go home and play the piano."

In an article ostensibly written by Teddy Rooney to help promote the film, he recalled fishing with Day: "We used to sit on the dock that sticks out into the pond, and fish. I think she's a real good fisherman, even if she didn't catch anything. I didn't either, but it was a good chance to talk.

"Everybody was so tired back in Connecticut," Rooney continued. "It was so hot, and the train yards were so dirty and sticky and all that steam made it worse. So between scenes, everybody would flop under the trees and try to cool off and get some rest. But not Dodo. She likes to walk, and we'd all be sitting there trying to breathe, and she'd go marching off into the woods. Even after she finished her lunch sometimes she'd take off and we'd watch her disappear down the road."

Crowds of people flocked to the small town of Chester to observe the making of the picture. Day would take fifteen-minute breaks to sign autographs and pose for photos with onlookers, who were roped off from the set. While shooting the scene in which Jane drives her station wagon to the general store, the shocked assembly looked on as it became clear that Day was going too fast to stop the car in time. She indeed crashed into a display rack but emerged from the vehicle unharmed. "I'm all right," she assured the crew. "Don't worry, I'm not used to this car and my foot must have slipped."

A New London housewife had written Day about a young neighbor who worshiped her. As arranged by the publicity department, the seventeen-year-old fan, Elva Newman, met her idol on location, arriving just in time to observe Day's minor collision. Later in Day's trailer, when Newman mentioned she was considering dropping out of school and becoming a model, Day responded: "I think that's the craziest, most foolhardy thing you could do. I left school early because I loved to dance and sing and now I regret it." As prearranged, Melcher arrived half an hour or so into their conversation to tell Day that they were ready to resume shooting.

In order to be able to handle "Sam," the Osgoods' pet lobster, Day received special instruction from a local dealer. As recalled by a script girl who observed the lesson, when he said it might be too much for her and suggested that the studio rig a fake, "Doris just burst out laughing and reached for that big, wriggling thing. 'C'mon, Sam,' she said. 'Let's get acquainted.'"

Though Joe Lubin's title song for *Jane* strove to be as jaunty as his "Teacher's Pet," it fell far short. Even less felicitous is "Be Prepared," which Day sings with a Boy Scout troop. But looking back, Day proclaimed *Jane* one of her favorite pictures, emphasizing how much she enjoyed working with Lemmon. Their rapport she felt was based on their both being "very spontaneous" and also their sharing a certain "naïve quality"—their being "just right out there in front, plain, honest."

Lemmon instinctively caught the essence of Day's technique as an actress. "I think she is potentially one of the greatest actresses I'll ever work with," he said, "because in every scene she is so open, simple and honest that I found myself in the position of having to play up to her. Which in the parlance of actors means she's so good that I automatically reacted to her. Doris gets a line on a scene and that's it—boom—she comes on so forcefully that she transports fellow actors right into the scene with her."

While Day and Lemmon formed an enduring friendship in the course of making *Jane*, their only picture together, their mothers bonded as well. Shortly after the completion of the film, Alma and Millie Lemmon were initiated into Hollywood's Motion Picture Mothers' Association and became fast friends. Given her daughter's phenomenal success, Alma extended her vicarious thrills as a stage mother by legally changing her surname from Kappelhoff to Day, embracing the name her daughter never liked. "She's met some wonderful women through the club," Day would say about her mother. "I always get a rundown of what everybody wore."

It was also soon after she finished *Jane* that Day wrote one of the most self-reflective—and revealing—essays of her life, when she was one of eight stars who responded to the implicit question behind "The Lesson that Electrified My Life," as posed by *Motion Picture Magazine*. (The other respondents were Joanne Woodward, Tab Hunter, Diane Varsi, June Allyson, Jerry Lewis, Natalie Wood, and Nick Adams.) Day's brutally forthright response focused on her lifelong difficulty confronting anything unpleasant. "My biggest fault, or weakness," said Day, "was my inability to communicate. When I was upset about something, I wouldn't discuss it. I'd avoid the issue, avoid the people, or both. Once, I even fired a woman who'd been with me a long time, when a heart-to-heart talk might have straightened out what was bothering me.

"Naturally, this showed up in my relationship with Marty," continued Day. "Small frictions arise in all marriages, ours included. They can grow into major disagreements if they are not ironed out. And we got pretty upset about one another more than once. Half the time when I was angry, I wasn't even sure why I was mad." After explaining that it hadn't been the first or the last misunderstanding, Day continued: "One morning, he walked into my dressing room just as I was putting on my lipstick. 'Don't forget to call your piano player,' he reminded me. 'You have a rehearsal at ten.' Before he left the room, he stopped, and turned back to me once more. 'Did you turn on the heat in the house?' 'No!' I snapped.

"Marty was puzzled. He didn't know why I'd suddenly grown so angry about nothing. When I joined him for breakfast a few minutes later, he took my hand in his, 'What's wrong?' he asked gently. 'Nothing!' I said irritably. 'Doris—we communicate now, remember?' Suddenly, I realized how silly I had acted, this day, and on many similar occasions. 'I don't feel like rehearsing today,' I said. He hesitated. 'So you got angry at me because I reminded you of it?' I squirmed uneasily. 'I guess so,' I admitted."

According to James Harbert, Day did not like recording with an orchestra. "She often said, 'Why don't we just record this with you and me at the piano? I feel very free when I'm singing with you. And then you can take it and add the orchestra.' She was comfortable with me, always. Dragging her to recording sessions became one of my responsibilities.

"A few times, I'd come over to get her, and she'd say, 'This is the wrong day.' I'd say, 'It is not the wrong day. The orchestra is sitting there, waiting for us.' She'd say, 'I have a hair appointment.' She really did not like going down to the studio and facing a roomful of musicians. Once she opened her mouth and got started, she was fine. But she was always nervous about it. She once said, 'Who are all those people over there?' I said, 'Dodo, those are the group singers you've been working with for the past 20 years. You need a pair of glasses—if Mary Baker Eddy will permit it.' I was always ready to kill the guard, if he let anyone come in [to the studio] who wasn't supposed to be there."

Though "On the Sunny Side of the Street" was one of the more than six hundred songs Day recorded, Harbert's view of her suggested it was far from a personal anthem. According to Harbert, more than once Day told him, "I can't stand to look at my films." Nevertheless, she preferred making movies to recording albums. When a friend asked Harbert if Day's disposition was as upbeat and bright as her image, he replied, "Only when she's in her better moods. . . . With one beer in her, she'd relax, and she could make great fun of herself. But she required TLC," he added. When she was with Harbert, Day did nothing to disguise her angry moods. Once, when he collected her in his car and arrived fresh from a Christmas party, she detected wine on his breath. Though he explained he had only had a lone glass of chardonnay, she let him know how upset she was and refused to get in the car.

This was something of an exception, however. Though she claimed to have learned her "lesson" about confronting colleagues with problems she might have with them, Day rarely did. Throughout her life, even after welcoming friends into her world, she remained nonconfrontational. She was particularly upset with her husband, at the time, because he refused to go along with her desire to adopt an orphan, one of the Boy Scouts she met making *It Happened to Jane*. (In the fall of 1958, rumors that Day was pregnant may have stemmed from one or two insiders who knew about this thwarted desire of hers.)

Nor was Melcher happy about Terry's return home from military school. Instead of reenrolling at Loomis, the sixteen-year-old Terry spent his junior year at Beverly Hills High, where he was less gawked at because of who his mother was. Back home, the enterprising Terry added handsomely to his allowance by selling advance pressings of his mother's records to classmates.

19

"Pillow Talk"

— a brief note

✳

"The First Couple of American Pop."
—JAMES WOLCOTT

Though Rock Hudson had been under consideration as a possible co-star for Doris Day in the past, the first time their names were linked in print was when they were declared the top box office attractions for the 1957–58 season in the tenth annual International Laurel Awards poll. This doubtless precipitated their making *Pillow Talk* together. It was producer Ross Hunter who recognized Day's potential to play a sensual character on-screen and cast her in the picture. And what better way to punch up that aspect of Day's nature than by pairing her with the six-foot-four Hollywood hunk Rock Hudson? In fact, Melcher had recognized his wife's sexiness from the beginning and briefly exploited it when they finally broke away from Warner Brothers—and from the girl-next-door image to which the studio had restricted her—with her portrayal of Ruth Etting in *Love Me or Leave Me*. But neither Melcher nor his wife seemed comfortable with that newly defined Doris Day, and a calcified image of the more pristine star continued to prevail in the public's mind—as well as in their own.

Film scholar James Robert Parish went so far as to say that after "such inept comedies" as *The Tunnel of Love* and *It Happened to Jane*, Day's career was at something of an impasse and that it had become increasingly difficult to "find vehicles that suited the cotton candy image of Day, whose persona as the screen innocent was reaching the point of tedium and absurdity." But now, with *Pillow Talk*, the girl next door became, in a sense, a thirty-five-year-old sex kitten.

Norman Jewison—who would direct Day in her third picture for Ross Hunter, *The Thrill of It All*—has offered one of the most succinct and perceptive summaries of the producer who came to her rescue with *Pillow Talk*. "[Hunter] loved everything about Hollywood. He loved the studios.

Loved the star system. He was so savvy about how the business worked that all the movies he made for Universal showed a profit—tear-jerkers, thrillers, romantic comedies. Ross was gay, and he and the man he lived with, a businessman named Jacques Mapes, were two of the most elegant guys in town. They threw bridge parties. People would kill to get an invitation to those parties. Not me—I didn't play cards much—but Rock Hudson and Claire Trevor were regulars." Hunter would prove to be a very hands-on producer who was a constant presence on the set.

In *Pillow Talk*, Day played Jan Morrow, a stylish interior decorator. The independent Jan's only problem is the party line (i.e., shared phone number) she has to share with a songwriting Lothario named Brad Allen (Rock Hudson). "This career girl had everything but love," began the voice-over for the trailer. "This bachelor had nothing else but. They had absolutely nothing in common, except a party line." Every time Jan picks up her phone to make a call, she is subjected to Brad's singing the same song for the benefit of a new conquest, "You Are My Inspiration." Screenwriters Stanley Shapiro and Maurice Richlin might have been thinking of George Gershwin, who famously had a special waltz with a standard lyric—and a blank for the girl's name—with which he lured each new attraction.

Though they are introduced as enemies on either end of the phone, Brad inevitably falls for Jan. In order to win her, he impersonates a Texan obviously named Rex Stetson, which is a good indication of how broad the script's humor could be.

In addition to helping redefine Day's image, Hunter had the insight to perceive Hudson's potential as a comedic actor. In fact, Hudson hesitated to confront the challenge. "Me? In a Cary Grant role?" he exclaimed when Hunter approached him about the part. "I just don't know. I may fall flat on my kisser." However, Hudson's reluctance hedged a subtext. Once he read the script, he had to have had some misgivings about playing a character that pretends to be gay in order to seduce Day's character.

Indeed, the notion of Hollywood as a "dream factory" does not reach higher heights than in this whimsical casting of a gay man who pretended to be straight, portraying a straight man pretending to be gay. These convolutions evoke Shakespeare's *Twelfth Night*, wherein a male actor portrays Viola, a woman, who, in turn, impersonates a man, Cesario. As James Wolcott would wryly write a half century later, "[Hudson] turns the gay closet into his own Superman phone booth, a convenient place to switch identities."

Certainly everyone involved with *Pillow Talk* was aware that Hudson was gay. (Norman Jewison would later refer to Hudson's homosexuality as an "open secret" at the time.) But in the same way the studios had colluded in preserving Day's girl-next-door image—up until then, that is—they had a vested interest in maintaining Hudson's status as a virile heterosexual. Having Hudson play a character only pretending to be gay ultimately was not viewed as a threat. But could a good part of Hollywood avoid perceiving the situation as an inside joke?

Hudson was persuaded to take on the comic role of Brad by Michael Gordon, the director who was making his Hollywood comeback with *Pillow Talk*. Gordon had been blacklisted in 1951, when he appeared before the House Un-American Activities Committee (HUAC) and refused to name names. He also took a dark view of the making of a light comedy. "No matter how absurd the situations may appear to the viewer, to the people involved, it's a matter of life and death," he told Hudson. "Comedy is no laughing matter."

Tony Randall was featured in the film as the foil who also wants but fails to get the girl, a generic type already introduced by Gig Young in two of Day's previous films (*Young at Heart* and *Teacher's Pet*). Though Randall would become known for portraying "goofballs" and "nerds," he was a well-trained stage actor who had studied drama with Sanford Meisner, movement with Martha Graham, and voice with Henry Jacobi. Randall became a part of Hunter's Day-Hudson formula and costarred in their two subsequent films.

The other principal player was Thelma Ritter, whose character's salt-of-the-earth values and sardonic comebacks graced many a memorable film of the mid-twentieth century, including *All About Eve, With a Song in My Heart, Titanic, Rear Window,* and *The Misfits.* Though Ritter never won the Oscar she—time and again—deserved, she would at least be nominated in the featured category for her winning performance as Jan's perpetually hungover housekeeper (it was the fifth of her six nominations).

Shortly before filming began in the first week in March (1959), Day revealed to Harbert that even though she felt "exhausted" when she had to do lighting tests with the assistant cinematographer, "I looked wonderful. I never looked so good." But Arthur E. Arling, the film's cinematographer, judged the tests "terrible" and reshot them himself. This time Day found them awful. "They made me look like Marjorie Main," she said, referring to the horse-faced character actress best known as Ma Kettle. "I told Marty, maybe we should use the assistant to make the picture."

Also before shooting began, the Melchers launched weekly informal dinner parties for cast and crew. "We became a family," recalled Hunter. "We began to know one another well, to react to the same family jokes, to know what to expect of our association. We were at ease with one another, a condition that created a climate of camaraderie on the set, an essential for filming a successful comedy." During preliminary rehearsals on the set, when Hudson "was busy on the phone," the stalwart character actor Jeff Chandler was spotted milling around. Day said, "Jeff, why don't you take Rock's place?" He did, "ad libbing whatever came into his mind in response to Doris's lines," said a reporter in *Modern Screen*. In her efforts to make the insecure Hudson feel more at home in a comic role, Day remained on the set when he filmed their split-screen, telephone scene to feed him her lines, which could have been just as easily cued by a script girl or by playing Day's previously recorded lines. And during the prerecording session for their song, in which Hudson was to join her in the chorus, the magnanimous Day spontaneously suggested to him, "Why don't you sing a verse?" Hudson, though not especially proud of his untutored baritone, went along with the idea. Like practically everyone who worked with her, Hudson found Day to be a perfectionist and added, "[T]hat comes through in her acting, as well as her singing."

When he anticipated working with Day for the first time, Hudson expected someone "as warm as a December night on an ice floe." But as Day herself recalled, "[T]he very first day on the set, I discovered we had a performing rapport that was remarkable. We played our scenes together as if we had once lived them." They quickly came to feel and behave as close with each other as they ever had with anyone else.

Hudson was especially surprised that they got along so well, since he fumbled during the first scene they shot together—a scene that would appear at the end of the film. "I was [supposed] to storm into her apartment, find her in bed and pull her out by grabbing her ankles and hauling her off the foot of the bed. I did all this, supposedly in the heat of anger, and it went very well until I pulled her off the bed. I forgot to let go of her ankles, with the result that my leading lady crashed to the floor. A real great start, wasn't it? But she just lay there on her back, grinned up at me and said, 'Would you please let go of my ankles?'"

After wrenching her from bed, Hudson's Brad had to carry Jan out of her apartment building and to the street. Since Hudson had chronic back problems, a special harness was rigged to his midsection with straps over the shoulders, which enabled him to lift Day with ease. (The cat following the dangling cord of Jan's electric blanket was a fortuitous accident that added to the scene's hilarity.)

Their compatibility should have been foreseeable, for Day and Hudson had much in common. Not only were they at the peaks of their careers, sharing number one box-office status, but they both enjoyed teasing and being teased. Moreover, like Day, Hudson was riddled with doubts and insecurities, his stemming from a truly miserable childhood. When he was still Roy Harold Scherer Jr., Hudson's father abandoned him; his stepfather and mother proceeded to abuse him, both emotionally and physically. Most important, they could relate to being icons whose images spoke falsely: He was no more the All-American Male than she the Girl Next Door.

According to Tony Randall, Hudson "didn't have the greatest confidence in his own ability. I always felt the reason was he'd become a star too fast and got so many bad notices. I think he really believed he wasn't such a great actor. And probably in the beginning it was true. But he had become damn good. . . . You saw how good he was in 'Pillow Talk.' He was so funny." Looking back on getting to know Day, Hudson said: "She is the same way I am about new people. We both creep along as though we were on the ledge of a 20-story building. Which is so nonsensical, really! If grown ups could be like kids about meeting new people, it'd be a better world. Kids look at each other and say, 'innocent until proven guilty.' We grown ups work it the opposite way, and it wastes a lot of time." Given Day's penchant for nicknames, they inevitably—if quickly—came up with new ones for each other. He became Ernie; she was either Eunice or Maude, depending on Hudson's mood.

Once shooting began, Day got a walk-on part in the picture for Miriam Nelson in order to have lunch with her in the commissary, an efficient way to fit an old friend into her hectic schedule. Nelson appears in the film as a patient in a doctor's waiting room when Brad sneaks in to evade Jan—without realizing he has entered an obstetrician's office, a situation providing a running gag in the picture.

In the course of shooting, Day caught Hudson's habit of doing crossword puzzles during downtime on the set. She, in turn, wanted to teach him how to play tennis, but he didn't take her up on the offer. He also intended to show her how to scuba dive, on a proposed visit to his house at Newport Beach.

They truly did get along famously. With great exaggeration, Hudson recalled that "[t]hey had to add a week on to the shooting schedule because we could not stop laughing. . . . I used to think about terrible things, to try not to laugh, but I think that's the wonderful part about when you see two people on the screen—if you like them, if they like each other, and you sense that they like each other."

The Melchers celebrated their anniversary on the set of *Pillow Talk* on April 3, and, three days later, as she had the year before, Day acted as a presenter during the Academy Awards. There were six emcees that year: Bob Hope, Jerry Lewis, Mort Sahl, Laurence Olivier, Tony Randall, and David Niven. "To present the awards for cinematography, the academy selected two of the camera's favorite subjects," Olivier said as he introduced Day and Hudson.

For the Oscars, Day wore a floor-length, form-fitting white gown, enhanced by sparkling earrings and a diamond necklace. Hudson wore a black tuxedo. There was no banter between the couple, who were surprisingly stiff as they read the nominees and revealed the winners: Sam Leavitt for *The Defiant Ones* (black-and-white) and Joseph Ruttenberg for *Gigi* (color). (*Gigi* set a new Academy Award record with nine awards.) Though she displayed her characteristic smile as she muttered congratulations to Ruttenberg, it was the only word Day uttered during the proceedings—apart from the names of the nominees—and one more than Hudson.

Fay and Michael Kanin's screenplay for *Teacher's Pet* received a nomination, but lost to *The Defiant Ones*. Gig Young, the costar of *Teacher's Pet*, was also in the running for Supporting Actor, but Burl Ives took the Oscar home for *The Big Country*. On his way to the stage to accept the award, Ives tapped the noticeably disgruntled—and possibly inebriated, from all appearances—Young on the shoulder.

* * *

Jim Harbert, who had written an unused title song for *Pillow Talk*, was invited to a beach house in Malibu the Melchers were renting. He discovered the reason behind the invitation as Melcher greeted him. "Rock Hudson's here," said Melcher. "See if you can teach him to sing. If we could get them on a duo together, it would sell like gangbusters."

"Later, Rock Hudson learned to sing pretty well," explained Harbert. "But at that point, he sounded like a howling wolf. I remember Doris peeking around the corner while we were at the piano, and snickering at my expense."

After their musical session, Day invited her guests to take a dip in the ocean. Harbert declined, saying he didn't have a swimsuit. In fact, he was petrified of the sea creatures he imagined in the water. Offering him a spare suit, Day insisted and Harbert finally relented. Sure enough, once in the water, Harbert felt a painful pinch on his foot and emerged with a crab dangling from his big toe. While Melcher and Hudson expressed concern, Day broke out in hysterical laughter. But as soon as Day noticed what she called a group of "tourists" approaching, they made a quick retreat. "I have not been back in the ocean since," Harbert remarked fifty years later.

Harbert recalled another time when he was visiting the Melchers at their Malibu house when Jack Lemmon was there. Though he was encouraged to show Harbert how well he played the piano, Lemmon proved too shy to do so.

Another frequent guest at the Malibu rental was the Melchers' Christian Science guru Martin Broones, who gave Day what she would later call her "favorite book," *Kinship with All Life*, by J. Allen Boone. The book was a memoir about his life with Strongheart, a German shepherd, which "was the greatest movie dog ever," according to Day. "But it also tells you much more than that. It tells you the story of how one man learned to communicate with one animal—communicate by building a bridge."

For all the leaks that Melcher had given Hedda Hopper for her column, he was now trying to get her to promote Broones, whom he called "the Billy Graham of Christian Science" in a letter to the great lady of gossip. In another letter, Melcher wrote, "His last few lectures were overflowing to such a degree that the churches involved are now installing special p.a. speakers so that people may listen in the parking lots while sitting in their cars." Day had also recently recorded a song with lyrics by Broones, "Let No Walls Divide."

* * *

Shortly after *Pillow Talk* was completed, the Melchers set out on a promotional tour for *It Happened to Jane.* They began by visiting Day's relatives in Cincinnati the first week in May 1959. They were slated to go
to Boston, New York, Philadelphia, Washington, D.C., and Chicago, but
such plans were abruptly curtailed when Day contracted mononucleosis
in Cincinnati and had to return home by train.

When it opened that spring, *Jane* fared poorly with the critics, who
simply didn't know what to make of it. "Up to a point, this is a funny comedy," wrote the reviewer in *Variety.* "The point is reached about three-
quarters of the way through when the film abruptly changes form and
loses momentum. . . .The story runs out of steam—much as the locomo-
tive that is a central point—because Norman Katkov's screenplay is not
clearly either farce or romantic comedy. It is farce through the major portion. . . . Miss Day, a beguiling figure of outraged womanhood, doesn't
lose her essential femininity in the glory of the cause. She is pugnacious
but perceptibly female."

Nor was Philip K. Scheuer too pleased in his review for the *Los
Angeles Times*: "[The film] is not as hilarious as Quine's direction of the
screenplay by Norman Katkov makes it appear to be, and there are sequences, like the one involving a fife-and-drum corps, that contribute
nothing but footage. . . . Miss Day looks a bit weather-beaten in some
shots but never lacks for pep." Nor was Scheuer alone in feeling that
Kovacs was "the one unqualified delight." "The picture is stolen from the
scenery-chewing leads by a bald Ernie Kovacs," wrote John D. Thompson
of the Toronto Film Society.

Even as provincial a paper as the *Beverly Hills Citizen* found much to
carp about. "Unfortunately," wrote Hazel Flynn, "in tailoring [the story]
to Doris Day's proportions some of the real flavor of New England has
been lost and a few things—principally Doris' ultra blonde Hollywood
appearance and flintiness—are completely out of line with the gentle
primness of that part of the country."

Jane also failed at the box office. The film's wry sensibility and relatively sophisticated story line just didn't go over well with Americans
who, fearful of an atomic bomb, wanted to go to movies to escape from
their everyday paranoia. The film did extremely well in London, however, where it was released as *Twinkle and Shine* and became the second-
largest grossing picture in five years, after *Around the World in 80 Days.*
Jane would flounder yet again, when it was rereleased with the newer

title in the United States. Regardless of its title, the picture has aged well, however. While declaring Day's role "one of her most characteristic," George Morris found it "a delightful movie, completely unassuming and consistently engaging. Director Richard Quine infuses the narrative with just the right mixture of bucolic whimsy and behavioral charm." In his recently published book on Day's career, *Considering Doris Day*, Tom Santopietro wrote that the film was "charming" and that "its box-office failure is hard to fathom."

20

Plain as Day

✳

"It was like coming out of heaven into chaos."
—DORIS DAY

Though *It Happened to Jane* failed to appeal to moviegoers when it opened in the spring, Doris Day would have an enormous commercial—if not critical—success with the picture she worked on—albeit not released—next, *Please Don't Eat the Daisies*. Produced by Joe Pasternak for Sol Siegel at MGM, it was based on a bestselling book by Jean Kerr about her experiences as the wife of Walter Kerr, the influential New York theater critic. (The Kerrs become Kate and Larry MacKay in the film.)

Having produced *Love Me or Leave Me*, Pasternak recruited that film's cowriter Isobel Lennart to create the screenplay for *Daisies*. Though he did not take credit, Pasternak had a hand in improving the script. "I particularly want to commend you about the final scenes between Kate and Larry," Siegel wrote Pasternak in a memo after reading his changes. "They have genuine emotion and should play beautifully." Alas, many film reviewers would not agree with Siegel's assessment.

In the course of working with Day when she embodied Ruth Etting, Pasternak developed a sharp grasp of her paradoxical nature. "Doris is a wonderful, wholesome girl," he said. "But she is complex and has uncertainties about herself. That's what makes her such a great performer. Simple girls can't act. If she were as uncomplicated as her publicity would lead you to believe, she wouldn't be the tremendous box-office draw that she is."

With Day as his lead, Pasternak called on Charles Walters to direct. A former choreographer and dancer, Walters was preparing for his directorial debut with *Jumbo* at MGM in 1947 when it was shelved and he made *Good News* instead. In the intervening years, he directed a number of major musical movies, including *Easter Parade, The Barkleys of Broadway, Summer Stock*, and *High Society*. Walters biographer Brent Phillips says the director was no fan of Day's when *Daisies* was given to him. "But when he read the book, he said, 'My God. This *is* Doris Day!' He instantly fell in love with her, from the very first day they worked together. There are a lot of on-set photos of Day and Walters laughing hysterically."

Phillips also asserted that Walters wanted Betty Grable to play Deborah Vaughn, the Broadway actress who, panned by Larry MacKay, first slaps him—at Sardi's—and then tries to seduce him. The part of Deborah went to Janis Paige, who had costarred in Day's first picture, *Romance on the High Seas*.

Day received $200,000 for fifteen weeks of work on *Daisies*. As associate producer, Melcher received $45,000, and their Daywin music company, a branch of Arwin, took in an additional $12,500 for the use of "Que Sera, Sera," "Any Way the Wind Blows," and Joe Lubin's title song. (Melcher originally wanted the title of *Pillow Talk* to be *Any Way the Wind Blows*—fortunately, he didn't get his wish.) Day was also given $5,000 to obtain "her own wardrobe," which would remain her property. Though David Niven had recently won the Oscar for *Separate Tables*, he was paid considerably less than his costar, $125,000. Hobo, the sheepdog, was rented at the flat rate of $170 per week. ("The cat works for $25 per day," said an item in Pasternak's private papers.) The total budget for the picture was $1,979,071, and it came in slightly over, at $2,021,406.

Several days before the cameras started rolling—August 3, 1959, with a two-month shoot ahead—Joe Pasternak had a "Get Acquainted Day," a picnic for the stars to meet the four children in the film. (Ten-year-old Stanley Livingstone, who was playing Gabriel MacKay, was on the verge of debuting in what would become a popular TV sitcom, *My Three Sons*.) For Day's big number—the title song with the kids—Walters taught her to play the ukulele. Whenever she practiced, her portable dressing room was roped off with a very effective sign on the door: "Quarantined!" (The musical arrangement for her recording of the title song was done by Bill Marx, Harpo's son. According to Jim Harbert, it was Marx's idea to set the song as a canon.)

Though the irrepressible Kate MacKay is archetypal Day—whether rolling up her sleeves to paint her house or elegantly dressed for a night on the town—her winning effect is enhanced by Niven's typically reserved performance. Unfortunately, no chemistry can be felt between the suave Niven—here too stiff and somewhat off his game—and the preternaturally vivacious Day. (According to film historian David Thomson, Niven "preferred to seem brittle, unreliable, a man whose banter and charm occasionally crumbled to reveal inadequacy.") As Niven biographer Graham Lord pointed out, both Day and Niven "broke two basic actors' rules—never to appear with children or animals—by taking on both." Lord also observed that Niven's accent "veered from English to American and back" throughout the film.

*　　*　　*

Shortly after *Please Don't Eat the Daisies* was completed in early October 1959, Day made personal appearances in New York with Rock Hudson to promote *Pillow Talk*, which the trailer extolled as "the most sparkling sex-capade that ever winked at convention." During their extensive autumn tour of the country promoting the picture, the Melchers took a vacation in New England. They admired the foliage and explored areas where they contemplated buying a home to spend a month or two every year. From New York, they went to Boston and visited the coastal Massachusetts towns of Rockport, Marblehead, and Gloucester, where Day fell in love with the seafood. They spent a night in Concord in the "governor's suite." "I exercised in the morning with the tall windows wide open," Day recalled, "and Marty laughed and said they'd be sending the cops." While in Concord, they went to see the big granite church in Mary Baker Eddy's nearby hometown, and observed the plaque hanging where Eddy was born. (The house itself had burned down long ago.) They visited Melcher's mother, sister, and brother-in-law in North Adams and took a side trip to Williamstown. There they stopped at the popular Mount Hope Farm, from which they had apples, honey, and jellies sent home.

Farther north, in New Hampshire, they stayed at an inn in the White Mountains that was owned by a friend. "[T]hey walked in the woods, saw the nearby river flood to a torrent in the heavy rains, came back and warmed themselves at great roaring fires. They helped cook on the wood stove and drove the jeep into the nearby town. 'I found that I love small towns,' Doris says. 'The pace is gentle, slow, and you have time to walk and to smell and see and hear.'"

Though they "fell in love" with Bennington, Vermont, the Melchers were thinking about buying a place closer to North Adams. "While the Melchers refused to be pinned down specifically as to where they will live, the implication was strong that nearby Williamstown will be the place,"

Edwin Matesky said in the *North Adams Transcript.* "They won't be full-time
residents. . . . But they will come to the Berkshires whenever they can and
stay as long as they can. And if Doris has her way, it will be often in winter."
According to Melcher, Day was particularly fond of the change of seasons,
which she missed on the West Coast.

Day regretted ending their vacation in New York, where they returned on November 5 for business matters, including a party that Columbia's Goddard Lieberson threw for the label's leading singer at the
popular 21 Club. "It was like coming out of heaven into chaos," she said.
"It was such a shocking contrast that I didn't want to stay so we didn't.
We left. New York seemed simply too hectic."

✳   ✳   ✳

When *Pillow Talk* opened in October 1959, the reviewers welcomed it as
a new modern comedy and embraced Day and Hudson as a natural team.
"A comedy to be laughed at—by adults, the juniors, and the exhibitor on
his way to the bank," Bill Weaver wrote in *Film Daily* after attending a
film with a preview audience that had "the time of its life. . . . Its co-stars,
Rock Hudson and Doris Day, have done nothing previously better—or
better for them. . . . The picture is rich, sleek, fast, modern, amusing in
concept and magnificently executed by all hands." In the *Hollywood Reporter*, Jack Moffitt forecast: "[I]t is sure to hit the target of high grosses.
This . . . production is a brightly ingenious example of stimulating cinematic know-how in all departments. . . . Miss Day is absolutely tops in
her combination of sophistication and naivete."

It is "the year's most sophisticated light comedy," Arthur Knight said
in the *Saturday Review*, adding, "It's one occasion where everyone concerned seems to know exactly what he is doing, and does it well." If Paul
V. Beckley cooed over the film's "smart, glossy texture" in the *New York
Herald-Tribune*, the review in the *New York Times* by Bosley Crowther—in
the past less than enthusiastic about Day—was even more over the top:
"[T]he film must be cheerfully acknowledged one of the most lively and
up-to-date comedy-romances of the year." Crowther added that Hudson met the challenge of his role "with surprising dexterity" and that
Day played her part "fiercely and smartly. . . . [She] has a delightful way
of taking the romantic offensive against a man. Her dudgeons are as
chic and spectacular as her nifty Jean Louis clothes, and her fall for Mr.

Hudson's deceptions is as graceful as a ski-run down a hill." (If producer Ross Hunter had the wit to have Jean Louis design Day's costumes for the picture, he also knew how to keep his star happy by "gifting" her the entire wardrobe once filming was completed.)

While pointing out that the picture paired the two box-office "champions" of the 1958–59 season, *Time* magazine turned them into commodities. "When these two magnificent objects go into a clinch, aglow from the sun lamp, a-gleam with hair lacquer, they look less like creatures of flesh and blood than a couple of 1960 Cadillacs that just happen to be parked in a suggestive position."

As confirmed by *Variety*, the picture remained box-office champion in its sixth successive week. In fact, it was the number-one film for a couple of months. Budgeted and brought in at $2 million, the film grossed $18 million in the United States alone. It was also voted the most popular picture of 1960 in Finland—over *Ben Hur*—and confirmed Day's star status throughout the world.

In his glowing encomium to the winning team of Day and Hudson, James Wolcott noted that *Pillow Talk* "coincided with the creation of Barbie and Ken, doll versions of Doris and Rock." He further invoked even loftier comparisons: "Day's helmet hair, her career-gal outfits and piquant hats, were a sneak preview of Jacqueline Kennedy's style as First Lady; Hudson's grinning rogues were light, early drafts of J.F.K. Without knowing it, Rock Hudson and Doris Day were shucking the Eisenhower blahs and ushering in the New Frontier. They were the First Couple of American Pop."

* * *

After they finished making *Pillow Talk*, Hudson visited the Melchers and brought along home movies he had made in 1955 in Ireland, when he was shooting *Captain Lightfoot*. He apparently knew that his *Lightfoot* costar, Barbara Rush, was going to be at the Melchers as well, with her husband, Warren Cowan. However, he discovered a larger gang than he was expecting, including Ross Hunter and Tony Randall. The group had such a grand time that they ended up meeting at the Melchers with some regularity on Saturday nights. "Barbara and Doris became great friends," recalled Cowan. "And that's where I first met Merv Griffin, at one of those parties." It was Cowan who proceeded to give the gang a name: the Crescents, referring to the Melchers' home on Crescent Drive.

The name stuck. According to Hedda Hopper, the Crescents succeeded the Rat Pack, which had originated as a label for a Holmby Hills gang, consisting of Humphrey Bogart, Lauren Bacall, Frank Sinatra, Angie Dickinson, Judy Garland, and Sid Luft, among others. This was before that tongue-in-cheek name made its comeback—and really took hold—to describe the famous newer "ring-a-ding" good-time Rat Pack consisting of Hollywood players, including Sinatra, Dean Martin, Sammy Davis Jr., Joey Bishop, Peter Lawford, Barbara Rush, and Shirley MacLaine.

Barbara Rush proved a link from the Rat Pack to the Crescents. According to Hopper, the Crescents were "beach rats" because they "rendezvous at a hideout at Malibu which has the best barbecued food in these parts." Hopper also reported that their number included Jack Lemmon and his soon-to-be-wife, actress Felicia Farr. Whenever they congregated at Crescent Drive, it was the Melchers who barbecued the steaks.

✳   ✳   ✳

Since Day liked her new rehearsal pianist, James Harbert, so much, she was only too happy to record a couple of his songs, "Daffa Down Dilly," a sprightly number with lyrics by his first wife, Charlene, and "The Blue Train," a country song with a Western twang. "I rewrote 'The Blue Train' at Marty's request," recalled Harbert. There was a snag, however. "When Marty insisted on publishing the songs, I said, 'That's not really fair. Sam [Weiss] is a publisher, too, and he's the one who introduced us. And you're old friends—you can't do this to Sam.' Marty said, 'You have a lot to learn about this business.' Then I went to Sam and said Doris wants to record these songs and Marty wants to publish them. And Sam said, 'Go ahead and give them to him. That's the way it always is with Marty.'"

Harbert served as orchestra leader for the Columbia recording sessions on January 25, 1960. Shortly afterward, A&R man Irving Townsend offered him a job at the studio. If Harbert came to appreciate that it was the Melchers who had sold Columbia on the idea of making him an A&R man, he later learned why from some engineers at the studio. "Mitch Miller had the habit of getting right in the booth with his singers and conducting in their face," Harbert said. "He did get performances that way, sometimes. But to do that with Frank Sinatra or Doris Day, who were consummate artists? She really didn't like it. The engineers told me that once, when Sinatra was making a recording, and something blew up in the booth, he said, 'Too bad Mitch Miller wasn't in there.' They also told me that Doris once said, 'Keep that bearded son of a bitch out of my booth and out of my face. I was singing songs when he was still playing snake charmer music [on his oboe].' That's why I became her A&R man, producing some of her stuff. She didn't want Mitch any more." But like the little ball that became his trademark, Miller bounced back hardily. By the following January, Miller was on the air with what would become his extremely popular *Sing Along* show. Though CBS had rejected his idea for the show, NBC swooped it up and feasted on its earnings.

Harbert recalled that whenever he was arranging material for Day, she would tell him: "Now don't put it up in too high a key for me. I can't reach 'C' any more." "I knew that she could still reach it," Harbert said, adding that many singers rise to the occasion when working with an orchestra. "When you have the feel of the orchestra behind you, and especially during a recording session, that lifts the voice. So I put her in the keys she sang in when she was younger—but she didn't know it." Indeed, Harbert added, "Sinatra used to have two sets of keys—one for singing in a club and one for recording."

Day clearly had the same level of confidence in Harbert's guiding her voice as she had had in Donald Saddler's overseeing her dance steps. "She will do anything you ask her," Melcher told Harbert. "She likes you, and trusts you, because she says you never lie." Melcher had exploited Day's faith in her accompanist by using Harbert's influence whenever he wanted her to record a particular song. "As far as Marty was concerned, I wouldn't push her enough to record new songs," said Harbert, who emphasized how odd it was, in meetings with the Melchers, to hear Marty refer in the third person to "Doris Day," underscoring that he looked upon her as more of a breadwinner or commodity than a partner.

It wasn't Melcher but Columbia that wanted Day to record "Far Away Boy," a tearful ballad from Frank Loesser's upcoming Broadway show *Greenwillow*. When Harbert tried to pursue the matter, he ran up against Melcher's ironclad rule: "We're not recording anything we're not publishing." At first, Day herself agreed. She told Harbert, "If there's a good song there, they'll give it to Johnny Mathis to do." However, after rehearsing the song several times with Harbert, Day shared his enthusiasm. "You're right. It's a terrific song. I want to be a part of this. To hell with Marty." But by then, Loesser had taken his *Greenwillow* score away from Columbia and given it to RCA.

Among the more tantalizing projects Harbert conceived of for Day was *I've Got a Right to Sing the Classics*, an album inspired by one that

Columbia had brought out that year, opera singer Eileen Farrell's *I've Got a Right to Sing the Blues.* If the hefty Wagnerian soprano could record Harold Arlen standards, Harbert reasoned, why couldn't Day record classical pieces? "I used to give Doris classical records," Harbert said. He introduced her to Wagner's "Lieberstod"–"one of the sexiest pieces ever written," he added. "And she loved this recording of George Szell and the Cleveland Orchestra. She asked for another copy to give to someone else. If she had gone the classical route, she would have ended up at the Met." Indeed, when asked on the set of *Calamity Jane* who her favorite singer was, Day included Wagnerian soprano Helen Traubel on a list that included "Gordon MacRae, Perry Como, Nat Cole, and Ella Fitzgerald."

But Day feared she wasn't up to the task of cutting such a record, and she was hesitant at first. Harbert softened her nerves by assuring her there were a number of well-known classical pieces that did not "require a huge operatic range." She warmed to the idea. Harbert remembered working with her on Mozart's 'Voi che sapete' (from *The Marriage of Figaro*). After Day said, "Well, that's simple," Harbert answered, "For you, it is. . . .We may have worked on a song by Ravel or Debussy as well," he continued. "She especially liked the idea of our just doing it with the piano, as opposed to with a big orchestra." The potential album did not particularly appeal to Melcher until Harbert told him, "Marty, they're all P.D. [public domain]. I will do new arrangements and then you can publish them."

Though it was Harbert's supervisor, Irving Townsend, who produced the Farrell crossover album, he proved instrumental in quashing *I've Got a Right to Sing the Classics.* "It's a cute idea," Townsend told Harbert. "But if the critics take her to task for daring into the classical field, she's going to get upset and we'll never be able to get her to record anything again.'"

Day did record her *Show Time* album during three sessions in February 1960. It had an archetypal selection of familiar tunes written for Broadway shows (except for the rousing title song, penned by Joe Lubin specifically for Day). It wasn't Harbert but Alex Stordahl who supervised the album, which included two hits each from *Annie Get Your Gun, Oklahoma,* and *My Fair Lady*–and singletons from a number of other musicals. None of the album's selections hit closer to home than "Ohio," from *Wonderful Town.* As she sings the song's plaintive refrain, "Why-o, why-o, why-o, why did I ever leave Ohio," Stordahl overdubbed Day, allowing her to add a second part, in effect singing a duet with herself. The combination seems to offer a different, sadder singer who, having left her Ohio home, here meets her original self.

A Woman in Jeopardy

✳

*"I don't want to do this. . . . I want to do gay and happy pictures.
I don't want to experience all this fear. I can't and I won't!"*
—DORIS DAY

ay maintained that she canceled plans to make *Who Was Sylvia?* at Columbia Pictures because she did not want to undertake another comedy on the heels of *Pillow Talk*. She chose instead a film version of *Matilda Shouted Fire*, a play by Janet Green that had been touring the British provinces on its way to London in the winter of 1958. It's a "sort of Hitchcock suspense murder mystery," explained Hedda Hopper, who further revealed that Ross Hunter would be producing it for Universal. The play's absurd title eventually became the far more provocative *Midnight Lace*. It was originally to be shot in London.

Focusing on a suave British businessman's attempt to drive his wealthy American wife (named Kit Preston) to suicide so he might enjoy her fortune with his mistress, the story is reminiscent of the classic film *Gaslight*. Though Rock Hudson was initially mentioned as Day's costar, Melcher wanted Laurence Olivier, and planned to meet with the great British actor upon Olivier's return to Hollywood to complete his work on the gladiator epic *Spartacus*, on December 23, 1959. In the meantime, Hunter flew to New York, where he saw Rex Harrison in Jean Anouilh's play *The Fighting Cock*. Hunter had already decided on two cast members from that Broadway production, Natasha Parry and Roddy McDowall, for *Midnight Lace* before he realized that Harrison would be ideal as Day's villainous husband. Accustomed to hiding his mean-spirited nature behind the comic roles he tended to play, in real life Harrison drove both a mistress (Carole Landis) and a wife (Rachel Roberts) to suicide.

The notoriously arrogant Harrison would later dismiss the film in his memoir, saying he "stumbled into" the role. The subtitle for his memoir,

My Life in Comedy, actually gets to the heart of his real complaint: Had the film been one of Day's "light comedies . . . I could have played the Cary Grant or Rock Hudson part," he wrote, adding, "though I did my best to make the villain of the piece seem debonair, there was not much humor in it."

Midnight Lace was shot at Universal on a forty-day schedule, beginning on March 22, 1960, and concluding on May 16. British character actress Hermione Baddeley, making her American film debut as Dora, the busybody barmaid, was also up for an Oscar (for *Room at the Top*) while working on the picture that spring. On the verge of winning a Tony Award for *The Fighting Cock*, Roddy McDowall went to Hollywood to shoot his scenes at Universal in less than a week. Doris Lloyd, who played McDowall's mother, Nora, in the picture, had played his mother twice before, in *Molly and Me* (1944) and two years later in *Holiday in Mexico*.

Despite working with a very familiar actress, McDowall was probably happier back in New York. Given the story's dark theme, the pedestrian director David Miller realized that his actors were finding the picture intense and "becoming depressed." He lightened the mood one day by rigging a phonograph player so that when Harrison—in accordance with the script—turned it on for a scene, the cast heard him singing "I've Grown Accustomed to Her Face," from his hit musical *My Fair Lady*.

Harrison recalled that Day "found the proceedings such a strain that she had a nervous breakdown during shooting, which stopped production for a bit, after which she credited me and my 'light sense of humor' for helping her keep her sanity while we shot the rest of the picture."

It's hard not to visualize Harrison's often acidic tongue in his cheek as he described Day: "[A] dear girl, a kind girl, and a Christian Scientist. We used to hold what amounted to Christian Science sessions on the set (or so it seemed to me), when all the lights would be put out and the director could be heard telling Doris sotto voce 'God is in the studio, God is in the flowers, God is on the set. . . .' At which point I would wander away and sit down to ponder life and death."

On the plus side, Day declared Universal her "favorite studio" with "the sweetest lot." She especially liked the "lovely" dressing rooms. But given the number of scenes calling upon her to be terrorized—coupled with her tendency to realize the emotions she portrayed in a role—Day's difficulties making *Midnight Lace* would become legendary. What is less well known is that Day had anticipated difficulties with the picture and, in fact, had been reluctant to make it. "I was with her just after she'd read the script of 'Midnight Lace'—the penetrating psychological study of a woman frightened," wrote movie reporter Laura Bascombe. "Well, it was Doris who was frightened. She read the script, reread it and panicked. 'I don't want to do this,' she told me, when I found her one day in her beautiful white den, in a mood as black as ink. 'I want to do gay and happy pictures. I don't want to experience all this fear. I can't and I won't!'"

However, as Day also told Bascombe, "Marty says I'm healthier and in better spirits when I'm working. He's forever manufacturing new things to do, and I'm always screaming about it, but of course he's right. Work for me is a sort of therapy, a way to release this tremendous energy of mine."

In her memoir, Day recalled Melcher being "so insistent" on her undertaking the role of Kit that she finally relented. For the second time, her husband was compelling her to play a character being stalked by her husband. "I should have known better," Day added, "the effect on me of playing the part was even more shattering than in 'Julie.'"

Referring to the most challenging scene for Day, when Kit is trying to convince her husband that she is not fantasizing about being stalked, Ross Hunter recalled, "I remember that she was so great in that scene that she became hysterical and we had to take her home." Before shooting that pivotal scene with Kit's collapse on the staircase, David Miller told Day: "This is the peak. This is where you break. There is no way out. You have to break emotionally, go into complete hysteria. Everything must become unhinged."

As described by Bill Davidson in a cover story on Day in *Look* magazine, her work on "the big scene in the picture" prompted not a "nervous breakdown" so much as a "near collapse. . . . She fell on a stairway, and director David Miller ran over to see if she was all right. She then continued with such frenzy of emotion that one of her co-stars, standing nearby, said to Miller, 'My God, that isn't acting. She really means it.' When the scene was over, the frightened cast and crew rushed over to the prostrate, sobbing form."

Day told Davidson that to project Kit's terror, she thought back to a "horrible experience" she once had when she was home alone. Like Kit, she received a threatening phone call. It was "from a man who had waited on me in a store," she recalled. "I was so frightened that I couldn't hang up the phone, and then I heard footsteps approaching the front door. I bolted the door and shouted, 'Who is it?' A voice said, 'Telegram.' I was afraid to open the door, and I cowered in my room until my husband came home. I nearly screamed with relief when I saw him. He had a telegram in his hand and he said, 'What's this doing out on the doorstep?' When I began to play the part in 'Midnight Lace,' I felt I knew what was going on in the woman's mind." In her memoir, Day also recalled that she "re-created the ghostly abuses of Al Jorden" to convey Kit's terror.

Melcher took his sobbing wife home and put her to bed. "He brought me my dinner on a tray," Day told Hunter the next day. "Then he sat on the edge of the bed, and for three hours, he sang hymns to me until I fell asleep."

* * *

At their annual Golden Globes event, on March 8, 1960, the Hollywood Foreign Press declared Rock Hudson and Doris Day the "world's favorite" actor and actress—"to almost no one's surprise," the *Los Angeles Times* said in its story on the awards. Later in the year, Day was chosen to receive the "Star of the Year" award by Theatre Owners of America. While previous winners included Rock Hudson, Jerry Lewis, William Holden, James Stewart, and Danny Kaye, Day was only the second woman to be so honored, following Deborah Kerr, who had won in 1958.

Day did not fare as well with her nomination for *Pillow Talk* at the 32nd Annual Academy Awards on April 4. She did, however, present an Oscar that year. After Gogi Grant sang a nominated song, "Strange Are the Ways of Love," host Bob Hope said: "Strange indeed are the ways of Hollywood. This year for the first time in the history of the Academy, a young woman is up for an award for putting her head on a pillow. Here's Miss Doris Day." Day wore a white suit designed by Irene for her in *Midnight Lace,* elegantly enhanced by white gloves. Though she was free of jewelry, her eyelashes were obviously false, and, in the style of the day, her hair seemed extra bouffant. She displayed her customary decorum and did not have to concern herself with a letter that Jerry Wald—who produced the ceremony that year—found it necessary to send to female guests: "There will be no cleavage on this year's Oscar Awards show. This was one of the major criticisms we received last year, that the necklines were too low. Most of the complaints came from the Middle West. If you need any help, a wardrobe mistress backstage is equipped with enough lace to make a mummy."

"Doris, you've come a long way since our radio days," Hope said as he greeted the star onstage and congratulated her on her nomination. Referring to her extensive work on his radio show, Day replied, "I owe it all to you, because you gave me my first lines on a stage." The remarks were as scripted as the joke that followed, when Hope mentioned that he thought Day was "going to give this award with Rock, tonight." "Would you believe it," responded Day, referring to *Pillow Talk*, "[t]hat man is still on the phone." Day then gave the Best Song award to James Van Heusen and Sammy Cahn for "High Hopes."

While Day was minutes away from losing the one and only Oscar she would ever be nominated for, *Pillow Talk* managed to win one of the few awards that did not go to *Ben-Hur* that night—for Best Story and Screenplay. (As Cahn and Van Heusen subsequently quipped, "We're glad 'Ben-Hur' didn't have a title song.") Though Audrey Hepburn (*The Nun's Story*) and Elizabeth Taylor (*Suddenly, Last Summer*) had been favored to win, Rock Hudson presented the Oscar for Best Actress to Simone Signoret for *Room at the Top*. "I can't say anything," said the voluptuous French siren. "I wanted to be dignified and all that, but I can't." The win by Signoret, with her openly leftist views, prompted a barrage from a disappointed and irate Hedda Hopper: "I drew the line when Simone Signoret hit the jackpot," Hopper wrote in her syndicated column. "I'm as broadminded as anyone, but that was ridiculous. Let her decorate her mantel with Picasso doves and the like. I got so mad, I upped and resigned from the Academy."

Nor was Day the only nominee for *Pillow Talk* who failed to win a statuette. Thelma Ritter lost in the Supporting Actress category, Frank De Vol lost for his music score, and Richard H. Riedel, Russell A. Gausman and Ruby R. Levitt lost in the Art Direction–Set Decoration category. Ritter, who had been nominated four times before without ever winning, stayed at home, where she had friends over to watch the ceremony on TV. Shelley Winters snatched the Supporting Actress award away from their hostess, for her role in *The Diary of Anne Frank*.

In May, *Modern Screen* ran another cover story on Day, focusing on Terry. A senior in high school, on the verge of graduating, Terry was far from the "Secret Child" the magazine's sensational headline meant to exploit. Though the entire article reads as bogus and unreliable, the reporter, Hugh Burell, did apparently track down Al Jorden, Terry's father, in Cincinnati and uncovered interesting tidbits. "Haven't seen the boy in 12 years now," Jorden said. "I'd like to see my boy. But I haven't been able to."

* * *

When *Please Don't Eat the Daisies* was released, Columbia Records designated the month of April as "Doris Day Month," to promote her records with reportedly "the biggest campaign" they had ever undertaken. And some dubious organization called the National Laugh Foundation selected the film as "the official motion picture for National Laugh Week, April 1–8."

As prominently displayed on the kitchen counter in several of the film's scenes, Melcher had negotiated a product placement deal with Quaker Oats. The film's release featured a national ad announcing the $500,000 tie-in with the breakfast cereal, granting one free movie admission for any child under twelve, accompanied by an adult. "This unique promotion is being kicked-off by extensive national advertising in all the media. The campaign is so designed that virtually every American family should be made aware of PLEASE DON'T EAT THE DAISIES. Here is just a portion of the campaign." It entailed a full-page ad in *Life, This Week, Parade,* and other Sunday supplements, as well as "45 newspapers in 34 key cities" and full-minute ads on TV episodes of *Ozzie and Harriet, Love of Life,* and *As the World Turns.* There were even more national tie-ins with Coca-Cola and North American Van Lines, and suggestions for still further tie-ins with toy stores and pet shops.

The Press Book featured tie-ins with local food stores, via the Quaker Oats connections, "to bring the news to the attention of every adult and child in town!" It also offered thoroughly laid-out suggestions for nine contests to be launched locally through a newspaper or a radio station.

The extensive publicity campaign for *Daisies* is a perfect demonstration that marketing savvy can determine a hit film. Although the movie was well received in the trade papers, reviewers tended to focus more on its box-office prospects than on its artistic ones. "A light and frothy comedy, and boffo family fare. Doris Day and David Niven in top roles will liven its excellent chances in all bookings," predicted *Variety.* "It has all the ingredients to insure it a solid box office reception," Mandel Herbstman wrote in *Film Daily,* where he also cited the "delightful breeziness" of Charles Walters's direction.

The mainstream reviewers were far less engaged. Though *Newsweek* had a feature on Day celebrating her "present exalted status," the accompanying anonymous review was summed up with the ominous phrase "Oopsy-Daisy." In the *New York Times*, the curmudgeonly Bosley Crowther wrote: "Some gentle people may love [these characters] and think the gaudy setting in which they are CinemaScoped and Metrocolored fully to be the ultimate in home felicity. We, an experienced resident in a house full of boys (and dogs), found them to be over-eager, over-witty and overwrought—and also undernourished with the substance of good solid farce. Furthermore, the situation on which the family trouble turns—Pop is a drama critic who develops a tendency to gags instead of honest criticism, which irritates Ma no end—is so completely preposterous that it is no situation at all. Might as well fight over politics."

"[T]he movie certainly isn't very funny," Philip K. Scheuer wrote in the *Los Angeles Times*, where he explained that "Niven makes Mackay an uncommonly truculent kind of fellow and Doris Day seems unusually cross at moments, too."

But given the enormous marketing push it received—and the wide family audiences it appealed to—*Daisies* became a huge hit and the second-biggest money earner for MGM in 1960. (*Butterfield 8* was the first, suggesting that the majority of filmgoers were becoming less inclined toward family fare already, at the beginning of the sixties.) In its "National Box Office Survey" for Easter Week, *Variety* reported that *Daisies* was "proving so strong in current round that it is grabbing first place away from another Metro pic, 'Ben-Hur.'"

Perhaps the single biggest fan of *Please Don't Eat the Daisies* was Paul Brogan, an eight-year-old who lived with his adoptive parents in Concord, New Hampshire. He recalled when his parents took him and his sister to see *Daisies* at a drive-in. "We took the station wagon so my sister and I could go to sleep on an air-mattress in the back, when the adult film came on." The "adult" film was *Psycho*, which made for one of the most unlikely pairings of movies of the period.

Paul already knew who Day was from her ubiquitous rendition of "Que Sera, Sera," and he was excited about finally seeing her on the screen. He recalled wanting to see her in *The Man Who Knew Too Much*, but his parents told him he was too young. He also acquired his propensity for becoming a hardcore movie-star fan from his mother, named Clara, no less, Day's pet name.

After he saw *Daisies*, Paul sent a letter addressed to "Doris Day, Hollywood, California," in which he wrote: "If I didn't have my own mother as a mother, I'd love to have you as a mother." In response, he received an 8-by-10, personally autographed still from the film. Far more valuable was the return address on the label, 713 North Crescent Drive. "From then on, I wrote to that address," recalled Brogan. Over the passing years, he received not only a response from Day to his every letter but also, eventually, a typewriter on which to write his own.

"We were corresponding at the time," recalled Brogan. "Everyone at school thought I had forged all the letters from her, because nobody in Concord, New Hampshire, could have Doris Day as a pen pal. Then, just before graduation, an enormous box arrived. There was a letter inside from Doris. It was a short note: 'Congratulations on your graduation. Here's a typewriter for you to use. I don't want to miss a single word in your letters, and this typewriter will help to make that possible. Love, Doris.' I spent the summer after graduation teaching myself to type with two fingers."

While she was recruiting a new foster son via the U.S. Post Office, Day's own Terry graduated from Beverly Hills High in 1960. There was no question about his going to college. It was a given. He told his parents, however, that he was interested in show business as a career. "Surprisingly, my mother had no objection to this," Terry recalled. "But she wanted me to be in the business end of the entertainment field. She didn't want me to be an actor or a singer." According to Terry, Day and Melcher "had many serious talks" on the subject, adding that, after finishing college, he could become his stepfather's associate. Day specifically wanted Terry to study law, thinking that would be helpful, no matter what else he did. "She didn't want me to be one of those spoiled kids who got ahead only through his parents' pull."

It was Melcher who chose Principia, a Christian Science university, in Elsah, Illinois, where Terry was enrolled in a liberal arts program. He proved more of a playboy than a student, however. He "shared a room, a pink-and-white jeep and some keen games of tennis" with a classmate named Mike Laughlin. "The boys sort of flipped the campus with their white sharkskin tennis shorts, their witticisms and their jeep." With his mother the number-one box office star in the world, Terry couldn't resist all the perks the situation provided, and he floundered as a student.

* * *

In conjunction with the upcoming release of *Midnight Lace, Life* magazine ran a cover story on Day by David Zeitlin with a three-page picture spread.

"She is the eternal freckled-faced girl next door—but with a difference," wrote Zeitlin. "She has more shekels than freckles." But it was in his research notes for the piece that Zeitlin really caught his subject: "[Day] is an enigma. . . . The Melchers eat health food, and are known as party poopers around town. They go to bed at ten o'clock. . . . You cannot categorize her with a phrase or a sentence. . . . She is not too popular socially. . . . A lot of Hollywood people regard her as a square . . . a make-up man hoped he would not be assigned to Doris, not because she was hard to make-up but because he knew she'd try to get him to give up smoking . . . doesn't want certain periods of her life discussed . . . no pix with 18-year-old son . . . frugal. . . . Doris is emotional and high strung. She cries when happy. [She] says she can also weep at the sound of music, a lovely letter or a moving poem.

"Saw 'Midnight Lace' last night, Ross Hunter's pretty successful attempt at tearing a page out of Hitchcock's book," Zeitlin wrote in a memo to his editor, John Stanton. "This is Doris Day's picture, her show. [She] is most convincing in her role. When she starts to crack up, you believe it. But when Doris breaks up and generates tears and hysteria, it is not acting. It is for real. She actually works herself into a state of hysterics, when the scene calls for her to be in such a state. She blows her top on a staircase in one scene in which the anonymous phone call comes through, and does it so thoroughly, they had to suspend shooting for three days afterward. In this respect, and in several others, Miss Day, the freckle-faced blonde with the sunny disposition is quite an enigma. She is a downright paradox."

In his response, Stanton advised Zeitlin to focus "completely on the enigmatical, paradoxical, just plain puzzling woman a la your suggestion cable." An early draft of his piece did just that: "The lady behind the sunshine face is a woman with a mind of her own. What she likes to do she does. What she doesn't want to do, she doesn't. She won't be pushed around. 'Working with Doris is like swimming in meringue,' an associate remarked. 'Everything is sweetness and light, but you can't get anything done. Doris never says 'no,' but she can look at you with a smile that is as negative and final as a Supreme Court decision.' Doris has very firm ideas about how she is photographed. She is concerned about how she looks in the picture, but extremely sensitive about the impressions certain photographs might give."

"I can think about tearing [up] and I do," Day told Zeitlin in the course of describing her acting technique. "I think whatever you need is within you, everything you need is there. I've never been taught how to act. I don't know what my method is. I can't explain it. But when I am called on to do something, I have to do it. And I know I can. I have complete confidence."

The *Saturday Evening Post* was also considering a piece in conjunction with the release of *Midnight Lace* to be written by Pete Martin. But, as revealed in an internal memo, the cost of doing business with the Melchers—who insisted on controlling whatever was written about Day—presented a stumbling block, and the magazine decided to pass up the story. "To get back to this approval bit—they also insist on approving all photos" appeared in an internal memo. Martin concluded: "To say that I don't like Mr. Melcher as much as I like Doris Day is to put it mildly."

In addition to *Life*, however, there were stories in *Look, Good Housekeeping, McCall's,* and *Redbook,* and many other magazines featured articles on Day. The picture had been "pre-sold" to "more than 135,000,000 potential movie-goers!" boasted the Press Book, promoting the film as "a complete change of pace for the number-one blonde actress." A "studio source" added that *Midnight Lace* was the first of Day's films that she had ever watched from beginning to end.

To help sell the picture, the Melchers went to Chicago and then to New York, before spending the weekend with Melcher's relatives in North Adams. Photos of Day arriving at Grand Central Station appeared in the papers on October 2, 1960. One particular fan met Day during this New York visit—a young man by the name of Howard Green. "I was living in the Bronx," recalled Green. "I had seen a centerfold in the Daily News of Doris arriving at Grand Central Station. I called Universal Pictures to try and find out her schedule. I tried to sound as professional as I possibly could. I was just an 18-year-old kid, [but] I wanted to meet her so badly. I spoke to someone in publicity there, and asked what her schedule was. And they actually told me that there was going to be a press conference for the foreign press the following day at the Plaza Hotel [where the Melchers always stayed in New York]. So of course, I made a point of being there early, before she was scheduled to arrive.

"As it turned out, that was the day that her Life Magazine cover came out: 'Sunny Doris Day in a Shivery Role,'" continued Green. "I had that magazine under my arm and I was waiting on the hotel floor where the conference was to be held. My back was turned, and all of a sudden I heard that all-so familiar voice. I turned around and sure enough, there she was, coming down the aisle with a couple of guys—probably from the publicity department at Universal. Oh, I was just shivering in my shoes—she looked so beautiful. I really didn't know what to say, as I held out the magazine, and said, 'Miss Day, would you please sign this for me.' And she gave me that dazzling smile of hers, as she said, 'Of course.' She signed it and then she went into this room for a luncheon."

While in New York promoting *Midnight Lace,* the Melchers had what was falsely reported as their first real battle. Without consulting his wife, Marty had committed her to modeling $150,000 worth of Irene gowns from the picture at a "fashion luncheon" on October 7. The independent Day refused to participate, though she did make what was described in numerous reports as a "6-minute fashion featurette" in "gorgeous color," which exhibitors were invited to show "as a Fashion Extra."

It was also during this New York visit that Day met a woman who, in a couple of years, would become her personal assistant. "When I met Doris, she had just finished making 'Midnight Lace,'" recalled Barbara Flicker. "And she was so frightened making one scene in particular, that she talked about never wanting to do another picture with that kind of terror in it."

Flicker became acquainted with the Melchers through her first husband, Robert Crystal, who was a music scout for Melcher in New York. "Bob and I lived in an apartment behind the Coliseum," said Flicker, referring to the area around Columbus Circle, "in a building that people referred to as 'Tin Pan Alley West.' He had an office in the house, and all these unknown singers were coming in. I don't think he ever got an act that really went somewhere. But then, I don't think Marty gave him any real authority, either."

More specifically, Melcher was keen on discovering a new male singing quartet—like the Four Freshmen, the Ames Brothers, the Four Lads, or the Hi-Lo's—and he recruited Crystal to try to manufacture a new one. According to Flicker, Crystal had jackets for the prospective singers to wear during auditions, and there was a continuous parade of candidates traipsing through their apartment. But according to Flicker, whenever the harmonizing worked, their movements failed to jibe—or vice versa—and Crystal never managed to put a group together.

After growing up in a large Irish family in South Bend, Indiana, Flicker did a stint as an airline stewardess for United Airlines in 1955—"when it was still fun and quite exciting," she said. She was a twenty-eight-year-old model who converted to Judaism before marrying Crystal in September 1960. "It was such an innocent time," recalled Flicker, who, with her husband, would see the Melchers whenever they came to New York. She remembered dining with them in their suite at the Plaza Hotel.

"I also remember when we all went to see 'The Sound of Music' [in October 1960], and we were sitting next to Mamie Eisenhower, who was sound asleep throughout the performance [across the aisle]. And Doris, in an effort to disguise herself, wore a brown wig and a large coat." As reported, Day used a black wig to get around Manhattan. But in contrast to his wife's desire to hide amid the throngs, Melcher assumed a promotional mode. "To take his movie star to the theater, Marty had rented a brown Rolls Royce," Flicker said. "That night, when we were leaving the theater, they all get Doris past this crowd, into the car, and drive away. But they forget me, and I'm standing on the curb.

"A few blocks later, Doris looks around and says, 'Where's Barbara?' And, like in an old slapstick comedy, they come back to the theater, open the back door, I jump in the Rolls, and we make our get-away. I should have realized then, that that was the beginning of Doris saving my life. Because after we moved to Los Angeles, we went to all the ballgames with Doris and Marty. I would go get the hotdogs and Cokes, and Bob and Marty would get Doris past this tremendous crowd, and then I'd have to fight to make my way back with the tray of food. And Doris was always saying, 'Where's Barbara now?'"

As Day herself recalled attending *The Sound of Music*: "I bought this brown wig, figuring nobody'd know me as a brunette. I was getting by just fine, and everything went well until I left my seat and went to the lobby for a cold drink after the first act. There I saw a woman peering at me, and word must have gotten around, because afterward we were mobbed trying to get into the car. The cops out front tried to help."

"She was a star," Flicker remarked, "and everything around her would just stop when she walked into a room. It made for this silence around us—regular noises would just stop. It was creepy. And I don't know how stars handle the loss of being able to go out without makeup on, or just in jeans and a sweatshirt."

According to Flicker, "Marty just wanted to elevate Doris to a whole other level. He told us that from the very beginning, he kept saying to Doris, 'You've got the greatest swayback and the greatest butt in the world. And I'm gonna make you famous, kid.' Marty took the responsibility for doing anything unpleasant. And Doris was this sunny, gifted lady, who didn't want to know about the business end of it. They really separated who did what: Marty had no desire to be a celebrity, and Doris had no desire to sign the checks.

Although Melcher wasn't "a mean man," Flicker contended, Day was "scared silly of him, because he was really big, and he had a kind of a hawk-like face. He was a big, clumsy schmuck, while Doris was just adorable." According to Flicker, long before the phrase "good-cop, bad-cop" was coined, "They really did have an act going. Doris and Marty were like a perfect team. I mean, Marty seemed more like a 'handler' than a husband. If Doris didn't like someone in makeup or hair or something, she'd just tell Marty, and that person would be gone the next day. Doris would never show any displeasure around anybody. She made her life all about playing a 'good' girl."

"Doris hardly ever came to New York," said Mitch Miller, who recalled taking her and Melcher to dinner at a fashionable French restaurant, possibly Le Veau d'Or on East 60th Street. "I get the check and sign for it, and then Marty says, 'Can I have the receipt?' You can't make up stories like that."

Melcher's rough façade, his strutting bravado—which frightened not only Flicker, but also many he worked with during his career as a Hollywood czar—was, to some degree, a defense mechanism and a tactic. He cultivated it over the years to go head-to-head with the cutthroats and backstabbers in the music and movie industries in which, thanks to his wife's talents, he quickly rose to the top. (Sam Weiss said Melcher was actually a "namby-pamby" and a "coward.") Even though he was a Jew in charge of a gentile who was an all-American icon, Melcher never felt fully comfortable in Hollywood. The greater irony is that the biggest thief and con man he dealt with turned out to be his own lawyer, Jerome Rosenthal, even though Melcher did not discover this treachery until shortly before his own premature death.

"Marty would always be telling you how important he was, and how powerful he was. But he wasn't," recalled Guy Webster, Terry's close friend since childhood. "He was riding strictly on Doris's charms. He was very crude. He was not a wheeler-dealer. He turned everything over to Rosenthal."

Day herself would allude to her husband's gullibility time and again during a series of interviews in the summer of 1960, which produced one of the most revealing stories about the Melchers. It appeared in the September issue of *Photoplay*. Day's face was blown up on the cover, her coiffed blonde hair appearing to bounce alongside a vertical headline that sounded even more provocative than the piece would prove to be: "Is Doris Sick of Being a Good Wife?" Based on talks with both of the Melchers, the article opens with Day's confiding, "I'm a difficult character to live with. . . . Marty should know, he's been living with me for nine years."

In the piece, Day emphasized, "I am too fanatic about cleanliness, I know it. I'm sure no man wants his wife to be all that clean—but I can't help it. I can't stand dirty ash-trays, and clothes lying around on chairs all over the place. I loathe messy kitchens. I can't bear to eat in a strange restaurant unless I can peep into the kitchen." The topic prompted her to confide problems she had raising a son. "Terry would come in dirty from playing outside and it bothered me out of all proportion. Marty would calmly send him up to wash and then he'd say to me, 'Hon, a boy has to get dirty. I used to get dirty all the time. It comes off in water.'"

During the interview, Day playfully tossed a pillow at her husband on the couch. Melcher confirmed that his wife was a "neatnik," but added that "her desk is such a mess that [I go] crazy trying to sort out bills and such." He was also annoyed by her "habit" of telling "little fibs." "You even lie about the ages of your dogs," Melcher said during a joint interview. "I can't bear to think of them as getting old," Day responded. The article also reiterated Day's lifelong tendency to "sometimes 'tune out' of a conversation," and was extremely revealing when Day reported, "I tell [Marty] everything—but I had to learn how. I didn't have what he calls the ability to communicate my secret feelings."

To another reporter, Melcher recalled driving with his wife when he was stopped for going through a traffic light as it was turning red. "The officer was very polite [and] I was very polite. No trouble at all. Then Doris suddenly starts talking to herself—out loud. 'Well!' she says, 'I'll never do another benefit show for the police around here!' So the officer peered into the window, gave her a look and said, 'I heard you, lady.' And he promptly added 'uncooperative,' on the ticket—which cost me an extra fine!"

*   *   *

Watching *Midnight Lace* with the foreknowledge that Kit's husband is the man stalking her makes the mechanics of the plot seem flimsy upon a second viewing, and the film has not withstood the test of time well. Though the initial reviews proved wide-ranging, most embraced Day's star turn in yet another genre—murder mystery. In the *New York Times*, Bosley Crowther said: "Miss Day gives a golden imitation of a love-struck heiress scared out of her wits, and Mr. Harrison is virtually sterling as her chin-up, stout-fellow spouse." Crowther, however, was less happy with the story, and felt that the film "shortchanges the wealth-bedazzled viewer only in the way it concludes." The review in the *New Yorker* was contemptuous and dismissive, claiming that the film "trifles with our emotions. . . . If you like tying to guess which of half a dozen weirdly assorted people is a potential murderer and if you like being scared an infinitesimal way out of your wits before you reach a happy, idiotic ending, then by all means join the long queue at the Music Hall."

Arthur Knight proved far more upbeat in the *Saturday Review*: "Doris Day switches from sunny charm to stark terror with virtuoso skill [and] the film's air of well-bred urbanity notably augments the shock value of each new turn of events." And so was John L. Scott in the *Los Angeles Times*: "While the whole business is pretty unnerving, Miss Doris Day remains one of our favorite film heroines—frightened or otherwise—and we suffered right along with her. . . . The feminine star scores heavily as a nice, jolly girl frightened almost out of her mind."

Day herself also wowed Archer Winston in the *New York Post*: "Doris Day, let us be early ones to confess it, gives one of her best performances, ranging from her usual well-dressed charm into phases of hysteria which she has never before achieved"; Harrison Carroll in the *L.A. Herald Express*: "Miss Day's forte may be comedy but she gives an outstanding dramatic performance here"; and Alton Cook in the *New York World Telegram and Sun*: "[Day is] so appealingly frail and fragile, she inspires a cheerleading interest in her ultimate survival."

It's surprising to learn—from Day herself, no less—that a number of fans complained about her undertaking the part of Kit. "It's funny that so many people seem to identify closely with me or with the roles I play. This really came home to me when I did a serious dramatic role in . . . 'Midnight Lace,' with Rex Harrison. In the picture, Rex was trying to do away with me and I thought it was a good change from the comedies but the fans didn't think so. We received so many letters telling us that they couldn't stand to see me suffer, that they were suffering with me. The letters made me feel terrible."

The role did, however, generate a good deal of Oscar buzz. Dorothy Kilgallen was one of the first to predict that Day "might well win an Academy Award for her emotional performance," as did Earl Wilson in his column, in which he claimed that Day "gives the kind of performance that Oscars are made of." In January, journalist Mike Connolly contributed to the Oscar buzz: "It's a little early to tell for sure but this seems to be the way the Oscar winds are blowing this year. Academy Award voters appear to favor Doris Day as best actress for 'Midnight Lace,' Burt Lancaster as best actor for 'Elmer Gantry.'" When Day failed even to be nominated, Louella Parsons expressed the outrage many felt: "The Academy Award nominations came out pretty much as expected with the exception of Doris Day missing for 'Midnight Lace.' She was on almost every published poll of possibilities. It's purely personal with me, but I'm sorry that Melina Mercouri won out over Doris [as a nominee]."

Yet Day's stardom emerged brighter than ever. Right after Christmas, the *Associated Press* announced that she had been named "Screen's Top Moneymaker" "by the men who run the nation's theaters." Given her three "blockbuster" pictures that year—*Pillow Talk, Midnight Lace,* and *Please Don't Eat the Daisies,* she "won the honor by a wide margin." Those three pictures had, in fact, already grossed $31 million. The runners-up, in order, were Rock Hudson, Cary Grant, Elizabeth Taylor, Debbie Reynolds, Tony Curtis, Sandra Dee, Frank Sinatra, Jack Lemmon, and John Wayne. "Miss Day is the first woman to win the top spot since 1943." She was also, in 1960, "the world's best-selling female vocalist."

Given the success of *Midnight Lace,* there was talk of Day doing a duets album with costar Rex Harrison. When she mentioned this to Harbert, Day jokingly said, "Rex will sing and I'll do the Sprechstimme"—or talk-singing, as Harrison famously did in *My Fair Lady.* "Many artists don't know what's right for them, which is why they need an A&R man," added Harbert. "But like Sinatra, Doris always knew." She also, unfortunately, always deferred to Melcher.

But at the time, Melcher parlayed his wife's success into what was promising to be a major arrangement with Columbia Pictures, "calling for $26,000,000 in two years." As further described in the *Hollywood Citizen News,* it involved an eight-picture deal, four of which had "Miss Day" as star, the other four with Melcher as producer. The first was to be *Roar Like a Dove,* directed by Richard Quine. But Columbia found Melcher's demands excessive, and in little over a month *Variety* reported that the negotiations with the studio were over. As Melcher explained to the *Los Angeles Times,* "We package and produce; the studios finance and distribute. We own half the picture in most cases." Melcher also said that his wife had offers "up to $1 million" to do a Vegas show, which Day wasn't crazy about. "'I don't think I'd enjoy working night after night,' Doris added. She smiled. 'After all, I'm a day girl.'"

But as *Variety* also reported, Day's new five-year contract with Columbia Records had gone through, with a $100,000 yearly guarantee and a separate arrangement for Melcher as "prexy of Arwin Records, whereby he'll produce recordings for Columbia (not those of his wife), which in turn will be distributed by that company." Day had been "romanced by several other top labels, and came 'very, very close' to handshaking a good deal at Capitol," added the story in the trade magazine, referring to the label whose top pop artists included Sinatra, Nat King Cole, Peggy Lee, and Dean Martin.

Such news was quickly followed by another significant event for Day—which proved a landmark. "The ghost of Hollywood's legendary glamour stalked the forecourt of the Grauman's Chinese Theatre yesterday drawing the largest turnout of press, photographers and people for the traditional 'footprint' ceremony since it was first started by the late Sid Grauman back in 1927," proclaimed the *Hollywood Reporter*. Day was, the story emphasized, "the magnet for the biggest gathering in the history of this event." According to George Gibson, who had staged the Grauman event for three decades, Clark Gable had previously drawn the largest crowd (in 1937) but Day "far outstripped that gathering." Simultaneously, the Hollywood Chamber of Commerce presented Day with its "Star of Stars" award.

In the midst of Day's success, elite director William Wyler considered her for Katharine Hepburn's costar in his remake of Lillian Hellman's daring play *The Children's Hour*. (Eventually the parts went to Shirley MacLaine and a different Hepburn—Audrey.) Moreover, Melcher was negotiating with David Stillman, who owned the rights to *Dark Victory*, for Day to do a remake of that classic Bette Davis 1939 tearjerker. Day also won her sixth consecutive Laurel Award, breaking the record held by Walt Disney.

The controversy over the Motion Picture Academy's failure to recognize Day's performance in *Midnight Lace* was reignited after Elizabeth Taylor took home the Oscar for *Butterfield 8* on April 17. Louella Parsons declared it "a rotten shame" that Day was not even nominated and mentioned that she had received "hundreds of letters" from fans, protesting the Academy's mistake in overlooking Day. The oversight would prove all the more galling, considering that much of Hollywood felt Taylor's victory had more to do with her personal ailments and travails than her overwrought performance. Though Day did not attend the ceremony, she lent a coat designed for her by Irene, who was nominated for the Costume Design award for *Midnight Lace*. It was worn by a model, and promptly returned to Day after the ceremony.

There was equally dismaying news on the home front, when Terry announced that he was dropping out of college after his freshman year. Terry's disgruntled stepfather got him an unwelcome, "jack-of-all-trades" job at the William Morris Agency—delivering mail, running errands, etc.—upon the young man's return to North Crescent Drive from Principia College. Terry wasn't happy there. "Most of the stars managed by the agency were chronic complainers and egomaniacs. Nothing suited them. Naively, I expected them to be like Mom."

There was one person associated with celebrity to whom the six-foot, two-hundred-pound, nineteen-year-old Terry did relate, Dean Martin's daughter Claudia, a high school senior. "The first time I dated Terry, he took me to my brother Craig's going-away party," said Claudia, who continued, "We go to dinner and go to a movie or stay home—do anything we feel like. He's nice. He has a very good sense of humor. He's very witty. He loves parties. I've gone to some with him." Claudia was also seeing Mike Laughlin, one of Terry's friends, at the time. "Terry went to school with him," Claudia said. "He introduced him to me. . . .Terry knows. It doesn't bother him."

*   *   *

During three studio sessions the first week of May 1961, Day recorded an album devoted to dreams and dreamers. It took its name from "I Have Dreamed," the soaring ballad written for *The King and I* by Rodgers and Hammerstein. The recordings were supervised by Harbert, who also wrote the album's first song, "I Believe in Dreams." Day's melancholy delivery of the slowly climbing melody underscores the song's complexity. The album also included "All I Do Is Dream of You," which Day projects in the voice of a little girl, as well as her wistful renderings of "When I Grow Too Old to Dream" and "I'll Buy That Dream." As usual, Day proved masterful at locating the sweetness of yearning.

The highest praise for the album arrived in the form of a letter from Richard Rodgers, the title song's composer, declaring it "the most beautiful version" he had ever heard. "Doris liked to take things at her own tempos, and no one had ever done ['I Have Dreamed'] quite that slowly before," James Harbert said. "I did something of a Delius-like arrangement for her on it." Day's decided preference for slower tempos accentuated the feeling she conveys at times that she is making love to her listeners. That sense of seduction was enhanced by the freedom and spontaneity she brought to her recording sessions. "I would arrange a song to be in rhythm, but she would decide to sing it freely, paying no attention to how long each note was supposed to be held," recalled Harbert, "just whatever suited her fancy, at the moment. She'd suddenly go out of tempo, and I had to completely re-write the arrangements right on the spot. Just try and count the way she sang 'Secret Love'—it's all over the place."

Harbert recalled Day's rejecting a song he proposed for the *Dream* album—Cole Porter's "Use Your Imagination," selected because it "hadn't been recorded to death," according to Harbert, and for the suitability of its lyrics. "If I remember correctly, she mentioned something about 'the song not being one of [Porter's] best,'" he added.

Day was being considered for the film version of Cole Porter's *Can-Can*. Harbert recalled that Melcher invited him to attend a meeting at Arwin's offices with Porter's agent to discuss the project. Melcher began, "You know, Cole Porter would be very fortunate to get Doris Day to do a film, but she doesn't come cheap." "Cole Porter doesn't care about money," replied his agent. "If you're going to speak to me on this level, I'm leaving. Very nice to meet you, young man." After he walked out the door, Melcher told Harbert, "Now that's an agent."

Shortly after she recorded her album, Day received letters from relatives and friends, sharing their distress over news out of Cincinnati. With the revealing headline "DORIS DAY DAD WED TO NEGRO," UPI reported on May 22, 1961, that the day before, William Kappelhoff had married Luvenia Williams Bennett, the black woman who helped run his tavern. (Their marriage license was dated May 16.) It was William's third marriage and Luvenia's second. She had only just obtained a divorce from her first husband, Harold Bennett, on March 24, and had a ten-year-old son named Adrian. (Kappelhoff's second wife, Freda, died in 1958.) "I sent her a telegram," Kappelhoff recalled, referring to his daughter. "We hoped to see Doris, and we sent our love. She didn't send us a note of congratulations or a gift."

"It wasn't so much the fact that she might not have approved of me," Luvenia said years later. "It was more the hurt my husband suffered when she didn't even acknowledge our telegram, or get in touch with us.

I hurt for my husband but, the truth is, I feel sorrier for Doris." Luvenia would also say, "We would have been happier if she had come right out and voiced her disapproval. . . . Not saying anything was worse."

While hoping to keep news about her father's marriage from gossip mongers, Day had another reason for her silence, as Kappelhoff revealed: "Doris tried to get me and her mother together again. I couldn't do it—even for her. But I love Doris. I admire her gumption and pep. I hope one day she'll accept Luvenia and me, because we're happy."

*   *   *

With her arms wrapped around a white rectangular column, a bemused Day, her face aglow with freckles, appeared on the cover of the June 20 issue of *Look* magazine. She sported a pixie-ish hairdo and wore a powder-blue cardigan sweater. While promising to reveal "[h]er fortune, her fears, her failures, her faith," the accompanying article by Bill Davidson set out to debunk Day's girl-next-door image by focusing on her "complexity."

Davidson reported the Melchers were "conservatively estimated" to be worth $6 million and added that they lived on a "comparatively modest scale." He further cited a $26 million deal that Melcher had made with Columbia Pictures for his wife to star in eight pictures—"in addition to several independent productions."

In his most surprising declaration—attributed to nameless "associates"—Davidson described Day's lifelong tendency to seem to suddenly go blank. "You can be talking to Doris, and she's gay and charming, and suddenly there's a vacant, faraway look in her gray-blue eyes, and you've been dismissed from her mind. She has tuned you out." And he quoted costumer Irene regarding a typical evening with the Melchers. "You're invited to dinner at their house, and generally there's another couple there—maybe Audrey Hepburn and Mel Ferrer. There are no cocktails. It's carrot juice at 5:45, dinner at 6, dessert from Doris's soda fountain—where the bar used to be—at 6:45, a movie shown on their living-room screen at 7, and home to bed at 9."

Day was becoming increasingly annoyed with the impossibility of living anything akin to a normal life. The Melchers visited North Adams early in October 1961. A crowd reportedly numbering 150 people gathered once Day was noticed "casually" visiting a clothing store in Williamstown late one afternoon. "Concerned that the large crowd pressing into the store might cause damage to the spanking new show cases or that someone might be pushed through a window in the crush, Williamstown police were summoned."

Having decided to purchase a second home in the Berkshires, the Melchers thought they had found just the place in Williamstown. It was a onetime dairy farm that featured a comfortable, rambling ten-room New England farmhouse, two barns, and garages on a 136-acre estate. "They were so favorably impressed that Harry Melcher, after their departure, began the negotiations which have led to its purchase by him," said a report in the local *Transcript*, referring to Martin's brother. "If they decide they don't like it and don't want it, I'll consider it just an investment," Harry explained. Melcher's "surprise" Christmas gift to his wife was not the house, but a poodle puppy, whom she named Tinker.

* * *

Back in Los Angeles, Day recorded a ravishing album called *Duet* with classical musician and top jazz pianist Andre Previn in only two studio sessions on November 30 and December 16 totaling nine and a half hours. But a good deal of rehearsal time had been spent preparing for these recordings during the winter with James Harbert. Although it was Irving Townsend who first signed Previn as an artist and then thought of pairing him with Day, Harbert initially rehearsed some of the songs with Day.

Sensing she was intimidated by the prospect of working with Previn, Harbert told her, "'Sure he may be a genius. But he's a person, just like the rest of us.' She was very nervous about the whole thing. She needn't have been. He stood in awe of her, as so many of us were."

According to Harbert, "Andre came back from their meeting saying, 'What is the scene at that house? Can't they afford a decent piano? I'm trying to play this thing and the notes stick. What do you do? How do you play for her?' He continued: 'these two dogs come in and they start farting, and I don't know what to do or say.'" Trying to make light of the situation, Harbert formed his response as a joke, telling Previn: "It's a new technique: You not only have to push the keys down, you also have to lift them up."

After returning to the house on North Crescent several times, Previn registered yet another complaint with Harbert: He had left behind the music for five or six songs, which disappeared. Day claimed to have no idea where they were. "There's a rule," explained Harbert: "Marty Melcher must publish all her new songs. He must have flushed them down the toilet." Harbert added, "I was having a little fun with the situation, but Andre was losing his sense of humor about it and it was getting pretty tense. He said, 'How do you deal with it when the music keeps disappearing?' I told him, 'I have ten copies of everything.'"

In the end, the album would include several of Previn's songs, with lyrics by his wife, Dory: "Yes," "Daydreaming," and "Control Yourself." *Duet* would also feature the spacious tempos Day was partial to, with "Wait Till You See Him" and "Falling in Love Again" proving particularly slow.

When Day arrived for the recording session on November 30, she had a pamphlet with her, "Voices of the Voiceless." It had heartbreaking photos of homeless animals, and clearly she had been crying. "She and I hugged," Harbert recalled. In contrast, Day and Previn's relationship remained "stilted." "Finally, Andre saw she was holding something, and he tried to break the ice by saying, 'What do you have there?' In an oddly serious tone, she said, 'I think this is something we should all read,' as she handed it to him.

"He opened it up, and he was speechless—I could see that it had thrown him. Well, they finally get out on the floor, and made a take or two, and it didn't go so well. They do a break, and he came up to me in the hall, and he said, 'What the hell is that pamphlet she gave me? Is she trying to tell me I'm an animal or what?' I said, 'Andre. For God's sake, she's an animal lover.'

"It took me a lot of doing with him to say, 'Listen, I've worked with her for three years and I know her very well. She was nervous about working with you.' And he said, 'Well, I'm getting nervous about working with her. She's trying to put me down.' I had to convince him that the pamphlet had no personal meaning.

"Well, after the false starts during the first hour or so, he settled down, she settled down, and they made a terrific album. But Irving Townsend was even concerned, at one point, that Andre might walk out."

*   *   *

In view of his wife's ongoing status as the number one star, Melcher became even more protective of her work time. In the process, he reduced still further any shred of a personal life she might have had—or yearned for. "During her heyday, Terry wanted to say 'good morning' or 'goodbye' to his mother," Guy Webster recalled of his daily visits with Terry. "But Marty wouldn't let him see her, and Terry could only talk to his mother by intercom. I witnessed this many times. That became the only way he could communicate with her. He had a need for love and tenderness, which he found with my mother. My mother became his confidante and surrogate mother. He was comfortable at our house, and spent a lot of time there, because his house was basically closed off to him. They had to keep it clean and white, and there was no place for him to mess it up.

"He grew up without any motherly love," continued Webster. "And Marty, being an authoritarian figure, taught him all of his worst traits, like never picking up a tab, and never having any money with him. When you don't have any money, somebody else has to pay the bill. So Terry was penurious his whole life, and never gave anything. He would join clubs on his mother's name, and never pay a thing. We used to have a term for such behavior, which was actually borrowed from Marty: 'America's Guest.'"

22

"Even More Shekels Than Freckles"

—✳—

"If I'm such a legend then why am I so lonely? If I'm a legend, then why do I sit at home for hours staring at the damned phone?"
—JANIS JOPLIN

Billed in the Press Book as "a champagne chaser" to *Pillow Talk*, *Lover Come Back* did all it could to duplicate the formula of its predecessor—in hopes of replicating its success. Not only did it pair Doris Day with Rock Hudson again, it also teamed them with Tony Randall as a sidekick once more. The story was even based on similar plot developments, with Hudson again playing a character pretending to be someone he's not.

One key person who rebelled against the formulaic nature of *Lover Come Back* was director Michael Gordon, who, having directed *Pillow Talk*, chose to pass on its clone. "It seemed so similar, I thought people would think they're just repeating themselves," explained Gordon, whose refusal of the assignment provided yeoman director Delbert Mann with his first opportunity to work with Day. Given the picture's huge success, Gordon would come to regret his decision. (While it cost approximately $2.5 million to produce, *Lover* grossed $8.5 million in domestic showings alone.)

Hudson's participation did not come cheap. Though Melcher had successfully blocked Hudson from receiving a producing credit on *Pillow Talk*, he now had to relent to win him back for the follow-up. *Lover Come Back* was coproduced by Universal and 7 Pictures Corporation, Hudson's recently formed independent company, which had already produced *Come September* starring Hudson, Gina Lollobrigida, Sandra Dee, and Bobby Darin.

Though Hudson continued to adore Day as much as she did him, like
many others who worked with her, he grew to resent Melcher. While referring to Melcher as "Farty Belcher," Hudson's manager, Henry Willson, won
an important battle for his client, who ultimately received a million-dollar
share of the profits on this particular picture.

In the fanciful farce, Day played Carol Templeton and Hudson played
Jerry Webster—advertising executives at rival firms, both vying for the
same big account. The plot revolves around a "miracle product" called
"VIP." After making TV commercials for this nonexistent item, Webster
is compelled to have it invented. As described by Linus Taylor, the scientist hired to create VIP, "It will bring relief to the suffering, joy to the
depressed, inspiration to the artistic and peace to the world. And, it will
sell for only ten cents." A brightly wrapped piece of candy, VIP has the
same effect as "a triple martini."

When Carol meets Webster, she mistakes him for Linus, and he plays
along with her folly. Carol wants to sleep with Linus/Webster and does
all she can to seduce him, flying in the face of the myth—which would
continue well beyond this film—that Day only played characters protective of their virginity. As in *Pillow Talk*—and indeed in several of the romantic comedies to follow *Lover Come Back*, in which Day portrayed married women—there was nothing virginal about her characters. It would
become a permanent cultural conceit that had no basis in fact.

Having hit it off so well on their first picture, Hudson and Day were
fully at ease when they began work on *Lover Come Back*. Their playful affection only deepened as evidenced by their pet names for each other, including Zelda, Murgatroyd, and Ernie. They also had a shared fantasy life,
pretending to be a couple on a bowling team, or having taken a hayride
with a gang the night before. In one game they played for months, they
kept inventing ridiculous-sounding names of places where they were ostensibly building summer homes, and they would give each other regular
progress reports on their development.

Whether they realized it or not, another game they played spoke directly to why they related—and identified—so strongly with each other.
It was during the making of *Lover Come Back* that Day and Hudson
started sending each other letters under false signatures, as if they had
been written by anonymous fans. As reported in a *Life* magazine cover
story on the thirty-seven-year-old Hudson, the two stars "broke down
in mid-kiss" while filming their beach scene in the picture, when Day

suddenly recalled a "fan" letter she had recently received from Hudson with the trite and "silly" question, "What do you think of when you act a love scene?"

There was a serious and subtle undercurrent to such playacting and tomfoolery, however. Not only were both Day and Hudson number one at the box office, they were now icons whose images were diametrically opposed to their real selves. Each knew that their fans believed them to be people they were not—he a macho male, she a perpetual virgin. By constantly changing their identities with and for each other, they were sending up the whole conundrum—the paradox in which they daily found themselves. The many false identities they gave themselves and each other became their humorous, if pathetic, way of trying to be "real" with each other. In this respect, as in others, Day and Hudson were the very embodiment of the myths that Hollywood was forever churning out.

But Day and Hudson could also be as genuine and "in the moment" with each other as they could be with anyone else. As Randall recalled, when they watched the rushes of the film's beach scene, "[T]here was one take, where [Rock] leaned over—and one ball came out of his trunks. And then went back in. We said, 'Hey, play that again.' We were just shrieking and screaming. It nearly got into the picture."

The film's title song, by Frank DeVol and Alan Spilton, caused problems when *Lover Come Back* was made in the winter of 1961. "Doris didn't even want to do a title song, but she always deferred to what she thought was Marty's superior business sense," said James Harbert, "even though she had good instincts of her own." While adding that DeVol did a lot of arrangements for Day, Harbert continued, "Frank was terrific: He was quick and businesslike. He called us up on the phone and said, 'Do you have that opening tune rehearsed? Would you just play it for me over the telephone so I could get the tempo?' He said he would make the arrangement so that each frame would be synchronized with the costly cartoon that was being made for the main title."

Unfortunately, when the cartoon was finished and they went into the studio to record the song, they discovered it was too slow. "I can't record it that way," Day said. "It stinks at that tempo." Melcher encouraged Harbert to tell Day it would be fine: "She says that if you approve, she'll do it." But Harbert hesitated. "Then the vice presidents started coming in," he recalled. "I remember Marty coming over and saying to me, 'Do you want a job at Universal with these VIPs here?'" But Harbert held his ground. He told Melcher, "If I tell her it will be fine, she'll know that I'm lying and she'll never trust me again."

While the bigwigs were hashing it out, the orchestra disbanded. "They knew there was a hassle and they turned into a bunch of kids—playing cards and telling jokes," Harbert continued. "They knew they didn't have to play for a while—if at all." Finally, Harbert told Day, "It *is* the wrong tempo. But I don't think it matters, because the song isn't going to go anywhere, anyhow. It'll be pleasant enough, but the song doesn't have a chance in hell of selling two records—not even to your mother."

Without a definitive decision, the executives had other business to attend to and left about an hour later. In the meantime, Day had gone into the studio, where the orchestra members were milling around, and sat by herself, sulking, while Melcher, Harbert, and the recording engineer were left in the recording room. Indicating the control panel, Melcher asked which switch would allow him to communicate with the orchestra. According to Harbert, "The engineer almost had a nervous breakdown, because he had all his balances set, and Marty was just like an elephant, punching buttons, when he happened to hit the right one." After Melcher announced, "Playback 401A"—assigning the song a "phony 'take' number"—the orchestra members began to pick up their instruments. Day rose from her chair, looked at Harbert through the glass window, and shrugged in resignation, her hands up in the air.

When the recording was finished, Melcher said to Harbert, "Ask me how you become a producer." Harbert played along and Melcher replied, "The first person that makes a move is the producer." "It's a line I've used a lot ever since," added Harbert. "Despite all the bad things that have been said about Marty, you had to enjoy his humor. I'm one of the people who, despite all, liked Marty. His I-have-to-own-everything tactics—that's just the way predatory capitalism works in this country. But I found him amusing."

When Day performed her second song for *Lover Come Back*, "Should I Surrender," she sang it live on the set while Harbert played the piano. "I used to play for her on the sets, because she preferred singing live than lip-syncing to a pre-record," he said.

✳   ✳   ✳

The promotional campaign for *Lover Come Back* was worthy of the Madison Avenue ad men the film was satirizing. *Wonderful Day*, a new album

featuring both songs from the movie, was promoted on "10,000,000 packages [of] Imperial Margarine on sale in every store and super-market."
The $3.98 album could be "yours for only $1 and 2 large crowns from
the fronts of 2 Imperial packages." Still another professional "disc" was
prepared for radio stations, containing "personal interviews" with Hudson
and Day, including "interesting anecdotes about their lives and the making
of 'Lover Come Back' . . . in their own words."

   All of the attention worked. As reported in *Variety*, *Lover Come Back*
took in $440,000 in one week, when it opened in February 1962. "Some
idea of how much biz this means is seen in the fact that it is about
$200,000 ahead of its nearest rival . . . 'West Side Story.'" It was also a
big hit with reviewers, a number of whom thought it superior to *Pillow Talk*, which they all knew it was imitating. In the *Los Angeles Times*,
Philip K. Scheuer found it "a much funnier picture. [It] is, like its predecessor, a sex comedy—only more so. . . . Both stars perform briskly and
perceptively."

   "Mr. Hudson and Miss Day are delicious," Bosley Crowther wrote
in the *New York Times*, "he in his big sprawling way, and she in her
wide-eyed, pert, pugnacious, and eventually melting vein." In his ecstatic
review, Crowther said that " 'Pillow Talk' was but a warm-up for this
springy and spirited surprise, which is one of the brightest, most delightful satiric comedies since 'It Happened One Night.' [The script] has some
of the sharpest and funniest situations you could wish and some of the
fastest, wittiest dialogue that has spewed out of a comedy in years."

                          *   *   *

Unhappy with his job as an apprentice at the William Morris agency,
Terry secretly pursued his real ambition to be a singer by making a demo
record of an original song called "That's All I Want." (According to one
report, he borrowed $300 from a college friend to make the recording;
according to another, his musically inclined friend Jack Nitzsche provided half of the advance.) "I broke the news to my mother at the dinner
table," recalled Terry. "She reacted as I was afraid she would. 'Oh, no,' she
said. 'You haven't really made a record, have you?'" It was only after Day
went to bed that Melcher listened to his stepson's recording. His positive
response emboldened Terry to approach his mother again. He went to
her bedroom and then brought her into the den. "She sat there, quite
tense, while we put on the record and started it," Terry said. "A look of

surprise came over her face and she began to relax. When it was over, she turned to me and there was that broad smile on her face. 'Terry, was that really you?' she asked. 'I can't believe it. It's good.'"

"My mother and dad didn't take my singing seriously until they heard my demo record," Terry told another reporter. "They were stunned. Neither of them knew I could sing a note." The twenty-year-old Terry also claimed, "I spent a year at Principia College . . . and decided I was wasting my time. I knew what I wanted—show business. . . . My folks told me I would regret leaving college, but so far I think I'm ahead."

At Day's urging, James Harbert took Terry under his wing at Columbia Records. "Doris was kind of like an older sister to Terry," reported Harbert, confirming what a number of other colleagues had already observed. "But I thought it was kind of a nice relationship for a mother and son. She was hipper than most mothers, and she was light-hearted with him." She was also, according to Harbert, "worried about Terry and his career. She would say, 'What is Terry going to do?' He would come in and plink at the piano, for me, and sing a little bit. I could see that he was really into the new pop, rock business. It was his era. He knew the groups. I could also see that he would have to become more disciplined. So I said, 'Why don't you come in and work as a trainee, under me?'

"I went to Irving Townsend and said it would be nice if we could hire Terry Melcher," continued Harbert. "You know, the whole business was changing in those days, and he hung out with those groups. For me, it was a little bit wild and woolly. I finally made some money for Columbia Records with the New Christy Minstrels, which I developed. But he was into the rock scene, going to all the clubs. I said, 'That's great. But you've still got to learn how the business works: Who does the promotions. . . . Who does the distribution. . . . How to handle a session and not to waste money while the clock's running.'"

Terry began by studying at Columbia's trainee producers program in New York. Before becoming a record producer, he recorded songs, initially under the name Terry Day. His first song, "That's What I Want," was released with "I Waited Too Long" on the flipside. His mother did her best to promote the 45, without much success. But he could not shake his mother's identity from his own. "When Terry did his own record, I told him, 'There's only one thing wrong: You've got to go on the road to promote it,'" recalled Harbert. "'You've also got to identify yourself as the son of Doris Day.'" As much as Terry wanted to avoid building himself up by relying on his mother's name, Harbert compelled him to do just that.

Terry would create the band Bruce & Terry with friend and songwriter Bruce Johnston, before they formed the Rip Chords and recorded a Top 10 hit with "Hey Little Cobra." (Johnston later joined the Beach Boys.)

* * *

Several people who had recently helped establish Day at the height of her powers and success teamed up again on her next picture, *That Touch of Mink*. Having helmed *Lover Come Back*, Delbert Mann returned as director and so did Stanley Shapiro as cowriter (now with Nate Monaster) and as coproducer (with Melcher). It may seem surprising that her good friend Rock Hudson would not make the film, Day's twenty-ninth, with her. But as Cary Grant biographer Marc Eliot noted, Melcher "felt that Hudson had gotten too much credit and Day too little for the previous films' successes, and as the Hudson characters were always described as Cary Grant types, he decided to go for the real thing."

Getting Grant, however, proved far more expensive than Arwin Productions had bargained for. After Grant turned him down several times, Melcher had to include him as a "partner" who shared in the film's profits, as he had with Hudson on *Lover Come Back*. For Grant, it was a shrewd maneuver; *Mink* would become the debonair star's second-highest-grossing film—after *Operation Petticoat*, which was also written by Shapiro. Grant would ultimately earn $4 million from his involvement with *That Touch of Mink*. But he was not happy working on the film.

Nor did he like the picture's title. He considered mink passé and preferred the alternate name, *Warm Heart, Cold Feet*, which had been under consideration. (Day gravitated toward another inferior working title, which offended people at the production code office, *Not Tonight, Catherine*.) Shooting then was delayed because Grant was unhappy with the set design. He tried to make the environment more familiar and comfortable by placing seven paintings from his personal collection—including several Utrillos and Bordins, as well as a watercolor by Noël Coward—in his character's office.

In the frothy picture, Grant plays Philip Shayne, a suave business tycoon who ultimately forfeits his bachelorhood to Cathy Timberlake, an unemployed secretary, portrayed by Day. In the film's opening scene, Philip's limousine drives through a puddle, soiling Cathy's raincoat. To apologize, Philip sends his assistant, Roger (Gig Young), who meets up with Cathy at the Automat, where her apartment mate, Connie (Audrey

Meadows), works. While *Mink* marked Young's fourth picture with Day, it was Audrey Meadows's first. As Alice in *The Honeymooners*, and also as a TV game-show panelist, Meadows was already a household name and a familiar face.

On July 7, 1961, came the announcement that the filming of *Mink* would be delayed two additional weeks in order for Day to attend the Moscow Film Festival. "The hurried invitation from Washington, D.C., stated that her presence at the Moscow Festival would be deeply appreciated because she 'represents the American image as it should be projected in foreign countries.'" (As Ross Hunter would soon say about Day, "[T]he sunny, funny, freckled, friendly, sensible, beautiful girl . . . has done more for the American image abroad than Coca-Cola and Pepsi-Cola combined.") Indeed, what Edith Piaf was to France, Day had become to America. More than just a singer or even a superstar, she was now a national emblem.

Although time has blurred the reasons, Day never did go to Moscow, and filming finally began on *That Touch of Mink* later that month. Even if they started shooting with a finished script, as Grant recalled, "[W]hen we got on the set, frequently what [had] looked sweet on paper appeared sour acting it out. So we huddled again, and improvised until we got something we hope is funny. . . . Good comedy still stems from improvisation, which is the most strenuous, demanding and difficult type of acting," the comic actor added, a tad immodestly.

Though Los Angeles was in the midst of an unusual heat wave, the loud sound of industrial air conditioners made them prohibitive when the cameras were rolling, so cast and crew suffered under wilting conditions. "What a week! So hot, Cary and I have mopped our faces every few minutes," Day told journalist John Whitcomb for his "On Location" story during the shoot. When she wasn't in front of a camera, Day found a little relief from a portable fan. Day was also constantly chewing gum. When asked what happened to it during a shoot, she said that it went "[o]n the north starboard side of one cheek."

While making the film, Grant remained cool and aloof with his co-star. "Of all the people I performed with, I got to know Cary Grant least of all," recalled Day. "He is a completely private person, totally reserved, and there is no way into him. Our relationship on 'That Touch of Mink' was amicable but devoid of give-and-take," Day would say in one of her more honest admissions about a costar. "For somebody who is as open and right out there as I am, it was hard at first to adjust to Cary's inwardness."

Grant's distance may have been due, in part, to the stars' twenty-year age difference. Though the discrepancy in their age wasn't as noticeable as it was when Day costarred with Clark Gable in *Teacher's Pet*, Grant was very self-conscious about his growing age gap with younger costars, and it apparently affected his working relationship with Day. It become even more of a stretch for Grant the following year, when he made *Charade* with Audrey Hepburn, who was twenty-five years his junior. But Hepburn was also more elegant than the down-to-earth, gum-chewing Day, who reminded Grant of his Cockney roots—roots that he had thoroughly succeeded, as far as the moviegoing public knew, in leaving behind while burnishing his image as a suave icon. "Even I want to be Cary Grant," the star once said.

There was yet another, more specific conflict between Day and Grant, as recalled by Barbara Flicker, whose husband, Bob Crystal, was a music scout for Melcher in New York. While visiting Los Angeles when *Mink* was being filmed in Hollywood, Flicker observed "this heavy, heavy atmosphere on the set. When I asked, 'What's wrong?' Marty said, 'Don't worry, I'm taking care of it.'" According to Flicker, the subtext to the tension was that both Day and Grant favored their right profiles, which made any kissing scenes impossible. One or the other would have to relent and brave the left side.

"Doris was in her trailer, and Cary was in his," continued Flicker. "There was a doorknob that was supposed to be painted a certain color, but it wasn't. And Cary [who was a finicky stickler for decor] wasn't coming out until it got painted. Marty convinced Cary to actually turn his right side to the camera, as a trade-off if they'd paint the doorknob. I remember thinking to myself, 'So this is what movie stars are really like.'"

There was also the ongoing question of whether to film Day with her freckles, as she preferred, or without, as the decision makers wanted, including cinematographer Russell Metty, who had recently won an Oscar for *Spartacus*. "In working out a compromise, it was found that scenes from day to day did not match," claimed reporter John Whitcomb. According to Day, "I don't like to wear grease paint. My skin is dark, and when I get a tan, my freckles get even darker. And I'm not just one color. I'm many colors. That's part of my personality, whereas when I put make-up on, I'm one color all over and to myself I look weird."

At Ross Hunter's prompting, Day's costumes had become an increasingly important component of her films. (Jean Louis had designed eighteen costumes for Day in *Pillow Talk*, and Irene had an $82,000 budget to provide her with an identical number in *Lover Come Back*.) Like many a "woman's" picture of the 1940s, *That Touch of Mink* would even include a self-contained fashion show with the top models of the day: Isabella Albonico, Doris Lynn, Bette Woods, and Sue Barton. The all-important raincoat that Day wears in the beginning of the picture was manufactured by Norman Zeiler and discovered in an ad by Cary Grant. "Cary called and told me he thought the coat was perfect for Doris Day," recalled Zeiler. "I didn't believe it was Cary Grant, so I told him if he wanted to see our collection, he'd have to come up himself. And he did."

With Barbara Flicker as a tag-along, Day and Grant also went on a shopping expedition in New York before they began shooting. "We all went down to Seventh Avenue," recalled Flicker. "We were at Ann Klein's because Doris was buying off-the-rack, readymade wear for this picture, where she was playing a working girl. When we went down to the street, there must have been thousands of people and you couldn't move. Doris was very concerned about me: She realized I had never been in that kind of situation before. You know, it gets very scary when people start pushing, and all of these people are coming at you. I remember them rocking the car, and yelling, 'Hollywood phony!'. . . . That was my first look at movie stars, and how they move around—and how hard it is for them just to live," said Flicker, who added that Day passed on her "entire" wardrobe from the picture, once shooting was over: "She just dumped it on a couch, when she gave it all to me."

Making it his business to help Day select her clothes for *Mink* was a sure sign of Grant's feeling that his costar was not classy enough for him. His impeccable taste would add to the "look" of the film, but it would not compensate for his listless performance. Predictably, so many behind-the-scenes dissatisfactions had an impact on the finished movie. What should have been a scintillating pairing of Day and Grant appears flat on the screen and fails to overcome a trite and forced script.

Still, *That Touch of Mink* proved to be another gigantic hit. It was presold as a "rollicking romantic comedy," and the publicity campaign emphasized—absurdly—that Day gets "inebriated" for the first time in a movie. When asked how she felt about engaging in on-screen behavior that so sharply contrasted with her personal convictions, Day replied, "I'm an actress—I hope . . . I'm playing a gal named Cathy—not one named Doris Day. As long as a scene is in good taste, I'll do it." Another publicity item revealed that the Bermuda sequence was shot at the new pool area of the Miramar Hotel in Santa Monica, where Greta Garbo lived during her first three years in Hollywood.

By referring to the "indefatigable Cary Grant" and his "remarkable popularity and longevity," the Press Book for *Mink* tried to turn the liability of Grant's age into an asset. It reported: "Asked his secret for staying young . . . the actor grins and says, 'Stop thinking about growing older. Think young and it shows.'" The Press Book also included a silly, hyperbolic item, exploiting the well-known fact that Day was a "frantic and dedicated" Los Angeles Dodgers fan: "Doris Day faced the hardest acting assignment of her career when she was called upon to root for the New York Yankees in a baseball sequence"—in which Mickey Mantle, Roger Maris, and Yogi Berra made cameo appearances.

On-screen, Grant ultimately does nothing to disguise his contempt for his costar's lack of sophistication. From beginning to end, he makes it clear that he regrets having overcome his disinclination to do the film in the first place. He also makes it impossible to imagine that Philip would invite Cathy to go to Bermuda with him—let alone relinquish his bachelorhood for her.

Considering how poorly *That Touch of Mink* holds up, as already noted, it went over surprisingly well when it first came out. On the basis of an early preview screening, 297 viewer cards were filled out. In a "Recap by Sex Groupings," 126 female and 78 male viewers rated the film "Excellent," and 31 of each gender checked off "Very Good." The picture also fared well in the trades. "'That Touch of Mink' will be lined with money," correctly predicted Lawrence H. Lipskin in the *Hollywood Reporter*.

"Theatergoers will see to it. A scouting patrol from the army of Doris Day and Cary Grant's fans at a sneak the other night rendered an advance verdict by howling into oblivion so many lines of dialogue. . . . Doris' role is richer than her co-star's, and this therefore tends to be her picture."

In his review for the *New York Times*, even Bosley Crowther was remarkably upbeat: "The adroit Mr. Shapiro has written a lively, lilting script, this one with Nate Monaster, that has as much glittering verbal wit and almost as much comic business as 'Pillow Talk.' . . . And Mr. Mann has directed it with that briskly propulsive pace and that pinpoint precision in timing sight-gags that are the distinction of his bright new comic style. . . . But Miss Day and Mr. Grant are finally the ones who carry the whole thing to success."

Jack Pitman, in *Variety*, was one critic who seemed to anticipate what many would come to feel—that *Mink* was inferior to Day's other sex comedies. While declaring that "the recipe is potent: Cary Grant and Doris Day in the old cat-and-mouse game," Pitman avered that "the gloss of '. . . Mink,' however, doesn't obscure an essentially threadbare lining. In seeming to throw off a sparkle, credit performance and pace as the key virtues of this Universal release. The rest of it is commonplace. . . . As written, Miss Day's clowning has the better of it; and she, by the way, certifies herself an adept farceur with this outing."

In his pan of the picture, the acerbic essayist Dwight Macdonald pointed out that the "film is riddled with commercials"—what would come to be common product placements: Greyhound Bus Lines, Pan American Airlines, and Bergdorf Goodman. And in terms of Day's ongoing ranking as "Hollywood's No. 1 box-office property," Macdonald surmised, "I suspect most American mothers would be pleased, and relieved, if their daughters grew up to resemble Doris Day. She has the healthy, antiseptic Good Looks and the Good Sport personality that the American middle class—that is, practically everybody—admires as a matter of duty. Especially the females. No competition." Nevertheless, as *Variety* reported, *Mink* was number one for the fourth week in a row at Radio City Music Hall, where it "hit $1,000,000 gross mark in its present week."

With his wife continuing as the number-one film star, Melcher was financially thriving. As announced that summer, he was chairman of Cabana Motor Hotels, Inc., which had recently built a $5 million motel in Palo Alto. The company already had a motel in Atlanta, and another was under construction in Dallas. There were plans to open still more in Louisville, Baltimore, and Birmingham. Each hotel had two hundred to three hundred rooms, "with elaborate recreations facilities." Though Melcher's brother Jack managed the new Palo Alto property, Melcher exaggerated when he suggested that his wife was actively involved in opening each hotel. "Doris is kind of an inspector general," he said. "She will not allow anything to be associated with her name unless it's perfect." Ross Hunter would add to the PR buzz about the Palo Alto property, saying Day was "frequently seen" there, when "one hundred new rooms" were being added and she saw to the decorating of them herself.

Nor could Day have been too happy about having her name associated with this line of hotels that fall, when—along with Toots Shor and his new Manhattan eatery—it was revealed that Cabana's hotels were financed with money from the Teamsters pension fund, and they became the focus of federal investigations. Indeed, the news was a cover story in the *Los Angeles Times* on October 22, 1962, revealing that the Teamsters had already loaned $1.8 million to the Cabana operation and "committed" an additional $5 million. "Shor's new restaurant in midtown Manhattan, a popular rendezvous for entertainment and sports luminaries, was financed by $4.2 million from the Teamsters fund," the story also divulged.

23

Low-Wire Act

———————— ✳ ————————

"I like joy; I want to be joyous; I want to have fun on the set;
I want to wear beautiful clothes and look pretty. I want to smile,
and I want to make people laugh. And that's all I want."
—DORIS DAY, 1962

illy Rose's Jumbo, Doris Day's first musical picture in five years, would also prove to be one of her most lavish. It was based on a Broadway extravaganza of 1935, which theater historian Stanley Green described as a "musical comedy-circus-vaudeville-revue-spectacle-menagerie." How better to summarize a massive entertainment that featured thirty-one circus acts, twenty-one principals, seventeen aerial performers, thirty-two singers, sixteen dancers, upwards of five hundred animals, and then some—all presented live at New York's cavernous Hippodrome, completely rebuilt for the event?

MGM had planned to make the film version of *Billy Rose's Jumbo* in 1947, with Charles Walters as director, and later, in 1955, with Stanley Donen directing. "When we purchased 'Jumbo' Mr. Richard Rodgers agreed to . . . write and compose together with a lyric writer of his choice, three complete original musical compositions," said an "inter-office communication" dated March 7, 1955. By 1961, when plans to make the film were revived, the studio's rights to the material had apparently lapsed. According to *Variety*: "Purchase culminates almost a year of negotiations during which time Warner Bros. and 20th-Fox were hot for the musical. Fox bid was also on the basis of securing Miss Day as star. . . . While no purchase price was announced, property was out on a $1,000,000 asking price last May." With Day as its star, the film would be produced by Joe Pasternak and Melcher—with Roger Edens as associate producer. Along with Arthur Freed, Edens had supervised many of the great MGM musicals, including *Easter Parade* and *On the Town*. Charles Walters wasn't confirmed as director of *Jumbo* until the end of March, shortly before the studio announced that Red Skelton had the role of Pop Wonder, in the end given to Jimmy Durante. Though producers wanted Richard Burton as Day's costar, he was still in *Camelot* on Broadway and committed to making *Cleopatra* with Elizabeth Taylor.

Once Burton was out of the picture, hope arose that sparks would fly between Day and Stephen Boyd as her leading man, to help recoup the huge investment *Jumbo* represented. As confirmed on June 4, 1961, in *Variety*, this hope was not unfounded. Even though Boyd had been an "unknown" only three years earlier, the role of Messala in *Ben-Hur* had given his career "a meteoric upward turn." The Irish actor would proudly display his chariot from that film in his living room and hang the red-and-gold whip he had used as the charioteer above his fireplace. In fact, following his success in *Ben-Hur*, not only had Boyd signed to play Marc Antony to Elizabeth Taylor's Cleopatra, he also had begun shooting the picture before his costar's highly publicized bout with pneumonia commenced a series of monumental delays. In essence, Boyd and Burton ended up exchanging roles.

The other two leads in *Jumbo* were Durante and Martha Raye. After fifteen years of being relegated to stage, television, and nightclub work, Raye was making her motion-picture comeback. The role of Lulu was created for the eccentric comedienne, whose parents were circus acrobats before turning to vaudeville. *Jumbo* also reunited Raye with Durante more than twenty years after they worked together at Billy Rose's Casino de Paree, a New York nightclub. Even more noteworthy, Durante had appeared in the original stage version of *Jumbo*—though his part was expanded for the film. The famous "Schnozzle" at least got to repeat his most celebrated moment in the show: When he attempted to sneak away with Jumbo, the circus's prized elephant, and when asked just where he thinks he's going with the pachyderm, he gamely replies, "What elephant?"

Though Sidney Sheldon endeavored to make some sense out of the original, sprawling makeshift book by Ben Hecht and Charles MacArthur, his screenplay emerged both belabored and ho-hum. The story concerns Pop Wonder (Durante), who is time and again at risk of losing the circus that bears his name, because of his addiction to shooting craps. If the titular Jumbo is one of Pop's star attractions, his aerialist daughter, Kitty (Day), is another. While Pop has a long-term fiancée and all-purpose circus performer named Lulu (Raye), Kitty begins to fall head over heels for a new roustabout, Sam Rawlins (Boyd).

Kitty Wonder provided Day with yet another opportunity to strut her tomboy stuff. Before Sam sings the infectious "The Most Beautiful Girl in the World," she has to wipe the smudge from her face and change into a more proper gown. But like the rest of the Wonder clan, Kitty is unaware that Sam is really the son of a rival circus owner, played by Dean Jagger, and that he is part of a surreptitious plot to eliminate his father's competition. Despite such adversities, Kitty and Sam are, of course, united in the end—as are Pop and Lulu.

The ringmaster in *Jumbo* was played by Joe Waring, a character actor who felt his life had been saved by Day. After a small role in *Please Don't Eat the Daisies*, Waring suffered a debilitating bout of hepatitis, its complications keeping him in and out of hospitals for nearly two years. At home in New York, unemployed and feeling miserable, he received a note from Day: "Joe, get out of bed and come out here as soon as possible. You're doing the part of Harry in 'Jumbo.'"

Another carryover from *Daisies* was costumer Morton Haack, whose work for Ringling Bros. and Barnum & Bailey Circus in the mid-1950s made him an ideal choice for the picture. Setting a ten-year studio record for the number of costumes created for a single star in a film, Haack would design thirty-one outfits for Day alone, and more than two thousand for the entire cast, employing fifty seamstresses. Haack's notes in his wardrobe book reveal Day's complete dimensions in July 1961: her neck, 12 inches; chest, 35; underbust, 31; waist, 24; and hips, 37. Not even Disney could have invented a more perfect creature.

Shortly before shooting began, the budget for *Jumbo* had reached $5 million, "the most expensive musical in the studio's history," claimed *Variety*. Among the unexpected developments that increased costs, Roger Edens wrote "a major new theme song," "Sawdust, Spangles and Dreams," which would constitute an "entire third act" in the picture. Although Richard Rodgers did not compose new numbers for the movie, two songs were interpolated from other shows he had written with Lorenz Hart, "This Can't Be Love" (from *Boys from Syracuse*) and "Why Can't I?" (from *Spring Is Here*).

Production was scheduled to begin January 8, 1962, and conclude mid-May. (*Variety* would report that the film came in a week ahead of schedule and approximately $200,000 under budget.) The extensive rehearsals began two months earlier, or the first week in October. Day studied trapeze work, bareback riding, and clown routines, and in good time became acquainted with Sydney, the 9,000-pound elephant that had been cast in the title role. "Silvers Madison, his trainer, and Benny White, his keeper, gave me a 'crash course' in elephant-handling," Day told a reporter, "and Syd himself was terribly encouraging to a beginner. Needless to say, a lot of peanuts passed between us." (Day apparently remained unaware that the pachyderm was, in fact, female.) As she worked with the various animals in *Jumbo*, Day began discussing buying a ranch to serve as a refuge for abandoned pets.

Along with Boyd and Raye, Day learned what might be called "the low-wire act" and trapeze work by practicing on bars suspended a few feet above mattresses. Their mentor was the sixty-two-year-old Barbette, a onetime international circus performer who also created the aerial routines for the picture. Day would have not one but two doubles during the making of the picture. In a long "on-location" story that appeared in *Cosmopolitan*, the star complained that her "arms ached from pulling on tights." "There's another set on under these," she explained, "and the top ones are hard to get on."

"Doris had been rehearsing trapeze and tight-wire close to the ground. But the point is, she actually did it," Barbara Flicker recalled with awe. Flicker had recently moved to Los Angeles from New York, with her husband, Bob Crystal. While Crystal continued working for Melcher's music business, Flicker became Day's personal assistant, tending to her every need. "I picked her up every morning at about 5:30 and took her to the studio to get her into make-up and her hair done," Flicker said. "I'd just hang out with her all day, sit in the room, and write letters for her, do shopping, or walk her dog. More than anything else, she really wanted a friend, or a companion, who was always there for her."

Flicker and her husband had settled in L.A. just in time for "all of the pre-production stuff" on *Jumbo*. As Flicker confirmed, Day tended to be both charmed and charming with new friends. "Doris was still enchanted with me," recalled Flicker, "even though I didn't know anything, at the time. I was practically right off the farm. But we'd go to production meetings, and I gave them my opinion on everything, and Doris was really great about it."

Day, who would turn forty in the course of making *Jumbo*, became acutely aware of her age while working on the picture. After watching early rushes and being displeased with the way she looked, Day went to Joe Pasternak and asked that cameraman William Daniels be fired—without getting her wish. Famous for having made Garbo look her greatest, Daniels's solution was to offer only one full close-up of Day that consumes the whole screen in the "Over and Over Again" number. Most of the time, he showed her in filtered medium shots.

According to Flicker, Day's age was an issue from the beginning. "The first day I walked on the set, Joe Pasternak asked Doris if I was her daughter," recalled Flicker. Though they "laughed about" Pasternak's faux pas, Flicker detected a bruised undercurrent to Day's reaction; she saw Day as very vulnerable and transparent. "It wasn't very hard to read her emotions," Flicker observed. "They were always right there, on that big, blue-eyed face. She wasn't very good at hiding anything."

According to James Harbert, there was someone else at MGM at the time whom Day would have liked to replace. "She was not happy with Georgie Stoll, the music director," said Harbert. "She said, 'You know, if you were over there [at MGM], I'd be a lot happier about it.'"

"Doris worries incessantly about everything," explained her director Charles Walters, "her hair, her dress, her performance. She's a marvelous Christian Scientist and talks about her religion intelligently. She says that we shouldn't have fears, that we should trust ourselves and our instincts, that God is always with us. But she doesn't apply one whit of this to her work. If she's unhappy about a scene, she'll stew all day."

In her more specific recollections of working on *Jumbo*, Flicker recalled, "After 'Ben Hur,' everybody thought Stephen Boyd had this great body. But when he showed up on the set [of *Jumbo*], he had incredibly skinny legs and they had to pad his tights. I remember Doris being disillusioned by that. He was a strange duck, to boot." Yet according to Flicker, Day and Boyd were "very touchy-feely" on the set. "But then Doris was touchy-feely with everyone, except for Marty, oddly enough," added Flicker.

Louella Parsons would report in her column that Day and Boyd "maintained surface friendly relations" during the making of the film. "But there was no love lost between them. Nothing in particular. Just not each other's type, except when the camera was turning. As someone on the picture said, 'I doubt if Doris and Steve would have a dinner date—much less a romance.'"

Flicker also pointed out problems with "the stupid, reddish-orange wig" Day wore in the film. "It was huge, and it was heavy, and she didn't look very pretty in it. What the audience wanted was Doris Day, but when they put her in that wig, she wasn't Doris Day. It changed both the audience's perception of her and her perception of herself. She decided to let her roots grow out—and they were not natural blonde. There was a lot more gray there than any of us expected, because she was relatively young."

However, there were moments of good humor—indeed, high spirits. As Flicker relayed, "Doris could be terrifically funny. She even made fun of herself. They'd be playing the music for 'Jumbo,' and she would deliberately sing it off-key, which is really hard to do. She also did great imitations of other singers. She did John Raitt better than John Raitt did—with all the mannerisms and the voice. Doris was really a lot more fun than most people gave her credit for."

Among Flicker's most vivid memories of making *Jumbo* was watching Busby Berkeley direct the big circus acts. "Everybody was assigned a group number," said Flicker. "They'd start the click track, and all the 'Ones' would be on the trapezes. And then they'd go, 'Twos,' and all the lions would run on. It was like solving a mathematical problem. It was all in his head, and he was quite old by then. His wife was there with him all the time—he had a cane. And Chuck Walters just beamed, you know." Though Berkeley was the second-unit director on the picture, his reputation for being a tyrant who treated actors as objects—coupled with his being frail and beyond his youthful, more creative capacities—compelled Day to insist that Walters carefully monitor the musical numbers.

As Flicker also recalled, the circus people parked their trailers near the sound stage and simply lived there during the shoot. "I spent a lot of time with the animals and the circus people, because Doris did not always want me around her," continued Flicker. "But she wanted me totally available, at all times."

One time when Flicker arrived on the set, she discovered Day crying. "I was so stupid because I hadn't taken any acting lessons yet, and I didn't know about 'preparation,'" Flicker observed. "There she was, standing to the side, facing the wall. So I walked up to her, like a jerk, and tried to make her feel better. If I were her, I would have fired my ass that second. But she was very kind about it."

Day was not always so "kind," however, and particularly had difficulties dealing with others' pain or suffering. "If Doris didn't like something about somebody, she'd give this big sunny smile, then go to her dressing room, and tell Marty, 'Get rid of them,'" Flicker recalled. "Jane, who did Doris' hair, came in a little late one morning, apologizing. One side of her face was drooping, and she clearly had had a stroke. When she was halfway through doing Doris's hair, Marty arrived. Doris excused everyone, and told Marty she didn't want to see Jane again. And we never did."

Angie Dickinson, who was about to costar in a Broadway play produced by Melcher, reinforced that aspect of his relationship with his wife: "I have to be the 'heavy,' because Doris is the power, but she's a woman," he told Dickinson. "And I have to go in and do her fighting for her."

Flicker also recalled a Friday when Martha Raye and Jimmy Durante asked her out for a drink after work. "And I said, 'Sure.' I mean it sounded like it would be a lot of fun—and it was. But Doris didn't do that [go out with colleagues] and she didn't particularly like my doing that, either. In fact, she was furious. Those were *her* co-stars, not mine. But she just kept work separate."

In time, after taking "a lot of acting classes," Flicker came to appreciate how one learns to do a job as an actor, and then leave it behind. "But it stayed with Doris the whole time she was working on a picture, and perhaps even longer, because she just didn't have the tools to finish with it when she walked off the set, or to not take it home with her. You know, I don't think Doris slept very much when she was working on a picture. She really worried about it all the time."

In lieu of Day's socializing with people with whom she worked, Flicker became a full-time companion who accompanied the Melchers to many a ball game. "In addition to the Dodgers, Doris loved basketball, and we went to see the Lakers. And back then, there were like a couple thousand people—it wasn't all that popular yet. And Bob Crystal managed to talk the Lakers into selling us four seats on the floor, which they had never done before. They gave us four chairs, and the guards would make a wedge for us to get there.

"We went to every single Lakers game—even some out of town—because Doris loved the players. And they, in turn, loved her—her enthusiasm and her delight. They treated her like a pet. Wilt Chamberlain was playing then, and Elgin Baylor and Jerry West—and a guy named Rudy LaRusso, who had such a crush on Doris, he used to just stand in the background and stare at her. And I think it just made Doris feel fragile—they just towered over everybody." Yet another player, Rod Hundley, is on record as saying, "I'd pull up beside Doris Day where she was sitting at courtside. I'd wink at her and tell her, 'This one's for you, baby.' Then I'd shoot a 30-foot hook. She was gorgeous."

There were other, less benign aspects involved in working for a star. "It came to feel like I had been sold into slavery," said Flicker, who remembered two particular instances when her requests for time off were not granted. "I had gotten a call from a friend of mine who was in advertising. He said, 'Hey, we're doing a new toy commercial. Can you get off Thursday and do it?' I asked Doris, and she said, 'Absolutely not. You be on the set. I need you, and this is your job.' Well, it was the first 'Barbie' commercial, and I would have made enough [in residuals] to buy a house. But what Doris wanted was what Doris got. Another time, I had broken a front tooth opening a package of baloney. And I said I had to go to the dentist. And Doris said, 'Wait and go on Saturday.' And by God, I did. I just kept my mouth shut for the rest of that week, until I could get to the dentist. You don't break a tooth on Doris's time."

Flicker remembers being on call for Day at a salary of less than a hundred dollars a week. Still other anecdotes reveal just how thrifty the Melchers could be. One year Flicker's husband was expecting his wife to receive a "huge bonus," but Day gave her a set of dishes instead. "Bob was furious with me," Flicker said about her then-husband's disappointment. "Doris was very tight with a buck," she explained. "We were Christmas shopping at Geary's, I think, or some wonderful shop in Westwood. And she was picking out all these $12 to $20 presents for everybody—which would be like hundred-dollar presents today. And she found this great pencil box for Ross Hunter. They wrapped it up. But when we got home, we discovered that the pencil box was $125. Man, I was back at the store with that in about four seconds flat."

(Hunter himself reported, "One year she sent each friend a decorated tin of chocolate-coated pretzels. Absolutely delicious and an unexcelled conversation piece"—if far less expensive than the pencil box Day originally had in mind for him.)

As Flicker recalled about Day's visits to New York, she would sometimes disguise herself so she wouldn't be recognized in public. A related memory of Flicker's emphasizes just how unself-conscious Day could be. "Sometimes when we'd go to the Farmer's Market for breakfast," Flicker recalled, "Doris would wear her big sunglasses and a big hat so that she wouldn't be recognized. And nobody would notice us, until suddenly, she would start humming 'Que Sera, Sera.'"

Given Day's at-times absentmindedness, Melcher had taken to calling his wife Gracie Allen, who became one of the most successful entertainers of the twentieth century by playing the dimwitted sidekick to her partner, George Burns. "In real life, I'm like [Gracie] is on stage," Day would explain. One example of Day's ditziness was when she would wear new clothes with price tags dangling from them. Another was her confusing another shopper's grocery cart with her own at the store.

Day would do her own shopping at the Safeway, which she came to prefer to the Farmer's Market because there were fewer tourists. "I go about four times a week because I forget things," Day recalled. "Marty can't understand my doing it. He thinks I'm out of my skull. He says 'You're just a sitting duck for autographs and people.' . . . Yesterday another woman and I got our baskets mixed up. You should have seen us! We both had baskets stuffed to the top before she suddenly realized the purse in the basket wasn't hers! She looked around, and there was her purse—in my basket! We'd just been piling things on and it took us an hour to get sorted out. The manager was hysterical."

*   *   *

While his mother was busy making *Jumbo,* Terry found a new girlfriend, who, like himself, was a child of Hollywood royalty. Candy Bergen was all of fifteen when she had a blind date with the twenty-year-old Terry. They had been fixed up by one of Candy's girlfriends, who said Terry had "a beige Chrysler and a great sense of humor." "His resemblance to [his mother] was striking," recalled Bergen, "[H]e was tall, blond, blue-eyed and freckled, with a great infectious grin."

"I liked him at once. He was special, someone whose luck would never run out," she continued. "There was a touch of Tom Sawyer about him in spirit as well as in looks—a taste for tricks and trouble, an instinct for truth. He was funny and furtive, foxy and playful. There was a sweetness and innocence about our time together, a sense of safety. Our parents thought it was darling. At last I was in love." Candy's father, Edgar Bergen, was one of the most beloved ventriloquists of the twentieth century—along with his monocled sidekick, Charlie McCarthy.

The teenage Candy resembled her potential mother-in-law in at least one respect: She satisfied her enormous appetite without gaining weight. "Because of the size of my appetite and the impressive volume of my food intake, Terry took to calling me 'The Sherman Tanker' ('Tanker' for short) as a term of endearment," Bergen wrote in her memoir. "And when, parked in his car in my driveway, Terry turned and whispered to me tenderly, 'I love you, Tanker, honest I do,' it was pure poetry to me, music to my ears."

Barbara Flicker recalled having a couple of meals with Candy, Terry, and his mother. "She said that she wanted to be a model, but it was like,

'Oh, golly. Do you think I'm going to be able to do it?'" Having been a model herself, Flicker had no doubts that Candy would be a success, if that's what she really wanted. "She was such a gorgeous creature," continued Flicker. "She was so sweet and kind." Candy was also very young, and no one had any idea she was poised to become a major film star in her own right.

James Harbert remembered Candy's presence at North Crescent during some of the times he rehearsed with Day on the piano. "They would be romping around the house, and once, Doris said, 'It's gotten awfully quiet. What do you think is going on in there? Let's go in and see what they're up to,'" recalled Harbert. "I said, 'We can't do that. How would you like it if I were to do that to you?' We both laughed, and she said, 'Okay. I guess you're gonna be my conscience.' Years later, when I saw Candy, I told her, 'You know, I saved you way back then.'"

Candy's puppy love with Terry proved short-lived, however, several years before it would be reactivated. According to Bergen, "Terry got itchy. Terry's friends were older, racier members of Beverly Hills' Junior Rat Pack—Frank Sinatra's kids, Dean Martin's kids, Danny Thomas's kids. Hollywood's young elite. His life was just beginning, becoming his own. It was fast, it was free; I was not. This was no place for a high-school senior in saddle shoes who was flunking Latin and getting grounded. I saw him less and less."

One summer in the early 1960s, Terry and childhood friend Guy Webster rented their own place in Malibu. "We had this great upstairs apartment overlooking the ocean," recalled Webster, who was on summer break from college at the time. "There was a little volleyball court, and we had lots of parties for friends. We always had women around." Webster particularly recalled inviting Melissa Brown to one of their parties. "We knew Melissa from high school," said Webster, "but I think that was the first time Terry really met her. Melissa's mother had posed for the Columbia Pictures logo, the woman with the torch." In a little over a decade, Melissa would become Terry's first wife.

Terry also started seeing the twenty-four-year-old rock star Jackie de Shannon. "She wore a hot-pink sheath with matching high heels," Bergen said. "She had a hit single. She did not have homework." Terry curtailed his budding relationship with Candy by sending her "a hastily written farewell citing irreconcilable age differences" but hoping they would remain friends.

In the midst of all the chatter about his parents' peccadilloes, Terry

Melcher was proving to be a randy twenty-year-old himself. While referring to Terry as "one of my best friends," Ned Wynn—the son of actor
Keenan and grandson of vaudevillian Ed—would recall the summer of
1962, when his mother compelled him to follow in his father's footsteps
by playing in summer stock. According to Wynn, Terry "was particularly
galling to me. When he found out I was going to do stock, he never let
up. 'Straw-hatting it this summer, Ned?' he grinned. 'Hitting the old silo
circuit there, are ya? Pancake number five and Albolene? We'll be thinking of you in Arrowhead. Too bad there won't be very many girls there
or anything.' Terry would be up in Lake Arrowhead at his mother's [new
weekend] house with two other friends, Gregg Jakobson and Eddie Garner, all summer. They had a speedboat. There were rooms all over the
place. I could see it all: drinking, water skiing, cadres of teenage wonder
kittens like so many bikini-clad guerrillas slipping out of the woods and
onto Terry's dock."

According to Wynn, "Terry and I had certain things in common, attitudes and experiences that made us able to communicate quickly and
easily. Terry wasn't always comfortable with people, which suited me
just fine. We understood that aspect in each other." As conveyed by both
Candy Bergen and Ned Wynn, the youthful Terry was acting his age and
developing into something of a playboy. Within a year, James Harbert
recalled, "[jazz pianist] George Shearing called Irving Townsend at three
in the morning, one Saturday, upset because his daughter was out with
Terry and hadn't come home yet." Townsend in turn called Harbert, who
knew that Terry liked to play poker for low stakes at Pokerino in Gardena,
in south Los Angeles, where it was legal, and where he tracked him down
by phone. Shearing's daughter was still with him.

*　　*　　*

With an emphasis on "BIG," the Exhibitor's Campaign Book for *Jumbo*
was itself extra large and indicates just how much MGM was banking on
the film: everything from the ninety-two-inch hat for Jumbo the elephant
to the "largest scenic backdrop ever constructed for a motion picture."
The book also claimed that the film had "many of the world's most famous circus acts," including Ron Henon, the Carlisles, the Pedrolas, the
Wazzans, the Hannefords, Billy Barton, Corky Christiani, Victor Julian,
and Richard Berg.

Quaker Oats was again part of the marketing plan, "with more than

7000 member grocery stores participating in a JUMBO DAYS tie-in backed by half a million dollars in advertising and promotion." The scheme included coupons in Quaker Oats packages enabling children under twelve to attend the picture free when accompanied by an adult. There was also a massive record campaign: "So confident is Columbia Records for the album's success that the company is making the LP its highlighted fall and pre-Christmas album. More than 100,000 copies were in the first pressing alone, and advance orders have indicated this will not be nearly enough to meet the heavy demand."

Indeed, the lush score by Rodgers and Hart made *Jumbo* an ideal vehicle for Day's musical comeback, and she, at least, sparkles in it. Her plaintive renditions of "My Romance" and "Little Girl Blue"—the show's two outstanding ballads—present Day at another singing and acting peak. The large circus numbers, "Over and Over Again" and "Sawdust, Spangles, and Dreams"—in "Panavision and Metrocolor"—helped the film become as big and beautiful as MGM had intended.

On the positive side, the sweep of William H. Daniels's camera is frequently the equal of the gorgeous soundtrack. Yet neither can entirely compensate for a basically flimsy story. Moreover, the lack of any palpable romantic connection between Day and Boyd proves a huge drain on the film's effect, vitiating the crucial romance at the heart of the plot and diminishing the impact of the songs, which alone justify the film's existence. Despite publicity claims that Boyd was making his debut as a singer in the picture, his voice was slated to be dubbed by Broadway singer Bill Hayes, but was ultimately filled in by a certain James Joyce. Several decades later, music critic Gary Giddins would, perceptively, refer to Boyd's "anti-charisma" in the film.

Still, the *Jumbo* marketing campaign seemed to work—at first, in any case. The National Screen Council members voted it the Box Office Blue Ribbon Award for January. It received *Seventeen* magazine's "Picture of the Month" award, and *Photoplay* declared it "Gold Medal Movie of the Month." The early trade reviews were also, in the lingo of the biz, "boffo": "The biggest puzzle 'Jumbo' presents is why they waited 27 years to film it," exclaimed Robert B. Frederick in *Variety*. "Whatever the reasons, movie-goers have plenty of cause to rejoice—it has been filmed and it's great! The overall excellent, professional handling of director Charles Walters is greatly responsible, though never obvious, for the 123 minutes going by in a hurry. . . . Doris Day has never sung better. . . . While the story is no challenge to her thespic talents, her return to the thing she does better than anyone in films could (and should) persuade her to make movie musicals."

The review in the *Hollywood Reporter* was equally rhapsodic: "A rousing musical trim-tailored for the holidays and dazzling enough to sustain playoffs in any season, MGM's 'Jumbo' is a thorough delight to eye and ear. . . . Miss Day's well-scrubbed, desirable portrait of a determined but rather addle-brained young woman is altogether perfect. She has the voice for the songs and the figure for the production numbers. Boyd unleashes a good singing voice and a more engaging manner than in most of his previous films, an air of nonchalance he has not always had."

At least two of the reviews were extravagant in their response. "'Jumbo' is a great big blubbery amiable polka-dotted elephant of a show, just the ticket for a holiday hoot with the wife and kiddies," claimed the critic for *Time* magazine. "[Walters] skillfully mingles cinemagic and circuspocus, and he almost always gets the best out of his players. . . . Day as usual is blindingly sunny, but in a circus the glare seems suitable." George H. Jackson was quick to chime in, in the *Los Angeles Herald Examiner*: "It is colorful, vivid movie fare, with strong appeal for all ages. Releasing it at this time of the year makes it a spectacular Christmas present. [Day] invests her role of the circus manager-performer, etc., with that sparkle and zest which has made her one of the screen's most popular personalities. For Doris not only carries the story line but is also called on for the romantic lead too."

Optimistic expectations were boosted by an early report in *Variety* that *Jumbo* was "heading for a sockeroo $165,000 for opening week" at Radio City Music Hall, New York's only remaining movie palace. Yet the film did not fare that well with a number of other critics nor, ultimately, with the public. "['Jumbo'] is hitting the screen about 25 years late," averred Bosley Crowther in the *New York Times*. "The aura of wonder and excitement it tries to throw around old-fashioned circus life . . . the sense of emotional exaltation it tries to pump into a dull tanbark romance—all are such stuff as was familiar in circus pictures that many years ago." In summary, Crowther called it "simply unoriginal, solemn, sluggish and slow." He found Day to be "something of a bore as she plows her way through the proceedings as the herd-rider on the dying show. . . . And her downright labored endeavors to sham a romance with Stephen Boyd . . . are as blunt as the driving of stakes to hold the tent."

"Sidney Sheldon has based his preposterous screenplay on the preposterous book of the original 'Jumbo,'" wrote the equally displeased

Brendan Gill in the *New Yorker.* "Even the Rodgers-and-Hart songs seem
alarmingly dated . . . and, to sharpen still further one's sense that something has gone wrong with the time machine, the young lovers, each
presumably on the threshold of a first romance, are played by Doris Day
and Stephen Boyd."

Nor was it just the New York critics who were contemptuous of *Jumbo.* "The point here seems to have been a family picture with something
for everyone," said a review in *Newsweek.* "But the way it works out, it is
not so much a picture for the whole family as hardly anything at all for
anybody in particular."

There was at least one very special person Day reached out to with
a letter—her young pen pal Paul Brogan. After he wrote his idol that his
parents wouldn't let him see *Midnight Lace* ("because it was too scary")
or *Lover Come Back* ("because it was too 'adult'"), Day wrote Paul that
she had a picture coming out at Christmastime that he would be able to
see, *Jumbo.*

Though Day nabbed a Golden Globe nomination for *Jumbo,* the
film's failure at the box office cost her what would have been one of
the most natural assignments of her film career: the title role in MGM's
upcoming *The Unsinkable Molly Brown.*

*   *   *

As if it were timed to arrive with the release of *Jumbo,* the first biography
of Day was published in December 1962. A slim, 139-page Monarch
paperback that sold for thirty-five cents in drugstores, it was written
by Tedd Thomey, a forty-two-year-old journalist and freelance writer
who had written *The Loves of Errol Flynn,* a "recent Monarch bestseller."
Thomey's title for his Day biography was even less imaginative—*Doris
Day*—without any subtitle. Monarch attempted to give it a little more flair
by adding above the title, "The Dramatic Story of America's Number One
Box Office Star." Nor was the cover photo of Day as enticing or effective
as it might have been: She's wearing a red dress and lurching forward on
a bed or a divan, her hands cradled in front of her, sporting a gaudy ring
on her wedding finger.

The embellished tone of Thomey's dramatic opening—describing the
car accident that broke Day's leg—is laden with superfluous and dubious narrative details: "It was a black, moonless October night in Ohio in
1937 and the two young boys and two young girls were bouncing gaily

along the street in a small sedan. They were on an important mission, driving to their favorite hamburger stand, a spot noted for the juiciness of its ground meat and the sweet sharpness of its pickles." Thomey's account reads like the worst of the countless movie magazine articles that, early in her film career, tried to reconstruct Day's life—a cut-and-paste job, based on journalists' imaginings.

Nor was his biography as sensational as readers probably expected in light of several scandals swirling around the Melchers in the fall of 1962, beginning with news of their pending divorce. Despite the lack of any chemistry between Day and Boyd on the screen, rumors began percolating about their having had an affair. Indeed, a story circulated that such rumors had been planted by the studio in an attempt to deflect attention from the even more incendiary and accurate rumor of Day's affair with the African-American Maury Wills. A celebrated base stealer for the Los Angeles Dodgers, Wills would later confirm that he stole Day's heart during this period. The girl next door was suddenly emulating her father in surprising ways.

24

The Imperfect Setup

✳

"Women have to pretend to feel a good deal they don't feel."
—GEORGE BERNARD SHAW

"It's not gossip when you know the person; it's news.*"*
—RICHARD GREENBERG

While his wife was tied up with her film and recording responsibilities in the summer of 1962, Marty Melcher took on a project that would exclude her. He produced his first—and, as it turned out, his last—Broadway show; it was called *The Perfect Setup*. Written by Jack Sher—the author of the magazine story that had served as the basis for Day's 1952 picture *The Winning Team*—*The Perfect Setup* concerned a public relations man with a wife in Westchester and a mistress in Manhattan, where he works. In spite of his firm belief in the permanence of the eponymous situation, the character is compelled to make a choice. In the end, of course, he chooses his wife.

Given its slightly risqué story line, *The Perfect Setup* might have appeared an odd choice for the seemingly priggish Melcher. Odder still, it was soon announced that his wife would star in a film version of the play. But then, the Melchers' life was not exactly the rosy picture of the all-American home they maintained it to be. Only days before *The Perfect Setup* opened on Broadway, on October 26, rumors were rampant about their separation, about Day's affair with Maury Wills, and about Melcher's affair with one of his leading ladies, Angie Dickinson. If the affair with Dickinson were true, the situation would have made for perfect typecasting: in the stage comedy, Dickinson played the mistress of the husband (Gene Barry), whose wife was portrayed by Jan Sterling. (Robert Cummings, Day's costar in *Lucky Me*, had initially been announced in the Barry role.)

"As I recall, he did not come on to me, at all, but he was sweetly avail-able—let's put it that way," recalled Dickinson, who was between mar-riages at the time, but claims not to have had an affair with Melcher. "If I had wanted to spend a lot of time with him, he would have been very happy about it. I liked him enormously. And when I like a man—a sexy, tall, good-looking, successful guy—then I would enjoy his company a lot. There's something about flirting that's fun. It's more exciting than bacon. I've always liked being in the company of men. There's an underlying danger there: adventure and excitement."

According to Dickinson, she didn't notice anything that suggested Melcher was unhappy or concerned about his marriage. "The play itself had taken all my energy. My career had stalled, and I was seeking a new direction," she said. "So I wasn't interested in someone else's problems. I had my own. I had just turned down a movie at Universal because I felt it would only prolong my career in the direction it was going—flat-lining. And I thought maybe I could stir up some interest by going to Broadway. It was a move designed to get my career going in a better direction."

The Perfect Setup did not prove a boon to Dickinson's career, however. It closed after its fifth performance on Broadway. Playwright Sher would blame the play's dismal reception on the Cuban missile crisis, which was mounting and seemingly out of control during the play's brief run. (The crisis in Cuba did not prevent filmgoers from filling movie-house seats and being introduced to Sean Connery as James Bond in *Dr. No.*) But clearly, Melcher was overextended, trying to contend with the mess in his personal life and hardly providing the focus a producer needs when opening a play on Broadway. As Dickinson recalled, "Mrs. [Ira] Gershwin came up to San Francisco to see the play [in previews]. And she said, 'Well, darling. It's not very good. The only way it's going to work is if one woman plays both parts.' And she was so right."

Though Melcher was sad when he told the cast they were going to have to close in New York, Dickinson for one "was kind of relieved it was over, because it was so torturous. All we did was work, morning till night. . . . It was the worst job I ever had in my life—opening in a new play—because they're rewriting all the time, trying to make it better. The actors have to constantly re-learn it and restage it." Indeed, *The Perfect Setup* would be Dickinson's first and last stage experience.

Having maintained the charade of a happy marriage for at least half a decade, the Melchers finally separated in the fall of 1962. In her memoir Day claimed this was "a propitious time to break up" because Melcher was about to go on the road with *The Perfect Setup*, before taking it to Broadway. She also explained that Melcher had become increasingly dictatorial and had begun slamming his fist against the wall often, evoking the unpredictable and fearful brutality of her first husband, Al Jorden. The final, violent straw for Day was the time she observed Melcher strike Terry, prompting her to ask him "to move out altogether" that very day. (She even explained, parenthetically, that Melcher relocated to the Sunset Towers.)

As she continued to account for the failure of her marriage in her memoir, Day revealed that their sex life had "deteriorated" and that she had been unable to please Melcher, or "fake a reaction," the way many wives do, during a one-sided sex act. Years later, Day further explained: "Good sex requires that each person be aware of the other, a mutually shared experience, but Marty had lost that ability and desire to create the kind of flow that is so vital to making love; his patience had become very limited and he was satisfied simply to gratify himself. But I'm not one of those women who can be a fixture. I simply can't. I can't fake it."

Though she added that, at the time, she still cared for Melcher, Day's growing list of complaints made it seem otherwise. She had become "contemptuous" not only of her husband's terrible temper and physical abuse of Terry, but also of his "keeping me constantly at work" and, what is perhaps the most revealing gripe of all, "his dependence on my career." (Neither Day nor Melcher had any idea they were both working primarily for their lawyer, Jerome Rosenthal, at their own expense.) Moreover, in contrast with the previous portrait of Melcher as a devout Christian Scientist, she mentioned increasing annoyance with his consistently falling asleep at services. Demonstrating just what a relief the separation represented for her, she added that she instantly knew she wanted it to be permanent, as opposed to the trial Melcher viewed it as.

The first indication that the Melchers' relationship had foundered seeped into print as a brief item in Sidney Skolsky's column on October 1, 1962. "Doris Day and Marty Melcher are having more dissension than Leo Durocher has with an umpire," said Skolsky, whose reference to the argumentative baseball figure—Durocher was known as "Leo the Lip"—might have been a sly way of telescoping more specific rumors about Day's relationship with Maury Wills.

Having transformed Day's image with *Pillow Talk*, gay producer Ross Hunter was also adept at glossing over reality and manipulating the media, and he rushed to the Melchers' defense. "Hollywood's sizzling with gossip about Doris Day splitting with her husband and business partner,

Marty Melcher," reported journalist Earl Wilson four days after the Skolsky item appeared. "But close friend Ross Hunter tells me it's a crazy tale. They're briefly apart. Marty went to Phoenix with his play, 'The Perfect Setup.' Doris, an incurable baseball addict since her Ohio childhood when she screamed for the Cincinnati Reds, stayed behind to emote in a film, and to root the Los Angeles Dodgers to the pennant and then the world championship."

Mike Connolly added to the chatter on October 10, claiming that an "announcement" of the Melchers' impending divorce was "due any day." Though, a week later, Wilson again denied that any such announcement was forthcoming, he nonetheless figured among the first to allude, in print, to rumors of "a third party": "Hollywood won't believe the rumor that Doris Day's sweet on a New York Yankee star—first, she and Marty Melcher are very rich and seemingly happy together; second, she's a Dodger fan."

On October 18, from both coasts came dire predictions from two of the nation's major gossipmongers: Broadway columnist Dorothy Kilgallen said that "Doris Day, America's favorite movie star, will be making headlines out of Hollywood in the near future," and Hollywood's Sheilah Graham divulged, "People close to the private attitudes of Doris Day say that her marriage with Marty Melcher will be a casualty before the new year dawns. Doris never discusses her private attitudes. But Marty has been away a great deal. Recently they paid $75,000 for their 'Tee Pee' place at Arrowhead Lake. It seems to follow that whenever a film couple buys a house, something drastic happens."

Once she became the number-one box office attraction, the pressures on Day to maintain her exalted status added a stress to the Melchers' already strained relationship. For years, they had been functioning primarily as business associates without really providing the emotional sustenance that everyone expects from a partner. (As Day herself would say time and again, Melcher had been more like a father than a husband.) Under the circumstances, the thought of a private retreat—where they might get away from it all and be able to work on becoming more intimate—suddenly seemed like a good idea. They found a weekend place in Lake Arrowhead, ninety miles east of the city in the San Bernardino National Forest, known for its year-round natural beauty and spectacular scenery. But any hope of repairing their deep-seated problems came to naught, and within a year Day would be asking Melcher for a divorce.

Barbara Flicker recalled a weekend that winter when she and Day, alone together, visited the house in Arrowhead. "Doris drove us up in her Lincoln. It started snowing, and we didn't have snow tires. So we pulled into this gas station, where there was this whole line of cars waiting for chains to be put on their tires. When the attendant saw Doris Day, it was like nobody else existed, and we had chains on the tires in about four seconds flat. They also brought us hot dogs from a hot dog stand. They were just thrilled to see her." According to Flicker, the Arrowhead house was "very plain, with nice, comfortable furniture. Doris wasn't an extravagant person at all. They rarely ate out at restaurants or entertained. In fact, Doris and I slept in the same room, on twin beds."

Also, according to Flicker, that weekend was the one time Day "really opened up. I brought my cigarettes and a bottle of Pouilly Fuisse. And even though Doris famously didn't drink, we sat up one night and polished off the bottle of wine. And she even tried a cigarette or two, for the first time in a while. She was talking about her [first two] marriages to the 'boys in the band,' and said it was the happiest time in her life. She talked about that time with such glee, and said it was so much more fun than making movies." She also told Flicker that she was having an affair with someone else, while she was married to one of them.

"But it all seemed like kid stuff, to me. It didn't seem like we had developed a real relationship. I just chalked it up to her being a movie star, and figured that maybe they were different, that they didn't need friends. Later, I found out that Doris was unique, that way, that she just couldn't get close to people. When we returned at the end of the weekend, Marty and Bob were standing out in front of my house, waiting, because they were really worried about their 'star.'"

The fact that Day both drank wine and smoked cigarettes that weekend—evidently for the first time in years—is a good indication of just how distraught she was, given what was happening between her and her husband, and the public's growing perception of the problems between them. Indeed, the rumors linking Melcher's name with Angie Dickinson had begun while he tried out *The Perfect Setup* in various cities before its Broadway opening. As the interrelated scandals built to a fevered pitch, the Melchers attempted to do what they could to rein them in. Melcher phoned Louella Parsons and asked her to report that he and Doris "have always had a nice calm, quiet life together and have never been apart throughout our marriage. Then I branch out a little and put my play, 'The Perfect Setup' into production, and all those dumb noises start. Just say it's what it is—nonsense.

"I guess it all started when I had to go to San Francisco for tryouts of my show," Melcher further explained. "Doris is a wild-eyed Dodger fan, and stayed in Hollywood. She doesn't fly, so I planed down to see her every couple of days. Now I am in New York making arrangements for my play which opens Wednesday, and then I'll be home. I talk to Doris not only once, but sometimes several times a day. Doris is now filming 'The Thrill of It All' . . . and she didn't come to New York because it would take too much time traveling by train. . . . [We] have no problems, and there's no foundation to all these silly rumors." "Doris agreed with her husband," Parsons added, "and said she was having a difficult time filming scenes with children in 'The Thrill of It All.'"

The columnists were all atwitter once again when they learned that Day—after the second game of the National League playoff—gave Maury Wills, the base-stealing star of the Dodgers, a portable record player so that he could play her records. Barbara Flicker was present for the photo op and gift-giving moment. By late November, Florabel Muir not only confirmed in the *New York Daily News* that the Melchers were separated, but that Day had "developed a romantic interest in a member of the Los Angeles Dodgers baseball team." She further divulged that Melcher had moved into an apartment in Hollywood, while his wife remained in their Beverly Hills home.

Walter Winchell had his say in his column on December 2, claiming that the Melchers had separated. "The rift-rumors have been a red-hot topic in the Hollywood hills for several months. Miss Day's only comment today came from a Universal Studio spokesman. Said he: 'She has nothing to say and will have nothing to say.' Hubby's statement sounded like an echo: 'Our policy is not to discuss our personal affairs.' Melcher moved out of their elegant home Tuesday. He is living at the Sunset Towers, a residential hotel on the Strip. Their joint wealth is said to be over $15 million. . . . Among the swain expected to bid for her heart and hand following the expected abrogation are movie actor Stephen Boyd, and one of the L.A. Dodgers handsomest home run stars."

Once the rumor regarding Day and Wills erupted, the studios were compelled to counter it. Since Day was a potential moneymaker for any one of them, they all had an interest in containing the scandal and preventing it from interfering with her number-one box-office status. And as explained subsequently by reporter Aaron Putnam, it was the MGM press agents who, "in desperation . . . tried to create a new love interest that might be more acceptable to DD fans. They came up with ruggedly handsome Stephen Boyd[,] her leading man in 'Jumbo.' Studio 'flacks' informed columnists that Steve, not Maury was the new knight for Day."

New York columnist Earl Wilson quickly took the bait. "Girl-Next-Door Doris Day's new heart interest isn't a baseball player, but her somewhat younger leading man, Stephen Boyd," wrote Wilson. "But Steve refused to be a smoke-screen. As soon as 'Jumbo' was finished, he flew back to England. Reporters mobbed the British actor at [the] London Airport and demanded to know if it was true he planned to wed Doris."

Louella Parsons relayed Boyd's dumbfounded reaction when he disembarked from the plane and found himself questioned about his putative romance with Day. "Flabbergasted," exclaimed Boyd. "I'm absolutely flabbergasted! It is so false and ridiculous [that] I have no words."

As the scandal consumed more and more ink in legitimate newspapers that winter, Parsons continued to attempt to strengthen her stand in the face of colleagues' wagging tongues. The first week in December, Parsons claimed that the Melchers had Thanksgiving dinner at home and went to a party together the following night. She also claimed it would "snow in Tahiti" before the Melchers got a divorce, and characterized their separation as "time out, a sort of breather, but a cordial one."

The following week, Parsons wrote, "There's an awful lot of 'togetherness' between these two for all the 'apartness' talk." Parsons further reported that the Melchers spent the entire Sunday together at their Beverly Hills country club, playing tennis and staying on for dinner. "[They] told friends who dropped by their table that they were looking around for a decorator to re-do their house at Lake Arrowhead and that they would be going to Palo Alto . . . early next month to co-host the opening party for the newest motel in their chain."

As well documented in a long investigative piece by journalist Jerry Paige that traced all of the above developments, Walter Winchell subsequently confirmed that the Melchers had, in fact, separated. But it's a reporter who refused to go on record—or possibly Paige himself—who offered keen insights into the Melchers' problems: "It seems to me that Doris did something that could have been fatal to her marriage, and may still kill it: She grew up. You see, all her life she's been looking for a father to replace the one she lost by divorce when she was 12. But her first two husbands . . . didn't fit the bill. . . . Then along came Marty Melcher, an experienced businessman and a strong personality who moved in and gave Doris not only security, but guidance. It was Marty who steered her to top stardom, and he was the tower of strength she needed. She was glad to let him run her life. But in climbing to the top, Doris gradually gained the experience that enabled her to mature," continued Paige. "And suddenly, as far as I can see, she wasn't content to let Marty make all the decisions anymore. Naturally Marty must have felt that things had worked out fine so far, and why change?"

Decades later, Day herself would say: "I should not have permitted Marty to be my personal manager and agent. This is not the role a husband should play. I should have been with a top agency that would have brought me interesting, challenging films to do, an agency which has writers and directors and studios to put together for a particular project. Marty just wanted to keep repeating the successes I had, so after *Pillow Talk*, Marty kept putting me into comedy after comedy of the *Pillow Talk* variety."

Paige's report also shrewdly conjectured that Terry was a compelling reason the Melchers remained together as long as they did. "A couple of years ago, Terry left for college," wrote Paige. "And though he soon changed his mind and came home, it wasn't long before he packed up again and moved out of the house to live with a friend. Then he moved to New York to work in Columbia Records' executive training program, after cutting a record which got nowhere. Later he returned to California. He had become an adult with a life of his own, and there was no reason to keep the marriage together for his sake.

"Now, having denied to the world that there's trouble in their marriage, Doris and Marty are on the spot. The separation confirms it. And to make such an admission, especially for Doris, is very hard."

Day would not deal with the separation—or publicly air the problems leading up to it—for well over a decade, when she wrote her memoir. Still, some of what she eventually wrote suggests just how accurate the perceptions of Paige, or his informant, were.

As she recalled her feelings, Day didn't seem to recognize that, at first, she may have colluded in making Melcher into a father figure—even though she made it very clear that in time she no longer appreciated him in the role. "One of the things that had gone wrong was that in many ways Marty had changed from being a husband to trying to be a father figure," Day said. "He was becoming more and more rigid and dictatorial, trying to make me into a child. He was telling me to do things, rather than discussing them with me. And when I showed any resistance, he'd have a temper tantrum."

It's revealing that Day, at the time, turned down the perfect opportunity to go to New York and see the first and last play her husband produced on Broadway. She had agreed to record *Annie Get Your Gun* as part of a series of classic Broadway shows with new "dream casts" for the lucrative Columbia Record Club. But she refused to make the recording in New York. "'Annie Get Your Gun' was the brainstorm of an A&R man in New York, who thought of pairing Robert Goulet with Doris," recalled James Harbert. Goulet was suddenly receiving a lot of attention because of "If Ever I Would Leave You," the hit he had just introduced in Broadway's *Camelot*. But according to Harbert, Day was not keen on working with the Canadian baritone. And given her new, more glamorous image, she was leery of harking back to her *Calamity Jane* role. Day relented, however, adding that she loved the Irving Berlin score.

Though Day recorded *Annie Get Your Gun* in one four-and-half-hour session on October 8, she also spent considerable time preparing for it with Harbert. Concessions were made for her to record her vocal contributions in L.A. and then send the taped sessions to New York, "where orchestrator Philip Lang wrote arrangements around Day's vocal tracks—an inside-out variation on the usual process." "It was hell for me because I had to make all the tracks with the piano," recalled Harbert. "She and I sat together in the Columbia recording studio [in L.A.]. I had to play as softly as possible so it wouldn't get into her microphone. I had that problem with her films, too, because she liked to sing live on the set, and I had to be very careful to avoid playing too loud."

Goulet joined Day and Harbert in the L.A. studio. Despite his reputation for being arrogant, "Goulet was the picture of modesty," according to Harbert. "He felt so lucky to be recording with her that he was on his very best behavior." Harbert received no credit on the album because it wasn't his project. "I was working as her rehearsal pianist, because that's the only way it was going to get done. I could have raised hell and said I wanted my name on the album, but neither of us liked it very much. I remember Doris saying, 'Well they wanted us to do it. We did it, and it's done!'"

The Perfect Setup proved to be the perfect alibi for the Melchers and their failed relationship. According to Harbert, even though he was seeing Day regularly during this period, he had no awareness of any problems they were having, and no idea that they had separated. Clearly, Day could be as consummate an actress offscreen as she could be on. On the other hand, there was no doubt in Harbert's mind that the Melchers' relationship had built-in limitations. "Their marriage had gone dry and seemed to me to be what they called 'a Hollywood arrangement,'" he said, "and all that that implies."

Day herself would basically allude to it that way in 1960, while putting as positive a spin on it as she possibly could. "You can't imagine," she told Philip K. Scheuer of the *Los Angeles Times,* "what it would be like to be in this business without [Marty's] protection, without someone very close to you looking after you. Ours is a most wonderful kind of arrangement, working together—great security in a business where there is often so little. It is just tremendous what he has done for me."

*   *   *

Though Day discussed her alleged affair with Maury Wills in her memoir, she patently denied it. "The only times I had seen Maury were at the games, at an occasional function given by the team's owner, Walter O'Malley, and at parties given by Barbara Rush and Warren Cowan, who were great fans [and married, at the time]," Day said. In an apparent later-day defense, the injured star relegated the gossip to "the fact that Wills and his wife were reported to be getting a divorce at just about the same time Marty moved out of our house."

Nearly thirty years later, Wills would devote a chapter to his affair with Day in his own memoir, *On the Run: The Never Dull and Often Shocking Life of Maury Wills.* Wills explained outright that "we made an agreement that regardless of what happened, we'd always deny it." He proceeded to justify his breaking that agreement by contending that one-time teammate John Roseboro had already spilled the scandalous beans in his autobiography in 1978.

But if the ostensible affair between Day and Wills boils down to a matter of "he-said, she-said," Wills might be an unreliable source. Roseboro wrote in *Glory Days with the Dodgers,* "I don't think there was anything to the story that Wills and Doris Day had a romance. . . . However, it helped make Maury a glamorous figure and it helped him get a lot of ladies. . . . But Wills was discreet. Whether he was seeing a star or a nobody, he kept it to himself and didn't brag about it."

He didn't, in any case, for several decades. In *On the Run,* Wills avoided imparting any prurient details, and his memory seemed a bit shaky on the specifics of his supposed affair with Day. But he firmly asserted that they were lovers and explained that they didn't begin sleeping together "until after the season." Wills also wrote, several times, that he was "scared" and "didn't know what to do." It wasn't just that he was married and had a family "up in Spokane," but also that he was "a young 29" and felt Day to be "more sophisticated than I. . . . It was bizarre to me because she was such a worldly person." Day was also eleven years his senior.

Wills recalled Day bringing him lunch "in a nice wicker basket," as well as the "battery-operated record player [that] looked like a little suitcase." Indeed, much of Hollywood took note of the phonograph. He also believed that "she really loved me" and "that only made me more scared. I didn't know what love was all about. The only love affair I'd had was with baseball." (Evidently the situation quickly changed; in *On the Run* he followed these remembrances with the observation that "Edie Adams was the favorite of all the women with whom I've been personal.")

"I'd have loved to have gone to dinner, but we couldn't go out in public," continued Wills in his recollections of his affair with Day. "That winter, the rumors began to fly. They started one night at the Friars Club when I was being roasted. She knew I was there and she called me. They told her I was in the middle of the program and couldn't come to the phone. She left her phone number and somebody recognized it. After that, when I went places, the interview was about Doris Day right off the bat."

"I was there when the rumors were going on about Doris and Maury Wills," recalled Barbara Flicker, who was unaware, at the time, that the Melchers had separated. "I honestly couldn't believe it had happened, because I knew how busy she was. I don't know when she would've had the time. There wasn't any. I mean, I was with her day and night. . . . Unless she got up at two o'clock in the morning, until three or four. . . . I just can't figure out when or how they physically could've done it."

In the course of promoting his memoir, Wills explained that that was precisely when they met. "I'd call Doris at three or four in the morning. I'd ask her to come over and sometimes she would. Then we'd make love." He also told a reporter that the Dodgers' general manager, Buzzy Bavasi, forced him to terminate the affair. "It was made clear to me that if we continued to see each other, we'd both be hurt. Doris cried when I told her it was all over. I've never seen her again. It's sad, now, to think of what might have been. If only we'd met 30 years later."

Confirming that far less damage had been inflicted than Day's handlers had anticipated, some months after the news of Day and Wills broke, Rock Hudson and Day were declared "the hottest film couple today

[and they] proved it by walking off with the top Golden Globe awards
as world film favorites." They received their awards at a dinner before
"more than 1,000" at the Ambassador Hotel's Cocoanut Grove on March
5, 1963. The awards were becoming "old hat" for the duo, observed a
report in the *Los Angeles Herald-Examiner* the next day, before explaining
that Hudson had already won it three times, as Day had twice.

*   *   *

The September 1963 issue of *Confidential* magazine tackled the controversial subject of interracial romance in Hollywood by focusing, at first, on
Sammy Davis Jr.'s marriage to May Britt, which came after his reported affairs with Kim Novak, Ava Gardner, and Lana Turner. But with a head shot
of Day preceding photos of both Britt and Novak on the cover—the three
of them peering over the sensational headline "Are White Stars Switching
to Negroes"—it's easy to surmise what really prompted the story. Such a
supposition is strongly reinforced by discovering Day's photo superim-
posed with a shot of Maury Wills on the first page of the lengthy and
provocative article by Aaron Putnam.

"Hollywood was shaken to its tinsel foundations last year by rumors
that its two Most Valuable Players had formed their own exclusive sports
club," wrote Putnam in *Variety*-like lingo. "These sizzling reports concerned the friendship between Doris Day, Hollywood's vestal virgin, and
Maury Wills, base-stealing shortstop of the Los Angeles Dodgers baseball
team. Maury was voted the National League's Most Valuable Player of
1962. And Doris, the world's biggest box-office attraction, has long been
Movieland's M.V.P."

Putnam allowed that since Day had long been a sports fanatic, "no
one was particularly surprised when she rented a season box next to the
Dodgers' dugout." He coyly added, however, "At first no one realized
she was rooting for the fleet-footed Negro shortstop more than [for] his
teammates." He also proceeded to quote his has-been forerunner, Walter
Winchell: "Sight-to-see at Dodgers Stadium when the Dodgers play . . . is
Doris Day (she never sits down at the games) rooting hard. She occupies
the field box next to the Dodgers' dugout. So she can greet the players
every evening with a blown kiss."

Far more damaging was Putnam's quote from Hearst columnist
Dorothy Kilgallen. "One of the 10 most famous females in show business can't convince her best friends that her interest in a ballplayer

is strictly professional. . . . She isn't having much luck convincing her husband, either."

Indeed, the swirling rumors about Day and Wills gained credence in light of the ongoing rumors about the Melchers' marriage being in jeopardy. "The whole thing is absurd," Putnam quoted Melcher as saying. "I love my wife. She's a wonderful girl."

"Then he packed his bags and moved out of their $250,000 Beverly Hills home," added Putnam with his one-two punch. "Doris also avoided the press, but by this time newspaper headlines informed the world that the separation rumors were true." Day herself would divulge just how accurate the rumors were in her memoir, published twelve years later.

"The movie moguls were stunned," continued Putnam. "They had spent millions molding Doris into the image of America's girl next door. Her publicity buildup made fans forget she was at least forty, had been married three times and had a twenty-one-year-old son.

"Her father, divorced from her mother, married a Negro a few years ago. The Hollywood rajahs feared Doris might follow his example unless they took drastic steps to prevent such a merger."

Putnam helpfully added, "An unwritten law in Hollywood is that interracial romance is okay, so long as it's kept quiet, but interracial marriage is taboo. Top Negro stars such as Lena Horne, Dorothy Dandridge, Eartha Kitt and Harry Belafonte have married outside their race. But no top Box Office white star has married a Negro, despite the current trend to integrated romance."

*　　*　　*

Day may have waited until the fall of 1962 to ask Melcher for a divorce, but to all evidence any love between them had ceased when they began to disavow it after the making of *Julie* in 1956, when she turned away from Melcher and toward her costar Louis Jourdan. But even if the 1962 separation immediately brought Day relief and a "sense of freedom," it would prove short-lived. When Melcher returned to North Crescent Drive, he explained that, according to Rosenthal, if they divorced they would "lose everything."

It's impossible to know exactly what Melcher had actually learned from Rosenthal at that point. But as described by Day, the stricken look on his face suggested that he knew quite a bit. Nor can there be any doubt that Rosenthal felt seriously threatened by an impending divorce, which was apt to expose what the courts would eventually deem as his criminal practices. As both time and the California court system would eventually reveal, Rosenthal was like a latter-day version of Rasputin—controlling Czarina Day's fortune by manipulating her spouse—and this was obviously a perilous juncture for the attorney.

In spite of her finally deciding that she wanted a divorce, Day was compelled to reconsider such wishes when Melcher, in effect, read her Rosenthal's riot act. As a tangible peace offering, Melcher gave his wife a $16,000 diamond ring. Though she would agree to take Melcher back for the sake of their financial investments, the nonconfrontational Day said that, once and for all, she confronted her husband with her "terms" for doing so. While forfeiting his conjugal rights with his wife, Melcher was free to see others, so long as he kept his dalliances to himself and remained discreet about them. Day was laying down the law, which meant she would be living less of a lie in private, while continuing to live one in public. But by agreeing to such an arrangement, she was also consigning herself to an unhappy regimen.

It was as a free agent herself that Day may have slept with blond, blue-eyed Yankee slugger Mickey Mantle, with whom she first mingled when he made a cameo appearance in *That Touch of Mink*—along with Yogi Berra and Roger Maris. A notorious womanizer, Mantle boasted to friends that not only had he slept with Day at his regular suite in New York's St. Moritz Hotel, but that she was "one of the best lays" of his life. Indeed, Day had apparently started acting like a free spirit some time before the Melchers' aborted separation. Barbara Flicker recalled that she never saw the Melchers being affectionate with each other and that Day began to show up at her place, sans husband, a number of times during this period.

"I remember playing charades with a whole bunch of people every week or so," said Flicker. "Suzanne Pleshette, and Artie and Coz Johnson, who were from *Laugh-In*, and Cliff Norton, who was a great comic. We just ended up in my living room, in this 'little house' on Santa Monica Boulevard. And Doris would come over and have the best time with everybody, and Marty was never with her. Our charades 'club' called her 'Dorn.' She had a really great laugh—it just exploded when she was really tickled. And Artie made her laugh about as hard as anyone I ever heard."

It was during this period that Flicker decided to leave her husband, Bob Crystal. "When I told Doris I was getting a divorce—which was a few months after *Jumbo*—she kind of smiled. But then, she just dropped me," said Flicker. "She just didn't like dealing with any problems, let alone someone else's." (Day had even once told Flicker, "I don't need anyone with problems.") "I think it was also the Christian Science attitude—that she wanted me to be perfect. Occasionally, she would flip a Watchtower on my desk with circles around certain articles. I would think to myself: 'Who is she trying to kid?' I mean, one time when Doris hurt her back, there were about 2,000 doctors in her dressing room.

"We had been so close," continued Flicker. "You know, when the basketball games were going on, I was spending maybe sixteen hours a day with her, for an intense period of time. And then suddenly it was over. And it made me sad, because I came to realize that you really only become good friends with someone when you work through disagreements and problems. And I don't think Doris ever really did that with anybody."

Flicker's divorce from Bob Crystal was handled by Jerome Rosenthal, and she settled for a single dollar. Several years later, Flicker spotted Day on her bicycle in Beverly Hills. "When I saw her on the street one day, riding her bicycle to a bakery, I went in, too. I said, 'Hi, Doris.' And she ignored me. Once she was finished with you, it's not just that she didn't want to see you anymore, but you had ceased to exist for her. She had changed so little."

Flicker returned home in tears after the episode. "I was really hurt. But I had seen it before, and I should have known better." Indeed, Flicker also recalled that Day "had an assistant after me named Peggy. And she got very close to Peggy. But after Peggy adopted a baby, Doris never spoke to her again."

But even if Flicker was inclined to perceive Day's behavior as a personal snub, it might have been a more benign gesture—one of the many examples of Day's sometimes tuning out the world around her. As Day would write in her memoir, she was once stopped by a man on Beverly Drive in the early 1970s. Day assumed he was a fan but was quickly corrected. "Don't you remember me?" he asked. "No," replied Day. "Should I?" "Well, you didn't have that many husbands." Day was stunned to realize it was George Weidler, husband number two.

Flicker recalled another incident demonstrating just how out of touch Day could be with people who worked for her. "Doris decided to cook one night, and we made cheese soufflés," said Flicker. "She called her housekeeper—a big, wonderful woman [Katie]. Doris thought she was living in the guest house in back. And we called her in to help serve, but she had gone home. She had been going home every night for some time, but Doris didn't realize it. That should have been someone she had gotten very close to. Doris should have known [Katie] was married and had a home of her own. But Doris had too much going on in her own life to bother with the details of somebody else's. She couldn't deal with anything that didn't make her own life run smoother.

"You know, Doris was the first one to play independent, working women in movies. But maybe she didn't know how to be one in real life," continued Flicker. "Maybe she was still learning. I think she really liked singing and acting, but I don't think she liked the rest of her life. Everything was about finding ways to get back on the set."

25

Some Inconvenient Truths

———————— ✳ ————————

"Doris was doing a lot of sexy stuff in her movies at the time,
long before the sexual revolution. And she knew it, too!"
—BARBARA FLICKER

While the public was becoming more aware of sexual shenanigans in the Melchers' private life, it was about to be treated
to a lustier side of Doris Day on-screen as well. A feature story on Stephen Boyd in *Modern Screen* remarked that his costar in *Jumbo* was about
to become a "veritable sexpot" in her latest picture, *The Thrill of It All*:
"Freckly Doris is draped in diaphanous nighties in several scenes with
Jim Garner. Beefcake, cheesecake—anything to keep the public happy."

The idea for *The Thrill of It All*, Day's thirty-first picture—her fifth for
Universal—arose at an L.A. party at which Ross Hunter met Carl Reiner.
Always on the prowl for a new vehicle for his leading female star, the
producer asked the writer of both the Sid Caesar and Dick Van Dyke
television shows if he had ever thought of writing a film. Reiner instantly
told Hunter about an outline he had created with Larry Gelbart a couple
years earlier. It was based on Reiner's idea for a send-up of television
commercials, which were becoming increasingly ludicrous. Hunter asked
Reiner to visit his office the next day, and this led to the TV writer's
first film script. (Gelbart was tied up with his latest Broadway venture, *A
Funny Thing Happened on the Way to the Forum*, and did not work on the
screenplay.)

Day once declared "Thrill of It All" her favorite script after "Pillow
Talk." "Nothing has to be changed, not one line," she told Melcher after
reading it. Although Day played a married mother named Beverly Boyer
in the film, the picture was in the mold of her recent phenomenally successful comedies. She had a new costar, James Garner, as her husband,
Gerald, a gynecologist. Hunter, who had become known for hiring re-

tired stars in featured roles, hoped to cast Jeanette MacDonald and Nelson Eddy as the Fraleighs, a middle-aged couple whose fertility problems Gerald resolves. Hunter had Jeanette and her husband, Gene Raymond, for dinner along with the Melchers.

"Jeanette and Doris were absolutely delightful together," said Day's pen pal Paul Brogan, who became the president of the Jeanette MacDonald fan club as well as a friend of Day's. "Personally, they just hit it off. Jeanette was a huge fan who never missed a Doris Day film when it played in Los Angeles. And Doris was very flattered she felt that way. But ultimately Jeanette got ill, and so they brought in Arlene Francis and Edward Andrews."

The movie included a spoof of a TV show, in which Reiner inserted a bit part for himself. It was an unmistakable parody of the inane skits Reiner used to perform on Sid Caesar's *Your Show of Shows*. Along with Reiner, director Norman Jewison knew a good deal about the film's subject. Though he would become far more famous as a film director of heavy-duty social dramas (such as *In the Heat of the Night*), Jewison got his start working on three hundred or so TV shows at the Canadian Broadcasting Corporation, before making high-profile specials for CBS. "Both Carl and I came from live television and were both natural rebels," Jewison said. "We wanted to parody TV's product spokespeople and present the sponsors as one-note egomaniacs."

Part of a seven-picture deal he had made with Universal, *Thrill* was Jewison's second film. (His first was *40 Pounds of Trouble*.) When he arranged a lunch between Day and Jewison, studio head Ed Muhl had to have been aware of Melcher's insistence upon controlling things and making them on the cheap. "Impress Doris," Muhl told the fledgling director, "and you'll shoot her next picture." But as Jewison recalled, it was Melcher he had to impress at lunch in Universal's commissary.

According to Jewison, Melcher "was loud, taking over the room as soon as he arrived. He had on a slick Sy Devore suit," said the director, referring to the top-of-the-line Beverly Hills tailor. Melcher opened with, "I like your work, Norm." When Jewison pointed out that he had made only one picture, "Melcher gave a dismissive wave of his hand, the one with the big cigar in it," continued Jewison. "I said I like your work and I mean it," insisted Melcher. It quickly became apparent that Melcher had done his homework and knew that Jewison had made many TV specials with some big stars—including Judy Garland, Jackie Gleason, Danny Kaye, even Frank Sinatra.

Jewison remembered Day at that luncheon: "very blond and peppy, though she looked her age, which was thirty-eight." (She was, in fact, forty.) She proceeded to ask her prospective director about his personal life, wondering, in particular, if he had a "spiritual" background. As pre-arranged with Melcher, Day then excused herself and joined another table, leaving him to close the deal. "Melcher leaned over to me," continued Jewison. "It wasn't just Melcher's suit that was slick. Most things about him were slick. Even his hair was combed straight back from his forehead, slicked down flat over his scalp."

"Don't worry about Doris on this movie," Melcher told him. "All you gotta do is keep telling her that she looks great. Remember that, she looks great. You won't have any trouble."

Jewison was about to learn just why Melcher had placed so much emphasis on his wife's looks. "They were Doris's weak point," said the director. "Not her looks per se, but the way she perceived them. Doris did not believe that she was an attractive woman. I thought she was beautiful. Millions of fans thought she was beautiful. Everybody she had ever worked with thought she was beautiful. Doris remained unconvinced."

According to Jewison, he realized what he was up against "the first minute" he arrived on the set and discovered enormous camera lights in place. He asked the cinematographer, Russell Metty—who had shot Day in *Midnight Lace* and *That Touch of Mink*—what they were for. Metty explained that they were necessary to compensate for the heavy-duty filters he was using on the cameras. "He knew what he was doing," Jewison soon came to realize. "The combination of strong lighting and soft filters would wash Doris clear of every wrinkle, every flaw, every blemish. She'd have the skin of a teenager."

But despite her cameraman's helpful tactics, Day was at first terribly insecure about her appearance. "She seemed uneasy in the first scenes we shot," said Jewison. "She couldn't relax into the role and I suspected it was her anxiety about her looks." Jewison proceeded to reconstruct one of his early conversations with Day in her trailer.

"If you're worried about how you're going to look in the movie," he told her, "why don't you take charge of everything?"

"What are you talking about, Norman?" replied Day. "Do it yourself. You know what you want. Do your own makeup. Take charge of doing your gowns. Take charge of the lighting, the camera angles."

"Oh, Norman."

"Who knows, take charge even of the directing."

"You're making fun of me."

"No, Doris, I'm taking you very seriously," explained Jewison. "What I'm trying to tell you is that all of us on the movie are dedicated to making you look great. You don't need to worry. Just let us take care of what we know how to do. Jean Louis, Russ Metty, me, the rest of the crew, we know our jobs. I want you to relax and concentrate on your job. Acting! Just give me a focused performance."

In all fairness to Day, any qualms she had about working with Jewison were not entirely out of place. Because this was only his second film, Jewison was far from the seasoned directors that Day was accustomed to working with, and she might have felt skittish about his being a relative novice. She also was becoming acutely aware that she was fast approaching middle age, and that filmmakers would be dropping her just as quickly and mysteriously as Michael Curtiz had first embraced her.

But according to Jewison, his "reverse psychology" worked on Day. His leading actress "got much less anxious about her looks. She started to have fun on the movie, which was the way it was supposed to be. She had terrific timing, a natural comedic rhythm." Given her background as a singer, Jewison added, "[S]he knew instinctively when to hit her lines and give them the right inflection. Rhythm and timing are vital for comedy, and Doris was better at them than just about anyone I have ever worked with." Day, however, remained more nervous about her appearance than Jewison imagined. During the making of the film, she even had the still photographer—whose job it was to take publicity photos on the set—replaced.

Jewison had had the brilliant idea of casting James Garner as Day's costar. The virile Garner—with a Clark Kent chin, complete with cleft— was born on April 7, 1928, making him six years Day's junior. He would prove every bit as natural a screen mate for Day as Rock Hudson. Though Garner was hardly known for his work in comedies, Jewison said he had detected his "comic presence" in TV's lighthearted Western *Maverick.* Offscreen, Day engaged in the same kind of playful games with Garner that she had with Hudson. "On the set we do takeoffs on the folks back home," Garner explained while they were shooting the picture. "She calls me Al and I called her Sylvia-honey."

But it wasn't all fun and games while Day was making *The Thrill of It All.* One evening, Day's beloved white poodle, Charlie, choked on a bone and died. Though she reported for work the next morning at 6 a.m. as usual, she proved inconsolable. Without explaining why, her dresser told assistant director Tommy Shaw that she wasn't going to leave her trailer. When Shaw reported Day's inexplicable delay to a disbelieving Jewison, the director said they should give her another twenty minutes. When still more time had elapsed, Melcher was summoned. He arrived with Ross Hunter, who told Jewison, "You're the director. It's your responsibility to keep this movie shooting." It's significant that Melcher himself refused to approach his wife, revealing just how strained their relationship had become.

Jewison went to Day's trailer and knocked on her door. She finally emerged and "fell" into his arms, sobbing. "It's Charlie, he's dead. . . . And it's all my fault. He choked on a bone. I gave him the lamb chop. I killed him." For Day, Charlie's death invoked the terrible time when she was an adolescent on crutches and her spaniel, Tiny, ran away from her and was struck by a car, triggering a lifelong guilt. Jewison sympathized with his star for another half hour, explaining that it really wasn't her fault. As he recently recalled, "Slowly, she stopped crying and returned to make-up. Half an hour later, she emerged, beautiful as ever. She had a deep love for animals but she was also a professional."

Hollywood columnist Harrison Carroll visited the set in December during the shooting of a sequence of the delivery of a baby, set in a traffic jam on Manhattan's FDR Drive, with the Queensborough Bridge in the background. "Isn't this a wonderful set," Ross Hunter boasted. "We went to New York and tried to shoot this sequence on the real expressway. It rained for 10 days. I called the studio and said I wanted to come back and build the set on a sound stage where we could control everything. . . .We can do anything in Hollywood. I figured I saved us $200,000 by building this set in the sound stage."

*　*　*

Essentially a send-up of commercial television, *The Thrill of It All* has a secondary focus on a woman's role as a homemaker. Invited to do a commercial for Happy Soap, Beverly (Day) responds, "I'm not an actress. I'm a housewife." But she makes the commercial, and it quickly launches a lucrative career that, much to her husband's consternation, interferes more and more with her home life. She's no longer there for Gerald, who becomes increasingly annoyed. During a serious argument, while he's packing to leave, Beverly asks, "Whatever happened to my rights as a woman?" "They grew and they grew until they suffocated my rights as a man," replies Gerald, who asks her to "[g]ive up this asinine career and go back to being a wife."

Mrs. Fraleigh, Gerald's patient who is trying to become pregnant, observes, "There's nothing more fulfilling in life than having a baby." Such sentiments were precisely what Betty Friedan railed against in *The Feminine Mystique*. The book had a seismic impact upon its publication in 1963, sparking the woman's lib movement exactly when *The Thrill of It All* was released. Friedan was outraged by "experts telling women their role was to seek fulfillment as wives and mothers." After interviewing a number of her peers, she identified a "nameless aching dissatisfaction" among them, "the problem," she declared, "that has no name."

When she wrote about a culture of women whose "only dream was to be perfect wives and mothers," Friedan might well have been describing the dilemma of both Beverly and Day herself. According to Friedan, "In the fifteen years after World War II, this mystique of feminine fulfillment became the cherished and self-perpetuating core of contemporary American culture. Millions of women lived their lives in the image of those pretty pictures of the American Suburban housewife, kissing their husbands goodbye in front of the picture window, depositing their station wagons full of children at school, and smiling as they ran the new electric waxer over the spotless kitchen floor."

*　*　*

Universal's high expectations for *The Thrill of It All* were well conveyed to exhibitors with a large, twenty-page Press Book. The picture was promoted with yet another two-page spread in *Life* magazine explaining, "She is subjected, as always, to slapstick indignities such as the pratfall and a crate of tomatoes. But she gets away with it because of her antiseptic freshness—and the fact that she is an uncommonly skilled comedienne." In fact, Day fell out of the crate, as the cameras were rolling, knocking her head on a steamer trunk and her elbow on the floor. Luckily, what might have proved a far more serious accident left her merely bruised.

The twenty-one-year-old Terry also contributed a long article to help sell *The Thrill of It All*, revealing, in the process, a common problem for children of celebrities: "All along, I've wanted to find my own identity as Terry Melcher—not simply as 'Doris Day's son.' In my teens, I dreamed of moving away from home, of living by myself or with pals." While acknowledging that he did poorly at Beverly Hills High, Terry added, "I was rebelling against being the son of a star. I wanted to be appreciated for myself and had little focus on my future." Terry was equally revealing when he said, "Mom worries about everything, from the freckles on her face to the food we eat, to whether her hair is squeaky clean. She worries about sly jabs in the daily press and about her tennis score. A perfectionist, she is fussier than a preening peahen about the way she looks, lives and behaves." He further divulged, "Mom doesn't make friends easily. She's withdrawn. Instead of letting conversation bridge a friendship, Mom reaches out in other ways."

Though the film hasn't aged well, it was well received by many reviewers when it originally opened. "Thank goodness," crowed Bosley Crowther in the *New York Times*. "Doris Day has finally got back to having a husband, some kids and is acting her age in her latest knockabout comedy . . . which bounced gaily into the Music Hall yesterday. [She] is best at domestic comedy when it's got a real bounce and bite to it. And that's what this one has." Crowther also described the star's customary techniques: "Miss Day is her usual explosive, indignant, disarming, pop-eyed self, full of sudden blurts and stammers and cuddly gurgles of joy."

The review in *Variety* acclaimed the film as being "the best" of her four recent romantic comedies, "in terms of having something more to say about contemporary life than 'gosh, ain't love wonderful.'" James Powers also penned a rave for the *Hollywood Reporter*: "Miss Day, of course, has few peers as the clean-cut, nice, but agreeably sexy wife. She is also now an expert at the throwaway line and throwaway glance. She is one of the screen's best comediennes and she has plenty of good material to work with in Reiner's bright script and with Jewison's inventive direction."

Variety also reported that the film was "soaring to a mighty $205,000, one of the big opening week totals for summer at the Music Hall." And on August 7, 1963, the show business paper reported that *Cleopatra* was "again No. 1 picture for sixth week in a row, [and the] 'Thrill' is finishing a strong second although playing in only 10 key [cities]."

✳   ✳   ✳

When *The Thrill of It All* opened in the summer of 1963, James Harbert was "packing his bags . . . for a five-week visit to Paris where he'll write the music and lyrics for the world-famous Lido de Paris revue," a local

Hollywood paper reported, in addition to revealing that he would be "the first American to compose a score for the 50-year-old French revue."

The new Paris show—*Bravo!*—was to be written and cast in Paris, with an American version to open in Las Vegas (at the Stardust Hotel, on October 23). According to Harbert, *Bravo!* was "loaded with special effects: ships sinking, earthquakes." It also transformed his career. In taking a five-week French leave, Harbert had forfeited more than he intended. In a comment demonstrating that Terry had truly become his stepfather's son, Harbert said, "When I got back from Paris, I discovered that Terry had gotten a hold of my artists and was recording them. And that's a no-no. I gave it to him, all barrels." Terry had taken particular charge of the New Christy Minstrels, the folk group that Harbert had put on the charts. Harbert also kept hearing that Day had been spreading a damaging tale: "He just went off to Paris and abandoned me." "We had had such a nice relationship in those years," continued Harbert. "And then, in the end, I heard that, 'She's had it with you, and all you did to Terry.'"

Harbert had, in fact, been growing restive at Columbia, where he felt that his work not only failed to tap his true creative talents, but also prevented his applying them elsewhere. "I didn't like being a midwife," recalled Harbert. "I'm a composer, an author, and a lyricist. And I just didn't like delivering other people's 'babies.' Also, my classical background began to erupt. I went to Goddard Lieberson and said, 'I can't take it any more, being a pop producer. You've got to send me over to Columbia Masterworks.' But Lieberson said, 'No way. You're the only one making any money on the west coast for the company.' And then Doris had gotten a little pissed off at me when I got the chance to do a show in France, where they regarded me as an important composer, and I went ahead and did it." Indeed, Harbert's cabaret shows in Paris and Las Vegas became something of an institution and emboldened him to leave Columbia early in 1964. It was shortly after Harbert returned to the States that John F. Kennedy was assassinated, transforming the world on both sides of the Atlantic.

26

"Something's Got to Give"

---------------- ✳ ----------------

*"Popular music in the USA is one of the few things in the
Twentieth Century that has made giant strides in reverse."*
—BING CROSBY

*"If Marilyn Monroe died for our sins, as a saying of the
time had it, then Doris Day smiled for them."*
—JAMES HARVEY

ilm historian Stanley Cavell coined the term "comedy of remar-
riage" for a subgenre of romantic comedy involving a couple who,
having separated, must overcome seemingly insurmountable obstacles in
the course of reuniting. This certainly describes *Move Over, Darling,* based
on the1940 screwball comedy *My Favorite Wife,* starring Cary Grant and
Irene Dunne. Yet an earlier and unfinished version of *Move Over, Darling,*
with the title *Something's Got to Give,* has a place in the history of this latest Day comedy. *Something's Got to Give,* begun the year before, was to
have been Marilyn Monroe's thirtieth picture and her first in more than
a year. George Cukor was set as the director, and Dean Martin and Cyd
Charisse had been cast as Monroe's costars. But eight weeks after filming began, the troubled and frequently tardy star, who could no longer
remember her lines, was fired from the project. Two months later, she
was found dead.

Melcher was willing for his wife to step into the blonde bombshell's
pumps up to a definite point. While announcing that Day would be the
successor to Hollywood's sex goddess, Melcher emphasized that she
would not have nude bathing shots like the "much-publicized ones" already released of Marilyn. "It will be sort of a married 'Pillow Talk,'"
continued Melcher, ". . . what we call 'clean sex.'"

Though *Move Over, Darling* was yet another attempt to duplicate the success of the Ross Hunter formula, Melcher now had as coproducer Aaron Rosenberg, a onetime all-American football star who had become a prolific Hollywood producer. The film was also the first of three that Day made with Twentieth Century Fox. According to film scholar Drew Casper, Fox thought of Day for the picture not only for her drawing power, but because she had just "spoofed" Monroe in *The Thrill of It All.*

A number of writers worked on what eventually became the final draft of *Move Over, Darling.* The first version was written by Edmund Hartmann in 1960, with the title *Do It Again.* Renamed *Something's Gotta Give,* it was revised by Arnold Schulman in November, and again by Nunnally Johnson—one of the most prolific and successful writer-producer-directors Hollywood would ever know—the following February.

Given Melcher's recent dismal failure with *The Perfect Setup* on Broadway, it seemed surprising that he then recruited the play's author, Jack Sher, to work on the screenplay (early in 1963). But both stories were basically the same. They describe a man torn between two women. In the case of *Move Over, Darling,* Nick Arden is literally—if inadvertently—a bigamist. His first wife, Ellen, disappeared in a plane crash and was declared legally dead, and Nick became free to marry Bianca. But Ellen, portrayed by Day, is only missing, not dead. She has been stranded on a desert island for five years and is then saved by the navy. Ellen returns home just in time to stalk Nick and Bianca on their honeymoon. As it plays out in adjacent hotel rooms, the farce quickly comes to resemble Noël Coward's *Private Lives,* and it may in turn have inspired Neil Simon's *The Heartbreak Kid,* also built around a honeymoon in jeopardy.

The *New York Times* reported that the script was "altered to suit" Day by reverting to elements of the Irene Dunne and Cary Grant version. There were, nevertheless, basic differences, according to Hal Kantor, who worked on the final version of the screenplay with Sher. "My feeling is that in the original, when Irene comes back, her attitude is that this is a funny situation and she makes Cary suffer. In this, while Doris understands there is some amusement, she suffers with him for a while and then she gets damned mad."

Michael Gordon returned as Day's director, and James Garner was reunited with the star. As Nick, Garner would prove again to be an ideal Rock Hudson substitute for Day. (Hudson was at the time busy doing the narration for a Twentieth Century Fox documentary about Monroe called *Marilyn* and making *A Gathering of Eagles* at Universal.) Casting the secondary players was not without problems, however. "I had, at that point, only starred in films," said Polly Bergen, who played Bianca. "And I said, well, I don't want to play 'second banana' to Doris Day, who was the biggest star in the world and has got to be a complete and total pain in the neck. . . . She'll arrive at noon, to be photographed. They'll be shooting me at six in the morning and the camera will never be on me in a shot that she's in: It'll be, you know, on the back of my head, on her, and I am not going to do this movie."

Michael Gordon, who had previously directed Bergen on Broadway in *Champagne Complex,* convinced her that she was perfect for the role, and she proved grateful. "I so fell in love with [Doris]: she was the most wonderful, funny, delicious, completely sharing, giving actress I had ever worked with—and I mean that sincerely," Bergen enthused. (As an interesting side note, Melcher was Bergen's agent in the beginning of her own multifarious career as another singer who became an actress.)

Ellen's desert-island companion was played by Chuck Connors, known for his years with the Los Angeles Dodgers. (In baseball parlance, he had been up "for a cup of coffee.") Six-foot-seven, Connors dwarfed his leading lady. And the indomitable character actress Thelma Ritter, who had played Day's alcoholic housekeeper in *Pillow Talk,* was elevated to portray the elegant mother-in-law.

Though originally scheduled to begin on April 1, 1963, production was postponed several weeks until Garner became available. The film was ultimately completed in fifty-three days. Its most talked-about sequence—when Day passes through a car wash in her open-top convertible—was shot last. (That set alone cost $40,000.)

Fully aware of Day's growing reputation as a temperamental worrywort, Twentieth Century Fox went to the unusual measure of assigning not the usual one but two on-the-job unit publicists. The "second man wasn't selected for his ability at the typewriter," revealed reporter Milt Johnson. "Unknown to Doris, he was picked because he was an avid sports enthusiast and knew the batting averages of the Los Angeles Dodgers by heart. The studio figured—and correctly so—that this man could keep the baseball-struck Doris so busy with sports talk that there wouldn't be any trouble." When shooting the department-store scene "with milling crowds of extras," the soundman was confronted with "a mysterious buzz [and] production was held up while the crew checked out everything down to the extras' squeaky shoes. It was discovered that Dodo—bless her sports-loving little heart—was carrying a transistor radio in her bosom. She was listening to the World Series."

Nothing, however, could distract Day from worrying about her appearance. Some days after shooting had begun, the star had the cameraman replaced, according to Milt Johnson, "suddenly" and "without notice." Early in the shoot, she suffered her third cracked rib during the making of a picture after Garner forcefully picked her up and carried her under his arm, as the script demanded. "The star's physician, Dr. Frederick Ilfeld, said she will have to wear an elastic brace for four weeks but will be able to finish the picture," the *Los Angeles Times* reported. In her memoir, Day explained that she made the balance of the picture "mummified with adhesive tape" and between takes was forced to rest in her dressing room.

Whenever Garner spoke about working with Day, he would emphasize how different she was from the girl-next-door image she sustained. "You can't miss with a girl like that," he once said. "I'd rather have Doris than Liz Taylor. Everything Doris does turns to box-office gold. And she is not at all the wholesome, malt-drinking, all-American girl everyone supposes.

"I think Doris is a very sexy lady who doesn't know how sexy she is. That's an integral part of her charm," Garner explained. "One other thing about acting with Doris—she was the Fred Astaire of comedy. . . . Whether it was Rock Hudson or Rod Taylor or me or whoever—we all looked good because we were dancing with Clara Bixby. . . . Making a movie with Doris was a piece of cake."

Like many other coworkers, Garner had special praise for Day's natural improvisational skills. Director Michael Gordon also discussed Day's tendency to be herself when she was making a picture. "One of the things that I remember with [special] pleasure and admiration is the unswerving dedication to truth that characterized her approach to comedy," he said. "It was her own unique comedic truth, to be sure, but it was comparable in its own terms [to what] she was able to draw on so movingly in films like 'The Man Who Knew Too Much' and 'Midnight Lace.'" Gordon evoked Day's vulnerability as well: "That kind of involvement yielded in 'Move Over, Darling,' a wonderfully surprising and delightful ad-lib. Visualize Doris trapped in a convertible with the top down, doused with detergent foam and drenched with spray. Then suddenly as the terrifying revolving cylinder of brushes is inexorably bearing down on her, over the horrendous din you hear her cry out faintly, in poignant desperation, 'My hair!' The screenwriters and I wished we'd thought of something like that. Doris spontaneously did—frequently."

But even if Garner was one of the many costars who admired Day's freedom when working on a picture, he found little to admire in her husband. "Marty was a hustler, a shallow, insecure hustler who always ripped off $50,000 on every one of Doris's films as the price for making the deal. . . . When we were making 'Move Over, Darling,' he was bragging a lot about money he had just borrowed from the Teamsters to finance some big hotel or other. A wheeler-dealer businessman, but of course we all knew where his clout came from and without Doris he couldn't have driven a truck for the Teamsters. I never knew anyone who liked Melcher."

*   *   *

Since *Move Over, Darling* was basically a farce about conjugal rights, the Production Code office gave Twentieth Century Fox problems with the script from its earliest incarnation, when it was called *Do It Again*. Even after the writers made adjustments to successive versions in order to secure approval, the Code office continued to raise objections, particularly to the proposed lyrics of the title song: "Oh, I yearn to be kissed/Move over darling/How can I resist/Move over darling/Come into my arms/ And be more than just company/Make love to me." Within two days, Joe Lubin supplied revised final lines: "You've captured my heart/And now that I'm no longer free/Please treat me tenderly/Move over darling/ Make love to me." Completely censored, they were deemed "acceptable." Lubin's collaborator on the song was Hal Kantor. But Terry Melcher, who was attempting to transform his mother's recording career by giving her a new and bouncier sound, rewrote their work. "They brought me the song for the film, and I didn't think it was so great," recalled Terry. "I said, 'We can do this title, but I'll have to rewrite the thing.'" (Country-star-to-be Glen Campbell played the guitar during the recording session of *Move Over, Darling*.)

Terry had his friend Jack Nitzsche supervise the recording. At Terry's bidding, Nitzsche also tried to give Day a new "rock" sound with "Let the Little Girl Limbo"—by Barry Mann and Cynthia Weill—several months earlier in April 1963, with his "wall-of-sound" arrangement, based on Phil Spector's technique, involving echo effects and tape loops. Though Melcher and Day liked the recording, Terry suppressed its release. "He decided it was definitely not [his mother's] style. . . . [H]e pointed out all the places that, as he said, 'were shady or suggestive.'"

According to James Harbert, "When Terry was trying to get his
mother to change her sound, I said, 'She could do anything. She could
sing middle-of-the-road rock as well as anybody.'" But Harbert also told
the up-and-coming A&R man: "Your mother's a great artist, and trying to
push her in the direction of a teen-age rock star isn't the way to go."

At the time, Terry was also producing records for TM Music, Inc.
Though the initials were his own, the company was owned by Bobby Darin, who had only good things to say about his newfound young friend
and recording adviser. A number of records produced by TM Music had
total sales exceeding two million copies. "He's a young genius," Darin
said of Terry. "He has the most infallible music sense of anyone I've ever
met. This guy's going to go a long way."

"As music was changing and getting more bluesy and funky, nobody at Columbia knew who were the musicians behind the hits, the
guys making the sounds that were taking over the radio," recalled Terry.
"Actually, as music changed, the fact that Doris Day was my mother was
not that much of a help. If anything, it made it more difficult to achieve
some credibility of my own. I was very lucky to meet Jack Nitzsche, who
introduced me to all the best players in town. He was the first guy with
any kind of an ear, with credibility 'on the street,' who decided that I had
some talent. Nitzsche kind of invented orchestral rock."

Marty Melcher resisted his stepson's impulses to update Day's style.
Though *Variety* would claim before long that "Doris Day reports she'll
attempt to crack the juke wax market for Columbia Records with some
'modified rock 'n' roll,'" she did not go far enough in that direction and,
within several years, brought her two-decade reign as a top-flight recording artist to a close. By failing to adapt to the revolutionary changes engulfing both the music and film worlds in the early 1960s, the backward-
looking Melcher squandered what might have been his wife's ongoing
career in both realms. As shrewd as he had been in managing Day's
career during the past two decades, Melcher, conservative at heart, failed
to keep up with the changing times.

A press release for *Move Over, Darling* presented a positive spin on
Melcher's increasing control of interviews with his wife. "He makes her
contacts, intimate or slight, swear that there are what he describes, as 'areas of sensitivity' which are not to be touched upon in conversation. This
protective cocoon of hard-shelled devotion leaves Doris completely free
to work on her pictures—the thing she likes to do most and does best."
The release, written by Don Prince, was surprisingly candid: "Those that

say that Miss Day is the girl-next-door on a golden treadmill don't know their Day. She is plagued by insecurity stemming from emotional trauma sustained in her past. She hates to make decisions, and will call Marty to ask him such trivial questions, as to what dress she should wear to dinner, but she is a compulsive worker."

*   *   *

With Fox's long overdue and extravagantly expensive *Cleopatra* on the verge of release, the studio was under enormous pressure to have a success with *Move Over, Darling*. In addition to the regular theatrical trailer, the marketing campaign offered "a teaser [i.e., briefer] trailer to tempt customers," as well as TV and radio spots, and a Dell paperback "novel" based on the film. This package to exhibitors praised Day's recording of the title tune "with the 'new beat' so popular today." *Life* magazine featured a three-page spread on the film, in which Day, referring to the car-wash scene, quipped, "In movies, I'm always getting dunked or man-handled. I should be paid by the fight."

When *Move Over, Darling* went into general release on Christmas Day 1963, the reviews were predominantly negative. "By now, for all of Miss Day's blond prettiness, I tend to think of her as the perfect den mother, industrious and highly non-inflammable, and I deplore any role that causes her to take an aggressive stand in respect to s-x," wrote Brendan Gill in the *New Yorker*. Gill's outright pan further accused Garner of playing "light comedy with a crushingly heavy hand" and claimed that Bergen and Ritter "ought to have been given lots of funny things to say and are often able to convey their awareness that they haven't been."

The reviewer for *Time* magazine was also far from pleased, declaring the film "a remake of a remake, but the new version doesn't half make it." While adding that Day "just can't bring herself to attempt [Marilyn Monroe's] celebrated nude bathing scene," the critic also pointed out that "James Garner appears to be playing the role long patented by Doris. Sex threatens him, and poor Jim has a tough time staying chaste." A. H. Weiler was even more dismayed in his review for the *New York Times*: "[The film] appears to be straining and shouting for effects that should be natural and uncontroverted. A viewer is constantly belabored by the obvious and the punches and punch lines are nearly always telegraphed." Even more blunt, the *Saturday Review* pronounced the film "a brightly colored mess," and found its sentimentality distasteful: "Those with weak stomachs should leave before the scene in which Doris Day and the children admit they belong to each other."

The trade reviews recognized the film's potential to be a hit and proved more generous, as they usually were. "The story is contrived yet delightful all the way. A slick production polish has been accorded the picture [which] has the ingredients of popular success," offered Mandel Herbstman in *Film Daily*. "It has generous doses of humor, romance and 'heart,' and high-power box office names, to make it a strong hit," observed James Powers in the *Hollywood Reporter*, who added that Day "gets her laughs. She is also briskly capable in the romantic scenes and the tender ones with two small daughters."

Film critic John Simon's vehemently negative review perfectly encapsulated the intelligentsia's growing aversion toward Day, particularly since she had become number one at the box office. Knowingly or not, Simon built his reputation for intelligence and discernment on being superior to what was mainstream, and Day became one of his principal victims. This was, after all, the time when foreign pictures and "art films" had begun to capture the highbrows' attention at the expense of Hollywood's escapist, commercial fare. If anything, the passion of Simon's disapproval seemed to reinforce the importance of Day's star power.

"It should give us pause that Doris Day has been, for years, the number one box-office attraction in the American cinema," Simon wrote. "It should start us thinking that her sickening films have been well received by the reviewers. . . . The only very real talent Miss Day possesses is that of being absolutely sanitary: her personality untouched by human emotions, her brow unclouded by human thought, her form unsmudged by the slightest evidence of femininity.

"What, I repeat, does this endemic Day-worship mean?" Simon continued a paragraph or so later. "It means that two or three generations of Americans are basking in witlessness and calling it wit, in facelessness and calling it radiance, in sexlessness and calling it sex, in total darkness and calling it Day. It means that until this spun-sugar zombie melts from our screen, there is little chance of the American film's coming of age."

In spite of the mediocrity Simon ascribed to Day—not to mention his arrogant critic's sense of superiority—the American film was very much on the verge of coming of age in the early to mid-1960s. Such movies as *Dr. Strangelove, Who's Afraid of Virginia Woolf?, Bonnie and Clyde,* and *The Graduate* were at the forefront of a revolution in American cinema. *Move Over, Darling* opened three years after Fellini's *La Dolce Vita* and Antonioni's

L'Avventura had an impact on filmmakers and audiences alike. Ingmar Bergman's films were well established by then as a regular fixture in American art houses. The more avant-garde filmmakers Jean-Luc Godard and Alain Resnais—who challenged viewers with their nonnarrative, abstractionist methods—had also come into vogue by the mid-1960s.

Among other impulses in the air was the disdain with which commercial success and public approval were increasingly greeted. A couple of decades before the so-called dumbing down of American culture, it was already perceived as being dumb. Precisely when Day was breaking records to become the most popular female star of all time, a cultural sea change was taking place.

If only Day's husband had resisted his inclination to follow the old and tired formulas and had been willing to surf the changing tide, his wife's film career may have thrived, instead of sputtering out in relative disgrace in the eyes of cultural commentators. In only a few years, director Mike Nichols would offer Day what might have proved the perfect transition to her senior years—the role of Mrs. Robinson in *The Graduate*. (Nichols's early dream cast also included Robert Redford, Candice Bergen, and Ronald Reagan.) Alas, Day and Melcher would turn it down without qualms or misgivings. After nearly two decades of burnishing her pristine, girl-next-door image, neither Day nor Melcher could envision any other. As James Harbert conjectured about the offer of the role of Mrs. Robinson: "I could hear Marty saying, 'We can't have Doris Day seducing an underage boy in a film.'" It was the continuing moral high road attitude of the Melchers that invited the wrath of the likes of John Simon.

"What bothers me so much about Doris's post–Warner Brothers career, is that she didn't step in and make more of a fuss about the mediocrity and the pabulum that she was force-fed, which she didn't mind passing on down to her public," Rex Reed averred with passion. "I think Marty forced her to do those films, and she couldn't possibly have been over ecstatic about those scripts, when she got them. I don't even think they were ready to be green-lighted. They were just works-in-progress. All she had to play was an attitude, in great clothes. She devoted a huge chunk of her career to mediocrity, and I think she should have made a much bigger fuss about it. It has always troubled me that she was not more aggressive about the quality of the work that she was involved in. She could have made better films if she had not wasted her time making mediocre ones."

But as always, moviegoers couldn't care less about film reviews—or reviewers—and *Move Over, Darling* was a huge hit. According to *Variety*, it was the sixth-biggest money earner in 1964, after *The Carpetbaggers*, *It's a Mad, Mad, Mad, Mad World*, *The Unsinkable Molly Brown*, *Charade*, and *The Cardinal*. But one of the most shocking signs of a backlash against Day's ongoing top box-office status appeared as a caveat on the jacket for the DRG reissue of her dazzling *Duet* album, made with Andre Previn: "It might be prudent at this point to advise those of you who are made uneasy—or even ill—by Miss Day's antiseptic screen persona to state emphatically herewith that the subject at hand is Doris Day the singer—not the movie star!" The rerelease of the *Duet* album appealed to a higher-brow segment of Day's audience.

Although he would prove an eloquent admirer, James Wolcott succinctly described the negative view of Day that came to prevail and clouded her subsequent reputation. Four decades after *Move Over, Darling*, he wrote in *Vanity Fair*, "Once the most popular female star on the planet, Day provokes a gag reflex today from those who equate her with the waxy shine and Waspy complexion of unliberated womanhood in the conformist 50s. Her gumption, optimism, and pep are considered corny, counterrevolutionary."

Even as big a fan of Day's as the celebrated mainstream critic Rex Reed would write, "The fresh scrubbed-nose wonder of the early Doris Day has all but been obliterated in the memory by the quagmire of cheapjack silliness her career has become, so that all that talent and freshness and delicious appeal I used to applaud in her early days at Warner Brothers have all but been forgotten by a public with a short memory. Doris Day has turned into a joke. The talent and energy and class are still there, but she prefers to keep them hidden under forty pounds of spray net."

In opposition to John Simon's high-handed stance, there were at least two other highbrow commentators who rushed to Day's defense—John Updike and Molly Haskell. "She just glowed for me," Updike claimed, when he was interviewed years later for a TV documentary devoted to her. "Not the only star in the sky, but certainly one of the brightest."

Citing the "proto-feminist boldness of some of [Day's] working-girl characters," film scholar Haskell wrote about her becoming "suspicious of the quickness with which most people dismissed her." In a lengthy appreciation of Day, Haskell rhetorically asked, "Was it that her all-American wholesomeness in the anti-America sixties had become an embarrassment? Her cheery optimism and determination were not only qualities we had lost but ones we felt ashamed of having entertained in the first place. . . . To many women, she was like a hundred-watt reminder of the excessively bright and eager-to-please feminine masquerade of the fifties.

"Day was more convenient than appropriate as a symbol of oppression of women," Haskell further observed. After referring to her work in *Pillow Talk*, *That Touch of Mink*, and *The Thrill of It All*, Haskell explained, "When I remember her roles in these films, it is as one of the few movie heroines (and one of the last) who had to work for a living. Grace Kelly and Audrey Hepburn, bless their chic souls, floated through life. Voluptuous Ava Gardner ran barefoot and bohemian through exotic places. Marilyn Monroe was the sexual totem for the various fetishes of fifties America. Kim Novak and Debbie Reynolds and Shirley MacLaine, who like Day, were not goddesses and hence had to exert themselves, still sought a man to lean on. One never felt in them the driving, single-minded ambition one felt in Day—the very strength that was used as a weapon, in the sex comedies, to impugn her femininity."

According to Haskell, "Doris Day ought to be treated with several degrees more seriousness than has characterized most articles and critiques of this—I think—underrated actress. Not only was I defending her talent, but, more preposterously, her movies—something not even her best friends would buy. 'If only her career had been different,' they would say, shaking their heads. 'If only Hollywood. . . .'"

* * *

Emphasizing just how successful Day was in disregarding her naysayers, she was named the top box-office star for the second year in a row, as announced on January 6, 1964—while *Move Over, Darling* was still in release. (This was based on the thirty-second annual poll of the country's theater owners.) The biggest male star was John Wayne, who came in second, after Day. It was also the seventh time that Day had placed on the list of the top-ten box-office attractions—and her third year as champ.

While Day was increasingly taking a critical drubbing from many a reviewer, the Melchers staged a swift retreat, as it were, and became less cooperative with—and even more manipulative of—the press than they had been. The Women's Press Club again gave Day its Sour Apple Award for being the Most Uncooperative Actress of the Year. In his cover story on this development for British *Photoplay*, Peter Howell rushed to point out that this was the second time Day had received the ignominious distinction. Yet he did not rush to the defense of the favorite American actress of so many fellow Brits.

"The truth is that, to a certain extent, Doris IS uncooperative," wrote Howell. "An interview with her—if you can get one—can be difficult. Her husband and manager, Martin Melcher, insists that interviewers portray Doris as the whiter-than-white-and-not-a-stain-in-sight type. Or nix. Before reporters even reach paper dart distance of the star, he briefs them on 'areas of sensitivity' they must not discuss with her. Questions that focus on the Doris who never smokes, drinks or swears are welcome. But any unwelcome probe brings down a wall that makes the one in Berlin look like an ant hill."

Howell proceeded to give specific stories "circulating" about Day's deteriorating relations with the press, including a reporter whom she "indignantly" abandoned when he lit up a cigarette. "The same reporter later got a shock when he visited the set of 'Move Over, Darling' and found her puffing away at one herself!" Howell also described Day's interaction with a photographer who "annoyed" her during a Dodgers game: "Doris registered disgust by exploding a huge bubble of gum in his direction and poking her tongue out. . . . Then there was the American journalist who flew to Hollywood to see Doris, only to be told he couldn't speak to her unless he gave complete control over everything he wrote to Melcher."

Howell himself managed to finagle an interview with her. "It isn't pleasant to read that you aren't a nice person. And it's all so petty and superficial," Day told Howell, in self-defense. "One writer tried to prove I was temperamental when I sent back a salad I had been served in the studio dining room. How trivial can you be? Of course I sent the salad back. I like good food and I admit I'm fussy about it. This particular salad was all wilted and sad looking. It wasn't temperament. It was good sense."

"Although there is some truth in what Doris says about the more sensational elements of the American Press, there can be no doubt that she is also to blame," continued Howell, who perceptively explained, "One of the reasons is that, despite the hard veneer Hollywood leaves on most of its denizens, just below the surface Doris is still sensitive."

Howell also quoted Ross Hunter on Day's dual nature: "For all her effervescence and apparent joie de vivre, I sometimes have the feeling that Doris is busting inside." Having produced three of her pictures and socialized with her for years, Hunter knew exactly what he was talking about.

In an article he wrote himself, provocatively titled "The Most Misunderstood Girl in Hollywood," Hunter felt compelled to defend his megastar against what he called "cesspool journalism." "During the past five years, Doris Day has been attacked by almost every magazine published," he wrote in the October 1964 issue of *Modern Screen*. "She has been criticized, ridiculed, misused and misrepresented in a hundred ways," he added, before offering a personal anecdote on the matter. "A New York writer once told me with a smirk, 'I've interviewed nine people and I've been able to get good digs about Doris from each one. You're my tenth and last source. I hope you aren't going to disappoint me.'"

According to Hunter, the "magnanimous" Day had been discouraging him from rushing to her defense for years. "Please don't. It's just a misunderstanding," she told him, "so let's forget it." And, "I'm sure the writer didn't mean it the way it looks in print."

In contrast with the notion that she could be difficult on the set—or that she often appeared late and unprepared—Hunter claimed that Day was "prompt and line-perfect." "She has an indefinable ability to be believable and intensely funny in preposterous situations," he said, explaining Day's penchant for comedy, a penchant Hunter had fostered. "Her round, blue eyes . . . bring dramatic credibility to the incredible.

"I call Doris 'Miss ReActor,'" Hunter added in what was a producer's transparent love letter to one of his most dependable stars. "She is the greatest reactor in the business, i.e., she responds electrically to other members of the cast. She vitalizes a scene. She listens to tired lines as if she were hearing them for the first time, and she responds freshly for each take.

"She is a good sport," he continued. "She will endure mud baths, soap suds torrents, and winds of hurricane velocity for the sake of a funny scene, and she will endure them with an air of incredulous, ladylike outrage that sends audiences into hysterics.

"Of course, she's a perfectionist," Hunter allowed. "After she has finished a scene she asks, 'Did I do it right? Did it ring true? Did I sound okay? Should we try it once more?'" The producer who had prompted what had been the most successful extended period in Day's twenty-year film career offered still more insights into his star.

It has been said that Doris wants her own way. Let's put it like this: she has the courage of her convictions, and she has a right to those convictions. This girl is a professional; she has an innate comedy sense and a backlog of experience. When a scene is disputed, she brings her keen instinct for laughter and her knack for inciting it to bear. However, in case of a difference of opinion, Doris wants to hear the other person's comments.

As often as not, she will change her mind about a scene, saying, 'Yes, I see. That's great. Let's do it that way. I hadn't thought it through. . . .' Doris can be led with logic to the ends of the earth; [but] she can't be coerced one inch. She's neither an automaton nor a green kid, but a seasoned, perceptive, creative human being.

Hunter refuted the media's suggestion that Day was friendless by resorting to cliché: "If Doris has no friends, Heinz has no pickles." But the producer's bouquets to Day eventually led back to his reason for writing the extensive article in the first place. "At this point you're probably thinking, 'Okay, Doris sounds like a livin' doll, but if she is, why did the Hollywood Women's Press Club once award her their Sour Apple as the year's most uncooperative actress?'"

After writing about the pressures of being a movie star with a home life to maintain, Hunter continued:

In Doris' case, she knocked herself out at first, trying to do everything asked of her. Gradually she discovered—to her confusion and dismay—that her efforts to please all segments of the press were unappreciated in some cases, misunderstood in others. Now and then something Doris said jokingly was reported solemnly, or blown up to be used as a scare-head title. Even worse, a controversial statement never made by Doris would be manufactured to give an interview 'excitement.'

Doris decided to give no more interviews,[Hunter went on], Between picture-making, record-waxing, personal appearances, traveling with Marty and running a household, she was testing her stamina to the limit. When she had a few days of free time, she wanted to live a simple, private life. She wanted to be inconspicuous. She wanted to relax and recharge her batteries. Then came the avalanche of criticism—and it was shocking.

Hunter then charged forward, bringing up the most painful gossip of all—"the recurrent rumor of possible divorce between Doris and Marty"—only to fall back to toe the party line. "The first time I heard that bit of gossip, I laughed out loud," Hunter observed. "I knew the background. Marty Melcher has been too closely associated with show business for too long to have escaped the bite of the play-producing bug. A few years ago he bought a fine Jack Sher script, and signed Jan Sterling and Angie Dickinson for two of the leading roles. After Los Angeles rehearsals, the play hit the road with Marty shepherding the production. Marty had been gone less than 48 hours when a columnist asked in print, 'Is there trouble in the Melcher household?'"

Considering that a dozen years later, Day would explain in her memoir that she had long wanted a divorce from Melcher, Hunter was merely another cog in her publicity machine's attempt at damage control. Besides, Day had been supportive by covering up the gay Hunter's long-term relationship with set designer Jacques Mapes, and he owed her the favor. (Hunter himself had tried to conceal the liaison by pretending to be engaged to Nancy Sinatra, an absurd tactic since most of the film community knew that he had been living with Mapes for twenty years.) Still, it seems odd for Hunter to be reintroducing the tired story about why Melcher had "flown the coop" to tour with the Sher play a full year after this manufactured defense first appeared in print.

The players involved had to be aware that Hollywood insiders knew the Melchers' marriage to be more of a business partnership than a love match. But they could also rely on the naive, movie-magazine reader to be deceived by sentimental marital hogwash. If the business of Hollywood was primarily about creating dreams on the big screen, it also often entailed maintaining illusions on the smaller screen of real life.

*   *   *

While more and more reviewers were trashing Day and her films, her superstar status was underscored when *Time* magazine approached her early in 1964 about doing a cover story on her. Aware of the rigorous research that went into such profiles, Day became concerned that her true age—forty-two—would come to light, and she rejected the project. When her publicist Pat Kingsley encouraged her to go ahead with the idea, Day asked why she should. "Because you're number one," replied

Kingsley. With irrefutable logic, Day cited her status as the very reason she need not be bothered.

Day was also about to have another tremendous hit with her next picture—her third and last with Rock Hudson—*Send Me No Flowers*. In January 1964, Day came down with a head cold that developed into a severe sinus infection. Though she showed up for the first day of shooting *Flowers* at Universal, a fever sent her home. Cured with antibiotics, she returned for work the following week, when filming got under way and continued for two months.

Julius Epstein created the screenplay for *Send Me No Flowers*. With his brother, Philip, he had written the screenplays for both *Casablanca* and Day's first film, *Romance on the High Seas*. Based on a Broadway comedy of the same name by Norman Barasch and Carrol Moore, *Send Me No Flowers* had its real roots in the seventeenth-century French master of farce Molière. Though Universal had acquired the rights for the film in April 1963, Day and Hudson's names did not become attached to the project until December.

The plot pivots around George Kimball (Hudson), a hypochondriac who overhears his doctor's fatal prognosis regarding another patient, which he mistakes for his own. Concerned about the welfare of his wife, Judy (Day), George sets out to find her a substitute husband. Unaware of his presumed fate, she, in turn, misinterprets his odd behavior as revealing his having an affair. Matters escalate in the manner of farce before everything gets ironed out.

As a vehicle for reuniting Day with Hudson, *Flowers* was trying, yet again, to repeat the winning formula they had established with *Pillow Talk* and duplicated with *Lover Come Back*. Those two pictures had been seen by more than fifty million moviegoers around the world and together brought in $25 million. But Epstein's dialogue lacked the sparkling wit of those earlier hits. Hudson had resisted playing George at first. "Right from the start I hated that script," he said. "I just didn't believe in that man for one minute."

Initially, Tony Randall was penciled in for Hudson's role. Given that Randall was more naturally cast as fussy and finicky types (such as Felix in the long-running TV version of Neil Simon's *The Odd Couple*), the film might actually have worked better with Randall as George. (Although Hudson had just played a similarly far from macho figure in his previous picture, *Man's Favorite Sport*.) Randall was ultimately cast in *Flowers* as George's neighbor and friend, Arnold.

Paul Lynde, the fey, funny character actor and TV personality, looked upon his bit part as a cheerful cemetery-plot salesman in *Flowers* as his favorite film role. Hudson, on the other hand, found Lynde's role unsavory and the scene in which George approaches Lynde's character to buy a plot for three—himself, his wife, and her future husband—"completely distasteful."

Since Norman Jewison had been so successful with the last variation on the romantic comedy formula, *The Thrill of It All,* he was entrusted with this latest mutation. Jewison recalled his reunion with Day: "Doris and I had become comfortable with each other. But working with Doris meant once again brushing up against her husband, Marty Melcher. This time Marty billed himself as the movie's executive producer and again collected his $50,000 fee for performing no visible service. I neither liked nor trusted Melcher and stayed out of his way as much as possible." (According to one report, Melcher's producer's fee for each of his wife's films had doubled, to $100,000, by the time of *Flowers.*)

Looking back, Jewison said he felt that *Flowers* "showed good pacing . . . was tight and had no wasted motion." The admiration he had expressed for Day after working on *The Thrill of It All* was enriched by their second collaboration. "Doris showed me a different side of her acting in this movie, or rather, two new sides," said Jewison. "One was her on-screen vulnerability. Not much of it was called for in a farce, but in a couple of scenes, she needed to project a wounded quality, and each time I asked it of her, she delivered. The other was a deft way with physical comedy that I hadn't entirely expected, so I kept inventing new, funny situations for her. In one, she turned a simple act, bringing in a morning delivery of eggs from the back porch, into a tour de force of small calamities. . . . She carried it off beautifully."

Befitting her superstar stature, Day had a new trailer—forty percent larger than her last—that accompanied her on location shoots. "If it were one inch wider," Day joked in a publicity report, "I'd have to leave it home. It just barely qualifies with the Vehicle Code to be permitted on a highway." In addition to its use for dressing and resting, the trailer featured a separate "conference room" and an "electric kitchenette." It provided her refuge at the Riviera Country Club during the filming of the scene in which Judy's golf cart careens out of control and she rides through lawn sprinklers. It was also where Day shared many a personal thought with hairstylist Barbara Lampson, who first worked with the star on *Move Over, Darling.* They became fast friends as Lampson proceeded

to style Day's hair for the balance of her film career and then her TV
series as well.

✳   ✳   ✳

While they clearly adjusted to their new relationship as a public "couple"—
albeit with private and personal agendas—the Melchers had an ongoing
interest in finding an alternative to their weekend house in Arrowhead.
Day placed the dissatisfaction with their getaway home on her husband: "A
weekend wasn't long enough to acclimate to Arrowhead—at least it wasn't
long enough for Marty. It takes him about four days to become acclimated
to the mountains, then he's fine." Shortly after Day finished working on
Send Me No Flowers (the first week in April), they finally found the perfect
replacement for their Arrowhead getaway—a beach house in Malibu, where
they had already spent many happy days in the past. For Day, Malibu had
been one place where she could truly relax.

The house belonged to Jane Russell, who had purchased it for $34,000.
Recent rental neighbors of the house included Dean Martin, Lana Turner, and Debbie Reynolds. Rita Hayworth had lived next door with Dick
Haymes, and Mae West owned a house just down the beach. Though it was
on the market with a realtor, the thrifty Melchers waited until the listing
expired, sparing themselves any fees. It was a two-story, stucco, rose-pink
affair on the beach side of the Pacific Coast Highway. Though the house
indeed faced the beach, one entered from the rear, walking through a garden, "planted in the New England fashion." The ground floor contained a
glassed-in living room with a fireplace "running the width of the house," a
large living room and dining room combination, plus a kitchen and powder
room. Upstairs were two bedrooms with separate baths, and another wing
had two guest bedrooms and a bath.

Day added a wraparound veranda, which became the house's most
striking and inviting feature. She also re-covered the downstairs beach
room walls in vinyl and modernized the kitchen. "I try to make my home
honestly reflect me," explained Day, whose decor combined antiques and
modern furnishings.

As before, Day enjoyed long walks on the beach early in the morning and no less in the evenings upon her return from work. Though
she did not do as much to promote *Send Me No Flowers* as she had for
other recent films, she prerecorded interviews for exhibitors to submit

to local radio stations ("all three are on one platter"). She also contributed to a half dozen "fashion features for newspapers and specialty shop promotion."

The film's larger-than-usual twenty-page pressbook for exhibitors clearly indicates just how much muscle Universal was putting behind marketing it. In addition to the "free" radio interviews, there were TV spots and the usual assortment of tie-ins. Moreover, Al Hirschfeld provided an elegant drawing of the film's three stars, available for free publicity in local papers.

When it opened at New York's Radio City Music Hall, *Send Me No Flowers* received mixed reviews. Bosley Crowther in the *New York Times* proved as pleased with the second Jewison-Day collaboration as he had been with the first. He prescribed it as a kind of cure-all for his readers: "If taken in one submissive gulp, with maybe a dash of skepticism in a glass of leniency to wash it down, [it] should do more to free the sluggish system of the poisons of hypochondria and set the old laugh organs humming than a medicine-cabinet full of pretty pills." Like Jewison, Crowther emphasized that Day had become a consummate physical comedienne, "full of puffs and splutters."

Comparing the film to the Broadway play it was based on, the reviewer in *Time* magazine also gave an almost full measure of praise: "Rearranged for moviegoers as a formula farce, the show still seems artificial but the artifice somehow seems right—in a puppet show, who needs reality? . . . Actress Day, who at 40 should maybe stop trying to play Goldilocks, comes off as a cheerful, energetic and wildly overdecorated Mama Bear." But the notice in *Variety* was, for a change, negative: "Perhaps it's because the possibilities inherent in a marital comedy with the same stars aren't endless, or because the basic premise here is too old-hat and not sufficient ingenuity is displayed in garmenting the familiar plot with necessary fresh habiliments, but whatever the cause, '. . . Flowers' doesn't carry the same voltage, either in laughs or originality, as Doris Day and Rock Hudson's two previous entries."

Anticipating James Wolcott's accolades in *Vanity Fair* by four decades, a Universal executive proclaimed Day and Hudson "the greatest box office team in the history of the industry—greater than Mary Pickford and Douglas Fairbanks, Pola Negri and Rudolph Valentino, greater even than Greta Garbo and John Gilbert. What these two have that the others lacked is a sense of humor. They make sex funny—not tragic."

Wolcott actually denigrated *Flowers* in his *Vanity Fair* tribute to "the country's top box-office team," but acclaimed Day and Hudson as "the best romantic-comedy team ever . . . far superior to Katharine Hepburn and Spencer Tracy, whose movies . . . strike me as creaky, talky, and dated. Doris and Rock seem to be more modern now than they did then—they throw off more light, there's more to read in their relationship."

"The Superb Technician"

✳

"I don't like to do anything that I can't do very well."
—DORIS DAY

While all Hollywood studios were suffering financial woes in the mid-1960s, none was more directly tied to the cost overruns of a single picture than Twentieth Century Fox. "[T]he catastrophic cost of 'Cleopatra' and its disaster at the box office broke Fox's back," wrote Darryl Zanuck biographer George F. Custen. Though Zanuck wanted Day to play Maria in what would become the most successful movie musical of all time, *The Sound of Music*—and many predicted she would—he no longer had the authority to make such an executive decision. Zanuck's son Richard was then in charge of the ailing studio. After Julie Andrews's agent showed him a few of her scenes in *Mary Poppins*, then in production at Disney, Richard Zanuck decided to cast the relative newcomer.

Instead of *The Sound of Music*, Day had to make do with a vastly inferior Fox film *Do Not Disturb*. Either Melcher was losing his eye for decent material or growing lazy and accepting whatever offers came his way. He increasingly subjected his wife to schlock. On the other hand, with shooting planned in London, Paris, and Germany, *Do Not Disturb* was apparently conceived as a much more lavish picture than it became. Given her fear of flying as well as her increasing desire for a home life, Day agreed to do the film only if it were shot exclusively in Los Angeles.

Certainly she was in a position to do as she pleased. In January, *Newsweek* reported her position as Hollywood's number-one box-office star for the fourth time. The article added that Day's record for filmdom's actresses had been matched only by Shirley Temple. (It was topped, in the male category, by Bing Crosby.) In his story on the development for the UPI wire service, Vernon Scott labeled Day "Queen of the Movies" and pointed out that in addition to being the strongest draw for four years, she also had been a "member of the top ten for more than a decade."

"The title [of the film she's working on] is apt," added Scott. "Few people have the temerity to disturb the reigning queen of Hollywood. Her trailer is beautifully appointed in light blue and white. It is here she retires between scenes to nibble on pretzels and hard candy. Publicists, assistant directors and other functionaries hang around outside as if awaiting an audience. But it doesn't match up. Once in the presence, Miss Day's natural friendliness evaporates expectations of regality. [M]en admire her sex appeal, and women would like to copy it."

Nonetheless, by 1965 Day's star was on the verge of plummeting to Earth in a number of ways. For one, with two extraordinary successes, *Mary Poppins* and *The Sound of Music*, Andrews would supplant her as the nation's leading box-office star. And despite Scott's pronouncements about her being friendly, Day earned her third Sour Apple Award for lack of cooperation with the press. The Melchers were so out of touch with Hollywood protocol that they even invited Richard Zanuck to a Lakers' game on Oscar night, when they should have known he would not be able to join them.

Producer Ross Hunter was not alone in rushing to defend Day against the "blow struck by" the Hollywood Women's Press Club when it gave her its "nasty" award for a third time. Cincinnati mayor Walton Bachrach showed up on the set of *Do Not Disturb* to present his city's native-born star with a counteraward, unimaginatively dubbed "The Sweet Apple."

Do Not Disturb was directed by Ralph Levy, who would become better known for *The Beverly Hillbillies* TV series than for his films. In fact, *Do Not Disturb* feels more like a TV sitcom than a romantic comedy, and that's how the studio pitched it. Based on William Fairchild's play *Some Other Love*, the story concerns Janet Harper whose husband, Mike, the executive of a woolens firm, is transferred to London. Once there, Janet opts to move to a country house while Mike, unwilling to commute, spends more and more time in the capital. When she suspects him of having an affair with his attractive secretary, Janet decides to arouse his jealousy by flirting with a debonair antiques dealer. The predictable rigmarole leads to an obligatory happy ending,

Macho Australian actor Rod Taylor initially turned down the part of Mike. "This is something more on the lines for Rock Hudson, Tony Curtis, Jack Lemmon or Cary Grant," he told himself when he first read the script. "I can't do this stuff, and I'm not too enamored with the chance of playing opposite Doris Day.

"Male co-stars with Doris always go the same route, I thought, and I had heard she takes herself quite seriously," Taylor further explained. "As it turned out—after I was persuaded to change my mind—Doris was one of the most womanly, interesting fun broads I have ever worked with. I couldn't wait to get up and go to the studio each morning."

In another article, Taylor went on to say that "she is certainly no prude. All that business you hear about her not drinking and such must just be part of an image set up for her security. We certainly had a lot of enjoyment having a few belts after work when I would mix up a batch of rum daiquiris."

Melcher, however, maintained his own squeamish attitudes concerning his wife's pristine image. There was a scene in which Taylor carries Day upstairs to bed, stops at the door to their room, gives her "a good deep conjugal kiss," and kicks the door closed behind them. Melcher, who was on the set when the scene was shot, objected strenuously to the kiss. He called Taylor aside and told him so, demanding that the scene be reshot. Taylor said, "For God's sake, man. In this script we're married people. Why shouldn't I kiss my wife?"

The film was made quickly during the spring of 1965. "I was surprised when I saw the first rushes," Taylor said. "It was there! Our 'chemistry' worked." Though provided with a chauffeured car to drive her from her bungalow at one end of the Fox lot to the sound stages at the other, Day preferred walking whenever she had enough time. Usually, her brown poodle, Muffy, could be seen at her side.

Acting upon a novel publicity idea, Twentieth Century Fox, in "hotels coast to coast," distributed "doorknob cards" that not only read, "Doris Day says DO NOT DISTURB," but also depicted a sexy image of Day snuggling with a pillow. When Lufthansa Airlines took up the idea and placed ads with a caption reading "Please Do Not Disturb," depicting Day asleep on a plane, Melcher sued.

Good Housekeeping did a cover story on Day with six photos of the star who, it reported, remained "the reigning box office queen of the world." Though geared to promote the upcoming release of *Disturb*, the brief story focused on Day's photo shoot with photographer Howell Conant.

"The bigger they are the easier to work with," reported Conant. "He had good reason to know," explained the unsigned article, "having worked with such people as Audrey Hepburn, Elizabeth Taylor, Grace Kelly, Julie Andrews. Of all these dazzling ladies, none has won his heart so quickly and so completely as the forty-one-year-old dynamo on our cover. . . . As soon as Doris saw that the man behind the camera knew as much about his business as she did about hers, she began to give out. She danced the watusi in a skintight gown that would have brought a lesser lady to her knees; she clowned as a one-man band; finally, and without a drop to drink, she became royally and delightfully smashed."

The biggest marketing gambit for *Do Not Disturb* was a "Doris-for-a-Day Look-Alike Contest," sponsored by the studio and the Wool Bureau, and held at theaters across the globe. "Newspapers and television stations all over the world paused in their recital of grim events to sponsor regional searches for the girl most resembling the golden girl next door," reported a lengthy story in the *Los Angeles Times.* "[Forty-three] local winners were flown to Los Angeles for a warm facsimile of royal welcome. Trips to Disneyland, a yacht club, a discotheque." The fifty worldwide finalists represented fifteen countries, and the winner, Tuula Mattila, was a twenty-four-year-old librarian from Finland.

Fox shot five trailers featuring Day's own voice in Italian, French, German, and Spanish—as well as English—emphasizing how much the film was designed to appeal to a growing international market. "There will actually be two different Spanish language trailers, one for Spain and one for Latin America," announced an article in *Variety.* The "look-alike" contest also affirmed Day's feeling, as she had recently told Vernon Scott, that women "see me and say, 'If she can be in pictures, so can I.'" His observation echoed what Al Levy, her first agent, told his colleagues at the very beginning of Day's film career.

Along with such a massive marketing campaign, Day's wholesome familiarity helped sell *Do Not Disturb* to her fans—but not to reviewers. (As George Morris succinctly put it: "Doris Day's collision with Continental culture would make Henry James blanch.") In his pan in the *New York Times,* Bosley Crowther pronounced the film "the most foolish piece of comic trivia [Day has] been caught in since her pre-Rock Hudson days. . . . It is without wit, in script and direction." "It has no real wit or bite to it," Margaret Harford echoed in the *Los Angeles Times.* "There are enough slow stretches so that you can count on getting in several good naps." *Do Not Disturb* nonetheless captured fifth place at the box office its opening week, behind the latest James Bond picture, *Thunderball, That*

Darn Cat, The Sound of Music (already in its forty-second week), and *The Agony and the Ecstasy.*

Sensing that Day was losing ground commercially, the Melchers began to look for new angles and twists to give her career a boost. She told Dick Kleiner for a story in the *Valley Times,* "We considered living in New York for six months a year, so I could join the Actors' Studio and do some real acting. You know, play psychopaths and cripples and that kind of thing. But I don't think I'd like it. I prefer my own things around me." Once again, her desire to be a homebody prevailed.

While his mother's film career showed signs of deepening erosion, Terry prospered as an A&R producer at Columbia Records. He was living in his own small house in Benedict Canyon in Beverly Hills. He produced the Byrds' amplified version of their hit single of Bob Dylan's "Mr. Tambourine Man," which was released in June 1965 and rushed to number one on the charts. The Byrds followed up with the huge hit "Turn, Turn, Turn," which arrived in November. Terry produced both of these recordings. He also presided over Paul Revere and the Raiders that year, in addition to cowriting songs with Bobby Darin and serving as a director of the first Monterey Pop Festival.

But despite his success and growing independence, it was still difficult for Terry to cope with being the son of such a huge star. He told John Maynard, a reporter, "Let's face it, it's like starting out with—well, not two strikes on you. Actually, it's more the opposite. Like being signed to a ball club because your father's Mickey Mantle. It's hard to say. I guess—well, there's this sneaky idea you might be getting a break the rest of the team didn't, and of course, for the wrong reasons. You've got to make it on your own, and if you don't, it's that much harder to get your teammates' respect. Mother and Marty know all this, don't think they don't."

When Terry was a few years younger, he had divulged more than his parents had desired during an interview, a circumstance prompting Melcher's presence at this one. Maynard conducted it at "one of Hollywood's best known restaurants," though it remained nameless in the piece itself. Melcher arrived late, however, and Maynard used his absence as an opportunity to ask Terry about his rumored engagement to Dean Martin's daughter Claudia. The twenty-year-old Claudia Martin had eloped two years earlier, but the marriage was annulled. According to Maynard, Terry's plans for this second marriage were "not formalized behind anyone's back," and "Terry's folks, as usual, had little or nothing to say to the press about what they considered the children's own private business. And this suits both Terry and Claudia just fine."

In fact, Terry had invited Claudia and her younger sister Deana to the Byrds' recording session of "Mr. Tambourine Man." Though Terry did not marry Claudia Martin—who, in a matter of months, was reportedly seeing Eddie Fisher—some time later he dated Deana. Not just the Martin sisters found Doris Day's son attractive. In a scene anticipating Mrs. Robinson's shenanigans in *The Graduate* and giving new meaning to the notion of "keeping it in the family," Terry would recall his raiding the refrigerator in the Martin home when the sisters' stepmother approached him from the rear. "Hey Terry," said Jeanne Martin. "Wanna fuck?" "Actually, Mrs. Martin, I was just getting some milk," he replied, with cool detachment.

*   *   *

While Terry was scoring a "ten" as a mover in the fast lane of the sexual revolution, his mother was further establishing herself as a celebrity sports fan. "I watch Doris Day through my field glasses at both the basketball and baseball games," Sidney Skolsky reported in his syndicated column during the first week of August (1965).

> It is a slightly different Doris Day at basketball than at baseball. This week, for the Cincinnati games, Doris wore a white blouse (edged with red one night, blue the next) and a white pleated skirt. At the basketball games, Doris usually wears slacks. At the baseball games, Doris always carries a lovely basket filled with colorful groceries. There's the white celery, the orange carrots, the red radishes. There are a few dainty sandwiches. At the basketball games, Doris . . . doesn't eat a thing. She chews. [Also] at the baseball game, Doris will cheer loudly or yell to the umpire [that] he is a bum. She usually leaves the game at the end of the seventh or eighth inning; it must be a super cliffhanger to keep Doris there for the complete game. . . . I often miss an important hit or basket because I'm watching Doris Day instead of the play.

As reported in *Variety* on October 2, 1965, Day, while attending the World Series, was "almost a better show than the ball game." "Every time somebody hits a ball in the air, she's out of her seat. She jumped to her feet in what looked like a frenzy when Maury Wills (Dodger shortstop) got caught stealing in the third inning." According to the same story, Melcher turned Dodger Stadium into a kind of an office. After the first couple of innings, he would roam around the stadium and kibitz with people he knew, while munching on their food.

In January 1966, Charles Maher of the *Los Angeles Times* deemed Day, no less a basketball fan, the "Lady of the Lakers." One of the players of the Baltimore Bullets, Johnny Green, blamed his team's recent loss of eight games on the potent distraction furnished by Day, who made the Lakers "bullet-proof" on their home turf. "They start you out shooting at her end of the court," complained Green. "They figure you won't get over the shock too quickly. By the time you switch sides in the second half, you're through." Green added that it was "tough driving at the basket with her staring at you." Day leapt to her own defense: "It definitely was not my intention to sabotage the enemy camp," she told Maher before dissembling: "It didn't occur to me that I was attracting any attention at all." Day's own attention was grabbed when her former costar Gordon MacRae spotted her at a Lakers game and had her alias, Clara Bixby, paged on the loudspeaker system.

While the Melchers had difficulty living with the media attention they attracted, they couldn't live without it, either. In response to her having won a third Sour Apple Award, Day resumed giving interviews to the movie magazines. But given the upheavals agitating and altering life in the midsixties and opening to question much of what Day's girl-next-door persona represented, Melcher's decision to preserve her wholesome image, both offscreen and on, continued to work against her. Shamus O'Hea touched on the subject by writing in *Modern Screen* that Day "has kept swimming against the current tide of raw and abnormal sex films." He proceeded to quote Day: "I think my pictures *are* sexy. 'Pillow Talk', for instance was all sex. But there's a difference between good, clean, farcical sex and sordid sex. I don't think a girl has to wear a low-cut dress or play a prostitute to be sexy on the screen. I wonder if there is such an interest in raw movie-screen sex among fans as some producers believe. Do the people want to see such things? Or do the producers just think they do?"

"Doris is angered by all the stories about her so-called dull home-life," O'Hea wrote, just before quoting her on the subject: "I guess my private life would seem dull compared to Frank Sinatra's or Dean Martin's. It's not dull to Marty and me." But, as would eventually be revealed, Day's private life was considerably less dull than the Melchers' portrayal of it.

Looking back, it is interesting to speculate how differently Day's film career might have played out had she divorced Melcher when she wanted to and been spared the series of lackluster films with which it was fast coming to an end. In contrast to Melcher's arguing that they needed to maintain her good-girl image—making a divorce out of the question—consider how many stars of Day's magnitude survived the scandals surrounding a Hollywood divorce without impeding their careers. If anything, Elizabeth Taylor's celebrity and salary flourished during this very period, when she divorced Eddie Fisher and married Richard Burton—with whom she then made one blockbuster film after another. Moreover, Day's two early divorces and Melcher's divorce from Patty Andrews had been common knowledge. Time and again, Terry would prove increasingly willing to comment on his stepfather's hypocrisy, even though his mother never would. According to Terry, Melcher was a "sanctimonious usher," and "what I brooded about most was Marty, trying to square the reality of finding out the truth about him with the image I had lived with."

✳   ✳   ✳

In 1966, one of Hollywood's most highly esteemed directors—particularly of female stars—sixty-seven-year-old George Cukor, was trying to recharge his stalled career by seeking a vehicle for Day. On June 29, Arthur Laurents wrote him regarding the possibility of adapting one of his Broadway musicals for the screen. "Silence on the 'Do I Hear a Waltz?' front," it began. "I hope not permanent silence because I think it could make a really marvelous musical film.

"The only other item I have which might work for Doris Day is 'Invitation to a March.' Obviously, her part would have to be built up and, in any event, the fantasy about the young kids would have to be eliminated and turned into a more realistic depiction of teenagers today. Still, I doubt if Miss Day would want to play the mother of a marriageable boy—even if he is twenty." Day was then forty-four, and indeed reluctant to play any middle-aged character.

Tempting as it is to imagine how she might have fared under Cukor's expert guidance—and many may have wished her simply to make another musical—posterity has to settle for what came next, *The Glass Bottom Boat*. It reteamed Day with Rod Taylor and, in fact, proved superior to their first ho-hum venture, *Do Not Disturb*. (When Hedda Hopper first referred to *The Glass Bottom Boat* in her column, she announced that they were trying to "snag" Cary Grant to play Day's "scientist boy friend" in the picture.) It was to be the first of two films Day made with the sixty-two-year-old Frank Tashlin.

Originally a cartoonist, Tashlin began his career as an animator and writer with Max Fleischer, creator of the iconic floozy Betty Boop, before moving on to Disney, Merrie Melodies, and Looney Tunes. His cartoonist's approach to human nature would limit to two dimensions all the live-action films he would write and/or direct, including *The Fuller Brush Man, Paleface, Will Success Spoil Rock Hunter?*, and *Cinderfella*. It has been said that if *Cinderfella* star Jerry Lewis hadn't existed, Tashlin would have had to invent him. His characters don't behave rationally or coherently. They come together only to explode on-screen.

Given his inability to render characters in full-bodied terms, it is surprising that Tashlin was viewed, at the time, as one of the most important directors with whom Day had worked, a line that included Curtiz and Hitchcock. *Saturday Review*'s Hollis Alpert described Tashlin as an "expert at farce," and film scholar Roger Garcia regretted that *Caprice*–Day's second picture with Tashlin–became a "maligned" film . . . overdue for reassessment." But Tashlin's reputation would quickly deteriorate, along with that of his films.

In *The Glass Bottom Boat*, Day plays Jennifer Nelson, a widow working as a tour guide at a space laboratory, presided over by Bruce Templeton (Taylor). It becomes his mission to seduce Jenny, and he recruits her as an aide in writing his memoirs, giving rise to complications. When Bruce's colleagues overhear the name Vladimir, Jenny's pet dog, they assume that he is a Russian spy. But when she in turn learns that Bruce's memoir is a scam and that she's suspected of being allied with a spy, Jenny plays along with the deception. Though it's impossible to take any aspect of the story seriously, the picture marks at least one major development for Day–she is, finally, playing a mature woman, decidedly not a virgin and even overtly seeking sex.

With its Russian-spy subtext, *The Glass Bottom Boat* may have been intended as a satire on the Cold War. But the film lacked the bite of Stanley Kubrick's *Dr. Strangelove*, which had been released only two years earlier. Written by Everett Freeman, the script of *The Glass Bottom Boat* exists as a flimsy excuse for inane sight gags and a few humorously effective situations. Despite its limitations, the picture went over well with the public and at least some of the reviewers, who appreciated Tashlin's cartoon sensibility.

Tashlin's slapstick provided opportunities enhanced not only by Day, but also by a fine team of supporting players, including Paul Lynde as a security officer who resorts to drag to try to entrap Jenny, Edward Andrews as a bumbling general, and Eric Fleming as a C.I.A. operative—who, of course, proves to be a true secret agent. (As Lynde told an interviewer, "The day I walked in fully dressed and made up—everybody was just raving—and Doris came over and looked me up and down and said, 'Oh, I wouldn't wear anything that feminine.'") The ukelele-strumming TV and radio star Arthur Godfrey made his film debut in the picture as Jenny's father, who operates the eponymous boat for tourists at Catalina Island. Robert Vaughn, television's *The Man From U.N.C.L.E.*, makes a cameo appearance in a party scene, and no less than the late film star Wallace Beery supplies the burp emitted by Bruce's robotic vacuum cleaner run amok.

The Glass Bottom Boat also launched the career of comic newcomer Dom DeLuise, who, as an increasingly exasperated and inept spy, steals practically every scene he appears in. "In essence, my appearance on the Carol Burnett show was my audition for 'The Glass Bottom Boat,'" DeLuise recalled, referring to *The Entertainers*, a weekly variety series starring Burnett, Caterina Valente, and Bob Newhart. (It appeared on CBS during the 1964–65 season.) Along with singer John Davidson and comedienne Tessie O'Shea, DeLuise was one of Burnett's regular guests.

According to DeLuise, Day herself offered him the *Glass Boat* job via a phone call to New York. "She said, 'We'd like to ask you to come to California to do a movie.' And as calmly as I could, I said, 'Okay'—without jumping out of my clothes. But my real response was, 'OH MY GOD! I'VE JUST TALKED TO DORIS DAY!' And I couldn't believe I was going to be in a movie with her." The fledgling comedian rented a car and drove to L.A.

"When I arrived at MGM," DeLuise continued, "I thought the man at the gate was going to say, 'Get out of here, and don't come back.' But he gave me keys to my cabin, and there was Doris Day. She greeted me warmly. I admit that I was nervous. I was clearly in awe of her. When I started to perform, within a couple of minutes, I made a mistake and I said, 'I'm sorry.' And she said, 'Sometimes, when you're ad-libbing around something, that's what they end up using. Wait for the director to decide.' So she gave me an important lesson right away."

DeLuise first appeared in arguably the film's funniest scene—involving a cake, a wastebasket, Day's left leg, and DeLuise's right. According to DeLuise, they spent nearly an entire week shooting that scene. "The director, Frank Tashlin, told me to take some [electrical] wire and throw it into the air, and let it land on Doris. I told him that you can't just throw loose wire on Doris Day—and I wanted to tell her about it. He said, 'No, no. Don't tell her. Just do it. She'll react.' So she opened the door, I threw the wire, and she dealt with it wonderfully. And I thought, Wow: she's very 'present' and very 'now,' because she wasn't anticipating the wire, but it became a part of the scene."

Though DeLuise was intimidated by a lot of "tough, physical stuff" they were called on to do, Day kept encouraging him: "Of course you can do it." According to DeLuise, "She makes you better. The safer you feel, the better the work you deliver." Day had relatively few scenes with DeLuise, but clearly felt responsible for helping him on this, his first picture. He particularly remembered the time Day invited him to lunch in her trailer. When he learned that Day had baked the brownie she offered him, he asked if he might have another to take with him. "When I got home, I sliced it every which way, and I mailed a little bit of that brownie to all of my relatives—it was like a communion [wafer]."

DeLuise also recalled an afternoon when Day was dismissed but he was still needed for filming. "Her make-up was off. She was in her clothes and ready to go home. And I said, 'Lucky you—you can go home, now.' And she said, ' I don't want to go home. I want to be here for you.' You know, I was this young kid, but she gave me her full attention."

When Day did go home, during this period, she returned to her Malibu house, where she regularly walked along the beach while Melcher stayed behind at the studio to look at the daily rushes. During her solitary walks on the sand, Day could observe Catalina Island, twenty-two miles away, where much of the filming was taking place. She would also retire early and be up at 5 a.m. to begin the day by walking on the beach and preparing for work. A privileged visitor to the Malibu beach house, DeLuise once asked what her social life was like. She simply replied that she had none.

Day arrived at 7 a.m. one morning for location shooting at Catalina Island with pastries for cast and crew. While they were shooting her in the water for the film's prologue, the waves were so choppy that Tashlin became seasick. The star was momentarily forgotten, left to flap around as the ailing director commandeered everyone's attention.

Among his more touching memories, DeLuise recalled casually conveying to Day his feeling humiliated to discover his name misspelled on the back of his canvas chair. At Day's behest, it was replaced the next day with a corrected version. DeLuise also remembered a pivotal time during the shoot, when he was undecided about marrying Carol Arata. He appealed to Day, who took both of his hands, looked into his eyes, and asked, "Do you love her?" When he answered that he did, she advised him not to hesitate. DeLuise married Arata once work on *Glass Bottom Boat* concluded, and they have remained together ever since. (Consuming sixty-one production days, the shoot of *Glass Bottom Boat* ran over schedule.) As she had been with her early Warner Brothers colleague Miriam Nelson, Day proved an ideal matchmaker for others, if never for herself.

DeLuise further recalled an accident when they were shooting the extensive chase scene near the end of the picture and Day slipped, hitting her face on the seat of a chair. "I asked, 'Isn't Doris Day going to go home?' But they simply moved the camera to avoid her swollen eye." During this mishap, Melcher arrived looking like a European director, his coat draped over his shoulders. In a proprietary way, he asked, "Who hurt the kid?" "We proceeded to finish that scene, even though she was visibly hurt," continued DeLuise. "Every day, my respect for her went up and up and up. . . . She was a technical, but wonderfully spontaneous, comedienne and actress." Like many others, DeLuise was also especially impressed when he observed Day prepare for a scene in which her eyes were supposed to be "welled up" with tears. "She stood there for a couple moments and then said, 'I'm ready,' and the tears were in her eyes."

When he introduced himself to DeLuise on the set, Melcher said, "I'm the executive producer of this whole movie." "He was like a little boy, wanting to make sure that I knew he was the producer," explained DeLuise. "He was often there, and seemed terrific. He was very, very playful, and energetic, and sweet. He was also a good foil for her."

Melcher was also showing signs of a rare willingness to tamper with the public's traditional view of his wife. While Jenny is dressed as a mermaid in the film's prologue, the notion of her as a secret agent prompts Bruce to visualize her as Mata Hari—and both of those exotic costumes figured prominently in the ads for the film. "Is This the Girl Next Door?" asked one of the ad's headlines, confirming that the film was intended to break with the star's virginal image. "The Spy Who Came in from the Water," another declared, suggestively. The film was also promoted with a special MGM short, *Every Girl's Dream*, featuring Nancy Bernard, the 1966 *Maid of Cotton*, who visited the studio for promotional purposes, as well as Day's modeling clothes from the film.

* * *

Although *The Glass Bottom Boat* has many contemporary detractors, it was actually a hit with the public and with some reviewers when it was initially released. Hollis Alpert, in *Saturday Review*, felt that "while this movie is as glossy and improbable as all the rest [of Day's generic pictures] it is easily the funniest. . . . Mr. Tashlin has done something else that is, perhaps, more remarkable. He has come close to unfreezing Doris Day. Instead of a slightly over-age virgin preserving her cinematic purity to the bitter premarital end, she is, this time, seen as a youngish widow, with quite normal sensual yearnings for Rod Taylor."

In the *Los Angeles Times*, Philip K. Scheuer described it as "one of those insane comedies that won't amuse anybody but us lowbrows. Reviewers have sneered at it generally around the country, but then Doris Day has become one of their prime targets anyhow." Another "lowbrow" reviewer, James Powers, went all out in his rave for Day in the *Hollywood Reporter*: "Miss Day, over the past few years, has been subjected to a critical assault for her film work seldom equaled. It is difficult to understand why. She is a superb technician. She can grab and milk a line or situation with pure technique as can few other film comediennes. She is graceful and pretty. She lights up a scene and invests it with charm and gaiety. Miss Day is an unique artist and the strong public response to her talents is no accident, nor is it due to anything but a shrewd display of those talents."

"The Spy Who Came in from the Cold Cream"

---- ✳ ----

"The really frightening thing about middle age
is that you know you'll grow out of it."

—DORIS DAY

After suffering a heart attack, Day's eighty-five-year-old father, William Kappelhoff, died on March 31, 1967, at the Jewish Hospital in Cincinnati. Her first husband and Terry's father, Al Jorden, would die a few months later (July 5, 1967), taking his own life with a .38 caliber gun to his head. His obituary noted his years on the musical staff of WLW, the Cincinnati radio station on which Day got her start as a singer. Jorden was survived by his second wife, Wiletta, and their sixteen-year-old son, Bruce. Though clearly significant, both deaths appeared to have had little if any impact on Day, who turned her attention to the diminishing returns from her recording and film careers.

Day's thirty-sixth picture, *Caprice,* was Melcher and Aaron Rosenberg's third coproduction, as well as her third film for Twentieth Century Fox. Her costar was a rugged young Irish actor, Richard Harris, who had made his breakthrough as a carousing English rugby player in *This Sporting Life* in 1963. After petitioning long and hard for the role of King Arthur in *Camelot,* the brawny actor had already won the part in Warner Brothers' big-budgeted film version of the musical when the part opposite Day in *Caprice* intervened. Though suddenly star material, Harris seemed an odd choice to play opposite Day. As many a reviewer would point out, he was far too young to play her costar. Still a powerful box-office draw, however, Day retained the clout to select whom she wanted. It's amazing to learn that her choice, according to Harris, was a matter of mistaken identity. "It turned into a bit of a nightmare, because

Doris made a mistake," Harris insisted. "She was the one who asked for me as her co-star, but she confused me with Sean Connery. They wanted to make a James Bond pastiche, as everyone was making at that time, and Marty Melcher had told Doris all about this great Irish hunk that Hollywood was chasing round. Day probably never saw a thriller movie in her life—she seemingly confused me with Sean Connery—and she said, OK, let's get this James Bond guy."

When Day once showed up at the Beverly Hills Hotel for an interview, a handsome man in the lobby gave her a knowing smile, but she had no idea who he was. After pointing him out to her interviewer, she learned he was Connery. (Years later, Day would identify Connery as one actor with whom she had always wished she had worked, Marlon Brando another.)

Day may have irredeemably harmed *Caprice* in another way by demanding from the outset that the two leading roles be gender-reversed. To make her into a female James Bond, the script's "Patrick" became Patricia, a secret agent seeking to avenge her father's murder. Harris, in turn, had to portray Christopher—originally "Christine"—a double agent who trails her.

Though *Caprice* went into production in the middle of the summer of 1966, work suddenly came to a halt when Day threw her back out during a chase scene on a fire escape. In traction for a week, she had to contend with the ensuing pain of a pinched nerve. Harris also delayed the shoot twice, each time collapsing on the set in a drunken stupor. According to biographer Michael Feeney Callen, he was downing two quarts of vodka a day, and on at least one occasion drank "vodka diluted with water from his swimming pool full of chlorine, bees, ants and spit." Given such behavior, it comes as no surprise to discover that while Harris was making *Caprice,* his wife, Elizabeth, left him for good. She returned to London from Los Angeles and filed for divorce. ("Star's Wife Says: I Am Scared of Him," ran the *Daily Mirror* headline on July 23, 1966.)

Shooting resumed in mid-August and ended on September 23, with postproduction work continuing throughout the fall. Though *Caprice* did its best to transport the viewer to ostensibly European sites, the scenes in a Paris cosmetics firm were actually filmed at the famed Bradbury Building at Broadway and Third Street in downtown Los Angeles. Mammoth Mountain in the High Sierras provided the backdrop for the Swiss skiing scenes.

While working on the picture, Harris was "warming up" for *Camelot* by singing between scenes, and Day could not refrain from joining in. "By the end of production they were making up songs of their own," Norman Lee Browning offered in an article he wrote after visiting the set. Harris enjoyed working with Day. "I liked her, she was fine, she was a ball," he said. But he would also prove dismissive of their love scenes, declaring that they made him feel as if he were "kissing my auntie." Harris found director Frank Tashlin "as odd and intriguing" as Day did.

Day's Patricia Fowler is unmistakably a feminine satiric James Bond. While DeVol's theme music evokes a John Barry score, the title images melt on the screen—just as they did in 007's *Goldfinger, Thunderball,* and *You Only Live Twice.* Set on those "Swiss" ski slopes, the picture's prologue is reminiscent of yet another popular comedy of the era, *The Pink Panther,* an unacknowledged parody of Hitchcock's brilliant *To Catch a Thief.*

As with many a Tashlin film, the overriding impulse of *Caprice* was to spoof the genre it was imitating. Having been caught for stealing "the top secret plans" for a "new, roll-on, underarm deodorant" in the opening scene, Patricia declares, "I'm a spy who came in from the cold cream"—referring to the bestselling John le Carré novel. And as the head of Patricia's firm is advised, "If you prosecute, there might be adverse publicity: The idea of cloak and dagger spies stealing underarm deodorants could strike the public as pretty silly. Our companies could be laughed out of business." Though such a line may have been intended to forestall any derision, unfortunately *Caprice* would prompt far more disapproval than laughter from moviegoers and critics alike.

Tashlin ultimately seized credit for the screenplay and from the beginning had his hand in rewriting the script. Fresh pages had been added as late as August 16, and reworking the film's climax spilled over into September. But Tashlin's gifts as a filmmaker had nothing to do with dialogue or story, and the convoluted plot evaporates even as it unfolds.

Though Patricia and Christopher initially appear to be working for rival cosmetic companies, the story line pushes "the tradition of the double-dealing double agent" too far, and after they have switched sides countless times, it's difficult to say which firm they're in league with, or why. Under the flip-flopping circumstances, Christopher's final line proves more ludicrous than cute: "How could I get the girl in the end, unless I'm a good guy?"

The scenario reaches an absurd and self-conscious height when Patricia follows a woman she's trailing into a cinema and pauses under the marquee advertising *Caprice,* starring Doris Day and Richard Harris. (It is during this film within the film that Day sings the nondescript title song by Larry Marks.) This is followed by yet another overly precious moment when a photo of Patricia's slain father appears on the screen in the person of Arthur Godfrey, who portrayed Day's father in *The Glass Bottom Boat.* In many ways, Tashlin wanted to have his satire and to be taken seriously, too, without achieving either goal very effectively.

Even the Press Book would present the picture as an "unusual suspense comedy" with important underpinnings. "Here is a film as current as the headlines: all about industrial espionage," the publicity for the film claimed. But like its title, *Caprice* was basically a lark, and its more serious ambitions compromised its whimsy.

Since Tashlin was a master of visual, as opposed to verbal, puns, *Caprice* would emerge as a highly stylized, if dispensable, film. In conjunction with cinematographer Leon Shamroy, Tashlin created a movie that is every bit as bold and "mod" as Ray Aghayan's costumes for Day. (The trailer for the film claims that "It Swings"—just like Christopher's bed, in the picture.) *Caprice* would be the last film released in CinemaScope, an otherwise throwaway fact, made all the more relevant only because thirteen years earlier Day had starred in the first musical film shot in the same technique—*Lucky Me.*

✳ ✳ ✳

While Day was working on *Caprice,* both of the Melchers had a series of interviews with C. Robert Jennings, for what would amount to a lengthy—and somewhat revealing—article in *Coronet* magazine. Day discussed her lifelong ambivalence about money. "I'm very funny about money," she admitted. "Marty'll bring home a check I have to sign for thousands of dollars, and it doesn't interest me. But if I catch him with a market bill that's off three dollars, I can't stand it." As Jennings added, "Doris once switched grocers in Beverly Hills because she spotted a small error on the tally slip."

"Doris is not tough but a very bright girl," Melcher told Jennings. "She's very objective and has the rare ability to understand quickly and clearly a rather involved situation. But she's too busy to become involved in the day-to-day operation. She comes to the office a couple of times a week to dictate letters, sign papers, and meet with me and the lawyers for any top-level decision which must have her approval. But her office is at home."

On the perennial question of Day's image, Melcher said, "[O]ddly enough, [Doris] always wants to play the other role, the other woman, *not* the girl next door. But I like that image of her, and her public wouldn't accept her any other way. 'Love Me or Leave Me' was the first picture in which Doris took a drink and a lot of people squawked." Here is further evidence that even if Day no longer wanted to continue embracing the image she colluded in creating, her husband would not let it go.

Jennings also divulged that the Melchers had made their Malibu beach house their full-time residence and even put the Crescent house up for sale. Whether he shared his concerns with his wife or not, Melcher was becoming increasingly restless about Day's career prospects. Not only was her recording career drawing to a close, but, as both of the Melchers knew, Hollywood was not kind to aging female stars—no matter how big they had ever been.

Nor were reviewers. Unsurprisingly, *Caprice* did not go over well with the critics. Many were particularly hard on Day and devoted a good deal of their shrinking print space to her having become a middle-aged actress. "If all the spy pictures modeled after James Bond were piled one on top of the other, 'Caprice' would be on the bottom," Paul Zimmerman declared in *Newsweek*. "Hollywood should stop casting Miss Day as the bubbly young girl. Her love scenes with an obviously younger Harris are unpleasant to watch and faintly ridiculous. Tashlin, who also co-wrote the script, undoubtedly intended it to be a spoof—with all the gadgetry of Bondiana turned to the conquest of the powder room. But nothing is funny."

"Although loaded with slapstick and labeled as a comedy, 'Caprice' is quite unfunny," echoed the critic of *Commonweal*. ". . . unfortunately this DeLuxe Color is cruel to Miss Day, whose hair-do, make-up, and mod dresses are all wrong for anyone even vaguely interested in cosmetics. But maybe she's supposed to be an anti-advertisement for the other firm." Arthur Knight concurred in *Saturday Review*: "It is difficult to describe 'Caprice' in terms of plot. One thinks of it rather as a conspiracy—a conspiracy directed, specifically, against the aging and unflatteringly gowned and photographed Miss Day. . . . She moved doggedly through the film from close-up to close-up that crudely revealed the puckered skin around her lips, the tired lines about her eyes."

In his dismissive review in the *Village Voice,* Andrew Sarris complimented Tashlin's direction as being "better" than the picture "deserves,"
before citing his real problem with the film: "the optical obscurities that
now enshroud any Doris Day project. Even the subject—cosmetics espionage—conspires to remind us that we have been on a long Day's journey
into naught."

Such vicious comments were, of course, painful for its star. When
Caprice came up during a retrospective look at her entire film career, Day
simply said, "I do not care to discuss 'Caprice,' so I won't. Thank you."

＊   ＊   ＊

Even before the *Caprice* reviews, Melcher had been trying to steer his
wife's career in another direction. For months he had been urging Day
to turn her talents to television, but she did not fancy being put out to
TV pasture and proved resistant. "Television, she insisted, was out of
the question because there was no time to perfect the details of a program, and Doris had always been known as a perfectionist among her
co-workers," explained reporter Eve Steele. In fact, however, Day had almost relented when NBC offered her the gargantuan sum of $1,600,000
for four specials. "Just when it seemed Doris was going to agree, she
refused because her contract called for the shows to be done in front of
an audience."

It was shortly before the release of *Caprice* that the *Los Angeles Times*
announced Day as "the first talent acquisition" of the new CBS theatrical
film division, an acquisition involving several films and vague "other duties in the CBS organization." Under the headline "CBS Grooming Doris
Day for Slot Lucy Ball Is Expected to Vacate," the following day (May 10)
Daily Variety ran a story providing more details. Finally convinced that
Lucille Ball was going to retire her long-running TV show, "CBS brass
[have] recently renewed their hot pursuit of Doris Day. . . . The chase
has paid off. Miss Day has been contracted for her own comedy series
to start season after next in the Monday slot Miss Ball vacates after next
season's finale."

Behind the scenes and apparently without his wife's knowledge,
Melcher had spent a year negotiating "one of the industry's all-time
plush talent deals" for Doris Day, including ownership of the negatives
and complete control over rerun rights—"on or off the network. The
show, moreover, will cost the web about $120,000 a segment in the ini-

tial cycle, a record for a half hour situation comedy, and roughly $10,000 a week more than the current champ in this respect, the 'Lucy Show.'" *Variety* further reported the expectation that the show would "generate video's highest priced commercial minute for a regular series, with a first-run tab understood already fixed at very near $100,000. Thus far the top-minute price on webs for a regular series is also collected by CBS, the $73,000 per it gets for 'Lucy.'"

That spring, Day was also under consideration to star in the film version of *Hello, Dolly*. Though the role hardly seemed right for her, Day was still more appropriate for the part than Barbra Streisand—as were at least two others under consideration by Twentieth Century Fox: Carol Channing and Ginger Rogers. (Before Streisand secured the role, Earl Wilson reported that Day was "stealing" it from Channing and Rogers.) Though Day's film career endured even as television was eager to embrace the star, her recording career with Columbia Records came to an end after nearly two decades. She would record her last two songs for the studio—"Sorry" and the theme to *Caprice*—on November 4, 1966.

"Columbia and Doris were having a hard time," Terry explained. "She wasn't at all happy with the kind of songs she was singing. They never found enough time to work on her recordings. They became something that was just kind of tossed in between the movies." While Terry's remarks were offered several decades later, he seems to have forgotten just how much he had tried to get his stepfather to change Day's musical approach. Her contract with Columbia had become a lost cause, given the huge changes sweeping American culture, in general, and the music world in particular. The Melchers made no adjustments, and Day's records and films were now passé.

Melcher did bring in arranger and contractor Don Genson, who would later claim that they had first worked together for the Andrews Sisters. They booked three studios where Day, taking pleasure in the leisurely tempos she preferred, recorded eleven of her favorite songs—including such chestnuts as "Street of Dreams," "Life Is Just a Bowl of Cherries," "Are You Lonesome Tonight," and "For All We Know." "I love those slow tempos," Day recalled years later. "That's the way I really enjoy singing more than anything. You usually can't get away with it, because the producer will invariably come out of the booth and say, 'You have to pick it up! People will go to sleep!' I didn't think so at all. I thought they were all wrong. They didn't think it was commercial, and they're so afraid not to be commercial."

Unfortunately, in terms of both business and critical perception, Day's record producers had been right. The cultural ground had shifted so rapidly beneath her that Day's arrangers—at her own urging—had not served her well. Suddenly she was singing for an older audience, though in a voice as pure and expressive as ever.

*   *   *

Terry was renting a house from a friend, Rudolph Altobelli, on Cielo Drive, high in the hills of Benedict Canyon in Bel Air—a gated community north of Sunset Boulevard. Previous residents included Lillian Gish, Cary Grant, and Henry Fonda. With its stone fireplaces and wood beamed ceilings, the house had been styled after a French provincial farmhouse. "It looked more Twentieth Century Fox than French," quipped Candice Bergen, who would soon be living there with Terry. "There was a cartoonlike perfection about it," she continued. "You waited to find Bambi drinking from the pool, Thumper dozing in the flowers." Since Terry had ended their budding relationship four and a half years earlier, Bergen had enrolled at the University of Pennsylvania in Philadelphia, where she had become homecoming queen her freshman year and cultivated her interest in photojournalism. A natural beauty, she became a high-profile, if reluctant, model. She neglected her studies and was asked to leave Penn after her sophomore year. By the time she reached twenty-one, Bergen had also made her film debut in *The Group* and starred in *The Sand Pebbles* with Steve McQueen (made in Asia) and *Live for Life* (a French film starring Yves Montand, made in Africa). She also became educated in aristocratic European ways through her alliance with a "tall and elegant" and "older" Austrian count.

The twenty-one-year-old Bergen had become a budding movie star and worldly sophisticate when she moved back to the United States in 1967. "After almost two years away, I found the country chaotic, often unrecognizable. [It] was a country divided: the new counterculture suddenly and sharply in rebellion against the old order; anarchy versus the status quo."

Bergen first saw Terry's house on Cielo Drive when she attended one of his parties. Pulling up to the house, she heard the Beatles' "Strawberry Fields Forever" blaring even before she located the gate. Music filled the rooms. "Always there was music," she recalled. "Beatles, Byrds, Stones, Mamas and Papas, Beach Boys, Janis Joplin, Doors—many of whom were there that night." A recent alumnus of Truman Capote's elegant black-

and-white ball at the Plaza Hotel in New York, Bergen felt out of her element as she encountered so many strange and foreign hippies in the dim-lit rooms, candles and incense burning.

If the Candice Bergen whom Terry suddenly encountered seemed different than the Candice he had last seen, he realized that it was not because she had changed but because she had not—unlike the rest of the world he knew. For years, and from afar, Terry had observed how Candy had become ever more entrenched in the mainstream culture his mother epitomized. It wasn't only the movie career she was forging for herself, but the modeling, the Revlon ads, the articles and items in the gossip columns. There was even a brand-new *Vogue* cover with Bergen's overly painted face peering out from beneath a bouffant hairdo. The magazine promised the inside "scoop" on "THE AMERICAN WOMAN 1967 . . . Love . . . Money . . . Husband-Stealing . . . Psychiatry. . . Art . . . Work . . . Fun . . . Entertaining . . . The Good Life Where the Action Is."

But now that Candice was with him, Terry instantly saw through what she called her "snappy New York repartee" and her "new suit of armor." "Gradually I gave up, seeing the silliness of the social game at which I had become too adept, remembering that it wasn't something to be played with Terry, who hated the hypocrisy and did not share my skills," Bergen recalled in her memoir, in which she describes nothing less than a transforming experience as the two of them retreated to a bedroom, leaving the party behind. "My life was everything Terry now condemned and rejected. . . . I realized that there hadn't been much honesty in my life of late. As we talked softly into the night, I began to feel the sense of safety I'd lost when life had gotten too fast. . . . I put away the arch grownup that I had invented."

Though she planned to return to New York to live a new life there, Bergen impulsively decided to stay with Terry—"at first on a day-to-day basis," she explained. Given that her parents' house was only five minutes from Terry's on Cielo Drive, she had to go to "great lengths" to prevent them from knowing that she was living with Terry and had not returned to New York, where she had been living alone. "To my father, Terry was not simply unsuitable; he was totally unacceptable," confessed Bergen, who proceeded to cite "his politics, his friends, his lifestyle and especially the influence he exerted on me."

Though neither Candice nor Terry had lived with anyone, their adjustments were eased with the help of a butler, a housekeeper, and a "houseman," whose duties included looking after fourteen cats and Nana, a Saint Bernard. Whether or not Nana was named after the sheepdog that looked after Michael, John, and Wendy in *Peter Pan*, Bergen compared life with Terry to being in Never-Never Land. "[W]e were starry-eyed kids on a big budget," she added. "As Hollywood's children, we instinctively did things larger than life. Just like in the movies."

Though she revealed her deception to her mother after several months, Bergen kept the truth from her father the entire two years she remained with Terry. The bigger surprise is that Edgar Bergen failed to discover the truth, given the many articles and stories written about the young couple. When asked whether she and Terry were going to marry, Candice replied, "I don't know. I don't like to talk about those things. If my private life can't be private I think I want to stop being a celebrity." Terry told the same reporter, "Yes, I'm in love with her. I'm crazy about her, in fact. She's the only girl I've ever been in love with like this." He would not discuss marriage plans, however. "Isn't that for the girl to answer?" he asked, rhetorically. Though Day, too, would not go on record, "close friends" reported "that nothing would make her happier than to have Candy Bergen as her daughter-in-law."

* * *

In the middle of June 1966, Melcher announced that he had bought *Red Eye,* an original "Western comedy" by Jack Guss. It was originally going to be made by Twentieth Century Fox, but the deal fell through. It led, however, to another Western picture, produced by Melcher and Norman McDonnell at Universal. With an original screenplay by Harold Swanton, the story centers around Josie Minick, a widow with an eight-year-old son who becomes "the first woman sheep rancher in Southern Wyoming." The film was originally called *The Epic of Josie,* but there would be nothing "epic" about the film when it was finally released as *The Ballad of Josie.*

The announcement of the picture in *Variety* (November 10, 1966) emphasized that *Josie* marked Day's first "oater" since *Calamity Jane* in 1953 as well as her return to Universal, where her "biggest hits [had] covered a five-year span": *Pillow Talk, Midnight Lace, Lover Come Back, That Touch of Mink,* and *The Thrill of it All.* "She checks [in] on the lot in January," *Variety* also reported, "after having been away for three years." Ads for the picture would even bill the star as "Doris (Calamity Josie) Day."

Day's *Josie* costar was Peter Graves, who had played a rancher in the long-running TV series *Fury.* Shortly after making *Josie*, Graves would return to television as the star of CBS's new hit *Mission Impossible.* According to a publicity report, Day chose Graves after seeing him on TV. The picture also featured two veterans of Westerns, Andy Devine and George Kennedy, and marked Elizabeth Fraser's fourth film with Day. *Josie* was directed by the prolific if pedestrian Andrew V. McLaglen, whose father, Victor, had won an Oscar for his performance in *The Informer* (1935).

It had been fourteen years since *Calamity Jane*, and, according to another press release, Day took a refresher course "in riding, roping, quick-drawing a six-shooter and handling a rifle." She practiced horseback riding on the beach at Malibu. Costumer Jean Louis made Day three sets of pants to show off her spectacular-as-ever figure: a tight pair for standing, a second and slightly looser pair for sitting, and a third "even roomier" pair to permit her to mount a horse without splitting them.

The film was shot primarily on the Universal lot, with some location shooting at Albertson's Ranch in the San Fernando Valley. Once in the midst of "an emotion-charged scene" with Graves, McLaglen suddenly yelled, "Cut!" "I thought it was going very well," Day reported. "I was puzzled and asked him what happened, assuming I might have goofed in the long dialogue, or maybe he disagreed with my performance," she added, displaying characteristic insecurity. "He shook his head to both questions, then pointed up the hillside to a spot back of me and above my shoulder and smack in the middle of the camera's view. . . . The whole cast and crew stood and watched in a little bit of awe and wonder, as we saw a baby [sheep] being born right in the middle of our scene."

Such episodes stopped production a number of times. The Press Book recorded that, having "hired" 1,500 sheep for one important sequence, the flock grew to 1,525 during the first nine days of shooting, "and was still growing when the director 'retired' the flock from acting chores."

If Rod Taylor had been surprised to discover that, contrary to her reputation, his costar in *The Glass Bottom Boat* took a drink now and then, Graves was even more astonished to observe Day drinking real brandy during the episode in which Josie becomes inebriated. "Before the scene, the prop guys came through, and they said, 'Doris, what would you like in there? You want some iced tea or Coke or something?'" Graves recalled. "She said, 'No, put brandy in there.' . . . She must have tossed off about six brandies . . . and her eyes were crossed, and she was stoned."

Though Day found the arrival of newborn sheep wonderful, she was far less amused by the treatment of horses at Universal. "They didn't even have a barn," she recalled. She went directly to Lew Wasserman, president of MCA, which owned Universal at the time. "I told Lew if he didn't do something about a barn I'd put it in the paper." Thanks to Day, the studio's horses finally had a barn for resting and grooming.

Though Day aficionados spend considerable time arguing over which is her best film, they would probably be quick to agree that, in addition to *Starlift*, *The Ballad of Josie* is among her worst. As a number of reviewers claimed, nothing rescues *Josie* from resembling a cheap and quickly thrown-together TV show. Day herself would come to disparage the film as just that, even though she retained a soft spot for it: "I think it should have been just a little TV film, and I think it was probably written with that in mind."

The critics unanimously panned the film. "There's enough wool on the hoof screenside to put a ward-full of insomniacs to sleep," quipped Edgar Driscoll Jr. in the *Boston Globe*. *Variety* dismissed *Josie* as "a pleasant, innocuous Doris Day oater comedy" and recommended that Universal pair it with a "strong dual bill mate for okay b.o. in general situations." In the *Hollywood Reporter*, John Mahoney was equally negative about the movie's prospects: "Both the comedy and drama of an interesting premise are diluted in a flow of weepy suds. . . . [T]his Universal entry may scratch its way to profits in general release, but it will be slim pickin's. . . . Miss Day has a number of moments in which to exercise her sure instinct for comedy, but the excesses of maudlin whimpering imposed upon her by the script ultimately drown sympathy."

Universal followed *Variety*'s advice and released *The Ballad of Josie* as a second feature with *Counterpoint*, an equally forgettable World War II action drama starring Charlton Heston. "Both [pictures] look as if they had been manufactured on the company's back lot to give Universal City tourists something to gawk at," offered Vincent Canby in the *New York Times*. "In fact each film, in its own way, is so incredibly unimportant that the suspicions of a sympathetic moviegoer must be aroused. . . . One might believe that the films had really been turned out for immediate television airing. They'll get to television soon enough anyway. In the meantime, it seems as if Universal were bent on setting back the art of the commercial American film by 25 years, as well as on destroying the money-making reputations of the stars involved."

"Doris Day, who used to fill the coffers at Radio City Music Hall is relegated to second place on a double bill at Showcase theaters," chimed in Wanda Hale, who gave the film only two stars in the *New York Daily News*. "It shouldn't happen to an unknown actress named Josie Doakes, much less to the star who made millions for her backers."

"There's nothing about *The Ballad of Josie* that couldn't have been taken care of in the 54 minutes allotted weekly to a Western series on TV," wrote Leo Sullivan in the *Washington Post*, who accurately saw the film as a harbinger of the end of Day's film career. "You might say that this Western outburst is Doris Day's first deliberate step into television, which, we are told, is to be her principal forum in the future."

Indeed, two months before work on *Josie* commenced, *Variety* announced: "A project, still in negotiation, could prove a major coup for [CBS], since it would mean the video debut of Doris Day. The 'perennial Puritan' of the celluloids would emcee a drama anthology, like Bob Hope's *Chrysler Theater Show*, that would have her actively performing in same every fourth week." The following April, a *Variety* headline summed up the latest development in the story: "CBS Dickers Doris Day for Both Pix and TV Series." Then, on May 9, 1967, came the announcement that Day would star in up to "four pix ('two plus two') of CBS theatrical films." And on May 10, the no less telling headline: "CBS Grooming Doris Day for Slot Lucy Ball Is Expected to Vacate."

*   *   *

No matter how disappointing her recent films, Day's hardcore fans remained as enamored of the star as ever. Born in Chicago in 1944 and reared in Indianapolis, Mary Anne Barothy fell in love with Doris Day when she was only ten. She eventually joined Day's British fan club—for its informative newsletters—and became particularly struck by the experiences of another club member, Ilene Freshwater, who had been encountering Day at Lakers and Dodgers games in Los Angeles. The brazen Freshwater also stopped by the house at 713 Crescent and chatted with Katie Sarten, the Melchers' cook. "She wrote about this in the fan club magazine, and I thought, 'Wow! She's actually met Doris Day and talked to her,'" recalled Barothy. "I was bold enough to write to Ilene. I said, 'Gee, on your next trip West, why don't you plan to stay overnight with us?' I was thrilled when I actually got to know somebody who had talked to Doris."

Barothy first visited Los Angeles in 1965, when she stayed with Freshwater and her roommate, Hilda Wilby—another Day fanatic. They lived on

Bundy Drive. "I would drop Ilene off at Van de Kamp's, where she was a waitress, and then have the use of her car," Barothy recalled. "No matter where else any of us was going, we would always drive by the house on Crescent Drive, hoping to see Doris. Ilene and Hilda and another girl, from Scotland, Helen Faye, had gone to Catalina, and had their pictures taken with Doris when she was making *The Glass Bottom Boat*. They took me out there [to Catalina] hoping to see her, but she had already left." Barothy also befriended two more Day fans on that trip: Lauren Benjamin, visiting from Colorado, and Mary Kaye Konrath, all of sixteen years old, the others four or five years older.

When Barothy returned to Los Angeles in 1967, Freshwater and Wilby arranged that she meet Day at Bailey's Bakery on a Saturday morning. "Marty and I will be coming down," Day told them. "He'll go to the office [on Canon Drive], so I can spend some time there." Day was particularly fond of the manager of Bailey's, another Hilda.

"Since Doris didn't give an actual time, we got there very early, like 9 o'clock," Barothy recalled. "We thought it would be better for us to wait for her, than for her to wait for us. A little after ten, I just took a bite of a roll, or something, and then I heard her voice. Since I was the one she didn't know, she came up and put her arm around me and said, 'You must be Mary Anne.' She sat down with us—Ilene, Hilda, and Mary [Konrath] and myself—and we were just sitting there. It was like she was one of us. There was nothing pretentious about her. It was like she was a friend from a long time ago—really amazing! Of course she didn't have all the makeup on, but she still looked great. I mean, that woman could wake up in the morning and look perfect without any makeup."

Barothy was, at the time, a reporter for the *Indianapolis News*. Melcher and Day had ridden their bikes into town together and he eventually came to fetch his wife and ride home with her. After he had been introduced to Barothy and told that she was a reporter, Barothy observed, "Right away, you could see him bristle, because he wanted tight control over everything. But Doris said, 'Oh, don't worry about her—she's a friend of mine.'" In fact, during their first meeting Day asked Barothy if she had ever considered moving to Los Angeles, planting a seed that blossomed that March, when Barothy secured a job as assistant PR director for the May Company department store. She moved to Los Angeles and took an apartment with Mary Kaye Konrath on Olympic Boulevard—"about a mile from Doris's home," Barothy emphasized.

One afternoon, out and about on her bicycle in Beverly Hills, Day met another fan. "It was the end of 1967, and I had just done a pilot of *Mothers-in-Law*," recalled actress, singer, and comedienne Kaye Ballard. "She was on her bicycle, looking adorable and talking to Billie Cheapwood in front of her little antique shop. And when I saw it was Doris Day I almost fainted, because I had always admired her." Ballard introduced herself and told Day about the pilot, and Day said, "Oh, I hope it goes, I hope it goes!"

Learning that Ballard was drawn to an antique magnifying glass in Cheapwood's collection, Day bought it for her. Ballard, who had met the Queen Mother in 1950, now detected "that same regal quality" in Day. "They have a charisma. When they talk to you, you have this feeling that they're only talking to you and only thinking about what you are saying. But they're probably wondering what they're going to be having for dinner that night."

"The Constant Virgin"

---✳---

"I knew Doris Day before she was a virgin."
—OSCAR LEVANT

*B*ased on a French farce, *Where Were You When the Lights Went Out?*, Day's thirty-eighth picture, must have lost a great deal in translation. The screenplay was cowritten by Everett Freeman, who had also written *The Glass Bottom Boat*. This time, Freeman served as Melcher's coproducer. *Lights* was yet another Day vehicle for MGM, where she always enjoyed working with both hair stylist Sydney Guilaroff and makeup specialist William J. Tuttle, respectively.

One advantage *Lights* had was its title, which, at the time, was instantly recognized as a reference to the New York blackout of November 9, 1965. (It affected more than thirty million people in New England and eastern Canada.) Written with Karl Tunberg, Freeman's flimsy story brings together fictional film star Margaret Garrison (Day) and Waldo Zane (Robert Morse), who has just stolen $2,400,000 from his company and is hiding out in her Connecticut house on the night of the blackout. When Margaret's husband, Peter (Patrick O'Neal), returns home and finds them together on the couch, he imagines the worst. In the end, Peter comes to realize that nothing happened between Margaret and Waldo the night before. Margaret, who had taken sleeping pills and quickly passed out, remains unsure.

The picture was directed by Hy Averback, who had worked with Day nearly two decades before, when they both toured with the *Bob Hope Show*. Averback had become famous for directing comedy series on TV—most recently *F Troop*—which may be why *Lights* comes across more like a sitcom than a feature film. O'Neal, who was also better known for his work in TV, played Peter Garrison, a role for which such major stars as Burt Lancaster, Marlon Brando, and Richard Burton had reportedly been under consideration.

Established as a Broadway star in *How to Succeed in Business Without Really Trying*—and having recently played in the film version—Robert Morse seemed an odd choice for Waldo, the embezzler. Though given a mustache, Morse's baby face and diminutive stature made him simply inappropriate as a prospective mate for Day's Margaret.

The picture was set to begin production at the studio on July 17, 1967, but Day suffered a pinched nerve while rehearsing with O'Neal, and filming had to be postponed for several weeks. Moreover, ninety-degree temperatures during location shooting in New York that summer made work almost unendurable for a cast that was obliged to wear winter clothing for their re-creation of a November night. (Fortunately for Day, her work on the picture was confined to the Hollywood studio—according to her wishes.)

New York mayor John V. Lindsay had recently made the city a more film-friendly town by establishing an office to help movie companies deal with clearing locations and security in the bustling metropolis. *Lights* was one of the first pictures made with the city's utmost cooperation. The scene in Grand Central—which figures so prominently when the lights in the picture, indeed, do go out—involved five hundred extras; other scenes required blocking traffic from Times Square.

Lights wanted to be something of a self-reflective spoof. Following a prologue and the opening credits, Margaret is seen being interviewed in her New York penthouse apartment by Roberta (Lola Albright), a pert journalist for a national magazine. "I was hoping Broadway would maybe give me a change of image," says Margaret. "What happens: I'm still 'The Constant Virgin,'" she adds, referring to the play she is starring in on the Great White Way. Margaret's husband, Peter, even calls his "Maggie" a "freckle-faced American sweetheart" and tells Roberta, "I knew her before she was a virgin." Lest anyone fail to make the connections between Day and her character, Margaret herself refers to her "corn-tassled, Yankee-Doodle, middle-class morality."

Clearly designed to exploit and send up Day's reputation, these remarks seem terribly belabored, and the halfhearted parody proves self-defeating. Further hobbled by an inane and predictable plot, *Lights* contributed mightily to making the conclusion of Day's film career so ignominious.

Perhaps the only one to benefit from the film's release was Hollywood character actor and resident wit Oscar Levant, who seized the opportunity to write a letter to the editor of the *Hollywood Reporter* concerning the use of his sarcastic remark, "I knew Doris Day before she was a virgin." "I originated that line back in 1964," wrote Levant, who had appeared in Day's first film, *Romance on the High Seas.* "[I] used it in my book, *Memoirs of an Amnesiac,* published in 1965. . . . As I have said before, imitation is the sincerest form of plagiarism."

*　　*　　*

While sending up her virginal image in her latest picture, Day was also becoming better acquainted with the sexual revolution engulfing the country—and particularly her son's generation, as college dormitories were becoming co-ed and the birth-control pill had such a liberating impact. She recalled a party at Terry's home. Candice Bergen prepared fried chicken and served it outdoors, while Pam Pollen, a member of the Gentle Soul, one of Terry's music groups, sang for the guests.

"Pam was in a long dress and she has long black hair. She is so spiritual looking, just beautiful," said Day—who was working extra hard to relate to the younger generation in the media—"and sang marvelously. Not a bit of being *on.* . . . She knew that we were there, and she hoped that we enjoyed it, but there was a complete lack of ostentation, a selflessness. She simply sang to this boy. Most of them were songs he had written. They sat there singing to each other, and the feeling was lovely, something that drew us all together, close. These young people communicate without talking, that's the most powerful of all communication. That oneness . . . that quiet. . . ." Day even resorted to the new slang: "This is how they communicate and I dig it, I know what they're doing."

Just as his mother's extraordinary recording career had come to an end, Terry became a prime mover in the renaissance in popular music that was transforming the culture. He was particularly close to both the Beach Boys' Brian Wilson and his wife and John and Michelle Phillips of the Mamas and the Papas. For her part, Bergen felt entirely out of her element while mingling with Janis Joplin, the Beatles, the Rolling Stones, the Lovin' Spoonful, and Jim Morrison. "These people astounded and amazed me," she recalled. "I was never at ease. I felt self-conscious and uncomfortable in their presence, unpleasantly aware of my pretensions, clumsy and awkward." She tried her best to fit in, donning "robes and beads" and smoking pot. But to all appearances, the handsome Terry and Candy were viewed as a happy and healthy couple. Rumors of their impending marriage abounded.

During the two years they lived together, Bergen made three films: the disastrous *The Adventurers,* the underrated *Getting Straight,* and the fiercely enigmatic *The Magus.* When Terry accompanied Bergen to Majorca, where *The Magus* was filmed, wedding rumors escalated. At least one report claimed that the couple had secretly married in Europe. But as Bergen would write two decades later in her memoir, not only was she not "meant to be married" to Terry, she was also even surprised that they were together—"so different were we from one another."

According to Bergen, as their basic incompatibility continued to surface, their relationship turned "testy and tense. . . . It was passive versus active; Terry, older, wanted contemplation, meditation, introspection; I wanted conversation, participation, discussion. . . . Denouncing life at a distance, an armchair social critic, he stayed aloof, while I, fired by his oratory, felt drawn into the thick of it."

Describing their deteriorating relations, Bergen made clear that her film work, entailing much location shooting, presented some of the hardships. But it was really the fundamental differences in their personalities that ultimately separated them. "If I sometimes resented Terry's anger toward my work, Terry resented social conventions and traditions and ridiculed my meticulous observance of them," Bergen recalled. "To him, it was sheer dishonesty. To me, it was mere manners."

✳   ✳   ✳

With Six You Get Eggroll, Day's thirty-ninth picture, was the first feature produced by Columbia Broadcasting System's new motion picture division, Cinema Center Films. Day's salary for the picture, estimated at $500,000, was but part of a much larger deal Melcher had been working on. "Doris Day and CBS still won't admit officially that she is set to star in a weekly half-hour situation series for the network next fall," Hal Humphrey wrote in the *Los Angeles Times* on February 7, 1968. "Yet producers Bob Sweeney and Dick Dorso have 15 script outlines all set, and as soon as Doris finishes a movie she's now doing for CBS she'll begin shooting for the series."

"We're still negotiating, and there are about 15 lawyers involved, but nothing is signed yet," Melcher told Humphrey. While acknowledging that for the TV show his wife would be playing a widow who meets various men, Melcher added, "She will still stand for morality. Everything will be wholesome, as it is in her movies. . . . Don't forget she is always the victim. She has an inner morality which prevents her doing anything wrong knowingly."

When Melcher discussed plans for the series with Day, she consented to go ahead with it, but with one caveat: "I'll do it, but only if you control the whole thing from beginning to end," she told Anne Fleming for an article in *Photoplay*. Fleming added that Melcher was "deeply involved in the writing of the first ten scripts." As early as January 1, 1968, Army Archer reported in *Variety* that "[Day] will play a widow with two kids on her CBS half-hour TV'er. After having read four scripts, she claims, 'I'll love working on TV.'"

"I don't really know when the show will go on the air," Day told yet another reporter, for the *L.A. Herald-Examiner.* "They're working on a format now, and I suppose I'll have some children in it. I do know what the work schedule will be, and it suits me fine. I'll rehearse a day, then shoot for three days. Then I'll have three days off. I'm not worried about the hard work in television. I enjoy working, and those three days off will be heavenly."

By having his wife play a widow with two sons in her TV show, Melcher was taking advantage of a cultural trend focused on single parents. After declaring television "the most potent force in mid-twentieth century American mythmaking," sociologist Karen Lindsey would write, "In the '50s, the model of the family was clear cut. Mommy, Daddy, and the kids. *Father Knows Best. I Remember Mama. Ozzie and Harriet. Make Room for Daddy. I Love Lucy. Life of Riley.* . . . In the '60s, things began to change. Divorce was a social reality, but a fantasy taboo, so TV compromised. The mortality rate among television spouses soared: suddenly widows and widowers with kids were the norm. *The Diahann Carroll Show. The Doris Day Show. The Andy Griffith Show. The Partridge Family.* And then the crème de la crème, *The Brady Bunch*: widow with cute large brood marries widower with cute large brood."

Given that she was forty-six and well into middle age, Day was practically compelled to play widows. Even before her TV show, Day portrayed a mature widow with children in what would prove to be her final film, *With Six You Get Eggroll.* Shortly before Cinema Center Films brought out *Eggroll* in August (1968), United Artists had an equally big family picture with *Yours, Mine and Ours.* It starred Lucille Ball and Henry Fonda as a widow and widower who bring stress to their many children in the course of turning two families into one.

In *Eggroll,* Day portrays Abby McClure, who runs her late husband's lumberyard while raising three boys. Early in the film, Abby falls in love with Jake Iverson, a widower with an eighteen-year-old daughter named Stacey. Abby and Jake elope to Las Vegas. That they tell the kids after the fact precipitates the turmoil. Jake was played by the rugged if low-key Brian Keith, whose father, Robert, had portrayed Day's father in *Young at Heart* and who also appeared in *Love Me or Leave Me.* Stacey was portrayed by Barbara Hershey, making her movie debut in *Eggroll—*as was Pat Carroll as Abby's sister, Maxine.

Director Howard Morris had worked on Sid Caesar's *Show of Shows* for a decade, perhaps the reason—just as with Day's two previous pictures—that *Eggroll* seems more like a TV sitcom than a feature film. It was based on the experiences of Gwen Bagni and Paul Dubov, who cowrote the screenplay.

Day's lifelong concern for animals was becoming more acute, manifesting itself here, as it had particularly when she made *The Man Who Knew Too Much* and, more recently, *The Ballad of Josie.* After shooting the scene in *Eggroll* where a vehicle crashes into a truck full of chickens, she required assurance that the squawking birds were all right. And, according to the *Los Angeles Times,* "When Doris saw a dog running around, she'd stop filming and ask them to give the dog water. She heard that CBS wanted to get rid of all the cats at its Cinema Center and she was up in arms. She's responsible for the cat population at the studio."

In spite of such stories, both cast and crew had fun making *Eggroll.* With a basketball hoop set up at the rear of the sound stage, some of them became adept at shooting baskets. And as others had reported over the years, Day would stay on the set even when she was no longer needed. "Doris was great to work with," recalled John Findlater, who played Abby's son Flip. "Anytime I had to do a scene with her, whether she was on camera or off, she was there to make sure that everything would go all right. A lot of times the stars will go home when you have your close-ups, and someone else will have to read their lines to you. But she was always there."

In addition to thirty-seven costume changes, Day had more hairdos in *Eggroll* than in any of her other films. "This was Doris' idea," explained her hairdresser, Barbara Lampson. "When you first see her, she's a little severe, then as the rapport develops between her and Brian, the styles change. It's kind of rough on Doris because Friday she had four complete wardrobe changes and hair changes. The week before she had eight wardrobe changes."

The screenplay for *Eggroll* strives for laughs primarily by inverting generational clichés, as when Stacey tells her father, "Don't you think you're a little bit old to be carrying on like this?" Or when Maxine tells Abby, "You know, one thing I don't understand is why parents never run away from home." (The Press Book actually pitched the picture as a "romantic comedy about the generation gap.") But even if the film appears to be embracing the massive changes sweeping through the culture, the results come across as gratuitous as the band of hippies that arrives near the end to accompany Abby to a police station. *Eggroll* emerged as a striking example of how what had been radical and nonconformist early in the decade was becoming mainstream and conventional by its end.

While his parents were doing too little too late to try and join the cultural bandwagon that would become known as the sixties, Terry Melcher continued to thrive in the music world. This young man who now epitomized the hippie in his dress and views enjoyed a major hit with a new Paul Revere and the Raiders album, *Rain, Sleet and Snow*. He was also in the midst of producing an album in partnership with the Beatles, *Dear Delilah*, featuring the Grapefruit. Later, he would boast that in the late 1960s, he was earning about $250,000 annually. He also had hopes that his mother would make an album with the Beatles. Like so many other projects planned for Doris Day, this one never came to fruition.

* * *

Before *Eggroll* was finished, CBS held a gala Chinese luncheon for the press on Valentine's Day 1968. "Turn On, Turn Up and Drop In CBS Films' Love-In Luncheon For Doris Day," read the invitation. Printed on a "psychedelic poster," it encouraged guests to "wear their mod, mad clothes and beads." The luncheon was held on a studio soundstage "decorated like a discotheque." As reported by Bill Kennedy in the *Herald-Examiner*, "Everyone was wearing love beads, including Lord Nelson, an English sheep dog who appears in the film. At least I think it was a sheep dog, but there were so many shaggy youths from Hertz-Rent-A-Hippie in the place that he could have been a rock 'n' roll guitarist." While some rushes from the upcoming film were projected, director Howard Morris described the action to the assembled throng. With Melcher at her side, Day appeared in one of her getups for the film—a pink quilted robe with matching pink satin slippers.

The event would prove to be the last time a large gathering saw the Melchers together. Ten days after their seventeenth anniversary, on April 3, 1968, Melcher entered Mount Sinai Hospital, suffering from bacterial endocarditis, an inflammation of the heart lining and valves. Within the week, he would die of a stroke.

30

Night for Day

---- ✳ ----

"Who can say what it is that makes a man die:
A sad heart that no longer wishes to go on beating."
—ERNEST LEHMAN, THE KING AND I

When her husband died on April 20, 1968, Doris Day was suddenly at a loss and incapable of moving forward. Looking back at this seismic moment in her life, Day would admit that it was "the one thing in my life that I handled badly. I had lived closely with Marty for 17 years, he had done everything for me. When he died it left a terrible void. I didn't know how to act, what to do, my tears never stopped, I couldn't talk to anyone on the phone." She also recalled, "For a while I didn't believe in anything. All I did was sit in my backyard and stare at the trees."

Given the business-like nature of her relationship with Melcher, Day's remarks might suggest an overreaction. But her shock appears thoroughly natural. Melcher was, after all, so young, his death so unexpected. As work on *With Six You Get Eggroll* was winding down, the fifty-three-year-old Melcher had felt increasingly ill and finally had no choice but to go to the hospital. Perhaps he would have survived the heart infection had he sought medical help sooner. But his faith in Christian Science barred his doing so.

As recalled by Jack Sher's widow, Moira, it was not long before his death that Melcher phoned her husband, desperately asking that he come over to the house, apparently to discuss a recent discovery regarding the Melchers' lawyer, Jerome Rosenthal, who in the past had also represented Sher. By the time Sher arrived, a stricken-looking, robe-clad Melcher had decided not to go into the matter. Sher returned home, baffled. Some years later, Day herself would recall coming home from the studio and discovering Melcher "sitting out on the curb in his robe and slippers, just waiting for me to come home," as if he had something urgent to tell her. But he never did. As Day would later claim, "I believe that Marty just wanted to die, because of the mess he was in."

"Jerry Rosenthal managed Stanley Kubrick, Kirk Douglas, and my husband as well, and he took them all, for all their money," Moira Sher recalled. "Jack ended up having to sell his house in Brentwood, and paid back taxes for years. It was just before I married Jack, after *Move Over, Darling*." According to Moira, Melcher knew that Sher had lost his home to Rosenthal's shady business practices. Sher speculated that Melcher had just discovered similar investment problems.

With private services, Melcher was buried at Forest Lawn cemetery, the final resting place for Hollywood royalty, which inspired Evelyn Waugh's classic satire *The Loved One*. A bystander caught a glimpse of Day as she entered the funeral parlor, her face "etched with sadness, but I noticed a hint of great strength and courage in her eyes," he reported, in what may have been publicity pabulum.

During the first year of her marriage to Melcher, Day had signed her checks, "Doris Day Melcher." But shortly thereafter she began signing simply "Doris Day." Upon Melcher's death, though, she returned to her married name, confirming that she most related emotionally to Melcher both at the beginning and the end of their marriage.

Some years later Day would acknowledge, "I wasn't too sure about being in love with him, but he was really a father image, the strong, protective figure that my own father never was because he left our house and divorced my mother when I was only eleven. Marty was protective, and that was something I needed at that time. He turned me into a dependent child. . . . I didn't know about the other side of him, his obsession with money, his deceit, his dealings." Day turned over the responsibilities for administrating her late husband's estate to the twenty-five-year-old Terry. Having always been more like a brother than a son to Day, Terry now took over Melcher's role, which had always been for her more like a father's than a husband's. Though Melcher's personal estate was worth $1,360,000, he had—astonishingly—left no will. Terry had to be appointed executor under an emergency order issued by the court on April 26. Still acting as the Melchers' attorney, Rosenthal instructed Terry to make large payments to several companies, which, it was later revealed, were really corporate entities designed to finance business ventures of his own.

Rosenthal proceeded to put up a host of barriers to all of Terry's examinations of Arwin's finances and would continue to do so for well over a decade. As soon as Terry began to suspect that his parents' long-term manager was crooked, he hired new attorneys and accountants. He formally terminated the association with Rosenthal on July 23, 1968. When Terry's new representatives requested business records, Rosenthal refused to supply them—"almost without exception," according to a court's ruling. Rosenthal claimed there were so many documents that it might take years to transfer them all. Terry and his mother had a receiver appointed to collect what documents they could. But even when Terry showed up with sheriff's deputies, Rosenthal refused to unlock the room containing the files, and a locksmith had to be brought in. And, as later determined by a court judgment, the records Rosenthal did turn over "were deceptive, calculated to mislead and delay."

For a month or so after Melcher's death, Terry, who went to his stepfather's office every day to examine the records, was surprised to receive phone calls at the office from "ladies in town," asking who would pay their rent now that Melcher was gone. "Of course I knew that Marty had an interest in outside ladies," recalled Terry. "Occasionally I'd find dollies in his office when I stopped in to see him about some music business. But it was still a shock to find that he was keeping a few of them around town."

Terry was unsure whether his mother knew of Marty's sexual peccadilloes. But as Day would explain in her memoir, when they had decided against getting a divorce in 1962, they also agreed that they would no longer sleep together. Moreover, they agreed never to discuss—with each other—their intimate relations with others. According to Terry, "It really wasn't all that important. What was important was discovering [Melcher's] hypocrisy, his lack of values, understanding his shallow rigidity." Like the 1950s—the era of his wife's heyday—Melcher, prudish and puritanical on the surface, was quite the opposite underneath. He had been, in reality, a prodigious womanizer.

Several years later, in an open reflection on this difficult period in her life, Day told Bill Davidson of *TV Guide*, "Our marriage wasn't perfect—whose is?—but there were many good things and suddenly there was a big black aching void. All I wanted to do was sit in my back yard looking at the trees. Nothing could compensate for the void, not even religion. . . . I couldn't even bring myself to face the fact that I was supposed to begin work on my new television series—the last deal Marty had made for me before he passed on. When I couldn't look at the trees in the back yard anymore, I went to Palm Springs to look at the desert."

For a month, Day rented a house in Palm Springs, where regular guests included Barbara Lampson—her hairdresser and close friend—Alma, Terry, Marty's brother Jack, and a good number of her dogs. (Jack Melcher lived with his wife, Rita, in Palo Alto, where he was general manager of one of the hotel operations owned by his brother and sister-in-law.) Unbeknownst to Day, Alma had given Jack some of his late brother's clothes. When he showed up one day wearing one of Marty's suits, Day became hysterical.

While the ghost of his detestable stepfather continued to hover over his mother, it was Terry who succeeded in reviving Day. "How about *The Doris Day Show*? It's the start of a whole new career for you," Terry said when he visited his mother in Palm Springs. "Terry, I just can't think of scripts and TV when I've lost Dad," she replied. "Mother, a deal is a deal," Terry insisted. "You made a deal and what are you going to do?"

"I got furious with Terry and began to cry," she recalled. "I said, 'Why did you say that?' He replied, 'This show isn't just you. It means a lot of work to a lot of people.' I thought Terry was cruel and inhuman at the time, but now I bless him for literally forcing me to go back to work."

Day's reluctance to undertake the show was due not only to her feeling despondent and inconsolable. Along with much of the rest of the world, she had always felt that movie stars resorted to starring in a TV series only when their film careers had hit rock bottom. (As Hedda Hopper wrote a decade earlier, "Doris makes no TV appearances, doesn't like it, and thinks people who make movies aren't particularly interested in it.") All along, Day had been ambivalent—at best—about having her own TV show. That may be why, in her memoir, she falsely claimed that she didn't even know the project was in the works at the time of Melcher's death. She had, in fact, discussed the idea with several reporters months before. Here was yet another dramatic detail in her autobiography that had no basis in reality.

"She didn't want to do the TV series," recalled her old friend Miriam Nelson. "But she had lost a lot of weight, and was quite thin, and I remember that later she realized the show was the best thing she could have done, because it got her up and going again. And she enjoys working. She loves the relationship she has with all the people behind the scenes, the crew. And she loved laughing a lot with everybody, and that gave her a new lease on life."

As Day herself told a movie-magazine journalist shortly before Melcher's death: "Marty says I'm healthier and in better spirits when I'm working. . . . He's always manufacturing new things for me to do, and I'm always screaming about it but, of course, he's right. Work with me is therapy, a way to release this energy."

*   *   *

By June 6, or only six weeks after Melcher's death, Day was hard at work on her television series. She found the new medium extremely challenging, at first. "I still don't know how I was able to do it," she recalled. "I was just lucky to get my lines studied and my make-up put on. Every day was an ordeal. There was a first assistant director named Bob Daley on the show. He was built just like Marty and dressed just like him. I'd be sitting on the set and every time I looked up and saw Bob, it was Marty. It was just shattering to me."

James Hampton, who played the hired hand in the series, recalled Day as "kind of empty" on the set during the first few weeks of shooting. "[She was] just kind of walking around, like lost. So sad." Fran Ryan, who played the housekeeper on *The Doris Day Show* its first year, reported that Jack Melcher was also a presence on the set when they began work. According to Terry, his mother had Jack move into the house on Crescent Drive so she wouldn't be "so alone." Though Jack Melcher apparently took time off to help Day adjust to her husband's absence, he would neither confirm nor deny it when interviewed by Ronald Crawford for a story in *TV Radio Mirror*. Their telephone conversation was a "frustrating one," according to Crawford, who added that Jack claimed he had "nothing to do with the show." Decades later, Jack Melcher would recall that he came by to look in on his sister-in-law only for a brief period, at the time.

According to Jack Melcher, Terry was in control of everything. "Sometimes," Day recalled about the early days of her TV show, "you'd think my son was my father! . . . He'd drop by, en route from the studio to his place at Malibu, to make sure I was okay, even though we'd seen each other at the studio not more than a couple of hours earlier."

Given all of the love that Day's character was showering on her two young TV sons, it was painful for Terry to observe his mother work on the show. "Terry would stand backstage and cry, because it was the mother he never had," recalled his good friend Guy Webster. "We talked about it a lot, because it was so upsetting to him to see her cuddling them and giving them the love and attention she never gave him."

Day found companionship at home with her Aunt Marie, who quickly replaced Jack Melcher as family member in residence. "Marty always called her Rocky," Day said of her aunt, "because she reminded him of a rock— strong, good and honest, like a pioneer woman. She also reminded Marty of an old actor named Ned Sparks, because of her dry wit. . . . When Marty passed on, I needed a rock, so I sent for Aunt Rocky, who was divorced and living alone in Cincinnati." Day also found consolation in her four French poodles: Bo-Bo, Big Red, Charlie Brown, and Muffy. "With Marty gone, they are the only living, physical reminders of how much he meant to her, for he had given them to Doris as presents," observed a reporter. And according to her fan Paul Brogan, who was clearly becoming more of an intimate friend, the letters he received from Day became much more extensive and more personal after Melcher's death. She increasingly urged him to visit her in Los Angeles, as he eventually would.

During the first year of *The Doris Day Show,* the cast had a read-through rehearsal on Mondays, began shooting on Tuesdays, and concluded the episode on Fridays. Each day of shooting, from 10 to 6, used one camera with film, as opposed to videotape. The first year's shooting took place on two vast soundstages at the old Goldwyn West Studios, at Gower and Sunset Boulevard.

After she began to lose herself in work and recover from her depression over Melcher's death, Day spoke with Cleveland Amory for his "Celebrity Register" syndicated column. When he asked how she was coping, she replied: "I like to walk on the beach. I like to meditate. But mostly I like to ride my bike. I ride my bike every day. I ride all over Beverly Hills—right in the traffic. . . . I like to do all my own marketing. I have a basket right on my bike—in fact I have two baskets. I like to visit with the shopkeepers." After a pause, Day resumed: "And I don't like the shopping centers at all. . . . I like little butcher shops and candy stores and groceries. When I'm not riding my bike, I like to walk."

✳ ✳ ✳

When *Where Were You When the Lights Went Out?* opened on May 30, the reviewers were every bit as cruel to Day as they had been upon the release of her previous picture, *The Ballad of Josie.* "It is almost pointless to complain about yet another Doris Day movie, except to underline what can happen when an actress chooses to freeze her image," complained Arthur Knight in a commentary in *Saturday Review,* typical of the lambasting the film took. "For all the soft-focusing and careful light-ing that her cameramen give her, the screen reveals that she is no longer a frolicsome lass in her twenties. Clothes, make-up, youthful hairdos, and outsized dark glasses can no longer conceal the lines of maturity. Not even her harshest critic is quite so pitiless as the camera's lens, and the time is obviously at hand (if not past due) when Miss Day must not only be, but act, her age." Knight was equally contemptuous of the film itself: "[It] is more of the old Day formula . . . she might well study it to determine where to go from here. I can't think of any reasons for anyone else to bother."

Renata Adler began her review for the *New York Times* with a unique interpretation of the formula that had marked Day's sex comedies. "Do-ris Day's honor, from movie to movie, was becoming a kind of drag as she tumbled from euphemism to innuendo. The beginning of each movie asked the question whether Anything was going to Happen, the middle raised the desperate possibility that something Had Happened, and then . . . she was married." Adler ended with the grim observation that "[Day] seems doomed to exclaim in every movie some version of the 'Oh, Peter, I'm tarnished' line she has in this one—a perennial, uncertainly comic in-spiration, by virtue of what doesn't happen to her." In the *New York Daily News*, Wanda Hale held the screenwriters and director "responsible for making the stars look like the least funny foursome ever assembled to pull off a laugh spree."

In a Sunday edition of the *Boston Globe*, Marjorie Adams defended Day while speculating about her upcoming TV series. "She has the chance to acquire a TV following as big as the one she had so many years as a screen star. Besides, TV critics are not as cruel as the New York magazine film critics, who long have assailed Doris as a sentimental nitwit."

Fifteen-year-old Paul Brogan felt the need to add to Adams's de-fense of his idol and long-term pen pal. Brogan wrote a letter to the *Globe* in which—after declaring himself "probably [Day's] biggest New England fan"—he called *Where Were You When the Lights Went Out?* "one of the funniest and finest films Doris Day ever made. . . . She makes you feel good and that is the wonderful thing about her. I hope that warm, happy glow comes across on the television screen, too." In her published response to Brogan's letter, Adams wrote that she had met Day several times, including once at a party at the Melchers' home. "I have found her all the things you like about her on the screen. But you'll have to admit there's an 'anti–Doris Day' contingent among 1967–68 movie goers."

The "anti–Doris Day" stance was all too real. As Day's film career was fast coming to a close in 1968, a harshly negative attitude became prevalent among cultural arbiters who lumped her vastly superior fare from the 1950s and early 1960s with the later dross. The anti–Doris Day attitude would inform her reputation for generations to come—except, of course, with her legion of fans.

As the great comic playwright and sceenwriter Garson Kanin succinctly wrote, "The basic mistake that was made in the handling of the Doris Day image was that she was asked to play the same age for a decade. Not only the same age, but the same undeveloped, undeveloping person." Following Melcher's instincts and dictates, Day herself contributed unwittingly to the problem by refusing to make any changes in her image. In spite of the way she was being treated in the press—or perhaps because of it—Day busied herself promoting her new TV series. "It's a warm, family show," she told Hal Humphrey of the *Los Angeles Times*. "You can call it corn, but I love it." Humphrey went on to say, "With the movies dealing today in less sham and more basic sex fundamentals, there aren't so many 'Doris Day parts' around, and she feels strongly about the type she's played all these years and doesn't want to change it."

"Marlon Brando isn't any one thing," Day said, once again embracing her old image rather than renouncing it. "He can be a hero or a heavy robbing a bank, but if I saw Jimmy Stewart or the late Gary Cooper doing that I think I'd cry because I feel as if I really knew them. Well, I think people feel that way about me, too, and expect me to be a certain way." Elsewhere, Day remonstrated, "If you had a store and people asked for certain things, you'd make sure you had them, wouldn't you? That's my answer. I'll make comedies as long as people seem to enjoy me best in them." Thus the calcification of Doris Day's image and her downhill slide into artistic irrelevance.

Though Day also told Humphrey that she didn't mind the pace of working for TV with only one day for rehearsals, she failed to mention that after the completion of the eighth episode, the powers-that-be complained that the show was consistently running a day over schedule. They recommended cutting time for rehearsals and cutting back in other ways. But Day would have none of it. For the first time in her life, and without Melcher to intervene on her behalf, Day took charge and simply refused. For the first time, she was finally taking control of her life. In lieu of attending a dinner party for CBS affiliates to promote the show,

Day prepared a video explaining that the "production schedule is just so tight, that it's impossible to be there with you."

Day acquired a number of behind-the-scenes aides, too. In addition to Terry, record producer Don Genson became more involved in her business affairs. Genson also became a father figure to Terry, who, given the calamitous business matters unfolding with Rosenthal, was not having an easy time managing his mother's finances. "It really griped my ass to have to deal with the CBS network executives," Terry recalled. "I was twenty-six, so compared to them I was a kid, but I wasn't used to being treated like a kid in my own business." In mid-August, Rosenthal filed suit in Superior Court to have Terry removed as administrator of Melcher's estate, claiming it was being mismanaged. As reported by Anne Fleming in *Photoplay*, "After five days of testimony in court, Judge Martin Katz ruled that Terry Melcher was not only to remain as administrator, but also certified to his competence on the basis of decisions Terry had made."

*   *   *

With Six You Get Eggroll was released in August, several months after Melcher's death and a month before the debut of Day's TV series. Judging from the flimsy marketing campaign, National General Pictures did not harbor high expectations for *Eggroll*. Lame publicity suggestions included tie-ins with local Chinese restaurants, florists, pet shops, and mobile-home dealers—and letting "Every Sixth Person Free" into the theater. There was also a silly gambit to offer free tickets to "the first twelve authentically costumed hippies and their dates if they are also in costume." This last proposal reinforced just how out of touch with the revolutionary culture Arwin—and other mainstream studios—had become.

The longing to appear "hip" and "with it" became a part of the publicity campaign, as indicated by the title of an article to promote the film in *Photoplay*—"If My Son's a Hippie Then So Am I!" Day was quoted as saying: "Adults make the mistake of looking for approval, constantly looking for approval, always trying to do the accepted thing so people will like us. We conform because we don't want the neighbors thinking poorly of us." This, indeed, had been Day's personal feeling for most of her life. But her disowning it in print was something new.

Years later, Day said her feelings about *Eggroll* were "very loving and warm" because it was Melcher's last film, and the only one he had pro-

duced independently. "I adore that movie." Perhaps out of sympathy for
Day's personal loss, she received some of her best notices in years for her
last film role. Many reviewers made inevitable comparisons with *Yours,
Mine and Ours.* "Screened as a sneak preview in a large suburban theatre,
the capacity house greeted Miss Day's name on the screen with heavy applause and audibly enjoyed the film throughout," Robert B. Frederick reported in his respectful review for *Variety.* While John Mahoney, in the *Hollywood Reporter,* found the cast "consistently superior to the material," he
also wrote, "A strength of the script is the credible flavor of that dialogue
which tries least to be funny, particularly the interplay between Miss Day
and Keith, who make an excellent team, albeit in need of a better game."

Calling it "the latest chapter in the continuing adventures of the
Widow Day," Vincent Canby dismissed the film in his review for the
New York Times. He was far less dismissive of Day, however. "There are
. . . some hints of the very real comic talent that has, over the years, become hermetically sealed inside a lacquered personality, like a butterfly
in a Mason jar." From his elevated perch at the *Saturday Review,* Arthur
Knight proved surprisingly well disposed toward the film. "A few weeks
ago I wrote—not too unkindly, I hope—a piece urging Doris Day to for-
sake her virginity (at least, her on-screen virginity) and grow up to her
capabilities. Without even waiting for my good advice, in . . . *Eggroll* she
has done just that—with a vengeance ([consider her] children, one quite
grown up). The point is that, with deft support from Brian Keith and a
wittily dialogued script from a quartet of writers, Miss Day has moved
brightly and engagingly into the area of character comedy."

A knockoff of old-fashioned family pictures as well as a TV show—
that came out while the world was changing around it—*Eggroll* has not
held up well. Nor does it have any place on a list of the far more popular—and edgy—films of 1968: *Planet of the Apes, 2001: A Space Odyssey,
Rosemary's Baby, Charly,* and *The Thomas Crown Affair.*

*   *   *

The Doris Day Show aired at 9:30 on Tuesday nights on CBS. It followed
The Red Skelton Show and preceded *60 Minutes.* Its major network competition was ABC's *N.Y.P.D.* and NBC's *Movie of the Week.* In her show, Day
played Doris Martin, a widow who has decided to leave "the big city" to
raise her two towheaded boys on her father's farm in Mill Valley, Cali-

fornia. The salty and bearded Denver Pyle played grandpa Buck Webb, a surrogate father to his grandsons. Fran Ryan was Aggie, the housekeeper, and James Hampton was Leroy B. Simpson, the hired hand. Fresh from his role as the family sheepdog in *With Six You Get Eggroll*—and recognizable as the sheepdog from the TV series *Please Don't Eat the Daisies*—was Lord Nelson.

Competing against five hundred other youngsters, ten-year-old Philip Brown won the part of Doris Martin's son Billy. The role of the younger son, Toby, went to six-year-old Tod Starke. According to Hampton, Day "spent her own money to make improvements on the set and with her wardrobe." With Melcher unavailable to comfort her, Day gradually began taking charge of her life in ways she never would have before. Melcher certainly would never have allowed his wife to shell out any of her own money for her set dressing.

But the conceit of the show, an attempt to turn back the clock, was pure Melcher. The Vietnam War, the assassinations of the Rev. Martin Luther King Jr. and Robert Kennedy—both of whom were assassinated in 1968—the civil rights backlash, and other cultural upheavals of the raucous late sixties were missing from this bland throwback to good old-fashioned fifties sitcom values. (Ironically, the show was set near San Francisco, the epicenter of so many radical developments including the so-called Summer of Love in 1967.)

With Day's rendition of "Que Sera, Sera" playing in the background, the opening title shots set the saccharine and nostalgic tone for the series, as "Doris" ran down a country hill with her boys—followed by their sheepdog—and the camera focused variously on a field, a pond, a butterfly, and finally a sunset. Each episode emphasized the salt-of-the-earth values Doris Martin instilled in her boys. The series might well have been called, as one reviewer put it, *Mother Knows Best*, and many of the half-hour segments included a moment, near the end, when Day's eyes would fill with tears of pride for her boys.

The first episode of *The Doris Day Show*, which aired on September 24, 1968, toyed with the issue of Day's age. As the clan celebrates Doris Martin's birthday and she counts the candles on her cake, Aggie announces that there are only twenty-two. Denver Pyle was himself clearly playing with age, as well. At forty-eight, he was only two years older than Day but was playing her sixty-two-year-old father. He even had makeup applied to his hands to make him appear significantly older.

In his review of the show's premiere for the *Los Angeles Times*, Don Page declared it to be "three parts Donna Reed, two parts Father (or Mother) Knows Best, a dash of *Petticoat Junction* and sprinkled lightly with *America the Beautiful*. And there she is, eternally lovely and girl-ish. Soft blonde hair, innocent eyes, the pink mouth forever framing a flawless set of white teeth. Doris Day makes Cinderella look like a truck driver."

While squeezing in his customary praise for Day in his syndicated review of the first episode, critic Rex Reed focused on Day's insecurity. "Doris is an enormously natural and personable performer, but she's nei-ther old nor ugly, so why, I'd like to ask, must all of her close-ups be shot with so many filters over the camera lens that she looks like she's being photographed through Vaseline? Everything about this show is so icky-poo sweet and jim dandy confectionery you might know the sponsor would be Duncan Hines cake mix."

Indeed, the first season featured scripts that exhibited the squeaky-clean verities and inevitable platitudes the world had come to expect from Day. While acknowledging in his review in *TV Guide* that "there are plots in this series," Cleveland Amory claimed that "they are buried under so many layers of cotton-candy writing, not to mention the thun-derous laugh track, that they deserve better. . . . Not only is this show no more interesting than anyone's everyday life, it's a good deal less so."

When the series was in its second month, film scholar John Hallowell wrote of his deep admiration for Day in the *New York Times*. "A couple of Saturday afternoons ago I watched *Calamity Jane* on television and it was even better than when I saw it 10 times as a kid," Hallowell said. "When the gods decide to let us blow ourselves up and save the best movies for themselves, surely in some great screening room on Olympus they'll be running Doris Day singing 'Secret Love.'"

Though Hallowell made it clear that he was a lot less fond of *Where Were You When the Lights Went Out?* as well as her new TV show, he visited Day on the set at Golden West Studios. "She occupies an enormous, air-conditioned trailer the television boys gave her, replete with white picket fence, trees and grass. Inside, there were daisies, daisies everywhere: a daisy candy plate, daisies on the table, and even daisies drawn on her star's canvas chair." "I mean she lives here," the show's producer Dick Dorso told Hallowell, "she works so hard, so we got together and gave her this."

When Hallowell mentioned to Day her reputation for being "Miss Niceness," she replied: "I couldn't do my work and worry about if I'm 'too sweet,' the way they say. 'The girl next door.' Me? Never. I just can't worry about everybody's approval. Maybe they don't like my hair. Or I smile a lot. I don't know. And I really don't care. I'm only concerned with what *I'm* thinking. O.K.?"

When he asked her why she had stopped making musicals, Day replied: "[M]ovies went away from that trend. Musicals are really hard work. . . . I seemed to do so many of them at Warner Brothers. We were contract players then. . . . I don't know—all those dance numbers, long rehearsal hours. When the trend changed, I was kind of pleased."

To further promote the series, Day consented to meet Betty Rollin for an article in *Look* magazine, which would open with a large, two-page spread of the star sitting on the deck of her Malibu beach house with her four poodles. Day is barefoot and wearing blue shorts, a white T-shirt, and a red-and-white gingham sun hat. "Everyone I know thinks Doris Day is a drip," wrote Rollin. "That's because, I hasten to tell them, they don't *know* Miss Day, and they are judging her from her largely sappy motion pictures, where her chief thing is saying 'no' and making it sound better than 'yes.'"

When asked by journalist Anne Fleming why she had deliberately lost twenty pounds for the TV series, a coy Day playfully responded, "I guess I wanted to hear some wolf whistles," before adding, "I wanted to be in top shape mentally and physically." For a feature in *Photoplay*, Day also told Fleming, "This series was a godsend for me. I realize how hard it must be for active women to adjust [to a double life]—like Mrs. John Kennedy and Mrs. Robert Kennedy."

Day did not tell Fleming that one wolf who more than just whistled at her was stalwart movie star Glenn Ford, her first "date" since Melcher's demise. Ford was a blind date for Day, arranged by a mutual friend who invited them both to a Sunday night dinner. "He wouldn't tell me who it was," Day reportedly told another friend. "He said he was a film star who had made many women swoon over the years. Don't tell Glenn, but I thought it was Cary Grant. But I knew Cary. He wouldn't go out on a blind date with me without calling."

Because the fifty-two-year-old Ford's divorce from fashion model Kathy Hays had not been finalized, his dates with Day had to be on the sly. But according to reporter Shirley Baker, after several months of seeing each other, Ford became "an almost nightly visitor to Doris' home." According to Paul Brogan, tap star Eleanor Powell (Ford's first wife) confirmed that Day and Ford had been an item for a short time.

* * *

The war with Rosenthal flared anew in 1969, when Day's son and "six companies they own" filed a million-dollar suit in Superior Court against Rosenthal. As Terry became more and more enmeshed in his mother's financial affairs, he grew to regret the circumstances he found himself in. "I had worked hard on turning her mind around and getting her interested in her television show," he recalled. "But as she responded to this and began to look happier, I got to thinking, goddamn it, she's going along fine now, whereas all I do is sit in lawyers' offices and in court for three months and it's only the beginning."

One of Rosenthal's standard tactics was to protract the lawsuit with his countersuits. He filed no less than eleven suits of his own—and as many as eighteen, according to another report—in a number of states, making the legal saga "one of the longest continuous engagements in California civil litigation" history. (*Day vs. Rosenthal.*) Terry particularly hated having to spend "three weeks in Dallas in a courthouse without any air conditioning."

While he became more and more engulfed in the Rosenthal morass, Terry did what he could to maintain his successful career as a record producer. He was introduced to a would-be recording artist named Charles Manson by their mutual friend Gregg Jakobson, a songwriter who had collaborated with Dennis Wilson and the Beach Boys. Manson was living on a commune at what used to be the Spahn Movie Ranch in the Santa Susana Mountains—where many Western films had been shot, as well as episodes of TV's *Bonanza* and *The Lone Ranger*. During his first visit, Terry observed Manson perched on a rock, "surrounded by [nude] 'family members,' who hummed and sang in the background as he talked and sang 15 or 20 songs." Terry would later say how "impressed" he was by the power and "leadership" that Manson exhibited over his disciples.

Candice Bergen recalled the night Terry returned from his first meeting with Manson. "[He was] intrigued by this man, by his apparent spirituality and lack of materialism. He admired the naturalness of their life on the ranch, the simplicity, the closeness. He returned and recorded them singing, coming home to tell of these 'soft, simple girls' sitting naked around this Christlike guy, all singing sweetly together."

* * *

A number of major changes were planned for *The Doris Day Show* in its second year. "[It] was hardly the world-beater CBS thought it would be in its initial season," Cecil Smith observed in the *Los Angeles Times*, "and the network is shifting it to a prize spot in its Monday night comedy lineup [at 9:30] following *Lucy* and *Mayberry RFD*, moving *Family Affair* to Thursday nights to accommodate it." The series would also leave Golden West Studio behind and be shot at a new CBS studio in Studio City—where Day proved much happier—and for a new sponsor, Bristol-Myers Co.

In addition to repositioning the show's weekly slot, its format was radically reconceived, opening up opportunities to expand the plot. No longer was Doris Martin confined to country life with her father and two boys. She now commuted to San Francisco, where she had a job as a Girl Friday to Michael Nicholson (McLean Stevenson), the editor of *Today's World* magazine. In the course of the season, the roles of her father and sons diminished. To prepare viewers for the new format, the new introductory titles showed Day leaving the ranch in a red convertible and then approaching San Francisco over the Golden Gate Bridge.

Some of the changes reflected changes in Day herself, after she recovered from the shock of Melcher's death and became more outgoing and vivacious again. Still other alterations were prompted by fans' suggestions. "People complained I never wore pretty clothes and had no romance in my life," explained Day, referring to herself as Doris Martin. "I just sat around night after night playing checkers." Moreover, she had no "girl friend" or character she could "talk girl talk to," a deficiency remedied by adding Rose Marie—a familiar TV face from both the *Dick Van Dyke Show* and *Hollywood Squares*—as Myrna, another secretary at *Today's World*.

"I was a little apprehensive . . . because her husband had just died, and my husband had just died," recalled Rose Marie. "[But] we hit it off right from the beginning. She was just wonderful. She's so easy to work with." The biggest change in the series was Day's taking control of the show. Now she made all the final decisions herself. And to do so, she even started watching the daily rushes.

But looking back, Day observed how the first year had been so close to Melcher's death that she was "just going through the motions," while many others had taken charge of production. She added that she hadn't wanted to contribute much because she was heartbroken and just didn't care about anything.

*   *   *

Day left the house in Malibu and returned to North Crescent, since it was closer to CBS's Studio Center in the San Fernando Valley, where she was now making her series. While Day was working on the second season of her TV show in the summer of 1969, Neil Armstrong took his "giant leap for mankind" on the moon even as the rock world staged its greatest celebration at Woodstock. Terry had become increasingly tied up with the Rosenthal imbroglio, which took a significant toll on his relationship with Candice Bergen. In her memoir, Bergen recalled the significant Monday when Terry informed her that they would be vacating the house on Cielo Drive later that week and moving into the Malibu beach house, which his mother had vacated.

"[H]e disappeared into endless daily legal meetings for months on end, slowly unraveling the threads of the swindle, unable to fathom the depths of the dishonesty," Bergen wrote. "For months we hardly saw each other. He was buried in financial briefs he struggled to understand, exhausted by the intricacies and the tedium, and seemed beaten by the betrayal. He never arrived at the beach before ten o'clock at night after the debilitating days of meetings and began taking sleeping pills for a few hours' unconsciousness before morning came and he got up to start again. He began to drink. . . . We saw each other less and less, until finally he confessed that he now saw me as yet another responsibility in his life, when he was collapsing under the weight of those he had just taken on. We agreed that I would soon move out. . . . The pills and the drinking increased, blotting out the painful confusion of a golden boy whose life had turned against him."

In the midst of these developments, Charles Manson kept trying to track down Terry in hopes of getting a record produced. According to Bergen, it was during her final weeks at the house in Malibu that a telescope disappeared from the porch. Some days later, a Manson colleague came by with a message that Manson knew they had moved from Cielo Drive. Manson had, "in fact, stolen a telescope from the deck of the Malibu beach house," recalled Terry, "to let me know he knew my whereabouts."

The following week, on August 9, Manson's gang of murderers descended on the Cielo Drive house recently vacated by Terry and Candice. Now rented by film director Roman Polanski, it became the site of one of the most infamous crimes of the century when four houseguests and Polanski's pregnant wife, Sharon Tate, were savagely slain.

* * *

The first episode of the second season of Day's TV show, "Doris Gets a Job," was built around Doris Martin's securing a job in San Francisco. The second, "A Frog Called Harold," focused on Toby's pet frog—which Doris Martin inadvertently transports in her purse to the office—demonstrating, yet again, that Day had no qualms about handling animals, be it this amphibian, the pachyderm in *Jumbo*, or the skunks and baby lambs in *The Ballad of Josie*. The sixth episode, "Doris, the Model," is a lame excuse for what can only be viewed as a fashion show.

Day reported that one of her favorite episodes from the second season was the seventh, "Doris Strikes Out" (November 24, 1969), in which Buck injures his back and Doris has to serve as the umpire for her boys' Little League game, nearly foiling her date with a French movie star. "You know baseball as good as any guy," Toby tells his mother, playing on the tomboy image Day had presented in several of her early Warner Brothers films.

Though Denver Pyle's role of Buck was virtually eliminated from the show during its second year, he was working behind the scenes, directing several of the episodes, two of which featured Larry Storch as Duke Farentino, a boxer whom Doris sets out to interview for *Today's World*. (The first, "The Prizefighter and the Lady," aired on January 5, 1970.) A familiar face from the idiotic Western spoof series *F Troop*, Storch enjoyed working with Day. Like many others, he emphasized that she was a "natural."

Having heard that Day was a perfectionist, Storch took his assignment very seriously. "I gave my wife a hard time, going over my lines so much," recalled Storch, who also remembered working on a particular scene with Day. "She was so unnerved by deer heads on the wall, that she just couldn't do the scene." Director Pyle was completely sympathetic and shot the scene on a different set. When Storch told Day that he was in the navy in 1942 with Al Jorden, her first husband, he was unprepared for her icy response. "She wasn't very happy even with the mention of his name," said Storch, "and she would have nothing to do or say about him."

Day nonetheless began to use her show as a vehicle for working with old friends and colleagues, even as she was making new ones. In "Doris vs. the Computer" (January 12, 1970), Billy De Wolfe makes his first appearance as efficiency expert Mr. Jarvis—a character who would become more of a regular the next three seasons. The last two episodes of the second season introduced Edward Andrews as Colonel Fairburn, the owner of *Today's World* (Andrews had appeared in both *Send Me No Flowers* and *The Thrill of It All*).

* * *

While shooting a picture in Mexico in November 1969, Candice Bergen picked up the phone one evening and called Terry, for what amounted to their first conversation in several months. Terry, who was at his mother's house on Crescent, told Bergen that the police had just come by to inform him that Charles Manson was behind the hideous Tate murders. Even though Manson knew that Terry no longer lived in the Cielo Drive house, Terry was convinced that he was the reason the crime had been committed—as Manson and some of his followers later confirmed, it was meant to send a message to Terry.

After recovering from the loss of her husband, Day was thriving by losing herself in work on her TV show. In the meantime, between the ongoing lawsuits with Rosenthal and the pending Manson murder trial, Terry's life was spiraling ever downward. Though Manson was in jail, the traumatized Terry had a growing paranoia that Manson's "family" members were after him. He hired round-the-clock bodyguards for his mother and himself. He left the house in Malibu and rented one in Beverly Hills, where he kept a shotgun by the door and a pistol by his bed. He not only became reclusive but increasingly reliant on drugs and alcohol.

"I myself rarely saw him and I couldn't get him on the phone," Day recalled. "In fact, [Terry] had developed a quiet hostility toward me. On those few occasions when I did get him on the phone, his conversation was often incoherent."

It was probably during this period that Terry showed up one day at

his childhood home in Toluca Lake. "Our doorbell rang, and this bearded individual was there, and he looked inside, and said, 'I'm home, at
last,'" remembered Tom Von Der Ahe, who, with his family, had moved
into the house two years earlier. "He seemed very familiar with the place
as he started to walk in. I put my arm up and said, 'You're not coming
in here.' He was confused and disheveled, and he just kept saying, 'I'm
home, I'm home.'" Though his uninvited visitor failed to identify himself,
Von Der Ahe assumed that it was Terry.

"It's All About Animals"

✳

"I'd take a dog over a man any day."
—EDITH BOUVIER BEALE

Since Terry was in no condition to supervise the third season of *The Doris Day Show*, Don Genson assumed control and was named co-executive producer. As with the second season, however, Day had ultimate control over everything. The third year of the series also introduced yet more format changes, the greatest of which was given away by the title of the first episode, "Doris Finds an Apartment." Doris Martin leaves her father—and the farm—behind her and moves to the city with her boys. Though "Que Sera, Sera" continued as the show's theme song, a new pictorial background accompanied the opening credits as Day appears racing down the spiral staircase of her new home, her face beaming. The sequence then resumed with the familiar opening from the previous season—Day driving over the Golden Gate Bridge and then frolicking in and around San Fransisco—all achieved in less than a minute.

Production on the third season of *The Doris Day Show* began on June 15, 1970. Day's great friend Billy De Wolfe became a regular guest star as Mr. Jarvis, a neighbor of Doris Martin's in her new home, and as an efficiency expert who appeared in an earlier episode. Having appeared in an inane episode during the second season ("Kidnapped"), Kaye Ballard also became a recurring guest star as Angie Pallucci. With her husband Louie (played by character actor Bernie Kopell), Angie runs Pallucci's Restaurant and rents the apartment above Doris Martin's.

"I played an Italian, like I had in *Mothers-in-Law*, and that kind of pigeonholed me," recalled Ballard. "As a matter of fact, it might have hurt my career a little, because she signed me to an occasional guest shot. Well, in two years, I did fourteen shows. Consequently, people thought I was a regular, when I wasn't, I was only a guest star."

But Ballard loved doing the show. "It was a joy working with her because she made everything so relaxed. It was the most ideal life in the world. She always gave you a nice dressing room. She knew what she was doing at all times. We'd have big lunches on the set, and we'd laugh. And there was never any tension.

"Like Loretta Young, she knew when the lighting wasn't hitting her right. And like Eve Arden, she could read a script just once, and she'd know the lines. During lunch, we'd ask her, 'Are you doing the lines, or are we just talking?' She was that natural. She was wonderful to work with. And it was a genuine thrill for me because, in my eyes, she was truly a movie star. But I don't think she knew how good she was. She never had any formal training in acting—and that made her feel insecure. . . . I think she was more confident about her singing than about her acting. But she definitely underestimated herself. In fact, if you told Doris how good she was, she got embarrassed."

Like everyone else who became a friend, Ballard called Day "Clara." "I think I called her Clara because I couldn't believe that I was talking to Doris Day—I was so in awe of her. She called me Melba Nerle: that was a girl she went to school with. She told me, 'Melba always wore black bloomers, and you're always in black slacks, so I'm calling you Melba Nerle.'" Over the years, Day and Ballard would sign their letters to each other Clara and Melba.

"Even before I was on the show, we had lots of dinners together," Ballard continued. "I kept trying to fix her up with somebody because she always seemed so lonely and sad to me. I remember trying with Peter Lawford and Flip Wilson."

Two years after Melcher's death, Day acknowledged to an interviewer that she was lonely. "I would like to marry again because I want that one-to-one relationship," she said. "I want to know that when I come home from the studio it won't be to an empty house and a lonely evening. I want to be a wife. If it sounds corny, it's too bad, but I want to be loved and to love someone in return. It's time for me to get back to being a complete woman."

But even if she craved companionship, Day still shunned large parties.

"When I was the hot new kid in Hollywood, making *Myra Breckin-ridge*, I was getting invited to all these parties, and I would call Doris and ask her if she wanted to go with me," recalled Rex Reed. "She'd say, 'Oh, you must be joking. There's not a drug strong enough that would get me to Edie Goetz's dinner party.'"

As Day wrote to hardcore fan Mary Anne Barothy, the holiday period was especially "strange" that year, since Aunt Marie, her beloved "Rocky," had died on Christmas Day. One way Day might have reduced her loneliness and stress was reportedly by having an affair with her TV show's producer, Don Genson, even though he was married. (Genson's wife, Arlyn, had played Simone, one of the French models who disappears in the "Doris, the Model" episode the second season.) Rumors linking Day with Genson seeped into print, as did reports that Arlyn Genson killed herself because of their affair. Strictly on the basis of observing their interactions, Kaye Ballard insists that their affair really happened. "If you were around the place, you just knew," Ballard said. "You can tell when people are flirting with each other. She wanted to trust some man all the time. You could feel that she needed to have a man around. She liked someone to take care of things. But then, they never did. The irony was, she did a better job taking care of herself."

Once she became more comfortable about working on television, Day agreed to do her first talk show with her old pal Merv Griffin, who a few years earlier had launched what would become one of the most successful game shows in TV history, *Jeopardy!* According to Griffin, he did not personally approach Day. "She was phoned by the show and told, 'Merv would love to have you on.' I didn't think she'd ever do a talk show and I didn't want to put her in the position of having to turn me down directly. But then, oddly enough, she accepted, and she showed up sporting a 'midi' dress for the first time.

"It was one of the funniest situations that ever happened on my shows. She walked on with a little female Irish setter, saying, 'Merv, I've brought you a gift.' It was at a time in my life when I had just gotten a divorce. I had moved out and was living as a bachelor. But because this was happening on television, I had to accept.

"The show was done at the Hollywood Palace, and at the stage door were all these people who wanted to see if I really took the dog," explained Griffin. "So I put the dog in my car and took her home." At the time, Griffin was renting a house in Bel Air from Broadway songwriter Fred Ebb.

"The dog was kind of friendly towards me, but not great at first," Griffin continued. "But a couple of nights later, I had to go to a big function. There was a giant bathroom—two complete bathrooms in one, really. So I put her in there. Well, when I got home, she had totally destroyed the bathroom. She was so mad. She had knocked things out and the sink was falling down. And I didn't know what to do. A couple of days later, I had her in the car and ran into a store to get some things. I put the windows down, appropriately, came out, and she had eaten the sun visor and torn up everything. And I thought, 'Good God, what kind of a dog is this?' I was ready to call and give her back, when suddenly, she and I became friends. And she turned out to be one of the greatest dogs I ever had in my life." Griffin named her Poochie. "In fact, I even bought her a 'Patrick,' a beautiful little Irish setter puppy. She raised him, and they became inseparable, and they traveled everywhere with me.

"Some time later, I told the story on the air to somebody," Griffin continued, "and Doris saw the beginning of the show and got furious. She called me up and said, 'If you don't want that dog, I'll take her back.' I said, 'Doris, that's a very funny story. And since then, Poochie and I have become inseparable. I love the dog.' Doris said, 'I thought you were making fun of her.' She had probably turned off the set. I said, 'You know, Doris, if you had listened to the whole program, you would have realized that I love this dog—and you're not getting her back.'"

*　　*　　*

Day had another television breakthrough on Sunday, March 14, 1971, when *The Doris Mary Anne Kappelhoff Special* appeared. It was the first of two that Melcher had committed her to in addition to her series, and it meant to convey a newfound intimacy by including her complete childhood name. Indeed, the title for the special was Day's idea. She even wanted to shoot the show in her spacious backyard, but the notion was rejected. Instead, a "garden" was built on a soundstage at CBS Television City.

Though it had been years since she danced professionally, Day claimed that she had no problem during rehearsals. "I suppose it's because I'm very active," the forty-nine-year-old Day told a *Variety* reporter for an advance story about the special. "I keep my pool at 96 degrees and swim three times a day. I'm the only one in Beverly Hills who swims, you know. My pool man, who takes care of all the pools around, told me that. I also ride my bike and I exercise to keep in shape. So there I am . . . me . . . Doris Mary Anne . . . doing all those dances!"

The hour-long program, which featured Perry Como and Rock Hudson, opens with Day riding her bicycle. Followed by a growing throng of children and a motorcade of policemen, she sings a medley consisting of "Secret Love," one of her signature songs, "Who Will Buy," from the musical *Oliver!*, Paul Simon's "Feeling Groovy," and the Beatles' "Ob-La-Di, Ob-La Da." Clad in a yellow skirt and matching kneesocks, with an orange bow in her hair and an orange sweater vest over a white blouse, Day is perched on a lawn chair when she introduces her menagerie of pets—Daisy June, Muffy, Beau, Charlie Brown, Tiger, and Bubbles—before singing a familiar song to them, with some new lyrics: "You must have been a beautiful baby, you must have been a wonderful pup."

According to co-executive producer Don Genson, the contemporary songs were Terry's idea, but Perry Como had his own plan. He agreed to appear on the show without pay if Day would, in turn, lend her presence—also without fee—to his next Christmas special. Como made his arrival on the show singing "Didn't We, Girl." This was followed by Day's rendition of "It's Just the Gypsy in My Soul," in Spanish gaucho attire, accompanied by two male dancers. Como next sang "When You Were Sweet Sixteen," and then joined Day in another of her hits, "Everybody Loves a Lover." After a medley of more duets, Day asked Como to sing her mother's favorite, "Summertime"—which turned out to be an obscure country song, not the familiar Gershwin tune from *Porgy and Bess.*

Donning a black bushy mustache, Rock Hudson made a surprise but brief appearance, which didn't amount to much. Day concluded the program by singing her biggest hits, including "It's Magic" and "Sentimental Journey"—with various costume changes.

Once Day learned that Como's Christmas special was going to take place before a live audience, she reneged on her reciprocal agreement, and her guest star reportedly sued her. She came up with other reasons, of course. "It was agreed I would do his show when we could," Day told hardcore fan Pierre Patrick. "It turned out that I was so involved with many things—knee-deep in everything! There was no time for me. I couldn't find time to rehearse because you . . . rehearse a lot when you do a special—it's every day."

"Doris Day has always been one of the most criminally maligned talents in Hollywood," wrote Rex Reed in his syndicated rave review of the special. "She is a first-rate comedienne, a sensitive and gifted actress, and she sings like a dream. But, somewhere along the way, her movies turned sour and people started accusing her of milk-shake hangovers.

[This is] the first time she's come out of her shell in years and certainly the first time she's shown on television, appearing as herself instead of in the disguise of something that just popped out of an apple pie. . . . Perry Como put in a dull but harmless appearance, and Rock Hudson materialized from behind a forest of peonies and dandelions she had just sung to long enough to kiss her for old time's sake, but mostly it was just Doris Day, getting realigned with reality and reacquainted with the world. . . . In my favorite part of the evening, her baby pictures led into a discussion of her film career during which she had a good laugh poking fun at herself in film clips of her old movies. . . .The girl could re-open the old Roxy tomorrow! . . . She is warm, winning, disarming, real, funny and thoroughly captivating."

"It's first class all the way, offering musical moments that are at times awash with romance and nostalgia, and at other times, happy, bright, fun," chimed in Aleene MacMinn in an advance review of the show for the *Los Angeles Times*. "To put it simply, it's good, solid, reliable entertainment."

* * *

The fourth season of *The Doris Day Show* entailed still more significant alterations in the format. "In talking to the principals involved in the new-look *Doris Day Show* it became evident the sweeping changes were partly influenced by the instant success of CBS' *All in the Family*," said the *Los Angeles Times*. "The words 'adult comedy' were often repeated."

Though Doris Martin was still working for *Today's World* magazine, she had been promoted from executive secretary to associate editor and had a new boss, Cy Bennett, played by John Dehner. Also new to the series was Jackie Joseph as Bennett's secretary, Jackie Parker. (Day would give Joseph the nickname Jocko.) Turning Doris Martin into a career woman left no traces of her sons or widowhood. "This was asking a great deal of loyalty from the viewing audience," Tom Santopietro said in his well-considered study of Day's career, *Considering Doris Day*. Santopietro proceeds to conjecture the producers telling viewers, "Hey, watch our show for three years but forget any interest you may develop in any of the characters—they're history. Doris is no longer anyone's daughter and she's no longer a mother." Doris Martin was also freer now to fall in love with Dr. Peter Lawrence, played by veteran movie actor Peter Lawford.

"By the fourth and fifth seasons, the story line concentrated almost exclusively on Doris as a beautiful young 'bachelorette,' and I was out of work again," explained Kaye Ballard. "That show was probably a mistake for me professionally, but personally it was wonderful to do," she also claimed, referring to the fact that it tied her up for two years without employing her as much as she would have preferred.

Long after Day had given her an antique magnifying glass, Ballard returned the gesture with two beribboned medals for Day's dogs. They were proudly displayed in Day's studio bungalow, along with paintings of clowns hanging on yellow burlap walls; and there was an "Old Salt" doll given to Day by Billy De Wolfe. "Completing the scene were three dogs sleeping with their little jaws flush with the floor," journalist Roberta Ormiston observed after visiting the star at the studio: Bubbles, which Day called a "schnoodle" (a combination schnauzer and poodle), Bambi, the malamute, and Rudi the dachshund.

Making a series was taxing work, but Terry softened the blows by hiring a car and driver for his mother, who shunned an attention-getting limousine for a less conspicuous Chrysler Imperial. Del Brown, her chauffeur, picked up Day every morning at 9—except on Thursdays, when the show was "put in the can," and he came at 6 a.m. She was usually home around 8 at night, after having watched the dailies at the studio.

Terry's own life in the fast lane took something of a U-turn in the summer of 1971, when it was announced that the bearded, long-haired record producer had reunited with Claudia Martin and that they would marry in the fall. The twenty-five-year-old Martin seemed to be redefining the notion of scandal. She was still married to her second husband, Keil Muller, the father of her two-year-old daughter, Jessie, when she turned to Terry. Taking more than one cue from her swinging parents, Dean and Jeanne Martin, Claudia reportedly told them: "Of course it would have been better if I'd filed for divorce before I started dating Terry. But you don't plan on falling in love, it just happens. And when it does, you don't always wait to do things according to the etiquette book."

* * *

Having finally met her idol several years before, Indianapolis fan Mary Ann Barothy had now moved to Los Angeles, where she was seeing Day regularly. "Doris invited me out to her home, with Linda [Ronnie and Warren Cowan's daughter]," recalled Barothy. "We went over, nervous as anything.

Linda was a nervous type, anyway. She was almost insecure, at times, and I think she made Doris nervous, too. I remember when we went there, the smell of eucalyptus was overwhelming."

Barothy inherited Biggest, an abandoned poodle that Day had rescued and nursed back to health. (Day would eventually take Biggest back, when Barothy's landlord told her she couldn't keep a pet in her apartment.) Day expressed an interest in the speed-writing course that Barothy had recently taken. In need of a new assistant and companion, Day was sizing her up for the job. She had her go with her to the Farmer's Market. "The point is," Barothy recalled, "she was starting to include me in things here and there, before I started working for her." Bestowing the surest sign of her affection, Day had also given Barothy a nickname, "Marzy Doats"—as in the popular song from another era—or "Mare," for short. In fact, Barothy was a guest at a surprise birthday party for Alma on July 6 at the studio, along with Day's hairdresser, Barbara Lampson, her wardrobe mistress, Connie Edney, Billy De Wolfe, and Alma's friend Olive Abbott, whose brother Bud was half of one of Hollywood's most famous teams, Abbott and Costello. It was a couple of weeks after that party that Day made a job offer to Barothy.

"Ruth, the lady who was helping her, was going to be out of town, and she wanted me to help her take the dogs to the set," recalled Barothy. "She always took about five or six with her. They stayed basically in the dressing room. Ruth would take them out, and feed them, and have a little lunch for Doris. I was thrilled that she had asked me. I was free and not working at the time—I was on disability [she had been in a car accident], so I could help out. Then, shortly after that, I had the pins taken out of my legs, and I went back to work. A couple of weeks after that, Doris had called me at my office and asked if I would like to come to work for her. Well, duh—oh, wow!"

Barothy became Day's personal secretary, a touchy situation in respect to her girlfriends who had introduced her to the star. "I was the last kid on the block to meet her. Their attitude, at first, was, 'Well, why didn't she ask me?'" Barothy received $135 a week for her labors. She had also moved to Sherman Oaks with her friend Mary Kaye Konrath. "We lived on Moorpark," said Barothy, "and Alma lived next door to us. She used to live in Studio City, but Doris wanted someone to look in on her. And Mary became very close to Alma."

* * *

On the basis of a particularly weak first episode, which aired on September 13, 1971, a reviewer in *Variety* pointed out that the fourth season of *The Doris Day Show* was trying to imitate *The Mary Tyler Moore Show*. But Dehner was no Ed Asner, the reviewer wrote. "The show has no place to go but up. . . . The writing level needs upgrading to get some basically funny relations going between the principals—or else Miss Day could be in trouble, despite the bright appeal of her own character within the context of the show."

But in a feature for the *Boston Globe*, Percy Shain turned what many others saw as a liability into a virtue. "Doris has earned the right to be regarded as a TV institution. She's in her fourth season of series stardom, is well entrenched in her Monday night slot, and commands a solid popularity with the viewing audience that has made her a model of consistency in the ratings. Yet this has been done with a vehicle so rickety that it tends to collapse with each run. No show in history has had to be fortified and renovated so consistently as hers. Every year there is a complete over-haul—in concept, in cast, in production, in looks. . . . You have to bow low to a lady who came into television as an established star, but had the grace and the will to adjust until she hit the right combination, and then to keep adjusting as flaws developed."

"I just pay close attention to my son's advice and heed my own instincts," Day told Shain. "I have developed an inner strength that serves me in good stead." Shain also provided a record of the show's "remarkably consistent" ratings over the years: 1968–69, a 20.4 rating and a 34 percent audience share; 1969–70, a 22.8 rating, 35 share; 1970–71, a 20.7 rating, 31 share. In its second week of the new season, the show was up to tenth position.

"The road behind her, though, is strewn with the bodies of those she toyed with and discarded," added Shain, referring to the various regular guest stars who were ousted each year to accommodate the ever-changing story line. Shain did not mention that all of Day's costars were under strict orders not to discuss their work with her without permission. Long after Marty Melcher had died, his widow demonstrated that she had learned a thing or two about controlling the media.

∗   ∗   ∗

Though Day was still busy with her TV show in the fall, animal rights were becoming a much larger part of her life. After hearing about a kennel in Burbank that mistreated diseased and abandoned animals, Day helped mobilize a troop to liberate the ailing creatures. "I stood there, covered in dirt and blood, while they handed each dog to me in a towel," Day reported, "and the tears just started streaming down my face." With her best publicity prowess, Day saw to it that TV reporters were on hand to capture this "tiny Dachau for animals" on film. "No animal kills for pleasure or sadistic blood lust," she said. "They kill to eat or protect themselves. I think there are human beings who should be placed in kennels instead of animals."

A special report on KABC-TV revealed the "Auschwitz-like" conditions at animal shelters in Los Angeles, galvanizing three women in particular to form a group they called Actors and Others for Animals: Gloria Grey; actor Richard Basehart's wife, Diana; and Johnny Carson's wife, Joanne. Day became involved by phoning her old flame California governor Ronald Reagan. "Of course, they said it was impossible to speak to the governor, and I said, 'You tell him it's his co-star from *The Winning Team.* I was married to him when he was only Grover Cleveland Alexander, the baseball player, and he'd better call me back if he knows what's good for him.' Well, he was on the phone in four minutes flat. I said, 'Ronnie, this is Doris, and we're in big trouble down here in L.A.' And he said, 'It's a city problem.' He hates Mayor Yorty, and all those politicians do is shift the blame. But the animals suffer. Animals don't vote."

Doris Day Show costar Jackie Joseph found a stray dog on the street, which Day took in and named Bucky because of its pronounced overbite. Rex Reed also recalled the time Day discovered a dog hitched to a meter post outside a bank. She entered the bank and discovered the dog's owner in a line, waiting for a teller. According to Reed, "She said, 'Give me the check. I'll take your place in line and cash the check, and you go and take care of the dog,' and he did—while the whole bank applauded."

According to drag performer Jim Bailey, the first time he met Day—at a dinner party at Kaye Ballard's—she wasn't interacting with anyone until the subject of pets arose. "It was a week after my first performance at Carnegie Hall [on February 5, 1972] and a few days before I was going to have my first really big concert in L.A., at the Dorothy Chandler Pavilion," recalled Bailey, who was most celebrated for his uncanny Judy Garland impersonation. "And at that time, I really didn't want to go out and party; I wanted to concentrate on the show. But Kaye said, 'Oh, Kid, come on over. We'll have dinner with a few other people.' She lived on St. Ives Drive in Beverly Hills. So I went up with a friend of mine. I got there, and there were about six of us. And of course, everything was happening in the kitchen, as it does with Italians. But I was suddenly aware of someone sitting on the couch in the living room. I noticed that she was dozing off. I said, 'Who is that?' And Kaye said, 'It's Doris.' I said, 'As in Day!'"

Bailey asked Ballard if Day was okay, and she replied, 'Yeah, yeah. She's just relaxing.'" (According to Ballard, "She was always yawning, always snoring. . . . She'd just fall asleep on the couch.") "She had no makeup on," continued Bailey, who noticed a glass of red wine on the coffee table next to her. "Her hair wasn't blonde, blonde. It was sort of a dish-watery blonde, and she had it in a twist. She was wearing a paisley-patterned granny dress, with a little lace collar, lace cuffs, and shapeless all the way to the floor."

When Ballard introduced Bailey to Day, she struck him as "very laid-back." "We had dinner, and when we went back into the living room, Kaye was talking to Doris about me, and about my upcoming concert. Doris said she had seen me on television recently. And that was about it."

But later, when Bailey was talking to someone by the piano about his schnauzers, Day suddenly joined the party. "The head came up," continued Bailey. "She said, 'What! You have a schnauzer?'" When he told her that he had three, Day arose from her chair, joined Bailey by the piano, and spent the rest of the evening discussing pets. Bailey explained that his were named Rudy, Bonnie, and Pola—after Valentino, Parker, and Negri.

"Of course it was Doris Day: I idolized her, and wanted to talk to her about her movies. But Kaye had warned me not to bring up anything from the past. When I said, 'You mean I can't even talk about the beautiful albums she did,' Kaye told me, 'Forget it, Kid!'"

"Where do you take your dogs?" Day asked Bailey. When he mentioned Miller Animal Hospital, she said, "No, no, no, no, no. Take them to Keagy and Keagy and Winters, in Beverly Hills." Day subsequently called Keagy and Keagy to prepare them for Bailey and his brood. "About a month later, she called me to say, 'I had one of my dogs in, and they said you had been there. How was it? How did you find them?' It was like she was doing PR for the vet.

"We'd chat every so often, and it was always about our animals. She called hers her 'kids.' They slept with her at nighttime, and once a week she covered herself with Vaseline before going to bed, and it was a mess because of the dogs' hair on the sheets mixing with the Vaseline. She told me that the maid really hated it."

Bailey also recalled meeting Terry at a party and telling him "how wonderful" his mother was. "You must have dogs," said Terry. When Bailey asked why, Terry replied, "She probably wouldn't have spoken to you if you didn't have dogs. It's all about animals now."

* * *

When Bernardo Bertolucci's *Last Tango in Paris* opened at the New York Film Festival in the fall of 1972, film critic Pauline Kael heralded it as a major cultural event. The sexually graphic film wasn't put into general release until some months later, when it opened amid controversy and commotion. After attending a benefit screening together on March 15, 1973, Day and Billy De Wolfe visited Kaye Ballard, who asked what they thought of the film. "Well, diarrhea's a part of life, too, but I don't want to see that on screen either," said Day, who was disparaging the degree to which nudity had infiltrated mainstream films. She added, however, that Marlon Brando was "brilliant in a couple of scenes."

Paparazzi took photos of Day with Mae West, who was at the same screening of *Last Tango*. According to Ballard, "No one was funnier than Billy De Wolfe. His real name was Billy Jones. He lived in Ravenswood, on the floor above Mae West. He used to say, 'I'm the only one who can say to Mae West, Why don't you come up and see ME, sometime?'"

Some days after she saw *Last Tango*, Day was sitting on the sofa in her living room, talking to Mary Anne Barothy, when she received a horrifying phone call. "Oh, my son . . . my son," Barothy heard Day say. Terry had just been in a serious accident, and Don Genson was phoning with the news.

As soon as she got off the phone, Day told Barothy they were going to Hemet, which was near Palm Springs. Terry had been riding on his motorcycle near there when he collided with a car and went flying into the air. He landed on his feet, shattering his legs and incurring thirty-seven fractures. "We took a couple of the dogs and drove down there. We stayed at the Ramona Inn and had adjoining rooms," Barothy recalled. "At first, they didn't know if Terry was going to live. They thought they might have to amputate his legs." While he was in intensive care at the Hemet Valley Hospital, Terry developed life-threatening embolisms. "Those long vigils through the endless nights brought me closer to Terry than I had ever been before," said Day, who shuttled between Beverly Hills and the desert for six months.

When Terry was finally released from the hospital, Day moved him into the guesthouse at Crescent, where she and her mother could tend to him as he continued to recuperate. He was in a wheelchair at first and then required a walker. "It took four months, casts on both legs, for Terry's legs to mend and grow strong, but it was also a time during which our family ties also grew strong," claimed Day.

Helping Terry recover made Day feel more like a mother than ever before. "Although he is thirty years old, it's the first time I've ever taken care of him," she recalled. She also came to realize that it was "the horror of that motorcycle accident" that rescued Terry from the dark place he had fallen into. Day would further credit her improved relations with her son to Charles Head, a psychologist with whom the two of them had regular sessions—and whom Day continued to see on a weekly basis.

While undergoing therapy on her own, Day offered some self-help advice in the course of publicizing her TV show—inadvertently revealing how self-critical she tended to be. "I feel that seeing and hearing myself on the screen has helped a great deal in my own self-improvement," she explained. "I've found many faults in myself that way. . . . And with home movies, tape recorders and even still photographs, most people can use this same method to improve themselves. . . . Like me, you may find that your voice is much too soft to carry. Or it may be too loud."

For British TV, Day agreed to make a commercial for Blue Band margarine, but only after she sampled and approved of the product. As put together by Len Taylor (a director at Ogilvy, Benson & Mather), the ad would be shot by Day's own cameraman but directed by the up-and-coming director Nicolas Roeg, who had recently begun to establish himself in Hollywood with the offbeat films *Performance* (starring another famous singer, Mick Jagger) and *Walkabout*. According to Taylor, Don Genson wanted to shoot the commercial in Day's CBS dressing room, "but we had a theoretical notion that we were more likely to find the 'real' Doris Day at her real home: the difference between the public and the private person was what we were interested in showing." After meeting with Day for the first time on North Crescent, "we left her home feeling like the people in *Reader's Digest* who met unforgettable persons," Taylor said.

Wearing a red-checkered shirt and white pants for the commercial, Day is first seen riding her bicycle home and then seated at a patio table, buttering her bread as several dogs leap up at her. "The shooting of the commercial went off without a hitch except we ran into overtime and that was not Doris's fault," Taylor said. "She ate her way with professional aplomb through two or three sliced loaves (a bite a slice) and only groaned towards the end."

Along with four other board members of humorist Cleveland Amory's Fund for Animals (Angie Dickinson, Amanda Blake, Jayne Meadows, and Mary Tyler Moore), Day agreed to pose in fake fur to prove that it was just as fashionable as the real thing. She waived her usual fees for the event. She also drew a lot of attention to the cause when she appeared at Lion Country Safari—a nature preserve for animals in Irvine, California—to support a boycott of fur coats. "Killing an animal to make a coat is a sin," Day told the media. "Once I bought real fur coats. Today when I look at them in the closet, I could cry." Tears indeed came to her eyes at the press event, as she described the inhumanity of animal traps, which compelled the tortured victims to gnaw off their own paws in order to hobble free.

32

Freedom at Last

---------------- ✳ ----------------

"I'm everything. You're everything.
We're all everything. We're all one."
—DORIS DAY

While she was working on what would prove to be the fifth and final year of her TV show, Doris Day appeared on the cover of the June 10 issue of *TV Guide* (1972), surrounded by four of her "furry friends": Rudy, Bubbles, Daisy, and Bambi. In the issue's aptly titled article, "The Dog Catcher of Beverly Hills," animal activist Cleveland Amory reported that Day had eleven dogs. "But don't put that in. . . . You're only allowed four, you know," she explained to Amory, referring to a Beverly Hills ordinance. "Just say my mother has three and, let's see, Mary Anne [Barothy] and Judy [Ruby] have two each—they're my secretaries."

According to Amory, Day was on a daily mission to place strays in good homes. While Terry had eighteen cats at the time, Don Genson—who "used to have just one little poodle"—now had a large number of dogs. "Just say four," Day warned, not wanting to get Genson in trouble either. "I'm working on producer Ed Feldman," Day added. "He says he has an older dog and can't have another now. But I'm beginning to get somewhere with him. He runs [away] every time he sees me."

When Amory asked Day about her religion, she did not reflexively refer to Christian Science, as she had frequently in the past. Instead, she spouted a vague New Age mumbo jumbo. "I'm not anything now—except just what I am," Day told Amory. "I've studied so many religions to get to the spot where I am now. I've studied metaphysics and Krishnamurti. To me, Albert Schweitzer is religion. I'm everything. You're everything. We're all everything. We're all one. We're all one with the universe—with God."

"Doris was very spiritual, in her own way," confirmed Mary Anne Barothy. "But she became less into Christian Science, and more into metaphysics. We used to go to Carmen Sawtelle's place on weekends. She was an elderly woman who had lived in Hawaii for years." Sawtelle was a spiritualist who had developed a more recent following in Los Angeles. "She had several people over, and she'd preach," continued Barothy, who added that Day also used to listen to tapes of the far more well known healer Edgar Cayce.

Day fell "completely" and "unexpectedly" in love with a guest star of her show during its last season, which was made in the summer and fall of 1972. In her memoir, she would identify him as an actor she had worked with in a film. "There had been nothing between us; we were acquaintances, not even friends." Though he was married and lived in the east, he was now in Hollywood, shooting a movie of the week for television.

According to Day, the picture he made became a weekly series, enabling their affair to continue for more than a year. "This man I fell in love with was totally different from the men I had known before," she recalled. "He wasn't a father figure, as Marty had been, a guardian telling me what to do and when to do it. . . . He was as interested in metaphysics as I was and we had a wonderful time talking and exploring each other's minds."

Day failed to mention that her new flame was the silver-haired, patrician actor Patrick O'Neal, who also owned two popular New York eateries near Lincoln Center, the Ginger Man and O'Neal's Balloon. Five years Day's junior, O'Neal had played Day's husband in *Where Were You When the Lights Went Out?* and was now a guest star on *The Doris Day Show*, in which he portrayed Jonathon Rusk, a TV news correspondent with whom Doris Martin falls madly in love.

"Patrick O'Neal was fascinated by her," said Paul Brogan, Day's life-long fan and increasingly good friend, "because he had pre-conceived notions about working with Doris Day, 'the girl next door.' Then, when he got to know her, all those notions went out the window. She's so sensual, especially because she's not aware of her sensuality. O'Neal really opened her up. She started going with the bra-less look, and started going out more, because of him."

Day admitted to being "amused" when the gossip columnists linked her with Don Genson, instead of with O'Neal. "I never denied the rumors [regarding Don Genson] or discussed them, thereby keeping alive a perfect cover for the affair I was really having," Day explained in her memoir. "That's the way it's always been about my rumored affairs," she added, inadvertently confirming that she had had a number of extracurricular trysts.

Day did such a good job of keeping her affair with O'Neal hidden that Mary Anne Barothy—probably the first to become aware of it—learned of it only when it was drawing to its messy conclusion, and failed to realize how long it had really been going on. Barothy picked up Day at the studio on a Friday in winter. "I took her over [to O'Neal's place] with her clothes, a candle and some other things. I dropped her off. I told her, 'Clara, you're asking for trouble: This man is married.'"

"Alma called the next day and demanded to know where Doris was," Barothy continued. "I said, 'I'm sure she's fine, but I don't know where she is.' Alma was mad, because she knew darn well I knew exactly where she was. But Doris told me not to tell anybody. Then on Sunday, Doris called me, sobbing on the phone, and told me to come pick her up. I just threw on some clothes and drove over there. The way home was like the scene in *Pillow Talk*, where Tony Randall is driving and she's crying."

Barothy had by that point moved into the house at Crescent to help Day with an increasing number of tasks. This was in December 1972. Earlier that month, after Day's maid, Nada, said she was returning home to Yugoslavia, Alma had moved back in with her daughter to take care of things around the house. "But then, Alma went to visit her daughter-in-law, Shirley, in Houston, where she lived with her children," recalled Barothy. "So Doris asked if I would move in with her, until she could make some other arrangements. I had the front bedroom, and the den became my little office.

"How she underestimated herself," Barothy further recalled. "I was looking for something in a closet in a little area off of the den, and I discovered all kinds of awards and certificates there. I asked her why they were all put away, why they weren't displayed. And she said, 'Oh, that was in the past.'"

Decades later, when season five of her TV show was released as a boxed DVD set, Day provided commentary for two of the episodes, recorded in 2007, when Day was eighty-five years old. Number seventeen, "The Hospital Benefit"—which originally aired on January 22, 1973—was essentially a fashion show, featuring a cameo appearance by Biggest, one of Day's favorite dogs. Day's remarks for this particular episode don't amount to much of anything. She became far more animated and emotional as she recalled working on the next episode, "It's a Dog's Life," the last one that Day shot, in fact, even though it appeared as the eighteenth of twenty-four that final season. "It's a Dog's Life" seemed like a chapter out of Day's own life as Doris Martin rescues two strays just before the dog catcher can impound them. They were portrayed by Biggest and by another of Day's poodles, Myra Muffin, better known as Muffy.

"There's my baby, my adorable one," remarked Day in her voice-over commentary, as she observed Biggest cradled in her arms thirty-four years before. "He was left on a porch in Los Angeles," she explained, when his owners vacated their home. A wistful Day enthusiastically applauded Biggest's performance in a scene when he arrives with Mr. Jarvis's wallet in his mouth.

Day's costume supervisor and fashion coordinator, Connie Edney, pointed out that every episode during the fifth season was the equivalent of a fashion show. "She has from five to ten changes per show," Edney told Army Archerd for a feature story in *Variety*. "If she weren't in such healthy shape, she wouldn't be able to get ready. It's like doing a fashion show every week." As Edney confirmed, most of Day's costumes came from Joseph Magnin, "where she's been gathering threads four years for the DD show from their Designers' Room, and other departments."

It was while Day was working on the fifth year of her TV series that Denver Pyle, who was no longer involved with the show, introduced her to two of his friends, John Shaw, an oilman from Midland, Texas, and Robert "Doc" Anderson, a "psychic reader" from Chattanooga, Tennessee. "Apparently they came out periodically to L.A.," recalled Barothy. "'Doc' did readings for celebrities. John was a real cowboy, with a cowboy hat and big boots, with his initials in the leather. John could have been in his mid-fifties. Doc was older, and kind of heavy-set. They came to the set, and Doris was interested in having a reading from Doc. They went into the parlor of her [trailer] dressing room."

Shaw and Anderson always arrived in tandem. "They would come back three or four times a year," Barothy continued. "The next time, they were staying at a hotel in Santa Monica. By then, I was living with Doris. Ruth Williams and Doris and I went to their hotel, and Doc was going to do another reading. Ruth went in first, then Doris, then me. . . .We only found out later that Shaw was married. I think he had 'a schoolboy crush' on Doris. All of a sudden, this antique Model 'T' car arrived on a truck-bed. Doris was dumbfounded when it just showed up. It was in mint condition, and totally unexpected."

* * *

During an interview for a London radio program (it aired on February 5, 1973), Day gave the first hint that her TV show might be coming to an end. "I've just finished my fifth year, you know, in television, and whether I stay on or not I don't really know," she said. "It's very hard and it's very confining and when you do have some time off you're so tired that you don't feel like making a film. You have to rest to get ready for the next season."

On March 15, *Variety* reported that *The Doris Day Show* would conclude with its current season. Having fulfilled the contractual obligation that Marty Melcher left her with at the time of his death in 1968, Day decided to retire. She didn't necessarily see it that way, however. "I'm tired," Day admitted in a lengthy statement issued on March 20. "Doing a [TV] series is extremely hard work and I feel that five years is enough. There are so many other things to be done and said, and doing a situation comedy week after week is no longer fulfilling for me. It's time to go on to something else."

As she continued to give her explanation, Day observed that she had become more serious-minded in recent years, which was an implied renunciation of the fluff her series had perpetrated, and she displayed a yearning to be relevant and useful. "There is really no reason why prime-time TV must devote so much of its time to pure entertainment. TV is the most powerful medium in the world; and Hollywood, its prime source of material, has used it almost entirely as an outlet for entertainment. Entertainment is a valuable and worthwhile commodity. It has provided me with a good living for many years. But it is not the alpha and omega of the world.

"Hollywood and the networks so often say, 'We are giving the public what it wants.' But the public never really knows what it wants until somebody gives it to them. It seems to me it is up to Hollywood and the networks to lead rather than follow. And I just don't think *The Doris Day Show* in its present form is going to lead anywhere except maybe to the bank. I have nothing against banks, either. We all need a source of income. I'm only saying that there must be a better way—and when and if I find it for myself, I'll be back."

Day was apparently aware of TV's growing influence on cultural and political developments, including its role in helping to end the Vietnam War. While the recently formed PBS network was exploding with documentaries, even a network series like *M*A*S*H*, which premiered in September 1972, had an important satiric edge that was simply missing from Day's retro TV show. (*M*A*S*H* was set in Korea, but there was no mistaking its sardonic message about the waste and carnage of a misspent war in another part of Southeast Asia.)

Though she typically underestimated her own influence, Day certainly had as much clout as Alan Alda of *M*A*S*H*, and she might have tried to maneuver her series into more meaningful territory. She chose instead to apply her bottomless energies to important causes offscreen. It was during the show's last season that Day and guest star Jackie Joseph joined forces with Actors and Others for Animals. One of its board members was Day's good friend Raquel Rael, whose husband, Jack, had been singer Patty Page's manager. Day became the organization's vice president and one of its principal spokeswomen.

"We met on evenings or weekends and discussed a course of action to improve the staffing of the animal shelters and to really change the way people treated their animals, encourage the spay and neutering of pets, and halt illegal puppy mills," recalled Joseph. "[Day's] activities with the group went from dramatic rescues, speaking to city councils and creating celebrity fund-raisers. All this during shooting *The Doris Day Show*, where she sold peanut brittle in nice tins to the crew in order to raise a few dollars for the cause. She was on the phone between shots getting personal goods to auction from James Garner and other pals."

Whether she admitted it to herself or not, one of the reasons Day might not have renewed her TV show for a sixth season was that she wanted to find a companion and settle down again. To that end, she wanted to look as young and attractive as she could. "As soon as work on her TV series ended, Doris told me she was pursuing the idea of having a face lift," recalled her assistant Mary Anne Barothy. "Of course, my comeback was, 'You don't need one.'"

According to Barothy, Day was prompted to have the work done by her friend Grace Emerson. "Grace was a numerologist to the stars," explained Barothy. "She did Rock Hudson many times, Burt Reynolds, and Doris, who became a friend. Grace had had a face lift, and Doris was surprised by how quickly she healed. So Doris found out who her doctor was [Steven Zax], and contacted him.

"I dropped her off for a consultation, and came back an hour later to get her. On the way home, she started talking about the doctor. I almost drove off the road when she said, 'I think I'm going to have breast enhancements first.' She wanted to do this when she knew her mother was going to be away." (Alma was visiting her daughter-in-law and grandchildren in Houston for the holidays.)

"They picked Doris up, in the morning [on December 29, 1972], and brought her back in the afternoon—maybe around three o'clock," Barothy continued. "A nurse came in and walked her to her room. And they said it would be best if someone stayed in the room with her. She had a large sofa, and I just slept there that night." They told Barothy that she should feel Day's breasts every few hours, to be sure nothing was hardening. "I said, 'Wait a minute! I'm not into that.' Thank God, things worked out, and everything went well. Facial surgery came a month or two later [on January 11, 1973]. Slits behind the ears to pull things, and some cuts under the eyes."

Kaye Ballard became acutely aware of the work that had been performed on Day's chest. "I used to be able to wrap myself around her and kiss her on the cheek, when we embraced. But after the enlargements, I could no longer reach her cheeks."

* * *

Given some steady petitioning from the Doris Day Society, British television finally aired *The Doris Day Show* on two networks—"with more to follow," as reported in the society's March newsletter. The U.K. was also treated to a reissue of Day's hit song "Everybody Loves a Lover." "After an awful lot of pressure by many of you plus regular phone calls from each one of us, CBS caved in and decided to re-release this great double-sided single," wrote Sheila Smith in the newsletter.

When Jacqueline Susann happened upon Rex Reed's syndicated profile of Day in the spring of 1973, a photo of Day with her black poodle, Bobo, compelled her to write to the star. Susann explained how much Bobo reminded her of her own poodle, Josie, the title character of her first book, *Every Night, Josephine!* Famous for introducing a new level of decadence in her fiction, the fifty-four-year-old Susann also mentioned that she was coming to Los Angeles in May to promote her new novel, *Once Is Not Enough*, which, like her *Valley of the Dolls*, would become a best seller. She added that she would be staying at the Beverly Hills Hotel. Day wrote back, asking Susann to call when she was in town and visit the house on Crescent.

"I was prepared not to like the woman," said Mary Anne Barothy, who was present at the first meeting between the two. "I thought she was just gonna be trash—like her writing. Anyway, she came, and Doris and she had an immediate liking for each other. And to my surprise, she was very nice—very kind, and very nice to me."

A number of common bonds made Day and Susann each other's "new best friend," as Susann phrased it. In addition to their obvious love for animals, they shared a philosophy of life. Susann always wore an ankh, the Egyptian symbol for eternal life. "The important thing isn't how long you live," she maintained. "It's *how* you live. I'm a hedonist. I like good food, good drink, good clothes, and good men." Indeed, Susann's beloved Josie died from a highly unusual and overindulgent diet for a poodle, including caviar, Bloody Marys, peanuts, and tangerines.

For her part, Day had told journalist Jane Ardmore a year or so after Melcher died, "I personally don't believe in death . . . I believe it's a bridge we cross over and instead of thinking about it, I think about life." Also like Day, Susann had one son. They could further relate to being superstars of their respective realms who were commercially successful, if critically derided.

In no time at all, Susann took to calling Day by her nickname, Clara Bixby, and Day called Susann "Opal Mandelbaum." Susann would proceed to exert a considerable influence on Day. With her skill in crafting one best seller after another, Susann recognized the makings of one in Day's own story and persuaded her to write her memoir. "You could help so many people who think life is rotten and without hope," Susann advised Day, alluding to the star's knack for bouncing back from one adversity after another. And given Susann's love of animals, Day was inclined to take whatever advice she offered.

Day could never bring herself to chastise her pets in private or public—not even when they occasionally injured her—and at least once, seriously. On May 13, 1973—Mother's Day—Mary Anne Barothy and Day returned from dinner. "I was driving and Doris was sitting in the backseat of her green Chrysler," recalled Barothy. "When we arrived at home, I got out, slamming the door, thinking Doris was getting out on the other side. . . . Instead, she was in the process of getting out on my side and the door slammed on her finger. It was her ring finger [on the left hand] and three quarters severed—right to the bone. She was in terrible pain."

That, at any rate, was the story that Day and Barothy devised for the press. In fact, when they returned from a Mother's Day dinner at the Magic Pan, they discovered some of the dogs fighting. "Biggest did not get along with the two dachshunds, Rudy and Schatzie," recalled Barothy. "They were all three males and they were territorial. We always had to keep them separate. Somehow, while we were at the restaurant they had gotten together. Doris tried to break up the fight, and one of them bit her. She had wrapped her hand in towels, but it was pretty bad. So I took her over to Cedars-Sinai." Given the severity of the gash, there was concern she might lose her finger, but Dr. Thomas Nicholudis saved it with fifteen stitches. To Day's dismay, Nicholudis died in a plane crash some days later on his way to a medical convention.

Though Susann and her manager-husband, Irving Mansfield, lived in New York, they were back at the Beverly Hills Hotel in June 1973 for the American Booksellers Association convention. To help raise money for what Susann called Day's "pet pet charity," the author gave support to the second annual fund-raiser for Actors and Others for Animals on the Warners lot on June 3, 1973. She contributed four hundred copies of *Every Night, Josephine!*, which she spent hours autographing on a hot, sunny day. She also set up a meeting between Day and Sherry Arden, the publicity director of William Morrow, Susann's publisher.

Morrow held a party in Susann's honor for hundreds of booksellers, and Day agreed to attend, unaware that Susann had an ulterior motive for inviting her. "The day of the party, Doris tried to beg off," wrote Susann's biographer Barbara Seaman. "Irving [Mansfield] had to get tough with her, and . . . sent Jay Allen to pick her up and make certain she got to the hotel." Neither Day nor Allen, Susann's publicist, knew how ill Susann was from cancer treatments she was receiving at Century City Hospital. In the end, Susann, propped up against a bar stool, greeted people at the party until she felt too weak and had to retreat to her room. Day then became the surrogate hostess, only learning the truth about her new friend's illness some months later.

After Susann took her new friend on their first outing in a rental car, an alarmed Day told Barothy, "The next time we go anywhere, you have to drive. Jackie doesn't pay any attention to stop lights. She just goes right through them." Barothy recalled being the chauffeur one night, when—with Alma and Raquel Rael accompanying them—they picked up Susann and her husband on their way to Hamburger Hamlet on Sunset Boulevard. "Jacqueline liked Bloody Bulls," which is a Bloody Mary made with beef bouillon broth. "We all had a couple of drinks," said Barothy.

During dinner, Susann mentioned that she was going to London in September to promote the British edition of *Once Is Not Enough.* "Clara, you've got to come with me," coaxed Susann. "You have a lot of fans over there." In spite of her trepidations about flying, Day consented when Rael said she would go as well, with her mother, Rose.

One afternoon, Susann invited Day, Rael, and Barothy to meet her at the Polo Lounge in the Beverly Hills Hotel. "It reminded me of girls in high school," recalled Barothy. "We were at one of the booths, drinking, when in walked David Janssen. He said 'hi' to Jacqueline. Always eager to find a man for Doris, Jacqueline said, 'Clara. Get up and go to the bathroom.' Doris protested, 'But I don't have to go to the bathroom.' Jackie continued, 'Get up and walk across the room and he'll notice you.' And as soon as she left the table, he got up and came over. Jackie not only introduced David to Doris but gave him her number."

Eight years Day's junior, the dark and handsome David Janssen had been catapulted to TV stardom in the mid-1960s with *The Fugitive*, and was now cast in the film version of *Once Is Not Enough*. He invited Day for dinner at his home in Century City. "When he came for Doris, she wasn't ready yet," Barothy remembered. "But I invited him in. We were sitting around the bar—the one that George Montgomery had made—waiting for Doris to get ready."

As they were leaving, Day informed Barothy that it would be a "late night," meaning that she need not wait up for her. But neither of them ever imagined how late. "At 4:30 or 5 in the morning, I could hear the dogs barking and carrying on when she came home. Poor thing: she had gotten so sick. Something didn't agree with her." "I spent practically the whole evening in the bathroom," Day told Barothy. "He'll never ask me out again." And he didn't.

Though her face and breast work suggested a yearning for companionship, once she retired, Day's desire to stay at home increased. Though she accompanied Ross Hunter to see Rock Hudson in the musical *I Do, I Do* (with Carol Burnett as his costar) she was reluctant to go to the private party after the performance. "He'll be so tired," she remarked, as an excuse to go home despite the importance of the night for Hudson. But there was no arguing with Hunter's comeback: "He'll be expecting you." In fact, Day had played a major role in getting Hudson a singing assignment in *Pillow Talk*—his first such undertaking. Thus Hudson's stage debut had a special piquancy for them both. Day had, at least, lent her particular glamour to the event, arriving at the Huntington Hartford Playhouse in a tight-fitting pink satin gown along with other celebrities, including Ed Ames, Suzanne Pleshette, Sally Kellerman, Ray Bolger, Art Linkletter, Ann Miller, and Roger Moore. Donald Saddler also attended the event, and he chatted with Day for the first time in decades.

It had been Carol Burnett's idea to approach Hudson to be her costar in *I Do, I Do*, which would mark his theatrical debut. "He'd never done a play and never sung on stage, and singing on stage is naked," recalled Burnett, "but he called me back in two minutes and said he'd do it." Hudson ended up enjoying his live experience in a musical so much that he went on to work in productions of *Camelot* and *On the Twentieth Century.*

As instigated by their erstwhile costar, Day and Hudson got together at the Polo Lounge in the Beverly Hills Hotel with Tony Randall around the time of *I Do, I Do.* Randall was hoping to persuade them to make a new picture with him. "I took her there, and when I went to get her, Tony had left," recalled Mary Anne Barothy. "Doris introduced me to Rock, and then she told me Tony's idea was that she would leave Rock for him in the movie. She said, 'The public would never buy that. No way!'"

*   *   *

More than a dozen years after beginning his long-term correspondence with Day, the twenty-year-old Paul Brogan met his idol for the first time shortly after she attended *I Do, I Do.* For years, Day had been encouraging her New Hampshire pen pal to come to Los Angeles and meet her. He finally did in June 1973, in conjunction with the annual meeting of the Jeanette MacDonald International Fan Club that month at the Beverly Hilton Hotel. (Brogan had become the director of public relations for MacDonald's fan club when he was sixteen.)

As prearranged with Day, Paul mustered the courage to walk up to the gate at 713 North Crescent and ring the buzzer on the left side, at 11:30 on a Monday morning. Day herself answered the intercom. When Brogan identified himself, "The front door opened, and there she was, with that gorgeous figure, running down the runway and giving me a hug and a kiss." Once inside, Katie gave them a couple of Cokes as they sat in the living room, gazing out at the pool and getting better acquainted. Day told Brogan that the cast on her hand had recently come off and that she was "just getting used to the freedom" again. "I got up this morning and went for a bike ride and I went swimming. I'm just loving the luxury of not having to do the series, and suddenly having all this free time on my hands." When Brogan said, "Well, yes. But what am I going to do on Monday nights, beginning in September?" She looked at him and said, "Well, I hope you're going to get a life."

When Brogan asked her what she had thought of *I Do, I Do,* Day replied: "It seemed like it would never end. But Ernie [Rock Hudson] was so wonderful in it; and I'm so proud of him for doing it. I don't know where he found the courage to." When Brogan pressed her for comments on Carol Burnett's performance, Day repeated, "Rock was wonderful," without saying a word about Burnett. According to Brogan, Day had been very hurt by a spoof Burnett had done of her on TV and also by Phyllis Newman's parody of her on *That Was the Week That Was.*

Brogan quickly learned that there were certain topics to be avoided with Day, who had spent decades ignoring anything unpleasant by changing the subject. "For example, you never discussed the age issue," he recalled. When Brogan told Day about actor Leon Ames hitting on him at a banquet dinner for Jeanette MacDonald, she seemed unfazed, and said, simply, "Well, we don't discuss Leon's personal life. Leon's a nice man and a good actor." (Ames had played Day's father in both *On Moonlight Bay* and *By the Light of the Silvery Moon.*) Brogan visited with Day for about an hour, when she announced that she was hungry and suggested they go to Nate 'n Al. "Actually, her secretary [Barothy] drove me there, while she rode her bike. We got there and parked in the lot, and we sat down in the booth that she always has. The minute she arrived, every head turned. She was wearing dark glasses and a hat, but the way she walked and moved, the way she presented herself."

Brogan was impressed that they allowed Day to park her bicycle inside the always teeming Nate 'n Al. Incredibly, this was the first time the small-town New Englander had ever been to a deli, and Day advised him to have "the Pastrami New York and a side order of potato salad." Brogan told her that he had recently gotten a job with the motor vehicle department of the state of New Hampshire. When he mentioned that he had seen *With Six You Get Eggroll* fifty-four times, she just stared at him, took his hand in hers, and said, "And you didn't get diabetes?" "It was very deadpan," added Brogan.

More a fanatic than fan, when Brogan went to see *The Trouble with Angels* (in February 1966), the theater's coming attractions featured the trailer to Day's *Do Not Disturb.* "I went back every day for a week, so that I could see that preview." When he learned that Day herself had never even seen *With Six You Get Eggroll,* he was taken aback, and asked why. "You know, I lived it every day on the set for three months, working on the picture. So what was the point?" She also told Brogan that they frequently failed to use the take she would have preferred. "She often felt that she did better in the first take, and was never satisfied with what was finally chosen."

As soon as Paul mentioned that he played the piano, Day said, "I really would love to sing again, but my voice is so rusty. You know, I haven't really sung in quite a few years." Brogan pointed out that she had been singing on her TV series in recent years, specifically recalling her versions of "I Left My Heart in San Francisco" with Tony Bennett and "Silver Bells" on the Christmas episode of the third season.

Day met with another fan she had been corresponding with while he was stationed in Vietnam. "She received, a couple times a week, a long, hand-written letter on small-lined paper, from this soldier, who was from Long Beach," recalled Mary Anne Barothy. "He would write faithfully—as though he were writing to his girlfriend—and she responded every so often. She had arranged for us to have lunch with him at Nate 'n Al once, when he was coming home on leave. He sat on one side of the booth, and we sat on the other. He was a nice young man, but nervous as anything, that he was actually getting to see his idol. He was so star-struck, in fact, that he couldn't talk or eat or do anything. I remember feeling sorry for him."

Day had named one of her dachshunds after yet another fan, Elsie Spray. "I always thought it was an odd name," recalled Mary Anne Barothy. "Until I once noticed in the fan mail a letter from England, from Elsie Spray. In a later letter, she mentioned that she was going to be coming to the States. Doris casually wrote back, saying how nice it would be to see her. Well, I was home alone one night, when Doris was in Palm Springs or somewhere. There was a knock at the door, and there was this kind of disheveled, middle-aged woman with a number of suitcases. She said, 'I'm Elsie Spray. Is Doris here?'

"I put her in the den, and had the maid make something for her. I took her to a hotel, where I thought I could check in on her. Doris told me to take her out: Mary and Linda and I took her to Nate 'n Al."

*   *   *

Almost exactly a decade after the gossip columns were filled with stories about her affair with Los Angeles Dodger Maury Wills, Day now had to contend with rumors about her sleeping with Sly Stone, the flashy, black singer with the spectacular Afro. Another recent guest at North Crescent, Stone was recording for Terry a new album called *Fresh*. "'Que Sera, Sera,' the 1956 platter, may sound a bit soupy and syncopated today," reported *Time*. "But when rock star Sly Stone, 29, of Sly and the Family Stone, heard the mother of record producer Terry Melcher sing it at her very own piano, he was turned on. He even decided to include an updated gospel version in his latest album, 'Fresh.' . . . How did the Bad Guy of Rock and the Golden Oldie hit it off so well? 'I told her, "Sit down, girl." I showed off,' Sly explained. 'She liked that. Yeah, she's very aware. She's very wise. Only thing—she started talking about the Baptist church, and she shouldn't do that.'"

Day told another reporter about plans for her to work with Stone. "We're discussing my doing an album with Sly," she said. "It would be such a departure for me, all that rock music, but that's what sells today, and I like rock music! People take me for the waltz type because they've never seen anything different, but they'll see it now."

As the rumors gathered momentum, Day tried to get the gossip-hounds off the scent by acting as if she had never even met Stone. "My son often brings friends home," she told a reporter. "Half the time I don't know who's even here because I have my own rooms and Terry has his. We respect each other's privacy." She also went out of her way to deny the rumors in the *Los Angeles Times.* "How do these things get started?" Day rhetorically asked columnist Joyce Haber. "I met the man once in my life, three years ago, and I haven't seen him since. And now, apparently cause he has used our 'Que Sera, Sera' in his new LP, I'm supposed to be having a romance with him. . . . Don't columnists check their material? Or am I being naïve?"

In fact, decades later, the powerful blues and jazz singer Etta James recalled having met Day at Stone's house in Bel Air, where he had a "fabulous home studio." James was going to perform "Que Sera, Sera" with Stone, but, according to her memoir, "it never came off; the night of the session he was too high to work." Also, according to James, Day was "going with" Stone at the time.

In her memoir, Day would muddle the issue of the possible Stone affair. In the prologue, when her collaborator A. E. Hotchner asked her about the rumor, Day replied that she "hadn't heard that one." But then, in the ensuing narrative, she identified Terry as the first to tell her about the story, in fact, as soon as it appeared in 1973.

Once Jacqueline Susann persuaded Day to write her memoir, the novelist's new publisher, William Morrow & Company, took on Day's book. Indeed, Susann's literary agent husband, Irving Mansfield, brokered the deal. Early plans calling it *Sentimental Journey* were eventually abandoned. As Day herself explained, her story proved far more "harsh" than "sentimental." She already had the contract with Morrow when Hotchner arrived in Los Angeles to meet her for the first time, in August, to discuss the possibility of his becoming her coauthor. They conversed in the quiet garden off the main dining room of the Beverly Hills Hotel. (A· five-minute walk from Day's house, the hotel's various dining rooms became akin to the retired star's office.) A prolific writer who was most celebrated for a memoir of his friend, *Papa Hemingway*, Hotchner had already met Terry, who indicated that his mother was prepared to discuss the most intimate details of her life. But even though *Her Own Story* would have a number of shocking revelations about America's girl next door, it would hardly prove the tell-all memoir it was promoted as being.

According to Hotchner, the Doris Day he first glimpsed was on the cusp of turning fifty, but her "incredibly youthful, curvaceous, sexy body" made her appear more like a thirty-year-old. She was five-foot-seven and claimed to weigh exactly what she did upon her arrival in Hollywood nearly thirty years earlier: 121 pounds. Hotchner told *Publishers Weekly*, "I flew out to California to meet Doris and I found her totally mystified about her image as an indestructible virgin. Sure, she'd made a lot of up-beat films, but what I didn't realize was that behind that sunshine figure was this awful life."

Day and Hotchner met for the second time in New York, where she also spent time with Billy De Wolfe before flying with Jacqueline Susann to London on September 17, 1973. Once they were airborne, Susann noticed Day looking out the passenger seat window and she humorously asked, "Looking for strays?"

"When we arrived at the Dorchester [Hotel], all the press had come to meet us and say hello," Day remembered of her arrival in London. "By the time we got our suite it was 10:30 a.m. I went to sleep and slept until eight, then we all got dressed and went to dinner. But that night at two a.m. we suddenly found ourselves awake. Raq and I talked until five, then she went to sleep but I was wide awake. I was still wide awake at nine but it was certainly time to try [and sleep], so I put a note under Raq's door asking her to let me sleep and tell the switchboard not to ring. I slept until six p.m. I did the same thing almost the whole time I was there. I never got to go sightseeing—I'm going to have to go back again and soon, because I love London; I've loved it ever since we were there to film *The Man Who Knew too Much*, but I could never get myself turned around to the time change."

Day received a lot of attention from the press when she appeared at the cocktail party and black-tie dinner dance that Mark Gulden, publisher of William H. Allen Ltd., gave to promote the British edition of Susann's *Once Is Not Enough*. But, according to Day, the highlight of her London trip was meeting members of her British fan club, which she referred to as the "only authorized" one. The Doris Day Society had upwards of five hundred members. It published a quarterly journal and was on the verge of winning first prize at the convention of the International Council of Fan Clubs.

"They sponsor the Animal Welfare Trust and are the dearest people you've ever met," Day observed. "Sydney Wood, Sheila Smith, Valerie Andrew and John Rainer are the directors of my 'Society.' They and some twenty others came to the hotel. We had champagne and all sorts of little goodies. They took pictures like mad and showed me pictures. They have some collector's items you wouldn't believe. I'd taken along a 'Mom's Brag Book' Mary gave me for the trip, filled with pictures of my dogs, and oh, yes, one picture of Terry. I answered all sorts of questions. They wanted to know when I was going to start recording again . . . to which the answer is, soon. And they wanted to know about my year off . . . which of course is the first time that has ever happened."

Sydney Wood recalled meeting his idol some days earlier at a high tea at the Dorchester. "I finished work on a Friday and I bought the *Evening Standard.* On the second page was a big picture of Doris arriving at London's airport. And I could not believe she was in town." After learning that she was going to be staying at the Dorchester, Wood just appeared there with another fan the next day. "Sitting on a chair, with both her legs crossed under her, was Doris, all dressed in denim, with a cap on her head.

"We realized she was with some friends, and we didn't know who they were. I was absolutely petrified. But eventually, when there was kind of a lull, I went over and introduced myself. And she was absolutely amazing! She knew who I was, and we were there for about two or three hours, just sitting there, talking to her." Day suggested they organize a get-together for her other British fans, and Wood seized the opportunity.

It was late one night at the Dorchester that Susann confided in Day about the debilitating treatments she was undergoing for cancer. Day admired and related to "Opal's" embrace of life, even in the midst of such dire circumstances.

Though she had planned to return to the United States via ocean liner, once aware that the hurricane season could make for a particularly stormy crossing, Day chose to fly back instead. (This was after a brief excursion to Paris with Rael.) Day ultimately left London for Los Angeles on September 27, and Barothy picked her up at the airport. "When she got back, Doris told me that Jackie had used her to get publicity in London," recalled Barothy. "That wasn't her attitude when she left. But she also had a good time, because she got to meet so many people. Nevertheless, she came to feel that there was an ulterior motive to the trip all along."

"There was a genuine fondness between Jackie and Doris," recalled Rex Reed. "They were gal pals, who liked each other, and trusted each other. But Doris never wanted to take it into a professional level. She never wanted to go into the career part of their relationship. And anything having to do with promoting a book would have infringed upon her trust."

Two days after Day left London, two officers of her British fan club, Sheila Smith and Val Andrew, flew to New York, where they visited family and friends. They next attended the International Council of Fan Clubs convention in St. Louis, followed by a trip to Los Angeles. They had breakfast with Day and Barothy at the Beverly Wilshire Hotel. They had dinner one night alone with Barothy, at Day's usual table at Musso and Frank's, one of the oldest restaurants in Hollywood. Day was busy at the time, ransacking her home for items she could auction off at the upcoming annual bazaar of Motion Picture Mothers, Inc.—clothes, pictures, records—dedicated to raising money for Actors and Others for Animals. As designed and managed by Alma, the booth was called "Doris Day's Dog House."

On October 20, the visitors attended a fund-raiser chaired by Day, Lucille Ball, and Mary Tyler Moore. The program for the event declared: "Beauty Without Cruelty: A Celebrity Fashion Show for Dogs." Smith and Andrew also recalled going with Day and her mother to the Farmer's Market, which Alma in particular loved. The stands and shops made it highly reminiscent of Cincinnati's Findlay Market, where Alma's brother had had a bakery. "Alma seemed a very nice lady. She joked a lot, and had a very distinctive laugh," said Smith. For the second half of their stay in Los Angeles, the young women transferred from a Hollywood apartment to Barothy's, where they stayed with Mary Kaye Konrath. Along with Day, Barothy, Konrath, and "Vicki"—an old friend of Day's visiting from Cincinnati—they also had dinner at Alma's apartment in Sherman Oaks in the Valley. A bright and cheerful couple, the British women impressed Day with their practicality and their willingness to pitch in. This led, in several years, to her employing them as all-around helpers.

*   *   *

When he filled in for Johnny Carson on *The Tonight Show* on November 26, 1973, McLean Stevenson invited Day to be one of his guests. "That is something I've wanted to do all my life," Stevenson remarked after he greeted Day on air by kissing her on the mouth. "In the two years we did *The Doris Day Show* together, I never once got to kiss you." "Well, you were my boss," countered Day. "I guess that's supposed to sort of limit things."

Mangling his words in his attempt to debunk Day's "goody two-shoes" image, Stevenson had to acknowledge how "nervous" he was. "I've started to talk funny." His awkwardness prompted him to recall how anxious he was "when I tested for the part of Mr. Nicholson on your show. . . . I never will forget how you relaxed me," he added, to gales of laughter from the audience.

Inevitably, Stevenson raised the subject of animal rights and Day's latest fund-raiser. "I think that we've made almost $70,000, which is fantastic," said Day, "when you think that we took over the back lot at the Warners studio. The people just really came out, and they were fantastic." She was particularly grateful to Joan Crawford for donating 30,000 Pepsi-Colas—plus helpers to dispense them. Day brought out two dogs, Tiger One and Tiger Two. To distinguish them, she explained, they became Big Tiger and Little Tiger, and then Biggest and Littlest.

"If I called you up on the phone and asked you for a date, would you go out with me?" Stevenson asked his guest near the end of their segment together. A flustered Day hemmed and hawed, before saying, "Of course, I would." When she added, "I have a little infection in my nose," Stevenson responded, "Oh, I'm sorry. Well, then let's not go out until after that gets cleared up, okay?"

After more banter and as an afterthought, Day recruited the audience's sympathy when she said, "Do you think the folks are interested in this?" For his part, Stevenson proceeded to anticipate the tabloids' response: "Virgin Finds Romance with a Guy in a Cheap Sport Coat and She's Got a Bad Nose," or "Nasal Drip Dates Drip." "We'll have dinner and we'll all let you know what happened," Day said to close the subject. Day had to leave before Stevenson's next guest, singer Nancy Wilson, arrived, because she was recording a duet with Terry of "These Days," a song written by Jackson Browne, and she was due at the studio.

After her appearance on *The Tonight Show*, the *National Tattler* ran one of a number of stories linking Day with Stevenson. Written by Bernie Brown, it told of a Sunday brunch they had at Day's favorite, Nate 'n Al, after which "Stevenson took her to a party at a friend's home in Malibu where they drank mai-tais, held hands and, as a friend put it, 'seemed very much taken with each other.'"

"It is very hard for a woman in my position, especially in my age bracket, to date in this town," Day said. "People are afraid to approach me because of who I am." Stevenson was not among them. As a caption below a photo of the two clasping hands on *The Tonight Show* explained, "He asked her out as millions watched."

Even if things went nowhere with Stevenson—according to Mary Anne Barothy—Terry was eager for his mother "to meet somebody and settle down." Day met Warren Beatty at a party hosted by singer songwriter Rod McKuen. Beatty was a famous lothario at the time who couldn't settle down with anyone. As his sister, Shirley MacLaine, once said, Beatty had trouble committing to a dinner engagement.

"She gave Beatty her phone number during the course of the evening," recalled Barothy. "He sent flowers, and then he called a number of times. But she wasn't really interested, so she had me talk to him. I had to make excuses all the time for her." In recent years, Beatty described Day as "the one that got away."

* * *

Paul Brogan paid his second visit to Day on a Saturday afternoon in December 1973. Since his previous visit, Day had introduced a black grand piano into her predominantly white living room. She had agreed to do a TV special with John Denver and needed to rehearse. When Brogan asked if he might play for her, she replied, "Sure. Go ahead." According to Brogan, "She was sitting in another part of the room, sipping a drink."

Brogan played "You Make Me Think About You." When he had finished, Day said, "That's so pretty, Paul. What is it?'" "I guess it's what you would call the love theme from *With Six You Get Eggroll*, when you and Brian Keith are carrying on in front of the fire," Brogan answered. "Really?" said a dubious Day. "Yeah, really. Remember I'm the one who saw the film fifty-four times." Brogan next played "The Kissing Rock," and this time, Day sang along on a couple of lines.

Brogan presented Day with the photo he had taken of the two of them during his first visit; it highlighted her prominent and recently enhanced breasts. Peering at it, Day said, "We should call this the 'Headlights' shot." "You always had the sense that vulgarity was not appropriate around her," said Brogan, "unless she herself made a slightly risqué comment."

As soon as he learned that actor Louis Jourdan lived directly across the street from Day, Brogan jokingly asked her if she had the gate put up in front of the house because he was still stalking her, as he had when he portrayed her husband in *Julie*. But it proved no joking matter, for Day, who apparently recalled how fond she had been of Jourdan. "Her eyes welled up, and she looked so sad, for a moment," recalled Brogan. "She said, 'I really don't want to talk about it.' And that was all she said."

When Day asked him what he had planned for the next day, a Sunday, Brogan replied that he would be attending Mass at the Good Shepherd on Santa Monica—the Catholic church where tourists often lined up to watch the arrival of regular celebrity congregants, including Loretta Young, Irene Dunne, Barbara Stanwyck, Rosalind Russell, and Jane Wyman. (It had been dubbed "The Church of the Religious Cadillac.") Day, in turn, remarked, "I used to go [to church], but I don't anymore. I just don't believe in organized religion." He immediately sensed that "it was one of those things where you just knew the subject was closed, and you didn't pursue it. If you asked a follow-up question, she'd just disregard it, and plunge into another topic."

Having agreed to cowrite Day's memoir, A. E. Hotchner also returned to L.A. in December and began to work with Day for five months, sometimes four hours a day in the guest house at 713 Crescent. "These people who have been superstars for so long know how to conduct interviews without telling anything important about themselves," Hotchner told *Publishers Weekly*. "I understood soon enough that I'd have to get away from the traditional way of interviewing, to forget about any sort of chronology. I substituted free-flowing, unstructured daily sessions that, in the end, became pretty much like psychoanalysis for her."

Hotchner continued, "With this kind of interviewing, you lose all organization and you get a lot of material that's of no value. But you do get the real emotions of a person going deep down inside herself." Indeed, while recalling the tragedies in her life, Day would often break down and retreat to the main house to compose herself before returning to Hotchner a half hour later. Hotchner made five more trips to L.A. He insisted that he did not ask her who else might be interviewed. "I never asked for her approval," said Hotchner, who tried but failed to secure the cooperation of both Hitchcock and Cary Grant. He flew to Washington, D.C., to interview Rock Hudson, who was there performing *I Do, I Do.* He also had conversations with Alma, Terry, and numerous others who had figured so prominently in Day's life.

With her mother in tow, Day spent Christmas Eve at a large party at Raquel Rael's. She was home for a quiet Christmas Day and New Year's Eve. She ushered in the 1974 new year with a "sauerkraut dinner" for Alma, Terry, Billy De Wolfe, and Rael and her mother, along with Hotchner and his wife.

Even though she was retired, Day could still command enormous sums for supplemental work, entailing less and less of her time and effort. Early in the new year, she signed a contract with General Foods giving her $1 million for what would amount to only seventeen days of work over a five-year span, making commercials.

In February, Day and her mother attended Terry's wedding at a friend's home in Rancho Santa Fe in Orange County. The thirty-two-year-old Terry married Melissa Elizabeth Whittaker, a self-described singer and actress—and a dark-haired beauty—who was three years his junior. "Melissa was the ex-wife of a tennis buddy of Terry's named Chris Whittaker," said Paul Brogan. "Her marriage to Terry was all very quiet. She was extremely pretty." She was also, according to her new mother-in-law, extremely nervous on her wedding day. Having introduced Terry and Melissa more than a decade before, Guy Webster now served as Terry's best man.

"Melissa and Chris had a beautiful daughter," observed Webster. "Melissa was a tender and emotionally delicate woman who had a hard time dealing with life. She was briefly married to someone before Chris, a young rich kid who was sweet, but completely crazy. Then, Terry came in as sort of a savior, who was there for her at the end of her marriage to Chris. But Melissa could be very difficult. She didn't trust Terry, or anybody, for that matter. She thought all men were scoundrels. They ended up having a very stormy relationship."

While his career as a record producer stalled, Terry tried relaunching himself as a singer with the release of his first solo album, *And Not to Mention Boarding School,* the month of his marriage. It featured his mother's harmony on "These Days," as well as contributions from members of the Byrds, and Spanky MacFarlane, of *Our Gang* fame. It is "an eccentric work that suggests he's given up not just on optimism but even on despair," wrote Bud Scoppa in his review of the album for *Rolling Stone*. "His duet with mother Doris Day on Jackson Browne's 'These Days' is so down and drained of life that I find it nearly painful to listen to." Another critic would define the album's genre as "Beverly Hills Country."

33

The $22.8 Million Decision

＊

"I am healthy, and I am rich."
—DORIS DAY

When Doris Day asked her old friend Billy De Wolfe to accompany her to London in September 1973, he turned down her last-minute invitation. De Wolfe did not tell Day that, concerned about a chronic cough, he had scheduled a battery of tests at UCLA Medical Center. In fact, when Day returned to Los Angeles from London later that month, De Wolfe instructed Mary Anne Barothy to tell her that he was in Santa Barbara, instead of in the hospital. But his resolve to keep the increasingly dire circumstances of his health from one of his closest friends did not last very long, and De Wolfe decided to tell Day what was going on.

"Doris and I went to visit him in the hospital," said Barothy, who recalled how sad he looked "without his toupee, and all hooked up to tubes and everything. I remember asking if he had a private nurse. When we discovered that he didn't, Doris signed him up for one. She also told his doctor not to tell Billy that he had cancer until he absolutely had to."

Barothy described how one Sunday that winter she and Day took De Wolfe for a "healing service" with TV evangelist Kathryn Kuhlman. "We sat up in the balcony," Barothy remembered. "June Allyson and her husband were sitting right in front of us. After the service, we met with Kathryn in her dressing room, and she prayed over Billy. There were two 'catchers' behind him, in case he fell."

Sometime in January 1974, after Barothy returned from spending the Christmas holiday with her mother in Indiana, Day asked her to move out. Given Alma's deteriorating eyesight, Day could no longer rely on her mother's ability to drive through Coldwater Canyon and back to her own apartment—especially at night. At Terry's prompting, Day felt compelled to invite the seventy-eight-year-old Alma to move back to Crescent Drive and set up in the front bedroom, which had been Barothy's for more than a year. It was hardly an ideal arrangement, however, as mother and daughter proceeded to make each other's lives miserable. Alma lived much of her life vicariously through her daughter, and now that Day was retired and so often at home, her mother's controlling nature proved overwhelming. Alma not only told her daughter what to do, but also wanted to know where she had been during her every sortie. If anything, the problems were exacerbated for Day because her mother could be terribly indiscreet.

"As soon as Alma moved [back in,] there was trouble," Barothy said a couple of years later. "Doris realized then that she'd made a huge mistake. She became very depressed and withdrawn, staying in bed for days at a time. Later, Doris started taking trips just to get away from her mother. She even had to keep many of her dates secret, because she knew that if her mother found out whom she was seeing, it would soon be all over town.

"Several times, Doris phoned me on the morning after a date and said, 'Would you believe my mother was sitting on my bed when I came home?'" recalled Barothy. "'She greeted me with a gruff, "Where have you been?" I was furious!'"

"My mother has been a thorn in my side all my life!" Day told Barothy. "Mother's main interest in life is running my life and trying to stick her nose in all my business. I purposely don't tell her everything because I know she will blab it. . . . All she wants to do is run my life—and I'm sick and tired of being treated like a child!" According to Barothy, not only did Alma enjoy "putting Doris down," she also enjoyed "embarrassing Doris in public by telling off-color stories and using foul language that would cause a truck driver to blush."

Given the escalating friction, Terry recommended that Alma return to her own place, but Day felt obliged to continue the arrangement even as she kept up her complaints to friends. "I've got to get mother out of my home," she griped. "She's driving me nuts. You just don't know what it's like to be trapped in my own home with her."

Barothy moved into a new apartment with her friend Mary Kaye Konrath on Clark Drive, about a mile from the house on Crescent, and continued to work as a social secretary for Day, who now also had her help Terry in the afternoons. Since the seemingly interminable court case with Rosenthal was finally coming to a head in 1974, Terry was grateful for her services.

Once, early in the spring, when Barothy was alone with Billy De Wolfe, he made a request: "You know, when Clara goes to the Jimmy Cagney tribute [on March 13], John Wayne will be there. I want you to ask Clara if she can get the name of John's doctor," he added, fully aware that Wayne, who also had cancer, was fighting for his life. "By God, I'm going to lick this illness," added De Wolfe for emphasis. But it was too late. De Wolfe was soon back in the hospital, where he died on March 4.

Day was not one to dwell on death, however, and she went ahead with the American Film Institute's tribute to Cagney at the Century Plaza Hotel a few days later, which was described at the time as "the most star-studded gathering in Hollywood history." Day was part of the program, following Frank Sinatra on stage to laud her old friend and mentor, who had costarred with her in *Love Me or Leave Me*, one of her best films. On the verge of tears, Day praised Cagney for his talent and underscored how grateful she was to have worked with him. A film clip of Day singing "You Made Me Love You" from the picture followed. John Wayne made a point of cornering Day at the event—not to discuss his cancer treatments, but to tell Day how sorry he was that they had never made a picture together. Rex Reed, who was at the event, recalled, "She looked like a million dollars. She was wearing a strapless dress, and the body was shown off better that night than I had ever seen it."

A few nights later, on April 1, Day had a pre-birthday dinner with Barothy and, among others, Paul Brogan. They went to Hamburger Hamlet on Sunset, one of Day's favorite restaurants. During dinner, Day told her companions how flattered she had been by Wayne's remark at the Cagney tribute. Brogan recalled being taken aback when he saw Day order a Scotch and soda. "Oh my God! You're drinking!" Brogan exclaimed. "What about the soda fountain?" Day laughed. "That was just about the fan magazines," she replied. "Besides, this has more kick." The exchange prompted Day to reminisce about a period during her marriage when she didn't drink or smoke because of her devotion to Christian Science. But she made it clear that those days were long behind her. "While I believe in a lot of what Mary Baker Eddy stands for, I don't follow any organized religion now," she told the table. "And there's nothing wrong with having an occasional drink." When the still-stunned Brogan responded, "My God. If the fan magazines got a hold of this, given your image, what would they say?" Day simply shrugged it off. "Well, Marty's dead."

On her birthday, April 3, Barothy discovered Day on her bed in tears. Although she was finally retired and free of most professional obligations,

Day was finding her life overwhelming, in particular, the recent loss of her beloved De Wolfe, the imminent loss of her newer friend Jacqueline Susann, the ongoing madness of the Rosenthal trial, and the uncertainty over its outcome. All these developments were affecting her. And then, there was her mother. Though Day had devoted her life to pursuing Alma's ambitions and dreams, she still didn't feel she had done enough for her. And Alma, who was in Houston with her daughter-in-law and grandchildren, hadn't even picked up the phone to acknowledge her daughter's birthday.

Barothy knew that Day's mood would change by the evening, because Terry had organized a surprise party for his mother with twenty-five guests at a new restaurant in Westwood—the Hungry Tiger. Guest Rex Reed managed to get Day to the restaurant without spoiling the surprise. Later that night, Alma finally called from Texas with birthday wishes.

✳   ✳   ✳

In June, Day went to Las Vegas with Raquel Rael seeking celebrity items to auction at a benefit for Actors and Others for Animals. They caught Sinatra's show at Caesar's Palace and asked him for a pair of his pajamas, which he promised, but then failed to deliver. "We went to see Tom Jones in his dressing room after his act," Day recalled, "and he took off his pants and gave them to us." "He split them in the seat during his wind-up number," added Rael. "That ought to fetch a pretty penny."

Having already procured a number of personal items from Liberace for the fund-raiser, Day regretted being unable to catch his show at the Desert Inn. She was committed that night to attend the opening show of Jack Cassidy and his wife, Shirley Jones. University of Southern California film professor Drew Casper attended the Cassidys' show as the guest of Barbara Stanwyck and Shirley Eder, both of whom knew of his "great love" for Day and her work. "This is going to be a gift for you, Drew," they had assured him, without mentioning that Day would also be there.

"We all sat in a booth," recalled Casper. "Then, before the show, Doris Day arrived. And of course, I couldn't look at Shirley or Jack during their show. I couldn't take my eyes off her. She was stunning. She had this midnight blue sheath on, with spaghetti straps. And she noticed me looking at her. She was there with Hotchner."

Afterward at a party, Eder introduced Casper to his idol. "I held her hand and told her what her films meant to me and how, in every course I teach at USC, I always show a Doris Day film. It's kind of like my trademark. She couldn't believe that her films warranted any critical introspection or that I would be teaching them at USC. And she literally cried when she heard me tell her this."

Day also looked quite fetching at the Actors and Others for Animals benefit itself, which was held later in the summer. She sported a hat jauntily cocked to the side, and the freckles on her face were enhanced by the glaring sunlight. She also wore an outfit with a plunging neckline that emphasized her cleavage. Paul Brogan was agog when he first saw her at the event. "Wow! What a knock-out outfit!" he exclaimed. "You never could have gotten away with that a few years ago." Without skipping a beat, Day picked up on Brogan's comment, confirming that she was well over Melcher's death and feeling liberated from his puritanical attitudes and domineering ways. "I know," she said, grinning. "Marty never would have allowed it."

Brogan recalled meeting both Alma and Hotchner for the first time at the fund-raiser, during which Day had a large trailer for more private meetings with friends throughout the day. "The bazaar itself was a phenomenal event, in that thousands of people came all the way to Warners' vast Burbank lot in the valley and paid three dollars a head primarily for the purpose of seeing Doris in person," recalled Hotchner. "Pilgrims to the Burbank Lourdes. There were a few other celebrities present—Bea Arthur, Lassie, Earl Holliman, Jonathan Winters, and McLean Stevenson—but from the moment she appeared, it was evident that Doris was the prime reason they had come."

Day arrived at ten in the morning for the benefit and remained until eight that evening. A number of girls were assigned to follow her wherever she went. They collected ten cents for every autograph Day signed and twenty-five cents for every photo for which she posed. "They did a booming business," continued Hotchner. "Everyone called her Doris, and everywhere she went they pressed and swirled around her so tightly she could hardly manage to write her name."

In addition to the myriad items she had collected in Las Vegas—and from her personal collection—Day helped auction dresses donated by Debbie Reynolds, Kaye Ballard, and Eydie Gormé, among others, as well as Paul Newman's pajamas and Robert Redford's hat from their recent hit movie *The Sting*. Day spent a good part of the late afternoon in an area set up for her to pose for photos for a dollar per person. "Immediately, a line formed that stretched halfway across the lot," Hotchner said. "It was terribly hot and Doris had not eaten all day, but she remained in the photo area until the last person in the line had been taken care of."

On his last night in Los Angeles, Hotchner accompanied Day to a party given by producer Gus Schirmer, "a very low-key guy, who lived very simply on Orange Drive in Hollywood," recalled Judy Garland impersonator Jim Bailey. "He was very instrumental in signing talent for variety shows. He was having a few people over for dinner, and Doris asked Kaye [Ballard] if I was going to be in town. We met at Kaye's house first, with Paul Lynde and A.E. Hotchner. I remember Doris looked fabulous. She had a figure to die for. She was wearing tight white pants, and an orange top. I also remember being nervous when I heard that Paul [Lynde] was going to be there. I knew Paul, and I knew he could be a very bitter person when he was drunk, and he got very blotto that night."

Indeed, Ballard, Bailey, and Lynde griped about the vagaries of show business and the uncertainty of getting steady work. Having been through it all herself, Day put a positive spin on the situation and turned around their attitudes with her encouraging remarks. "Oh, that Clara Bixby," Ballard said to Hotchner, as they were leaving. "You know something—I think God did a little dance around her when she was born."

* * *

Though Day had already appeared on *The Tonight Show* with McLean Stevenson as the guest host, her first time with Johnny Carson came on September 2, 1974. Others appearing that evening included the bawdy stand-up comic Rodney Dangerfield and ninety-year-old character actor Burt Mustin, who had played Reginald Owens's decrepit butler in *The Thrill of It All.* It was Carson's first show after a layoff of almost six weeks following an exercise accident that had landed him in the hospital with a severely pinched nerve in his neck.

"Do you know what's happened since I've been gone?" Carson asked rhetorically during his opening patter. "Do you believe it? We have a new president and a new vice president." In the seismic conclusion to the Watergate scandals, Richard Nixon had resigned and been replaced by Gerald Ford, who selected Nelson Rockefeller as his second-in-command.

Carson proceeded to introduce Day, his first guest, as "one of the best-known entertainers in the entire world." Day, dressed to feature her

left: Day and Jack Lemmon in Connecticut filming *It Happened to Jane*. When she was given lobster-handling instructions by a local dealer: "Doris just burst out laughing and reached for that big, wriggling thing. 'C'mon, Sam,' she said. 'Let's get acquainted.'" (34)

above: Given Rock Hudson's back problems, a harness with a seat was rigged under his coat for him to carry Day in the climactic scene in *Pillow Talk* (35).

left: Day in *Midnight Lace*—"the penetrating psychological study of a woman frightened," wrote movie reporter Laura Bascombe. "Well, it was Doris who was frightened. She read the script, reread it and panicked. 'I don't want to do this,' she told me, when I found her one day in her beautiful white den, in a mood as black as ink." (36)

above: Day and Hudson—who called each other Eunice and Ernie—during the beach scene in *Lover Come Back*. As Tony Randall recalled, when they watched the rushes of the scene: "There was one take, where [Rock] leaned over—and one ball came out of his trunks. And then went back in. We said, 'Hey, play that again.' We were just shrieking and screaming. It nearly got into the picture." (37)

right: Day's 62-year-old father, William Kappelhoff, with his third bride, Luvenia Williams Bennett, who managed his tavern in downtown Cincinnati. (1961) (38)

below: Cary Grant, visiting his co-star at her trailer during the making of *That Touch of Mink*, and telling her an animated story. (39)

above: Cavorting on the set of *That Touch of Mink* with three baseball legends, left to right, Yogi Berra, Mickey Mantle, and Roger Maris. "A notorious womanizer, Mantle boasted to friends not only that he had slept with Day at his regular suite in New York's St. Moritz Hotel, but that she was 'one of the best lays' of his life." (40)

left: Though they both denied the rumors of their fling at the time, Day and Maury Wills—famed base-stealer for the Los Angeles Dodgers—had a clandestine affair in 1962, when the number-one box office star requested a divorce from her husband. (41)

above: That's Barbara Flicker (née Crystal) to the right of Day, at a Lakers' game. Despite his wife's obvious enthusiasm, Melcher, arms crossed, is clearly displeased. (42)

below: Day herself holds center stage in the international Doris-for-a-Day Look Alike contest, held in December 1965, as a promotional gimmick for *Do Not Disturb.* (43)

above: Tooting around the set with co-star Rod Taylor while making *The Glass Bottom Boat*. (44)

right: Day modeling her mermaid costume from *The Glass Bottom Boat*, which she wore for the film's opening scene, which was shot on location in Catalina. (45)

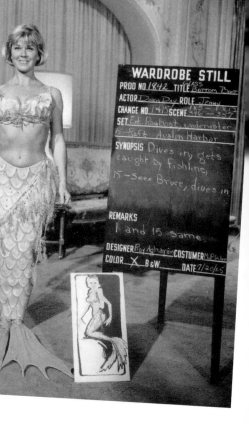

above: Day in *The Ballad of Josie*. Costumer Jean Louis made Day three different sets of pants to show off her spectacular-as-ever figure: a tight pair for standing, a second and slightly looser pair for sitting, and a third "even roomier" pair to permit her to mount a horse without splitting them. (46)

left: Terry Melcher with Candice Bergen at the Whiskey A Go Go, a "happening" place, in the summer of 1967, when everything in Terry's life was still on an upswing. (47)

Day enjoying the warm embrace of actor Patrick O'Neal, a co-star in
Where Were You When the Lights Went Out? Day would later claim O'Neal
was a true love of her life. (48)

above: With Kaye Ballard, who played Angie Pallucci in fourteen episodes of *The Doris Day Show*. According to Ballard, working with Day "was a genuine thrill for me because, in my eyes, she was truly a movie star. But I don't think she knew how good she was. She never had any formal training in acting—and that made her feel insecure. . . . I think she was more confident about her singing than about her acting." (49)

right: Mary Anne Barothy (l) with good friend Lauren Benjamin. Barothy lived with Day on N. Crescent for a year, serving as secretary and companion. (50)

left: One of Terry's first outings after his motorcycle accident and long convalescence, accompanying his mother to the March 1973 premiere of Ross Hunter's disastrous musical version of *Lost Horizon*—the producer's last feature film. (51)

right: Life-long fan Paul Brogan with Day in June 1973. When he next visited L.A. and showed Day this photo, she said: "We should call this the 'Headlights' shot." "You always had the sense that vulgarity was not appropriate around her," said Brogan, "unless she herself made a slightly risqué comment." (52)

Day in London with her new best friend, best-selling author, Jacqueline
Susann, in September 1973. Susann persuaded Day to write her memoir,
Her Own Story, published in 1975. (53)

left & below: Day's appearance on Johnny Carson's *The Tonight Show* in 1974, shortly after she had breast enhancement surgery—and it shows.

. . . beginning to cover the evidence after Carson made some suggestive remarks. (54)

above: With Hugh Hefner at his Playboy mansion in Hollywood for an Actors and Others for Animals benefit, September 1975. (55)

above: Day is keeping pace with her fourth and last husband, Barry Comden. "It was like making love standing up, full of passion and promise," wrote Comden, referring to their first kiss. (56)

above: With Bitish fans Sheila Smith (left) and Valerie Andrew (middle), who moved into the house on N. Crescent for what they would later call "The Comden Years" (57)

left: Emanuel "Buz" Galas with a Doris Day Pet Food grocery-store display he designed and helped construct. (1975 or 1976) (58)

right: British fan Sydney Wood stayed with Day at N. Crescent in 1978, prior to moving in and becoming a long-term caretaker. (59)

Day and Hudson—"Eunice" and "Ernie"—reunited for a press conference to announce Day's new cable TV show, *Best Friends,* in 1985. The event prompted the media to uncover and report on Hudson's having AIDS, which helped alter the world's perception of the illness. (60)

right: Day with life-long fan Howard Green, who first met his idol in October 1960, when she was in New York promoting *Midnight Lace*. Photo was taken at the Doris Day Convention in Carmel, in 1987. (61)

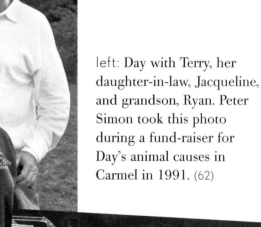

left: Day with Terry, her daughter-in-law, Jacqueline, and grandson, Ryan. Peter Simon took this photo during a fund-raiser for Day's animal causes in Carmel in 1991. (62)

right: A rare recent photo of Day, taken in April 2000, buying groceries near her home in Carmel. (63)

spectacularly enlarged breasts in a powder-blue, bell-bottom pants suit
with no bra under her thin blouse, played right into Carson's relentless
penchant for wry—yet obvious—sexual innuendo.

Commiserating with Carson about his medical condition, Day said
that her own pinched nerve had recently flared up and that she had
considered wearing her cervical collar on the show, but decided not to.
When Carson mentioned that his doctors told him not to play tennis
for three months, Day gave her characteristic devil-may-care, Christian
Scientist advice: "That's silly. . . . They'll have you in bed for six months.
. . . You should get out and do what you want to do, and forget it," she
added, while motioning with her hands for the audience to agree, which
they did with enthusiastic applause.

As they continued to discuss their shared ailments, Day mentioned
that she imagined there were no differences between the neck verte-
brae of men and women. Carson replied, "Below the neck, the changes
start rapidly." As the audience laughed and hooted, Day, in a seemingly
unconscious reaction, sat up abruptly in her chair and covered her glar-
ingly protruding nipples with her loose-fitting jacket. Day dismissed as
something made "out of nothing" Carson's observation that in the wake
of her appearance on *The Tonight Show* with McLean Stevenson, "fan
magazines" had linked them romantically. She added that the magazines
claimed she was engaged to Stevenson, even though they had never even
been out for a meal together. (They had, in fact, dined at Nate 'n Al since
doing the show together.)

When Carson broached the subject of her fame as a vocalist, Day
replied that she was feeling "rusty" and refused to sing. She added,
however, "I'm going to start singing again, because I really love it." The
subject prompted Day to say "hello" to trumpeter Jimmy Zito in Doc
Severinsen's band and chat with him about their days together with Les
Brown. When the inevitable subject of pets arose, Carol Wayne, a regular
on NBC's then-new game show *Celebrity Sweepstakes* who was sitting in
for Ed McMahon as Carson's sidekick, provocatively said that she was
"not fond of animals." "I don't want anything to lick me that's not going
to marry me," she added for a laugh. Day replied that she was fine with
that, but the daggers shooting from her eyes suggested otherwise.

Though Day appeared to be at ease during her first appearance with
Carson, she was generally just too self-conscious to ever really be herself
in such a public setting. Though she learned how to let herself go and

perform before a camera, *The Tonight Show* was recorded before a live audience, which had always intimidated her.

Two days after her appearance on *The Tonight Show*, Day sent Jacqueline Susann a letter, saying it had been a failure. In addition to her customary insecurities, she wrote that a heavily medicated Carson had not been up to his usual humorous standards and that she would have preferred appearing on Dick Cavett's show, where he would have engaged her in more intelligent conversation.

A week later, Day flew to New York with Raquel Rael to see Susann, who was fast approaching the end of her life at Doctors Hospital. Day stayed for several days and visited Susann frequently. "I wanted to be at Opal's side, but I was called back to Los Angeles to testify in court," she recalled.

In the midst of so much sadness, Day finally had a cause for rejoicing. On September 18, after a six-month court battle, Superior Court judge Lester E. Olson announced his decision, awarding Day $22,835,646 in damages for malpractice and fraud perpetrated by Jerome B. Rosenthal. Olson declared Rosenthal's practices to have been "gross and outrageous," adding that his management of Day's estate "oozes with client-attorney conflict of interest" and "stinks to high heaven." The judge further accused Rosenthal of taking advantage of the Melchers by accepting "kick-backs and rebates in the guise of attorney fees." The damages "were awarded as the culmination of 13 consolidated civil suits that included 14,451 pages of transcript from 67 witnesses, encompassing 3,275 individual exhibits, 68 boxes of financial records, and lawsuits that had been dragging on for five years. Given such gargantuan proportions, the case cost California taxpayers an estimated $250,000." Day's attorneys' fees amounted to $850,000, which became a part of the court's award.

For her part, Day went on record as saying, "My husband trusted Rosenthal and I trusted my husband." She also broke out in tears upon hearing the ruling. "I knew that justice would prevail. Re-living it all has destroyed me. As the judge recounted it all, it just wiped me out."

Rosenthal was compelled to pay $1 million in punitive damages when Olson also declared as bogus his claim that there existed an "oral agreement" making him half-owner of "the Day-Melcher empire." Further, Olson condemned Rosenthal for his "tortured effort" over the years to maintain an "indentured relationship" with Day, a relationship he had enjoyed—indeed, exploited—up to Melcher's death and, then, until his dismissal by Terry.

Even more remarkably, Olson divulged that armed sheriff's deputies had picked the locks in order to gain access to Rosenthal's financial statements and that he had resisted "virtually at gunpoint." Olson further judged Harland Green, Rosenthal's partner from 1961 to 1968, to be "vicariously liable" for damages concerning "negligent investments."

"I am healthy and I am rich," crowed Day, even though Olson reprimanded her for having been "too busy making movies to pay attention to her own affairs." He also criticized Melcher for having been in "blind awe" of Rosenthal, claiming that the attorney had "misled clients about their financial holdings, failed to turn over their records to them, used confidential information for his own gain, lured them into sham transactions and then charged exorbitant fees for bailing them out."

"I was so busy at the time I really didn't know what was going on," Day admitted, inadvertently echoing the judge's criticism. "I couldn't be at the office and the studio, too."

Though many would come to believe that Melcher had deliberately diverted his wife's fortune—and even buried the bulk of it in Swiss bank accounts—Olson did not deem that to be the case. "I think really, in his heart, Marty meant well by her," offered James Harbert, Day's long-term accompanist. "I was never totally convinced that he ripped off the money. I think it was just bad investments by Rosenthal. But Marty had a kind of naïve business streak. My impression was that he wished the best for her."

Though Olson "further enjoined" Rosenthal from taking any legal actions "anywhere in the world that involved the complex Day-Melcher-Rosenthal business and financial dealings," Rosenthal's attorney, Craig F. Dummit, declared, "This is only the first round," adding that the judge's ruling would be appealed. And, alas, it was. And as newspaper stories covering the verdict were quick to point out, Rosenthal had also rooked other celebrity clients of his, including Ross Hunter, Van Johnson, Kirk Douglas, and Gordon MacRae.

But given the protracted six-year ordeal of the Rosenthal imbroglio, Day was understandably relieved—ecstatic, even—with the verdict. She threw a celebratory lunch at Yamato, a new upscale Japanese restaurant directly across from the Twentieth Century Fox studios in Century City, during which she just glowed. Day was still feeling on top of the world some days later, when columnist Dorothy Manners saw her having lunch with Ross Hunter at another restaurant in Beverly Hills. After Day left her table to visit with a seeing-eye dog seated alongside his master's chair, Manners asked Hunter, "Does Doris know that man or that dog?" "Doris knows all dogs" was Hunter's witty and wise response.

* * *

That fall, Day attended a fund-raiser for Cat Care at a private home in Beverly Hills. A noticeably drunken Alma showed up late in the afternoon with an equally inebriated John Shaw, the wealthy Texas oilman. In Los Angeles on business, Shaw had dined with Day the night before, when his wife was expecting him home. At the fund-raiser, Shaw seriously injured himself when he fell over a table trying to get up from a sofa. Though Day wanted to take him home to Crescent to help him recover, Shaw was taken to the hospital, where doctors suspected that he might have had a stroke.

"I think it was Midway Hospital," recalled Barothy, who added that Day went by herself to visit Shaw in the hospital the next day. Late that night, Barothy received a call from Ruth Williams, Day's new friend and helper, telling her, "You've been terminated. The locks are being changed on the doors, and your stuff will be out of the house."

"Apparently, when Doris arrived at the hospital she found a woman in John's room," continued Barothy. "Doris didn't know that she was John's wife. Somehow, Doris thought I had set them up for this confrontation she didn't want to have. And I was fired for it." Or so Barothy construed, without ever really being sure of what had really happened.

The episode showed up, at the time, as a blind item in Rona Barrett's gossip column "about a blonde movie-TV doll (not Connie Stevens) who fired her secretary for having interfered with her private life." But according to Barothy there were probably additional reasons for Day's eliminating her from her life so abruptly.

"I figured that Alma was behind some of what happened," said Barothy. "Alma resented me, because I had been doing what she used to do and still wanted to be doing. She also resented the fact that I had gotten close to Doris." Once she was through with Barothy, Day would have nothing more to do with her, as was the case with so many others who "got close." "Some time later, I ran into Doris at Nate 'n Al," recalled Barothy. "I said, 'Hi, Clara,' and she was very nice." But as much as Barothy felt she never really understood just what had come between them, and as much as she wanted to discuss it with Day, she realized she would never be given the chance.

* * *

Despite the ongoing problems with her mother and the loss of dear friends, Day increasingly grew to enjoy her retirement. Though she rarely went to see a movie, she did attend, with Raquel Rael and Ruth Williams, that winter's blockbuster, *The Towering Inferno*. When the theater's manager noticed the retired star in the long line, he said to her, "There's no reason for you to stand out here and wait. You and your party can come right in." The egalitarian Day replied, "If they have to stand in line, then I do, too," and everyone in earshot broke into applause.

But Day was not completely finished with contractual assignments. Though it had been two years since she worked on her TV show, Day remained obligated to make a second TV special for CBS. Before this appearance, in the beginning of 1975, she also agreed to be a guest star on ABC's *The John Denver Show* on December 1, 1974. Denver's other guests included Dick Van Dyke and George Gobel.

During his introduction of Day, Denver plugged her work for Actors and Others for Animals. He also told her, "When I was a troubled teenager, you saved my life" to set up an inane skit that was built around Day, as Denver dreams that he costarred with her in several of her early Warner Brothers pictures. It was nothing more than a lame excuse for them to sing duets of the films' title songs. "By the Light of the Silvery Moon," "On Moonlight Bay," and "I'll See You in My Dreams."

Day's second TV special, *Doris Day Today*, aired on February 19, 1975. It was produced by George Schlatter, sponsored by Kraft, and directed by Tony Charmoli, a longtime Broadway dancer who had started as a choreographer in the early days of television, before he became the regular director of *The Dinah Shore Show* for five years. "On Dinah's show, we had a lot of guests," recalled Charmoli. "I got to work with Cyd Charisse, Betty Hutton—just about anybody who was a star at the time was on her show. We had lots of meetings at Dinah's house, and we used to wave at Doris when we saw her [in her yard next to Shore's]. I had never met Doris but I felt like I knew her from all of her movies."

Charmoli had already worked with producer George Schlatter on a number of programs, including a couple of Shirley MacLaine specials and a children's show that featured a five-year-old newcomer named Ron Howard. "George called me 'Wonder Wop' because I saved many situations—and the name stuck," said Charmoli.

"When George called me in to talk about the Doris Day show, he said, 'Well, you've worked with all these women,'" he continued. "And I felt like I knew Doris, so there was no hesitation." Though Schlatter told him he'd be "perfect" for the show, Charmoli may have been salvaging another "situation": They began rehearsing the very next day.

"We had several days of rehearsals, which was a luxury for me, because I was used to doing everything in one day," continued Charmoli. "Doris had quite a bit of input. She knew her capacities extremely well. Because I was new with her, I listened very carefully. Our costume designer was Michael Travis. We were up in George's office when Michael brought in some gowns. We liked one and said it was pretty. Doris said, 'I like that too. But it's going to look terrible on me.' It was a black gown with feathers around the bottom. She put it on, and when she came out of the dressing room, we could see that she was so right. She knew what was good for her, and she brought in some of her own gowns."

When Charmoli asked Day if she wanted to see how a particular number had turned out, she said, "Are you happy with it?" When he said he was, she added, "That's all I have to know." "I never worked with any other star who turned down such an invitation," Charmoli remembered. But then, Day asked to sit in on the final edit of the show. When Charmoli declined, he explained, "Day said, 'I'll come and sit in the back and be very quiet. I won't say a thing.'

"She came to the edit with my assistant director. We began by looking at a couple of different close-ups. I decided to go with the second one, and from the back, I heard, 'You're gonna use the second one, aren't you?' I just turned in my chair, and looked at her. I just kept looking at her. I said nothing. She was silent, too. Then she got up and walked out with my assistant, and came back with tons of lunch for all of us, and a stray dog she had found. She put all the lunch down and never came to another edit." As written by Schlatter and Digby Wolfe, the show worked hard to convey that the retired star was up to date with the latest trends. It opened with Day on a swing, clad in an old-fashioned lace and frilly dress, singing "Anything Goes." As Day continued the song, her costume changed into a sparkling blue pants suit with flared bottoms, and she forsook her prim and sedate posture for some disco hand waving. She proceeded to introduce the viewers to "some friends of mine" (i.e., her guest stars): Tim Conway, Rich Little, the "fabulous" Lockers dance group, and "that Colorado cutie," John Denver—all of whom joined her in a brief reprise of "Anything Goes," replete with disco movements.

Next came Day's rendition of "Day by Day," the hit song from *Godspell*, accompanied by a bongo drummer and electric guitarists in contemporary garb, as well as violinists in black suits. Day was wearing a brown, sequined gown that again highlighted her voluptuous breasts. As everyone who had seen her in recent months and years reported, she certainly did not look like a fifty-three-year-old performer. Her voice was also in wonderful shape as she performed a series of duets with Denver, beginning with "Exactly Like You" and, later, a "Sunshine Song" medley with a sunshine theme including "You Are the Sunshine of My Life," "Sunshine, Lollipops and Roses," and Denver's new hit, "Sunshine on My Shoulder." After joining with Rich Little in an arrangement for a duet of "Everybody Loves a Lover," Day sang segments from a number of her films while he, a celebrated impersonator, offered rapid-fire impressions of a number of her costars, including Sinatra, Gable, Grant, Cagney, Harrison, Douglas, Lemmon, and Stewart. If the low points in the show were two tasteless skits designed to fill out the hour, a highlight was Day's moving version of "The Way We Were."

"When we did the taping of the show, 'The Way We Were' took a long time," recalled Charmoli. "She couldn't get through it. She would break down in tears. Even when she couldn't see the pictures [which were projected behind her], the sentiment of the song with the knowledge of all these dead stars floating past her, got to her. She had to stop a couple of times, because she was so choked up and it was affecting her vocally."

According to Charmoli, "Day liked John Denver a great deal, which was a plus, because two stars don't always get along so well. It was a joy to see them rehearse and enjoy each other. And I think that comes across—you can see that they're both totally comfortable with each other." Indeed, Day enjoyed spending several days at Denver's home in Colorado that winter, and taking skiing lessons—though she would never ski again.

In the end, however, Charmoli had absolutely no idea how Day felt about the finished show. "The night it aired, I called the house after the show, to see how she liked it. The maid answered. She said, 'Oh, Doris went to bed. She didn't see the show.'" Even though Charmoli sent Day a tape, he added, "I don't know if she ever looked at it or not."

But now that she was retired, Day was clearly eager to move on. She decided to divest herself of memories of the Malibu house by putting it on the market in the summer of 1975. When entrepreneur David Geffen first saw the house on August 10, 1969—the day after the Manson murders on Cielo Drive—he fell in love with it. Geffen had been walking along the beach with his friend Lou Adler when they came upon Terry

Melcher and Candice Bergen, who were standing in front of the property. While Terry explained why he might have been the real "target"
of the crime that captured many a headline, "Geffen's eyes," wrote his
biographer Tom King, "roamed up to the beach house. He was struck by
its simple beauty and fell in love with it at once. Compared with some
of the other homes along Carbon Beach, it was rather small, but it had
large windows and a deck that faced the ocean. It did not have a large
yard and in fact was situated right off the Pacific Coast Highway." Geffen
bought the house from Day for $425,000. In the course of turning it into
his primary residence, Geffen significantly enlarged the house.

*   *   *

One person who managed to get onto the set of the *Doris Day Today* special was life-long fan Howard Green, who had first met Day fifteen years
earlier, when he was eighteen and she was in New York promoting *Midnight Lace*. In the intervening years, Green had worked for Paramount,
United Artists, and Fox, in New York, and was, by 1975, a publicist at
Twentieth Century Fox in Los Angeles.

"Tony Charmoli was a friend of mine," recalled Green. "As soon as I
saw that announcement in the *Hollywood Reporter*—well, nothing could
stop me from getting to the telephone! 'Tony—you've got to get me on
that set.' I had seen her a number of times before then at Nate 'n Al, and
stuff like that. But now, I did get on the set. I brought her a poodle-
shaped Styrofoam object covered with licorice nips. I presented it to her,
and she was just delighted, and she kissed me on the cheek. She was
everything any Doris Day fan expected her to be. We chatted for a while,
and we got some coffee from the percolator. I asked her if she was doing
any contemporary music for the special." When she told Green she would
be singing "Day by Day," he realized she was referring to the 1971 song
from *Godspell*. But it reminded him of the original "Day by Day" that
she had recorded in the 1940s, and he told her how much he loved her
rendition. "She started singing it," recalled Green, "and I joined her. And
before I knew it, I was looking in her eyes, and she was looking in my
eyes, and we were singing 'Day by Day' together. About halfway through,
I had to hit my forehead when I suddenly realized I was doing a duet
with Doris Day. And right after that, they called her to the set to do a
number with John Denver."

Day sent Howard Green a "lovely" thank-you note for his licorice gift. In his reply, Green mentioned that he was doing freelance writing for the *National Enquirer*. Day wrote back, saying, "Howard, you're a nice man, and if you'd like to do a story with me for a magazine like 'Good Housekeeping' and talk about the animals, I'd be happy to do it." Though nothing ever came of her proposal, they began a regular correspondence. "I was very surprised because her letters to me were very open, and she spoke to me as a friend. In one letter, she mentioned that she might not ever work again."

With her newfound freedom from any professional responsibilities, Day had more time to devote to her fans. Paul Brogan recalled paying his idol yet another visit in May, when they met for breakfast. "It was at a place on Rodeo Drive called Elizabeth's Tea Room, and Alma joined us," Brogan recalled. Alma and Brogan arrived before Day, who rode her bike to the restaurant. According to Brogan, "Doris would stop and speak to every animal between home and the restaurant. When Doris finally arrived, Alma said, 'Well, it's about time you got here. I've been holding this table for us, and it's been getting very heavy.'"

Early in September 1975, Brogan spent an afternoon with Day at another benefit for Actors and Others for Animals. The event, called Wine Country Safari, was at Hugh Hefner's Playboy mansion in Los Angeles. While taking a photo of Day—who posed with Hefner sporting a fine-feathered friend on his shoulder—Paul Brogan felt that the king of playboys himself was "foaming at the mouth over her breasts. She didn't look a day over thirty and he was clearly amazed. Even with all these Playboy bunnies running around, he couldn't take his eyes off of her. He was like a little child." Brogan recalled that this was the first time Day recommended he try a place called the Old World Restaurant. It was owned by Day's dentist, Robert Franks, who had invited her to have lunch with him there one day in May 1975. It was at that lunch that she met the restaurant's manager, Barry Comden. Ten years her junior, Comden, who proceeded to live with Day for five years, would become her fourth—and last—husband.

34

"The Comden Years"

✳

"There's something about the animals. . . .
I just can't do enough for them."
—DORIS DAY

"If so many people love me, why am I all alone?"
—DORIS DAY

When Doris Day first dined at the Old World Restaurant in Beverly Hills, Barry Comden recommended both the eggs Benedict and the coffee ice cream. "I don't know if she fell in love with the hollandaise, the ice cream, or me," Comden recalled, adding that Day returned frequently to the restaurant during the next month with various friends. "My mother was in the hospital," Day remembered. "My secretary and I would visit her, and instead of cooking at home, we'd eat in the Old World."

Comden said he first met Day in 1960, when he was walking on the beach in Malibu with his good friend Jerome Rosenthal who introduced them. Fifteen years later at the Old World, the dapper Comden instantly appealed to Day. He was twelve years her junior and prematurely gray. "I remember meeting Barry Comden at a restaurant at the Aware Inn, a health place on Sunset, after having dinner with Doris," recalled Kaye Ballard. "He would always come over and say hello. I thought he was attractive. I also thought he looked a lot like Patrick O'Neal, who was the one she said she really loved."

Having been married once, Comden had a young son, Daniel, and a stepson, David. Comden took pride in being related to the famous Broadway writer Betty Comden, who, with her partner, Adolph Green, created a number of the most beloved American musicals for stage and screen, including *Singin' in the Rain, Peter Pan, Bells Are Ringing,* and *On the Town.* Barry Comden's Romanian mother, Natalie, had married Betty Comden's uncle, David. A brazen "flapper" during the roaring twenties, the nineteen-year-old Natalie had published nude "girlie" magazines.

Barry Comden added to his allure by giving Day special treatment at the Old World. "Whenever Doris visited the restaurant, she was never presented with a check," reflected Valerie Andrew, who, along with Sheila Smith, lived with Day on Crescent to help out during what they later called "the Comden years." "He would always have her favorite wine chilled and waiting for her; and he'd always be bringing round leftovers from the restaurant for the dogs to eat," added Andrew.

For their first date, Comden took Day to Trader Vic's, the popular Polynesian restaurant in the Beverly Hilton Hotel. When Comden took her home after their second date, Day rebuffed his advances in the car, and he thought their budding romance was over. But Day continued a flirtatious mating dance by appearing for brunch at the Old World the next day—with another man. Several weeks passed before Day returned to the restaurant with Raquel Rael and Alma in tow. Before leaving, she met with Comden in the parking lot behind the restaurant, where they kissed for the first time. In a 1997 proposal for a memoir—which Richard Johnson of Page Six in the *New York Post* dubbed a "tell-all book"—Comden compared the sensation to "making love standing up, full of passion and promise." "Barry and I have been seeing lots of each other," Day confirmed some months later in a cover story in *Parade.* "He's gotten to know my son very well, and they really like each other."

Having bagged a kiss, Comden again tested his luck when he accompanied Day home to Crescent after another date. As relayed later by Johnson in his Page Six column, Comden wrote: "I sat on the end of her bed while she took a quick shower. On an impulse, and as a joke of course, I opened the shower door. She let out a yell, and for the first time I laid my eyes on the most beautiful body I had ever seen." They made love that very night, after which Day asked him to move in, and he did.

Sometime before or shortly after they met, Comden conceived of a line of pet food and related products that would use Day's name. Actors and Others for Animals had difficulty coping with the overload of injured and homeless creatures, and Day wanted to help by establishing her own nonprofit foundation for pets; she seized upon Comden's pet food idea as a way of realizing her plan. Comden wrote that they could envision their dream becoming a reality with "a great financial future for her foundation" via the pet food business. From the very beginning of their time together, Comden thought that Day's attitude toward pets would extend to him. "Little did I know I'd be the one who ended up in the doghouse!"

In the course of developing the pet food operation, Comden signed up three associate entrepreneurs for the venture: Roy Rodde, Al Sheppard, and Sol Amen. The last had worked with a graphic designer named Emanuel "Buz" Galas in the early 1960s, and called him in the spring of 1975 with an invitation to become art director of the new enterprise. "We want to make a presentation to Doris Day," Amen told Galas. "I want you to draw up a complete line of products and services under her image, and I want it, like yesterday."

"I did the presentation and handed it over to him," recalled Galas. "He came back to me and said, 'She signed a seven-year contract, on the basis of what you did, to show her. Now we're opening an office in Beverly Hills, and I want you to come and work there.' Barry also had his office there.

"As for the start-up date, it was definitely springtime 1975," added Galas, "because we were well in our offices on Wilshire by the time summer arrived. I believe we moved into Carson industrial park, just off I-5 [at 871 Artesia Boulevard], in July or August."

Once Day gave her consent, the Doris Day Distributing Company grew to encompass far more than just pet food. In addition to the canned morsels, there would be pet bowls, jewelry, collars, and leashes. Large display units for grocery stores were manufactured as well. "We went scouting for a factory to produce all this stuff, and ended up with a hundred-thousand-foot facility in Carson," continued Galas. "It had a five-thousand-square-foot office space. We started building the displays in the warehouse. We hired cabinet-makers to come in, and I got involved in that directly—designing and building them at the same time, and doing all the packaging and setting up the photos for the promotional material. There were even going to be pet spas and motels, and veterinary services."

While Comden busied himself supervising what he would come to call "the great dog food disaster," A. E. Hotchner was finishing his work on Day's memoir. When he presented Day with a completed manuscript of *Doris Day: Her Own Story* in the fall of 1975, Hotchner wasn't sure what to expect. "A person will say a lot of things when poking around in memories, but when they show up in cold hard type, it's easy to withdraw, refuse to acknowledge that those words were indeed spoken," Hotchner explained. "When I returned with the manuscript, I wasn't certain how Doris would react, but she took the whole thing very well. We did make changes for the sake of accuracy or to alter things that might hurt others, but she didn't say of anything, 'I don't want that mentioned in the book.'" At least not until after it was published.

Hotchner's prologue to *Doris Day: Her Own Story* was meant to lure readers by promising a no-holds-barred, "tell-all" memoir. Hotchner played up his own misgivings about doing the book, explaining how he thought Day's story would turn out to be "all sweetness and light." But if, according to Hotchner, Day "had always been rather circumspect" about interviews, she now mustered the candor to tell him, "I'm tired of being thought of as Miss Goody Two-Shoes . . . the girl next door, Miss Happy-Go-Lucky. You doubtless know the remark dear Oscar Levant once made about me—'I knew her before she was a virgin.' Well, I'm not the All-American Virgin Queen and I'd like to deal with the true, honest story of who I really am. This image I've got—oh, how I dislike that word 'image'—but it's not me, not at all who I am. It has nothing to do with the life I've had." But getting at the truth was not entirely natural or easy for a woman who had spent the past twenty-five years dissembling some aspects of her life and being confused about still others. After all, Day once claimed that she had given out so many versions of her age that she no longer knew how old she really was.

Upon the book's publication, Hotchner pushed her to undertake an extensive book tour. Day was hesitant, but finally overcame her reluctance when Comden agreed to accompany her. Before the tour began, Day taped *The Merv Griffin Show* in Los Angeles. There she first met Barbara Walters, who later interviewed Day in NBC's New York studio for *The Today Show*, the first TV interview about the memoir. "Through the years Doris Day has become ingrained in the public mind as the virgin, the wholesome girl next door," Walters announced in her introduction, before adding that the book was full of surprises. While she declared *Her Own Story* "compelling," Walters emphasized that "this is not the Doris Day you expect."

Day had been anxious about her session with Walters, who was famous for raising topics that her guests preferred to avoid. "I didn't sleep all night," she told Walters during their early-morning chat. In what was probably a strategic maneuver to make her appear natural and revealing, Day did not wear much makeup either. But she looked remarkably fresh in a blue turtleneck sweater and bell-bottom pants, her blonde hair peeking out of a blue knit cap. She proceeded to give short, pert answers to most of the questions. When Walters asked her to talk about her failure to get along with Kirk Douglas when they made *Young Man with a Horn,* Day responded that, in fact, it was the film they made together that she did not enjoy. That answer prompted Walters to quote from the book—"Kirk never makes much of an effort towards anyone else, he's pretty much wrapped up in himself"—before adding, "I have a feeling I'm going to tell more of [what's in your] book than you are."

When asked about her future, the "Que Sera, Sera" gal responded: "I don't know if I want to get married again. I don't know if I want to work again. . . . I'm really enjoying my life, as it is now." Day did not mention that she was practicing something she preached in her memoir by living with someone before marrying him. Though far from a daring thing to do in the wake of the ongoing sexual revolution unleashed in the sixties, such conduct represented a surprising contrast with the good-girl image that clung to Day—even if, now retired, she had lost interest in maintaining it.

In a syndicated column, Diane White reflected upon how evasive Day had been with Walters. In her memoir, Day "spills everything about her unhappy childhood . . . her three marriages, her sex life," White wrote. But during the interview with Walters, Day had given "only the most perfunctory and oblique answers to questions about her marriages and sex life. She confessed it all in the book, but she wouldn't talk about it on television. Ms. Walters, in desperation, began reading certain passages from the book and asking Ms. Day to comment on them. 'Did I say that?' she asked innocently, flashing that million dollar grin."

Day was still playing the part of "Doris Day," in other words, and contradicting herself as the occasion demanded. While she spent more and more of her life disassociating herself from the image she had helped create, she was now subtly disavowing her own autobiography—and particularly the negative ways in which it portrayed Melcher—at the same time she was promoting it. When Mary Murphy of the *Los Angeles Times* asked Day about the interview with Walters, Day became defensive. "Well for one thing I hadn't slept all night and I was tired. When I met Barbara out here [in Los Angeles] she was warm and friendly, but in *The Today Show* environment she was different," complained Day, who added that Walters was "tough." Day also shared her misgivings about the portrayal of Melcher in her memoir: "I couldn't believe it when I saw galleys of the book and read what people had to say about Marty," Day cried out. "It almost broke my heart. I never knew. I almost stopped publication."

In still another feature about the memoir for the *New York Daily News,*
Kathleen Carroll homed in on Day's own characterizations of Melcher
in the book, which now dismayed her. In Carroll's opinion the book
described Melcher "as a weak, venal man, and curiously, this shocked
even Doris herself. The information as to Melcher's true character came
from sources other than Doris, and, when she heard about it, she was
astonished. 'Did you consider your husband a fool or a heel?' someone
asked. 'I don't know,' said Doris, looking sad for a moment. 'I don't really
know. It just proves I never really knew him.'" Day said in an interview
with Merv Griffin that she was shocked by what others had to say about
Melcher in her book and was "sorry" she had published it.

It was becoming obvious that Day had never read *Her Own Story*
before—or even after—its publication. Though, in the book, she discussed
at some length her affair with a married man (only confidants knew
that her nameless paramour was Patrick O'Neal), she called Hotchner to
complain after a San Francisco reporter asked her about it. But by the
time Day returned to *The Tonight Show* to plug the book in the middle
of January 1976, she seemed to be over whatever jitters had led to those
strained and confused answers about her own memoir. Now, leading
off the show in a very seventies pink maxi-skirt set, she appeared ready
for anything Johnny Carson might lob her way. "You've been known as
a very private individual most of your life," Carson began his softball
pitch. "Now, all of a sudden you've come out in a book and said, 'Hey,
I'm gonna tell you all about me.' How come all of a sudden?"

By now, Day had perfected the story about why she had decided to
write the book. It was her "very good friend" Jacqueline Susann who
had encouraged her to write it. "When she got to know me," Day told
Carson, "she said, 'You know, with all that's happened to you, you're very
good humored—and cheerful and happy. And I can't understand how
you could be that way.' And the more we talked about it, she said, 'You
really should put it down in a book.'"

Day had even developed a new party line on why reading the book
would provide a valuable experience—it would be "a good influence"
on others. As an afterthought, she told Carson, "One other thing, maybe
. . . is [that my] image has been so boring: you know, the virgin, and
the Goody Two Shoes and all that nonsense: You know, it's not human.
And I wanted to straighten the record." Day went on to reminisce about
the Ross Hunter comedies she had made a decade and a half earlier,
calling them "sexy" because "everything was left to the imagination."

Times had changed, she agreed with Carson, as they bandied about the then-new terms for distinguishing levels of pornography—"hardcore" and "softcore."

The conversation wound back to her book. While Day worked on the memoir with Hotchner, she recalled, "Some days were really emotional for me. . . . When you start talking, and you're gonna tell all, you re-live it. And there were many, many sad times in my life," she said, referring primarily to her parents' miserable relationship and her own disappointing marriages. When Carson asked Day if she was going to marry again, Day responded, "Do I know? You know, I don't know what I'm going to do tomorrow. . . . I may not marry again ever—three times and you're out. Isn't that the way it goes?. . . . I like to really get to know someone," Day also said. "But you know, having been married three times, it's obvious that I did not know them. You always think you know them." When Carson asked her if she traveled with anyone, Day said, "That's rather personal," making no mention of Comden. She also stressed how much she loved Carmel, the Eden-like environment she first got to know while filming *Julie*, in 1956, and further declared herself to be "a very happy lady now. . . . I love my life. I don't care about working. I don't need it."

As Carson prepared to introduce his next guest, Rex Reed, Day referred to him as "a very, very dear friend of mine." The acerbic film critic emerged wearing a purple crew-neck sweater and white bell-bottom pants. He was very animated as he, too, tried to debunk Day's enduring image. "I thought people, for years, thought Doris Day didn't go to the bathroom," Reed said. "I mean, she's real." When he emphasized that Day's memoir was the story of a survivor, she plunged right in with a rhetorical eureka. "You know what you have to have? A round bottom. . . . You know the [inflatable] dolls that have round bottoms, and you knock them down and they bounce back again? You just can't keep them down. Right? Okay. That's what you have to have, a round bottom. And I've got one."

"If ever there was a victim of other people, it's Doris," added Reed. "And yet, there is a unique ability there, to bounce back. . . . She's like a cat: throw her off the top of a bridge, and she'll land on her feet." Speaking for her enormous fan base, Reed also told Day, "I don't think you have ever realized how important your talent has been. You have never really enjoyed these films that I grew up loving, and still love." When Day said she would like to "remake them now," Carson asked her what she would change. "The scripts," replied Day, "because they're trite."

Carson's other guests that night included singer Donna Theodore and Dale Alexander, the self-help author of *Healthy Hair and Common Sense.* Reed recalled that he and Day "hopped in a car the minute the show was over" and went for dinner at a place that easily crossed a number of international borders. "It was at a Mexican restaurant called the Swiss Chalet, and the hostess was Miko Taka from [the movie] *Sayonara*. Only in Hollywood!" exclaimed Reed.

As Day continued to give TV interviews to promote her memoir, her responses grew more rehearsed. She stuck to many of the same comfortable themes when she appeared on *The Mike Douglas Show* in Philadelphia, telling her host, "I don't miss not working. . . . Just living and getting up in the morning is fun. . . . I don't know who the girl next door is? What does she do? . . . Everything is part of a plan. . . . God is in charge." Dressed all in white, offset by gold hoop earrings and a gold link belt, she again compared herself to those "round bottom" inflatable dolls— a good line. Another of Douglas's guests, TV personality Steve Allen, echoed Rex Reed by observing that Day had not received the "critical appreciation" she deserved. Day had asked that a car be ready for a quick getaway after Douglas's show. But she ended up so thoroughly enjoying herself that she remained at the studio after the end of the show, chatting and singing songs with her host.

Day also went to Chicago for Phil Donahue's show and then returned to L.A. for Regis Philbin's. But of the half dozen TV shows on which she ultimately appeared to promote her memoir, Day seemed the most open and relaxed on the first one, which she had prerecorded with Merv Griffin in Los Angeles. Day and Griffin had been friends for two decades, and there were many things they could discuss without her having to worry about curve balls hurled her way. In a canary-yellow blazer over a white turtleneck sweater and white bell-bottom slacks, she appeared more casual than she would be on subsequent shows. Their chat also occurred before Day discovered—or claimed to have discovered—the book's revelations about both Melcher and her affair with a married man. What's more, she had already been a guest on Merv Griffin's show twice before.

The retired star received a standing ovation from the studio audience when she arrived on the Griffin set. After introducing Day as "a true friend," Griffin asked her why she had written her memoir. "When I read the galleys, I wondered myself," Day responded. "It's like going through analysis. . . . I had no intention of writing my story," she also told Griffin.

"You don't want to divulge your life to the world." But despite giving voice to such hesitations, Day seemed fully at ease with Griffin, the one-time singer whom she had helped break into Hollywood, and, indeed, their conversation elicited some of the most self-revealing remarks of her life. "I've never been ambitious," she said, and "I'm not that pretty. I'm average. . . . I'm an average-looking lady." She also asserted her conviction that God "really is running the show" and explained that she had gone ahead with her second and third marriages because she thought she had grown "so much wiser" and learned from her mistakes. And, in keeping with the image she otherwise disavowed, she discussed her unease watching *Last Tango in Paris*, which she had seen with Billy de Wolfe. "We were both embarrassed," she recalled.

No matter how routine the questions and answers on her book tour may have become, Day was still unenthusiastic about the interviews she gave. She had spent much of her life selling her films, her recordings, and, finally, her TV show. Now, here she was, supposedly retired, back out in public selling what was ostensibly the true story of her life and herself. It was an unwelcome imposition on the first real sense of freedom she had known in nearly three decades. And it was backfiring on her—getting her into sensitive areas she never wanted to visit in public.

＊　　＊　　＊

However uncomfortable Day might have been with the revelations in *Her Own Story*, they were crucial to making the William Morrow book—which featured a cover shot of a smiling Day standing on a hillside with her hands planted firmly on her hips as well as an $8.95 price tag—a best seller. (A full-page ad for the book appeared in the *New York Times Book Review*, declaring, "For the first time—the 'girl next door' talks about her astonishing life.") Many of the reviews were sensational.

In a rave for *Variety*, Foster Hirsch hit upon several key points about this "quintessential middle American shiksa," emphasizing just how much Hotchner's prodding his subject for behind-the-scenes stories had paid off. "Unlike many film star biographies, this wonderfully candid chronicle doesn't read like a glossy publicity handout because Day transcends the fake intimacy and superficial self-revelation that are the customary currency of the celebrity book," Hirsch wrote. "Narrated in a sensible, no nonsense manner, Hotchner's portrait discovers new energy in such standard show business themes as the conflicts between romance and career and between life and art, the early struggles and the mid-career letdowns. . . . As the heroine of her own story, Day is immensely likable. She's more passionate and vulnerable, more complicated, than in any of her movies. . . . Her estimate of her career is wholly unpretentious since she seems content to be known as a star personality rather than a serious actress."

A big fan of Day, literary giant John Updike offered an intriguing perception of her serial marriages in his review of the book for the *New Yorker*. "The same strong personality behind her professional success has no doubt contributed to her personal problems," Updike wrote. "Al Jorden's jealousy, George Weidler's walkout, and Marty Melcher's disastrous dealing can all be construed as attempts of a male ego to survive an overmatch with a queen bee." Updike's sense of an ambitious, overachieving Day contradicted the more self-effacing image she had of herself and preferred to promote. But it also seemed a valid perception that accounted for much of her husbands' behavior toward her. Such a deep-seated motive might help explain, for instance, why Melcher twice had his wife portray a woman whose husband was trying to murder her, in *Julie* and again in *Midnight Lace*.

Only Robert Kirsch—in his review of the book for the *Los Angeles Times*—seemed to recognize that the memoir did as much to maintain Day's image as to debunk it. "Somehow, I don't think that the revelations here will really shatter the image," wrote Kirsch, "because I am not so sure after reading this candid account that, films and appearance aside, Doris Day is really very different from the image. . . . Nor, paradoxically, do I think that this book is the whole story, either. I am not questioning the honesty and candor in it but rather suggesting that honesty and candor are not automatically sufficient to explain and evoke. I have a strong feeling that Miss Day felt the experience a violation of an intrinsically decorous nature; there is evidence of a certain distaste at the revelation. . . . If she is at pains to correct some of the gossip about her . . . some of the most interesting parts of the narrative are slighted. . . . In short, what happened is here—why it happened is only partially explained. [T]he relationship between image and persona is only hinted at. When, at the end, Hotchner tells her that he has watched people watching her and 'I've never seen so much love,' she asks, as we might: 'If so many people love me, how come I'm alone?' That plaintive question hangs in the air at the end of the book."

Day also consented to two consecutive days of interviews with film scholar Molly Haskell. When she met with Day at her home on Crescent, Haskell found "a woman totally in command of herself and her every utterance." Haskell fairly swooned, adding that Day "consciously projects not so much a self as a state of mind: one of unalloyed harmony, joy, mental health as its own reward. This determined euphoria, or mind control—for it is a product of will, not intuitive faith—is the end result of Christian Science principles adopted early but since modified to a less orthodox and more personal code."

Her Own Story made its first appearance on the *New York Times* best-seller list at No. 6 on February 15, 1976. Two weeks later the book had climbed to No. 2, and then hit the top of the list on March 14. It remained at No. 1 for a month, before slipping back to No. 2. All told, it was on the best-seller list for twenty-one weeks in 1976.

Among the more personal responses to her memoir, Day received a long letter of appreciation from Ethel Eisenberg, née Ann Perry, who wrote that the book had brought back her memories of their working together at WLW in Cincinnati in 1944. In her thank-you letter of June 26, Day wrote that the response to the book had been an "exciting experience" for her, adding that she had already heard from "hundreds and hundreds of people." In her efforts to keep up with all the mail, Day was staying up later and later. Indeed, it was one in the morning when she penned her note to Eisenberg. Day even placed a white wicker writing table next to her bed for composing such notes whenever the whim struck.

Perhaps the greatest indication of the book's success was the size of the paperback printing, which Bantam brought out in October 1976. The initial print run was increased by 100,000, making the first printing a record 700,000. Within three weeks, the book had reached No. 8 on the paperback best-seller list, and climbed to No. 6 by the beginning of December. Day promoted the paperback edition by giving a number of radio interviews, all conducted by telephone from her home.

In conjunction with her retirement, the arrival of Day's memoir prompted the publication of three other books focused on the star's film career. The first, and most astute, of them, *Doris Day* by George Morris, was a 157-page paperback published in 1976 as part of a Pyramid series of books devoted to individual movie stars and their films. Christopher Young's *The Films of Doris Day* and Alan Gelb's *The Doris Day Scrapbook* followed the next year. The last two were large picture books examining Day's career film by film and include only a minimum of biographical information.

✳ ✳ ✳

Shortly after the publication of *Her Own Story*, Day decided to marry for the fourth time. The decision came upon her spontaneously in her beloved Carmel. Having supervised the Old World in Beverly Hills, Comden had Day accompany him for the grand opening of a new branch of the restaurant in Palm Springs, in what used to be Jilly's, on Palm Canyon Drive. As soon as the festivities concluded, Day and Comden left for Carmel, where they spent several days at the Tickle Pink hotel. They had their own private suite, which included a fireplace and a view of the ocean. Long in love with Carmel, her idyllic time there now with Comden sealed their relationship.

Day and Comden had frequently returned to Carmel during their first year together. They planned on spending a week there in April 1976, but because the Tickle Pink could accommodate them for only two nights, they decided to extend their stay at the Ventana Inn just south of Carmel. During a lunch at the inn's highly rated restaurant, they met and befriended its owner, Larry Spector, who invited them to spend time at his personal cottage in Carmel. This is where, one morning before breakfast, Day blurted out, "Comden, let's get married!" He instantly agreed, and they were almost as instantly married.

The wedding took place at Spector's home on April 14. A last-minute decision turned their "bike-riding weekend" into a honeymoon. "I laid out cake, fruit, flowers, hors d'oeuvres and decorations," Spector told the *Los Angeles Herald-Examiner*. "The judge forgot to bring his wife [as witness], so we dragged in the court clerk. We sat around and talked and told jokes. With proprietary discretion, everyone left [the couple alone] about an hour later." Eight people had witnessed Day, clad in a beige pants suit, marry Comden, who was wearing a fashionable, for the times, light blue leisure suit.

As soon as Day and Comden returned home to Beverly Hills, they discovered that Terry had moved in to the house on Crescent to get away from his volatile relationship with his wife, Melissa, from whom he would soon be divorced. After the failure of his second solo album, *Royal Flush*, Terry moved to London and tried to relaunch his career as a music producer there.

A month or so after they married, Day and Comden traveled to Jackson Hole, Wyoming, for a proper honeymoon, spent outdoors as much as in, picnicking on the banks of the Snake River, where they enjoyed white-water rafting. Day invited her British fan-club friends Sheila Smith and Valerie Andrew to come and tend to things at the house while she and Comden were away. "She thought we might want to come for a vacation, and use the house, and look after the dogs, while they were on their honeymoon," recalled Smith. "They were surprised to discover that we didn't drive and wondered how we would get around," Andrew added. Smith also remembered that Day always called her fourth husband "Comden," and he referred to her as "the missus."

When Day and Comden returned to the house on Crescent, they were so pleased with how well everything had been cared for that they invited the British couple to move to Los Angeles to work for them. "They took us to the office and let us see what was going on, including some of the pet food samples," recalled Andrew. "I think it's because they wanted us to come out and work, and be helpful in any way." "I told them I had to think about it," added Smith. "I was working for a magazine, in accounting. I was happy there. I had friends and all my family in London, and I never thought of leaving." Andrew was working for a travel agency at the time.

Before returning to London, Day's British guests accompanied her and Comden to the Beverly Hilton Hotel for a meeting of potential distributors of Doris Day pet food. Whatever hopes Day had had for the operation that bore her name, she now grew increasingly dismayed about how it was evolving. Comden later acknowledged that only after the discussions at the Beverly Hilton did he realize that the enterprise had grown into a pyramid-type scheme. Comden recalled feeling "had" when they entered the meeting room and saw "dozens of people" in "ugly green jump suits" with Doris Day logos milling around. Day shot him an angry, disgruntled look as she prepared to speak, but once she took the stage to address the employees of the new company, she reverted to her sunny, welcoming self. She gave a light pep talk, and finished by saying "I hope you all join with us." "Those eight words," he recalled later, "sealed our fate forever."

The following month, the California Department of Corporations sued the "Doris Day Distributing Co." for having "sold more than $150,000 worth of pet food distribution franchises since April 4 without applying for registration required by state law." Since Day was not listed as a shareholder, officer, or director of the makeshift company, she was not named a defendant in the suit. But as she herself would later explain, it was her fateful participation in the event at the Beverly Hilton Hotel that connected her to the operation and implicated her in all that transpired. "I remember her saying that the fact that she went to one of the meetings and got up and spoke to the audience nailed her for being a part of the company," recalled Sydney Wood, the British fan club friend who soon came to work for Day. "Up until then, it was just her name, not her person."

"The conflict came about between Doris and Sol Amen, over the quality of the dog food—and cat food too," recalled Emanuel Galas. "Doris was testing them on her pets, and it was very frustrating that we kept getting non-approvals from her. But Amen was concerned with the profit factor. He wasn't going to spend more making the food. He said to me, 'What she wants to do with the dog food will cost us more than we can possibly collect on the retail end.' She wanted people-quality food. They wanted a very broad distribution.

"I got worried at that point," Galas continued, "but we kept on building the display units, and they kept on selling the distributorships. They had distributors come into the facility to see what was going on. They kept signing them up. I think some of them were paying fifty grand a crack for a distributorship. They all lost every penny."

So did many other investors who responded to an ad in the *Los Angeles Times*, inviting them to "[m]ake a substantial income from the pet food industry and help your favorite pets" by sending $2,500 to the Doris Day Distributing Co. Adding to the come-on was a photo of Day with her dog Biggest, also the chosen eye-catcher for the pet food can labels, which Galas had designed. After $300,000 had been raised, Amen performed what for him was a typical vanishing act. Amen had already served a year in prison in 1971 "on mail fraud charges arising from a work-at-home franchise scheme that netted his former employer some $500,000." Lawsuits that "went on for years" and legal fees running more than $20,000 a month doomed the Comdens' marriage practically from the beginning.

Sheila Smith recalled, "We realized there was trouble. I remember sitting around the bar with Doris and Barry, having a drink and having a conversation about the pet food. And I remember one of them calling someone about it and having a very heated conversation. On the way to the hotel, in the car, she suddenly got very upset. Maybe it was the idea of those distributors, and that she didn't know about them. But it seemed like Barry was surprised about it, too."

"She probably didn't believe that he didn't know about it," added Andrew. "But I think Barry was naïve." Day and Comden eventually filed a civil suit in November 1976, claiming "they unilaterally canceled an agreement with the company because she was not permitted prior approval of the products." It wasn't until the following February that Day, as revealed by *Variety*, won a court order "to keep a pet food products company from using her name as a sales gimmick, but it could prove costly in the end. . . . She and her husband, Barry Comden, have to put up a $1,000,000 bond before the order can go into effect." The judge "turned down Day's request for a list of the firm's distributors."

"They invited me to participate in suing Doris," continued Galas. "I said, 'No, I really don't want to get involved in that.' I didn't feel that she was the real problem. I knew these guys by then, and what they were like—Rodde, Barry, and Amen—all three of them. They made quite a team."

Day had no idea that her fourth husband's past included involvement with such characters. "Barry was very charming," recalled Nan Case, whose first husband, Mike Robert, had grown up with Comden in Brookline, Massachusetts. Comden and Robert became fellow students and roommates at Tufts University. "Barry knew how to talk to people," continued Case. "He could charm the skin off a snake. My impression was of a somewhat slippery kind of a guy. I never thought of him as being very intellectual. But in those days, to get into Tufts, he had to be smart. Still, there was a lot of show, but little substance.

"Bob and Barry were quite close through their college years. They were a couple of ne'er-do-wells, who gravitated toward each other. Barry's mother, Natalie, married a very, very wealthy man. They lived in this magnificent house on Chestnut Hill. They were one of the richest families in Brookline. He was brought up like a little prince—exactly. So he thought he could do anything he wanted to. And he always dressed very flashy—he was swishy."

As with Marty Melcher, Comden's bluster was in all likelihood something of a front. He "tried to act like a tough guy," said Nan Case's son, Miles Robert, who grew up in New York, and was friends with Comden's stepson from his previous marriage, David. Once again, Day had attached herself to a man who was sometimes in over his head, and not always capable of controlling forces he had unleashed.

"I thought Comden was good looking, and I thought he would have been a great addition to her arm, like Queen's Elizabeth's purse," recalled

Rex Reed. "But I think he wanted more than that. He wanted to become a part of the scene. He did not want to be Mr. Doris Day. And yet, I think he was incapable of doing the kind of deals to further her career that Marty was capable of. He got involved in other aspects of her life, which were disastrous. Even he said that the dog-food business was the biggest rip-off."

Terry's friend Guy Webster concurred. "Barry was very handsome and charming, a little bit smarmy, maybe. He was perfectly cast as a restaurant host. Doris wanted him to have a legitimate job, and helped create this pet-food business to give him street credibility, so he wasn't just living on her largesse. But he was no businessman."

Comden eventually came to realize that what A. E. Hotchner would describe as a "franchise scheme" was, in Smith's words, "the beginning of the end. I think if that hadn't happened, they would still be together. I think that she loved him, really and truly, and he definitely loved her. It was a shame that that happened. When we first were there, they were very happy." Moreover, Smith remembered Day as being "very enthusiastic about the pet-food deal"—in the beginning.

"I was lured into it by being told that all the profits would go to my foundation," Day explained years later. "That's the only reason I did it. There was nothing in it for me. It was all going to be for the animals."

*   *   *

The thirty-nine-year-old Sheila Smith decided to move from London to Los Angeles and work for Day. On her own, at first, she settled into the guesthouse on Crescent Drive in July 1976 and, within six weeks of her arrival, obtained a California driver's license. "I share my little abode with five of the Day canine family, namely Schatzie, Rudi, Muffy, Charlie Brown and Bobo," Smith wrote in the next Doris Day Society newsletter. In addition to their "canine family"—or what Day herself had taken to calling her "Canine Country Club"—the household included several felines: Sneakers, Lucy Brown, and Lucky Day.

Having suffered a series of strokes, Alma, long in the hospital, was rapidly deteriorating by the time of Smith's arrival. "She was quite sick," recalled Smith. "She had something like Alzheimer's, but nobody talked about it." After lingering in this condition for well over a year, the eighty-one-year-old Alma died on October 9, 1976. Given the difficulties she had recently had in adjusting to her daughter's retirement, Alma's ailment may have been a blessing in disguise. Having lived much of her life vicariously through her daughter's success, Alma, as the present increasingly slipped away from her, spent her fading days remembering the past. "We visited almost every day," Day wrote in a "letter" to her British fans. "I miss her very much but I'm happy in the knowledge that she is having a grand reunion with her son (my brother Paul) and all her dear family and friends who she missed so much."

"I think Doris treats death differently from other people," Smith observed. "There's never a funeral. She mourns in a quiet way. It's as if she doesn't really want to know about it. But whenever one of the dogs died, it was a really big thing, with candles and photos and a kind of a shrine. She always said that she thought dogs were more important than people." Smith recalled that when Alma died, "Barry was there for Doris all the time."

"She's never put people first," said Rex Reed. "She's always put animals first. And I think it's all about her needing guidance and help from people who would solve her problems for her, but never get too close."

By November, Valerie Andrew, who was thirty-six, joined her partner Smith at the house on Crescent. Day had an employment agreement drawn up providing $800 a month for each, plus room and board. They would also receive $7.50 an hour for overtime work. "Two hundred dollars a week seemed fine to me, because it was all mine," Smith remembered. "I mean, we had our accommodations and our food taken care of, as well." Given their backgrounds as officers of her British fan club, the extensive duties listed in the agreement began with responsibilities that drew on their related skills, in order to help them secure green cards: "Answering fan mail; preparing biographies and news releases for newspapers and magazines; writing newsletters; attending to social business and personal affairs of employer; confirming with employer on contemplated social functions; managing financial affairs of household including all bookkeeping responsibility; assist in care of employer's dogs."

Although it appeared as the last item on their list of duties, caring for the dogs quickly came to consume most of the couple's time. According to the agreement, the forty-hour week consisted of "8 hours per day [based] on a 5 day week"—Monday through Friday. As stipulated, the hours ran from 10 a.m. to 3 p.m.; a "rest period" from 3 to 6 followed, and work resumed from 6 to 9 p.m. In reality, Smith and Andrew worked much more than that, and their chores simply became a part of the rhythm of their everyday life.

"We did absolutely everything: housework, cooking, looking after the dogs—18 of them—bathing them, taking them to the vet, driving her around sometimes, handling the fan mail," recalled Smith. "There were also the cats, and there was a bird, in Terry's bedroom. We just did a bit of everything.

"You had to cook for the dogs," she continued. "You never opened a can. You had to make brown rice and ground beef, or cubed chicken and vegetables. She would go to the markets in the mornings and get all the vegetables and things that they couldn't use at the end of the day, and bring them back early in the morning for us to chop and prepare. She did a lot. She would cook. But then you had all the dishes to do—and they were very big pots. It was a daily ritual. And then getting them to exercise in the yard and playing with them—apart from doing the housework. But she would wash the dogs, too. She really wouldn't ask you to do anything that she wouldn't do. She was always very fair, that way."

Longtime cook Katie Sartin also provided some relief with the housework. "She was coming once or twice a week. She used to do all the silver, and Doris's bathroom." There was also a Mexican man named Jesus who helped with work in the house and the yard. "His back was always bad," Smith recalled, "but Doris loved him." "He was a touch un-reliable, to say the least," added Andrew, who recalled often discovering him lying down in the laundry room.

"Doris loved to sweep the yard, and to putter—watering the plants," continued Smith. "She didn't sit and do nothing. But then, she spent an awful lot of time by herself—in the bedroom as well. Hardly any friends came by: Raq [Rael] every now and then. . . . Ronnie Cowan." Another regular visitor was Day's longtime costumer and friend Connie Edney. She made costumes for the dogs, and Comden photographed them, quaintly attired, as part of a larger project—a calendar or a book—that never materialized. Andrew remembered Muffy, for one, being dressed up as an angel.

✳   ✳   ✳

As the pet food business continued to unravel, Day and Comden did their best to distract themselves with trips to Carmel, where they had decid-ed they wanted to live. Once, while they were in Carmel, another British fan club officer, Sydney Wood, accepted Smith's open-ended invitation to come to Beverly Hills for a vacation. "I came out for three weeks, and stayed with Sheila and Valerie," recalled Wood. "I didn't drive, so I stayed around the house the whole time I was there, playing with the dogs in the yard and messing around in the garden." Having grown up in an old farm-house in the English countryside, Wood had learned how to be useful with his hands, and, as a matter of course, he applied his skills to items in need of repair anywhere he went. "I remember there were gas lamps around the pool, which I dismantled and cleaned, and I fixed some swings."

With his shy young son, Daniel, in tow, Comden took Wood shopping to get equipment to fix the swings. At Smith and Andrew's instigation, Day asked Wood if he, too, might like to work for her. This was suggested dur-ing Wood's last night in the States, when Day and Comden took him for a farewell dinner at Hamburger Hamlet. "I said my dad was still alive and that I would never leave him," Wood recalled.

After the death of Wood's father two years later, he moved to Cali-fornia to work for Day. By then, the dogs were taking up more and more of Smith's and Andrew's time, and they needed the extra set of hands. "It was totally against the law to have more than three dogs in the house, and part of our job was to keep moving them around," recalled Andrew. In addition to the backyard, there were enclosed areas on either side of the house. Smith and Andrew had to make sure there were never more than three dogs in any of the three outdoor areas at any given time.

"The police came by a number of times," Smith remembered, "but they never knew how many dogs were there—or acted like they didn't know." "They loved Doris," Andrew explained. Day was compelled to pay a $35 fine the following spring, when her neighbor Evelyn Johnstone filed a complaint. Evidence consisted of a photo Johnstone's daughter had taken of five dogs romping in Day's backyard. "Does entertainer Doris Day have more than 11 dogs living at her home on N. Crescent Drive?" began a story in the *Los Angeles Times* in the fall of 1977.

No matter how much Comden and Day devoted themselves to find-ing their dream house in Carmel, the pet food operation had opened an ever-widening chasm between them. Always relying on others to look after her financial affairs, Day left the business end of the venture en-tirely up to Comden, who came to feel it would be much easier for her to blame him when it all—inevitably—fell apart.

Though the pet food scheme remained a nightmare for Day, her dream of an organization that would look after the needs of animals became a reality with the formation of the Doris Day Pet Foundation in the beginning of 1978. Its principal goal was "to assist humane organizations by providing funds where they are most needed for the welfare of animals." A secondary ambition was to recruit pet caretakers by supplying pet food ("and generally helping with other expenses") to people who otherwise were in no position to care for animals on their own.

"She had this kennel in Canoga Park because she couldn't keep all of the rescued dogs at the house. I was on the phone all the time," recalled Andrew. "And that's how it started. It was rather small at first, run from the home, without any office or anything. But it was extremely time-consuming. There were days when I was constantly on the phone dealing with pet foundation things, and didn't have time for anything else."

"I really stopped doing the fan mail for Doris a few months after I came, because of everything else," Smith added. "We used to get our evenings off, but sometimes there were urgent calls to rescue animals and strays under cars, and then we'd stay up with them all night so they wouldn't bark. We could literally spend hours trying to coax dogs from under cars." Abandoned dogs were routinely placed through the house's front gate. "Many a morning, there were fresh strays in the yard to be cared for."

One of these dog rescues involved the police. "We learned of this sweet lady, Wanda, who had a retarded son, a man-friend who was an ex-Vietnam vet, and three dogs," recalled Andrew. "They lived in a skid-row hotel, and Doris wanted to take care of the dogs. One night, we went to get the dogs. Sheila had let me out of the car at the corner. There had been an incident in the lobby, and there was a man in the elevator covered in blood. I went to see Wanda in her very tiny little room, and she didn't want to let the dogs go. She maintained that the dogs had saved her life, when some hovel she was living in had caught fire. And two of the dogs had gotten burned." When Andrew returned to the street, there was no sign of Smith or the car. "She was afraid to park the car, so she kept driving around and around, and the police stopped her, wondering if she were a hooker."

Smith recalled a bizarre night on Crescent while Day and Comden were in Carmel. "We were looking after the house and the dogs. We had been out to dinner, and we came home. There was a taxi outside the house, but we didn't take much notice. We opened the electronic gate and drove the car in. And the next moment, this man ran in, with a suitcase. He could barely speak English. But he had a letter from you-know-who. She had said, 'If you're ever in town, please stop by.' And he did. He was from Montreal, and he said he had come to stay."

"We took him down to Beverly Hills, and we put him on a bus and told the bus driver to take him to the YMCA," said Andrew. "He came back the next day, and we spoke to him through the gate, saying, 'She isn't here. She's out of town,'" resumed Smith, who, along with Andrew, used to type Day's letters. "She would dictate letters to fans on tape. They would go on and on. Pages of it. And it was always the same thing at the end: 'If ever you're in town, come by the house, and we'll go to breakfast.' I remember thinking to myself, 'Oh, Doris. I wish you wouldn't say that.' Because of course, they took her literally, so they all used to come. It seemed like every day people would show up at the gates, armed with photos and records, and we'd take them in for her to sign. Sometimes, they would wait forever, and we'd take water to them, because it was so hot. And they'd just be standing there until she came out."

Since their excursions to Carmel had become increasingly frequent, the Comdens bought a van for the journey. On the eve of taking it there for the first time, they tested out their new "home away from home" by taking Smith and Andrew with them. They pulled up alongside a small park in Coldwater Canyon and had pizza and wine for dinner in the van, as part of its trial run.

Smith emphasized how charming Comden could be. "Barry was always eager to please. But being married to a star is pure hell. At restaurants, everyone would make such a fuss over her and give her all the attention. I remember Barry saying once, 'What about the peasants?'" Smith and Andrew also recalled going with Day and Comden and his mother and sister to a Lebanese restaurant in Westwood—a family-run "hole in the wall"—that Day frequented. "When they first took us there we loved it," said Andrew. "But I think Barry's mother and his sister were surprised because they were expecting a more upscale Beverly Hills restaurant." Day "also liked an even 'funkier' place—her very word for it—called Harry's Open Pit, where they had barbecued ribs, and you washed your hands in an old bathtub," added Smith.

*   *   *

Day and Comden made twenty or so trips to Carmel before they found the perfect setting for their new home there. It was a ten-acre hilltop expanse—a paradise on top of a hill—offering spectacular vistas of Carmel Valley. The property was situated directly above the recently opened Quail Lodge and overlooked the eighteenth hole of the resort's golf course. They discovered the site fortuitously, after having dinner at the lodge's restaurant with their new friends Gwen May, the head of the local chapter of the Society for the Prevention of Cruelty to Animals, and her husband, Jim, a real estate agent. When Jim May asked Day to describe the ideal location for her new residence, she replied, "Right up there," as she gestured beyond the restaurant window. He explained that the land belonged to a woman whose late father, a farmer, once owned much of Carmel Valley, adding that she had no interest in selling. But then, some months later, May phoned Day to report that the property was available after all, and could be hers for $300,000.

Hotchner, who visited Day there several years later, gushed over its natural splendors. "The imposing hills and streams and little roads of Carmel Valley are wrapped all around it, stretching to infinity in every direction," he wrote. "Off in the distance, approximately three miles away, is the ocean." The existing estate included a house perched up on a cliff, much of which Day and Comden tore down in the course of putting up their own complex of buildings. In keeping with a promise made to the owner, Day retained a portion of the original house, which became the entrance to the main building and the master kitchen. In addition to a guesthouse and yet another house for the dogs—with its own kitchen—Day built a spectacular, glass-encased bedroom cottage with a cathedral ceiling.

But Day's marriage to Comden ended long before construction on her dream house was finished. Items about the couple's deteriorating relationship began to appear in print by the spring of 1979. "Rumor of the week! Doris Day and her husband, Barry Comden, will be splitting shortly," announced the *Los Angeles Free Press* in mid-April. The couple separated in August of that year.

Wood, who by this time had moved into Crescent Drive, remembered that Comden returned to the house late at night, despite the crumbling marriage. "Even though Barry had been kicked out of the house, he would still come and spend the night," he recalled. "Doris told us that she had said 'goodbye' to him and that it was the end, but he would sneak back in—and this went on for some time. He'd arrive late, when none of us saw him, and then she'd kick him out again around 5 o'clock in the morning, before we were up. Valerie would say, 'His shaving gear and his toothbrush are wet.' The domestics always know what's really going on."

Over dinner at Hamburger Hamlet, Day would divulge to Paul Brogan at least one reason she continued to see Comden after they supposedly broke up. Having met a good number of Brogan's potential boyfriends, Day was discussing his problems maintaining a relationship and asked him what he looked for in a man. After Brogan's litany of positive qualities, it was Day—sipping her third Dewars' on the rocks—who said: "Don't you also think he should be well-hung? You know, Barry was, and it made up for a lot of other deficiencies."

Though Day's separation from Comden had become public knowledge, the couple spent the better part of a year trying to reconcile their differences. But to all evidence, Day was deeply ambivalent about Comden and may have been tolerating him because, with Terry abroad in London, she needed someone to look after her increasingly complex financial matters. In addition to supervising the construction in Carmel, ongoing court battles with Rosenthal suddenly required renewed attention.

"Miss Day never got her $23 million and she won't," Myrna Oliver reported in the *Los Angeles Times* on October 26, 1979. "In this case, Rosenthal's liability insurer settled with Miss Day for about $6 million payable in 23 annual installments, rather than drag the case out on appeal."(Comden proudly claimed to have negotiated the deal with the insurance company himself.) "Rosenthal, however, continues to dispute the ruling, and he has charged that his insurance company settled with Miss Day behind his back," Oliver added. "Thus his appeal continues in the 2nd District Court of Appeal. Meanwhile, he has filed another half-dozen suits related to the case. Two are libel suits, one against Miss Day and her publishers over comments she made about Rosenthal in her book . . . and another against writer John Updike and New Yorker magazine over a review of the book. The suits seek about $20 million in damages." Oliver predicted that, given the court's heavy backlog of cases, it would be at least three years before Rosenthal's case would come to trial.

By slow degrees, Comden managed to become more of a presence in Day's life again. At the beginning of 1980, columnists reported that the couple were back together. Their clandestine late-night meetings the previous fall had evolved into public sightings by spring, as written about in the *Hollywood Reporter* on February 4: "Am tipped that Doris Day & hubby Barry Comden reconciled, good news to their many friends."

However, by this time, Comden seemed to have developed what Day remembered as a "fortress mentality." One day in April, when Brogan was driving in Beverly Hills, he caught sight of Day and Comden riding their bicycles. Day, who was somewhat ahead of Comden, stopped for Brogan as he pulled over and rolled down the window. "How wonderful to see you," she greeted him. But then, as soon as Comden caught up with his wife, he scolded her for stopping, according to Brogan, and urged her to press on.

Given their on-again, off-again relationship, there were at least several "final straws" that marked its prolonged conclusion. In more recent years, Comden threatened to sue Rex Reed for reporting on the *E! Entertainment Network* that, "out of jealousy," Comden deliberately "poured scalding coffee all over" Day's close friend, Raq Rael, severely burning her arm. "She sued him, and won," added Reed.

Despite her personal problems in the spring of 1980, Day's legacy as a film star was shaping up in ways no one might have imagined at the beginning of her career. There were even signs of her becoming a feminist icon. The British Film Institute was one of the first organizations to take Day seriously as an artist by presenting a festival of her films that spring. "BFI staffer Jane Clarke [is] credited with originating the idea for a retro and for pursuing it despite what she says was a lot of 'prejudice within the local film culture' for whom, apparently, Day and her films are too camp for serious revival purposes," *Variety* reported on April 12. Clarke's "treatise" for the festival, written with Diana Simmonds and Mandy Merck, emphasized that Day was "particularly relevant today in prefiguring a less repressive, more equal sexuality. Day frequently plays an independent-working woman who confronts the male and forces him to modify his attitudes and behavior. Moreover, saying 'No' to manipulative sexual situations . . . is not the same as clinging to one's virginity."

*   *   *

With their relationship again increasingly shaky, Day and Comden still continued to oversee the preliminary work on her Carmel estate. They lived in the van during their trips north, and Day regularly took a number of dogs with her for consolation during an otherwise miserable period. "Barry was always staging fights so that he could leave me in the van and go out to a bar," Day later told Wood. Frequently left alone on what was still a construction site—set off from the road by only a chain-link fence—Day was understandably nervous about being stranded and isolated on the property at night.

Smith and Andrew recalled flying up to Carmel one day to inspect the property. They joined the Comdens for breakfast in the restaurant at the Pebble Beach clubhouse, where *Julie* had been shot. "We visited the property and all we could see were the bare outlines of the home and of the gatehouse, where our home would be," Andrew said.

Comden could be alternately penny-pinching and generous with the staffers. Wood recalled going with him to buy a lawn mower, and Comden balked when Wood suggested a motorized one. "He wanted to buy me one you would push, which would have taken all day," Wood said. But Comden gave Wood castoff boots, pants, and sweaters. He also fought for bonuses for Smith and Andrew. More than Day, he seemed to look out for their welfare.

By the spring of 1980, Day's core staff began to break up when Andrew received an urgent call from England notifying her that her father had fallen seriously ill. Andrew rushed home to England in March, and her plans to return to Crescent later were foiled. For some months, Meg Howard, a contributor to gossip queen Rona Barrett's entertainment magazine, had been coming by early in the morning and at the end of the day after work to walk the dogs. She also ran errands for Day.

"Meg Howard was gradually more and more a part of the picture," Smith recalled. "Then, one day [probably in May], I went up to the house and Meg informed me that she was going to be working there in place of Valerie. And that shook me, because Doris hadn't mentioned a word about it." After Smith confronted Day, who confirmed that Howard would be coming to work full time, Smith refused to work with Howard. "I didn't move out of the guesthouse right away, though," continued Smith. "In fact, Doris never asked me to leave, which was really funny, because I wasn't doing any work anymore, either."

A couple of weeks later, Smith moved in with a friend in Santa Monica—taking nine cats with her. Over breakfast one day, Terry, who had returned to Beverly Hills from London in the winter of 1980, told her that his mother wanted her to come back. "I'm sorry, but I really can't work with Meg," Smith recalled telling Terry. "Besides, it's up to your mum to ask me. But she didn't have the guts to tell me about Meg, nor now to invite me back.

"I've always thought it was a shame, the way that things ended,"

Smith added, describing the same sort of trailing off, or lack of closure, that many a long-term assistant had experienced with Day.

By mid-July, the stressful revival of Day and Comden's marriage was collapsing anew, and what Day herself would later call "the biggest mistake of my life" was about to come to its end. The tabloids announced that even though the couple could still be seen out together, the Comdens went their separate ways at the end of the day. "No pillow talk between Doris Day and estranged hubby Barry Comden—because after they go out on the town, Barry flatly refuses to set foot in Doris' home. He says it's because of the 12 dogs that run loose in the house. So both go home solo."

"It was only when Terry came over for a visit that Doris revealed to him that her marriage was through, and that she didn't know what to do about it," recalled Wood. Since his attempts as a record producer in England hadn't amounted to much, Terry was back managing his mother's affairs. By the winter of 1980, Terry had left London—as well as a woman to whom he was briefly married—and taken up residence at Crescent. "Once Terry moved back, Doris no longer needed Barry to help with the new house in Carmel," Wood observed. "If Terry had not come back, it's possible that she would have stayed with Barry for a bit longer, because she had no one else."

Still others felt that it was Terry who ultimately came between his mother and her fourth husband. "As far as I was concerned, Terry was afraid he wouldn't get any money if the marriage had continued," claimed Sheila Smith. "Terry felt that Barry Comden was out of his element as a businessman," added Guy Webster. "Terry himself was innately smart—brilliant, really—and a great manipulator. He understood the bullshit about show business and knew how to play it to his advantage. But not Comden. He was no businessman." Even Comden himself felt that Terry "planned my exit scene from the day Doris and I met."

Day and Comden played a final little drama at Crescent Drive one night at the end of their marriage. Day was in the kitchen, with Terry and Wood, when Meg Howard came rushing in to say she had just noticed the lights of the van through the living room windows. Comden was driving it away.

"Barry called me many times after then," recalled Smith. "He was so distressed. He didn't know who to blame, so he was blaming everybody.

He just went on and on." "He was really upset, and wanted to know if she was upset, too," added Andrew. "For years, he would still talk about it."

By the time the divorce petition was filed in Superior Court in Los Angeles in January 1981, there was little left for Day and Comden to clash over. "Comden's court papers state there is no community property to divide and because of that legal assistance in a property settlement is not necessary," reported the *Los Angeles Herald-Examiner*. What Andrew and Smith referred to as "the Comden years" were now over. To confirm their finality, Day would frame their divorce agreement and hang it on a bathroom wall in her new Carmel home, where she could be reminded of it every day.

Carmel-by-the-Sea

※

*"Her life and celebrity confused her. She didn't know
quite what to make of it all. It frightened her."*

—MARY CLEERE HARAN

The turbulence that marked the prolonged fade-out of Doris Day's last marriage gave way to the more tranquil life she had long desired. Once she made a comfortable new home for herself in Carmel, Day had less and less interest in ever leaving it. Despite Day's long-term success as a singer and film star, her life had nevertheless been filled with much adversity and unhappiness. Though her retirement years would not be entirely without hardship and tragedy, the serenity and relative isolation she found in Carmel would make them easier to endure. And while the tabloids periodically portrayed her as a recluse, Day continued, though sporadically, to entertain old friends while making new ones in Carmel. She even had a new cable TV series—albeit a quirky and short-lived one. And she has continued to work as a tireless crusader for her pet causes.

When Day and Barry Comden finally went their separate ways, the new buildings at the Carmel estate were still in the early stages of construction. In response to the oil shortages and long gas lines of the seventies, Comden had had the foresight to have an underground gas tank installed on the property. By the summer of 1981, the complex was finally coming together and landscapers began working on the gardens. "I flew up with Terry, and we got the property situated, putting up the beds and getting everything organized," recalled staffer Sydney Wood, who bonded with his benefactor as work on the property progressed. "Terry was great," said Wood. "He always treated me like a brother.

"When we first came to Carmel, I started giving everybody a 'Day' at the end of their name," Wood recalled. "The dogs became 'Snowy

Day' and 'Barney Day,' and Terry started calling me 'Woody Day' and I called him 'TPMD.'" (His full name was Terry Paul Melcher.) "Doris used to call me 'Woody' because she heard Terry call me that. And I used to call her 'Janie Osgood' because to me, she really is that character from *It Happened to Jane*. She left no stone unturned—she wanted to get to the bottom of everything: that was Doris. It might take her a while, but she'd always come back to it. I'd send birthday cards to 'Janie O.,' and she just loved it."

As work continued on the four other buildings in the complex, Day stayed in the guest cottage, the first dwelling to be completed. Wood lived in the gatehouse, which would become his home. Day's private house, set away from the main house, was spectacular. Encased in glass, through which she could see the magnificent views of the Carmel Valley, her enormous bedroom had her bed at one end set on a two-step, fourteen-inch platform of light coffee-colored stone, decorated with pillars and curtains. Behind the bed were two bathrooms and dressing rooms. (What would have been Comden's bathroom became the cats' habitat.) Up a set of stairs was an exercise room equipped with a treadmill and a stretching machine, geared to help Day with her chronic back problems. The other side of the bedroom complex featured a huge fireplace as well as a spiral staircase—the very one that had been used as a background for the opening credits of her TV show. Here it led to a reading room.

A long, glass-enclosed walkway connected the bedroom to the main house, which featured two guest bedrooms upstairs. Day would take her meals and entertain in the main house. In addition to a compound for the dogs, the property had a swimming pool. "It was in the front yard, outside her bathroom window, overlooking the golf course," said Wood. "She used to go in quite regularly. The whirlpool jets were so forcible that you could swim against the current in place." A four-foot adobe wall at the edge of Day's estate prevented the golfers at Quail Lodge from seeing into her yard. Nevertheless, she commanded a nice view of the golf course below. "The funny thing about her property, if you'd go around the back area, because of the wind through the valley from the ocean, it could be very cold," Wood recalled. "But if you'd go around to the front of her bedroom, looking down to the valley, south, it was hot as could be."

Day and company moved to Carmel in November 1981. "When they came up, it was with five different cars, with four or five dogs in each car," recalled Wood. "It was like a big caravan of the Day household." After she moved in, Day wrote Rex Reed describing the "Barnum and Bailey" troupe's arrival in Carmel—"safe and sound, tired but happy." She was, she added, "wading" through boxes. The note was signed "Clara and the critters."

Carmel immediately became Day's fortress, her refuge from the world—and from her past. "Whenever she entered the property and those huge gates closed behind her, she was in her own world," said Wood. "She could do exactly as she pleased. She had the love of the dogs and cats, and all the plants and flowers, which she adored. And she didn't have to get dressed up."

* * *

As Terry was getting his mother settled in Carmel, he was also pursuing Jacqueline Carlin, an attractive, ethereal woman on whom he had first laid eyes at his friend Guy Webster's wedding in September 1980. "There were maybe a hundred people," recalled Webster, "including Terry and Jacqueline. She was very beautiful and at that point very svelte. She looked a little bit like Doris and he had an immediate attraction to her, circling her at the party like a shark and asking me about her." Carlin was a good friend of Webster's and his wife, Leone. A model, Carlin had recently divorced comedian Chevy Chase.

But Terry didn't meet Carlin officially until some months after the wedding. "I met Terry at Guy and Leone's house in Ojai, California," she recalled. "They frequently invited a lot of Hollywood types, who I was trying to stay away from at the time. They said, 'Just come up for the weekend,' and they promised they wouldn't have anybody else there. So I drove up. It's about an hour and a half from L.A. Then Terry came, just for the day. He played tennis and we talked about our Morgans—an antique car, like an MG. He had a Morgan when he was in London, and I got mine in Paris."

"He drove all the way down from Carmel to hang out with us when he found out that Jackie was going to be a houseguest," Webster recalled. He and his wife then arranged another meeting between Terry and Jacqueline in New York. The four met for dinner at Gino's, a popular Italian restaurant on New York's East Side, famous for its wallpaper of zebras cavorting on a red background. "We invited Terry and Jacqueline," Webster remembered, "not to set them up, but just because we all happened to be in town at the same time. We noticed Terry's absolute interest in

Jacqueline, and when it came time to go, he said he wanted to take her home. And he did. And that was the beginning of their relationship."

"Terry started calling me back in Los Angeles, and he would come by on Sundays for breakfast," recalled Carlin. "That's how we got to know each other, over a period of six months—he would visit on Sundays. He was living at the time in the guesthouse, behind the big house on Crescent Drive. He was getting the house ready for it to be rented."

(Day hung on to the 4,300-square-foot house on Crescent Drive, turning it into a lucrative celebrity rental property. A constant stream of stars, industry executives, consul officials—even O. J. Simpson defense lawyer Robert Shapiro—rented it over the years, until it was finally put up for sale in 2006: the asking price, $5.25 million.)

What most appealed to Carlin about Terry was that he was direct and down to earth. "We never talked about dating, or anything like that. I was still stunned from the Hollywood life I had had with Chevy [Chase]. And Terry seemed so levelheaded and intelligent and straight and on point as to what he said. He never beat around the bush. He just said, 'Oh, that's what happens in Hollywood.' We didn't really date at the time. But I liked him," she added, explaining how they had become friends before they were lovers.

Jacqueline and Terry took their first trip together to Hawaii. "He surprised me when we were there, and he said, 'Let's get married.' I said, 'What! . . . I want you to tell me everything about your whole life, first, and I want to tell you everything.' And that went on for hours. I remember that we went up the top of a mountain, to a little church. I think it was on the Big Island [Hawaii]. It was very sweet." Jacqueline claimed later that "We always joked about how we didn't know when we got married. I always thought he really did know, but that it was just Terry's way of trying to be as cool about the whole thing as me." By May 1983, when their son, Ryan, was born, the newlyweds were living on Woodrow Wilson Drive in Los Angeles.

*　*　*

Once she felt comfortably situated in her new home, Day consented to giving interviews again, apparently in a low-key effort to maintain her stardom. A. E. Hotchner visited Carmel for what became a cover story in *Ladies' Home Journal* (June 1982). In contrast to what the tabloids had been describing as a "bitter recluse" and a "ragged and disgusting old lady," he found the sixty-year-old Day "as healthy and radiant and beautiful and chic as when last I had seen her. And, incredibly, looking not a day older."

On May 23, 1983, just two days after her grandson, Ryan, was born, Day began a weeklong appearance on ABC's *Good Morning America* with host David Hartman, which served as a retrospective of sorts of her long career in music and movies. "Long hesitant about invasions of her private life and thoughts, Doris Day agreed to the 'GMA' inspection strictly because of Hartman, a former teammate (1968's *The Ballad of Josie*) and trusted friend ('I feel safe with David')," wrote Robert Osborne in an advance story on the show for the *Hollywood Reporter.* "The new, rare look at one of Hollywood's classiest representatives begins airing next Monday when Rock Hudson joins the conversation, then continues all week with input from such other Day costars as Jack Lemmon, Gordon MacRae, John Raitt and Tony Randall, plus former band boss Les Brown and son Terry Melcher."

In addition to the shared recollections of costars and colleagues, the segments featured clips from Day's films and recordings of her songs. "I may work again," Day told Hartman, before emphasizing, "I probably *will* work again. . . . I might do TV, I might do a movie. . . . I'm getting homesick for everybody, the people, the crews, all the people I worked with. I miss them so much." While acknowledging that she remained in touch with many of her colleagues via letters, Day added, "but it's not the same as seeing them." In her interview with Osborne, Day told him that anything she would shoot next would have to be made in Carmel.

Day was indeed sought for many film and TV projects over the next two decades. In 1984, television producer Jimmy Hawkins proposed a sequel to *Pillow Talk* and even recruited Delbert Mann to direct. (Mann had directed Day and Hudson in *Lover Come Back.*) Together with writer Bruce Kane, they hatched a convoluted plot set two decades after the original *Pillow Talk.* Jan (Day) and Brad (Hudson) have gotten a divorce, and Jonathan (Tony Randall) once again hopes that Jan will marry him. But Jan schemes to win Brad back, and Brad concocts a scam of his own. He pretends to have amnesia and his doctor compels Jan to take him to various places that might revive his memory.

"This is terrific," Hudson told Hawkins that spring. "People have pitched so many ideas for us over the past twenty-five years, but this is a wonderful project. Let's get Doris involved right away." A tape describing the plot was sent to Day, who was enthusiastic and wanted to proceed.

Changes were made according to Day's wishes, and Hawkins even secured the approval of an executive at Universal.

Tantalizing as it might have been to imagine the mature Day and Hudson in such a picture, it's not surprising that the retired actress never followed through on plans to actually make the film. By 1984, Day had entertained numerous offers and seemed amenable to a good many of them, only to withdraw at the last minute. In fact, in September, CBS announced that Day would receive $300,000 to star in the pilot of a new show, and then $100,000 per episode if the show became a series. It was called *Murder, She Wrote*.

"CBS had that show earmarked at the time for Jean Stapleton," recalled Ron Stephenson, who was the director of television casting at Universal. "She had the offer on the table after *All in the Family* went off the air. When she turned it down, we had a list of about six viable actresses. Doris Day was at the top, then Loretta Young, June Allyson, and then Angela Lansbury." It was Lansbury, of course, who ultimately took on the role of Jessica Fletcher, and had great success with it. (*Murder, She Wrote* ran for a dozen years.) According to Lansbury, Fletcher was conceived of as a "ditzy" character, and she had to gradually work on the show's producers to make her less addled.

Stephenson had first met Day a few years earlier at Nate 'n Al, one of her preferred restaurants in Beverly Hills, when he and a friend were seated at an adjacent table. Day was there with two young women. "She had a voracious appetite," recalled Stephenson. "I sat and watched her consume maybe six bagels and rye bread and butter. When there was a lull in their conversation, I said something like, 'I'd just like to say hello to you, and what a great fan I am of yours, and all the wonderful things you do for animals.' That was all I had to say, and we were there for four hours. And that was when we began talking about much more than her career. To be honest, I think she was bored talking about her career.

"She was making a disciple for Actors and Others for Animals," explained Stephenson, who went on to "work a booth for her" at fundraising events. "She was incredibly loved by people. And when I met her, I knew why. When I was talking to her, I just generally got the feeling that this woman was a wonderful person. She was 'out there'—it was all there for you to see."

In 1984, Stephenson offered Day the role of Jessica Fletcher in *Murder, She Wrote*. "But I must say, nobody thought she would accept the offer, anyway. Everyone knew her reputation for not wanting to work. I think she actually had considered it, if they had been willing to film the show in Carmel. But of course, they would never have done that."

If one of the things holding Day back was insecurity about her age and appearance, she decided to remedy that with a new facelift in the fall of 1984. Terry took his mother to San Francisco for a consultation with a plastic surgeon. When Sydney Wood learned that she was going ahead with the work, he was genuinely concerned and asked, "You're not going to risk losing your smile, are you?" Having already had successful work on her face a decade earlier, Day replied with great confidence, "Oh, no. It'll be fine."

"They lifted the forehead, around the neck, and under the chin," recalled Wood. "There was lots of scarring." A nurse came home with Day to help her recuperate. "Doris was all very bruised, of course. But within a couple of days, she was cooking breakfast for the nurse," Wood remembered. "I took the nurse to church on Sundays. She was there for a couple of weeks, just standing around, waiting for something to happen. But Doris was going about her daily business, so she finally left." Day was terribly annoyed, because the surgeons had failed to remove a black mole from her lower right lip, as planned. "She would always cover it up with make-up and lipstick," Wood recalled.

* * *

At one point, Day entered into negotiations to join the cast of *Dallas*—to raise still more money for her animal advocacy. But then she decided instead to go along with Terry's plan for a small new TV show called *Doris Day's Best Friends*. It came about after the Christian Broadcasting Network (CBN)—a cable network that combined new programs with reruns of old sitcoms—approached Terry with the idea. As co-executive producer, Terry knew that concessions would have to be made for his mother: not only would the show have to be shot in Carmel, but there would have to be a focus on animals. The program was, in fact, created as a vehicle to educate the public about pet care and was sponsored by Kal Kan dog food. In addition to her guest visitors—past colleagues and familiar faces—the segments featured veterinarian Tom Kendall discussing such topics as health insurance for pets, the importance of ID tags, and the hazards of generic dog foods. There was also an emphasis on the need to neuter pets.

As Day would say in an interview for *USA Weekend* to promote the show, "If I were on a big ego kick and wanted to start a whole big thing with me again, I certainly wouldn't be doing this kind of show. I'd be doing a network series, which has been offered. But that is not what my goal is.

"I love people and animals—though not necessarily in that order," Day also told Stu Schreiberg for the article. "I've never met an animal I didn't like and I can't say the same thing about people." Indeed, by this time Day was caring for forty-eight dogs, "at the high point," said Wood, and "over a period of time, all of them were sick, or had something wrong with them. There was once a tramp walking along the road with a dog, and she gave him a check. She said, 'Go to Safeway. They know me there and will cash the check.' If she was at the supermarket and noticed dogs in the back of a car in a parking lot, no matter who it was, she would go and reprimand them. We would tell her, 'Just get the [license] number. Because you don't know who you're dealing with.' I think it's because the animals were more important to her than herself, that she'd always take risks."

The Christian Broadcasting Network hired publicist Linda Dozoretz to work on promoting *Best Friends*. Both Terry and his mother liked the straight-talking Dozoretz so much that they hired her to become Day's personal publicist, working primarily on promoting Day's animal foundation to the present day.

One of Dozoretz's first assignments was to put together a news conference at the Pebble Beach Country Club to drum up interest in the first installment of *Best Friends*. Though scheduled to tout a low-scale cable TV show, the event would have unexpected social repercussions of monumental proportions. Day reached out to Rock Hudson to be her first guest—the first "best friend" on her new show—and he agreed not only to appear, but also to help promote the show by attending the news conference. The anticipated reunion of America's real-life Barbie and Ken was major entertainment news, prompting two dozen reporters to come to the sleepy little Monterey community on July 15, 1985, to cover it. "Not since the hey-day press days/daze of Liz & Dick has there . . . been quite the noisy, and genuine, journalistic fuss over a Hollywood superstar as what happened in Carmel on Monday," Robert Osborne reported two days later in his column for the *Hollywood Reporter*. The press reps were already assembled when a beaming Day arrived at 4 p.m. Hudson was late, however, and Day began making excuses for him to the increasingly testy reporters, some of whom left before his arrival.

Those who remained were aghast at the sight of Hudson when he finally appeared more than an hour later. Instead of the gorgeous hunk who had been Day's three-time costar, the emaciated man who now made his way to her side was cadaverous and gaunt, his cheeks hollow, with sunken eyes and a gray pallor. He looked far older than his fifty-nine years. He shuffled unsteadily on his feet and appeared exhausted, even dazed, as he tried to banter with his old friend. Since Hudson had already looked somewhat haggard and listless on the popular prime time soap opera *Dynasty*, rumors about his health had started buzzing throughout Hollywood earlier in the year. Was he dying of cancer? Aware he was gay, industry insiders had even been whispering that he had AIDS, which, in 1985, was still a mysterious and controversial ailment, as well as highly politicized. For the reporters who had trooped off to Carmel to see what shape Hudson was in, the verdict was stunning.

"At the time he agreed to make the appearance, Rock was in the very final stages of AIDS," wrote his co-biographers, Jerry Oppenheimer and Jack Vitek. "He had lost so much weight that he had to purchase a new wardrobe—his waist size had dropped about six inches. He had no energy or strength left and spent long hours napping. He was sweating profusely and suffered constantly from nausea and diarrhea. His mind rambled and often his words were slurred, his statements incoherent." Given his grave condition, Hudson's consenting to the news conference— no less than to doing the show—was a powerful testament to the depth of his fondness for Day.

With wan results, Day and Hudson did what little they could to re-capture some of their fun and magic from two decades earlier, when they ruled the box office together and laughingly called each other "Eunice" and "Ernie" on the sets of their romantic comedies. Day did her best to maintain a smile as they stood before the media, trying to put a happy spin on the grim affair. Beneath it all, she was deeply concerned about one of her truly "best friends." Their love remained as intact and palpable as ever. They hugged, kissed, and tenderly nuzzled each other. But the news conference only ratcheted the rumors and frenzy about Hudson's condition to a fever pitch. That night in Carmel, he finally admitted to his friend and publicist Dale Olson that he indeed had AIDS.

Hudson managed to participate in the taping of the show over the next two days. But given the severity of his condition, the shoot was always stop and go. "In truth, it wasn't *Pillow Talk* they were reprising, but *Send*

Me No Flowers, this time for real, with no last-minute reprieve," critic James Wolcott observed, looking back at the episode fifteen years later. "History had repeated itself, the first time as farce, the second as tragedy."

Day invited Hudson to remain with her in Carmel, where she hoped to nurse him back to health. He went to Paris instead, in pursuit of new and promising AIDS treatments. Though neither Day nor Hudson knew it at the time, their appearance together at the news conference was the beginning of his final decline that would generate first controversy and then public sympathy for people with AIDS, even as the epidemic was still careening out of control. The physical plight of the once devastatingly handsome movie star served to prompt some understanding for others afflicted with the virus, who until then had been reviled by many as victims of their own behavior. Once he was ensconced in France, Hudson courageously made an official announcement that he was suffering from AIDS. He died two months later, back in California, on October 2, 1985. Olson subsequently referred to him as "the hero of AIDS awareness."

Though originally intended as the first episode of *Doris Day's Best Friends*, the segment with Hudson was broadcast by CBN eleven days after his death. In a special introduction to the program, Day paid heartfelt tribute to her erstwhile costar. "All his friends, and there were so many, could always count on Rock Hudson," said a lachrymose Day. "His favorite thing was comedy, and he always said to me, 'The best time I've ever had was making comedies with you.' And I really felt the same way. We had a ball." Even while acknowledging Hudson's death, Day mustered her more familiar optimism. "I feel that without my deep faith, I would be a lot sadder than I am today. I know that life is eternal, and that something good is going to come from this experience." Following this touching prelude came the episode they had shot in July.

What had been the show's silly premise became positively surreal, given the interim developments and Hudson's death. It begins with Day phoning Hudson to invite him to be on the show. The split-screen image of them in conversation is an obvious reference to their famous scene in *Pillow Talk*. After he accepts, she tells him that they're on a "tight budget with this new show" and implores him to take the bus, instead of flying to Carmel. After he arrives at a dusty intersection, the camera proceeds to follow the costars along a garden path, as Day's version of Gus Kahn's "My Buddy" plays in the background. Despite the bizarre premise, it's a genuinely poignant moment, made all the more so by Hudson's withered appearance and the real affection between them. ("My Buddy" went on to become something of a standard at AIDS memorials.) When they ask each other to choose a favorite among the films they made together, Day picks *Pillow Talk* while Hudson pauses before citing *Ice Station Zebra*—in which Day did not appear.

Though she quickly suggests that he is pulling her leg, apparently Hudson's mind had slipped. He was simply too ill to muster any strength—physical or mental—for more than minutes at a time. The segment ends with photos of the two of them at their prime, accompanied by an encore of "My Buddy."

In the end, Day was right. Some good did come from Hudson's startling death. AIDS now had a famous face, which helped erode the hypocrisy and prejudice against its earliest casualties. Hollywood, which had, in effect, created him, began to respond to the epidemic with increased awareness. Elizabeth Taylor, another good friend of Hudson's, became especially active, raising millions to fight AIDS through benefits and galas. Though Day never became involved with activism around AIDS, lost in the ongoing hoopla was the quiet, publicly affectionate way she had stood by the man whom she loved, perhaps as much as anyone she had ever known.

Best Friends featured twenty-five additional episodes with celebrities and colleagues who demonstrated their affection for Day by making the trek to Carmel for what amounted to frivolous chatter on a small cable network show. They included Les Brown, Robbie Benson, Denver Pyle, Earl Holliman, Joan Fontaine, Cleveland Amory, Gretchen Wyler, Howard Keel, Kaye Ballard, Angie Dickinson, Tony Randall, Robert Wagner, Jill St. John, Tony Bennett, Leslie Nielsen, and astronaut Alan Shepard. Each episode opened with aerial shots of the gorgeous Carmel coastline, as Day sang the banal theme music written by Terry.

* * *

According to Jacqueline Melcher, Terry reveled in having a son and they had an idyllic family life when Ryan was growing up. "Terry was so enamored of Ryan, he couldn't put him down," said Jacqueline. "We'd take turns reading him stories every night until he was about eight years old. Our family life was having other families with their kids come over after baseball or soccer games, and going to church on Sunday. We were all just one big happy family, including my parents and Doris."

During their early years together, whenever Terry and Jacqueline visited Ryan's grandmother they stayed in the guest cottage. In time, they found their own place in Carmel, only three or four miles down the road from Day. They were usually to be found at one of their various homes in Los Angeles or Martha's Vineyard. "It was so great to meet sophisticated people that lived in my neck of the woods," recalled photographer Peter Simon. Brother to Carly and son of Robert Simon—of Simon & Schuster publishing—Peter Simon is also a longtime resident of Martha's Vineyard. "Through a series of summer parties and cocktail parties, Terry and Jacqueline had developed a very close coterie of friends on the Vineyard. They used to stage these wonderful croquet events and were definitely a social focus of really fun times. They were also the first Hollywood people to really wind up here, and they imported all the Hollywood types. I would play a lot of tennis with Terry in the summertime. And Jacqueline was always extremely generous, opening up her beach to so many people."

With bills outpacing his income in the mid-1980s, Terry proposed to his mother that they buy the Cypress Inn in the center of downtown Carmel—a fifteen-minute drive from her home. He shrewdly suggested they turn the quaint Spanish mission–style property into a pet-friendly hotel, inducing his mother to go along with his proposal. Originally opened as La Ribera in July 1929, the inn has a lovely courtyard and a large front room with a welcoming fire burning year-round. Renamed Cypress West and, finally, the Cypress Inn, it became a landmark in Carmel's 1978 Historic Resources Inventory. Under Day's influence, Carmel would evolve into one of the most pet-friendly spots in the country. Street corners in the middle of the village offer "Pet Pick-Ups," or plastic bag mitts, to help keep the sidewalks clean. "The Responsible Thing to Do" is printed on them, along with illustrated instructions for their use.

For Day, both the Cypress Inn and the restaurant at the Quail Lodge functioned much as the Polo Lounge at the Beverly Hills Hotel had in earlier years. They were her places for meeting people to discuss business matters. After becoming the mayor of Carmel in 1986, Clint Eastwood declared that the local supermarket was her real "office."

"She always used to shop at Albertson's," recalled Wood. "But as she said, 'With all the cat food I buy there, you would think they'd give me a discount.'" When she finally asked for one and they refused, Day switched her allegiance to Safeway. It was at a Safeway that a timid clerk once told Day, "I have to make an announcement to let everybody know that our fresh French bread is ready, and I can't do it." Day replied, "Give me the microphone, and I'll do it for you"—and she did. "It's as if she doesn't have a care in the world," added Wood, recalling the anecdote.

In October 1985 Day finally won her seventeen-year legal battle against attorney Jerome Rosenthal, when the state Supreme Court turned down his appeal of an earlier judgment against him for malpractice. Rosenthal's appeal of that multimillion-dollar finding was essentially, as the *Los Angeles Times* reported, "an effort to clear his name, lawyers involved say." His attorney, Gerald Goldfarb, had requested that his client's name be "depublished" or erased "from official volumes of appellate court cases"—a request that was not acted upon. According to the *Times,* Day's attorney, Peter J. Gregora, claimed that the case was probably, at the time, "the oldest active case in the [state] court system." But it had come to an end at last.

* * *

In 1987, beginning with a celebration of her films, fourteen of which were shown over three consecutive weekends at the University of Southern California (February 28 through March 15), there were a number of major developments for Day. The retrospective was coordinated by professor Drew Casper, who long felt that Day and her films had not been taken seriously enough. The retrospective was almost like a birthday present for Day, arriving a month before she turned sixty-five.

"She had a fit when there were papers for her to sign for Social Security, and she wouldn't admit to being sixty-five," Wood recalled. Aware of his mother's reluctance to acknowledge her real age, Terry tried slipping in the necessary documents among other papers he gave her to sign. As Terry later told Wood, his mother discovered the Social Security forms and refused to sign them, denying herself two years worth of payments. This was the same woman who could prompt a drugstore cashier to apologize on her behalf to customers on line who had to wait while she redeemed her voluminous coupons.

"Whenever Terry came to see his mother on business and it was my day off," Wood recalled, "he would throw a pebble up at my window, and he'd say, 'What are you doing Woody?' And I'd say, 'I'm trying to sleep.' And he'd respond, 'I'm going to see Mom for an hour. Do you want to get a bite of breakfast after that?' If there was anything that they needed to talk about, Terry would take her down to the golf course, and they would walk around there and work things out." Day was still an early riser, up every day before dawn.

On June 4, 1987, Rosenthal held a "news conference" to put forth the preposterous notion that he had had Day's best interests at heart all along, and to announce that he would be filing a lawsuit against Day's attorneys. "Because of bad legal advice by over-zealous bad faith attorneys who succeeded attorney Jerome B. Rosenthal, and collected an estimated two million dollars in legal fees from Doris Day... Day and her former attorney, Jerome B. Rosenthal, became dupes and innocent victims of her subsequent attorneys," his "news alert" proclaimed. "To recover Doris Day's losses as well as his own, Rosenthal has filed a 30 million dollar lawsuit in the Los Angeles Superior Court for Breach of Fiduciary Duty, Intentional Infliction of Emotional Distress, and violations of Federal statutes, among other counts."

This was little more than a ploy to stave off the oral arguments for the state's disbarment case against Rosenthal, scheduled for June 12. But the tactic failed and Rosenthal was disbarred in July. The decision ended "an arduous, 19-year legal-ethics dispute," observed *Los Angeles Times* reporter Philip Hager. The disbarment panel had heard eighty days of testimony before accusing Rosenthal of thirteen acts of misconduct. The panel unanimously upheld the state bar's recommendation that Rosenthal be disbarred. He was seventy-six.

* * *

The first—and last—Doris Day fan convention was held in June 1987 in Carmel. Conceived and organized by Mike Doyle, president of the U.S. Doris Day fan club, and hosted by Joe Niagara, a onetime Philadelphia disc jockey who had befriended Day in 1959, the event centered around a luncheon at the Carmel Mission Inn, several miles from Day's home. "The hotel ... wasn't exactly five-star, not even close. But when Doris arrived, who cared?" wrote Howard Green in a report on the affair. "The roomful of Doris Day fans couldn't have been more excited. ... She entered the room and took our collective breaths away. ...We broke out into wild applause, and Doris signaled modestly for us to stop. But there was no stopping us." Among those applauding were Green himself, Frank Hale, Lauren Benjamin, Ray Lyons, Bruce Deal, Donald Chang, and Alan Milnes, who had come from England, where he presided over the *Friends of Doris Day* journal. Meeting each other for the first time, many of the fans formed lasting bonds.

Once the gathering of some fifty "Dayniacs" settled down, Niagara introduced two women "who have been associated with Dodo for a long time"—Connie Edney, her costumer, and Meg Howard, who helped Day "with everything at home"—and who now joined her on the dais. In her preliminary remarks, Day added that it was "a shame" Sydney Wood couldn't be there, but since it was Meg's "day off," he had to remain at home with the animals.

In December, columnists announced that Day would "play a nasty, scheming society matron" in *Dynasty* and that the producers were "prepared to match Joan Collins' salary" to win her. Earlier in the year CBS announced that *Falcon Crest* had offered her more than $1 million to join that popular series, set in northern California wine country, no less, and starring Jane Wyman. Somewhat later, Day turned down "$500,000-plus to star in a two-hour pilot" for a new series, a spin-off of *Falcon Crest*.

Day stepped up her activism on behalf of animals in 1988, when she formed her second nonprofit organization, the Doris Day Animal League, a national lobbying group headquartered in Washington, D.C. Its mandate was to cover a much wider spectrum of animal concerns than the pet foundation, as it sought to influence government policies toward animals.

* * *

Day called upon her daughter-in-law, Jacqueline, to help select a gown for the Golden Globe Awards on January 28, 1989, when she received the Cecil B. DeMille Award for Lifetime Achievement. "We went up to San Francisco to find the gown," recalled Jacqueline. "It was all creamy, and really nice." Former Carmel mayor Clint Eastwood presented the award to her at the Beverly Hilton Hotel. "I don't understand why I got this, but I love it," Day said during her acceptance speech. "This business has given me great happiness. I've worked with the cream of the crop." She also had her typical jitters about appearing in public and excused herself. "I'm a wreck," she confessed. "I don't do this anymore. I've got to come to town more often."

While his mother was being honored by the Golden Globes, Terry was up for an award himself that night, for Best Original Song—"Kokomo," performed by the Beach Boys in the Tom Cruise movie *Cocktail*. Jacqueline recalled Terry's disappointment when he failed to win. (Wood remembered that the melody of "Kokomo" had originated with John Phillips of the Mamas and the Papas, who first sang it for Terry in Wood's gatehouse apartment.) Since settling in Carmel in 1981, Day had returned to Los Angeles only one other time, when Wood drove her to a birthday celebration for Les Brown. The 1989 Golden Globe Awards actually marked Day's last time in Los Angeles.

With his then-partner, Gregory, an interior decorator, Paul Brogan visited Carmel in the spring and stayed at the Cypress Inn. Day joined the couple for breakfast and gave them a tour of the hotel. "It was shortly after she had purchased the place, and she was in the midst of redecorating," recalled Brogan. "She was very much alive and thrilled and delighted in ways that she never seemed whenever career matters were discussed." When Brogan asked Day about her possible appearance on *Dynasty*, she was utterly dismissive, saying, "Oh, that's just a rumor."

Day also entertained Dom DeLuise and his wife, Carol, one afternoon at her home, where they gathered for a meal in the courtyard patio. "We were about to have lunch, and we were talking, and laughing, and reminiscing," recalled DeLouise. "There was a garden, and there was a bowl for stray cats. We were having iced tea, and everything seemed wonderful. Then this cat came out, and Doris explained, 'About a month ago, we put a pill in the food for that cat, to sedate him, so we could take him to the vet and have him fixed.' And I looked at the cat: he didn't seem to realize that his testicles were gone forever. Then, when Doris said, 'Would you like some lunch?' I said, 'I think I'm gonna pass.'"

Meg Howard decided to stop working for Day and left Carmel in December 1989. "She adored Doris and would have done anything for her," said Sydney Wood. "But Meg's mother, who lived in Memphis, told her she was wasting her life, and that her career was going nowhere. Then, after Meg left, new people came and went, and I felt it was time for me to leave, because some of them were poisoning Doris against me. And then, I suddenly had the opportunity to move to Florida." He left early in 1990.

*　　*　　*

The first TV documentary about Day, *I Don't Even Like Apple Pie*, aired in Great Britain in March 1989. It was made by Christopher Frayling for the BBC and produced by Margaret Sharp. Day had appeared before their cameras at her Carmel home in January of that year, saying, "There's something about the animals. . . . I just can't do enough for them," as she reminisced about her life.

Two years later, the first American TV documentary, *Doris Day: A Sentimental Journey*, was made by independent producers James Arntz and Glenn DeBose, who had worked with singer Mary Cleere Haran. An elegant New York cabaret performer who builds her shows around insightful anecdotes, Haran particularly admired Day's "concentration" as a singer. "It comes from directly inside of her," Haran observed. "And her tone is so gorgeous, her pitch so perfect. She sings right in the middle of the notes. Her only embellishments have to do with when she caresses a certain lyric."

"We were fishing around for projects for a documentary, and I was such a diehard Doris Day fan, so I suggested her," continued Haran. "They were immediately excited about the idea. But through the grapevine, we expected that she wouldn't participate or be interviewed."

Haran phoned her friend and mentor, singer Margaret Whiting—"another old pro"—who knew Day and spoke to her on Haran's behalf. "After that, Terry agreed to meet with us," Haran recalled. "He was a major fan of his mother's singing, and really came alive talking about how she had put together her albums in the living room. We had this terrific rapport and he realized that we were not just interested in the campy Doris Day, that we would be bringing some substance to the project. But he still didn't know if his mother would get involved."

To entice Day they agreed to focus on what had long been the one thing she most cared about—animal rights. When they met with her the first time—in the front room of the Cypress Inn—Day was two hours late. According to Haran, "She was so rattled when she arrived. On the way over, she had found two stray dogs on the highway and had to be sure they were taken care of. That's all she talked about when we first met. She was beautiful. She wore a skirt with boots, and looked amazing. But it was obvious she didn't want to do the show. She seemed very guarded—and dutiful. And she was so real. She didn't have any movie star persona at all, or pull any rank. She was battling with doing this. I could see that her heart wasn't in it, and it was hard for her to get into the meat of a story. She had a certain diffidence. She seemed distracted, as if she wanted to be somewhere else. But she was also being a good sport about the whole thing."

Nevertheless, Day did not want to talk about her movies—at all. "She said she never watched them," Haran said, adding that when she broached the subject, Day became "very nervous" and started "crying a lot." "She had just closed the door to that part of her life and it was difficult to open it. And when she was uncomfortable, she showed it.

"Around the end of the interview," Haran continued, "when I was setting up a question about *Romance on the High Seas,* I said: 'Your first movie. . . . You became a star overnight. . . . You were number one on the hit parade. . . . You signed a seven-year contract. . . .' She just became wild-eyed. She said, 'You just don't get it, do you, Mary? It was not a dream come true. All I ever wanted is what you have right now: a baby, a husband who really loved me, a home, all the happiness that they could bring. I never got that, and that's all I really wanted.' And then she started to cry—a lot. I was nursing my baby at the time. And there was some anger and some jealousy in what she was saying. It was as if she hadn't talked about these things in years and years and years.

"I also think her life and her celebrity confused her—that she didn't know quite what to make of it all. It frightened her. To get her to talk about her life was very unsettling for her. I got this sense she had this complicated and unresolved relationship with her celebrity. She was bewildered by it. She kept herself from it. She had never embraced it. And when I realized that, it made me appreciate and admire her all the more."

When *Doris Day: A Sentimental Journey* aired on PBS in November, Andy Klein gave an accurate assessment in the *Hollywood Reporter*: "There are a few wry peculiarities here—who would have expected John Updike to be a fanatical Doris Day fan?—but mostly this is an appreciation . . . pleasant nostalgia and nothing more. . . . It makes a case for Day as both an underappreciated talent and an icon of independent womanhood during the pre-feminist 1950s. . . . A pleasant reminder for fans, the show speeds through Day's personal travails as lightly as though they had never happened."

While Day was still participating in the preservation of her legacy, not all of the attention she received in 1991 was welcome. Under the headline 'Doris Day, 67, Lives Like a Bag Lady!,' the July 23 issue of the supermarket tabloid the *Globe* ran a story on the retired star with bulletins at the top reporting: "She's absent-minded and roams the streets in a daze. . . . She wears ratty old clothes." The caption under an unflattering photo of Day claimed, "The faded star seems to live in a world of her own. Things have gotten so bad, says one friend, that she didn't even recognize her own voice singing one of her hits [in a restaurant.]" And, as another, nameless "longtime friend" ostensibly said, "I've seen her at three o'clock in the morning, rummaging through trash cans looking for food scraps to make stew for her dogs."

A furious Day demanded a retraction from the *Globe*, and when she didn't get it, she launched a $25 million suit against the publication in Los Angeles Superior Court on August 6. Day told *Variety* columnist Army Archerd, who reported on the suit, "This has to be stopped. We (in showbiz) are all being battered. We have to get together and put them out of business. People are being lied to."

"People need to know that tabloids like the *Globe* are really cheating and deceiving the public," Day said in a statement sent out by her publicist Linda Dozoretz, the day after actor Tom Selleck settled a $20 million lawsuit against the same weekly paper. "Many people, unfortunately, believe the lies these people print. I want to add my voice to those others who are suing the tabloids to reinforce the message that reckless, irresponsible journalism does a disservice to everyone—celebrity victims and innocent readers alike." The case was dropped after the *Globe* printed a retraction.

✳   ✳   ✳

"Doris Day is probably the most sought-after over-50 celebrity around today," Robert Osborne observed in the *Hollywood Reporter* in the spring of 1993, shortly after she had, in fact, turned seventy-one. "Everybody keeps trying to get her to come accept awards and/or present them, to do guest shots, make appearances, join benefits, anything she wants as long as she shows up (and contributes the mystique her name still holds). D.D. turns 99.9% of those offers down, however; she wasn't kidding when she decided to live a private life up in Carmel." But as Osborne further reported, Day agreed to participate in a fund-raiser for Crime Stoppers of Monterey County by attending an April 17 screening of "her own favorite Doris D. film"—*Calamity Jane*. Terry was the emcee for the event, and Clint Eastwood and Berry Gordy made appearances as well. They also "attended Day's reception at her Cypress Inn where everyone asked the ever young-looking Day, 'When are you going to go back to work?' Her usual answer, 'When the right script comes along.'"

In what would prove to be one of her last two public appearances, Day consented to be a guest on Vicki Lawrence's TV talk show, *Vicki*, in October 1993, talking about her pet foundations as well as her career.

That same month, she was also interviewed by Joan Lunden for a segment on *Good Morning America*. And, as reported in *Variety*, Day had earlier entertained an offer to star in three "telefilms per year as a recurring character" on ABC. Archerd announced that Day was "mad about" the idea for the series. "When will Day know if she's going ahead?" Archerd asked rhetorically in print. "'When it's written,' she said from her home in Carmel. 'When it's completely finished.'"

In 1994, a British record company released a compact disc titled *The Love Album*, which finally brought to light the eleven songs Day had recorded in rented studio spaces after losing her Columbia Records contract back in 1967. Sydney Wood had discovered the sheet music for the recording sessions in the garage at Crescent while packing everything for the move to Carmel. This led, years later, to the discovery of the master tapes in producer Don Genson's possession. To promote the album, Day had agreed to an interview with British reporter Chrissy Iley for a story in the *Sunday Times* of London. But once Iley arrived in Carmel, she found her subject less and less cooperative. "The American PR, Linda Dozoretz, called to confirm that Doris would have photo and copy approval," Iley wrote in a piece that appeared in the paper in lieu of the planned one based on an interview with Day. "I said that we didn't do that sort of thing in Britain. She [Dozoretz] said she understood and would go back to Doris's agent, who is Doris's son, Terry Melcher."

Obstacles seemingly overcome, the interview was then set for Tuesday, November 1. "We bought our plane tickets only to discover that she doesn't like Tuesdays," continued Iley. "On Wednesday, we discovered that Doris liked [photographer] Terry O'Neill less than Tuesdays." (O'Neill, actress Faye Dunaway's ex-husband, had photographed Day for an issue of *Life* magazine in 1986.) After further machinations, Iley said, "Melcher came back via Dozoretz. Would O'Neill sign away the rights to the photographs and say they would not be used anywhere without her approval? Could he be controlled? Yes, he could. The interview was back on again for Friday. But then it couldn't happen on Friday, because the make-up lady Doris has used for 40 years couldn't make it."

Though the interview was then apparently set to go ahead, in the end it never happened because Iley refused to sign the contract giving Day complete control. "It was a contract between Doris Day and Chrissy Iley, in which I was not only to give her approval over the text, but over headlines and picture captions as well," Iley wrote. "Not only was I not to be allowed to syndicate the interview, I was not allowed to tell any story resulting from the interview with Miss Day or 'conversations with Miss Day's agents or representatives.' So I was to be deprived of freedom of speech, censored. Shut up. What was the point of doing the interview?" Iley chose not to sign the contract, preserving the right to tell the story, instead, about why her interview with Day never happened.

Prodded by Terry in 1996, Day came close to making what would have been her first film in nearly thirty years, *Mother*. Filmmaker Albert Brooks met with Day at her Carmel home to discuss the movie. But given her increasing reluctance to be seen by the public, the seventy-four-year-old Day declined to play the domineering title character, and the part went to Debbie Reynolds. (Nancy Reagan had also been under consideration.)

In 1998, the Arts & Entertainment network produced *It's Magic*, the third TV documentary devoted to examining the career of Doris Day. Her personal life made news of sorts in March the following year, when the *Star* tabloid offered a story—plus one of the last public photos—of "the first man Doris . . . has been pictured kissing in years." Day's new beau was Sam Beard, a seventy-nine-year-old retired "labor negotiator" and neighbor. They were seen leaving the Rio Grill on a spring afternoon. With a doggie bag in hand, Beard reportedly escorted Day to her car and smooched with her before she drove off. "Sam was thrilled with the kiss," claimed reporter Alan Shadrake. "It even looked as if he was almost skipping across the parking lot after Doris drove away."

In April, Day met for lunch at the Quail Lodge with a group of her fans and colleagues; they included Pierre Patrick, Jackie Joseph, Bill Glynn, and Howard Green. "She looked terrific," recalled Green, who felt privileged to sit next to his idol, "years younger than her years. I couldn't contain my happiness. I turned to her and said, 'Doris, I'm so happy to be here today.' And modest gal that she is, she didn't realize that I meant, 'being with her.' She looked around the restaurant, thinking I meant being 'there,' at the restaurant, and said, 'Isn't it neat!'"

* * *

Sydney Wood received a call from Terry in the summer of 2000, inviting him to Carmel. "Doris took me to dinner," Wood recalled. "It was just like our first meeting, with lots of hugs and kisses. Then, when we were saying goodbye in the parking lot of the restaurant in Pacific Grove, she said, 'I'd love for you to come back.' And she started crying. Terry promised me the earth," continued Wood, "health insurance, good salary, my own place on the property. . . . He also said, 'You won't have to do any work. We'll get other people to do that. All you'd be doing is just taking Mom to lunch, every day.' Well, who could turn that down?"

At the time, Terry was living at Pebble Beach with his new wife, Teresa. "She had been a yoga instructor," Wood recalled. By the fall of 2001, Wood said, Terry "was going through a lot of troubles with Ryan, because his son couldn't cope with Teresa. He couldn't stand her, and because of that, Doris turned against Ryan." (Teresa Melcher doesn't comment publicly about her relationship with Terry's son or other family matters.)

Upon his return to Carmel, Wood discovered that much of the dream property was in need of repair. All the red awnings were encrusted with mold and algae from the sea air. The gas pump was corroded with rust and unusable. Moreover, shortly before his return to Carmel, Day had seriously injured her back when she tripped over a mattress in the cat room. She began going to a chiropractor for weekly treatments.

Whenever Day would arrange to meet someone for lunch, she would then regret it and complain beforehand about having to get dressed up to go out. But inevitably she would return appreciative of the lovely time she had just had, catching up with old friends. Wood recalled the afternoon some new friends, Paul and Heather McCartney, visited. "She told me to come and get her an hour into their meeting. But then she ended up spending close to five hours with them." Beyond their shared superstar status they had a mutual commitment to animals. After the meeting, Day told Kaye Ballard—who often told friends how "thrilled" she was just to be speaking to Doris Day—the same thing about her time with Paul McCartney.

After the chiropractor's ministrations failed to bring Day relief, she decided to have back surgery the following year. She was in the hospital for more than two weeks. After her release from the hospital, she continued her recuperation at a nearby nursing home with a couple of her beloved dogs. Terry was concerned about his mother's falling again on the hard stone floors of her bedroom. During her convalescence, he had the entire floor carpeted along with other renovations. When she returned home, Day found she did not like the overhaul and moved into the living room of the main house. She has made her headquarters there ever since.

Early in the fall of 2003, on one of his visits to see his mother, Terry stopped to chat with Wood, who was working by the pool. "I instantly got his voice and his smile, but I really didn't recognize Terry at first," Wood confessed. "His neck had become so wide and he had put on so much weight. He was clearly in pain. He started trembling, and I thought maybe it was because he needed a drink. I knew he was an alcoholic. Then Teresa came to get him and take him home."

While Wood failed to recognize Terry, Day failed to recognize her grandson, Ryan, when, accompanied by a friend, he approached Day in a grocery-store parking lot. Upon her return home, Day told Wood about the episode. "I had no idea what they wanted from me," she explained. "And even when one of them told me he was Ryan, I still didn't realize who he was. I thought he was just another silly fan," said Day, referring to her only grandchild. When Ryan later tried to visit his grandmother, he was barred from passing through the gate of the estate. The staff had been instructed not to let him in because they anticipated he might be serving papers connected to a long-standing divorce dispute between his mother and father and grandmother.

✳ ✳ ✳

After Ronald Reagan's death in 2004, right-wing commentator Bill O'Reilly spoke to Day about her memories of the president for the Fox News show *The O'Reilly Factor*. In addition to pointing out that Reagan was a Democrat when she met him, Day reminisced about the time Reagan was president and she learned that he and Nancy had left one of their pets behind at their ranch in Santa Barbara when they returned to the White House. "I thought that's terrible to do that. I think that's very sad for that dog," Day told O'Reilly. Day had told the same story years earlier, during an interview for *Parade* magazine. After reading the article, Reagan had called Day, telling her, "I was furious about that, and I'm calling you to tell you that [the dog] loves Santa Barbara. He loves the ranch [and] has lots of doggie friends there."

On June 23, 2004, President George W. Bush awarded Day a Presidential Medal of Freedom. "I am deeply grateful to the president and to my country," Day told the Associated Press. "But I won't fly," she added, explaining why she would not accept the award in person. In a more characteristic mode, Day added, "My first reaction was, 'For what?' . . . I'm not being coy, or looking for a laugh. I have never thought about awards, whatever I do." Indeed, Day had been approached several times to receive a Kennedy Center Honors Award, but her unwillingness to appear at the event prevented her from receiving one.

In her syndicated column on July 16, Liz Smith wrote that Elizabeth Taylor was "trying to lure" Day out of retirement for "one last hurrah." According to Smith's "Hollywood sources," Day was "interested but wants to see a script."

In September, Sydney Wood left Day and Carmel for good and moved to Virginia. "There was a lot of back-biting going on among the staff that I wasn't aware of at the time," Wood recalled. "Doris went through phases where she stopped talking to me. She'd just ignore me. And all my instructions were coming through somebody else. I had become a 'nobody,' and the atmosphere had gotten really bad. After one year of being God's gift, and then a year and a half of being ignored, I had had enough."

During Wood's final confrontation with Day, she told him, "Syd, I think your problem is that you don't like women." Wood replied, "I get on very well with women. It's rather the women you employ that are a problem for me." Day "froze," according to Wood, who left several weeks later. Though Wood had every intention of saying goodbye to Day, he learned, at the last minute, that she was crying and too upset for him to see her.

Part of the problem was that Terry, Wood's true friend who had always run interference between him and Day, had become less and less involved with his mother's affairs during this period. After living in Santa Monica with Teresa, Terry had recently moved back to the house on Crescent with her, where he was in the process of dying.

✳　✳　✳

After his divorce from Jacqueline, for a period Terry secretly visited his ex-wife late at night. "Terry would call in the middle of the night," she recalled. "He was distressed, lonely and miserable. He'd show up here, in tears, saying he didn't mean for [the divorce] to happen. This went on for a long time. But there was nothing we could do, because he was kept isolated. We couldn't get through to him. He had huge swings between anger, rage, and sadness. He didn't remember how he got to where he was, when he found himself at a new home in Pebble Beach. He was terribly confused because of his drinking problems and mood swings. And Ryan and I took the brunt of that confusion." Indeed, Jacqueline also remembered that when they were still married Terry checked himself into a clinic and that she and Ryan went to Al-Anon together to try to cope with his alcoholism.

"Terry's breakup with Jacqueline was a terrible blow to all of us, because he never came back to the Vineyard again," said Peter Simon. "It was seen as Jacqueline's turf. And we missed him terribly, because he was such a wonderfully vibrant, fun person in the focus of the Vineyard social world. He was such a kind soul. But their fights had become very public and embarrassing. People would cringe around them a lot."

"Terry was a very loving friend for me, but I lost him in the mid-1990s, when he became an alcoholic," recalled Guy Webster. "When his son was born, he just loved him unconditionally." According to Webster, Terry grew more and more distant from his son. "And that was unconscionable to me," Webster said. "It became increasingly difficult for Ryan to see him, because he was kept isolated. He lived behind walls, which Ryan literally climbed over trying to see his dad."

"Terry had become very weak and he wasn't in charge of his own life anymore," said Jacqueline. "I know that from Ryan. Terry was chemically destroyed, and probably reverted back to childhood. He didn't want any information going back and forth between Doris and Ryan and me, because then the truth [regarding his alcoholism] would have come out. Divide and conquer: If you keep people separated and there's no communication, you can change the reality of the situation with your lies."

After suffering prostate cancer and undergoing surgery, Terry died from melanoma on November 19, 2004. He was sixty-two years old. More of a brother and a father figure than a son to his mother, he had always said that it was only from Alma, his grandmother, that he had known true motherly love. "Terry told me how much his grandmother loved him, and how she took care of him," said Jacqueline Melcher. "Then one day, she wasn't there, and Terry's life stopped in a way. He missed not having a mother."

Though Day had endured disappointments and tragedies through the years, the loss of her only son proved devastating. Terry's various ailments had him slipping away months before his death, and he could no longer fill the crucial role of tending to his mother's needs. Now her friend and protector—if never exactly a son—was gone. She proved inconsolable and failed to attend his private funeral as well as the subsequent memorial that Ryan held for his father at the Carmel Mission on December 7. Day's strong conviction in eternal life leaves no room for funerals—or farewells of any sort. Indeed, whenever a dog needed to be put to sleep, Sydney Wood or another gardener would see to the job and then bury the dog on her property. But Day never wanted to know where they were buried. It was her way of keeping them alive.

Hoping to provide Day with some relief from her grief, Kaye Ballard and Rex Reed visited her in Carmel in the spring. Though she seemed keen for them to come—and even picked up the tab for their stay at the Cypress Inn—Day refused to see these old friends once they arrived. Having devoted so much of her life to wounded animals, Doris Day appeared to have become one herself.

"Everything Is Fine"

---------- ✳ ----------

"Tell him I'm feeding the doggies, and I'll call him back."
—DORIS DAY

"Oh, for heaven's sake. You're always calling me on my birthday," Doris Day said to Liza Minnelli on April 3, 2007, as her fans around the world listened in on their conversation. Magic 63, a Monterey-based radio station, was celebrating Day's birthday by playing her songs and taking calls from friends and fans.

"All of us are so damn lucky you were born," Judy Garland's daughter responded to Day. "I've been thinking about you the last few days and hoping you're as happy as you've made all of us." Minnelli then told Day how she had been an icon for her since she was a child. "You know my parents loved you so much. Especially my daddy," she added, referring to director Vincente Minnelli. "He was crazy about you. He took me to see every movie in the world you ever made."

Minnelli reported that she had mated her schnauzer with one of actress Arlene Dahl's dogs, "and she's now in labor"—one of the many animal stories that made the airwaves on Magic 63 that day. She added that she planned to name one of the "girl puppies" Doris.

"Everything is fine," Day told her, "and it's sweet of you to call."

The program—actually celebrating Day's eighty-fifth birthday although that went unacknowledged—had three segments, each hosted by a different DJ and each featuring a live phone-in from Day. The idea for the tribute initially came to Kevin Kahl, operations manager at Magic 63, when he was jogging one day early in 2001. Day has participated ever since, but 2007 marked the first time the gala streamed live on the Internet, prompting calls from around the world. The first few phone-ins came from British fans, followed by Ray Lyons, a Rhode Island man who, in 1993, had actually danced with Day in Carmel at a fund-raiser for pets. Kaye Ballard phoned in to wish her "Clara" a happy birthday. Paul Brogan was another early caller, before Day herself called in for the first time at 9:45. She sounded sharp, mentioning her "old" and "dear friend Paul," and recalling that dance with Ray Lyons. She also sounded warm, happy, and very much like her younger self, ready to laugh at a moment's notice.

Mike Cleary, the first of the three DJs who oversaw the festivities, had a surprise for Day as he put James Garner on the phone for what he announced was a "conference call." "We haven't talked in over a year," Garner said, adding, "Honey, I've had a bad year [but] I'm doing good now." While they reminisced about filming *The Thrill of It All* in 1963, Day took special delight remembering some of their ad libbing when they were at work on a fight scene. "There's a lot to laugh about," she said. While she added that her voice was not as "off" as it had been in recent years, Day also explained that she had been having allergy problems the past year due to the "pollen" and that she was "hoarse all the time." Still, her voice sounded remarkably supple and robust.

Day called in again at noon, when DJ Ed Dickinson had taken charge of the program. During that segment, fans Annie Mann and Sue Gökgör called from England and chatted with Day, who thanked them for the basket they had sent with Milk Bones for the "doggies." A decade before, Gökgör had established the Friends of Doris Day club. Born in Istanbul in 1937, Gökgör moved to England in 1966, where she lives in Oxford. With regular contributions from Mann as well as other international members, Gökgör produces and disseminates *The Magazine for Friends of Doris Day* three times a year. The publication, usually about forty pages, is crammed with anecdotes from Day's past and, based on Gökgör's ongoing conversations with Day, contemporary choice morsels. "She's given us joy, and she's showed us the way, with her philosophy of life, to never look back or forward," Gökgör said. Other Day fan clubs with an international reach have sprung up on the Internet, too, with Web forums permitting fans to communicate with one another on a daily basis: Discovering Doris, begun by Stephen Munns in 1998, and The Films of Doris Day, which Bryan James started seven years ago, both in England.

The day before Day's eighty-fifth birthday, Howard Green joined with ten other fans at the Cypress Inn in Carmel to celebrate and listen together to the Magic 63 program the next day. "But since we knew the radio show would be streamed over the Internet for the next thirty days, we didn't just sit around and listen all day," recalled Green.

That night the gang of devoted "Dayniacs" gathered for dinner at the Cypress Inn's restaurant, which had recently been renamed Terry's Bar, in her son's honor. More than any other major star, Day has always worked diligently to maintain a close relationship with her fans, and once again they were the ones who were there for her, and thrilled to be in such close proximity.

"Everything is fine," Day had declared to Liza Minnelli, and everything was, indeed, fine. Day had recovered from Terry's death and continued to be showered with affection from around the globe. It's as if she finally realized that her legion of fans have been her true family for most of her life.

"You're loved worldwide," DJ Kevin Kahl exclaimed to Day as the Magic 63 birthday celebration drew to a close. "And thanks to our Internet streaming, your fans got to hear you all over the world."

"I think that's really something," Day answered, her voice echoing her younger self again as she used a phrase that could easily have tripped off the lips of the adolescent Doris Kappelhoff in Cincinnati in the thirties. "You know," she said, "that's just a kick in the pants."

Acknowledgments

---- ✳ ----

$\mathcal{T}$his biography of Doris Day is indebted to a team of collaborators, beginning with my partner, Ken Geist, whose vast cultural knowledge and authorial wisdom were a boon to every phase of its development. Even as I turned our living environment into something of a Doris Day factory for the last four years, Ken shared my delight in many a discovery. Two other top-flight authors, Robert Gutman and Karl Johnson, were major players on what Karl came to call "Team Doris," supplying me with invaluable input as the book was written. Robert is a brilliant friend and mentor who devoted a good deal of the last few years to saving me from many an embarrassment with his meticulous advice, as he did with my previous biography.

Robert was a friend who became an editor; Karl was my editor at the *Daily News* who—with his wife, Mira—has taken a place among my closest friends. Karl's levelheaded approach influenced this book in both concrete and intangible ways. Above all, his probing questions helped me clarify Day's story.

This book would not have come together as efficiently as it has without the oversight of Ann Espuelas, my Virgin Books editor, always there for me, especially during the nerve-wracking endgame, when I despaired of meeting deadlines. In addition to Karl and Robert, Ann helped me shape the manuscript and tell Doris Day's surprisingly complex story as clearly as "Team Doris" could. She also handled all the notes with her customary care and good cheer.

I also hasten to include the name of another dear friend, Ann Schneider, who performed a labor of love—working many a night and over many a weekend—tracking down rare photos for the book. As always, Ann brought her impeccable visual sense to the project, and her ongoing love boosted my confidence and spirits whenever they flagged.

I owe a great deal to Fred Morris, my friend and agent, who proceeded with certainty when I had misgivings about ever being able to place this biography. Happily, my publisher Ken Siman believed in the project from the first day. I am particularly indebted to him for viewing it in terms of a big book. I am further grateful for his bringing together a number of talented pros to help. In addition to Ann Espuelas, they include Amy Hitt, whose copyediting posed any number of valuable questions; Jason Snyder, whose design of the book and photo inserts surpassed my most extravagant wishes; Laura Lindgren, whose striking cover captures Day at her height; and Devin Ness. While Ken was orchestrating our every move with precision, Devin was a behind-the-scenes stage manager, helping coordinate it all, particularly the permissions. I must thank Ellis Levine and Lisa Digernes for their painstaking legal advice as I was completing the manuscript, Judith Hancock and her nephew Mel Hancock for their meticulously detailed index, and Don Kennison, whose eagle-eyed, last-minute proofreading of the galley pages caught still more corrections for the final book.

I am also indebted to Liz Smith and Denis Ferrara for trumpeting this project, when still in its infancy, with much fanfare in the summer of 2005, thereby galvanizing the crucial support of many, in particular Howard Green and Paul Brogan, lifelong fans and acquaintances of Day's. Paul drove from his home in New Hampshire to mine in New York to bring me several boxes of his Doris Day memorabilia, encompassing the twelve scrapbooks he started in 1960. With daily phone calls, countless e-mails, and numerous get-togethers in Los Angeles and New York, Howard supplied me with rare CDs, DVDs, magazines, and information—in fact, much that was needed to tell Day's story comprehensively. Given the amount of detection involved in writing a biography, Howard took to calling me "Sherlock" and referring to himself as my "Hollywood correspondent." He also introduced me to another fan, Lauren Benjamin, who, with the aid of Mary Anne Barothy, helped me get Day's story straight.

Though it was never less than a privilege to work on this biography with a battalion of so many talented people, a special gift arose from forging new friendships with several of them. In addition to Howard and Paul, they include Kaye Ballard and Myvanwy Jenn, Donald Saddler, Val Andrew and Sheila Smith, Sydney Wood, Harvey Evans, and Barbara Flicker.

For sharing their memories with me, I am grateful to a still-larger parade of individuals who either knew and/or worked with Day: Jim Bailey, Mary Anne Barothy, Drew Casper, Tony Charmoli, Barry Comden, Warren Cowan, Dom DeLuise, Jason Derer, Angie Dickinson, Ethel Eisenberg (aka Ann Perry), Jim Fitzgerald, Matthew Gabriner, Emanuel "Buz" Galas, Lillian Glickman, Sue Gökgör, Peter Graves, Merv Griffin, James (Jim) Harbert, Mary Cleere Haran, Kevin Kahl, Fay Kanin, Harold and Marilyn Less, Ray Lyons, Annie Mann, Jack Melcher, Jacqueline Melcher, Mitch Miller, Robert Morse, Miriam Nelson, Janis Paige, Annette Pearson, Jim Pierson, Moira Sher, Peter Simon, Ron Stephenson, Larry Storch, David Towler, Tom Von Der Ahe, Guy and Leone Webster, Warner Weidler, Joe Welz, Paul Welz, and Elizabeth Wilson. I also thank Candice Bergen for giving permission to quote from her memoirs.

I owe yet another debt to Harry Haun and Charles Nelson for helping me track down many who added to my tale of Doris Day, and to Kenny Nassau and his wife Lee Hebner—two more close friends—who supplied frequent help with computer and research questions. And, for making me feel entirely at home when I stayed with them during my numerous trips to Los Angeles, I extend heartfelt thanks to Daniel and Katharine Selznick and to Dan Adler, my nephew, and his wife Jenna. Dan and Jenna's wonderful young sons, Eli and Jakob, roused me many a morning to begin my days conducting interviews and pursuing my research at the Warner Bros. Archives, the Margaret Herrick Library, and the Cinema Library at the University of Southern California.

There is yet another list of friends, associates, and advisers to thank, including Jim Baldassare, Lois Battle, Claire Bernheim, Sandy Brokaw, Michael Buckley, Nan and Richard Case, Donald Chase, Graham Dennie, Jehed Diamond, Ed Epstein, Michael Feingold, Suzy Fisch, Ann and Don Freeman, Meg Freeman, Jamie Gallagher, Corrine Geist, Fran Geist, Debbie and Rick Green, Sandy and Leonard Gubar, Gloria and Walter Hastreiter, Betty Hawari, Bryan James, Leandro Katz, George Kim, Walter Koenig, Martie Labare, Jim Lambert, Kevin Lewis, Guy Little and Kirk McNamer, George and Rosemary Lois, Bruce Lowy, Gary and Renee Manacher, Howard Mandelbaum, Tom McCormack, Ann and Dan Miller, Stephen Munns, Ellis Nassour, Ken Norwick, Brent Phillips, James Rosenthal, Marian Seldes, David Sheward, Andy Sichel, Stephen Silverman, Al Simmons, Suzy Troy, Ann and Jack Waananen, Vicky Wilson, and Sherman and Joan Yellen. Special thanks, as well, to my *Vanity Fair* editor Wayne Lawson and his assistant Matt Pressman for their masterful condensation of this large book into an excerpt for the magazine.

I also extend warm thank-you's to a number of librarians, beginning with Ned Comstock, Jenny Romero, and Haden Guest, each of whom proved an important research assistant, making my trips to Los Angeles all the more valuable. In addition to drawing my attention to the Constance McCormick, Roger Edens, Joe Pasternak, Andrew Stone, Jack Warner, and Universal Collections at USC's Cinematic Arts Library, Ned provided me with far more than I requested. Haden guided my every maneuver through the well-maintained Warner Bros. Archives, also at USC. Jenny introduced me to the Sidney Skolsky, David Zeitlin, and Alfred Hitchcock papers within the special collections at the Margaret Herrick Library. She also provided me with access to the Ronald L. Davis Oral History Collection of the DeGolyer Library at Southern Methodist University, and presented me with the single most important cache in reconstructing Day's life: Jane Ardmore's papers, also in the Margaret Herrick Library.

Rare for a journalist, the late Jane Ardmore befriended many of her subjects, and perhaps none more so than Doris Day. In fact, for well over a decade, Day frequently revisited her past, discussed her present, and talked about her future with her friend "Jane," and even wrote corrections in the margins of many of Ardmore's rough drafts of unpublished Doris Day articles. For permission to quote from Ardmore's many working notes and published pieces, I am deeply grateful to her niece Carol Hauer as well as to her cousins Susan Updike and Jack Behrend.

I also thank the always helpful staff members of the Margaret Herrick Library, the USC Cinematic Arts Library, and the Warner Bros. Archives. Among the other librarians and archivists I cite with gratitude: Gail Bailey of the *North Adams Transcript,* Thomas Branigar at the Dwight D. Eisenhower Library, Cindy Hill and Sharon Knieper at the Public Library of Cincinnati and Hamilton County, Brian Meacham, public access coordinator at the Center of the Academy Film Archive, Susan Morgan of the New York Public Library, Eric Reany of the *Cincinnati Inquirer,* and Shirley Smith and Carla Basinger at Hamilton County Probate Court. Thanks go, too, to Gina Blumenfeld of the Directors Guild of America.

Bibliography

NOTE: This bibliography does not include the many magazine articles, television shows, and DVD commentaries that were also used for research, but information pertaining to them can be found in the notes section and/or the text itself.

Alleman, Richard. *The Movie Lover's Guide to Hollywood.* New York: Harper & Row, 1985.

Arden, Eve. *Three Phases of Eve: An Autobiography.* New York: St. Martin's Press, 1985.

Ballard, Kaye, with Jim Hesselman. *How I Lost 10 Pounds in 53 Years.* New York: Back Stage Books, 2006.

Basinger, Jeanine. *Silent Stars.* New York: Alfred A. Knopf, 1999.

Beard, Lanford, editor. *E True Hollywood Story: The Real Stories Behind the Glitter.* New York: Chamberlain Bros., 2005.

Bergen, Candice. *Knock Wood.* New York: Linden Press/Simon & Schuster, 1984.

Berkman, Ted. *Around the World in 80 Years: Newsrooms, Soundstages, Private Encounters and Public Affairs.* Carpinteria, California: Manifest Publications, 1998.

Bloom, Ken. *The American Songbook.* New York: Black Dog and Leventhal Publishers, 2005.

Braun, Eric. *Doris Day.* London: Orion Books Ltd., 1994.

Brooks, Tim, and Earle Marsh. *The Complete Directory to Prime Time Network TV Shows.* New York: Ballantine, 1979.

Brownlow, Kevin. *Behind the Mask of Innocence.* New York: Alfred A. Knopf, 1990.

Butler, David. *David Butler: Interviewed by Irene Kahn Atkins, January 14– June 22, 1977,* A Directors Guild of America Oral History.

Cagney, James. *Cagney by Cagney.* Garden City: Doubleday & Company, 1976.

Callen, Michael Feeney. *Richard Harris: Sex, Death & the Movies.* London: Robson Books, 2003.

Colacello, Bob. *Ronnie and Nancy: Their Path to the White House.* New York: Warner Books, 2004.

Comden, Betty. *Off Stage,* New York: Simon & Schuster, 1995.

Connelly, Robert B. *The Motion Picture Guide: Silent Film 1910–1936.* Chicago: Cinebooks, Inc.,1986.

Cooke, Alistair. *The American Home Front.* New York: Atlantic Monthly Press, 2006.

Corey, Melinda, and George Ochoa. *The Man in Lincoln's Nose: Funny, Profound, and Quotable Quotes of Screenwriters, Movie Stars, and Moguls.* New York: Fireside, 1990.

Crist, Judith. *The Private Eye, the Cowboy, and the Very Naked Girl.* New York: Paperback Library, 1970.

Custen, George F. *Twentieth Century's Fox: Darryl F. Zanuck and the Culture of Hollywood.* New York: Basic Books, 1997.

Bibliography

Eliot, Marc. *Cary Grant: A Biography.* New York: Harmony Books, Random House, 2004.

Eyman, Scott. *Lion of Hollywood: The Life and Legend of Louis B. Mayer.* New York: Simon & Schuster, 2005.

Frank, Rusty E. *Tap: The Greatest Tap Dance Stars and Their Stories.* New York: Da Capo Press, 1994.

Freedland, Michael. *All the Way: A Biography of Frank Sinatra.* London: Weidenfeld & Nicolson, 1997.

———. *Doris Day: The Illustrated Biography.* London: Andre Deutsch, 2000.

———. *Jack Lemmon.* New York: St. Martin's Press, 1985.

Fuchs, Daniel. *The Golden West: Hollywood Stories.* Boston: David R. Godine, 2005.

Garcia, Roger, editor. *Frank Tashlin.* British Film Institute, 1994.

Gavin, James. *Intimate Nights: The Golden Age of New York Cabaret.* New York: Grove Weidenfeld, 1991.

Gottfried, Martin. *All His Jazz: The Life and Death of Bob Fosse.* New York: Bantam, 1990.

Granata, Charles L. *Sessions with Sinatra: Frank Sinatra and the Art of Recording.* Chicago: Chicago Review Press, 2004.

Green, Stanley. *Ring Bells! Sing Songs! Broadway Musicals of the 1930s.* New Rochelle: Arlington House, 1971.

Griffin, Merv. *Making the Good Life Last.* New York: Simon & Schuster, 2003.

Harmetz, Aljean. *Round Up the Usual Suspects: The Making of Casablanca—Bogart, Bergman, and World War II.* New York: Hyperion, 1992.

Harris, Andrew B. *The Performing Set.* Denton, Texas: University of North Texas Press, 2006.

Harrison, Rex. *A Damned Serious Business: My Life in Comedy.* New York: Bantam Books, 1991.

Haskell, Molly. *Holding My Own in No Man's Land.* New York: Oxford, 1997.

Havers, Richard. *Sinatra.* London: DK Publishing, 2004.

Hemming, Roy. *The Melody Lingers On: The Great Songwriters and Their Movie Musicals.* New York: Newmarket Press, 1999.

Henreid, Paul, with Julius Fast. *Ladies Man.* New York: St. Martin's Press, 1984.

Hirschhorn, Clive. *The Warner Bros. Story.* New York: Crown Publishers. 1979.

Hofler, Robert. *The Man Who Invented Rock Hudson.* New York: Carroll and Graf, 2005.

Hopper, Hedda, and James Brough. *The Whole Truth and Nothing But.* New York: Doubleday, 1963.

Hotchner, A. E. *Doris Day: Her Own Story.* New York: William Morrow and Co., 1976.

James, Etta, and David Ritz. *Rage to Survive: The Etta James Story.* Cambridge, Mass.: Da Capo Press, 1998.

Jessen, Lloyd K. *The Complete Guide to Doris Day.* Unpublished manuscript, dated 2000.

Jewison, Norman. *This Terrible Business Has Been Good to Me.* New York: Thomas Dunne Books, St. Martin's Press, 2005.

Kael, Pauline. *Deeper into Movies.* Boston: Little, Brown and Co., 1973.

———. *I Lost It at the Movies.* Boston: Little, Brown and Co., 1965.

Kanin, Garson. *Together Again!* Garden City, N.Y.: Doubleday and Co. 1981.

Keel, Howard, with Joyce Spizer. *Only Make Believe: My Life in Show Business.* Fort Lee, N.J.: Barricade Books, 2005.

King, Tom. *The Operator: David Geffen Builds, Buys, and Sells the New Hollywood.* New York: Random House, 2000.

Lahr, John. *Sinatra: The Artist and the Man.* New York: Random House, 1997.

Lax, Roger, and Frederick Smith. *The Great Song Thesaurus.* 2nd edition. New York: Oxford University Press, 1989.

Leamer, Laurence. *Make-Believe: The Story of Nancy & Ronald Reagan.* New York: Harper & Row, 1983.

Lewis, Jerry, and James Kaplan. *Dean & Me.* New York: Doubleday, 2005.

Lindsey, Karen. *Friends as Family.* New York: Beacon Press, 1982.

Lord, Graham. *Niv: The Authorized Biography of David Niven.* New York: Thomas Dunne Books, St. Martin's Press, 2004.

Lucas, John Meredyth, and Cari Beauchamp. *Eighty Odd Years in Hollywood: Memoir of a Career in Film and Television.* Jefferson, North Carolina: McFarland & Company, 2004.

Macdonald, Dwight. *Dwight Macdonald on Movies.* Englewood Cliffs, N.J.: Prentice-Hall, Inc., 1969.

Mann, William J., *Edge of Midnight: The Life of John Schlesinger.* New York: Billboard Books, 2006.

Marmorstein, Gary. *The Label.* New York: Thunder's Mouth Press, 2007.

Martin, Deana. *Memories Are Made of This: Dean Martin Through His Daughter's Eyes.* New York: Harmony Books, Random House, 2004.

McCabe, John. *Cagney.* New York: Alfred A. Knopf, 1997.

McGee, Garry. *Doris Day: Sentimental Journey.* Jefferson, North Carolina: McFarland & Company, 2005.

McGilligan, Patrick. *Alfred Hitchcock: A Life in Darkness and Light.* New York: Regan Books, 2003.

Melnick, Ross, and Andreas Fuchs. *Cinema Treasures: A New Look at Classic Movie Theaters.* St. Paul, Minn.: MBI Publishing Co., 2004.

Morris, Edmund. *Dutch: A Memoir of Ronald Reagan.* New York: Random House, 1999.

Mosley, Roy, with Philip and Martin Masheter. *Rex Harrison: The First Biography.* London: New English Library, 1987.

Navasky, Victor S. *Naming Names.* New York: Penguin, 1981.

Nelson, Nancy. *Evenings with Cary Grant.* New York: Warner Books, 1991.

Oppenheimer, Jerry, and Jack Vitek. *Idol: Rock Hudson: The True Story of an American Film Hero.* New York: Villard Books, 1986.

Parish, James Robert. *Hollywood's Great Love Teams.* New Rochelle, N.Y.: Arlington House, 1974.

Patrick, Pierre, and Garry McGee. *Que Sera, Sera: The Magic of Doris Day Through Television.* Albany, Ga.: BearManor Media, 2006.

Perry, Dick. *Not Just a Sound: The Story of WLW.* Englewood Cliffs, N.J.: Prentice-Hall, Inc., 1971.

Reed, Rex. *Big Screen, Little Screen.* New York: Macmillan, 1971.

Rhomer, Eric, and Claude Chabrol. *Hitchcock: The First Forty-four Films.* New York: Frederick Ungar Publishing Co., 1979.

Rico, Diana. *Kovacsland.* San Diego: Harcourt Brace Jovanovich, 1990.

Robertson, James C. *The Casablanca Man: The Cinema of Michael Curtiz.* London and New York: Routledge, 1993.

Robinson, David. *Hollywood in the Twenties.* New York: Paperback Library, 1970.

Roseboro, John, with Bill Libby. *Glory Days with the Dodgers.* New York: Atheneum, 1978.

Sarris, Andrew. *Confessions of a Cultist: On the Cinema, 1955–1969.* New York: Simon and Schuster, 1969.

Schickel, Richard. *James Cagney: A Celebration.* Boston: Little, Brown and Co., 1985.

Seaman, Barbara. *Lovely Me: The Life of Jacqueline Susann.* New York: Warner Books, 1987.

Sforza, John. *Swing It! The Andrews Sisters Story.* Lexington, Kentucky: University Press of Kentucky, 2004.

Shipman, David. *Judy Garland: The Secret Life of an American Legend.* New York: Hyperion, 1993.

Shipman, David. *Movie Talk.* New York: St. Martin's Press, 1988.

Silverman, Stephen M. *The Fox That Got Away.* Secaucus, New Jersey: Lyle Stuart, 1988.

Silvester, Christopher, editor. *The Grove Book of Hollywood.* New York: Grove Press, 1998.

Simon, John. *Private Screenings: Views of the Cinema of the Sixties.* New York: Macmillan, 1967.

Sperber, A. M., and Eric Lax. *Bogart.* London: Phoenix, 1997.

Spoto, Donald. *The Art of Alfred Hitchcock.* New York: Hopkinson and Blake, 1977.

———. *The Dark Side of Genius: The Life of Alfred Hitchcock.* New York: Ballantine Books, 1983.

Strait, Raymond. *James Garner.* New York: St. Martin's, 1985.

Thomey, Ted. *Doris Day: The Dramatic Story of America's Number One Box Office Star.* Derby, Conn.: Monarch Books, 1962.

Thomson, David. *The New Biographical Dictionary of Film.* New York: Alfred A. Knopf, 2002.

Editors of Time-Life Books. *This Fabulous Century: 1950–1960.* New York: Time-Life Books, 1971.

Tosches, Nick. *Dino: Living High in the Dirty Business of Dreams.* New York: Doubleday, 1992.

Ward, Geoffrey C., and Ken Burns. *Jazz: A History of America's Music.* New York: Alfred A. Knopf, 2000.

Wiley, Mason, and Damien Bona. *Inside Oscar: The Unofficial History of the Academy Awards.* New York: Ballantine Books, 1987.

Wills, Maury, and Mike Celizic. *On the Run: The Never Dull and Often Shocking Life of Maury Wills.* New York: Carroll & Graf, 1991.

Wilson, Steve, and Joe Florenski. *Center Square: The Paul Lynde Story.* Los Angeles: Advocate Books, 2005.

Wynn, Ned. *We Will Always Live in Beverly Hills: Growing Up Crazy in Hollywood.* New York: William Morrow and Co., 1990.

Zehme, Bill. *The Way You Wear Your Hat: Frank Sinatra and the Lost Art of Livin'.* New York: HarperCollins, 1997.

Notes

✳

Unless otherwise indicated in the text or in this section, all quoted statements in this book are based on the author's personal interviews with the subjects cited.

Chapter 1: *"Living Photographs"*

1 "I never got such a thrill in my life . . . " Melnick and Fuchs, *Cinema Treasures: A New Look at Classic Movie Theaters,* 13.

2 "I don't believe the motion picture . . . " Brownlow, *Behind the Mask of Innocence,* xxi.

2 "Why on earth . . . " Ibid., xvii.

3 "I think that she would have liked performing . . . " *Doris Day: I Don't Even Like Apple Pie,* Christopher Frayling, BBC documentary, April 3, 1989.

4 "The only thing they could say about me as a baby . . . " *Photoplay,* March 1952, 88.

4 "In 1921, when Alma was pregnant . . . " George Scullin, "Escape to Happiness," *Photoplay,* May, 1957, Part II.

5 "the center of the U.S. radio industry." *Encyclopedia Britannica,* volume 5, 711.

5 "It was an arduous program . . . all equally bitter." Scullin, "Escape to Happiness," *Photoplay,* May 1957, Part II, 105.

5 "Go back to bed at once . . . " *Photoplay,* March 1952, 55.

5 "That crazy girl, always imagining things." Ibid., 87–88.

6 "Some of the happy musical bedlam . . . [For her own part,] Doris was too young to care." Scullin, 105.

6 "All the kids wanted to come to our house . . . " Ardmore papers, Margaret Herrick Library.

6 "To a large extent . . . her playtime." Scullin, 105.

6 "He belonged to my mother and me . . . " "Lady's Circle," *The Magazine for Friends of Doris Day,* December 1999, 17.

6 "My mother tells me . . . " Shirley Eder, Detroit radio program, second of three interviews on a CD prepared by Howard Green.

7 "When my mother . . . " *Motion Picture,* August 1954, 68.

8 "I got mad . . . could I beat Doris." Ibid., 27.

8 "Most everybody liked Doris . . . " Ibid., 27–28.

8 "When we wouldn't allow . . . " *Movie Stars Parade,* November 1952, 77–78.

8 "Her father was one of those rigid, too-strict fathers . . . " Jane S. Carelton, "What Really Happened to Doris Day," *Modern Screen,* January 1954, 80.

8 "Since my father had to practice . . . " *Photoplay,* January 1961, 68.

9 "After school . . . " Doris Day, with Jane Kesner Ardmore, "I'm on My Way," *American Weekly,* November 17, 1957, 4+.

9 "I loved my bangs . . . " Doris Day, as told to Jane Ardmore, "What I Want Most for Christmas," *Photoplay,* January 1961, 68.

9   "[She] walked up and down each aisle . . . " Ardmore papers, Margaret Herrick Library, and "What I Want Most for Christmas," Ibid., 30+.

9   "Doris was an awful little snob . . . " Harold Heffernan, *Detroit News*, October 2, 1952, 51.

9   "powder blue with white pique trim . . . " Ardmore papers, Margaret Herrick Library.

9   "But it was as a stage mother . . . ." *Photoplay*, March 1952, 88.

10   "Of course I used to dress up . . . " Ardmore papers, Margaret Herrick Library.

10   "Sometimes Doris changed dresses . . . " *Movie Stars Parade*, November 1952, 77.

10   "After that, I used to run all the way . . . " Day, as told to Jane Ardmore, *Photoplay*, January 1961, 68.

10   "I so wanted loving things . . . " A. E. Hotchner, *Doris Day: Her Own Story*, 22.

12   "My father got in the car . . . " Ibid., 25. 12 "was the only real ambition I ever had . . . " Ibid., 25.

12   "When William Kappelhoff left Alma . . . " Edwin Schallertt, *Los Angeles Times*, May 25, 1947.

12   "But two months later, another court document . . . " Hamilton County court documents, second dated December 2, 1935.

12   "We kept trying . . . " Ardmore papers, Margaret Herrick Library.

13   "I'd go out on the porch . . . " Jane Wilkie, *Motion Picture*, October 1959, 80.

13   "I've never forgotten it . . . " Cleveland Amory, "The Dog Catcher of Beverly Hills," *TV Guide*, June 10, 1972, 38.

13   "At home we'd gather . . . " *Movie Stars Parade*, November 1952.

14   "Doris recalled that the first boy . . . " *Photoplay*, March 1952, 88.

14   "Want to play softball with the gang?" Mary Goodwin, *Photoplay*, February 1953, 43.

14   "She had trouble . . . " Ibid., 103.

14   "She was always dressing like a grown-up . . . " *Motion Picture*, August 1954, 28.

14   "Doke was an awful tomboy . . . " Ibid., 28.

14   "the little girl who always wanted to be a big girl . . . " Paul Kappel, "I Remember 'Doke,'" *Movie Stars Parade*, November 1952, 77, 38.

14   "I had a real mad crush on Clark Gable . . . " Elva Newman, "If I Were 17 Again," *Photoplay*, May 1960, 94.

15   "According to Mary Goodwin, Day . . . " Ibid., 104

15   "We were paid a few dollars . . . " Hotchner, 30

16   "As a rule . . . " Kappel, 77, 38.

16   "I suppose it was the . . . " Hotchner, 32.

17   "First, I had to see . . . " John Whitcomb, "The Freckle-faced Kid From Cincinnati, Ohio," Paul Brogan scrapbook #2.

17   "About 10 o'clock, Lawrence . . . " Doris Day, with Jane Kesner Ardmore, "I'm on My Way," *American Weekly*, November 17, 1957, 4+.

18   "I was in the way . . . " Scullin, 106.

18   "I couldn't have asked . . . " Hotchner, 37.

18   "You could have a career . . . " Wynn Roberts, "Atom Blonde!," *Photoplay*, June 1955, 39+, 80.

19   "Sometimes my audience . . . " "Doris Day: The Three Toughest Decisions in My Life," *Movie Life*, Brogan scrapbook #4.

19   "It would be a waste . . . " *Motion Picture*, August 1954, 68.

19   "I got off to a bad start . . . " William Lynch Vallee, "Day Break for Doris," *Silver Screen*, March 1948, 45+.

19   "I had heard her sing . . . " *Motion Picture*, August 1954, 68.

19   "Don't crowd the microphone . . . " Scullin, 107.

20   "If Doris thought . . . " *Motion Picture*, August 1954, 68.

20   "There was a screech of brakes . . . " Hotchner, 42.

Chapter 2: *"Day After Day"*

21   "people went to see the band . . . " Ward and Burns, *Jazz*, 311.

22   "We held auditions . . . " Scullin, 107.

22   "too much space on the marquee . . . " Frayling, BBC documentary.

22   "lovely new gown . . . in the club." Hotchner, 44.

22   "I looked pretty poised . . . " Ardmore papers, Margaret Herrick Library.

22   "She had a voice of her own . . . " Scullin, 107.

23   "It was at the Butler county . . . " Dick Perry, *Not Just a Sound: The Story of WLW*, 64.

24   "It was one night soon . . . " Hugh Burrell, "Doris Day's Secret Son," *Modern Screen*, May 1960, 29+.

24   "The surprise was that . . . " Hotchner, 49.

24   "only one real ambition . . . " Burrell, 66.

25   "Being on the road . . . " Simon, *The Big Bands*, 33.

25   "There were other factors . . . " Ibid.

25   "As Day herself would . . . " Hotchner, 53.

25   "Simon described the difficulties . . . " Simon, 35–36.

25   "I often did eighteen shows . . . " Shirley Eder, Detroit Radio interviewer, second of three interviews on disc prepared by Howard Green.

26   "Bob Crosby wired Day . . . " *Photoplay*, June 1955, 80.

26   "But Day's time with Crosby . . . " Ronald L. Davis Oral History Collection, DeGolyer Library at Southern Methodist University.

27   "A song plugger told me . . . " This first part of the quote is from Les Brown Web site.

27   "I sent for her . . . " Davidson, *Look*, June 20, 1961.

27   "Day began . . . " Simon, 102.

27   "I liked Doris, really liked her . . . ." Hotchner, 79.

27   "And there's Doris Day . . . " Simon, 102.

27   "Instead of 'ah,'" . . . " Hotchner, 56.

29   "was the clean, handsome . . . " Ardmore papers, Margaret Herrick Library.

29   "You've got to let kids . . . " Jaye Moore, "Doris Day's First Husband Dies!" Brogan scrapbook, #5.

Chapter 3: *An Unsentimental Journey*

31   "I had never . . . " Helen Louise Walker, "The Happy Life of Doris Day," *Screen Guide*, '51–'52—from Constance McCormick Collection at USC.

32   "What had been . . . " Hotchner, 59.

32   "The minute we walked . . . " Ibid., 60.

32   "We were married . . . ." Day, with Ardmore, 4+.

33   "110 miles per hour . . . " Hotchner, 66.

33   "Incredible, too . . . " Hotchner, 66.

33   "One of the cruelest things . . . " Ibid., 70. 34 "There was a religious problem . . . " Burrell, 66.

34 "hometown kid who had made good . . . " *Photoplay*, March 1952, 87.

34 "It was really quite touching . . . " Hotchner, 77.

35 "Neither mother nor I asked . . . " Schallert, May 25, 1947.

35 "We were in Dayton . . . " Simon, 104.

35 "The strike went into effect . . . " Bloom, *American Songbook*, 151.

35 "Whoever planned Les's tour . . . " Hotchner, 79

35 "We'd have to call . . . " Ibid., 79–80.

36 "After Terry was born . . . " Day, as told to Ardmore, 68.

36 "Once when Terry . . . " Ardmore papers, Margaret Herrick Library.

36 "Alma would also . . . " Ibid.

36 "We stayed at this small . . . " *Photoplay*, January 1961, 68.

36 "I was in New York . . . " Ibid., 68–69.

37 "Whereas she used to be . . . " Anne Fleming, *Photoplay*, January 1969, 79.

37 "Day did look back . . . " Mike Connolly, *Photoplay*, October 1955, 4.

39 "we all thought it was going to be a big hit." Hotchner, 78.

39 "It was at one of those . . . " Simon, 105.

39 " 'Sentimental Journey' was number . . . " Havers, *Sinatra*, 109.

39 "I can't possibly describe . . . " Hudson, *Motion Picture*, October 1959, 28.

39 "I don't believe it's . . . " *Movie Stars Parade*, November 1952, 77.

40 "I told him . . . " William Lynch Vallee, "Day Break for Doris," *Silver Screen*, March 1948, 45+.

40 "I have a photographic mind . . . " *Doris Day Society Journal*, Spring 1977, 11.

40 "According to Day . . . " *Modern Screen*, July 1954, 72.

40 "gentle" and "just the opposite of Al [Jorden]." Hotchner, 82.

40 "(In her memoir, she claims to have been in her "late teens.")" Also, according to Day, they quickly began sleeping together, and their sexual relationship was particularly good. Ibid., 82.

41 "If we had taken time . . . " Hoyt and Alice Barnett, "She's a Real Warm Day," 16, Brogan scrapbook.

41 "Knocking herself out . . . " Cal Grayson, "All in a Day's Work," *Band Leaders*, March 1946, 22+.

43 "Not really . . . " Hotchner, 83–84.

44 "George didn't have much money . . . " Ibid., 84.

44 "She was a girl . . . " Hopper and Brough, *The Whole Truth and Nothing But*, 159.

44 "Al Levy came around . . . " Hotchner, 84.

44 "Al brought Doris to say . . . " Hopper and Brough, 160.

45 "Whatever comes along . . . " Hotchner, 85.

45 "Sacks knew I was going . . . " Ibid., 86.

46 "The funny thing is neither of the two . . . " Ibid., 86.

46 "Whatever it was Al . . . " Day, with Ardmore, 4+.

46 "Day's song list included . . . " James Gavin, *Intimate Nights*, 72–73.

46 "Day's daisy voice was deceptive . . . " Marmorstein, *The Label*, 187.

47 "Right now she's a shade too 'sweet,'" and "On the other hand [she is] a fetching personality who will more than hold her own in class or mass nighteries." Eric Braun, *Variety*, 75–76.

47 "I'm sure the audiences . . . ." Hotchner, 88.

Chapter 4: *"Her Sex Sneaks up on You"*

50   "I know the best in the world . . . " Bear Family Records, Hambergen, Germany, vol. 1, 23.

51   "I knew Doris very well . . . " Hotchner, 26.

51   "one of the most unlikely auditions . . . " Scullin, "Escape to Happiness," *Photoplay,* June 1957, Part III, 69.

51   "That's the date, in any event . . . " Robertson, *The Casablanca Man: The Cinema of Michael Curtiz,* 99 and note on163.

51   "Not now," growled Curtiz . . . " Ida Zeitlin, "The Heart Is Everything," *Modern Screen,* July 1954, 74.

52   "by taking her hips . . . " Bloom, *American Songbook,* 48.

52   "I'd been working before people . . . " William Lynch Vallee, "Day Break for Doris," *Silver Screen,* March 1948, 45+.

52   "But Day would also . . . " Steve Cronin, "Happy Talk," *Modern Screen,* December 1952, 84.

52   "In his autobiography, *Casablanca* . . . " Henreid and Fast, *Ladies Man,* 126.

53   "We were all resting . . . " Ibid., 126.

53   "I sank down lower and lower in my seat . . . " Jay Dee, "A Great Day for Miss Day,"unidentified newspaper article, Warner Bros. Archives.

54   "But as explained three days later . . . " *Hollywood Examiner,* May 12, 1947.

54   "The studio wanted a star name . . . " *Los Angeles Times,* May 10, 1947.

54   "As soon as Mike Curtiz . . . " *Los Angeles Times,* May 23, 1947.

54   "One of the first behind-the-scenes . . . " *Hollywood Citizen,* May 19, 1947.

55   "simply be Ingrid Bergman and play the same . . . " Harmetz, *Round Up the Usual Suspects: The Making of Casablanca—Bogart, Bergman, and World War II,* 91.

55   "You have very strong personality . . . " Hotchner, 98.

55   "'For me,' she would recall . . . " Vallee, 45+.

55   "How naive I was when I made my first . . . " Carl Schroeder, *Screen Stories,* April 1956, 59.

55   "Doris was quite nervous . . . " from Sue Gokgor, *The Magazine for Friends of Doris Day,* December 1997, 6.

56   "On her solo numbers . . . " Scullin, "Escape to Happiness," Photoplay, June 1957, Part III, 69, 111.

56   "I liked it . . . and that's good enough for you." Ibid., 111.

56   "watching her shuffle . . . " Jane S. Carelton, "What Really Happened to Doris Day," *Modern Screen,* January 1954, 81.

57   "The man actually . . . " Vallee, March 1948.

57   "Jack had an innate strength . . . " Linda Griffith, "Bittersweet Memory of Love," *TV Radio Mirror,* May 1970, 91.

57   "I'm crazy about Jack . . . " Ibid., 91.

57   "Jack and Doris . . . " Ibid., 91.

57   "Doris was . . . " Ibid., 91.

58   They met at Day's "first" Hollywood party . . . " Reba and Bonnie Churchill, "Her Best Friends Wouldn't Tell Her," *Silver Screen,* June 1957, 17.

58   "Curtiz decided Day . . . " Vallee, March 1948.

60   "hated every minute of it . . . " Hotchner, 144–45.

60   "Perhaps the competitive Sinatra . . . " Havers, 130, 138.

Chapter 5: *Daydreamer*

61 "Though preliminary wardrobe . . . " Warner Bros. Archives, publicity files.

62 "had to fight . . . " Robertson, 99.

63 "Warner Brothers' newest sweetheart . . . " Thomey, *Doris Day: The Dramatic Story of America's Number One Box Office Star*, 76–77.

64 "Separation took place . . . " *Los Angeles Times*, June 16, 1948.

64 "[she] wants to make sure she really desires." Ibid., August 7, 1948.

64 "Something's happened to you . . . " Steve Cronin, "Happy Talk," *Modern Screen*, December 1952, 54.

64 "because I'd been thinking . . . " Haskell, *Holding My Own in No Man's Land*, 29.

64 "I wondered how it was going to be—having Terry with me . . . " Jack Wade, "How Doris Day Won Her Son," file at Margaret Herrick Library.

65 "The fact is, I wasn't quite sure . . . " Hotchner, 149–50.

65 "It was shortly before they left . . . " Constance McCormick Collection at USC.

65 "I was crazy about him . . . " Louella Parsons, "In Hollywood," *International News Service*, July 4, 1948.

66 "Day would have four hits . . . " Havers, 135.

67 "In the *Detroit News*, Al Weitschat wrote . . . " *Detroit News*, July 24, 1948.

67 "an engaging young singer and comedienne . . . " *Washington Post*, July 2, 1948.

67 "Miss Day is not only introduced . . . " *Los Angeles Times*, June 26, 1948.

68 "Marty became the second partner . . . " Hopper and Bough, 160.

68 "got into the habit of dropping . . . " Ernst Jacobi, *Photoplay*, February 1955.

69 "[Doris] needed a lot of direction then . . . " Butler, "David Butler: Interviewed by Irene Kahn Atkins, January 14–June 22, 1977" A Directors Guild of America Oral History," 227.

70 "Another thing that Doris Day . . . " Ibid., 370–71.

70 "Of course, things changed rapidly for Doris . . . " Warner Bros. Archives.

70 "spent the evening talking . . . " Leamer, *Make-Believe: The Story of Nancy and Ronald Reagan*, 147. 70 "My research cards show . . . " Morris, *Dutch: A Memoir of Ronald Reagan*, 281–82.

70 "There was a little place on . . . " Hotchner, 121.

71 "I thought it was lovely . . . " Ibid., 121.

71 "college football hero . . . " Robert Osborne, "Rambling Reporter," *Hollywood Reporter*, May 19, 1983, 2.

71 "They came to cheer up mother . . . " Day, as told to Ardmore, 68.

Chapter 6: *"It Seems Like I've Always Known Him"*

74 "he started at $18.80 per week . . . " Edwin Matesky, "Marty Melcher Hits Jackpot in Filmland, Plans Area Home," *North Adams Transit*, November 5, 1959.

76 "Gosh," said Day, "he was my agent . . . " *Modern Screen*, January 1951, 73.

76 "The first date [between Marty and Doris] wasn't a date . . . " *Modern Screen*, July 1954, 74.

76 "Neither of them was in the mood . . . " Jacobi, 104.

76 "At rehearsals I sang . . . " Doris Day, with Ardmore, 4+.

77 "People could identify themselves . . . " Hopper and Brough, 162–63.

77 "She agreed, as usual then, but . . . " Ibid., 164.

78 "It seems his office was constantly . . . " Jane Ardmore papers, Margaret Herrick Library.

78   "when he had a chance to better himself . . . " Hotchner, 126.
78   "Sam," she said, "I'm scared to death . . . until Andrews finally left." Ibid., 126.
79   "I don't want to bother Doris," explained Day's mother, "so I hope you can help me . . . " Brogan scrapbook #2.
80   "In fact, Alma's baked goods brought pleasure . . . " "Hollywood at Home," *Movie Spotlight*, April 1950, 14–15.

Chapter 7: *The Beating of Publicity Drums*

81   "Contracts were written for actors . . . " Knight, *The Warner Bros. Golden Anniversary Book* ("Fifty Years of Warner Bros."), 21.
82   "one of the funniest men in the whole world." Margaret Herrick Library.
82   "turned green." Johnny Carson show, September 2, 1974.
82   "[She] returned a few days ago . . . would be a ten-strike." John L. Scott, *L.A. Times*, February 27, 1949.
82   "After only one movie . . . sounding like a frog." *Daily News*, February 18, 1949.
83   "Warner Brothers seem singularly fortunate in Doris Day . . . " *Sunday Mirror*, April 10, 1949, 28.
83   "The voice of Doris Day should be well known . . . " *Daily News*, April 16, 1949.
83   "Another ordinary musical . . . " *Citizen News*, April 20, 1949.
84   "Hollywood, usually deadly . . . " *New York Sun*, August 13, 1949, 5.
85   "Those feuding inseparables . . . " *Daily News*, August 13, 1949, 21.
85   "sleeper . . . close to the truth for comfort." *New York Herald Tribune*, August 13, 1949, 4.
85   "A press agent once . . . that the saleslady now lives in the Day house." *New Liberty*, January 1949, 24–25.
86   "Virginia MacPherson for United Press . . . and a conscience." Roger M. Grace, "Perspectives Column-Uncle Jerry–Jerome B. Rosenthal–Is Dead," *Metropolitan News Company*, October 1, 2007.
86   "Lee likes doing all the things . . . " Pauline Swanson, "Oh, What a Wonderful Day," *Photoplay*, July 1949, 46+.
87   "I remember when I was first at . . . ." From a letter by Jane Ardmore to Elizabeth Otis, proposing a piece on Day. Ardmore papers, Margaret Herrick Library.
88   "waited for the right . . . " *Photoplay*, February 1950, 43.
88   "After a preview screening . . . " Robertson, 103.
88   "You couldn't do that then." Douglas, *The Ragman's Son*, 168.
88   "Kirk was civil to me . . . " Shipman, *Movie Talk*, 59.
88   "That face that she shows . . . " Hotchner, 273.
89   "Whether Doris will marry again soon is a matter . . . " Don Allen, "It's a Great Feeling," *Motion Picture*, March 1950, 66.

Chapter 8: *All Talking, No Singing, No Dancing*

91   "Mike Curtiz signed her . . . " John L. Scott, *Los Angeles Times*, February 27, 1949.
91   "The evil of studio . . . " Lucas, *Eighty Odd Years in Hollywood: Memoir of a Career in Film and Television*, 195. Lucas's mother was the silent screen star and screenwriter Bess Meredyth.
92   "didn't hesitate in accepting . . . " Hotchner, 118.

92   "I don't think I can handle it . . . *Family Weekly,* September 15, 1957, 14.

92   "In fact, Rogers was, herself, a last-minute replacement . . . " Elza Schallert, *Los Angeles Times,* October 10, 1949.

92   "We saw Miss Day's wardrobe tests . . . make her look just right." Warner Bros. Archives.

93   "The theme is not developed . . . " Warner Bros. Archives, August 29, 1949, memo to Jerry Wald.

94   "one serious encounter . . . cavernous, rococo office." Hotchner, 116.

95   "I don't have it . . . " Darr Smith, *Daily News,* January 3, 1950.

95   "The boys at the Warner office . . . " April 14, 1950, letter to Robert Taplinger in New York, from Warner Bros. Archives.

96   "as enjoyable as any picture I ever made." Hotchner, 128

96   "there had been a great improvement . . . " Butler, 230.

98   "Day also told Padgitt . . . I'll continue singing and . . . dancing." James Padgitt, *Dallas Herald,* June 1, 1950.

98   "She looks so unbelievably happy . . . " Betty Craig, *Denver Post,* March 30, 1950, 22.

99   "I know some hostesses . . . ." *Silver Screen,* June 1957, 17.

100 "look for a man who will be your lover . . . " Arden, *Three Phases of Eve: An Autobiography,* 72.

100 "romantically inclined" and "had been seen together . . . " *Motion Picture,* March 1950, 63.

100 "When it came to romance . . . " manuscript of *There's Nothing Simple About the Girl Next Door* by Laura Bascombe, written when Day was working on *Move Over, Darling.*

101 "The place was a wreck . . . " manuscript of *For Every Woman There's a Time to Grow Up,* by Doris Day, as told to Jane Ardmore, Margaret Herrick Library.

101 "liked yellow, printed fabrics . . . displaying their bounty." Drew Casper, "Doris Day: Elegant Authenticity for the Singer and Actress," *Architectural Digest,* March 2006, 172+.

102 "Williamsburg green," "Marty wooed me with a hammer," "Sometimes I think . . . " Kirtley Baskette, *Modern Screen,* October 1950, 74.

102 "head over heels in love . . . door with her." Hedda Hopper, "Sunny Doris Day Swinging to Drama," *Los Angeles Times,* July 23, 1950, E1.

103 "Doris Day wanted her husband to get me out . . . " Freedland, *All the Way: A Biography of Frank Sinatra,* 56.

103 "Though ultimately disappointing, the film would not be without its charms—even though Day would never acknowledge them." McCabe, *Cagney,* 259.

104 "Terry takes a rather proprietary attitude . . . " Don Allen, "A New DAY Tomorrow," *Motion Picture,* April 1951, 71.

104 "Marty used to come to dinner . . . " Jim Henaghan, "Love Sneaked In," *Modern Screen,* June 1951, 75.

104 Henaghan went on to say . . . " Ibid., 76.

105 "You didn't marry me because you loved me . . . " *Modern Screen,* October 1951, 74

106 "I wasn't even really a mother . . . " Laura Bascombe, "Last Words to Her Husband," *Photoplay,* July 1968, 47.

105 "Make believe is their business and home is where they leave it behind." *Modern Screen,* October 1951, 74.

105 "When you don't drink . . . " Ibid., 76.

106   "Why should I compete . . . " Ibid., 76.

106   "departed in a huff . . . " Marmorstein, 175.

106   "While acknowledging that . . . in the country some weeks." Granata, *Sessions with Sinatra: Frank Sinatra and the Art of Recording*, 69.

107   "The enormous success of the label . . . " Ibid., 69.

108   "She says she isn't up to . . . " *Examiner*, August 12, 1950.

109   "Marty Melcher kicked like seven steers . . . " *Variety*, February 26, 1952.

109   "In musicals, you're never through . . . " Johnson, *News*, October 10, 1950.

110   "Somebody gave me a red T-shirt . . . " Frank, *Tap*, 201.

111   "She was professional." Butler, 239–40.

111   "He's always lying in the way . . . " *Photoplay*, August 1955, 90.

112   "Dear Disk Jockeys: I am very . . . " *Billboard*, October 21, 1950.

112   "Under the headline . . . with all the trimmings." Harrison Carroll, *Herald*, November 16, 1950.

113   "Doris Day showed up . . . " Johnson, *News*, August 2, 1950.

113   "[a] charming piece of musical froth . . . " John L. Scott, *Los Angeles Times*, September 4, 1950, Part II, 7.

113   "a light-hearted filmusical . . . " Frank Quinn, *Daily Mirror*, September 2, 1950, 16.

113   "Hollywood—Data on delightful . . . " Gene Handsaker, AP "Newsfeature," March 9, 1951.

114   "If everything about . . . " Bosley Crowther, *New York Times*, December 23, 1950.

114   "One could wish that . . . " Otis L. Guernsey Jr., *New York Herald Tribune*, December 23, 1950.

114   "worthwhile entertainment . . . " *Variety*, November 15, 1950, Brogan scrapbook.

115   "another one of my 'un-favorites.' . . . " Margaret Herrick Library.

116   "permits a fine selection of players . . . " *Film Daily*, December 7, 1950.

116   "[a]bsorbing, biting and violent drama . . . " Dorothy Manners, *Examiner*, January 27, 1951.

116   "In *Helen Scott*, she was to . . . " Hedda Hopper, *Los Angeles Times*, January 31, 1951, A6.

117   "Jimmy Starr gave his readers . . . in the picture business." Jimmy Starr, *Herald*, March 1, 1951.

118   "Let me tell you about this lovely Day . . . " Jim O'Connor, *New York Journal-American*, March 27, 1951, 17.

118   "In her review for . . . I'm her fan." Louella Parsons, *Examiner*, March 24, 1951.

119   "Her Marjorie Winfield is a formative role . . . " Morris, 50.

119   "[Mel] Shavelson and [Jack] Rose, who conceived . . . source." *New York Times*, December 10, 1950.

120   "a Los Angeles mother of three . . . bottling in the summer, you know." Editors of Time-Life Books, *This Fabulous Century: 1950–1960*, 25.

121   "remains one of the screen's freshest personalities . . . " Margaret Harford, *Hollywood Citizen-News*, July 26, 1951.

121   "The picture is strictly summer-weight . . . " *Time*, August 20, 1951.

Chapter 9: *A Cunning Suitor*

123   "by way of Colorado . . . married in blue jeans." Margaret Herrick Library.

123 " . . . had to shoo them out of the house for their honeymoon." Ernst Jacobi, *Photoplay*, February 1955.

124 "but not without some difficulty . . . " unsigned, "Doris Day Gets Birthday Gift, A New Husband," *Los Angeles Times*, April 4, 1951, A1.

124 "It's Official—Marriage . . . " back side of publicity photo.

124 "They then enjoyed a posed . . . " This and the preceding paragraph were based on Peer J. Oppenheimer, "Doris Day: My Honeymoon Night," *TV and Movie Screen*, June 1958, 16–17+.

125 "Larkin replied that he was a personal friend of Melcher's . . . " Memo from Steve Brooks to Alex Evelove, May 1, 1951, Warner Bros. Archives.

127 "Housewives of America . . . I won't permit it." Press release, Warner Bros. Archives.

129 "Hedda Hopper's column had announced that Day would be starring in the film." Hopper, "Songwriter Story to Star Doris Day," *Los Angeles Times*, March 14, 1951.

130 "[Kahn would] frequently . . . " Warner Bros. Archives.

131 "Yesterday Mrs. Kahn . . . " Ibid.

132 "He sits on the bed beside me . . . " Hotchner, 127.

132 "I told Mike Curtiz, on the set this morning . . . " Warner Bros. Archives.

133 "soon realized that Thomas was no actor . . . " Robertson, 113.

134 "We have lots of fun at the piano on my show . . . " Hedda Hopper, *Los Angeles Times*, May 1, 1952, 26.

134 "the picture was originally called *Alex the Great*, then *Alexander*, and next, *The Big League*." Jack Sher, "The Ups and Downs of Old Pete," *Sport*, 49+.

136 "on whose name rests the film's chief marquee draw . . . Alexander's wife." Brogan, *Variety*, May 28, 1952.

136 "'The Winning Team' loses out . . . " *Time*, July 14, 1952.

136 "most persuasive when it interjects . . . " *Newsweek*, July 7, 1952.

137 "the happiest chapter," "something of a hero." Jim Burton, *Modern Screen*, May 1952, 89.

137 "very much like that young couple down the block from you." Ibid., 35.

137 "go into Beverly Hills and do a bit of shopping . . . " Ibid., 90.

Chapter 10: *"Dynamite" Doris*

139 "She has been working constantly . . . ." April 11, 1952, Warner Bros. Archives.

139 "Ray Bolger, who wasn't judged pretty enough . . . " *Daily News*, April 24, 1952.

139 "Hollywood has changed its feelings entirely . . . " Warner Bros. Archives

144 "Doris Day, beginning today, will devote . . . " *Hollywood Reporter*, June 16, 1952.

144 "It is an average round of comedy . . . " *Variety*, November 13, 1952.

144 " . . . Fairly pleasant, breezy filmusical, short on story but long on laughs." *Hollywood Reporter*, November 13, 1952.

144 "the rambling, much too complicated plot . . . " Philip K. Scheuer, *Los Angeles Times*, January 1, 1953, 21.

144 "It's easy on the eyes . . . " Kay Proctor, *L.A.. Examiner*, Januray 1, 1953, sec. II, 7.

148 "The studio is giving her the real grand treatment . . . " Hedda Hopper, *Los Angeles Times*, August 12, 1952.

148 "It's a harmless, entertaining . . . " *Seattle Times*, April 29, 1953.

148 "Choice, long-tested corn . . . zestfully than Doris Day." Archer Winston, *New York Post*, March 27, 1953, 56.

148 "Miss Day is thoroughly charming . . . " *Hollywood Reporter*, March 25, 1953, 3.

149 "a typical day . . . fan club officials from Seattle." Mary Goodwin, *Photoplay*, February 1953, 42–43+.

150 "There's nothing in the world . . . checked with her an hour before." Ibid.,

Chapter 11: *"Secret Love"*

151 "Both Doris and Curtiz . . . " Dorothy Manners, *Chicago Herald American*, June 22, 1948.

151 "I think 'Calamity Jane' is the real me . . . " Christopher Frayling, BBC TV documentary, first broadcast in Great Britain in 1989.

151 "I am Calamity Jane, didn't you know that?" Ronald L. Davis Oral History Collection.

151 "Day's definitive characterization . . . " Morris, *Doris Day*, 64.

152 "By the time we did 'Calamity Jane,' Doris had . . . ." Butler, 251.

152 "In 1876, Jane, by a daring feat . . . " Online encyclopedia entry on Martha Canary.

154 "I lowered my voice and stuck out my chin a little . . . " Hotchner, 131.

154 "by far the best picture Doris Day ever made." Hedda Hopper, October 19, 1953.

155 "Bands, Indians, stage coaches . . . " *Daily Journal*, Rapid City, South Dakota, October 26, 1953, 3.

155 "A rollicking musical filled with humor . . . " Milton Luban, *Hollywood Reporter*, October 28, 1953, 3.

155 "Doris Day has given Warners one of its best . . . " *Film Bulletin*, November 2, 1953, 8.

155 "In 'Calamity Jane,' Warners borrows . . . " Philip K. Scheuer, *Los Angeles Times*, November 1953.

155 "a lusty, zestful musical . . . " Irene Thirer, *New York Post*.

156 "Doris Day, having climbed to the No. 1 . . . she'll probably get them." Inez Wallace, *Cleveland Plain Dealer Pictorial Magazine*, May 17, 1953, 32.

Chapter 12: *"There's No Place Like Home"*

157 "When the family gathers at the old home . . . " Carl Schroeder, "Sentimental Journey," *Modern Screen*, September 1953.

158 "We looked out the window . . . " Ibid.

158 "dilapidated-looking" clothing factory. Peer Openheimer, "Having a Memorable Time," *Photoplay*, August 1955, 90.

158 "What's the matter? I'm nothing special . . . " *Motion Picture*, August 1954, 68.

159 "If we can't see it my way, I'm going to pack up and leave . . . " Schroeder, 63.

159 "Destined to win an Oscar . . . " BBC.

160 "was a brilliant musician . . . " Ronald L. Davis Oral History Collection.

160 "Even so, everything is organized . . . " Fred Brown, "What Marriage Has Taught Doris Day," *Movieland*, 66, from Constance McCormick Collection at USC.

161 "I don't know . . . . I'm never nervous making a picture . . . " Hedda Hopper, "Doris Day Gets Real Glamour Treatment," *Los Angeles Times*, December 22, 1954, B6.

162 "I tried to take a full breath . . . " Hotchner, 131–32.

162 "Doris had been working very hard . . . " Bill Davidson, *Look*, June 20, 1961, 45.

163 "I am not a physician . . . in a nice, middle-class neighborhood." Jane S. Carelton, "What Really Happened to Doris Day," *Modern Screen*, January 1954, 32+.

163 "The pictures and records . . . ." Joe Hyams, "Starring Doris Day," *Los Angeles Times*, September 11, 1960, TW13.

164 "Within a few years, Warners would claim . . . of $4.6 million." Harmetz, *Casablanca*, 191.

164 "I never dreamed I would be battling . . . " Ibid., 191.

165 "dismayed at how bad it was . . . ." Hotchner, 142.

165 "I think TV is here to stay . . . " eBay scrapbook, July 1953, 29.

166 "both had been in show business . . . pretenders." Shipman, *Judy Garland*, 383.

166 "that Garland had much less confidence . . . " Ibid., 383.

167 "When I first met [Doris] I didn't know who she was . . . "" *Silver Screen*, June 1957, 17.

168 "Doris Day is not as lucky . . . the magic star." Otis L. Guernsey Jr., *New York Herald Tribune*, April 10, 1954.

169 "[It] glitters harmlessly . . . " Archer Winston, *New York Post*, April 11, 1954, 27.

169 "With the help of director Jack Donohue . . . looking forced and tired." George Morris, *New York Times*, 67.

169 "In Palm Springs she had befriended . . . as an all-purpose companion." *Photoplay*, March 1956, 58–59.

170 "the key to the Doris Day illness . . . " Ibid., February 1954, 34+.

170 "I want you all to know . . . during the production." Doris Day, "I'm Well Again," *Photoplay*, May 1954, 46–49.

171 "I simply couldn't take . . . in which I would appear." Edwin Schallert, "Doris Day Needs No Song to Get Others to Listen," *Los Angeles Times*, April 25, 1954, D3.

172 "I was so nervous before I met Hitchcock . . . " Hopper, "Doris Day 'Grows up' in Etting Role," *Los Angeles Times*, June 12, 1955, E1.

Chapter 13: *"Fairy Tales Can Come True"*

174 "A year earlier, his wife, Ava Gardner . . . he had commanded." Lahr, *Sinatra: The Artist and the Man*, 49.

176 "if that creep Melcher is anywhere . . . " Hotchner, 148.

176 "[i]t was the intention of the agreement . . . " August 2, 1954, memo, Warner Bros. Archives.

176 "Saw M. Melcher . . . " Warner Bros. Archives.

177 "the said Martin Melcher . . . whatsoever." August 2, memo.

177 "With Ava [Gardner] having gone . . . " Freedland, 216.

179 "Frank lunged for the guy . . . " Zehme, *The Way You Wear Your Hat: Frank Sinatra and the Lost Art of Livin'*, 157–58

179 "Miss Barrymore became too ill to work . . . " Production book, Warner Bros. Archives.

179 "When you've been as broke as I've been . . . " Jim Ashe, "The Fights and Loves of Doris Day," *Hollywood Screen Parade*, November 1959, 25.

180 "a musical with a Western background . . . as her protector." Ibid., September 30, 1954.

180 "typically American . . . living conditions in America." *North Adams Transcript*, October 1, 1954.

180 "The sentiments of this wide-eyed romance . . . cruelty to strays." Bosley Crowther, *New York Times*, January 20, 1955.

181 "No objection is here made to their performances . . . " Archer Winston, *New York Post*, January 20, 1955.

181 "a study in contrasts . . . gentlest men I've ever known." Ernst Jacobi, "If You Like What You Love, You're in Luck," *Photoplay*, February 1955, 48–9+.

Chapter 14: *"A Perfect Motion Picture"*

183 "approval from the principals in the Ruth Etting deal." April 23, 1952, memo from Kenneth MacKenna to Pasternak, Pasternak papers at USC.

184 "at liberty to do with the names, and with each of the names, whatever we desire." July 31, 1952, Pasternak papers at USC.

184 "For her part, Etting 'refused to approve . . . .'" August 24, 1954, Margaret Herrick Library.

185 "Jane Russell, too, refused . . . " As told to Robert Osborne during an interview for Turner Classic Movies.

185 "There was apparently . . . " Dwight Whitney, "All Sugar, No Spice," *TV Guide*, December 28, 1969.

185 "I took one read-through . . . " Cagney, *Cagney by Cagney*, 134.

186 "I saw something in her . . . " Ibid., 136.

186 "wide open as a barn door . . . " Ibid., 136.

186 According to a memo dated November 10, the total budget for the film rose from $2,346,000 to $2,587,000. Pasternak papers at USC.

186 "I had a lot of glasses . . . " Ardmore papers, Margaret Herrick Library.

187 "On the few occasions . . . " Cameron Shipp, "Hollywood's Girl-Next-Door," *Cosmopolitan*, April 1956, 58+.

188 "I was frightened . . . " Lydia Lane, "Doris Day Learns How to Relax," *Los Angeles Times,* June 19, 1955, C11.

188 "Dear Joe: I was invited last night . . . produced in flawless taste." Pasternak papers at USC.

188 "performances that command Academy Award attention . . . "merely feeling sympathy towards her." *Motion Picture Herald*, May 21, 1955.

189 "unsavory romantic story . . . to that story." "The Gimp is Back, Still Rough on Ruth," unsigned article, *Life*, 67–68.

189 "Personally, [Day's] a far cry from the girl next door . . . " Hedda Hopper, "Doris Day Grows Up in New Movie Roles," *Los Angeles Times*, June 12, 1955, E1.

189 "reported that the early press response had prompted MGM to offer her $1 million for four pictures . . . " Edwin Schallert, "Doris Day Signing Deal for $1,000,000," *Los Angeles Times*, June 11, 1955, A7.

190 "[A] stinging but entertaining film . . . " Bosley Crowther, *New York Times*, May 27, 1955, 14.

190 "One of the most strongly dramatic . . . " Alton Cook, *New York World-Telegram and Sun*, May 27, 1955.

190 "A tremendously powerful drama . . . " William K. Zinsser, *New York Herald Tribune*, May 27, 1955.

190 "Filmgoers rousingly agreed . . . " Pasternak papers at USC.

191 "[i]t is one of those rare instances . . . " McCabe, 281.

192 "Still another reporter quoted Day as saying . . . her own young son." Shipp, 58+.

192 "Why do I always have to be the girl-next-door? . . . " Ibid., 58+.

Chapter 15: *"Whatever Will Be, Will Be"*

193 "the first . . . was the work of a talented amateur . . . " Rhomer and Chabrol, *Hitchcock: The First Forty-four Films*, 227.

194 "[Hitchcock] was not content . . . " Ibid., 138.

194 "I know I'll love working with [Hitchcock] . . . " Howard Thompson, "On a Dawn of a Bright, New Day," *New York Times*, Brogan scrapbook #3.

195 "The reception for Miss Day . . . " Edwin Schallert, "Doris Day Signing Deal for $1,000,000," *Los Angeles Times*, June 11, 1955, A7.

196 "That went over big with me . . . " Schroeder, 59.

196 "There wasn't much she could do about the poverty . . . " McGilligan, *Alfred Hitchcock: A Life in Darkness and Light*, 518.

196 " 'In the beginning,' recalled Stewart . . . " Spoto, *The Dark Side of Genius*, 392.

196 "I loved him personally . . . ." McGilligan, 518.

197 "It seemed they knew . . . " *Screen*, August 1956, 72.

198 "But, dear Doris . . . " McGilligan, 519.

198 "Now, I'm supposed to cry . . . " Schroeder, 59.

198 "What happened to me . . . " Spoto, 392.

199 "got such a performance . . . It was Doris." *Architectural Digest*, March 6, 1956, 251.

199 "One really good scream . . . " Schroeder, 59.

199 "the quintessential summary . . . " Spoto, *The Art of Alfred Hitchcock*, 276–77.

200 "first to its exotic . . . " unsigned article, *Life*, 95–96, Brogan scrapbook #1.

200 "Before I met Jimmy, I often wondered . . . " Doris Day, "I Married Jimmy Stewart," *Film Life*, February 1956, 14+, 63.

201 "In some of the terror scenes . . . " Scullin, Part III, 111.

201 "a natural flair for style" and . . . "lament." Shipp, 58+.

202 "Hitchcock fans have reached the . . . " Don Gillette, *Hollywood Reporter*, 81.

202 "We go out more than we used to . . . " Dorothy O'Leary, *Screen*, August 1956, 72.

203 "Melcher was the ringleader . . . " *Modern Screen*, July 1956, 65.

203 "It was a gold loving cup . . . " Reba and Bonnie Churchill, "Her Best Friends Wouldn't Tell Her," *Silver Screen*, June 1957, 17.

203 "Pastel place mats, flickering candles . . . " Ibid., 18.

203 "Before work began on *Julie* . . . in the wooded hills." *Modern Screen*, 64–65.

203 "loves music and plays piano . . . " Dorothy O'Leary, "One Wonderful Day," *Screen Magazine*, August 1956, 17+.

204 "more like a cook book than a travelog . . . " *Silver Screen*, 19.

204 "You know, Marty and I are going . . . " Schroeder, 42–43, 59.

Chapter 16: *Day Noir*

205 "We're going to Pebble Beach . . . " Schroeder, 59.

205 "documentary technique . . . " Philip K. Scheuer, *Los Angeles Times*, January 5, 1956, B11.

208 "Since Day was convinced . . . " *Modern Screen*, July 1956, 64–5.

208 "tendency in dramatic pictures to speak in low tones," Ardmore papers, Margaret Herrick Library.

208 "He's always after me to talk louder . . . " Reba and Bonnie Churchill, "Day is Night Club Star," *Beverly Hills Citizen,* May 31, 1956, 7.

208 "It was the first time I couldn't come home . . . " Ardmore papers, Margaret Herrick Library.

209 "constant, rather intense stabbing pain . . . " Hotchner, 172–3.

209 "very jealous." Ibid., 171–72.

209   "Louis and I had long talks about our problems . . . " Ibid., 172.

209 "Both Doris and I hated the director . . . " and "wanting to be sexy . . . " Jourdan shared these comments with Daniel Selznick, who put questions to him on behalf of the author.

209 "The romance goes out the window when you suddenly feel that you're married to your father." Beard, *E-True Hollywood Story,* 258.

209 "not a conversationalist" and "never really talked about us." Hotchner, 172.

210 "The complicated, four-hour . . . " Ibid., 173–74.

211 "By virtue of the attorney-client relationship . . . " DORIS DAY et al., Cross-complainants and Respondents, v. JEROME B. ROSENTHAL et al., Cross-defendants and Appellants. No. 50472. Court of Appeal of California, Second Appellate District, Division Three. August 8, 1985.

211 When *Julie* was about to be released . . . " Unsigned article, "Fearful Female on the Run," *Life,* 113–14, Brogan scrapbook #4.

212 "lovely black lady" and "one of the sweetest . . . " Hotchner, 179–80.

212 "The casting of Miss Day . . . " Philip K. Scheuer, "Tension Drawn Drum-Tight in 'Julie,'" *Los Angeles Times,* September 30, 1956, Part V, 1+.

215 "Female follow-ups were Susan Hayward . . . " *Los Angeles Times,* August 28, 1957.

215 "Doris Day is one of the most written . . . It's somebody else." Scullin, 105.

215 "They know more about me than I know myself . . . " Ibid., 107.

216 "In most businesses . . . " Ibid., 106.

Chapter 17: *"I'm Not at all in Love"*

219 "I'd like to go back to Warners . . . " Louella Parsons, *Los Angeles Examiner,* March 17, 1956.

220 "Doris likes the music in 'Pajama Game' so much . . . " Ibid., April 26, 1956.

220 "Doris Day, whose career has zoomed . . . to be called *Christie.*" Dick Williams, *Mirror-News,* March 21, 1956.

220 "reportedly one of the largest [deals] made in the record . . . business with a singer." *North Adams Transcript,* May 12, 1956.

220 "picture price these days is $300,000" and "[s]he and Marty Melcher . . . they liked a lot." Hedda Hopper, *Daily News,* May 16, 1956.

220 "Talks are understood to have stemmed . . . film as well." *Variety,* May 25, 1956.

221 "Columnist divulged that . . . " Sheilah Graham, *Citizen News,* May 28, 1956.

221 "more than $250,000" and "When Doris started at this studio eight years ago, her salary was $250 a week." Ibid.

222 "I don't know if I can handle the songs . . . . They require an Ethel Merman type," "Doris' Dancing Daze," *Photoplay,* August 1957, 48–49.

222 "Warners took over what amounted to a package . . . " Arthur Knight, *Dance Magazine,* August 1957, 36.

222 "Doris just jumped in . . . " A & E *Biography* of Doris Day, 1998.

224 "We had done a lot of costume . . . " Harris, *The Performing Set,* 94–95.

226 "It is unacceptable to show . . . '" Warner Bros. Archives, December 7, 1955.

227 "I told her one time that I had heard . . . " Butler, 230.

228 "told somebody that this was the perfect setting for Halloween . . . " Doris Day, tape recording for British fan club, December 7, 1957.

228 "improved [on the Broadway show] in practically every department . . . " Sylvia Ashton, *Show Business*, April 28, 1957, 3H.

228 "With zip and zest and a proper, precise knowledge . . . " James Powers, *Hollywood Reporter*, August 7, 1957.

229 "perfectly hectic two weeks . . . quickly spread." *North Adams Transcript*, September 16, 1957.

229 "box-office champ among the Broadway first-run films . . . " *Variety*, September 9, 1957.

229 "Curious neighbors . . . " Publicity report in Warner Bros. Archives.

229 "It is fresh, funny, lively and tuneful . . . " Bosley Crowther, *New York Times*, August 30, 1957.

230 "[e]verything about the show, in fact, looks fresh . . . " William K. Zinsser, *New York Herald Tribune*, August 30, 1957, 6.

232 "I plan to pull a Garbo . . . " Elva Newman, "If I were 17 Again," *Photoplay*, 94.

233 "When I started making 'Teacher's Pet' with Clark . . . " Ibid.

233 "was anything but macho . . . " Christopher Frayling, BBC documentary.

233 "Underneath it all [Clark] was delicate . . . I think, and didn't know how he was adored in this world. He had no idea. He was insecure." Ronald L. Davis Oral History Collection.

233 "there were times when Doris seemed a bit nervous playing opposite the great Gable." Gelb, *The Doris Day Scrapbook*, 100.

234 "They were a most unlikely couple . . . " Berkman, *Around the World in 80 Years: Newsrooms, Soundstages, Private Encounters and Public Affairs*, 132–33.

235 "Paul's death hit Doris very hard . . . " "Don't Believe Everything They're Saying About Me," *Photoplay*, October 1958, 91.

235 "When Marty suggested he come into this business . . . " Ardmore papers, Margaret Herrick Library.

235 "My mother and I felt his death very deeply . . . " Hotchner, 190.

235 "the way I saw Marty treat Paul . . . " Ibid., 190–91.

237 "The normal relationship . . . " Samuel D. Berns, *Motion Picture Daily*, March 17, 1958.

237 "is more fun than the funnies . . . " Philip K. Scheuer, *Los Angeles Times*, March 9, 1958.

238 "We loved [the house] the very first time we clapped eyes on it . . . I had always wanted." Doris Day, "If Time Stood Still," *Motion Picture*, July 1958, 70.

239 "office-den, something I've been dying to have . . . " *Photoplay*, June 1958, 48.

240 "When I went through the hot rod craze . . . " Terry Melcher, as told to Hortense Rich, "The Truth About Mother and Me," *Modern Screen*, August 1962, 55.

241 "to make time stand still for 24 hours," "I wouldn't think about the day to follow or the day before." Doris Day, "If Time Stood Still," *Motion Picture*, July 1958, 25.

241 "After lunch, I'd like to revisit all the places . . . " Ibid., 70.

243 "It was something that happened at the last minute . . . wrong for the role." Michael Buckley, *Films in Review*, June/July 1986.

244 "Kelly told both Day and Widmark that they looked . . . " Ardmore papers, Margaret Herrick Library.

244 "Well, he's very quiet . . . " *Photoplay,* 1966, as reprinted in *Doris Day Society Journal,* volume 1, #1, March 1970, 2.

245 "One of the year's funniest pictures . . . " *Variety,* October 9, 1958.

245 "It's a rollicking sampling . . . She's as wholesome as wheat germ, as bubbly as champagne." Jack Moffitt, *Hollywood Reporter,* October 9, 1958.

245 "[t]asteless and not very funny comedy, somewhat miscast." *Halliwell's Film Guide,* 2003, 877.

245 "one of the star's weakest." Morris, 95.

245 "People don't have to understand your words to know . . . what you sing," Sidney Skolsky papers, Margaret Herrick Library.

246 "In looking for Doris in future pictures . . . " "Reporter Finds Doris Day Warm, 100% Real," *Los Angeles Times,* December 13, 1958, C6.

246 "The audience won't accept me any other way . . . ." Philip K. Scheuer, "Doris Day Tops as Girl next Door," *Los Angeles Times,* December 16, 1960, A1.

246 "I've planned to take my son out of school in April . . . " Ardmore papers, Margaret Herrick Library.

246 "When I got there, they had all the German kind of food . . . " Jane Wilkie, *Motion Picture,* October 1959, 80.

247 "There was a lot of antiblack . . . " Hotchner, 181.

Chapter 18: *"Sticking Keys and Farting Poodles"*

248 "They've been three and five almost as long as Jack Benny . . . has been thirty-nine," *Photoplay,* August 1955, 90.

249 "At three o'clock every afternoon . . . " Freedland, *Jack Lemmon,* 56.

249 "We used to sit on the dock . . . " Teddy Rooney, "I'm in Love with Doris Day," *Motion Picture,* February 1958, 70.

249 "Everybody was so tired back in Connecticut . . . " Ibid., 70.

250 "I think that's the craziest, most foolhardy . . . " Newman, 94.

250 "Doris just burst out laughing . . . " *Photoplay,* October 1958, 91.

250 Their rapport she felt . . . "honest." Ronald L. Davis Oral History Collection.

250 "I think she is potentially one of the greatest actresses I'll ever . . . " Howard Green.

250 "She's met some wonderful women through the club . . . " Ardmore papers, Margaret Herrick Library.

251 "My biggest fault, or weakness . . . 'I guess so,' I admitted." "The Lesson that Electrified My Life," *Motion Picture,* February 1959, 74.

Chapter 19: *"Pillow Talk"*

253 "'such inept comedies' as *The Tunnel of Love* and *It Happened to Jane* . . . , Day's career was at something of an impasse and that it had become increasingly difficult to find vehicles that suited the cotton candy image of Day, whose persona as the screen innocent was reaching the point of tedium and absurdity.'" Parish, 749.

253 "[Hunter] loved everything about Hollywood . . . Rock Hudson and Claire Trevor were regulars." Jewison, *This Terrible Business Has Been Good to Me,* 78.

254 "Me? In a Cary Grant role . . . " Ross Hunter, *Modern Screen,* October 1964, 64.

254 "[Hudson] turns the gay closet into his own Superman . . . " Wolcott, 146+.

255 "Norman Jewison would later refer to Hudson's homosexuality as an 'open secret' at the time." Jewison, 86.

255 "No matter how absurd . . . " Oppenheimer and Vitek, 70.

256 "We became a family . . . " *Modern Screen,* October 1964, 64.

256 "was busy on the phone," and "Jeff, why don't you take Rock's place?" He did, "ad libbing whatever came into his mind in response to Doris's lines," said a reporter in *Modern Screen.* Brogan scrapbook #4.

256 "Why don't you sing a verse . . . " Kanin, *Together Again,* 193.

256 "I was [supposed] to storm into her apartment . . . " Hudson, *Motion Picture,* October 1959, 28–9+.

257 "didn't have the greatest confidence in his own ability . . . " Oppenheimer and Vitek, 71.

257 "She is the same way I am about new people . . . " Rock Hudson, *Motion Picture,* October, 1959, 29.

257 "In the course of shooting, Day caught Hudson's habit . . . of doing crossword puzzles during down time on the set." *Screen Stories,* March 1960, 58.

258 "[t]hey had to add a week on to the shooting schedule . . . " Beard, 261.

259 "But it also tells you much more than that . . . " Cleveland Amory, *TV Guide,* June 10, 1972, 40.

260 "They were slated to go to Boston . . . " *Los Angeles Times,* May 12, 1959.

260 "Up to a point, this is a funny comedy . . . " *Variety,* April 21, 1959.

260 "[The film] is not as hilarious . . . one unqualified delight." Philip K. Scheuer, *Los Angeles Times,* June 4, 1959.

260 "in tailoring [the story] to Doris Day's proportions . . . " Hazel Flynn, *Beverly Hills Citizen,* June 5, 1959.

260 "The film did extremely well in London, however, where it was released . . . " Hedda Hopper, *Los Angeles Times,* June 2, 1959, 26.

261 "one of her most characteristic" and "a delightful movie . . . " Morris, 97–98.

261 "'charming' and that 'its box-office failure . . . is hard to fathom." Santopietro, *Considering Doris Day,* 116.

Chapter 20: *Plain as Day*

263 "Doris is a wonderful, wholesome girl . . . " Peter Howell, "The Sweet Day Turns Sour," British *Photoplay,* April 1965, 68.

264 "But when he read the book, he said, 'My God. This *is* Doris Day!' He instantly fell in love with her, from the very first day they worked together. There are a lot of on-set photos of Day and Walters laughing hysterically." Phillips's biography of Walters is a work in progress. Comments were shared with author.

265 "preferred to seem brittle, unreliable, a man whose banter and charm occasionally crumbled to reveal inadequacy." Thomson, *New Biographical Dictionary of Film,* 356.

265 "broke two basic actors' rules . . . " Lord, *Niv: The Authorized Biography of David Niven,* 206.

265 "veered from English to American . . . and back." Ibid., 207.

265 "[T]hey walked in the woods . . . " Jane Ardmore, "Stop! Look! Live!," *Motion Picture,* April, 1960, 74. (The interview was conducted at Day's "Tennis Club," following a game.)

265 "While the Melchers refused to be pinned . . . " Edwin Matesky, *North Adams Transcript,* November 5, 1959.

266 "It was like coming out of heaven into chaos . . . " Ardmore papers, Margaret Herrick Library.

266 "A comedy to be laughed at . . . " Bill Weaver, *Film Daily,* August 12, 1959.

266 "[I]t is sure to hit the target of high grosses . . . " Jack Moffitt, *Hollywood Reporter*, August 12, 1959.

267 "When these two magnificent objects . . . " Parish, *Hollywood's Great Love Teams*, 751.

267 "coincided with the creation of Barbie and Ken, doll versions of Doris and Rock . . . First Couple of American Pop." Wolcott, 146–58.

268 "the famous newer 'ring-a-ding' . . . " *Motion Picture*, October 1959, 8.

270 "Gordon MacRae, Perry Como, Nat Cole, and Ella Fitzgerald." In private scrapbook from eBay, July 1953, 30.

Chapter 21: *A Woman in Jeopardy*

271 "Day maintained that she canceled . . . " Sheilah Graham, December 14, 1958.

271 "sort of Hitchcock suspense murder mystery . . . " December 17, 1958, *Los Angeles Times*, B12.

271 "stumbled into" and "light comedies . . . humor in it." Harrison, *A Damned Serious Business: My Life in Comedy*, 168.

272 "becoming depressed." *Screen Stories*, November 1960, 57.

272 "found the proceedings such a strain . . . " Harrison, 168.

272 "[A] dear girl, a kind girl . . . " Shipman, 52.

272 "favorite studio . . . with windows all around." Ronald L. Davis Oral History Collection.

273 "I was with her just after she'd read the script . . . " Bascombe manuscript is in Ardmore papers, Margaret Herrick Library.

273 "so insistent . . . " Hotchner, 201.

273 "I should have known better . . . " Ibid., 201.

273 "I remember that she was so great . . . " Mosley with Masheter, *Rex Harrison: The First Biography*, 203.

273 "This is the peak. This is where you break . . . There is no way out. You have to break emotionally, go into complete hysteria. Everything must become unhinged." From David Zeitlin's early draft for *Life* article, Margaret Herrick Library.

273 "the big scene in the picture . . . in the woman's mind." Bill Davidson, *Look*, June 20, 1961, 40.

274 "re-created the ghostly abuses of Al Jorden . . . " Hotchner, 202.

274 "He brought me my dinner on a tray . . . until I fell asleep." James Gregory, "Doris Day in Seclusion," Brogan scrapbook #6.

274 "'world's favorite' actor and actress—'to almost no one's surprise," *Los Angeles Times* March 9, 1960.

275 "I drew the line when Simone Signoret hit the jackpot . . . " Hedda Hopper, Brogan scrapbook #6..

275 "Haven't seen the boy in 12 years now . . . ." Hugh Burrell, "Doris Day's Secret Son," *Modern Screen*, May 1960, 29+.

276 "It has all the ingredients to insure it a solid box office reception," Mandel Herbstman, *Film Daily*, March 22, 1960.

276 "present exalted status," "the accompanying anonymous review was summed up," "Oopsy-Daisy." "Where Hollywood Begins," *Newsweek*, April 11, 1960, 121.

277 "Some gentle people may love . . . " Bosley Crowther, *New York Times*, April 1, 1960.

277 "[T]he movie certainly isn't very funny . . . " Philip K. Scheuer, *Los Angeles Times*, April 14, 1960, B7.

278 "Surprisingly, my mother had no objection to this . . . " Terry Melcher, as told to Hortense Rich, "The Truth About Mother and Me," *Modern Screen*, August 1962, 55.

279 "shared a room, a pink-and-white jeep and some keen games . . . and their jeep." Jaye Moore, "Doris Day's First Husband Dies!" Brogan scrapbook #5.

279 "She is the eternal freckled-faced girl next door . . . " David Zeitlin, *Life*, October 10, 1960.

279 "[Day] is an enigma. . . . The Melchers eat health food . . . " Zeitlin's research notes, Margaret Herrick Library.

279 "Saw 'Midnight Lace' last night, Ross Hunter's pretty successful attempt . . . " Ibid.

279 "completely on the enigmatical, paradoxical, just plain puzzling . . . And I know I can. I have complete confidence." Ibid.

280 "To get back to this approval bit—they also insist on approving all photos" This appeared in a July 27, 1960, letter from "Ursula" to Bob Sherrod, at the *Post*, as archived at the Margaret Herrick Library.

282 "I bought this brown wig . . . " John Whitcomb, "The Freckle-faced Kid from Cincinnati, Ohio," Brogan scrapbook #2.

283 "namby-pamby" and a "coward." Hotchner, 158.

284 "I'm a difficult character to live with . . . ability to communicate my secret feelings." "What Kind of Wife," *Photoplay*, September 1960, 48+.

284 "The officer was very polite [and] I was very polite . . . " Ann Masters, *Chicago American*, October 1, 1960.

285 "Miss Day gives a golden imitation of a love-struck heiress . . . " Bosley Crowther, *New York Times*, October 14, 1960.

285 "While the whole business is pretty unnerving . . . " John L. Scott, *Los Angeles Times*, November 17, 1960, B17.

285 "Doris Day, let us be early ones to confess it, gives one of her best performances . . . " Archer Winston, *New York Post*, October 14, 1960.

285 "Miss Day's forte may be comedy . . . " Harrison Carroll, *L.A. Herald Express*, November 17, 1960.

285 "[Day is] so appealingly frail . . . " Alton Cook, *New York World Telegram and Sun*, October 14, 1960.

285 "It's funny that so many people seem to identify . . . " Peter Bart, "All in a Day's Work for Mr. Melcher," *New York Times*, February 14, 1965.

286 "It's a little early to tell for sure . . . " Mike Connolly, *Valley Times*, January 30, 1961.

286 "The Academy Award nominations came out pretty much as expected . . . " Louella Parsons, *Los Angeles Examiner*, March 2, 1961.

286 "Miss Day is the first woman to win the top spot since 1943." *North Adams Transcript*, December 29, 1960.

286 "calling for $26,000,000 in two years." Louella Parsons, January 8, 1961.

286 "We package and produce; the studios finance and distribute . . . " Philip K Scheuer, "Doris Day Tops as Girl Next Door," *Los Angeles Times*, December 19, 1960.

287 "The ghost of Hollywood's legendary glamour . . . " "Doris Day Foot-Printing Revives Glamour Days at Grauman's Chinese," *Hollywood Reporter*, January 20, 1961, 1–X.

287 "William Wyler considered her as Katharine Hepburn's . . . " Paris, *Audrey Hepburn*, 176.

287 "Moreover, Melcher was negotiating . . . " Louella Parsons, *Los Angeles Examiner,* January 31, 1961.

287 "a rotten shame" and "hundreds of letters," Ibid., March 16, 1961.

288 "Most of the stars managed by the agency . . . " Terry Melcher, as told to George Christy, "The Doris Day I Know," 88+, Brogan scrapbook # 3

288 "The first time I dated Terry . . . " Ardmore papers, Margaret Herrick Library.

288 "the most beautiful version . . . arrangement for her on it." Bear Family Records, 1960–67, 20.

289 "It wasn't so much the fact that she might not have approved of me . . . " Tom Walker, "Doris Day–Diahann Carroll: The Negro-White Love That Haunts Each of Them," *Screenland,* June 1969, 54.

290 "Doris tried to get me and her mother . . . " Roger Kahn, "Is There a Doris Day?" Brogan scrapbook #5.

290 "[h]er fortune, her fears, her failures, her faith . . . complexity." Bill Davidson, *Look,* June 1969, 36+

290 "conservatively estimated . . . several independent productions." Ibid., 46.

290 "You can be talking to Doris . . . " Ibid., 49.

290 "You're invited to dinner at their house . . . " Ibid., 46.

291 "Concerned that the large crowd pressing into the store . . . " *North Adams Transcript,* October 11, 1969.

Chapter 22: *"Even More Shekels Than Freckles"*

295 "It seemed so similar, I thought people would think . . . " Oppenheimer and Vitek, 73.

296 "Farty Belcher . . . " Robert Hofler, *The Man Who Invented Rock Hudson,* 361.

296 "They also had a shared fantasy life, pretending to be . . . " Oppenheimer and Vitek, 71.

297 "[t]here was one take, where [Rock] leaned over . . . " Ibid., 71.

299 "10,000,000 packages [of] Imperial Margarine . . . in their own words." Pressbook.

299 "a much funnier picture . . . " Philip K. Scheuer, *Los Angeles Times,* December 15, 1961.

299 "Mr. Hudson and Miss Day are delicious . . . out of a comedy in years." Bosley Crowther, *New York Times,* Brogan scrapbook, no date given.

299 "I broke the news to my mother . . . " Terry Melcher, as told to Hortense Rich, "The Truth About Mother and Me," *Modern Screen,* August 1962, 55.

300 "My mother and dad didn't take my . . . " Vernon Scott, "Doris Day's Son Cuts First Record," UPI Hollywood correspondent, *Citizen News,* April 26, 1962.

300 "His mother did her best to promote the 45, without much success." *Los Angeles Times,* May 27, 1962. (This was also when Day proudly announced that Candy Bergen was Terry's girlfriend.)

301 "felt that Hudson had gotten too much . . . " Marc Eliot, *Cary Grant: A Biography,* 335.

302 "The hurried invitation . . . " *North Adams Transcript,* July 7, 1961.

302 "[T]he sunny, funny, freckled . . . " *Modern Screen,* October 1964, 65.

302 "[w]hen we got on the set . . . " Pressbook.

302 "What a week! . . . " John Whitcomb, "The Freckle-faced Kid from Cincinnati, Ohio," Brogan scrapbook #2.

302 "Of all the people I performed with . . . " Hotchner, 204.

303 "In working out a compromise . . . ." Whitcomb, Brogan scrapbook # 2.

304   "Cary called and told me . . . " Nelson, *Evenings with Cary Grant,* 263.
304   "'That Touch of Mink' will be lined with money," Lawrence H. Lipskin,
        Hollywood Reporter, May 9, 1962.
305   "Theatergoers will see to it . . . " Ibid.
306   "the recipe is potent . . . an adept farceur with this outing." Jack Pitman,
        Variety, May 9, 1962.
306   "film is riddled with commercials . . . No competition." Dwight Macdonald,
        Dwight Macdonald on Movies, 110–13.
306   "with elaborate recreations facilities." *North Adams Transcript,* July 23, 1962.
306   "Doris is kind of an inspector general . . . " Ibid., August 11, 1962.
306   "frequently seen," "one hundred new rooms," *Modern Screen,* October 1964,
        65.
307   "Shor's new restaurant . . . " "Doris Day and Toots Shor Figure in Teamster
        Loans," *Los Angeles Times,* October 22, 1962.

Chapter 23: *Low-Wire Act*

309   "musical comedy-circus-vaudeville-revue-spectacle-menagerie . . . " Green,
        Ring Bells! Sing Songs! Broadway Musicals of the 1930s, 122.
309   "Purchase culminates almost a year . . . " *Variety,* April 2, 1962.
310   "The Irish actor would proudly display his chariot from that film in his living
        room and hang the red-and-gold whip he had used as the charioteer above his
        fireplace." *Modern Screen,* March 1963, 72.
311   "Joe, get out of bed . . . " Helen Weller, "Doris Day Brought Me Back to Life,"
        Screen Stories, May 1963, 44+.
311   "Setting a ten-year studio . . . " Pressbook.
311   "the most expensive musical in the studio's history," *Variety,* October 5, 1961.
311   "would report that the film . . . " *Variety,* May 22, 1962.
312   "Silvers Madison, his trainer . . . " Pressbook.
312   "arms ached from pulling on tights" and "There's another set on under
        these . . . " Jon Whitcomb, "Hollywood's Biggest Star," *Cosmopolitan,* October
        1962, 12–14.
312   "After watching early rushes . . . " Pressbook.
313   "Doris worries incessantly . . . " Lotta Alexander, "I'm Afraid to Grow Old,"
        1968, Brogan scrapbook #5.
313   "maintained surface . . . less a romance." Louella Parsons, *Modern Screen,* March
        1963, 12.
314   "his reputation for being a tyrant who treated actors as objects . . . ." As told to
        author by Brent Phillips.
316   "One year she sent each friend . . . " *Modern Screen,* October 1964, 64.
316   "In real life, I'm like [Gracie] is on stage," Ardmore papers, Margaret Herrick
        Library.
317   "I go about four times a week . . . " Jane Ardmore, "Why Doris Rides by Day—
        Hides by Night!" Brogan scrapbook #5.
317   "a beige Chrysler and a great sense of humor . . . " Bergen, *Knock Wood,*
        116–17.
317   "Because of the size of my appetite . . . " Ibid., 117.
318   "Terry got itchy . . . " Ibid.
318   "She wore a hot-pink sheath . . . " Ibid., 118.
319   "one of my best friends . . . onto Terry's dock." Wynn, *We Will Always Live in
        Beverly Hills: Growing Up Crazy in Hollywood,* 164.

319   "Terry and I had certain things . . . " Ibid., 197.
320   "anti-charisma," Gary Giddins, *New York Sun*, May 3, 2005.
320   "Picture of the Month," *Seventeen*, January 1963.
320   "Gold Medal Movie of the Month," *Photoplay*, February 1963.
320   "The biggest puzzle 'Jumbo' presents . . . " Robert B. Frederick, *Variety*, December 5, 1962.
321   "A rousing musical trim-tailored . . . " *Hollywood Reporter*, December 5, 1962.
321   "'Jumbo' is a great big blubbery . . . " *Time*, December 12, 1962.
321   "It is colorful, vivid movie fare . . . " George H. Jackson, *Los Angeles Herald-Examiner*, December 22, 1962, A12.
321   "heading for a sockeroo $165,000 for opening week," *Variety*, December 12, 1962.
321   "Sidney Sheldon has based his . . . " Brendan Gill, "Elephantiasis," *New Yorker*, December 15, 1962, 135.
322   "The point here seems . . . " *Newsweek*, December 17, 1962.

Chapter 24: *The Imperfect Setup*
326   "a propitious time to break up . . . Sunset Towers." Hotchner, 207.
327   "deteriorated . . . I can't fake it." Hotchner 1985 British paperback edition, 352.
327   "contemptuous . . . as opposed to the trial Melcher viewed it as." Ibid., 207–9.
327   "Doris Day and Marty Melcher . . . " Jerry Paige, "Doris Day: The Story Behind the Divorce Rumors!" *Motion Picture*, February 1963, 34+.
329   "have always had a nice calm . . . " *North Adams Transcript*, October 23, 1962.
330   "developed a romantic interest . . . " Ibid., December 1, 1962.
330   "The rift-rumors have been a red-hot topic . . . " Walter Winchell, "Doris Day-Melcher Marriage on Rocks: Producer Moves Out of Home" *L.A. Herald Examiner*, December 2, 1962.
331   "New York columnist Earl Wilson quickly took the bait. 'Girl-Next-Door Doris Day's new heart interest . . . planned to wed Doris.'" As quoted by Aaron Putnam in "Are White Stars Switching to Negroes?" *Confidential*, September 1963, 14+.
331   "Flabbergasted . . . " Louella Parsons, *Modern Screen*, March 1963.
331   "snow in Tahiti . . . cordial one." *North Adams Transcript*, December 5, 1962.
331   "There's an awful . . . " Louella Parsons, Ibid., December 12, 1962.
331   "As well documented in a long investigative piece by Jerry Paige . . . " and "It seems to me that Doris did something . . . " Jerry Paige, "Doris Day: The Story Behind the Divorce Rumors!" *Motion Picture*, February 1963, 35+.
332   "I should not have permitted . . . " Hotchner, 1985 British paperback, 350.
332   "A couple of years ago, Terry left for college . . . is very hard." Jerry Paige, *Motion Picture*, February 1963.
332   "One of the things that had gone wrong . . . " Hotchner, 207.
333   "where orchestrator Philip Lang . . . " Marmorstein, 285.
334   "You can't imagine . . . " Philip K. Scheuer, "Doris Day Tops as Girl Next Door," *Los Angeles Times*, December 19, 1960, A1.
334   "The only times I had seen Maury were at the games . . . " Hotchner, 214.
334   "he-said, she-said . . . didn't brag about it." Roseboro with Libby, *Glory Days with the Dodgers*, 162.
334   "In *On the Run*, Wills . . . right off the bat." Wills and Celizic. *On the Run: The Never Dull and Often Shocking Life of Maury Wills*, 197–99.

335 "I'd call Doris at three or four . . . " Ellen Grehen, "Maury Wills: I Made Doris' Day—and We Were Both Married," *Globe*, April 30, 1991, 12–13.

336 "'old hat' for the duo . . . won it three times . . . " Gerry McCarthy, "Rock Hudson, Doris Day Win Golden Globe Awards," *L.A. Herald-Examiner*, March 6, 1963, A15.

336 "Hollywood was shaken to its tinsel foundations . . . despite the current trend to integrated romance." Putnam, *Confidential*, September, 1963.

337 "lose everything." Hotchner, 210.

339 "Don't you remember me . . . " Ibid., 286.

Chapter 25: *Some Inconvenient Truths*

341 "Freckly Doris is draped . . . " *Modern Screen*, March 1963, 72.

342 "Both Carl and I came from . . . " Jewison, 75.

342 "was loud, taking over the room . . . slicked down flat over his scalp." Ibid., 76–77.

343 "Don't worry about Doris on this movie . . . unconvinced." Ibid., 78.

343 "the first minute . . . Just give me a focused performance" and "But according to Jewison, his reverse psychology worked on Day. His leading actress got much less anxious about her looks." Ibid., 79.

344 "On the set we do takeoffs . . . " Brogan scrapbook #2.

345 "You're the director . . . she was also a professional." Jewison, 81.

345 "Isn't this a wonderful set . . . " Harrison Carroll, "Baby Comes By Telephone," *Los Angeles Herald-Examiner*, December 30, 1962, D1+.

346 "In the fifteen years after World War II . . . " *New York Times*, February 5, 2006.

346 "She is subjected . . . " "The Tomato on Top Is Doris," *Life*, September 27, 1963.

346 "All along, I've wanted . . . " Terry Melcher, as told to George Christy, "The Doris Day I Know," 88+, Brogan scrapbook #3.

347 "the best . . . ain't love wonderful." *Variety*, June 10, 1963.

347 "packing his bags . . . French revue." "Studio City Man to Write Paris Revue," *Valley Times*, August 22, 1963.

Chapter 26: *Something's Got to Give*

349 "It will be sort of a married . . . " *Los Angeles Times*, February 27, 1962, B16.

350 "spoofed," Drew Casper, Fox DVD of *Move Over, Darling*, 2007.

350 "My feeling is that . . . " Murray Schumach, "Hollywood 'Darling,'" *New York Times*, June 9, 1963.

351 "I so fell in love with . . . " *Move Over, Darling*, Fox DVD, 2007. (As an interesting side note, Melcher was Bergen's agent in the beginning of her own diverse career.)

351 "second man wasn't selected . . . listening to the World Series." Dwight Whitney, "All Sugar, No Spice," *TV Guide*, December 28, 1969.

352 "suddenly" and "without notice." Milt Johnson, "Is Doris Day Giving Up Her Religion?" *Photoplay*, May 1964, 85.

352 "The star's physician . . . " *Los Angeles Times*, July 12, 1963.

352 "mummified with adhesive tape . . . " Hotchner, 221.

352 "You can't miss with a girl like that . . . " Peter Howell, "The Sweet Day Turns Sour," British *Photoplay*, April 1965, 68.

352 "I think Doris is a very sexy lady . . . " Hotchner, 196–97.

352 "One of the things that I remember . . . " Sue Gogkor, *The Magazine for Friends of Doris Day*, August 1993, 6.

353 "Marty was a hustler . . . " Hotchner, 218.

353 "They brought me the song for the film . . . " Bear Family Records, volume 4, 23.

353 "He decided it was definitely . . . " Jan Landy, "Doris Day's No. 2 Son," Brogan scrapbook #4.

354 "He's a young genius . . . " Marlene Stratford, "Stop Hounding My Mother!," *TV and Movie Screen*, 30+.

354 "As music was changing . . . " Bear Family Records, volume 4, 22–23.

354 "Doris Day reports she'll . . . " *Variety*, November 27, 1964.

355 "a remake of a remake . . . " *Time*, December 27, 1963.

356 "It should give us pause . . . " Simon, *Private Screenings: Views of the Cinema of the Sixties*, 101–102.

358 "Once the most popular female star . . . " Wolcott, 146–58.

358 "The fresh scrubbed-nose wonder . . . " Rex Reed, *Big Screen, Little Screen*, 98.

358 "proto-feminist boldness . . . " Haskell, *Holding My Own in No Man's Land*, 22.

359 "Day was more convenient . . . " Ibid., 26.

359 "Doris Day ought to be treated . . . " Ibid., 27.

359 "she was named the top box-office star for the second year in a row, as announced on January 6, 1964 . . . " Vernon Scott, "Doris Day Picked Top Boxoffice Star," *Los Angeles Herald Examiner*, January 6, 1964.

360 "The truth is that, to a certain extent, Doris IS uncooperative . . . Hunter knew exactly what he was talking about." Peter Howell, "The Sweet Day Turns Sour," (British) *Photoplay*, April 1965, 62+.

361 "During the past five years . . . " Ross Hunter, *Modern Screen*, October 1964, 33–4, 64–65.

363 "Hunter himself had tried to conceal the liaison . . . " Mann, *Edge of Midnight: The Life of John Schlesinger*, 452.

364 "Right from the start I hated that script . . . " Oppenheimer and Vitek, 75.

365 "Paul Lynde, the fey, funny character actor and TV personality, looked upon his bit part as a cheerful cemetery-plot salesman in *Flowers* as his favorite film role." Wilson and Florenski, *Center Square: The Paul Lynde Story*, 92.

365 "completely distasteful." Ibid., 92.

365 "Doris and I had become comfortable . . . " Jewison, 85.

365 "showed good pacing . . . " Ibid., 84–85.

366 "A weekend wasn't long . . . " Ardmore papers, Margaret Herrick Library.

366 "I try to make my home honestly reflect me . . . " From Sidney Skolsky, Margaret Herrick Library.

367 "Rearranged for moviegoers . . . " *Time*, November 20, 1964.

367 "the greatest box office team in the history of the industry . . . " Lloyd Shearer, "They Only Make Money," April 12, 1964, Brogan scrapbook #2.

368 "the country's top box-office team . . . in their relationship." Wolcott, 146+.

Chapter 27: *"The Superb Technician"*

369 "[T]he catastrophic cost of 'Cleopatra' . . . " Custen, *Twentieth Century's Fox: Darryl F. Zanuck and the Culture of Hollywood*, 367.

370 "The title [of the film she's working on] is apt . . . " Vernon Scott, "Queen of the Movies," *Citizen News*, February 22, 1965.

370 "And despite Scott's pronouncements about her being friendly, Day earned her third Sour Apple Award for lack of cooperation with the press." *L.A. Herald-Examiner,* December 21, 1964.

370 "The Melchers were so out of touch . . . " Silverman, *The Fox That Got Away,* 121.

371 "I can't do this stuff . . . " *Doris Day Society Journal,* Winter 1977.

371 "Male co-stars with Doris . . . " *Screen Stories,* January 1966, 52.

371 "she is certainly no prude . . . " C. Robert Jennings, "Doris Day: It Pays to Be Pure," *Coronet,* September 1966, 24.

371 "a good deep conjugal kiss . . . " Jane Ardmore manuscript, "I'm in Love, I'm in Love, I'm in Love," Margaret Herrick Library.

371 "I was surprised when I saw the first rushes . . . " *Doris Day Society Journal,* Winter 1977.

371 "the reigning box office queen of the world . . . she became royally and delightfully smashed." "Doris Day Cuts Up," *Good Housekeeping,* October 1965, 72+.

372 "Newspapers and television stations . . . " Art Seidenbaum, "Hollywood Look-Alike Stunt All in a Doris Day's Work," *Los Angeles Times,* January 5, 1966, D1.

372 "see me and say, 'If she can be in pictures' . . . " Vernon Scott, "Queen of the Movies," *Citizen News,* February 22, 1965.

372 "Doris Day's collision . . . " Morris, 131.

372 "the most foolish piece of comic trivia . . . " Bosley Crowther, *New York Times.*

372 "It has no real wit or bite to it . . . " Margaret Harford, *Los Angeles Times,* December 27, 1965.

373 "We considered living in New York . . . " Dick Kleiner "Doris Day Keeps On Being Herself," *Valley Times,* June 8, 1965.

373 "Let's face it . . . " *Photoplay,* November 1965, 38–39.

373 "one of Hollywood's best known restaurants . . . " *Photoplay,* November 1965, 39.

373 "In fact, Terry had invited Claudia . . . " Martin, *Memories Are Made of This: Dean Martin Through His Daughter's Eyes,* 137.

374 "keeping it in the family . . . " Ibid.

374 "I watch Doris Day through my field glasses . . . " Sidney Skolsky, "Hollywood Week in Review," *Citizen News,* August 2, 1965.

374 "Every time somebody hits a ball in the air . . . " Bob McNamara, *Albany Knickerbocker News.*

375 "bullet-proof . . . any attention at all." Charles Maher, *Los Angeles Times,* January 28, 1966.

375 "has kept swimming against the current . . . producers just think they do?" Shamus O'Hea, "Love, Marriage and Movie Magazines," *Modern Screen,* 68.

376 "sanctimonious usher," Hotchner, 249.

376 "what I brooded about . . . " Ibid., 248.

377 "she announced that they were trying to 'snag' Cary Grant to play Day's 'scientist boy friend' . . . " Hedda Hopper, *Los Angeles Times,* October 8, 1964, D14.

377 "'maligned' film . . . overdue for reassessment." Garcia, *Frank Tashlin,* 176.

378 "The day I walked in fully dressed . . . " Wilson and Florenski, 94.

381 "one of those insane comedies . . . " Philip K. Scheuer, *Los Angeles Times,* August 17, 1966.

Chapter 28: *"The Spy Who Came in from the Cold Cream"*

383 "It turned into a bit of a nightmare . . . " Callen, *Richard Harris: Sex, Death and the Movies,* 168.

384 "vodka diluted with water from his swimming pool . . . " Ibid., 169–70.

384 "She returned to London from Los Angeles . . . " Ibid., 170.

384 "Shooting resumed in mid-August . . . " Garcia, 194.

385 "By the end of production they were making up . . . " Norman Lee Browning, "Mod-Clad Harris Discovers Comedy—and Doris Day," Brogan scrapbook #2.

385 "I liked her, she was fine . . . " Callen, 168.

386 "I'm very funny about money . . . drink and a lot of people squawked." C. Robert Jennings, "Doris Day: It Pays to Be Pure," *Coronet,* September 1966, 19–24.

387 "If all the spy pictures modeled after James Bond . . . " Paul Zimmerman, *Newsweek,* June 26, 1967.

387 "Although loaded with slapstick . . . " *Commonweal,* June 23, 1967.

387 "It is difficult to describe 'Caprice' in terms of plot . . . " Arthur Knight, *Saturday Review,* June 6, 1967.

388 "better . . . journey into naught." Andrew Sarris, *Village Voice,* June 29, 1967.

388 "I do not care to discuss 'Caprice,' so I won't. Thank you." Ronald L. Davis Oral History Collection.

388 "Television, she insisted, was out of the . . . " Eve Steele, "Can She Keep the Last Promise She Made to Marty?," Brogan scrapbook #5.

388 "the first talent acquisition . . . CBS organization." *Los Angeles Times,* May 9, 1967.

389 "Columbia and Doris were having a hard time . . . " Bear Family Records, volume 4, 27.

389 "I love those slow tempos . . . " Ibid., 27–28.

390 "It looked more Twentieth Century Fox than French . . . " Bergen, 184.

390 "After almost two years away, I found the country chaotic . . . " Ibid., 173.

390 "Always there was music," she recalled . . . " Ibid., 177–78.

391 "'scoop' on THE AMERICAN WOMAN . . . " *Vogue* cover, as reproduced in photo insert of *Knock Wood.*

391 "snappy New York repartee . . . first on a day-to-day basis," Bergen, 179–80.

391 "great lengths . . . the influence he exerted on me." Ibid., 185.

391 "houseman . . . to being in Never-Never Land." Ibid., 184.

392 "[W]e were starry-eyed kids on a big budget . . . " Ibid., 185.

392 "I don't know. I don't like to talk about those things . . . " Sheila Ellsworth, "The Daughter Doris Day Wants to Have," *Screen Stories,* April 1968, 71.

393 "in riding, roping, quick-drawing . . . " Brogan scrapbook #2.

393 "I thought it was going very well . . . " Abe Greenberg, *Citizen News,* February 14, 1967.

393 "Before the scene, the prop guys came through . . . " Beard, 263.

394 "They didn't even have a barn . . . " Joyce Haber, "Doris Day: She's More Than Just Apple Pie," *Los Angeles Times,* November 15, 1970.

394 "I think it should have been just a little TV film, and I think it was probably written with that in mind." Ronald L. Davis Oral History Collection.

394 "a pleasant, innocuous Doris Day oater comedy . . . situations." *Variety,* December 22, 1967.

394 "Both the comedy and drama of an interesting premise . . . " John Mahoney, *Hollywood Reporter,* no date given.

394 "Doris Day, who used to fill the coffer . . . " Wanda Hale, "It Ain't Fittin' for Doris Day to Play Josie," Brogan scrapbook #2.

395 "There's nothing about *The Ballad of Josie* that couldn't have been taken care of . . . " Leo Sullivan, "Doris Day a Loser in the Old West," *Washington Post*, Brogan scrapbook #2.

395 "A project, still in negotiation . . . " *Variety*, October 12, 1966.

Chapter 29: *"The Constant Virgin"*

401 "before she was a virgin . . . form of plagiarism." Oscar Levant, *Hollywood Reporter*, June 10, 1968.

401 "Pam was in a long dress and she has long black hair . . . ." Jane Ardmore, "If My Son's a Hippie Then so Am I!" 1968, Brogan scrapbook #5.

401 "These people astounded and amazed me . . . " Bergen, 183.

402 "meant to be married," "so different were we from one another." Ibid., 187.

402 "testy and tense . . . drawn into the thick of it." Ibid., 194.

402 "If I sometimes resented Terry's anger . . . " Ibid., 195.

402 "Doris Day and CBS still won't admit . . . ." Hal Humphrey, "Wholesome Series for Doris Day," *Los Angeles Times*, February 7, 1968.

403 "I'll do it, but only if you control the whole thing . . . " Anne Fleming, "Doris Day: I Want to Hear Some Wolf Whistles," *Photoplay*, January 1969, 80.

403 "deeply involved in the writing of the first ten scripts." Ibid.

403 "I don't really know when the show will go on the air . . . " Bob Thomas, "Names Make the News in Television: DAY," *Los Angeles Herald-Examiner*, February 5, 1968.

403 "the most potent force in mid-twentieth century American mythmaking . . . " Lindsey, *Friends as Family*, from the Introduction.

404 "When Doris saw a dog running around . . . " Joyce Haber, *Los Angeles Times*, November 15, 1970.

404 "Doris was great to work with . . . " James Gregory, "Doris Day in Seclusion!," Brogan scrapbook #6.

404 "This was Doris' idea . . . " Ardmore papers, Margaret Herrick Library.

405 "Everyone was wearing love beads . . . " Bill Kennedy, "Off to an Egg-Roll Love-In," *Los Angeles Herald-Examiner*, February 26, 1968, B9.

Chapter 30: *Night for Day*

407 "the one thing in my life that I handled badly . . . " Mary Murphy, "Doris Day Comes in on the Upbeat," *Los Angeles Times*, January 29, 1976.

407 "For a while I didn't believe in anything . . . " "Everything's Coming Up Day-Skies!," *Screen and TV Album*, August-October, 1971, 2+.

407 "sitting out on the curb in his robe and slippers" and "I believe that Marty just wanted to die . . . " Both anecdotes and quotes were recalled by Sydney Wood.

408 "etched with sadness . . . " Tom Keys, "Doris Day's Husband Dies," 1968, Brogan scrapbook #5.

408 "I wasn't too sure about being in love with him . . . " Hotchner, 1985 British paperback, 350.

408 "Rosenthal instructed Terry to make large payments . . . one of the companies at the time." *Day vs. Rosenthal*, August 8, 1985.

409 "almost without exception . . . calculated to mislead and delay." Ibid.

409 "Of course I knew that Marty had an interest in outside ladies . . . " Hotchner, 249.

409 "It really wasn't all that important . . . " Ibid.

409 "Our marriage wasn't perfect . . . " Bill Davidson, *TV Guide*, February 10–26, 1971.

410 "where regular guests included Barbara Lampson . . . " Patrick and McGee, *Que Sera, Sera: The Magic of Doris Day Through Television*, 361.

410 "How about *The Doris Day Show* . . . " Davidson, 6.

410 "Doris makes no TV appearances . . . " Hedda Hopper, *Los Angeles Times*, July 6, 1958.

410 "Marty says I'm healthier . . . " Laura Bascombe, "Doris Day's Last Words to Her Dying Husband," *Photoplay*, July 1968, 88.

411 "I still don't know how I was able to do it . . . " Bill Davidson, *TV Guide*, February 20–26, 1971.

411 "[She was] just kind of walking around, like lost. So sad." Ardmore papers, Margaret Herrick Library. Interviewed by Jane Ardmore on September 5, 1968.

411 "you'd think my son was my father! . . . " Adele Whitely Fletcher, "My Son Acts Like My Father," *Photoplay*, February 1971, 54.

412 "Marty always called her Rocky . . . " Davidson, 11.

412 "With Marty gone . . . " Roger Elwood, "Doris Day: Her Tears, Triumph and then . . . Tragedy!," September 1968, Brogan scrapbook #4.

412 "I like to walk on the beach . . . " Brogan scrapbook #2.

412 "It is almost pointless to complain about yet another Doris Day movie . . . " Arthur Knight, *Saturday Review*, August 24, 1968.

413 "Doris Day's honor, from movie to movie . . . " Renata Adler, *New York Times*, August 9, 1968.

413 "She has the chance to acquire a TV following . . . " Marjorie Adams, *Boston Globe*, June 2, 1968, A23.

414 "The basic mistake that was made . . . " Kanin, *Together Again!*, 198.

414 "It's a warm, family show . . . " Hal Humphrey, "She's Still the Same Doris Day," *Los Angeles Times*, August 12, 1968, C25.

414 "Marlon Brando isn't any one thing . . . enjoy me best in them." Roger Elwood, "Doris Day: Her tears, triumph and then . . . Tragedy!," September 1968, Brogan scrapbook #4.

415 "It really griped my ass . . . " Hotchner, 248.

415 "After five days of testimony in court . . . " Fleming, *Photoplay*, January 1969.

415 "Adults make the mistake of looking for approval . . . " Jane Ardmore, *Photoplay*, June 1968, 70.

415 "very loving and warm . . . I adore that movie." Ronald L. Davis Oral History Collection.

416 "Screened as a sneak preview . . . " Robert B. Frederick, *Variety*, August 7, 1968.

416 "consistently superior to the material . . . " John Mahoney, *Hollywood Reporter*, August 7, 1968.

416 "A few weeks ago I wrote—not too unkindly . . . " Arthur Knight, *Saturday Review*, September 7, 1968.

417 "spent her own money to make improvements . . . on the set and with her wardrobe." "Bonus Features" in the boxed DVD set of *The Doris Day Show*, Season 1.

418 "three parts Donna Reed . . . " Don Page, "Doris Day Show Debuts," *Los Angeles Times*, September 26, 1968.

418 "Doris is an enormously natural and personable performer . . . " Reed, *Big Screen, Little Screen*, 91.

418 "A couple of Saturday afternoons ago . . . I was kind of pleased." John Hallowell, "Will the Real Doris Day Sing Out," *New York Times*, October 27, 1968.

419 "Everyone I know thinks Doris Day is a drip . . . " Betty Rollin, "Doris Day: Miss Apple Pie Hits TV," *Look*, November 26, 1968, 54.

419 "I guess I wanted to hear some wolf whistles . . . " Anne Fleming, *Photoplay*, January 1969, 28–9+.

419 "an almost nightly visitor to Doris' home." Shirley Baker, "She's a Hell of a Woman!" Brogan scrapbook #3.

420 "I had worked hard on turning her mind . . . " Hotchner, 248.

420 "one of the longest continuous engagements in California civil litigation" history. *Day vs. Rosenthal.*

420 "three weeks in Dallas in a courthouse without any air conditioning." Hotchner, 248.

420 "surrounded by [nude] 'family members,' who hummed . . . " John Kendall, "Doris Day's Son Testifies on Manson's Voice, Personality," *Los Angeles Times*, October 24, 1970.

420 "[He was] intrigued by this man, by his apparent spirituality . . . " Bergen, 195.

421 "People complained I never wore pretty clothes . . . " Cecil Smith, *Los Angeles Times*, July 28, 1969, C21.

421 "I was a little apprehensive . . . " "Bonus Features" in the boxed DVD set of *The Doris Day Show*, Season 2.

422 "just going through the motions . . . ". Ronald L. Davis Oral History Collection.

422 "[H]e disappeared into endless daily legal meetings . . . " Bergen, 196–97.

422 "in fact, stolen a telescope from the deck of the Malibu beach house . . . " Hotchner, 249.

424 "I myself rarely saw him . . . " Ibid., 250.

Chapter 31: *"It's All About Animals"*

428 "I would like to marry again . . . " Scott, Brooke, "Doris Day's in Love! Does Her Son Approve?" *Photoplay*, October 1970, 88.

430 "I suppose it's because I'm very active . . . " *Variety*, March 17, 1971.

431 "It was agreed I would do his show when we could . . . " Patrick and McGee, 361.

431 "Doris Day has always been . . . " Rex Reed, *Dayton Daily News*, March 21, 1971.

432 "It's first class all the way . . . " Aleene MacMinn, *Los Angeles Times*, March 12, 1971, E22.

432 "In talking to the principals . . . " Paul Hennir, "Doris Day Series Gets 'Adult' Image," *Los Angeles Times*, September 10, 1971, F22.

432 "This was asking a great deal of loyalty from the viewing audience . . . " Santopietro, 286.

432 "By the fourth and fifth seasons, the story line concentrated . . . " Kaye Ballard, *How I Lost 10 Pounds in 53 Years*, 142.

433 "Completing the scene were three dogs sleeping . . . " Roberta Ormiston, *Lady's Circle*, August 1972, as reprinted in *The Official Doris Day Society Journal*, December 1972, 4.

433 "Of course it would have been better . . . " Bridget Walsh, *Photoplay*, August 1971, 46.

435 "The show has no place to go but up . . . " *Variety*, September 23, 1971.

435 "Doris has earned the right to be regarded as a TV institution . . . controlling the media." Brogan scrapbook #1.

436 "I stood there, covered in dirt and blood . . . " Seaman, *Lovely Me: The Life of Jacqueline Susann*, 446.

436 "tiny Dachau for animals . . . kennels instead of animals." Brogan scrapbook #1.

436 "Of course, they said it was impossible to speak to the governor . . . " Rex Reed, *Chicago Tribune*, January 16, 1972.

436 "She said, 'Give me the check' . . . whole bank applauded." Beard, 267.

438 "Those long vigils through the endless nights . . . " Hotchner, 252–53.

439 "It took four months, casts on both legs . . . " Ibid., 257–8.

439 "Although he is thirty years old . . . " Seaman, 446.

439 "She also came to realize . . . " Hotchner, 255.

439 "I feel that seeing and hearing myself . . . " Brogan scrapbook #1.

439 "but we had a theoretical notion . . . three sliced loaves (a bite a slice) and only groaned towards the end." *Doris Day Society Journal*, September 1972, 3.

440 "Killing an animal to make a coat is a sin . . . " Brogan scrapbook #1.

440 "Tears indeed came to her eyes at the press event . . . " Cleveland Amory, *TV Guide*, June 10, 1972, 36.

Chapter 32: *Freedom at Last*

441 "I'm not anything now . . . " Cleveland Amory, "The Dog Catcher of Beverly Hills," *TV Guide*, June 10–16, 1972, 34–40.

442 "There had been nothing between us . . . " Hotchner, 269.

442 "This man I fell in love with . . . " Ibid., 270.

442 "I never denied the rumors . . . " Ibid., 271.

443 "Day did such a good job of keeping her affair with O'Neal hidden that Mary Anne Barothy . . . "A couple years after the author's interviews with Barothy, she published a memoir, *Day at a Time*, in which she suggested that she knew about Day's affair with O'Neal for a much longer period than she originally conveyed.

444 "She has from five to ten changes per show . . . " Army Archerd, "Hollywood Style," *Variety*, July 31, 1972.

445 "I've just finished my fifth year . . . " *Doris Day Society Journal*, March 1973, 3.

446 "We met on evenings or weekends . . . " Patrick and McGee, 3.

447 "After an awful lot of pressure . . . " *Doris Day Society Journal*, March 1973, 2.

448 "The important thing isn't how long you live . . . " Beverly Linet, "Jackie Susann's Brave, Brave Battle," *Motion Picture*, January 1975, 42.

448 "I personally don't believe in death . . . " Ardmore papers, Margaret Herrick Library.

448 "You could help so many people . . . " Seaman, 446.

448 "I was driving and Doris was sitting in the backseat . . . " *National Enquirer*, Brogan scrapbook #1.

449 "The day of the party, Doris tried to beg off . . . " Seaman, 468.

450 "He'd never done a play and never sung on stage . . . " Oppenheimer and Vitek, 137.

453 "But when rock star Sly Stone . . . " *Time,* July 9, 1973.

454 "We're discussing my doing an album with Sly . . . " "Guess Who's Coming to Dinner?" *Modern People,* Brogan scrapbook #1.

454 "My son often brings friends home . . . " Brogan scrapbook #1.

454 "How do these things get started . . . " Joyce Haber, *Los Angeles Times,* May 3, 1973.

454 "fabulous home studio . . . Stone at the time." James and Ritz, *Rage to Survive: The Etta James Story,* 195.

455 "I flew out to California to meet Doris . . . " "Story Behind the Book," *Publishers Weekly,* February 2, 1976, 54.

455 "When we arrived at the Dorchester [Hotel], all the press . . . " Ardmore papers, Margaret Herrick Library.

456 "They sponsor the Animal Welfare Trust . . . " Jane Ardmore, "Meet Clara Bixby!" manuscript in Ardmore papers, Margaret Herrick Library. (Interview was conducted December 7, 1973, at Day's N. Crescent home.)

459 "It is very hard for a woman in my position . . . " Brogan scrapbook #1.

460 "These people who have been superstars for so long . . . " *Publishers Weekly,* February 2, 1976, 54.

461 "Melissa was the ex-wife of a tennis buddy . . . " Hotchner, 288.

462 "an eccentric work that suggests he's given up not just on optimism but even on despair," Bud Scoppa, *Rolling Stone,* June 1974.

Chapter 33: *The $22.8 Million Decision*

464 "My mother has been a thorn in my side all my life . . . " Mary Anne Barothy, "Movie Star's Former Secretary Tells of . . . THE WOMAN WHO MAKES LIFE HELL FOR DORIS DAY—HER MOTHER," *National Enquirer,* December 23, 1975.

464 "I've got to get mother out of my home . . . " Ibid.

465 "the most star-studded gathering in Hollywood history." McCabe, 331.

466 "We went to see Tom Jones in his dressing room after his act . . . " Hotchner, 1985 British paperback, 339.

467 "The bazaar itself was a phenomenal event . . . so tightly she could hardly manage to write her name." Ibid., 343.

468 "Immediately, a line formed that stretched . . . " Ibid., 344.

468 "Oh, that Clara Bixby . . . " Ibid., 344.

470 "Two days after her appearance on *The Tonight Show,* Day sent Jacqueline Susann a letter . . . " Mary Anne Barothy, *Day at a Time,* 132.

470 "I wanted to be at Opal's side, but I was called back to . . . Los Angeles to testify in court," Seaman, 486.

470 "My husband trusted Rosenthal and I trusted my husband . . . " and "I knew that justice would prevail . . . " These quotes come from the *Hollywood Reporter* and the *Los Angeles Times,* both dated September 19, 1974.

471 "I am healthy and I am rich . . . " Myrna Oliver, "Court Awards $22.8 Million to Doris Day," *Los Angeles Times,* September 19, 1974, 1.

471 "I was so busy at the time . . . " *North Adams Transcript,* September 19, 1974.

471 "further enjoined . . . business and financial dealings," *Los Angeles Herald Examiner,* September 18, 1974.

471 "This is only the first round . . . " *Hollywood Reporter,* January 19, 1974.

471 "Does Doris know that man or that dog?" "Doris knows all dogs," *Los Angeles Examiner.*

472 "about a blonde movie-TV doll (not Connie Stevens) who fired her secretary for having interfered with her private life." Barothy, 167.

476 "Geffen's eyes . . . " King, *The Operator,* 120.

Chapter 34: *"The Comden Years"*

479 "I don't know if she fell in love with the hollandaise . . . " Barry Comden, proposal for *Secrets Behind the Smile: Memoirs of My Life With Doris Day,* 4.

479 "My mother was in the hospital . . . " Lloyd Shearer, "Doris Day–The Woman Behind the Image," *Parade,* February 8, 1976, 9.

465 "A brazen 'flapper.'" Comden, *Off Stage,* 39–40.

480 "making love standing up, full of passion and promise." Richard Johnson, "Page Six," *New York Post,* August 3, 1997.

480 "Barry and I have been seeing lots of each other . . . " Lloyd Shearer, "Doris Day: The Woman Behind the Image," *Parade,* February 8, 1976.

480 "I sat on the end of her bed . . . " Johnson, *New York Post,* August 3, 1997.

481 "Little did I know I'd be the one who ended up in the doghouse!" Barry Comden, Part II of his proposal for a memoir, "The Great Dog Food Disaster," 1.

481 "A person will say a lot of things . . . " "Story Behind the Book," *Publishers Weekly,* February 2, 1976, 54.

482 "had always been rather circumspect . . . " Hotchner, 9, 11–12.

483 "spills everything about her unhappy childhood . . . " Diane White, "Can This Be Doris Day?" Brogan scrapbook, loose papers.

483 "Well for one thing I hadn't slept all night . . . " Mary Murphy, *Los Angeles Times,* January 29, 1976.

488 "The same strong personality behind her professional success . . . " John Updike, *New Yorker,* February 23, 1976, 109–14.

488 "Somehow, I don't think that the revelations . . . " Robert Kirsch, "Miss Goody Two-Shoes Kicks Back," *Los Angeles Times Book Review,* January 11, 1976.

489 "a woman totally in command . . . more personal code." Haskell, 29.

489 "The initial print run was increased by 100,000 . . . " *Doris Day Society Journal,* Winter 1976, 6.

490 "Comden, let's get married!" Comden proposal for a memoir, 14.

490 "I laid out cake, fruit, flowers, hors d'oeuvres and decorations . . . everyone left [the couple alone] about an hour later." *Los Angeles Herald-Examiner,* April 17.

491 "I hope you all join with us . . . sealed our fate forever." Comden proposal for a memoir, Part II, 10.

491 "sold more than $150,000 worth of pet food distribution franchises since April 4 . . . without applying for registration required by state law." *Los Angeles Times,* July 17, 1976, C7.

492 "[m]ake a substantial income from the pet food industry and help your favorite pets" Hotchner, 1985 British paperback, 355.

492 "on mail fraud charges arising from a work-at-home franchise scheme that netted his former employer some $500,000." Ibid., 356.

493 "to keep a pet food products company from using her name . . . " *Variety,* February 4, 1977.

494 "franchise scheme . . . There was nothing in it for me. It was all going to be for the animals." A. E. Hotchner, "Doris Day Today," *Ladies Home Journal*, June 1982, 127.

494 "I share my little abode with five of the Day canine family . . . " *Doris Day Society Journal*, Winter 1976, 2.

497 "Does entertainer Doris Day have more than 11 dogs . . . " Gerald Faris, "Too Many Dogs for the Girl Next Door," *Los Angeles Times*, November 10, 1977, WS1.

498 "to assist humane organizations . . . " *Doris Day Society Journal*, Winter 1977, 11.

500 "The imposing hills and streams and little roads . . . " Hotchner, *Ladies Home Journal*, 77.

500 "Rumor of the week! . . . " *Los Angeles Free Press*, April 18–24, 1979.

501 "Miss Day never got her $23 million and she won't . . . " Myrna Oliver, "Postscript: Doris Day Still Hasn't Found Happy End to 11-Year Dispute," *Los Angeles Times*, October 26, 1979, D1.

504 "the biggest mistake of my life . . . " Stu Schreiberg, "Doris Day," *USA Weekend*, January 10–12, 1986.

504 "No pillow talk between Doris Day and estranged hubby Barry Comden . . . " *National Enquire*, July 15, 1980.

504 "planned my exit scene from the day Doris and I met." Comden proposal, part II, 13.

505 "Comden's court papers state . . . " *Los Angeles Herald-Examiner*, January 7, 1981.

Chapter 35: *Carmel-by-the-Sea*

510 "bitter recluse . . . not a day older." Hotchner, *Ladies Home Journal*, 75, 77.

511 "Long hesitant about invasions . . . Les Brown and son Terry Melcher." Robert Osborne, *Hollywood Reporter*, May 19, 1983, 2.

511 "I may work again . . . " Ibid., 2.

511 "This is terrific . . . " Oppenheimer and Vitek, 155–56.

512 "Fletcher was conceived of as a 'ditzy' character, and she had to gradually work on the show's producers to make her less addled." (Lansbury shared this observation during a tribute to her at the Museum of Broadcasting in NYC, 11/14/07.)

513 "If I were on a big ego kick . . . I can't say the same thing about people." Schreiberg, *USA Weekend*, January 10–12, 1986.

514 "Not since the hey-day press days/daze of Liz & Dick . . . " Robert Osborne, *Hollywood Reporter*, July 17, 1985, 3.

515 "At the time he agreed to make the appearance . . . " Oppenheimer and Vitek, 186–87.

515 "In truth, it wasn't *Pillow Talk* they were reprising . . . " Wolcott, 146+.

519 "an effort to clear his name . . . " Dan Morain, "Doris Day Wins 17-Year Battle with Ex-Attorney," *Los Angeles Times*, October 17, 1985, A29.

520 "Because of bad legal advice . . . " Roger M. Grace, "Perspectives" on "Uncle Jerry," *Metropolitan News-Enterprise*, October 22, 2007, 7.

521 "$500,000-plus to star in a two-hour pilot," Brogan scrapbook #6.

521 "I don't understand why I got this, but I love it . . . " Braun, 2004 edition, 30.

525 "Doris Day is probably the most sought-after over-50 celebrity . . . " Robert Osborne, *Hollywood Reporter*, April 2, 1993.

525 "attended Day's reception at her Cypress Inn . . . " Robert Osborne, *Hollywood Reporter*, Brogan scrapbook #5.

526 "telefilms per year as a recurring character . . . completely finished." *Variety*, October 2, 1990.

526 "The American PR, Linda Dozoretz . . . why her interview with Day never happened." Chrissy Iley, "Oh Dear, What a Calamity," *Sunday Times*, November 20, 1994.

527 "the first man Doris . . . parking lot after Doris drove away." Alan Shadrake, "Doris Day Falls Made in Love Again—at age 73," *Star*, March 9, 1998, 25.

529 "I thought that's terrible to do that . . . " Brogan scrapbook #5.

530 "trying to lure . . . wants to see a script." Liz Smith, *New York Post*, July 16, 1998.

Index

Photo Credits

---------------------------------- ✳ ----------------------------------

Page ii: By Ed Clark/Time & Life Pictures/Getty Images.

Endpapers: Collection of the author

Photo inserts (by caption number)

1: From Photofest; 2: From MPTV.net; 3: Collection of the author; 4: From Ronald Grant Archive; 5: From Bettmann Corbis; 6: From Metronome/Getty Images; 7: From Globe Photos; 8: By James J. Kriegsmann/Frank Driggs Collection; 9: From The Everett Collection; 10: Collection of the author; 11: From Lester Glassner Collection; 12: From Bettmann Corbis; 13: By Murray Garrett/Graphic House; 14: By Jack Albin/Lester Glassner Collection; 15: From Bettmann Corbis; 16: Courtesy of Academy of Motion Picture Arts and Sciences; 17: From The Everett Collection; 18: From Photofest; 19: By Tom Caffrey/Globe Photos; 20: by Bert Six/ MPTV.net; 21, 22: Collection of Sheila Smith and Valerie Andrew; 23: Collection of the author; 24: From MPTV.net; 25: From Bettmann Corbis; 26: By Mac Julian/ MPTV.net; 27: Collection of the author; 28: Courtesy of Academy of Motion Picture Arts and Sciences; 29: © Paramount Pictures/Zuma Press; 30: Collection of the author; 31: © Warner Brothers; 32: From Lester Glassner Collection; 33: From Frank Driggs Collection; 34: From The Everett Collection; 35: © Universal Pictures; 36: By Bert Reisfeld/dpa/Landov; 37, 38: From Photofest; 39: By Milton H. Greene © 2008 Joshua Greene/www.archiveimages.com; 40: Collection of Sheila Smith and Valerie Andrew; 41: From Photofest; 42: Collection of the author; 43: From Bettmann Corbis; 44. 45: Courtesy of Academy of Motion Picture Arts and Sciences; 46: From Lester Glassner Collection; 47: By Phil Roach/Ipol/Globe Photos; 48, 49: From Photofest; 50: Collection of the author; 51: By Phil Roach/Ipol/Globe Photos; 52: Courtesy of Paul Brogan; 53: From Mirrorpix.com. (54) Both, from Carson Entertainment; 55: From UPI Corbis; 56: By Ron Galella; 57: Collection of Sheila Smith and Valerie Andrew; 58, 59: Collection of the author; 60: By Peter C. Borsari; 61: Collection of the author; 62: By Peter Simon; 63: By Mike Carrillo/ Online USA/Getty Images.

Permissions Credits

✳

SPECIAL FEATURE
DORIS DAY
LIFE STORY
Also, Hollywood's Mystery Girl
By Hedda Hopper

in this issue
Bill Campbell
Shirley Jones
Tab Hunter
Janet and Tony

Picture Show
& FILM PICTORIAL
THE PAPER FOR PEOPLE WHO GO TO THE PICTURES
3D

SCREEN
MAGAZINE
MARILYN MONROE
Answers 15 Intimate Questions

£20
To Be Won
"The Young at Heart"

MOTION
PICTURE

Why Eddie MUST Marry L
BY SIDNEY SKOLSKY

Novak: ONE MAN IS NOT ENOUGH!
odern screen
DELL

BURT REYNOLDS: MY OWN FATHER
SENT ME TO JAIL
movie
TV PHOTO
STARS
LEONARD NIMOY, LESLIE WARREN VANISH!
35¢
DORIS DAY:
THE AGONIZING SHAME SHE MUST HIDE FROM HER SON
THE 30 SEXIEST WOMEN IN HOLLYWOOD HISTORY
HOW MARLO THOMAS HURT CAROL BURNETT
JOHN WAYNE and GOLDIE HAWN—JUST HOW SERIOUS IS IT?

DICK C
"I make at a gir who wears

Doris Day

映画の友

mplete story of
S DAY'S
CAPE
M HELL

readers— THE ELVIS PRESLEY RING

th about Liz and Eddie's baby...
HOTOPLAY
OCTOBER 25¢

EDDIE'S
eard
ooners
N
tell

Motion Picture
MAGAZINE
Only
10¢
March